The Suspended Disaster

Columbia Studies in Middle East Politics

Columbia Studies in Middle East Politics
MARC LYNCH, SERIES EDITOR

Columbia Studies in Middle East Politics presents academically rigorous, well-written, relevant, and accessible books on the rapidly transforming politics of the Middle East for an interested academic and policy audience.

Syria Divided: Competing Narratives and the Performance of Violence in Civil War, Ora Szekely

Shouting in a Cage: Political Life After Authoritarian Cooptation in North Africa, Sofia Fenner

Classless Politics: Islamist Movements, the Left, and Authoritarian Legacies in Egypt, Hersham Sallam

Lumbering State, Restless Society: Egypt in the Modern Era, Nathan J. Brown, Shimaa Hatab, and Amr Adly

Friend or Foe: Militia Intelligence and Ethnic Violence in the Lebanese Civil War, Nils Hägerdal

Jordan and the Arab Uprisings: Regime Survival and Politics Beyond the State, Curtis Ryan

Local Politics in Jordan and Morocco: Strategies of Centralization and Decentralization, Janine A. Clark

Religious Statecraft: The Politics of Islam in Iran, Mohammad Ayatollahi Tabaar

Protection Amid Chaos: The Creation of Property Rights in Palestinian Refugee Camps, Nadya Hajj

From Resilience to Revolution: How Foreign Interventions Destabilize the Middle East, Sean L. Yom

Sectarian Politics in the Gulf: From the Iraq War to the Arab Uprisings, Frederic M. Wehrey

The Arab Uprisings Explained: New Contentious Politics in the Middle East, edited by Marc Lynch

The Suspended Disaster

Governing by Crisis in Bouteflika's Algeria

THOMAS SERRES

Columbia University Press

New York

Columbia University Press
Publishers Since 1893
New York   Chichester, West Sussex
cup.columbia.edu

Original title : *L'Algérie face à la catastrophe suspendue. Gérer la crise et blâmer le peuple sous Bouteflika (1999-2014)*. © Editions Karthala, 2019.
By arrangement with Words in Progress. Translation copyright © 2023 Columbia University Press. All rights reserved.

Library of Congress Cataloging-in-Publication Data
Names: Serres, Thomas, author.
Title: The suspended disaster : governing by crisis in Bouteflika's Algeria / Thomas Serres.
Other titles: Governing by crisis in Bouteflika's Algeria
Description: New York : Columbia University Press, [2023] |
Series: Columbia studies in Middle East politics | Includes bibliographical references and index.
Identifiers: LCCN 2023003162 (print) | LCCN 2023003163 (ebook) |
ISBN 9780231212021 (hardback) | ISBN 9780231212038 (paperback) |
ISBN 9780231559171 (ebook)
Subjects: LCSH: Algeria—Politics and government—1990- | Bouteflika, Abdelaziz, 1937–2021.
Classification: LCC DT295.6 .S4713 2023 (print) | LCC DT295.6 (ebook) |
DDC 965.05/4—dc23/eng/20230315
LC record available at https://lccn.loc.gov/2023003162
LC ebook record available at https://lccn.loc.gov/2023003163

Cover design: Elliott S. Cairns
Cover image: Nacerdine Zebar/Gamma-Rapho via Getty Images

To my parents, Marie-Christine and Frédéric

Contents

Preface ix

1 A Never-Ending Crisis? 1
2 Struggles at the Heart of the State 32
3 Cronies and Labyrinths 72
4 Fragments of Order 110
5 The Regulation of Freedoms 152
6 The Crisis as a Lived Experience 190
7 In Search of Lost Meaning 231
   Coda 274

   Acknowledgments 295
   Appendix A: Methods of Inquiry 299
   Appendix B: A Time Line for Bouteflika's Algeria 301
   Glossary of Terms and Abbreviations 305
   Notes 309
   Bibliography 357
   Index 389

Preface

Na Nigerian government, ee-oh
Dem dey talk be dat, ee-oh
"My people are us-e-less, My people are sens-i-less, My people are indiscipline"

—*Fela Kuti*

Never has an electoral campaign displayed such cynicism, in a country that is nevertheless familiar with power grabs... When talking to us, they resorted to the intimate language they use in the hushed atmosphere of their living-rooms, to speak about their drivers and their maids. "Chaʿab erkhiss," "people of nothing," "bare-footed," "ʿaryens," "digestive tubes," "raʿi," "shepherds" who only understand strength.

—*Ghania Mouffok*

Sitting in front of a fireplace, candidate Abdelaziz Bouteflika is answering the questions of a French journalist before the first round of the 1999 Algerian presidential elections. The frontrunner explains his incomprehension, as his six challengers have decided to collectively withdraw from a race that they consider to be rigged in his favor. "Abandoning and yet having the feeling that you have won. It's a bit much. You really have to be Algerian to dare doing something like that," he explains with his blue eyes wide open and a large smile on his face. Bouteflika presents himself as a solution to a decade of turmoil. While the country is in the midst of a bloody civil conflict, the former minister of foreign affairs demands broad popular support: "If I don't have clear and massive support from the Algerian people, I'll consider that they are happy with their mediocrity. And after all, I am not in charge of making them happy against their will."[1] He poses as a providential man. A few days later, Bouteflika will be elected with 73.80 percent of the vote from an overall voter turnout of 60.91 percent. This is the beginning of a twenty-year period of rule. Throughout this time, the man who has just been voted president of the republic will never really put an end to the crisis faced by the country. Rather, he will contribute to making it the core principle of government.

Fifteen Years Later

Fifteen years have passed, and Abdelaziz Bouteflika is now unable to walk or speak after suffering a transient ischemic attack in April 2013. He nonetheless remains head of state, as no viable alternative has emerged within the ruling coalition. After the uprisings of 2010–2011 in neighboring Tunisia and Libya, and the French military intervention in Mali, regional uncertainty prevails. Moreover, Algeria's economy remains dependent on increasingly unstable hydrocarbon prices. Popular discontent is widespread, yet state officials present the ailing president as the guarantor of peace and development. It is remarkable to see a political charade embodied so perfectly by a single personality. What better allegory of a system of government based on the possibility of an imminent collapse than a head of state unable to take his presidential oath?

In Algeria, certainly, the head of state played his role as the representative of a flickering order. Yet if this allegory seems remarkable, it is also too convenient. Abdelaziz Bouteflika certainly acquired a great deal of power over the years, but he was just a man in a fragmented ruling coalition that controlled a modern and sectorized state. Accordingly, this book studies Algeria under the rule of Bouteflika (1999–2019), not the president himself. It describes a specific mode of government by crisis, one that draws on the most vivid form of existential threat: the catastrophe. It studies the strategies of those who govern, but also the lived experience resulting from this mode of government. The following observations describe Algeria in the spring of 2014.

A DEMONSTRATION PREVENTED

I have not been to Algeria since June 2013. Seen from France, the past political year has been most peculiar. Following Bouteflika's stroke, observers were expecting him to withdraw from the presidential race in favor of an heir selected by the groups that constitute the ruling coalition. Yet an unlikely team of cronies and ministers has nonetheless managed to bring about his candidacy. Thus, the man who can barely utter a word is making his bid for reelection as a front-runner. In the meantime, public figures share expletives in broad daylight. Associates of the presidency denounce the shortcomings of the powerful military intelligence, the Department of Intelligence and Security (Département du Renseignement et de la Sécurité, DRS). Meanwhile, allies of this department reply that the leader of the largest party in the country, the National Liberation Front (Front de libération nationale, or FLN), is an agent working for the French secret services.[2]

On the way from the airport, the urban landscape unfolds before my eyes. The frenzied construction policy supported by the government has altered the fabric of the city. In addition to the plethora of new hotels lining the road to downtown Algiers, I can see the future Great Mosque—one of Bouteflika's signature projects—slowly taking shape. Around the mosque, there is already a parking lot. On the other side of the freeway, a new mall has been built and hundreds of cars testify to consumers' enthusiasm. A little further, along the bay, a freshly finished boardwalk offers a welcoming space for joggers and strollers. The capital is acquiring the features of a global city. A metro and a tramway were inaugurated in 2011 and a new opera house is under construction. Overall, the investment of public funds continues steadily and allows for the proliferation of construction sites across the city.

Later, in downtown Algiers, I meet with two activists belonging to the Youth Action Rally (Rassemblement Action Jeunesse, RAJ), an organization founded in the 1990s. One of them is Nidhal, a founding figure of RAJ and a friend who is hosting me. While organizationally autonomous, the association is linked to the Socialist Forces Front (Front des Forces Socialistes, FFS), the country's oldest opposition party.[3] Under the arches along the seafront, the two men stay a couple of meters away from each other. They speak elusively and use obscure nicknames ("you-know-who," "our friend"). Their discussion is shaped by caution. In their eyes, internal tensions within the ruling coalition could lead to rapid changes.

A sit-in staged by Barakat (Enough), a movement that denounces Bouteflika's bid for reelection, is planned for 4:00 p.m. near Maurice Audin Square. My companions notice bitterly that the organizers of the rally decided to hold it on their doorsteps. They imply, with a degree of accuracy, that Barakat's core activists belong to Algiers's educated upper-middle class. Indeed, the founders of the movement are journalists, lawyers, and doctors. According to RAJ's members, the authorities will tolerate the protest of the *barakistes*, as has been the case so far, to please international media. "All this is for the cameras," says one of them. As we walk past the entrance of the Faculté Centrale, we can see a dozen journalists waiting for the protest to begin. One detail attracts Nidhal's attention: according to him, the colossuses in blue uniforms who are waiting on the other side of the street come from the south of the country. He thinks that these policemen were brought here to take part in a brawl.

Suddenly, the first signs of the protest can be heard further up on Didouche Mourad Street. Following the shouts and cries, we are passed by the policemen, who run with long bludgeons in their hands. Just before Maurice Audin Square, a mass of pedestrians has formed. A handful of Barakat members make their voices heard. One after the other, they come out of the crowd and shout slogans hostile to Bouteflika's fourth mandate before being rapidly apprehended. As two officers are rounding up an activist on the stairs of a nearby street, a journalist and her cameraman rush toward the scene to record footage of the crackdown. This infuriates a group of young men who had until then witnessed the protest quite stoically from a nearby restaurant. "Get out! Go back to your country!" shouts one of them to the journalist. As the tension grows, neighboring shops begin shutting down. Meanwhile, agents of the General Directorate for National Safety (Direction Générale de la Sûreté Nationale—the Algerian police) take pictures of those who remain in the square.

After the police have removed the arrested protesters, the atmosphere slowly reverts to normal. Activists from diverse backgrounds, standing between police cars, are deep in discussion. A smiling man shows up and starts ostentatiously shaking the hands of known faces before leaving. A *barakiste* explains that this is the head of the city's police intelligence trying to sow doubt. Worried, Nidhal points at the weapons of the officers who monitor the square. "They carry automatic rifles (*klash*) in the middle of Algiers. The last time we saw something like that, it was in 1988," he says, referencing the bloody repression of the October uprising. Eventually, two men and a woman appear on the square brandishing posters of Bouteflika. A small crowd gathers around them as they shout slogans glorifying the president. They will disappear as easily as they arrived less than ten minutes later.

This first fragment illustrates the difficulty of apprehending the reality on the ground. Indeed, the scale and speed of the repression surprised even those who followed the campaign closely. One can also grasp the feeling of exhaustion and annoyance among some of the population, who have been the captive audience of a tense electoral process. Finally, it is important to note that actors draw on past episodes (here the uprising of 1988) to interpret the present situation and evaluate the possibility of a rise in violence.

RAJ IN TURMOIL

Well-known figures express their fears publicly. This is notably the case with Mouloud Hamrouche, a former reformist prime minister (1989–1991) who has become a common point of reference in liberal circles. During the campaign, Hamrouche intervenes repeatedly to share his concerns. In a widely discussed press conference, he speaks of a "crisis inside the regime" leading to "serious threats." A few weeks later, he reiterates his position and evokes the risk of increased violence. He suggests that the head of state (Abdelaziz Bouteflika), the army's chief of staff (Ahmed Gaïd Salah), and the head of the DRS (Mohamed Mediène) should conclude a settlement to resolve the current political impasse.[4] If this statement suggests an exceptional emergency, it also illustrates what I call the suspension of the catastrophe: year after year, presidential election after presidential election, political actors warn of the risks of a major political upheaval. Indeed, Hamrouche's call is in fact largely redundant. Already in 2002, the prime minister at the time, Ali Benflis, explained that the country was facing "a multifaceted crisis [going beyond] factual and conjunctural factors that might have a lasting impact on its future."[5] In 2002, as in 2014, these political figures emphasize the precariousness of the country's situation in order to promote their reformist agenda.

What really happens on Election Day? Nidhal and I decide to go to Bab El-Oued, a neighborhood associated with the great uprisings of Algiers's past: during the War of Liberation (1954–1962); in 1962, against the OAS (Organisation Armée Secrète, or Secret Armed Organization), a pro–French Algeria armed group; during the popular uprising of October 1988; and again in January 2011. A freelance journalist is coming with us. On this spring morning, Bab El-Oued is remarkably calm. Polling stations are sparsely occupied, and the exit polls improvised by our journalist friend indicate a rather flattering preference for the sitting president: no less than 100 percent of the vote would appear to be in his favor. This is far from surprising. In Algeria, citizens demonstrate their rejection of the "System" through abstention, which expresses both a lack of faith in the electoral process and a mistrust toward the country's putative representatives.[6] A surprise is unlikely, as it would mean that the state apparatus has turned against Bouteflika. Thus, after making sure that I am not myself a journalist, a man starts to reveal in front of me the orders that he claims to have received directly from Ali Haddad, CEO of a construction company and fervent supporter of the president. According to him, the election is already won. It is not even noon. Therefore, it is time to start mobilizing the fans of USM Algiers, a football club in which Haddad is the majority shareholder, to celebrate the victory. This kind of "spontaneous" celebration aims to demonstrate the democratic nature of the political order, and it is a performance directed at Algerians as well as international partners.

The following day, the government-owned newspaper *El Moudjahid*, which was the voice of the FLN during the War of Liberation, celebrates a "remarkable" official voter turnout of 51.7 percent. Emphasizing the legality of the election, the editorial presents Algeria as "the right example to follow with regards to human rights and democracy for countries that aim to take this path."[7] Yet Bouteflika's reelection is by no means uncontroversial in Algeria. Responding to the official praise, the private daily newspaper *Liberté* dedicates its front page to "the pictures that have traveled around the world." They show the president in a wheelchair while his personal physician "whispers in his ears," "seizes six ballot papers," and "accompanies him in the booth"—a situation that is only legal in cases where a voter can prove infirmity.[8] As for the *Soir d'Algérie*, another private daily, it echoes the denunciations coming from various opposition parties. It also publishes an op-ed by Amin Khan, a "poet and former public servant," on the ruling coalition's illegitimacy, its inability to solve the country's crisis, and the place of dirty money in its internal functioning.[9] If the criticism is harsh, it remains nonetheless nebulous, targeting the "System" rather than specific individuals or institutions.

Political opponents are striving to regroup and offer an alternative path. Leftist activists from RAJ and the Socialist Workers Party (Parti Socialiste des Travailleurs, a Trotskyist formation) who I meet over the next couple of days follow these maneuvers from a distance, without great enthusiasm. The widespread discrediting of politicians and parties undermines any attempt to unify the country's myriad opposition movements. On the one hand, official opponent and former prime minister Ali Benflis announces the creation of a "front bringing together the forces of change." On the other, various parties who have boycotted the presidential election prepare a "national conference for democratic transition" that will soon give birth to a "Coordination for Liberties and Democratic Transition." As for the FFS, it calls on other actors to "seek consensus," and leaves the door open to both the government and opposition forces. One must also take into account the actions of Mouloud Hamrouche and his emissaries, who are exploring their options, as well as an attempt to create an alternative among members of the Left. In short, areas of convergence proliferate, which paradoxically reveals the fragmentation of the political field and makes an actual reunion unlikely. "They all hate each other," a Trotskyist activist affirms abruptly while we are having coffee.

RAJ's leaders have decided to join a coalition of associations and unions whose aim is the creation of "a democratic, autonomous and inclusive space of civil society for convergence and struggle." To justify this strategy Abdelouahab Fersaoui, the association's president, tells me that "it is necessary to act on the social and economic aspects first, in order to mobilize people and bring them back to political demands." This effort nonetheless takes on a secondary importance when an unexpected blow changes RAJ's priorities. Following the protest in Maurice Audin Square, a member of the association was arrested along with a Tunisian friend. The reasons for the two young men's detention are unclear. As the authorities have not provided any information regarding the charges against them, where they are being held, or the date of any hearing before a judge, uncertainty increases and strategies diverge. While RAJ's leadership struggles to advance its project of convergence among social movements, grassroots members demand immediate street actions to free the prisoners. Former members, outraged by the length of the two men's detention, decide to get involved and start an online petition. The lawyers, linked to human rights associations, prioritize a legal approach to this conundrum. Finally, villagers from the detained activist's hometown protest his detention in the mountains of Kabylia, not far from Algiers. None of these actions prevent the judicial apparatus from imposing its rhythm and provoking concern about the possibly severe punishment the two men could face. They will eventually be sentenced to a suspended prison term two weeks later and released immediately. For RAJ, this unexpected crisis has revealed internal disagreements between former members, new leaders, and grassroots activists, which were in turn exacerbated by the unpredictability of state coercion.

This second fragment illustrates several key issues, starting with the redundancy of alarmist discourses nourished by political deadlock and repression.[10] This type of emergency rhetoric can be instrumentalized by reformist elites to advance their own agendas. Opponents, whether they belong to political parties, associations, or trade unions, are active but fragmented. While they have the ability to denounce the government in virulent terms, they are also constantly limited by an arbitrary and unpredictable coercive machine.

IN CHLEF

It takes about three hours to reach Chlef from the Agha train station, in the center of Algiers. The medium-sized town is situated in the Tell Atlas, between the capital and Oran, the second-largest city in the country. Surrounded by agricultural lands, it lies in the Chelif Valley and is known for the devastation it suffered as a result of two earthquakes in 1954 and 1980. After the last one destroyed most of the city, roughly twelve thousand emergency trailer units welcomed those who had lost their houses. More than thirty years later, these "temporary" neighborhoods remain, fueling denunciations of the precarious living conditions that are said to prevail in the *wilaya* (governorate).[11]

In Chlef, my interlocutors' questions underline a widespread mistrust toward strangers and politics. Beyond the refusal to be recorded—which is nothing new—the self-censorship and the will to remain anonymous are especially strong in spring 2014. The elections justify an extra dose of cautiousness. When I meet with Karim, an architect who has agreed to introduce me to the basics of local urban planning, he explains that he cannot give any names. Those responsible for the problems he identifies (corruption, mismanagement, lack of political will) will remain anonymous to avoid getting him in trouble. Similarly, Mansour, a representative at the People's Assembly of Wilaya (Assemblée populaire de wilaya, APW), belonging to a small nationalist party, describes the bureaucratic deadlock and his difficulties communicating with the local administration. Yet he refuses to speak politics and limits our exchanges to technical details. Before leaving me after our first encounter, he insists on giving me a warning: "We live in troubled times, with everything that is going on at our borders. You need to understand that everybody here has a history, and we don't want to live this history again." He is referring to the so-called Dark Decade (*al-ʿUshriyya as-Sawdāaʾ*) of the 1990s, a time when Chlef and its surroundings were plagued by the extreme violence perpetrated by Islamist insurgents, state security forces, and unknown criminal elements.

The last time we see each other, Mansour explains that if I am to come back to Chlef, I will need an official document from the Ministry of Higher Education. Such a letter would dissipate the doubts surrounding my motivations. I certainly cannot blame him for thinking that a researcher could be a spy. One must admit that both professions produce a form of power-knowledge that benefits the state, among other entities. Nevertheless, the spy fever is particularly acute in this month of April 2014. Increased international attention linked to the presidential election, coupled with fears of destabilization by foreign agents after the Western military interventions in Libya and Mali, accentuate the suspicion inherited from the anticolonial struggle. A Franco-Moroccan freelance journalist who came to cover the election without a press visa was denounced publicly as a spy by the cable news channel Ennahar TV. She was rushed out on a plane by the French embassy on April 16. More generally, the uncertain political context revives a defensive nationalism inherited from the era of colonization.

To be fair, negative discourses do not only target foreigners and members of the ruling coalition. In this Tellian city, I witness the recurring tendency of my interlocutors to criticize their fellow citizens. As we leave Nidhal's house in the morning, one of his neighbors, an old lady who knew him as a kid, asks about his sister. After Nidhal explains that she is now living in Canada and has no desire to come back, the woman welcomes this decision. According to her, "the further away you stay from Algerians, the better you are." She associates the hardships of everyday life with what are sometimes described as the population's intrinsic flaws. The same day, I am walking in downtown Chlef with a member of the General Union of Algerian Workers (Union Générale des Travailleurs Algeriens), who is also an employee of the local social security office. As we discuss the ongoing strikes, he doesn't hide his annoyance: "Workers are always demanding more money. This is the Arab way. They don't work, they make claims." The labor organizer lambasts an ongoing social movement, which he presents as a symptom of "Arabness."

The following morning, I have an appointment with Karim, who promised to introduce me to the subtleties of Chlef's land use plan. As we talk about the proliferation of irregular housing and the appropriation of sidewalks, he launches into a comparison with Paris. According to him, the difference in terms of cleanliness is once again a "problem of mentality" (*mushkila ʿaqliyya*). "If the people litter or if they leave their bags of potatoes, it is not only because of the city's public services. We don't have this notion of common interest as you do in Europe," he explains. It goes without saying that these discourses respond to different motives. Yet they also share a couple of commonalities. Firstly, they direct their criticism toward the Algerian population to explain what they perceive as a pervasive state of anomie. Secondly, they echo a set of caricatures that reflect colonial discourses (the Algerian as lazy, dirty, troublesome). The presence of a French researcher likely encourages this negative depiction. Disparagement serves to establish a sense of connivance with an interlocutor,[12] especially when they are expected to endorse pejorative representations of the target. Yet as we will see throughout this book, these caricatures were also fueled by the feeling of a never-ending crisis.

This third fragment allows us to discern in Chlef various iterations of a nationwide effort to elucidate this long-standing crisis. Actors designate those who are to be held responsible, whether they incriminate external enemies or blame the whole population. This moment of judgment, in Arendt's sense, is essential to the quest for meaning inherent to any critical situation.[13] This effort can lead to criticism of the "culture" of the people in a way that is reminiscent of colonial discourses. Thus, the Algerian case illustrates the need for a postcolonial analysis of the government of the crisis; only then can we distance ourselves from preconceived markers of political modernity.[14] Far from being a caprice or a merely performative claim, such a decentering is essential: if ever a space could be characterized by radical political, social, and epistemological crisis, structured by a long-term existential threat, it was the colonial space.

The Book

In the pages that follow, I pursue a set of pragmatic objectives, starting with an elucidation of Algeria's recent trajectory. As the country was the object of considerably less outside attention prior to the 2019 uprising (or "Hirak," which means "movement"),[15] this work aims to restore intelligibility to the analysis. In this respect, it studies Bouteflika's Algeria as a polity shaped by a long-standing systemic crisis, one that has impacted every domain of social life. While the Algerian government has pursued a form of institutional amnesia in the name of reconciliation, I demonstrate that the extreme violence of the Dark Decade remained the bedrock of the subsequent political order. Moreover, the reforms engineered in the name of preventing additional calamities allowed for the reconfiguration of that order, the co-option of new social groups, and the management of dissent. Paternalistic ruling elites coerced the masses in the name of disciplining a society prone to chaos. The prevention of an imminent disaster guided the process of state restructuring, from the transformation of security apparatuses to the erection of clientelist networks. In other words, this book also studies an extreme version of the government of the crisis. Invoking a "social imaginary of emergency,"[16] this *governance by catastrophization* is based on the anxious wait for a disastrous turning point and serves to manage a population and a territory.

The first chapter starts with a historical overview of the Algerian crisis, from the mid-1980s to the uprising of 2019. To familiarize the reader with the country's recent trajectory, I propose a periodization in four phases: premises, climax, latency, revolution. Then, I present the current state of the field, namely by reviewing the literature dedicated to Algeria as well as recent works on the restructuring of Arab "authoritarian regimes." Finally, I introduce recent theoretical debates on the notion of crisis and discuss the definition that will be used in subsequent chapters.

Chapters 2 and 3 focus on the ruling coalition and the role of the crisis in its progressive reconfiguration since the end of the 1980s. While the ruling coalition is not the focus of this book, its internal dynamics exacerbate the fear of a political collapse and are essential to understanding the objective and subjective dimensions of the impending catastrophe. Chapter 2 looks at the most powerful institutions in the ruling coalition, the presidency and the army, and analyzes their respective roles in producing and mitigating the suspended disaster. It shows how they justified their dominant positions by claiming to protect the nation from a potential repetition of the Dark Decade. After dissecting the institutional and symbolic bases of their power, I investigate the moments of conflict in which military leaders opposed their civilian counterparts. This chapter introduces the cartelized power structure that allowed for the relative cohesion of a diverse set of actors and agencies within what is commonly labelled the *Pouvoir*. I contend that the ruling coalition is best understood as a cartel aimed at securing for its members privileged access to state power and limiting the risks resulting from external competition. At the same time, the cohesion of this cartel was undermined by internal competition, notably between the presidency and high-ranking army officers. The illegibility of these struggles fueled social anxiety and discredited the political authorities. Chapter 3 looks at how various reform initiatives enabled the transformation and extension of the cartel, beyond a core group of state elites. In order to provide a clearer understanding of its structure before the Hirak, I present a diagram of the cartel, with its different components, as well as their positioning vis-à-vis the state field. The final sections of the chapter focus on the role of corruption and clientelism, and the relationship between the state and society. They also describe the increased entanglements of public and private actors, thereby elucidating a power structure that seems both pyramidal and diffuse, and ensures both exclusion and integration.

Chapters 4 and 5 focus on the consequences of successive political and media openings since the late 1980s. They show the weaponization of liberal representative institutions and how the resulting discontent with formal politics contributed to the advent of the 2019 uprising. Chapter Four turns to the adoption of a pluralist party system from the perspective of the so-called Presidential Alliance. The first section highlights the main rhetorical and organizational features of the two ruling parties (the FLN and the RND—the Rassemblement National Démocratique, or National Democratic Rally), as well as the peculiar trajectory of former prime minister Abdelaziz Belkhadem. The chapter then focuses on a moderate Islamist party that participated in the government coalition from 1999 to 2012, the Movement for the Society of Peace (Ḥarakat Mujtamaʿa as-Silm). It shows that the violence of the 1990s facilitated the latter's co-option in the name of saving the country. At the same time, the increased commodification of politics resulted in the discrediting of established political actors and their pervasive inability to produce legitimacy. Chapter 5 continues the analysis of pluralist politics by focusing on opponents in the political and media fields. It shows that the regulation of freedoms under Bouteflika was based on the articulation of a top-down process of democratization with a state of exception legitimized by the possibility of a catastrophe. Critical actors faced a hybrid and unpredictable repression based on nonlethal "democratic" policing and extralegal punishments. Nonetheless, the contentious form of local politics showed the limits of this "upgrading." Facing intense domestic pressures, the ruling coalition regulated the expression of dissent but was unable to fully suppress it. While seemingly unable to achieve meaningful change, opponents contributed to the circulation of highly contentious discourses. As such, they maintained pressure on the cartel even if their fragmentation prevented them from presenting a credible alternative. As the ruling coalition was constantly depicted as a criminal organization in the public space, its "resilience" remained effectively limited.

The last two chapters look at the social impact of the model of governance by catastrophization. Chapter 6 investigates the seemingly never-ending crisis not only as a principle of government but also as a lived experience. Following a group of young men in the small town of Ain Bessem, in northeastern Algeria, it describes a quotidian existence marked by boredom, unemployment, and a feeling of entrapment and structural injustice (ḥogra). The chapter then describes the struggle of the National Committee for the Defense of the Rights of the Unemployed (Comité national pour la défense des droits des chômeurs), thus illustrating how social movements came increasingly to emphasize pacifism and patriotism and prioritize socioeconomic claims, while simultaneously drawing on a virulent anti-system narrative. Grassroots actors thus adapted to the model of governance by catastrophization and crafted new strategies to occupy public spaces that proved to be essential in the advent of the Hirak. Structural inequalities nonetheless contributed to the fragile status quo of the early 2010s, as the government responded to social unrest by prioritizing security-based policies and economic redistribution. In this context, activists persevered despite their exhaustion and testified to their experience of the catastrophe. Finally, chapter 7 focuses on the symbolic and epistemic violence resulting from this mode of governance. While subjected to the possibility of collapse, individuals proposed competing diagnoses in order to save their country. Despite widespread confusion, two distinct narratives emerged, both centered on the nature of the Algerian people. The first one was based on the continued assertion of an ideal of political sanctity inherited from the War of Liberation. Meanwhile, a competing narrative depicted an undisciplined, violent, and childish people who had allegedly failed to assimilate the principles of political modernity.

Reading Bouteflika's Algeria through the prism of governance by catastrophization, this monograph presents Algeria as a paradigmatic example of a system of government that has now spread around the globe. It shows how the routine management of multifaceted crises is based on a combination of paternalistic discourses, securitization, and reformism. At the same time, far from lamenting the powerlessness of the masses, this book testifies to the dilemmas and strategies of active resistance in an environment saturated with uncertainty and haunted by the ghosts of past violence.

The Suspended Disaster

1

A Never-Ending Crisis?

The crisis consists precisely in the fact that the old is dying and the new cannot be born; in this interregnum a great variety of morbid symptoms appear.
—Antonio Gramsci

There is in our country a genuine war of meanings. This war of meanings will continue for a long time because Algeria, as an observation field, remains a fascinating topic despite the difficulties faced by researchers and the grip of a political society that prevents access to information and stages a distorted truth in order to protect its power.
—Mohammed Harbi

There is sometimes something vertiginous in the act of scrutinizing Algerian politics. It is not that what is happening there is radically different from what is happening elsewhere, or incomprehensible, or unsettling. Rather, dizziness comes from the confrontation of divergent analyses that proliferate without ever achieving hegemony. The resulting maelstrom of competing realities will confound those who perceive the world as a block, a mass of cold and polished rock. Algeria, which is often reduced to the category of a rentier state, doesn't have this mineral simplicity. It is not even limited to a few asperities. Careful observers, whether they are journalists or researchers, proclaim their discordant analyses with the strength of definitive opinion. Yet their diagnoses often fail to achieve the status of a shared truth that prevails in the public space. This is where vertigo catches you, when the quest for certainty faces the abysmal lack of reliable information.

The ground of reality is moving. The waves of uncertainty are breaking. Analysts must be confident to resist the whirlwind of facts. They must have the courage of their convictions, even if this sometimes means being bound by them. Thus, not everything is unstable. There are some recurring themes: the *Pouvoir* is corrupt and omnipotent; Algerians lack discipline; the revolution was confiscated; Kabyles are more democratic; the state is unfinished; hydrocarbons are a curse. All these statements are at best simplistic, as I will show in this book. Simplistic assertions are part and parcel of the war of meanings described by Mohammed Harbi. Each of these peremptory statements carries a dose of violence. Together, they illustrate the tensions and conflicts inherent to any system of domination. In a context where reliable information is missing, where facts are slippery, clichés can nonetheless become new realities.

When Algeria is not reduced to preconceived categories (authoritarianism, rentier state, terrorism), it is often shrouded in mystery. Preconceived categories limit our imagination and mysteries foster fatalism. Instead, one needs to bring complexity and nuance back into the analysis. Mohammed Harbi did this masterfully by shedding light on the anticolonial revolution.[1] At the same time, there is no reason to develop a savior complex. The object of every research project gives much more than it receives. As Harbi suggests, Algeria "remains a fascinating topic" for political science and theory, notably because of the continuous transformation of its political and economic structures over more than forty years. After Houari Boumediene's death in 1978, the once socialist system slowly adapted under foreign and domestic pressures, notably by adopting political pluralism and a market economy. This gradual evolution turned Algeria into a remarkable example of selective conformity to globalized norms. As in many other countries, reformism became a mode of legitimation, management, exclusion, and integration.[2] Beyond the defense of vested interests, these selective transformations also demonstrate the continued relevance of one of the core themes of the revolution that threw off the colonial yoke: the defense of sovereignty. As sovereign power is often circular—it creates, protects, and restores power—state reformism cannot be disconnected from its self-reinforcing logic.

This chapter offers a description of the seemingly never-ending crisis that allowed for the restructuring of the Algerian system of domination. It then proposes a methodological and theoretical discussion of the notions of crisis and catastrophization. The historical overview that opens the chapter testifies to the limits of control, as the process of transformation was conjunctural. This crisis brought together an economic depression, a popular uprising, and a decade of violence, followed by twenty years of conflict between ruling elites, socioeconomic unrest, and residual terrorism. Prominent actors tried to manage successive upheavals but were also affected by them. Continuous instability impacted the calculations of rulers as well as ordinary citizens, all of whom were forced to improvise. Widespread uncertainty gave institutional politics a taste of the post-truth moment now so familiar around the world. Eventually, the uprising of 2019 came as a logical and yet unpredictable outcome of a transformative sociopolitical process that prioritized short-term resilience over long-term sustainability.

A Crisis in Four Steps

Beyond the polysemous nature of the notion of crisis, one of its defining characteristics is that it has an existential stake. In political terms, the existential threat exists at different levels: the country, the ruling coalition, the party or the association, the individual, etc. Such an existential threat was a key feature of Bouteflika's Algeria, as the government allegedly strove to preserve stability and prevent the liberation of the morbid forces hidden deep inside the national psyche. This shared representation of an enormous peril was certainly a legacy of the 1990s, but it was also more than just a simple trauma. Indeed, the possibility of a new break in the continuum of history seemed genuine. In its original Greek etymology, *krisis* at once evokes a disruptive action (judgment, choice, contestation) and a decisive event (the end of a war, the acute phase of a disease).[3] Paradoxically, the long-standing crisis that I describe in this book is also a matter of postponed disruption. In a context of unresolved tensions and catastrophic expectations, events remained potentially decisive until proven to be nonevents. The exceptional became residual and the existential threat merely an unbearable routine.

PREMISES

In its objective dimension, the crisis does not appear ex nihilo. It is the consequence of imbalances already existing in a system. Algeria became independent on July 5, 1962. At the time, society was profoundly destructured by more than 132 years of colonial occupation and eight years of bloody asymmetric war. In addition to the division of the country's new ruling elites, its economy was largely dependent on French capital and the population suffered from dire material conditions.[4] Nevertheless, Algeria was immediately caught in the Third Worldist whirlwind, which promised a future characterized by emancipation and international respectability. The country was at the forefront of a utopian effort to rebalance global geopolitics for the benefit of formerly colonized countries.[5] Following a series of setbacks, the idea of a political failure became commonplace in analyses of the decades that followed independence. This judgment should not be understood as a historical fact. Under Bouteflika, rather, this alleged failure was a contentious representation of history, a politicized understanding of the country's postcolonial trajectory.

Conversely, one must also be weary of an enchanted representation of the 1970s. While the ambition of the developmentalist programs implemented under the rule of Houari Boumediene (1965–1978) was to ensure the country's complete independence, they also contributed to the brutal transformation of society under the guidance of bureaucratic planning. The productive apparatus built by state-driven industrialization policies was never able to fully integrate the population surplus resulting from a period of tremendous demographic growth (from 11.8 million inhabitants in 1966 to 16.6 million in 1977). The focus on industrialization at the expense of a de-structured rural economy also fueled internal migration and caused housing shortages in rapidly growing urban centers.[6] Facing multiple challenges, the country was never in a position to "accomplish its industrialization," to use economist Gérard Destanne de Bernis's phrase.[7] This explains its continuous dependency on hydrocarbon rents. Thus, far from appearing suddenly in the 1980s under Chadli Bendjedid's fiercely criticized presidency (1979–1992), the first signs of a structural imbalance were noticeable from the end of the previous decade. According to sociologist Saïd Chikhi, the progressive deterioration of urban space and the increase in workers' protests were the first signs of a "general crisis of the Algerian social system."[8] This does not mean that subsequent developments were unavoidable.

A precarious equilibrium is a long-standing feature of Algerian politics. Even Houari Boumediene failed in unifying the country's ruling elites, who had remained profoundly divided since the beginning of the struggle for independence. To be sure, he managed to achieve the highest degree of concentration and personification of political power in the history of modern Algeria.[9] Yet his dominant position implied both his isolation and the rapid weakening of the equilibrium that prevailed after his untimely death in 1978. The fate of then minister of foreign affairs Abdelaziz Bouteflika is telling. Once considered Boumediene's heir, he was rapidly indicted for embezzling public money and forced to leave the country.

In parallel to the conflicts dividing ruling elites, the beginning of the 1980s witnessed the revitalization of political contestation. Against a backdrop of cultural malaise, identity-related mobilizations succeeded in challenging the grip of the single-party system.[10] The Berber Spring of 1980 and the first great Islamist meeting organized in Algiers in 1982 marked the revival of direct challenges to the government. The first jihadi maquis appeared under the command of Moustafa Bouyali. A former anticolonial fighter (or *mujāhid*), Bouyali saw this new jihad as the continuation of the struggle for independence against an "atheist" government that had abandoned its population and especially the urban *Lumpenproletariat*.[11]

After President Chadli launched an economic *aggiornamento* in the early 1980s, the ostentatious wealth of the rising bourgeoisie provided a brutal contrast with the pauperization of the urban working classes, which in turn nourished a widespread feeling of betrayal. In fast-growing cities, socioeconomic conditions continued their steady deterioration. The rising unemployment rate met with shortages of all kinds (drinking water, housing).[12] As the state was essential in addressing popular demands, it remained economically dependent on hydrocarbon rents. Yet the collapse of oil prices in 1986 put a stop to this financial manna. The ensuing contraction of government earnings resulted mechanically in a rapid augmentation of the country's external debt, a drop in imports, and skyrocketing inflation.¹³ In this context, recurring riots and strikes unveiled a growing discontent that was soon going to flood the streets.

CLIMAX

The structural conditions for the outbreak of the crisis had been established. It took root in the colonial period, in the conjunction between macroeconomic and political factors, as well as in the changes affecting Algerian society (demographic growth, cultural conflict). Nevertheless, structures cannot explain everything. The acceleration of the critical conjuncture (i.e. the crisis) and the rise in violence were also the consequences of unpredictable events that undermined the legitimacy of the country's political leaders and the principles organizing the polity. In other words, the crisis in its objective dimensions brought together accidental phenomena and underlying conflicts. It was fueled by events that were both symptomatic and conjunctural.

After the oil counter-shock, the country's crisis reached a climax in 1988. The dramatic and unexpected sequence of events that unfolded over the course of that year demonstrates the role of contingencies in this process.¹⁴ Following a waterskiing accident, Chadli spent the summer recovering from his injuries. Given the president's absence, there were pervasive rumors that various factions within the ruling coalition were fighting against each other to appoint a new head of state. On September 19, 1988, Chadli ended a long period of silence and delivered a remarkably virulent speech. Here is an excerpt from that speech as published by the government newspaper *El Moudjahid* the following day:

> We must not fool ourselves with the reports that are published, since duty requires . . . that we fight the evils and flaws that plague all sectors. We will list wastefulness, bureaucratic sluggishness, inertia, the monopoly on authority, the absence of state agencies allegedly supposed to monitor and sanction those who speculate on prices. It is fair to remark that state institutions are rather inefficient at monitoring these questions, which results in an inability to manage the national economy. The question of skill appears at every level [of the state].¹⁵

These words evoke the speeches of Mouloud Hamrouche and Ali Benflis, both of whom were mentioned in the preface. Indeed, the tendency to present a catastrophic situation in order to promote a reformist agenda has long been a strategy of Algerian politicians. It illustrates the intimate relationship between the imaginary of emergency and reformist governance. In September 1988, nonetheless, Chadli's speech also unveiled the deep fractures dividing the state apparatus. Ongoing socioeconomic conflicts were now expressed in clearly political terms, as the presidency and its reformist advisers opposed the FLN's old guard.

In the fall of 1988, Algeria entered a phase of intense dramatization fueled by actors in both the government and opposition movements. Throughout the year, the repressive machine had already turned against leftist activists who organized dissent in the factories. On October 4, 1988, hundreds of youth from the working-class neighborhoods of Algiers took to the streets to express their anger and fight the police. On the following day, the unrest spread to the rest of the capital. It then reached the Mitidja region and the commuter towns where shanty dwellers had been relocated, before rapidly sweeping the country from Annaba in the east to Oran in the west. The government established a curfew and requested the intervention of the National People's Army (Armée Nationale Populaire, ANP). This was a major symbolic break. Until then, the ANP had been portrayed as the heir of the National Liberation Army and its revolutionary struggle against the French. In October 1988, it fired on its own people and took part in the arrest and torture of thousands. On October 10, after an Islamist-led demonstration in the center of Algiers ended in a bloodbath, Chadli committed to a series of profound reforms.[16]

The popular uprising of October was also the outcome of a gradual rise in contention and coercion. Since the early 1980s, football stadiums had become hot spots for the expression of dissidence and were increasingly subjected to state repression.[17] Moreover, the country experienced more than fourteen hundred strikes between October and December 1988, resulting in recurring clashes between protesters and riot police. Workers' disenchantment had spilled out of the factories and into the streets, where it met with the anger of disaffected youth.[18] The uprising of October thus appears to represent a confluence of political contingency, structural imbalances, and the development of new contentious and repressive practices.

A new constitution, adopted in February 1989, enacted the reforms promised by Chadli. After trying to depoliticize the unrest, bureaucratic and military elites accepted an opening under the pressure of various opposition groups. The subsequent dramatization of national politics was thus intertwined with the transition to partisan pluralism and the resulting intensification of political competition. The newly formed Islamic Salvation Front (al-Jabha al-Islāmiyya li-l-Inqādh, though the group is normally called by its French abbreviation, FIS, for Front Islamique du Salut) positioned itself as the main challenger to the ruling coalition. This heterogeneous Islamist movement was initially "undetermined," meaning it emerged opportunistically and was able to embody the contentious message preached in mosques.[19] Its spokespersons revived the nationalist rhetoric inherited from anticolonial struggle to denounce treacherous elites within the state. After their victory in the municipal elections of 1990, Islamist leaders drew on their own security services, which were partly made up of veterans coming back from Afghanistan. These militias patrolled the neighborhoods under their control in order to enforce an "Islamic order." The FIS claimed the right to define what was licit and illicit, to exercise legitimate violence, and to promote its own education model. Accordingly, despite its participation in pluralist politics, it also positioned itself as a radical enemy of the ruling coalition, thereby contributing to the dramatization of national politics.[20]

Throughout 1991 and 1992, a series of strategic choices fueled these tensions. During the first Gulf War, the reformist government of Mouloud Hamrouche decided to remain neutral, a choice that was decried by the FIS in the name of pan-Islamic solidarity. At the national level, the government passed a new electoral law in preparation for the upcoming legislative elections, which included substantial gerrymandering for the benefit of the FLN. In retaliation, the FIS launched a month-long insurrectional strike to obtain the law's withdrawal and trigger an anticipated presidential election. This mobilization resulted in the declaration of a state of siege, the resignation of Mouloud Hamrouche, and the arrest of the FIS's two main leaders, Abassi Madani and Ali Belhadj. Tensions decreased over the summer of 1991, following government-led consultations and the FIS's appointment of a more pragmatic leadership embodied by Abdelkader Hachani. Eventually, both sides agreed to facilitate the upcoming legislative elections.

Despite announcing the participation of the FIS less than two weeks before the elections, Islamist leaders ran an effective blitz campaign, and the party was successful in the first round of the elections.[21] Hachani urged

Islamist supporters to show moderation and respect for democratic procedures. He also tried to demonstrate the party's commitment to negotiation with the army and the presidency, without renouncing its Islamist agenda. In early January 1992, the press reported a secret meeting between Hachani and President Chadli.[22]

The generals of the ANP had other plans. Supported by much of the secular middle and upper classes, the military occupied the streets of Algiers on January 11, 1992, and forced Chadli to resign. The second round of the elections was cancelled the next day. On the fourteenth, a High Committee of State (Haut Comité d'État, HCE) was created to avoid a power vacuum at the executive level. In response, Hachani called for peaceful opposition to the coup. He was finally arrested after publishing a call for soldiers and policemen to "give up their allegiances to despots" and respect "the choice of the people."[23] Meanwhile, Mohamed Boudiaf, a leader of the historic uprising of 1954 against the French, had returned from almost thirty years in exile to head the HCE. Saying that the country was facing a crisis "of considerable magnitude" and calling for "radical change,"[24] Boudiaf decreed a state of emergency in February 1992 (it lasted until February 2011). He also launched a massive crackdown on Islamist activists, banning the FIS in March 1992. But this only fueled a progressive rise in violence. Boudiaf was assassinated three months later by a member of his security detail. The first terrorist attack targeting civilians occurred at Algiers International Airport in August 1992. This crescendo of violence was the consequence of a series of variously pragmatic, cynical, or idealist calculations made by a wide range of actors (state and non-state, civilian and military, self-proclaimed defenders of secularism and more or less radical Islamists).

It would be futile to try to summarize the ensuing Dark Decade in a paragraph. The goal of this overview is to show the entanglements of unpredictable events, strategic choices, and structural factors in the advent of the crisis. As for the civil conflict, it caused the death of between 150,000 and 200,000 people and was accompanied by forms of extreme brutality that are exceptional for the region.[25] It also fueled the atomization of the political field, a security-motivated exodus toward northern cities, a pervasive confusion regarding the identity and motivations of violent actors, and the fragmentation of society. In an economic context marked by massive inflation and nonexistent growth, the government also signed an agreement with the International Monetary Fund and the World Bank for the implementation of a structural adjustment program in 1994. At the end of the 1990s, the country, deprived of credible civilian leadership, was facing a multifaceted crisis.

LATENCY

The first steps toward a settlement of the conflict were achieved under the rule of retired general Liamine Zeroual (1994–1999). Appointed president of the HCE and therefore de facto head of state, Zeroual promoted the law on *raḥma* (forgiveness) for repentant jihadis in 1995. The same year, he was elected president of the republic in the first election since the coup. This political normalization allowed for the marginalization of the ruling coalition's fiercest critics.[26] In 1997, negotiations with the political wing of the FIS lead to the temporary release of Abassi Madani. A few months later, the Islamic Salvation Army, the FIS's armed wing, declared a unilateral ceasefire. Nevertheless, a series of civilian massacres perpetrated by the Armed Islamic Group (Groupe Islamique Armé, GIA) and a major political scandal—to be discussed in the next chapter—led to Zeroual's resignation. This is how Abdelaziz Bouteflika became president of the republic in April 1999.

Closing the painful chapter of the Dark Decade, which official discourses prefer to call by the apolitical term "National Tragedy" (*al-Māʾsāa al-Waṭaniyya*), was the cornerstone of Bouteflika's political platform. Bouteflika based his legitimacy on his ability to pacify the polity, notably through the organization of two referendums on "Civil Concord" (*al-Wiʾām al-Madanī*) in 1999 and "National Reconciliation" (*al-Muṣālaḥa al-Waṭaniyya*) in 2005, both of which benefited from massive popular support. During Bouteflika's first three terms, the government also carried out highly symbolic projects such as the East–West Highway and the Algiers Metro. It implemented large, state-driven programs to compensate for housing shortages and youth unemployment. From a macroeconomic perspective, the situation improved greatly. Between 2000 and 2010, the country's nominal GDP almost tripled, and this growth also included non-hydrocarbon-related activities. The official unemployment rate was at 10 percent in 2010, having reached nearly 30 percent ten years earlier.[27] This economic success nonetheless relied largely on public investments. Thus, high inflation and hydrocarbon dependency remained defining features of the country's economy. As a result, businessmen and pro-market economists often echoed the catastrophist political discourses with their own pessimistic predictions. According to the think tank Nabni, an economic reversal or the exhaustion of oil and gas reserves could lead to a return to the dark years of recession.[28] Such persistent economic fragility was nonetheless insufficient evidence to support the argument that the crisis remained latent.

Indeed, Bouteflika's rule was also characterized by perceived security threats and continuous expressions of dissent. After the Dark Decade came the era of "residual terrorism." The GIA was replaced by the Salafist Group for Preaching and Combat (al-Jamā'a al-Salafiyya lil-Da'wa wal-Qitāl), which later turned into al-Qaeda in the Islamic Maghreb. Moreover, the reestablishment of an ostensibly civilian government did not put an end to the questions regarding the cohesion and legitimacy of the ruling coalition. From this perspective, Bouteflika's first mandate saw at least two episodes suggesting a sudden intensification of the political order's contradictions. In the spring of 2001, the assassination of high school student Massinissa Guermah in a gendarmerie barrack prompted a major uprising in Kabylia. The mountainous region located about a hundred kilometers east of Algiers had already been the epicenter of the Berber Spring in 1980. In 2001, the combination of bloody repression and political inaction led to the radicalization of the protesters. A mass demonstration in the capital, home to an important Kabyle community, was again violently suppressed. The unrest lasted more than a year, caused more than a hundred deaths, and exacerbated identity-based claims in Kabylia, further isolating the region. It also exposed the continuation of state violence and alienated Berberist parties.[29]

A second period of instability followed the rebellion staged by Ali Benflis, the prime minister and the general secretary of the FLN, against Abdelaziz Bouteflika in 2003. The party, formerly the country's sole legal political group, had just returned to its dominant position after being "punished" for refusing to support the 1992 coup. Despite the sacking of Benflis and the judicial takeover of the FLN executive by members of the presidential entourage, antagonisms in the state persisted, notably between the presidency and members of the army who supported Benflis. Bouteflika's crushing victory in the 2004 presidential elections eventually ended this particular challenge to his authority. Nonetheless, these tensions at the top of the state revived the specter of conflict that had plagued Chadli's presidency. According to legal scholar Chérif Bennadji, the country was then confronted with a conjunction of "political, security and financial" crises.[30]

Taken separately, political instability and economic fragility are not intrinsically critical. Neither are the quasi-daily repetition of strikes, riots, infighting within political parties, or catastrophist discourses from public figures. Yet all these pervasive structural imbalances and recurring troubles maintained the possibility of a major upheaval. Moreover, they nourished a feeling of anomie and continued danger for the national community in a context of post-conflict stabilization. It is then that the idea of a latent crisis makes sense, appearing as it does at the crossroads of objective and subjective factors, when concrete and repeated episodes made an imminent collapse plausible. This latency is only made meaningful, however, through its relation to the previous climax, which remains the standard of an existential threat to the entire community and provides the relevant actors with exemplary and potentially recurring episodes of violence (the October 1988 uprising, the military coup of 1992, the massacres of 1997–1998).

The possibility of an imminent catastrophe reappeared at the end of Bouteflika's third term following a series of domestic upheavals (the corruption scandals of 2010, an urban uprising in 2011, the president's stroke in 2013) and regional turbulence (the Arab uprisings of 2011, Western military interventions in Libya and Mali). In this uncertain context, the seemingly never-ending nature of the crisis was a matter of perception rather than a definitive state of affairs. In a situation marked by structural uncertainty, one must not overlook the "social potential for ending as well as unending history."[31]

THE HIRAK

After a wave of urban clashes in January 2011, social unrest did not diminish. A very active yet fragmented society gave birth to multiple peaceful initiatives and incessant social movements, mixing economic and political claims.[32] Until late 2013, the Algerian government was to an extent able to address the population's socioeconomic demands and contain domestic pressures by drawing on hydrocarbon rents. The widespread discrediting and fragmentation of the forces of political opposition prevented the emergence of a genuine alternative. Yet, following a rapid drop in hydrocarbon prices in 2014, the government's ability to mitigate the effects of rising inequality quickly eroded. With the first signs of budget scarcity and a government turn to austerity, the mismanagement of national wealth became impossible to ignore. The economic and political dimensions of the latent crisis merged with public denunciations of a corrupt oligarchy that had plundered the country's national wealth. On social media or in the independent press, journalists and citizens described a national emergency resulting from a mix of incompetence and predation. The scandal over the East–West Highway, uncovered in 2010, became synonymous with the moral failure and greed of government officials.

A now incapacitated Bouteflika was reelected in 2014 with 81 percent of the vote. As I already mentioned in the preface, this electoral race saw multiple expressions of growing discontent. In addition to the protests organized by the Barakat movement, Bouteflika's campaign team was repeatedly met by angry protesters, and was even forced to cancel some rallies. Over the next five years, the political leadership's lack of legitimacy, combined with the ongoing budget crisis, continued to nourish tensions. In 2015, the powerful military intelligence services were dismantled and their long-standing chief, Mohammed Mediène, forced to retire in an attempt to assert presidential hegemony. In 2017, the government's inability to propose a coherent economic strategy led to the sacking of two prime ministers in three months, followed by the return of the widely hated Ahmed Ouyahia as chief of the government. Finally, in 2018, chief of national police and pillar of the ruling coalition, Abdelghani Hamel, was discharged following a drug trafficking scandal.

In early 2019, most economic indicators were negative: unemployment (11.7 percent), inflation (4.2 percent), and the trade deficit ($1.14 billion) were all on the rise. Meanwhile, government officials systematically associated dissent with immaturity at best and sedition (*fitna*) at worst. Ahmed Ouyahia routinely invoked the fate of Libya and Syria as a reminder of what could happen in the case of a popular uprising. Nevertheless, this catastrophist narrative was increasingly challenged in the public space. In football stadiums, fans denounced the cost of living and chanted their rejection of the ruling class with slogans like "Niktu l-blad, yā siraqīn!" (You fucked the country, bunch of thieves!). When attending meetings across the country, Ouyahia was regularly met by angry protesters, whom he in turn portrayed as anarchists (*fawḍawiyīn*). Bit by bit, the society shattered by the Dark Decade reconnected with the dichotomous politics once deemed essential to the anticolonial struggle. Algerian youth came to play a central role in the construction of a new antagonistic repertoire. As a heterogeneous sociological category, the youth signified the common experience of a generation that came of age in the 1990s and their aftermath. It also had an essentially negative meaning, constructed in opposition to the ruling coalition and the never-ending crisis, which by now had become a sort of *modus vivendi*.[33]

After weeks of sporadic protest across the country, the Algerian Hirak started on February 22, 2019, in opposition to the announcement of President Abdelaziz Bouteflika's intention to run for a fifth term. On every Tuesday and Friday after that date, millions of citizens demonstrated across the country. Bouteflika was eventually forced to resign on April 2 of that year. Yet the Hirak did not stop, and Algerians continued to denounce the "System," which they said still had to be uprooted. After twenty years of latency, another unexpected intensification of the critical conjuncture resulted in a revolutionary movement.

Studying Bouteflika's Algeria

A handful of questions emerge from this rapid historical overview: What is a latent crisis, in concrete terms? How is it reproduced on a daily basis, and what are its social, political, and economic manifestations? How can it become a principle of government and a resource for the durability of the ruling coalition? There are other, more pragmatic questions too, about the internal dynamics that shape the ruling coalition, the hybridization between authoritarian rule, economic restructuring, and democratization, and the strategies of the political opposition and various social movements. These questions go to the very core of both the relevant scholarship on the Algerian crisis and the methodological concerns that underpin this research. (Readers interested in a more fact-based analysis of these issues might skip the following methodological and theoretical sections and go directly to chapter 2.)

THE ALGERIAN CRISIS IN THE ACADEMIC LITERATURE

Since the collapse of the single-party system and the economic meltdown of the late 1980s, commentators have sometimes described Algeria as a country that resists analysis. Yet the country's trajectory has also inspired many works emphasizing one or several dimensions of its multifaceted crisis. Despite the confusion on the ground, scholars have studied the meanings, origins, and functions of violence during the Dark Decade through a variety of lenses, including those of social psychology, political sociology, and cultural anthropology.[34] Some have focused on a specific social group, as is the case, for example, in Tristan Leperlier's study of the conflict's impact on writers.[35] Others have looked at its significance from the perspective of humanitarianism and conflict management.[36]

In order to elucidate the root causes of the country's descent into chaos and the persistence of the "System," researchers have often followed dominant trends in comparative politics and economics. For example, many have read the Algerian crisis through the prism of failed development and rentier states.[37] Works in political economy have notably focused on the limits inherent to the developmentalist policies promoted under Boumediene in a context of intense ideological and/or sociological divisions among ruling elites.[38] They have also tried to understand the dismantling of the state-driven productive apparatus and the rise of new predatory behaviors in the context of economic restructuring.[39]

Another major trend in this scholarship has studied Algeria through the twin lenses of democratization and authoritarian resilience. Many of these works appropriated the normative categories of liberal comparative politics without questioning their heuristic dimension in non-liberal, postcolonial political environments. Some authors have sought to understand the short-lived political opening and the rise in violence by focusing on the emergence of political Islam as a challenger to the government,[40] by looking at institutional politics in a comparative fashion,[41] or by trying to offer a more complex and multidimensional reading of the crisis.[42] In the 2000s, scholars became increasingly interested in the question of authoritarian resilience in a seemingly democratic context. Some focused on the role of international factors in the "failed" transition to democracy.[43] Others looked at the composition and strategies of ruling elites,[44] the link between corruption and elections,[45] or the engagement with pluralist politics.[46] After 2011, Algerian researchers also systematically questioned the ambiguity of the political reforms implemented by the government.[47]

More recently, researchers inspired by political sociology and anthropology have renewed our understanding of Bouteflika's Algeria by moving away from a state- and democracy-centered approach. By looking at social movements and migrations, these scholars have provided some key insights into the strategies of marginal social groups confronted with widespread precariousness and uncertain legal frameworks.[48] By prioritizing fieldwork and returning to direct observation, despite the difficulties underlined by Harbi, they restored the legibility of the Algerian trajectory in the last years of Bouteflika's rule. While this book is broadly indebted to these scholars' insights, it nonetheless differs by combining extensive fieldwork with a theory of the crisis. In so doing, it draws on the Algerian case to offer an innovative framework for thinking about the future of governance.

Algeria once occupied a central place in theoretical innovation, providing as it were the raw material for a series of important intellectual projects, from Frantz Fanon's seminal works to the development of critical sociology with Pierre Bourdieu and Abdelmalek Sayad. Algerian thinkers such as Mohamed Arkoun and Malek Bennabi also developed original ways, situated at the crossroads of diverse philosophical traditions, of thinking about Islam, politics, and culture. While the study of Algeria still allows for the production of ambitious theoretical reflections,[49] more recent works tend to focus on questions of philosophy, literature, and aesthetics, and have a historical rather than a contemporary focus. With the exception of several recently published volumes,[50] the study of politics in Bouteflika's Algeria has too often been limited to questions traditionally attached to area studies: authoritarian persistence, social movements, clientelism, violence, the place of women and youth, and economic restructuring. Each of these issues are fundamental to understanding Bouteflika's Algeria, and they will be discussed in this book accordingly. All the same, my own account also draws on a more critical approach to propose an original analytical framework. As a case study located in the Global

South and informed by theory, this research is notably influenced by the works of Fernando Coronil, Achille Mbembe, and Béatrice Hibou.

This return to critical theory is made necessary by the historical overview presented here. The seemingly never-ending crisis came with its share of economic, physical, and symbolic violence. It created confusion and uncertainty and legitimated fatalistic representations of the polity, in both Algeria and the West, even after the remarkably peaceful uprising of 2019.[51] In response, critical theory resounds with the imperative to transform crisis into knowledge, and to overcome fatalism by reaffirming the possibility of a future free of the present violence.[52] It is necessary to develop a heuristic framework to study the country, without being constrained by pessimistic expectations and cultural exceptionalism.

THE RAGPICKER'S QUEST

The idea of a return to theory could suggest an abstract endeavor detached from the realities of fieldwork. Conversely, Kuhnian and Latourian epistemologies have developed a robust critique of an understanding of research limited to concrete facts and a-sociological truths. To be sure, the debate opposing abstractionism to positivism is a dead end. Rather than separating the idea from its material roots, I propose an immersive, qualitative, and participative approach to better discover the object of this study and its stakes.[53] To this end, the book draws on ethnographic fieldwork conducted between 2008 and 2014. It relates first-hand observations and recounts the experiences, reflections, and strategies of more than thirty interviewees representing a wide social and political spectrum. As such, it is entirely structured by the search for an equilibrium between theoretical generalizations and empirical observations.

Once confronted with the difficulties identified by Mohammed Harbi, the researcher becomes an integral part of the study. In my case, it goes without saying that this research was deeply impacted by the postimperial configuration that characterized my position as a French scholar in Algeria. Moreover, as a "Westerner" in an "Arab" country, the outside researcher is invariably caught up in the context created by the "war on terror."[54] From this perspective, once again, the suspicions of some of my interlocutors, as related in the preface, were not only normal—they were symptomatic of a political culture shaped by two centuries of European and American interference. From a pragmatic perspective, this means that it was more challenging, in a country marked by strong bureaucratic and police control, to access certain restricted places and to convince people to trust me with possibly sensitive opinions. As Algeria implements a visa policy based on reciprocity, the prospect of my being banned from the country was very real (indeed, it became a reality after 2014). I was thus systematically forced to assess the possibilities of fieldwork and to second-guess the rules imposed by the state on foreign researchers. Over the course of my work, I was never able to locate the limits of state tolerance with certainty, probably because these limits were not meant to be legible. As such, the reflexive approach proposed in this book aims to recognize the researcher as an admittedly secondary object of their study, even when it comes to one's prejudices and discomfort.[55]

This approach to research might generate legitimate questions. How can one claim to draw on empirical fieldwork when studying the trajectory of a country over some twenty years, especially when this country has more than forty million inhabitants and is the largest by geographical area in Africa and the wider Arab world? As I made the choice to conduct most of my semi-structured interviews with opponents of the ruling coalition, I was primarily exposed to their perspectives. In a political environment marked by surveillance and repression, developing trust and social proximity proved essential to documenting my interlocutors' political struggles and lived experiences. At the same time, it also meant that their political discourses, notably their appropriation of the normative language of human rights and liberal democracy, influenced my fieldwork. In this regard, the privilege of social proximity also came with the challenge of maintaining a critical distance and the need to constantly reinterpret the data collected.[56] This work was certainly made easier by the fact that, despite the alleged inaccessibility of Algeria as a field of study, I was not alone in developing such familiarity with these actors. Discussions with colleagues conducting their own research during the same period was key to understanding the ethnographic relationship that I had built with my interviewees and informants. These exchanges were also essential in testing my hypotheses. This certainly doesn't mean that the work presented in these pages is devoid of flaws. Despite my best efforts, the heroic narratives and normative expectations of those who kindly accepted to speak with me may well rise to the surface on occasion. This is probably inevitable, given that one of the purposes of this book is to make their voices heard. Nonetheless, following labor organizers, students, and politicians allowed me to observe their actual practices more freely. And it lowered the risk that I might be confronted with standardized and institutional discourses. This approach was also a matter of pragmatism, as I had neither the resources, the information, nor the authority required to ask challenging questions of more prominent actors and state officials.[57] As a result, the individuals interviewed in this book were not ministers or prominent businessmen. Most of them were grassroots activists and mid-level politicians. Many had another profession in addition to their political activities. In their own way, they faced the effects of the seemingly never-ending crisis and tried to formulate an alternative. They came from various ideological backgrounds (Berberist, Islamist, liberal, Trotskyist), and some even abandoned politics or radically reconsidered the form of their activism. To capture their daily practices and experiences, the book complements these interviews with impromptu observations that allow for the depiction of a fragmented reality.

The impressionistic portrayal of a social and political landscape requires additional interpretative work. This study is not about imposing the arbitrary truth of theory; rather it is about uncovering an assemblage and its unlimited complexity. Pieces of the field must be brought into dialogue with one another, juxtaposed and rearranged, so that a semblance of cohesion can emerge. From this perspective, such a research practice echoes the peripatetic habits of Walter Benjamin's ragpicker, the collector of historical leftovers who brings back meaning to better understand critical times.[58]

This book was largely written before the uprising of 2019. As such, it owes most of its substance to the fragmented testimonies of those who tried to escape domination. Together, from Tizi Ouzou to Algiers, from Ghardaïa to Chlef, interviewees described the routine of the latent crisis that choked Bouteflika's Algeria. Far from belonging to one coherent social class or to a category of actors targeted consciously, they often emerged spontaneously, in the course of mundane discussions. It was in moments like these that my role as a ragpicker, as an organizer of various experiences "in tatters," was most obvious. These discontinuous testimonies are the humus out of which the reflections presented in the following pages ultimately took root.

From Crisis to Catastrophization

Reflecting on May 1968, sociologist Edgar Morin pointed out that the notion of crisis had "spread to every horizon of human consciousness in the 20th century" and was therefore "emptied from the inside."[59] Despite this haziness, the notion of crisis remains essential when thinking about rapidly changing social structures and the subjection of entire populations to the rule of emergency and uncertainty. The notion helps make sense of politics in "dark times," as disastrous forces seem to obliterate light and destroy reason in the Middle East and beyond.[60] At the same time, critical processes can also become strategic resources. Actors can benefit from emergency and uncertainty to promote their agendas. From this perspective, the management of crisis can become a tool for social control and capital accumulation.

DEFINITION

In order to overcome the polysemous nature of the notion and offer a conceptual bedrock for further discussion, I propose the following definition of crisis: a multifaceted and undetermined political process, synonymous with the exacerbation of the contradictions and violence already existing in the social system, that endangers the dominant order and results in securitizing discourses and policies.

Firstly, as a *multifaceted political process*, the crisis is not limited to one sector but rather affects multiple social spaces in diverse ways.[61] As a result, the consequences of the process are neither limited to the "economic crisis," understood as combination of economic breakdown, budget scarcity, and rising unemployment, nor to the "political crisis," which results in the empowerment of extremist movements and the rejection of prevailing authorities. Rather, the crisis implies a succession of contingent failures that impact various interdependent elements of a social system. This results in a situation of general instability. As Michel Dobry points out in his seminal study, during "critical conjunctures," the increased fluidity of social relations provokes multiple "sectoral interferences."[62] The crisis spreads among sectors, whether this is because actors reproduce their conflicts within state institutions or because economic contradictions lead to a crisis of hegemony for the ruling coalition.[63] The multifaceted dimension of the process thus reveals the entanglements of different social fields (in Bourdieusian terms) or the codetermination of the base and the superstructure (in Marxian terms). The ability of actors to occupy various positions in different social sectors (i.e., multi-positioning) affects their capacity to resist the crisis and even benefit from it. The fluidity characteristic of the critical conjuncture thus offers strategic opportunities.

Secondly, the process is *undetermined* insofar as it unfolds outside of any predefined historical, political, or cultural logic. It is even possible that the crisis might result in nothing more than the status quo ante, or something approaching it. This indetermination turns the notion of change into a central stake for political debates, even for those who strive to maintain order. Actors speculate constantly on the outcome of the process to craft appropriate strategies. Dobry considers structural uncertainty to be one of the most essential features of the crisis, which means that the tools of evaluation previously used by actors in their daily calculations lose some of their efficacy.[64] Yet the historical overview proposed here suggests a slightly different interpretation. Indeed, once the crisis lasts for any length of time, and includes a period of latency, structural uncertainty itself becomes part of actors' routines. The difficulty of accurately assessing the state of political struggles and economic conjunctures is therefore integrated into their daily calculations.

The third element of the definition is the *exacerbation of the contradictions and violence already existing in the social system*. During a critical conjuncture, social fluidity and uncertainty allow for the radical questioning of preestablished power relations. In a context marked by a shortage of available resources and an intensification of related struggles, antagonisms sharpen and are expressed publicly. Changes in terms of who can access resources and under what conditions can result in the diffusion of violence throughout society, for strategic purposes.[65] In addition, the crisis exacerbates the systemic violence that usually serves the reproduction of social relations and particularly relations of domination. Far from being limited to its physical dimension, systemic violence can be economic (e.g., precariousness), institutional (e.g., the arbitrariness of the law), or symbolic (e.g., paternalism). As the critical conjuncture unfolds, the intensification of violence can lead to a hypothetical point of no return, after which it becomes impossible to prevent a catastrophe.

This brings us to the fourth element of our definition: *the endangering of the dominant order*. As an undetermined process, the crisis represents a threat to the established organization of society. The social world is shaped by relations of power that arrange its inherent plurality; it is structured in a way that reproduces the unequal distribution of resources and positions of influence between its members. I use the term "political order" to describe the system that institutionalizes relations of power, resource inequalities, and social divisions by drawing on categories and hierarchies. At the national level, the state is the main entity in charge of enforcing the rules, norms, and inequalities that structure the political order. As a multifaceted and cross-sectoral moment that renders social relations fluid, the crisis questions the order that divides and organizes society. For this reason, a key existential stake resulting from the critical conjuncture is the survival of the political order. But it is not the only one: the rise in violence, whether it is real or merely perceived, makes survival a key concern for individual and collective actors as well.

This, in turn, leads to the fifth and final element in our definition: *securitizing discourses and policies*. These responses demonstrate the defensive orientation of politics, as the government and opposition parties, and also independent think tanks and/or journalists, integrate the crisis into their daily calculations. Securitization has become a mundane way to shape public policies around the world.[66] It relies on the social construction of specific issues as major threats to the polity. This results in the constant growth of security apparatuses and the routinization of exceptional procedures in order to cope with a situation of alleged emergency. As it shapes subjectivities, the critical conjuncture allows for the securitization of entire sectors of human life. At the same time, securitization is not merely a form of fearmongering, as various upheavals can produce a context that objectivizes this security-based rationale (economic meltdown, terrorist attacks, mass protests). Moreover, previous critical events can serve as concrete references for securitizing discourses and policies (in the Algerian case, the uprising of October 1988 or the 1992 military coup). The crisis is therefore at the same time a sociohistorical process and a guiding rationale for securitized forms of governance.

STRATEGIES AND REPRESENTATIONS

For actors, the crisis is synonymous with constraints and opportunities. Strategies evolve according to the fluidity of positions and the unpredictability of events. According to Dobry, "structural uncertainty must have an impact on the psychological state of individuals."[67] If this is true for short-term critical conjunctures, it is certainly the case when crises continue over more than three decades. The impact is nonetheless different. If structural uncertainty can be perceived as a radical opening of possible futures, it can also result in more conservative behaviors. Dobry describes a "regression to the habitus," a return to ingrained habits that compensates for the crumbling of institutions.[68] As uncertainty lasts and is incorporated into the daily functioning of organizations, conservative behaviors become conscious strategies. Once it becomes latent, the crisis is paradoxically normalized. Actors can establish alliances, adapt their repertoires of action, and craft appropriate policies. Consequently, contradictions within the ruling coalition, the unpredictability of repression, false flag operations implemented by the intelligence services, or a potential rise in violence all became familiar terrain for Algerian activists, who conceived their strategies accordingly.

Actors can progressively rationalize the possibility of violence, as the unstable political and social equilibrium makes a confrontation between competing groups more likely. Gramsci once described a crisis as a "situation [that] becomes sensitive and dangerous, because a space opens for power grabs and the activity of obscure forces."[69] During the climax, the possibility of a generalized confrontation between two competing blocs exists, following the Turkish example.[70] Yet this antagonistic configuration is not the only threat. The collapse of state legitimacy can lead to the proliferation of groups using violence to pursue various motives. The crisis thus allows for the brutal resolution of long-standing conflicts.

In parallel, radical discourses, violent acts, and the illegible strategies of political organizations popularize representations of a society caught in a maelstrom of irrationality. For instance, Marnia Lazreg described Algeria in the 1990s as being in a "state of cultural and political delirium."[71] This does not mean that individual and collective choices stopped responding to logical calculations, yet the protracted crisis nourished depictions of a society that had lost its ability to reason. Without taking them at face value, discourses that uphold the population's cultural confusion influence politics. There lies the symbolic dimension of the critical conjuncture. As the multifaceted crisis impacts the whole social system, it also affects actors' representations, conditioning their understanding of the impending disaster as well as the reforms that could prevent it. The entire process can thus be understood as a moment of learning and resocialization that can eventually contribute to stabilizing the political order.

TEMPORALITIES

The question of the length and pace of the crisis underlies the overview presented in the first section of this chapter. The chapter's title itself invokes the notion of a "never-ending crisis," and might therefore rightfully fuel skepticism. The critical conjunctures studied by sociologist Michel Dobry can last a few weeks to a couple of months. Dobry focuses his gaze on the climax, without paying much attention to what follows. Yet here I contend that the climax of the crisis enjoys an afterlife during a period of latency, when critical dynamics are still at work and continue to influence the daily functioning of society. Consequently, it is possible to think about a critical conjuncture that continues over several decades, assuming the status of a seemingly permanent social state.

The idea itself seems to be an oxymoron. If the critical process is "an evolutive state, conceived as transitory," it seems "absurd to speak about a 'permanent crisis.' "[72] At the same time, the process is undetermined and therefore has no necessary end point. It is impossible to base our reasoning on the hypothetical end of the process, whether it is a return to normalcy or a collapse. Moreover, the crisis is not limited to a phase of transition, an exceptional moment between two periods of normalcy. It can also be a fragile state of equilibrium. Dobry himself insists on the necessity of thinking about the normalcy of a social process before analyzing it.[73] As a result, uncertainty and indetermination remain essential factors. The external observer can never completely reject the hypothesis of the "unpredictable survival of a system in perpetual crisis," a situation where "the breaking-point ... is continuously postponed," as was the case for the Italian system described by Norberto Bobbio.[74] As we already saw, the Algerian configuration was precisely characterized by such an "equilibrium of instability," which allowed for the resilience of a political order structured by an accumulation of contradictions.[75] It is thus logical to think of the critical conjuncture as having an indefinite (which is not to say *infinite*) quality.

Moreover, what is transitory from the perspective of history can seem permanent from the point of view of the individual. As much as it is an objective reality, the crisis also has a subjective dimension to it; indeed, it is a lived experience, a specific relationship to time that prevents one's projection into the future.[76] As the length of the critical conjuncture makes it a constant condition of human experience, its existential stakes are felt at the individual level. In addition, the crisis assumes a specific temporality. It can impact entire generations, for whom it is the dominant form of socialization. The transitory state has thus become a social condition, a routine where seemingly exceptional features have been normalized, whether it is the terrorist attack, the riot, or the state of emergency. For this reason, if a critical conjuncture lasts for more than thirty years, as is the case in Algeria, it may be perceived as "never-ending" by those who endure it.

The hypothetical end point remains a central stake that structural uncertainty charges with hopes and fears. The socially shared question is therefore *how* rather than *when* it will end, as critical events fuel contradictory expectations regarding the future of the community. The indetermination of the process makes a stabilization or a collapse equally likely. Beyond the finality of the critical conjuncture, observers who try to decipher its underlying logic also assess its tempo. Nicos Poulantzas sees the crisis as an "effective process with its own rhythm, with highlights and lowlights."[77] The recent history of Algeria shows moments of acceleration and stagnation, repetition and reflux. These variations in intensity resonated with widespread catastrophist expectations echoing the memories of the Dark Decade. Each acceleration could be the alleged point of no return, the imaginary threshold beyond which a rise in violence can no longer be prevented. In this context, the suspension of the process before this threshold became a key political stake and the core of a totalizing strategy of securitization based on the suspension of an impending disaster.[78]

The temporalities of the crisis echo the specific history and political culture of the polity that is affected by it. In Algeria, the Dark Decade was a crucial reference for those trying to anticipate the future of the country and the potential outcome of the critical conjuncture. Competing understandings of time were also inherently postcolonial, in that they give a considerable place to notions of tradition and modernity, progress and failure, development and backwardness. The future was understood through the prism of the absolute catastrophe of colonialism as well as the ideal of sovereignty inherited from the Third Worldist struggle of the 1960s and 1970s. Meanwhile, the past was scrutinized to understand recurring patterns and determine responsibilities. In short, during a crisis, representing the polity's historical trajectory becomes a highly politicized endeavor, which can legitimate both lasting forms of domination and radical emancipatory projects.

REVELATION AND RE-ENCHANTMENT

Crises are associated with spectacular events, especially as they reach their climax. Yet they do not necessarily lead to radical turning points. Political crises can result in dramatic changes in the power structure while still allowing for certain forms of continuity. For example, Tocqueville notoriously shows that the centralization inherited from the ancien régime was appropriated by French revolutionaries and became an essential feature in the new political order.[79] This continuity is also suggested by Dobry's diagnosis of a "regression to the habitus." The crisis thus sheds light on underlying dynamics that can suddenly be seen in broad daylight.[80] The process can be studied for its specificities, as the outcome of a set of disruptions. But it can also be understood beyond these discontinuities, in a deeper historical context. Indeed, the Algerian critical conjuncture was rooted in colonial occupation and postcolonial bureaucratic-military governance. Yet the crisis also brings together structural and conjunctural factors. It is shaped by the system's inner contradictions as well as by opportunism and chance. Consequently, one must not overinterpret the role of preexisting structures.

In any case, the crisis reveals usually hidden realities, such as the inner struggles that have undermined the cohesion of the Algerian ruling coalition. Undoubtedly, these revelations help elucidate what has often been described as an opaque system dominated by shadowy military figures.[81] They show the specificities and mundane aspects of Algeria's trajectory, and allow us to understand how a country that was portrayed as an "exception" after 2011 has recently experienced what some observers have described as a "new Arab Spring."[82]

The revealing power of the crisis is not without its share of ambiguities. The myths undermined by the critical conjuncture are not merely lies that hide the arbitrary nature of any system of domination. These fictions also organize the social world to make it practicable. Therefore, their dissipation leads to considerable difficulties when it comes to producing an analysis that makes sense, a shareable understanding of the situation. It is certainly puzzling—and even sometimes frightening—to come face-to-face with the truths revealed by a crisis. As a result, such revelations can call for forms of re-enchantment, as observers and actors alike attempt to reorganize the world and fill the vacuum left by vanished myths. This explains the proliferation of diagnoses, rumors, and conspiracy theories that compete with the once hegemonic myths that supported the old order. This process of re-enchantment also involves the formulation of new meta-narratives, often articulated with those already circulating in the polity. The critical conjuncture thus results in an intense struggle for what in Weberian terms would be called "symbolic domination," or in Gramscian ones "cultural hegemony."

Governance by Catastrophization

Since the mid-1980s, a "crisis of governmentality"[83] has undermined the procedures that had hitherto allowed for the management of the population and the economy, leading to a profound restructuring of the Algerian order. I will show in the following chapters that this restructuring drew on a selective conformity with globalized technologies of power, such as democratization, nonlethal policing, economic restructuring, and the inclusion of civil society. This kind of reorganization of the state and its peripheries has been described as an "authoritarian upgrading," and has resulted in the reconfiguration of governance "to accommodate and manage changing political, economic, and social conditions."[84] This transformative process and its limitations will be discussed in chapters 3–5.

In the Arab world and beyond, the restructuring of domestic political orders has accompanied a succession of crises. The ongoing process of neoliberalization has undeniably been a crucial factor, one that has "reshaped the contours of inherited institutional landscapes and rewoven the interconnections among them."[85] In addition to economic restructuring, successive crises have also accompanied the diffusion of a new militarized form of policing.[86] Born out of modernity, "risk societies" have become increasingly motivated by anxiety, shaped by defensive and negative concerns, preoccupied with preventing the worst rather than fostering collective emancipation.[87] New forms of governance have instrumentalized economic, political, and security threats to manage populations and territories. In cities, an urbanism of disaster has allowed for continued speculation and profiteering at the expense of poor neighborhoods and public budgets.[88] At the global level, sociopolitical upheaval, environmental catastrophe, and economic breakdown have been crucial in the expansion of neoliberal governance,[89] in what has been described as a process of "accumulation by dispossession" in the service of "disaster capitalism."[90]

In Algeria, the rise of crisis governance has followed an economic collapse, the implementation of a structural adjustment program, and the privatization of public assets. Yet it was also centered on the prevention of a new conflict. After 1999, the exceptional nature of the threat associated with a potential repetition of the Dark Decade generated an imaginary of emergency based on an anxious waiting for a disastrous turning point. The Algerian case thus represents an extreme example of a totalizing securitization aimed at preventing the most absolute threat: the collapse of the polity and the rise of senseless mass violence. It is an example of governance by catastrophization, a system of government that allows for the management of society in the name of preventing a disaster.

Like securitization, catastrophization is at the crossroads of a host of subjective and objective factors. While it is partly discursive, it is also a response to concrete social, economic, environmental, or political conditions.[91] As I showed in the historical overview that opened this chapter, the fear of a new wave of violence cannot be understood as a mere trauma. In Algeria, it was also a consequence of persistent "evils" (residual terrorism, social unrest, the illegitimacy and fragmentation of the ruling coalition, economic fragility, etc.). A totalizing form of securitization, catastrophization draws on the permanent dialectic between chaos and order and allows for the bureaucratic regulation of survival.[92] It is a comprehensive operational framework for policy making that aims to prevent an unfolding disaster. As such, both state and non-state actors quantify the number of "evils," monitor the impending catastrophe, and fix a threshold above which it can no longer be prevented.[93] In so doing, they can suspend the unfolding disaster before the turning point is reached, thereby permitting the daily management of a population and a territory.[94] Even though the fierce defense of sovereignty remains a key feature of Algerian political culture, governance by catastrophization also facilitates transnational partnerships. The shared imaginary of emergency encourages repeated interventions, merging managerial, humanitarian, and security-oriented approaches to preserve the linearity of development.[95] Local and foreign actors alike seek to avoid crossing the threshold of catastrophe.[96] In the name of stability and growth, catastrophization thus facilitates the polity's insertion into the global system.

By placing the catastrophe at the center of my analysis, I do not aim to propose a normative assessment of the political order in Algeria, or to suggest that a transparent, democratic, liberal order is the solution to an alleged failure. At its core, governance by catastrophization is a matter of political and social indetermination. As it justifies the state of exception conceptualized by Giorgio Agamben, it makes the distinction between war and peace, between civil war and revolution, impossible.[97] Indetermination thus means both stabilization and confusion, both of which bolster sovereign power. Moreover, following Walter Benjamin's insights, the catastrophe also signifies both a horizon of possibility and a lived experience. As such, its indetermination is also synonymous with a threshold prefiguring both destruction and redemption, the complete collapse of the order and the hope associated with this collapse.[98]

The conversation between Benjamin and Agamben takes place at the crossroads of domination and revolution. While his state of exception prevents a catastrophic potentiality and allows for the limitation of individual rights,[99] Agamben is constantly grappling with the tension between the perspective of the state and that of the oppressed.[100] Meanwhile, Benjamin famously opposed a "bastardized" mythical violence, the "bloody power" of the executive "over mere life for its own sake," with a "pure" divine power, the truly sovereign power "over all life for the sake of the living" that can abolish state power and found a new historical epoch. But he reckons that the latter remains almost impossible to identify with certainty, while the former is immediately perceptible.[101] Agamben endorses Benjamin's effort to push back against the annexation of exceptional violence by the state, but he sees pure violence as "the stake in the conflict over the state of exception."¹⁰² From this perspective, governance by catastrophization is not merely a top-down effort to control and discipline the subject in the name of preventing the disaster. It is also the process through which the possibility of a transformative expiatory catastrophe emerges. This tension becomes obvious at the grassroots level, once the catastrophe is conceived as a subjective emergency, a catastrophic experience of domination that nurtures a "weak messianism," which is to say the possibility of an emancipatory disruption of time.¹⁰³ The ambiguity of the suspended disaster is thus captured by Benjamin's "tradition of the oppressed," which is based on the confrontation between a state violence that obliterates the individual, and a "destructive character" whose revolutionary violence responds to the risk of obliteration.¹⁰⁴

We should appreciate Benjamin not only for his ability to imagine a governance by catastrophization that goes beyond state power and biopolitical management. His philosophy of history also sheds light on to the contradictory subjectivities of a nation shaped by anticolonialism and Third Worldism. At the heart of this philosophy lies the critique of a continuum of progress that is supposed to drive history. This critique allows us to think about the process of catastrophization as a particular temporality, as a disastrous stagnation contradicting the promises of modernity.¹⁰⁵ The notion of a missed opportunity after independence is thus central to understand the meaning of the catastrophe in the Algerian context, and notably the profound sense of cultural alienation produced by the deterministic modernizing machine of the developmentalist state. Yet at the very same time, the process of catastrophization animates the possibility of a redemption through a moment of destruction.¹⁰⁶ Indeed, the anticolonial revolution that overthrew French colonialism can still be saved and its radical potentialities once again actualized.

During the twenty years of Bouteflika's rule, Algeria was seemingly reinstalled in a continuum of security and progress. In the name of survival, development, and curing an "Algerian personality" (*shakhsiyya jazāi'riyya*) shattered by colonialism and the Dark Decade, population and territory were to be reinserted into the "homogeneous, empty time" characteristic of modern governance and nation building.¹⁰⁷ Yet this effort to normalize politics under the shadow of the suspended disaster cohabited with another understanding of the emergency, not as an impending repetition of the 1990s but as a routine of hopelessness and stagnation that invalidated the narrative of careful development promoted by the ruling elites. In this context, another temporality of emergency appeared, marked by the necessity of immediate and radical change. The catastrophe was thus situated at once in a traumatic past, an unbearable present, and a dreaded future. It was potentially synonymous with both an obliteration of the polity and a messianic release. To understand how the structure of the ruling coalition fueled this ambiguity, the next chapter will present its main institutions and the competing dynamics that undermined its cohesion.

2
Struggles at the Heart of the State

This is the time of adventure and war, when the masters of the cyclical society traverse their personal history ... History thus arises in front of men as an alien factor, as something they didn't want and they believed they were sheltered from.

—*Guy Debord*

This regime is afraid of clarity, like the night birds who can only fly in the dark.

—*Mohamed Boudiaf*

In the cozy atmosphere of his Tizi Ouzou apartment, while his wife prepared fresh pastries and coffee, Mohand lectured me about the origins of the "System."[1] Like many of my interlocutors, this former top-level member of an opposition party went back to the roots of the political order to explain its resilience. Along with other nebulous labels ("mafia," "*Pouvoir*," "*Nidhām*" and later "'*Iṣāba*"), the "System" served to describe the coalition that controlled the Algerian state. In Mohand's depiction, the "System" was intrinsically corrupting, unpersonal, and tentacular. Its resilient and ubiquitous nature seemed to make it impossible to reform, let alone defeat. A few months after Zine el-'Abidine Ben 'Ali's infamous flight from Tunisia, this veteran of Algerian politics reiterated that overthrowing Bouteflika would not change anything. Mohand's discourse did not say much about the social reality of the "System," but it suggested a radically uneven relationship with its opponents.

In this chapter, I present the internal dynamics within the ruling coalition under Bouteflika. After 1999, the tensions between the military and civilians resulted in a series of confrontations pitting the presidential entourage against high-ranking military officers. Thus, I analyze the role of the presidency, the institutional and symbolic bases for its gradual reinforcement since 1999, as well as the limits to this process. The second section looks at the military components of the ruling coalition in order to understand the reasons behind the systematic interference of generals in national politics. Their repeated interventions were notably justified in the name of the survival of the nation. The chapter then describes the cohabitation of these key actors within a cartel that controlled the Algerian state, regulated competition, and organized the distribution of resources. As we will see, this cartelized organization didn't prevent the tensions that constantly roiled ruling elites, and which fueled a paranoid understanding of politics.

To understand the place of the ruling coalition in the process of catastrophization, I propose a relational and institutional analysis coupled with a study of grassroots representations of its main actors. As governments strive to "control and manipulate the symbolic world,"[2] Algerian ruling elites weaponized the Dark Decade and the possibility of a repetition of this past disaster. Yet their public discourses failed to secure hegemony. Situated in "a grey zone between the real and the unreal," these contested fictions were nonetheless essential to the exercise of power.[3] They also contributed to the production of subversive or depoliticizing narratives that shaped grassroots experiences of domination.

The Presidency and the "System"

Notwithstanding the widespread criticism denouncing the corruption of the "System," the Algerian state is modern. In other words, it is divided into different sectors of activity and institutionalized, as the "governing institutions are conceived as independent from the individuals who occupy a function in their structure."[4] This does not mean that there is no opportunistic privatization of the power that individuals receive from the state. Nonetheless, each state agency, department, or institution has its own logic, its own tools, and its own norms with which actors must comply. The Algerian state is not the neo-patrimonial structure described by some specialists of postcolonial African politics, in which legal-rational processes are a mere cover for traditional forms of clientelism.[5] Beyond the fictions attached to the person of the president, the key to comprehending presidential power remains the institution, not the individual.[6] Given Bouteflika's condition, the crucial role played by influential figures in his entourage became obvious over the years. This evolution emphasized the tension between the personification inherent to presidential power and the reality of its collective exercise.

THE PRESIDENCY AND POLITICAL INSTABILITY

Since independence, the Algerian presidency has alternated between periods of reinforcement and weakening. After decolonization, presidentialization was a central stake in the establishment of stable civilian governments in newly independent countries.[7] In Algeria between 1962 and 1965, Ahmed Ben Bella strove to expand his power at the expense of his challengers. This is one of the reasons why a broad coalition reunited around colonel Houari Boumediene to overthrow Ben Bella in 1965.[8] Subsequently, the country's new strongman concentrated political legitimacy in a newly formed Council of the Revolution. Boumediene nevertheless paid more attention to the control of the armed forces than to constitutional procedures. While he remained minister of defense during his thirteen-year reign, he was only elected president in 1976. The presidential office was thus revived and given extended prerogatives. After Boumediene's premature death, Chadli Bendjedid was appointed as his successor. Lacking political stature, the new president needed to solidify his position once again. With his attempts to increase his political autonomy, he progressively angered some of his allies. The presidency became one institution among others, caught in the power struggles fracturing the ruling coalition.[9] Eventually, Chadli was "sacked" by a group of generals in January 1992. After the coup, the HCE replaced the presidency. Former nationalist hero Mohamed Boudiaf was appointed to lead this co-opted executive body dominated by the military. But Boudiaf's revolutionary legitimacy did not prevent him from being assassinated, nor did it protect his ephemeral successor from ridicule. Ali Kafi, another war hero who was notably the commander of Wilaya II after 1957,[10] rapidly earned the nickname "Johnny Walker" for his alleged penchant for hard alcohol.

In January 1994, the nomination of retired general Liamine Zeroual as head of the HCE opened a new phase in the restoration of executive authority. Receiving more than 60 percent of the vote in the first round of the 1995 presidential elections, he saw a further strengthening of his position. In April 1996, Zeroual forced hundreds of military officers into retirement. The same year, he pushed for a constitutional revision expanding his powers. Relying on his supporters in the administration and self-defense groups (*groupes de légitime défense*; they were also known as "patriots"), he also supported the creation of a new party, the RND, led by his minister and personal adviser, retired general Mohamed Betchine. The RND was founded in order to "support the president's strategy" and benefited from massive fraud to prevail in the legislative and local elections of 1997.[11] Once again, a co-opted president and his entourage used their central institutional position to increase their power at the expense of their challengers in the ruling coalition.

A reaction from the core of the state apparatus quickly followed. During the summer of 1998, a judicial storm echoed by national media led to the fall of the president and his close-knit guard (I will return to this episode later in the chapter). In any case, less than three years after embodying the return of electoral legitimacy, Zeroual was forced to resign. At this point, the Algerian ruling coalition had used up four heads of state in seven years. This highlights the peculiar role of the presidential institution in the reproduction of political instability in Algeria. It is both central to the state and particularly exposed to assaults coming from within it. Thus, the head of state sometimes appeared paradoxically as the last resort against the "System."

BOUTEFLIKA'S RETURN

In 1999, one man positioned himself as the providential solution to the country's ongoing crisis. Almost twenty years after being forced into exile following accusations of financial wrongdoing, Abdelaziz Bouteflika returned as an independent candidate in the presidential election, with the tacit approval of the army staff and the support of the FLN and the RND. A clear favorite, he received some 73.79 percent of the vote, a score that he described as "honorable" given the peculiar circumstances. Indeed, despite official promises of transparency, his six challengers had withdrawn from what they claimed was a rigged election. Bouteflika thus became president of the republic on April 27, 1999, following a truncated yet legal electoral process.[12] He appeared as a credible solution to the many problems encountered by Algerian society. In the words of a former member of the FFS, Bouteflika embodied some of the qualities that his predecessors were allegedly lacking:

> Seriously, I don't hate Bouteflika. Because for once, we had a president who wasn't a soldier and who was kind of smart. Not like Chadli or Zeroual. For once, we had a president who could at least represent us correctly outside the country, without causing shame. He is a short man, but he still has charisma and the ways of a president. We have also known him for a long time, as minister of foreign affairs, and he tried to do things, even if it wasn't always great. This was a welcome change.
> (LOUBNA, FORMER JOURNALIST AND MEMBER OF THE FFS, PARIS, SUMMER 2010)

This testimony expressed a satisfaction in reconnecting with a familiar figure. The new president's main asset was definitely his past as Boumediene's personal secretary and minister. As a well-known figure, Bouteflika was in a position to reestablish the historical continuum of development after the abyss of the Dark Decade. A key personality during the era of Boumedienism, at the time he was considered the informal heir of the deceased president, and even delivered his eulogy in December 1978. In one of his inflammatory books targeting Bouteflika, former ANP chief of staff Khaled Nezzar offers a biting account of the sympathy enjoyed by the future president during the 1999 campaign: "One listens to Bouteflika with hope," he writes. "He is the absentee who reappears, the resurrection of the dead. He carries the scent and the aura of a prestigious past."[13] Indeed, after the climax of the crisis, Bouteflika embodied the glorious past of the developmental state and the promise of a normalization of the country's trajectory.

The new president was also associated with a set of positive features. In Loubna's testimony, his skills and experience contrasted with the negative epithets often attached to the ruling elites ("ignorant, ridiculous"). This enthusiasm was echoed overseas and notably in France, where Bouteflika enjoyed sympathetic media coverage. On French television he was depicted as a "political wonderkid" and a "subtle but determined man."[14] In Algeria, his diplomatic experience and his alleged ability to restore "Algerian prestige" abroad generated higher expectations.[15] These hopes were also shared by many academics who saw Bouteflika's election as a sign announcing political reforms and improved diplomatic relations, notably with Morocco and France.[16]

Bouteflika's return reveals some of the traits made valuable by the crisis. The parallel with Boudiaf indicates that the marginalization of former revolutionaries forced into exile following power struggles became synonymous with probity and potential reforms. In addition, the new president benefited from the symbolic and political capital inherited from the Boumediene era, which allowed him to resume the virtuous continuum of modernization and growth. To foster such a restoration of historical continuity, Bouteflika offered to close the bloody parenthesis of the 1990s (in his words, to "allow all sides to head home without losing face").[17] To change people's perception of time and history in such a way, it helps to be some sort of illusionist. And if there is one thing that can be said about Abdelaziz Bouteflika in 1999, it is that he appeared to be up to the challenge of conjuring the illusion of a pacified and respected Algeria.

THE INSTITUTIONAL AND SYMBOLIC BASES OF PRESIDENTIAL POWER

To understand the past twenty years, it is not enough to focus on Bouteflika's image. Presidential power can only be exercised by drawing on the resources inherent to the institution. These resources were mobilized by the president himself, as well as by the many individuals active in the presidency and at its periphery, such as Bouteflika's brother and adviser Saïd, his personal secretary Mohamed Rougab, or former prime minister Ahmed Ouyahia, who also acted as his chief of staff between 2014 and 2017.

A network of interpersonal and professional relations trickled down from this source of power. As it benefited from the highly centralized structure of the Algerian political system, the presidency placed its appointees in all key public institutions. In this way it was able to monitor semiautonomous parts of the state apparatus (army, intelligence services, administrative sectors). It appointed members of the government, key public servants (including the governor of the Central Bank of Algeria and the CEO of the giant public oil company Sonatrach), *walis* (prefects), ambassadors, and directors of security agencies.[18] These appointments secured the influence of the president and his entourage over the administrative apparatus that covered the country. In reaction, local opposition figures denounced a form of state control that undermined their efforts, even when they managed to seize control of a regional assembly:

> Since Bouteflika was elected, he has centralized everything. The law allows him to use presidential decrees to appoint prefects and vice-prefects, as well as the directors of local administrations. The presidential staff selects those who will serve as regional antennas for the central power. At the national level, Bouteflika has built an administration that can act as if without constraints. With his decrees, he can decide everything, even the identity of the director of a local housing agency.
>
> (HAMID FERHAT, PRESIDENT OF THE APW
> AND MEMBER OF THE FFS, BEJAÏA, AUTUMN 2010)

The presidency also benefited from a strong hold on the legislative branch thanks to the Council of the Nation, one of the country's two parliamentary chambers. The president appointed one-third of the council's members.[19] For a law to be adopted, it needed to be supported by an absolute majority in the People's National Assembly (Assemblée Populaire Nationale, or APN, the other legislative chamber) and to receive three-quarters of the votes in the Council of the Nation. Enough senators (members of the latter council) were thus directly co-opted to block any project opposed by the president. For this reason, Mohammed Hachemaoui describes the council as a "tool for defusing the Assembly" and an "authoritarian enclave."[20] The election of its president was held under the direct control of the presidency, which allowed Abdelkader Bensalah to retain the second-highest office in the state from 2002 to 2019.[21] In April of 2019, Bensalah became interim president following Bouteflika's resignation.

The head of state could draw on his executive powers and his legislative influence to grant substantial benefits to his parliamentary clientele. Louisa Dris-Aït Hamadouche and Yahia Zoubir suggest that the raise offered to Algerian deputies in 2008 was a way to "create, if not political cohesion, at least allegiances."[22] Despite the sharp criticism coming from opposition parties and private media outlets, this measure was adopted following a presidential order. Algerian deputies thus received a raise of approximately 300 percent a few weeks before they approved the constitutional reform allowing Bouteflika to run for a third term.

The presidency also exercised oversight over the judicial branch of government, as it appointed four of the twelve members of the Constitutional Council, notably its president.[23] The head of state presided over the Superior Council of Magistrates, the entity that oversees judges and prosecutors.[24] Moreover, the president was often viewed as a kind of paralegal court of appeal for those who suffered from injustice.[25] Before Bouteflika's stroke in 2013, it was thus fairly common for individuals in conflict with the administration or the security forces to publish an open letter calling for the president to intervene personally. One high-level human rights advocate explained the president's paradoxical position in the following terms:

> People clearly make a distinction between the administration, the army, the regime in general on one side, and the president on the other. The president created an image of himself in the collective imaginary. Bouteflika, for many Algerians, is a kind of counterexample to the "System" that put him in place. Everybody knows that he is there because the *décideurs* wanted it,[26] but he is allegedly a victim who cannot implement his reforms properly. The "System" is the deadlock and Bouteflika a solution, and it is necessary to overcome the deadlock and speak directly to the solution.
>
> (ABDELMOUMÈNE KHELIL, GENERAL SECRETARY OF THE ALGERIAN LEAGUE FOR THE DEFENSE OF HUMAN RIGHTS, ALGIERS, SPRING 2011)

Bouteflika was thus portrayed as an alternative to the "System," even though his position was proof that he was part and parcel of the ruling coalition and benefited from the outspoken support of its most prominent civilian components.

This is a mystery that deserves to be elucidated. As a political institution, the presidency depends on its holder embodying the powerful myth of state neutrality. After he had sworn his oath, Bouteflika became the "president of all Algerians" and testified to a universalism that collided with the actual origin of his power. The fiction of state universalism is a classic of political theory. In his famous study dedicated to medieval England, Kantorowicz demonstrates the central role of the head of state. According to him, the king has two bodies. One belongs to the individual who became king and is physical, idiosyncratic, mortal, natural. The other is an embodiment of the nation, the state, and its power. It is symbolic, political, immortal, and mystical.[27] This foundational fiction was retained in an altered form by the modern nation-state exported by colonization, which homogenized the condition of its subjects, who now also became theoretically equal citizens. For example, Fernando Coronil explains that "the Venezuelan state has been constituted as a unifying force by producing fantasies of collective integration into centralized political institutions."[28] In Algeria, this legal-rational ideal of the homogenizing state collided with visible power struggles, unequal access to national resources, and corruption. The victims of structural injustice therefore relied on another fiction, this one rooted in the Islamic political tradition: that of the "prince" as a supreme arbitrator, even against state agents. The mistake here would be to limit this intervention to a mere form of neo-patrimonialism. Indeed, the role of the prince goes far beyond his personal position as a paternal alternative to a failing legal-rational system. The Muslim prince must reaffirm the existence of a kind of universal justice for all his subjects, without exception.[29]

The president remains the "symbolic head of state."[30] A co-opted figure, Bouteflika was the fetish presented by the ruling coalition to the population. As such, he was expected to validate the monolithic myth of state power by personifying the overcoming of internal contradictions and the unification of diverse components in the name of the greater good. His symbolic duty was to demonstrate the transubstantiation of private interest into public interest. In other words, beyond the reference to the ideal of justice embodied by the Muslim prince, the fiction of neutrality and universality defining the role of the nation-state still prevailed. The War of Liberation, the most essential reference in Algerian political culture, assigned this function to the state after 1962.

This is how one can understand the paradox of the Algerian presidency: at once a symbol of justice external to the state and a neutral figure of authority expected to overcome the division of those who control that very state. This ambiguity eventually became its weakness, as the resilience of such a fiction depends on the illusionist's abilities as much as on the underlying context, notably the capabilities of his physical and mortal body. After 2013, the impotent president was unable to embody a plausible alternative to the system. Meanwhile, the privatization of the state was made obvious by a series of scandals. Before that, Bouteflika was nonetheless able to capitalize on the narrative of national reconciliation.

THE PRESIDENT OR CHAOS

Before his stroke in 2013, Abdelaziz Bouteflika relentlessly played the part of a pacifying authority, a paternal figure whose only motivation was to protect the national community. By drawing on his constitutional powers, the presidency sought to transform elections into mere validation processes increasingly limited to a simple alternative: the president or chaos. Beyond the banality of such fearmongering, this narrative also resulted in the implementation of exceptional policies linked to the figure of the president.

After the 1999 election, critiques of Bouteflika portrayed him as "badly elected." In response, he argued that a candidate should not receive 99 percent of the vote, thereby bolstering the impression that he might be more supportive of democratic processes. In the following months, the presidency promoted a policy of National Reconciliation to compensate for its initial lack of legitimacy. In this endeavor, the organization of a referendum for "Civil Concord and Peace" linked the support for a particular policy to the individual who implemented it.[31] Given the arrangement of electoral results and the overrepresentation of the government in the media, the referendum allowed for the transformation of the presidency's administrative grip into political capital. With this initial advantage and the support of the main parties in the parliament, the outcome of the process merely indicated the "amount of legitimacy" produced. With an official voter turnout of 85 percent, of which 98 percent voted in favor of the project, the president managed to attach his person to the return of peace. While the referendum of September 1999 left many key problems unresolved (such as the ANP's political role or the banishment of the FIS), it was undoubtedly adapted to socially shared expectations.[32] As a result, Bouteflika was able to consolidate a narrative of himself as a peacemaker.

In 2004, he was reelected with 84.99 percent of the vote, despite fierce competition from Benflis and the reluctance of a portion of the military aristocracy. Just before the poll, Bouteflika stated that "a president who is not elected with an overwhelming majority should just stay home."[33] After tightening its grip over the FLN and the army by pushing out the most troublesome elements, the presidency positioned itself as the only significant political authority in the country. Bouteflika was free to continue his policy of National Reconciliation by convoking a new referendum. The announcement fueled some expressions of discontent. Nevertheless, a popular consultation aiming to restore "civil peace" was difficult to contradict. The campaign did not leave much space for the associations representing the families of missing persons or for human rights activists. The state apparatus, ENTV (the government-run television channel), the army's monthly periodical *El Djeich*, former members of the Islamic Salvation Army, as well as civil society leaders linked to the presidency—all expressed their unconditional support for the so-called Charter for Peace and National Reconciliation. On September 29, 2005, the referendum resulted in a crushing victory for the "Yes" side, which garnered some 97.36 percent of votes. The turnout was massive throughout the country, with the exception of Kabylia, where a general boycott followed the 2001 Black Spring. This new plebiscite turned out to be another crucial step in the reinforcement of the presidency, at the expense of the constitutional checks on it.[34]

The Charter for Peace and National Reconciliation, promulgated in 2006, granted immunity to state actors involved in the violence of the 1990s. It also banned further inquiries into past violence, which might have incriminated security agencies. Bouteflika's presidential being was attached to a constant state of exception that served to maintain peace and prevent a new disaster. As he "endorsed the biopolitical tradition of autorictas," he became a "law that blurs at every point with life."[35]

The referendums of 1999 and 2005 were undeniably successful in bringing peace to the country, with the general support of the population.[36] In addition to the full amnesty granted to members of the security forces, the charter notably offered state subsidies to the families of war victims and a conditional reintegration for former insurgents. It also attached Bouteflika's image to the reconciliation of the "Algerian family," while invocations of the "national tragedy" became a ritual in official discourses. After the 2005 referendum, it was time to reinsert the national community into the pacified, continuous, and cumulative time of development. The conjunctural improvement of the country's economy served this effort of legitimation, and Bouteflika was portrayed as "being at the forefront... of the process of modernization."[37] High hydrocarbon prices allowed the government to implement redistribution policies, presented as "gifts from the president," who posed as the guarantor of stability and growth.

To further consolidate the presidential grip on power, one last constitutional limitation had to be removed. The Algerian Constitution of 1996 stated that the head of state could only be reelected once.[38] Rather than convoking a new plebiscite, the presidency only sought to validate its project of constitutional revision in the APN. The rapidity of the process demonstrated the presidency's grip on the lower chamber. Bouteflika announced his desire to revise the constitution on October 29, 2008. Less than two weeks later, on November 12, the APN voted by show of hands: 500 parliamentarians supported the constitutional revision, 21 opposed it, and 8 withheld their vote. From now on, the permanence of the presidential figure was portrayed as a virtue.

Six months later, Abdelaziz Bouteflika was in position to run for a third mandate without any serious challenger. He benefited from the tacit backing of the army's chief of staff, Ahmed Gaïd Salah, whom he had appointed in 2004, as well as the vocal support of the so-called presidential alliance and the business community. In his official program, the president-candidate evoked "the powerful call coming from numerous citizens of all categories, asking [him] to continue [his] mission."[39] The message was clear: by erasing the constitutional limits on a lifetime presidency, he was merely responding to popular demands. In his campaign rhetoric, Bouteflika promised to "put out the fire of *fitna* [sedition]," and to help the people to grow up and become a "lion." He also invoked the memories of the Dark Decade: "Algeria is calling you in the name of its injuries, of those who were killed, all these victims, she is calling you. Stand up to save her, to save my country."[40] Eventually, the electoral battle ended with another crushing victory. Abdelaziz Bouteflika received 90.23 percent of the vote.

His supporters in both the government-owned and private press expressed their enthusiasm as the official voter turnout reached 74.54 percent. The day after the election, an editorial in the private daily *L'Expression* claimed that

> citizens have made the choice of stability and continuity, for the return of peace and security. Changing direction would have been a step into the unknown . . . Their message expresses a form of perspicacity, memory, and the ability to judge. There is also a will to grant the President of the Republic a power of representation that will allow him to make the voice of Algeria heard loud and clear. This being said, one should not think that our adversaries' disarray will last long. They just need to get over the blow and they will come back and try again. This means that April 9, 2009, is not an end. It is a step, a really important one, on the path to reconstructing the country. There is still a lot of work to do. A lot of work. President and people.[41]

Alternatives were portrayed as dangerous leaps into an unknown future, a way of invoking the specter of the 1990s. The author of this editorial justified the one-dimensional political offering in the name of the alleged alliance between the hero-president and the reified people.[42] He also reminded his readers of the threat of a potential comeback by the "adversaries" who opposed both Bouteflika and the policy of National Reconciliation—the former being the living manifestation of the latter. Electoral processes thus served to turn the lack of alternative into a necessity. It was a representation, in every sense of the word, of a unique, rational yet exceptional choice made in a pluralist framework. When facing the continuous threat of chaos, the people had to preserve order, rebuild the country, work harder, and, in order to do all of this, grant Bouteflika "a power of representation."

The climax of the crisis therefore remained an essential resource for the presidency under Bouteflika. It authorized a succession of plebiscites that restored a minimalist social contract, one based on a vertically oriented, security-based political fiction reminiscent of the Hobbesian Leviathan. It served the implementation of reconciliation policies, which permitted the distribution of various stipends while preserving impunity for the security agencies and ensuring the end of all legal proceedings linked to the war.⁴³ The 1990s also served as a bedrock for the formulation of political and media discourses that contributed to a "discursive catastrophization" and objectivized the need for security.⁴⁴ The official narrative was clear: the heroic old man had paved the way for the future by suspending the catastrophe. The renovated order was made to stand the test of time, by benevolently limiting the political possibilities. Yet the obvious tensions that shattered the ruling coalition undermined this seemingly flawless message.

Praetorian Shadows

The presidency was not the only location from which state power emanated. Even before Algeria's independence, the bureaucratic-military apparatus had achieved a dominant status in the nationalist movement. As a result, political figures had long denounced the premature corruption of the revolution.⁴⁵ After 1962, high-ranking officers of the ANP retained a central position in the ruling coalition. Even if their role fluctuated depending on the conjuncture, colonels and generals came to represent the real *décideurs* in the collective imaginary. Despite the advent of political pluralism, many observers considered the order's only purpose as preserving the vested interests of a bunch of obscure military figures. Essays published by authors from Berberist and Islamist backgrounds described high-ranking military officers as the main protagonists in the country's political life.⁴⁶ Former members of the ANP also became dissidents and published testimonies accusing their superiors of various atrocities.⁴⁷ Often published in France, some of these works gave birth to intense controversies. Undoubtedly, recurring military interference in Algerian politics had major consequences for the country's trajectory.

THE IMMUNE DEFENSE AND TUTELARY FUNCTIONS OF THE ANP

In the early summer of 2012, I was on my way to the 5 July 1962 Stadium with two American colleagues. Located on the western periphery of Algiers, the venue was hosting the celebrations of the fiftieth anniversary of the country's independence. In an almost full stadium, organizers offered a composite show, which combined music, taekwondo, a procession of children dressed as flowers and butterflies, trampoline artists, as well as representations of modern Algeria—emphasizing the role of schools and vocational training—and traditional Algeria—reduced to an amalgam of regional folklores. The audience was thrilled by the succession of stunts and the promise of the upcoming "mega-concert." Yet behind the festivities' seemingly incoherent features, the show delivered its share of political messages emphasizing, notably, the central role of the army. It started with a representation of the French occupation, described as a series of struggles and humiliations. At the end of the colonial night, a group of soldiers arise to ambush and decimate French troops. The National Liberation Army (Armée de libération nationale, ALN) came into being before our eyes to force the occupiers out of Algeria. It did so with the support of the people, represented by extras dressed as peasants walking in a line toward an adversary in disarray. The message was straightforward: armed struggle was instrumental to Algeria recovering its independence. The heroism of the mujahideen and the martyrs (*shuhadā'*, sing. *shahīd*) confirmed the military institution in its position as a liberator intimately linked to the people. This official history centered on military action offered a unanimous version of the revolution based on the sacred union between the army and the people. It overlooked the political tensions and compromises inherent to the nationalist struggle. It also provided military leaders with a double historical mission that legitimized their repeated interference.

Firstly, the ANP has an immune defense function. It is expected to protect the national community from internal and external threats that could imperil its integrity or autonomy. This function is common to armies across the world, but its meaning is further reinforced in a postcolonial environment. The imperative to protect the national body finds its seminal example in the War of Liberation and the subsequent militarization of the nationalist struggle. Hamit Bozarslan notes that the militarization of a revolution is accompanied by the rise of a "vitalist narrative of survival."[48] The Dark Decade revived this narrative, which has remained a key theme in the discourse of high-ranking officers. Because of its immune function, the army has the duty to protect civilians, even against themselves. As the constitutional guarantor of the polity's survival,[49] the ANP can take over its political destiny.

The immune defense function of the military is thus intimately tied to a second function, this one tutelary. The ANP is entitled to a right of scrutiny that can evolve into a right of ownership over the state. Far from being automatically synonymous with illegitimacy, this claim is the legacy of a political tradition sometimes known as "military radicalism." This approach was widespread in the Middle East, Africa, and Latin America in the mid-twentieth century, when left- or right-wing officers often supervised state policies aimed at guiding the nation on the path to development, modernity, and prosperity.[50] In the 1970s, the ANP's National Directorate of Cooperatives was the largest employer in the country, testifying to the sustained involvement of the military in the planned economy.[51] More recently, the Directorate of Military Factories has been instrumental in reindustrialization efforts promoted by successive governments since the mid-2000s.[52] In general, military supervision applies to all sectors, from security to the economy to politics. It is symbolized by the allegorical statue of a soldier holding a torch placed at the bottom of the Maqām ash-Shahīd, the Algiers Martyr's Memorial. While less common than its immune defense function, the military's tutelary function remains widespread across the world. It is generally attached to the notion of "praetorianism," used by political scientists to describe the unconstitutional dominance of the military over politics.[53] It applies, for example, to the Pakistani officers rallied behind Pervez Musharraf, who portrayed themselves as guardians of the country's destiny and justified the 1999 coup in the name of the common good.[54]

In critical times, the tutelary and immune defense functions of the praetorians merge. Ahmet Insel has argued, for instance, that the Turkish military routinely "claim a status of ownership over the state, notably during internal political tensions, especially when they feel that their power over the state is threatened."[55] As we will see in the next section, their Algerian counterparts have repeatedly acted in a similar fashion.

PRAETORIANISM AND CRISIS

The army staff occupied center stage during the climax of the crisis. In his memoirs, former chief of staff Khaled Nezzar (1988–1990) describes military interference as an attempt to "manage" or "settle the crisis" in order to protect "unity" and "national sovereignty."[56] Praetorian discourses used

48 STRUGGLES AT THE HEART OF THE STATE

FIGURE 2.1 Statue of a soldier "holding the light" under the Maqām ash-Shahīd. Algiers, autumn 2010. (Photograph by author.)

the progressive rise in violence as a pretext for the extension of the officers' prerogatives and the implementation of strategies aiming to protect order at all costs (coup, mass repression, infiltration of dissident groups). The explanations given a posteriori by another chief of staff, Mohamed Lamari (1993–2004), to a (fiercely anti-Islamist) French weekly illustrate this rationale. According to him, putschist generals knew what was good for the population and were ready to use force so that their vision of the common good prevailed:

> In 1992, we were confronted with a very simple choice: either witnessing the establishment of a theocratic and totalitarian regime similar to what happened in Afghanistan a few years later; or saving republican institutions, which is what we did . . . They are even pretending to prosecute me for this in front of an international court. I don't give a damn. What matters is that my country was saved. Then, so be it . . . Let's go back to what really happened. At the beginning of the 1990s, a fringe of our population fell into [a trap] when it was offered the establishment of a theocratic regime. But thanks to us, they eventually understood that it was just a strategy to seize power and they stopped supporting terrorists.[57]

In Lamari's eyes, the situation of emergency proscribed any compromise. He read the configuration in dichotomous terms: on the one hand, the proponents of the state and the common good (i.e., the military and civilians who supported the coup); on the other, the zealots promoting an archaic Islamic theocracy. The praetorians' monopoly on the common good enabled them to reject any political alternative to their strategy of eradication. The chaos of the 1990s merely demonstrated that a segment of the population had been misled. State violence was thus cast as a therapy for a frenzied national body, a purge to reestablish the balance of its humors.

Collective and individual actors are often wary of getting involved in a crisis, and the military is no exception. Indeed, praetorian interventions are not without cost. Going back to the Turkish example, while the army was able to preserve its position as the arbitrator of politics after the crisis of the 1970s and 1980s, it lost part of its prestige and influence.[58] In Algeria, praetorians intervened directly to protect the political order and their individual and collective interests. But this interference also resulted in human losses and tarnished the reputation of high-ranking officers, as suggested by the vast literature accusing them of war crimes. The 1992 coup was only possible as the result of a situation of extreme tension inside the state and in the entire society, as the outcome of a "long process of dramatization."[59] Outside this exceptional moment, during the phase of latency, the ANP's leadership focused on its immune defense function (responding to natural disasters, fighting terrorism). Its tutelary grip diminished as it lacked either a constitutional basis or a political justification.

This highlights the difference between praetorianism and praetorian systems. The first refers to the Roman archetype and describes "situations in which the military, specifically, exercises independent political power, either by using force or threatening to do so," resulting in different institutional arrangements and ideological orientations.[60] As for the second, it suggests that the army exercises direct control over the political system.[61] While praetorianism is a political impulse emanating from all or a section of the army, the praetorian system places the military directly in control of the government. In Algeria, such direct rule only happened for a short period, after the 1992 coup, with the active support of key civilian figures. The situation during the period of latency was far from meeting these standards.

Comparing Algeria under Bouteflika with Burma before 2016 can help us understand this contrast. First, in both countries, the military's political role is a legacy of the anticolonial struggle. As such, one cannot view praetorian politics simply as a sign of political decay or a mode of government fit only for underdeveloped societies. The political involvement of the army can be historically legitimate and can promote stability and development in postcolonial contexts.[62] The Burmese and Algerian cases are nonetheless different. In Algeria, high-ranking officers were among the most prominent players in the country's power struggles. In Burma, they exercised direct control over the state, without any real challenger.[63] While the Burmese army only shared political power on the margins, Algerian politicians and technocrats became major players in national politics. Bouteflika and his entourage are a telling example. Despite their tutelary function, high-ranking officers were obligated to form social coalitions and to leave civilians in charge of the government. This highlights the ambiguity of the suspended disaster, which maintains the possibility of a praetorian takeover in the name of necessity, and which is also synonymous with the political catastrophe represented by such a takeover.

PRAETORIAN CONTRADICTIONS

The contradictions of the military institution fueled the overall instability of the political order. In theory, the historical legitimacy and the tutelary positioning of the ANP placed it above mundane national politics. For Khaled Nezzar, the army was no less than "the soul of the country's political and administrative structure."[64] The retired general was here echoing a well-established representation of the institution. In his PhD dissertation, defended in 1973, future ambassador Khalfa Mameri stated, "Like all armies, the ANP's role places it by definition above and outside politics. It is at the same time a part of national heritage and its unfailing guardian."[65] Yet far from occupying this lofty theoretical position, the ANP was actively involved in the social and political reproduction of the existing order. Under Boumediene, "the army [performed] functions of political and military mobilization by training student conscripts."[66] The ANP already acted as a partisan actor, which was in sharp contrast with its allegedly neutral position as a "guardian of national heritage."

Because of its active involvement in the production and reproduction of the political order, the ANP suffered from internal divisions. The first cracks appeared during the War of Liberation. They pitted components of the ALN located inside the nation's borders against those who were based outside the country, and French-trained officers against those trained by Arab states. After these initial tensions, the army was chronically divided. After the 1965 coup, tensions followed the reinforcement of Boumediene's position, which was at odds with the collegial management prioritized initially. As a result, opponents of the country's new strongman naturally emerged from the army.[67] In 1967, the new chief of staff, Tahar Zbiri, engaged in a failed rebellion against Boumediene, arguing that the latter was putting in place a system of personal rule opposed to the national interest.[68] Conflicts affecting the army's leadership continued, notably with the disgrace of a subsequent chief of staff, Mostefa Beloucif, who was infamously forced to retire in 1987 and convicted for the misappropriation of public money in 1992.[69] Between 1988 and 1992, the political discord among civilians affected the general cohesion of the institution.[70] Meanwhile, top-ranking officers actively took part in the struggles for state control that contributed to the advent of the Dark Decade.

In 1990, the military intelligence services were unified under a single command, the DRS. Until its dissolution in 2016, the DRS represented a third dominant locus of power within the ruling coalition, one that competed with the presidency and the army command. The DRS was made of several subdivisions, including the Special Intervention Group and its infamous "ninjas" in charge of counterterrorist operations. It was sometimes described as a "super-ministry of security that [controlled] all structures dedicated to intelligence gathering."[71] Unlike a real ministry, though, the DRS acted as an autonomous structure and had the ability to influence politics outside of any legal framework.[72] The department relied on one of its subdivisions, the Center for Communication and Diffusion, to influence the private press. It also infiltrated and monitored state-owned companies. The DRS occasionally clashed with the army command, notably during major security-related upheavals such as the 2013 hostage crisis in Tingentourine, near the Libyan border.[73]

High-ranking military officers also routinely engaged in feuds with top government officials. This power relation is often described as a kind of vassalization. Well-informed observers tend to deny any autonomy on the part of civilian actors.[74] Yet after the return to electoral competition in 1995, politicians progressively expanded their margin of action, especially when they achieved a national reputation. Some openly questioned the scrutinizing role that military actors had claimed for themselves. Consequently, the increasingly public character of the conflicts between military and civilian figures under Bouteflika further invalidated the alleged neutrality of the ANP.

In addition to its internal divisions and its direct involvement in politics, the army was notoriously involved in acts of economic predation. In 1962, the appropriation of national wealth was linked to a general context of economic revenge that led former members of the ALN to reap the bounties of war.[75] After independence, the pattern of embezzlement was also a consequence of the military's systematic involvement in the planned economy.[76] With the economic liberalization of the 1980s, officers enjoyed privileges that allowed them to benefit from the looming crisis.[77] Their progressive reconversion and inclusion in the private sector resulted in a form of "economic encystment" as they used their position to "break into legal and informal economic networks in search for financial privileges and alternative cash crops."[78] In the 2000s, the children of key praetorian figures, such as Ahmed Gaïd Salah or Khaled Nezzar, benefited from their family connections to invest in real estate projects. As a result, rather than an institution exclusively preoccupied with the national interest, the army was increasingly portrayed as a "mafia of generals."

A CRITICIZED INSTITUTION

Some of the criticism targeting the ANP is encapsulated in the following anecdote. I first met Ali in Taghit, in the western part of the Algerian Sahara, in the fall of 2010. Following an unexpected event, I had to travel north in an emergency. As he was himself on his way up to Mascara, the thirty-five-year-old doctor proposed we travel together. On the way, between observations on the beauty of the granite landscape that interrupted the otherwise endless horizon, Ali spoke about his personal life. He described the difficulties he encountered in his daily activities as a physician, notably because of the mafia-like practices of some of his colleagues. He also complained about the country's pervasive corruption and lamented not being able to leave for France because of his family.

As we stopped at one of the many gendarmerie checkpoints on the road to Mascara, one of the young men in uniform suddenly erupted. He was furious at Ali for not braking early enough. The atmosphere in the car immediately became tense, as the soldier kept lecturing him, with his hand placed carelessly on the stock of his automatic rifle. After he allowed us to go on our way, Ali stated with a grim tone: "The less you see these green uniforms, the safer you are. They say that they are here to protect us, but everybody knows in this country that the generals are gangsters who are stealing public money." He then rehearsed a well-known script by explaining the origin of the "System" and the role of the generals.

Ali's criticism of the "mafia" that had allegedly confiscated power was soon interrupted by repeated phone calls. His parents were worried since he had not yet returned home. From then on, his mood became gloomier, and the discussion shifted to his main problem: family pressure. He was going home somewhat reluctantly. As we approached Mascara, he drove slower and slower. That same night, I was officially introduced to his father, Mohamed. The patriarch was watching the news in his bedroom, located on the third floor of their large family house. As I shook his father's hand, I understood Ali's predicament. Despite being thirty-five years old, he admitted that he was still intimidated when he approached his father's bedroom. To be sure, this former high-ranking public servant in a state-run bank was an imposing man.

During the dinner that followed, the conservation soon turned again to the army. After he learned that I was a researcher, Ali's father proceeded to explain the country's situation. He quickly started talking about corruption and the military. I reproduce here his explanation of what led him to pay to spare his sons from conscription, as I wrote it down later that night:

> When you have sons, you cannot let them go do this kind of thing. What happens there is inhuman. These are illiterate people who claim to be superior and who order young college graduates around, who insult them and who hit them if they feel like it. They don't even know how to read, and they get their revenge by forcing these kids to clean the toilets. When my sons had to do their military service, I paid for each of them. A lot of money—I didn't count. For the second one, it didn't work; they kept him for one month. You can imagine how hard it was. In a month, terrible things can happen.

Mohamed was a fierce supporter of the centralizing state and the single party as historical necessities. Yet despite his nationalist views and the relative wealth he had secured thanks to his career as a senior civil servant, he was extremely critical of those who came after Boumediene, especially in the military, because of their alleged violence and ignorance. He used corruption to spare his sons from military service. Physical threats were his main concern. He depicted ruthless military instructors whose ignorance and frustration resulted in a desire to humiliate young people. According to him, military service had turned into an ego-crushing machine, a cruel rite of passage allowing a brutal institution to force his sons into submission. Educated, living in comfort with his family, Mohamed linked his rejection of conscription to his sons' status. As bankers and physicians, they belonged to an educated elite that the defenders of the established order had to break in order to preserve the status quo.

The harshness of the former civil servant's discourse was certainly class-based. His words were nonetheless concordant with other analyses that underlined the growing mistrust toward the ANP. During the 1990s, the brutality of the ANP's methods and the failure of its leaders to prevent terrorist attacks undermined the institution's founding myths.[79] Under Bouteflika, military leaders' public image remained tarnished for the most part, because of their political interference and alleged corruption. Mohamed's rejection of conscription indicated the ANP's loss of prestige. Once associated with the integration of the citizenry and social promotion, the army had become an institution that forced young Algerians to put their lives on hold in the name of a never-ending struggle against terrorism. The ANP faced a crisis of authority, a rejection of its right to be obeyed without question. This fueled attempts to evade military service through various legal loopholes. And it is certainly no coincidence that Abdelaziz Bouteflika himself exempted several cohorts of conscripts.

THE INDISPENSABLE ANP

Does this mean that nothing was left of the ANP's revolutionary legitimacy? Faced with statements such as "Milosevic is a choirboy compared to Nezzar and his companions,"[80] the military aristocracy did not remain silent. Retired officers frequently spoke out to defend the institution—and themselves—against such accusations. General Yahia Rahal was among the first officers to publicly defend the ANP against criticism, while admitting that his colleagues may have committed "mistakes."[81] Without taking these justifications at face value, a nuanced understanding of the army's role is necessary. Under Bouteflika, a generational renewal led to the departure of key praetorian figures. Some died (Lamari, Belkheir). Others retired (Nezzar, Mediene). They were replaced by younger military officers, many of whom were trained during the 1990s. A relative feminization, symbolized by the appointment of the first female generals, also contributed to the renovation of the ANP's image.

The old revolutionary routine presenting the ANP as the "worthy successor of the ALN" remained, however. At the end of 2009, a qualifying game for the World Cup demonstrated the persistent link between the population and the army. After a couple of extremely tense matches between the Algerian and Egyptian national football teams, marked by exceptional fervor and acts of violence in Cairo,[82] the decisive game was to be played in a neutral stadium, in Omdurman, Sudan. The army organized a special airlift to facilitate the travel of Algerian supporters. As Algerian streets filled with ecstatic fans after their team's final victory, an old motto of military radicalism came back to life, as the crowd sang, "Jaysh, shaʿab, maʿa al-khaḍrāʾ!" (The army and the people with the green!). If football had replaced development as a reason for popular mobilization, the army and the people were nonetheless linked in this cathartic moment. While the historical alliance had been weakened by the crisis, its meaning persisted, erupting in the wake of a symbolic threat after the bus transporting the national team was assaulted by Egyptian fans.

In addition to its persistent alliance with the people, the ANP also retained genuine economic power. In 2009, military expenses amounted to 15 percent of state spending and 3.9 percent of the country's GDP. In comparison, at the same time, Tunisia dedicated 1.3 percent of its GDP to military spending, a rate similar to most European nations. As of 2018, the ANP's budget was the largest in Africa, representing almost 25 percent of state spending and more than 5 percent of the country's GDP.[83] In recent decades, the Algeria's military budget has almost always been drafted without political oversight. The one exception was in 1991, just before the coup.

After collapsing in the 1990s, the myth of the army was reformulated. The key stakes of professionalization and the withdrawal from the country's political life became recurring themes in official discourse. In parallel to its continuous war on "residual terrorism," the ANP was portrayed as an institution that was mostly preoccupied with public good. In 2005, for instance, the pro-government daily *L'Expression* dedicated an article to the military's efforts to make isolated villages accessible following winter storms. The journalist wrote that the ANP was "involved every day a little more in missions of humanitarian and public interest, offering the image of a faultless institution, after its complete disengagement from politics."[84] In the wake of various emergencies linked to climate change, or security threats at the country's southern border, scholars have likewise highlighted the army's efforts to prevent actual disasters by fulfilling its humanitarian duties, strengthening civilian-military partnerships, and supporting the economic integration of the spatial margins of the country.[85]

At the same time, the latency of the crisis meant that the tutelary impulses of high-ranking officers never disappeared. Politicians, opponents of the government included, kept seeing the army as a reference and a resource for settling their disputes. The legal conditions for direct military intervention remained and were still justified in the name of preventing an impending catastrophe. When it cleared the snow on the roads to isolated villages, the ANP acted under Law No. 91-23 of December 6, 1991, the same one used to justify the coup of January 1992. After the state of emergency ended in February 2011, an opportunistic addition to this law legalized "the intervention of units of the National People's Army in order to respond to imperatives linked to terrorism and subversion." Successive reforms maintained a space for military intervention, as repression drew on a mix of imposed exception and non-lethal policing. In April 2019, after more than six weeks of protest, it was the army chief of staff, Ahmed Gaïd Salah, who gave the final blow to the presidency by publicly demanding Bouteflika's removal.

The Cartel That Controls the State

The presidency, the army staff, and the DRS were the main nodes of power in the ruling coalition during Bouteflika's rule. Yet how exactly these entities related to each other was unclear. Observers described a "factionalized and opaque decision-making apparatus" that reinforced the structural uncertainty.[86] In the following section, I aim to make this power structure more legible by explaining the dynamics shaping the coalition. I also show how the public expressions of its internal contradictions contributed to the social and political construction of the suspended disaster.

A CARTEL

Bourdieu explains that the "state is not a block but a social field."[87] It is a "social space where actors compete with each other to control scarce resources."[88] A social field enables the creation of networks shaped by institutional hierarchies, tacit alliances, patronage, business relations, or competition. The fiction of the monolithic state nonetheless denies this internal fluidity and heterogeneity. This founding myth is made even stronger by the ethos shared by state agents. The state is a "strategic action field," which means that it is characterized by the copresence of individuals who interact based on a shared understanding of the objectives, rules, and relations that structure it.[89] Inside the state, these actors enter in competition for a specific capital, a "kind of meta-power, a power over all powers."[90] By drawing on their meta-power, state agents and institutions acquire the ability to intervene in surrounding social fields (economic, cultural, sports, media, political, and so on). This ability to act upon the entirety of society is legitimized by the universalizing fiction mentioned already. In the name of the people and the nation, state agents can shape social space. Because their action is directed outwardly and based on a fictitious unanimity, they are not supposed to enter into competition. The state field is thus a space of negotiation, an "arena for compromise."[91] In this arena, the groups competing for meta-power regularly bargain and occasionally clash, while striving to preserve order and their own vested interests.

The relative permeability of the state field and constant internal tensions therein fuel the lability of the coalition that controls it. The changing and heterogeneous nature of this collection of groups and individuals does not mean that it is not organized according to a guiding logic. In the 1990s and 2000s, ruling coalitions in the region evolved under the combined effects of bureaucratization, economic liberalization, and democratization.[92] Their ideological cohesion decreased, as was the case in Algeria under Bouteflika. To make sense of these divergent interests and sociological components, Hamit Bozarslan spoke of a cartelized state structure.[93]

The idea of a cartel captures the logic of collusion that structures the relations among actors in a social field. In economics, a cartel aims to regulate competition in a specific sector and to secure the business shares and profits of its various parties.[94] It is a mutually beneficial structure based on an agreement between competing entities to influence prices and prevent the entry of new challengers in the market they dominate. Here, the term "cartel" captures the idea of a coalition aiming to maintain its dominance by lowering the risk resulting from competition. I will henceforth use this moniker to designate the collective that controls the Algerian state, enforces the status quo, and secures the interests of its members.

These benefits result from their monopoly on the meta-power produced in and by the state. Because of the ubiquitous nature of this meta-power, members of the cartel can enjoy a diverse range of advantages: economic (wealth) or political (promotion of a conservative agenda); symbolic (being recognized as the spokesperson of a community) or material (financing infrastructures in one's hometown); collective (defending the interests of the ANP) or individual (becoming president for life). Thus, the notion of a cartel should not be understood merely as a negative phenomenon, most obviously as a reference to Latin American drug-trafficking organizations. In its political sense, the cartel describes a collective that aims to secure a set of advantages resulting from their control over the state, as is the case, for example, in the analysis of European governing parties proposed by Richard S. Katz and Peter Mair.[95]

To secure these advantages, the Algerian cartel ensured the reproduction of the political order. Nevertheless, internal contradictions led to confrontations between its members. In this context, competitors instrumentalized state institutions to monopolize resources (means of violence, money, manpower). They transformed acts of regulation (anticorruption campaigns, forced retirement, debt collection) into attacks against their adversaries.[96] As the crisis continued, recurring disagreements exposed the competition between different factions within the cartel. The deep chasm between the claims of the ruling elites, who pretended to govern in the name of the public interest, and their appropriation of state power became obvious. If this contradiction is hardly surprising, its revelation nonetheless had remarkable consequences: the effort to produce hegemony collided with unavowable truths. Meanwhile the socially shared fear of a rise in violence increased steadily.

OLYMPIAN QUARRELS

Specialists of postindependence Algeria have underlined the tendency of political leaders to criticize each other publicly.[97] The exposure of their quarrels intensified with the transition to political pluralism, revealing a recurring theme in the settlement of internal disputes. The fall of Liamine Zeroual offers a telling first example. Mohamed Betchine, a retired general and former head of military intelligence, was the president's closest aide. A ubiquitous figure, he was appointed "minister-adviser" to the presidency and a member of the RND's executive. When Zeroual informed his circle of confidants that he was not going to run for a second mandate, Betchine logically appeared to be his natural heir. However, the selection of the head of state had historically been a matter of compromise within the cartel, rather than a matter of "dynastic" succession.[98]

Between the summer of 1997 and the winter of 1998, the country faced a dramatic epidemic of civilian massacres. At the same time, internal struggles inside the cartel resurfaced with renewed vigor, as officials fought openly in the media. The presidential entourage was quickly steamrolled. Benefiting from leaks, the press revealed that Betchine and the minister of justice, Mohamed Adami, were involved in a corruption and car-trafficking scheme. Liamine Zeroual announced that he was calling much-anticipated presidential elections, invoking his "desire for [an] alternation" of power. Yet the leaks continued. Adami and Betchine eventually resigned in October 1998, in hopes of limiting the risk of prosecution.[99]

Judicial mechanisms had long been instrumentalized in the process of internal regulation. Following a liberalization in 1990, the private press became another tool for competing actors. Revelations in the media were weaponized, as leaked files served to tarnish reputations and justify prosecutions. Whereas internal struggles were previously limited to military-bureaucratic spheres, they now became a spectacle directed at public opinion. Consequently, the fear of a coup routinely resurfaced in moments of extreme tension. Previous examples showed that the head of state could be sacked (Ben Bella, Chadli, Kafi) or killed (Boudiaf). Yet the Adami-Betchine scandal told a different story: rather than endangering the status quo by taking down the president, opponents within the cartel could also target his close allies. The disclosure of corruption cases was enough to undermine the reputation and power of the presidency and its entourage.

Conflicts were not limited to the ANP-presidency dichotomy. From 2003 to 2004, as Prime Minister Ali Benflis strove to unseat Bouteflika, the country saw a polarization of its political leadership. During the Eighth National Congress of the FLN, organized in April 2003, Benflis benefited from massive support to become the party's general secretary. In response, Bouteflika first resolved to cancel the weekly meeting of the cabinet, then to sack his unruly prime minister. Eventually, the balance of power proved to be in favor of the president. According to the 1997 law on political parties, the interior minister, Noureddine "Yazid" Zerhouni, enjoyed the power to oversee political organizations. A Bouteflika ally, Zerhouni demanded an investigation into the 2003 congress, which in turn led to the cancellation of Benflis' election as general secretary. Politicians affiliated to the presidency then took over the FLN after Bouteflika's crushing victory in the 2004 presidential election. Given their respective institutional positions, the prime minister could not compete, at least not alone.

This momentary polarization of politics testified to a growing hostility between the presidency and a section of the military aristocracy. Since July 2002, Khaled Nezzar had been fighting a judicial battle in Paris, where he had initiated a libel suit against former officer and whistle-blower Habib Souaïdia. Supporters of one of the figureheads of the *éradicateurs* expressed their disappointment in the insufficient support from the presidency. Nezzar himself became increasingly hostile. In 2003, he described what he saw as Bouteflika's spinelessness for having refused to become head of the HCE in 1992, when the country needed him most. The president was a "a tiny heart and a tiny soul," he wrote, who "only appeared great in the shadow of a great man" (i.e., Boumediene).[100] Nezzar also belittled Bouteflika's participation in the nationalist movement, while making explicit reference to his height: "this claim to rewrite history, to revisit it, to resize it in such a way that it can fit him nicely, reveals suddenly his clumsiness, as he wears an ALN outfit that is wider and taller than his actual size."[101] During the same period, Chief of Staff Mohamed Lamari also intervened publicly to warn the head of state. He stated in the private daily *Le Matin* that "anyone who exercises the prerogatives of President of the Republic and tries to change the Republican order, to question political pluralism, to promote a tailor-made constitutional reordering, or to look down on the people and society, will find the army in their way."[102] As had been the case for the FLN, the army was nonetheless disciplined after Bouteflika's reelection. Lamari was forced to resign in August 2004 and Ahmed Gaïd Salah took over. The presidency continued its purge of high-ranking military figures, and key praetorians such as Larbi Belkheir and Mohamed Touati were also ostracized.

The purge implemented by the presidency was not simply the revenge of civilians against the army. It benefited from the support of military figures such as Gaïd Salah and Mohamed "Toufik" Mediene, the long-standing head of the DRS. Military intelligence maintained its ability to intervene in politics and destroy personal reputations. Efforts to curb its influence were made all the more difficult thanks to its strategic role in managing society and gathering compromising information, notably regarding corruption. As in former Eastern Bloc countries,[103] the reinforcement of the presidency faced a major structural limitation: the imperative now was to bring the "super-ministry of security" under presidential control.

After six years of cold peace, a series of scandals revolving around corruption and embezzlement targeted key members of the presidential entourage. In October 2009, Minister of Public Transportation Amar Ghoul was involved in a scandal linked to the taking of secret commissions during the construction of one of Bouteflika's signature infrastructure projects, the East–West Highway. After being questioned by investigators, Ghoul saved his career by sacrificing his chief of staff. In January 2010, another major scandal broke out, this one involving the oil and gas company Sonatrach, some of its top managers appointed by the presidency, and Minister of Energy and Mines Chakib Khelil. A key member of the presidential entourage, Khelil was officially indicted in 2013, after which he fled the country for the United States. The DRS was instrumental in revealing both scandals, even though it benefited from the key insights of Italian investigators in the second case. The corruption cases came at a tense time, marked by the uncertainty around presidential succession and recurring efforts to reform military intelligence. Shortly after Khelil's dramatic escape from the country, the government announced a project aimed at restructuring the DRS. Many of its high-ranking officers were forced to retire, including its number two, Athmane Tartag, infamous for his role as director of the Ben Aknoun interrogation center during the 1990s.[104]

Tensions between the DRS and the presidency continued. During the 2014 campaign, the newly appointed general secretary of the FLN, Amar

Saâdani, accused the DRS of interfering in the country's political life and blamed it for repeatedly failing to prevent terrorism. In response, retired general Hocine Benhadid raised the stakes by suggesting that the behavior of the presidential entourage amounted to high treason. Meanwhile, rumors of a conflict between Gaïd Salah and Toufik gained traction, as Gaïd Salah allegedly supported Bouteflika's assumption of a fourth presidential mandate, something to which Toufik seemed opposed. The president himself had to intervene. In an official statement released by the official news agency, he reminded everyone of the importance of the army's cohesion and denounced "fictitious conflicts fomented" by enemies of the country.[105] Bouteflika's reelection in 2014 seemed to settle this quarrel in favor of the presidency and its allies in the army command. During the summer of 2015, former head of counterterrorism General Abdelkader Aït Ouarabi, a Toufik ally, was arrested and indicted for destroying official documents. In October 2015, Toufik himself was forced to retire. By the beginning of 2016, the DRS had been dismantled. Some of its directorates came under the direct control of the army staff. The remaining subdivisions were integrated into a new structure, the Department of Surveillance and Security, which was placed under the command of Athmane Tartag and attached to the presidency.

Internal struggles and the reversal of existing alliances thus punctuated Bouteflika's four mandates. The public disclosure of these tensions fueled the constant rumor of a conflict among ruling elites that could jeopardize Algeria's stability.[106] As they revived memories of upheavals linked to the downfall of past presidential figures, these Olympian quarrels contributed the latency of the crisis and objectivized the existential threat faced by the country.

THE POLITICAL RATIONALE OF SUSPICION

Because of their illegibility, the constant struggles within the cartel fueled a social and political imaginary that became a key feature of governance by catastrophization. This imaginary can be understood in a historical perspective, as the continuation of the *peur bleue* (blue scare) instilled in the nationalist movement by French counterinsurgency forces. During the anticolonial revolution, the French Army relied on false flag operations and fraudulent lists of "traitors" to spread suspicion among its adversaries. The notion of *bleuite*, once used to describe the paranoia resulting from French manipulation, was later appropriated to depict the climate of total insecurity and uncertainty during the 1990s. The memories of these two wars—the War of Liberation, and the civil war that eventually followed—served as a bedrock for the construction of a dominant political rationale of suspicion in Bouteflika's Algeria.

Over the past twenty years, competition within the cartel has fueled a similar *peur bleue*. At the beginning of 2010, as corruption scandals destabilized the presidency, the head of the DGSN, Ali Tounsi, was shot dead in his office by one of his aides, who was accused of being involved in a corruption scheme. Adding to the confusion, the alleged killer's lawyers argued that this murder was in fact part of a plot organized by then interior minister Yazid Zerhouni.[107] As intense disagreements divided the core of the ruling coalition, Tounsi's death seemed to be motivated by obscure forces. As Bourdieu puts it, "inside a social field, one can kill for motives that are far from obvious to those situated just on the other side."[108]

Journalists and experts also contributed to the *peur bleue*. Confronted with a chaotic political spectacle, they attempted to understand the balance of power between key actors and predict the future direction of the polity. Their efforts were nonetheless often at odds. After the 2012 legislative elections, for instance, political scientist Lahouari Addi argued on the francophone website *Le Quotidien d'Algerie* that "Bouteflika was the biggest loser" of the electoral process because he had been "abandoned by the army."[109] Other outlets offered diametrically opposed analyses, as was the case, for example, when journalist Mohamed Cherak emphasized the crushing victory of the president's side and the disarray of its Islamist opponents in the Arabic-language daily *El Khabar*.[110] Contradictory readings could be found in the public and private press, on the Internet, and social media.

The DRS was assigned a central role in the rationale of suspicion that explained the country's recent upheavals. In his book *Algérie: Un système politique militarisé* (Algeria: A militarized political system), Madjid Benchikh, former dean of the Law Faculty at the University of Algiers and member of the FFS, argued that military intelligence was able to create and manipulate phony organizations so as to undermine real opposition parties.[111] Portrayed as an omnipotent agency, the DRS was suspected of manipulating protesters, controlling deputies and businessmen, and instrumentalizing al-Qaeda in the Islamic Maghrib. According to an Algerian political scientist who spoke at a conference organized in Paris in 2014, the services already had a well-planned strategy to create a state of emergency after the upcoming election and legitimize a new praetorian takeover. Indeed, experts contributed to reproducing a rationale announcing the unfolding disaster.

"Toufik" Mediene came to represent the occult forces active at the heart of the state. He was an alumnus of the infamous "red carpet" cohort, a generation of military intelligence officers trained in the Soviet Union after independence. Portrayed as possessing almost telekinetic abilities, he allegedly "had a complete hold on politics, economic activities and the administration."[112] Appearing to embody the very idea of power, Toufik seemed deprived of a physical self. For years, only one old and blurry picture of him circulated online. Under Bouteflika, he became a quasi-magical figure, someone who allegedly controlled everything and everyone, even the events that seemed to weaken him. After the DRS failed to prevent a terrorist attack in Tingentourine in January 2013, rumors assigned the authorship of this major security breach to the department's Machiavelli. Even though he was forced to resign in 2015, he remained a ubiquitous figure until the Hirak, a mastermind who was said to wield a secret influence over a shadowy network of affiliates. This representation of an almighty deep state symbolized by Toufik's spectral presence was also echoed in international media by experts, journalists, and researchers. According to some of them, the DRS was the obscure force behind most terrorist groups in the Sahel.[113]

The dominant political rationale of suspicion functioned as a regime of truth that served to organize the uncertainty and mistrust directed at the country's ruling elites. At the same time, it also exaggerated the role of intentional actions and cold-blooded calculations at the expense of structural causes and contingencies. Such a rationale reinforced the notion of a disembodied and omnipotent "System" and fueled an imaginary of conspiracy.[114] Combining disenchantment with re-enchantment, this imaginary can produce powerlessness in the face of an almighty enmity and legitimize fatalistic postures, such as the one adopted by Mohand at the beginning of this chapter.[115]

The consequences of this rationale were not only subjective. Political actors had to take the constant meddling of the security services and the military in politics into account. For instance, Asaf, a member of the Rally for Culture and Democracy (Rassemblement pour la Culture et la Démocratie, RCD), explained that party leaders had no other option but to consult high-ranking officers:

> We know that those who make the decisions are in the DRS and the army staff. Who doesn't know it? So I am saying that one might as well deal with the Lord as with his Prophet. We have obviously met with the military, not only with Toufik but with other generals . . . This doesn't mean that we agree with them. But we need to talk to them because they are the real decision makers.
>
> (ASAF, LOCAL OFFICIAL OF THE RCD, TIZI OUZOU, SPRING 2011)

This former high school principal presented his conclusion as common sense, and this was certainly not the last time I encountered an activist or a party official who evoked the necessity of maintaining communication channels with the praetorians. Engaging in talks with the DRS, accounting for military interference in political strategies, anticipating the possibility of a coup—these were necessities that shaped the actors' calculations. Military tutelage was a structuring reality of the Algerian system. At the same time, political debates under Bouteflika were also saturated with (sometimes slanderous) accusations of collusion and manipulation. For observers and activists alike, reality itself seemed to be on shaky ground. Even major events such as the uprising of October 1988 were often portrayed as elaborate plots. The rationale of suspicion thus contributed to a systematic infantilization of the population, which had seemingly lost its autonomy to be constantly manipulated by the inner circles of the *Pouvoir*.

Public discourses depicting almighty "forces of evil" acting inside the state—to borrow the phrase used by former prime minister Sid Ahmed Ghozali in his 1992 resignation letter[116]—were ambiguous. They revealed the divided nature of the cartel and the recurring manipulation of social and political groups by the secret services. Yet it was also a regulatory fiction. Once confronted with the relentless corrupting influence of the deep state, political activism seemed futile. Challenging the might of the military appeared to be either unrealistic or not worth the risk. In short, the political rationale of suspicion was simultaneously a revelation, a mystification, and a prescription.

NECROPOLITICS

Key actors at the heart of the state were often physically invisible. After he was hospitalized for cancer in 2005, Bouteflika's condition became a hot topic for mockery and conjecture. Shortly after his televised speech on April 15, 2011, in which he announced upcoming reforms, I was with two students in the dorms of the University of Tizi Ouzou. The young men ridiculed what they described as the president's "living dead" look. "We could see the puppet strings they used to make his lips move," one of them mocked. Back in Algiers a few days later, I heard the same jokes deriding the president. Some suggested that he might not be able to present the trophy to the next winner of the Algerian Cup at the beginning of May. Following a long-standing pattern, popular jokes (ḥikāyāt) already served as a mode of counter-sovereignty undermining political authorities.[117] This was before the ischemic attack that made Bouteflika unable to walk or speak. After April 2013, the president's body was showcased during elections or for the visit of a U.S. secretary of state, and in an official picture (French: *le cadre*; Arabic: *as-ṣūra*) adorning the walls of government buildings. He seemed to be kept alive artificially, waiting on the threshold of the afterlife until his Great Mosque was completed. Very much like Franco in another time and place, Bouteflika symbolized the encounter between the right to kill and the regulation of life.[118] Moreover, because he was the biopolitical sovereign embodying the exceptional policies that had brought peace back to the polity, his biological death, by threatening the fiction of authority, could lead to "the political death of the juridical order in its totality."[119]

Governance by catastrophization is a largely necropolitical matter, in the sense that the management of the population and the exercise of power assigns a central role to death, as a promise and a performance.[120] Under Bouteflika, Algerian necropolitics included the instrumentalization of the memory of the martyrs of the revolution in order to organize the distribution of financial resources. Other necropolicies were directly linked to the climax of the crisis, such as the use of mass violence and collective punishment by the security forces during the Dark Decade. Likewise, the legal obliteration of the crimes perpetrated in the 1990s served to generate obedience and cohesion within the cartel. Both the ANP and the presidency were instrumental in the necropolitical management of the country.

Death was not merely a threat or a resource—it was also a promise of transmission. The "Revolutionary Family," which had occupied center stage since Algeria's independence in 1962, was expected to hand over the baton to subsequent generations. This theme was repeated ad nauseam during official events. Celebrating fifty years of Algerian independence at the 5 July Stadium, for instance, the official ceremony concluded with a display entitled simply "Transmission": it showed two high school students, a boy and a girl, ascending a long ramp while holding aloft a torch; in this way they were to revive the flame symbolizing the memory of the revolution and its martyrs.

Yet generational renewal was more of an anticipated horizon than an actuality. While former revolutionaries filled the highest offices in the state, many young Algerians experienced the never-ending crisis as an all-encompassing condition of existence. They complained about living in an unbearable country, where they were exhausted by the city, their job (or lack thereof), and their fellow citizens (see chapter 6). Confessions sometimes evoked a state of mental distress similar to the experience of "daily death" (*mort quotidienne*) that Fanon diagnosed among North Africans living in France.[121] The transition away from the Revolutionary Family—its *death*—was a constantly deferred promise. Thanks to its mastery of biopower, the generation of Bouteflika, Toufik, and Gaïd Salah remained solidly attached to the realm of the living, protected by the sprits of its martyrs. To ensure its infinite survival, political time was frozen. For those who took part in politics, this glaciation generated a form of powerlessness. In 2008, a member of the Movement for the Society of Peace described just such a sense of disillusionment when talking about the debates surrounding the upcoming constitutional revision:

> In France, you start speaking about the presidential election two years before; in Algeria, the election is in little more than six months, and there is almost no discussion. As a member of a party belonging to the presidential coalition, I have no knowledge, to this day, about the president's decision and about the [constitutional] modification currently underway.
>
> (ABDELKRIM DAHMEN, MEMBER OF THE MSP'S NATIONAL COUNCIL AND FORMER DEPUTY FOR TIPAZA, ALGIERS, AUTUMN 2008)

Because of its ongoing mutism, the presidency fueled the political glaciation. In November 2010, more than a year and a half after the end of the presidential campaign, the giant posters of Bouteflika were still adorning Martyrs' Square, in the center of Constantine, the third-largest city in the country. The banners displayed the same motto: "A Strong and Safe Algeria" (*Jazāʾr Qawiyya wa Āmana*). The biological life of the sovereign seemed to defy natural laws and political life was frozen. In order to obscure the dreaded truth of the president's mortality, the results of his physical exams were kept secret. Shrouded in mystery, the country was characterized by a "lag time" (*temps mort*) that paralyzed history, as had been the case under colonialism.[122] Consequently, some awaited Bouteflika's death, believing it would bring about the fall of the "System." As Nassim, an RCD representative at the Tizi Ouzou APW told me in 2011, "when Bouteflika, who prolonged the life of the 'System' in 1999, dies, they [the *décideurs*] won't be able to survive. It's impossible." Others were amazed by the vitality of the spirit that continued to haunt the president's failing body. In 2014, as we watched the images of Bouteflika casting a ballot from his wheelchair, Nidhal noticed the brightness in his pale blue eyes and exclaimed, "This is the first time we've seen him like that since last year! He is back! He is going to eat them all!"

FIGURE 2.2 Electoral posters still adorned Martyrs' Square in Constantine more than eighteen months after Bouteflika's second reelection. Constantine, autumn 2010. (Photograph by author.)

Far from being limited to Bouteflika, the Algerian necropolis was built on a state of constant imperilment for the polity and its members. As the glaciation of politics became synonymous with survival, a thaw would have therefore implied the return of the law of death. Government officials could thus reduce their legitimation effort to the *ultima ratio* of state discourse: "it is us or chaos." Behind the constant securitization of public life, the cartel merely proposed a heterogeneous vulgate, bringing together nation, progress, and Islam. While allegedly settled by Bouteflika's Charter for Peace and National Reconciliation, the "national tragedy" remained the underlying reason for the forced insertion of the polity into a continuum of security, discipline, and growth. A few days before the beginning of the *Hirak*, former prime minister and newly appointed director of Bouteflika's campaign team Abdelmalek Sellal offered the following explanation:

> A lot of people forget that we faced a grave crisis at the end of the 1990s, a lot of them forget the tragedy we faced. Nobody even imagined that we could win and become a family again, but we survived thanks to President Abdelaziz Bouteflika's reconciliation policy. We must remember what was done, at a political, social, cultural, industrial, and agricultural level. The numbers are clear, and we will show the figures during the campaign.[123]

Until the very beginning of 2019, proponents of the established order thus relied on the symbolic violence characteristic of necropolitics, which consists of "maintaining the morbid spectacle of what [had] happened in front of the eyes of the victim—and the people around him or her."[124]

Eternal Return

Between 1999 and 2019, the cartel that controlled the Algerian state experienced a succession of internal conflicts. Despite tense episodes, the general equilibrium prevailed. The cartel was able to limit the risks resulting from the competition between its members and to secure their advantages on the market of meta-power. Instability persisted and disruptive events dissolved in a repetitive routine: corruption scandals, public quarrels among state officials, promises of reform, and warnings against a new rise in violence punctuated the country's political life.

The eternal return of the promise of transmission was a redundant manifestation of the latent crisis. On November 1, 2004, for the fiftieth anniversary of the beginning of the War of Liberation, Abdelaziz Bouteflika gave a speech in front of the National Organization of Mujahideen. "Revolutionary legitimacy is over," he proclaimed. The cryopreserved order survived nonetheless. Eight years passed. On May 8, 2012, for the anniversary of the massacres perpetrated by the French in the spring of 1945, Bouteflika, still president, addressed the crowd in Sétif. In what appeared to be a farewell speech, he pronounced the iconic phrase, *Jili tab jnanu*—literally, "My generation is a ripe garden," which is to say, it has given everything. A couple of days later, the FLN secured a crushing victory in the legislative elections.

Tab jnanu became a slogan decrying the persistent grip of the ruling gerontocracy.[125] For decades, familiar figures retreated in disgrace before reappearing with a new position. Forced to retire in 2005, General Mohamed Touati, a.k.a. "Al-Mukh" (The Brain), returned six years later as adviser to the presidency in charge of political reforms. Ahmed Ouyahia and Abdelaziz Belkhadem, respectively heads of the FLN and the RND, were ousted from their parties in 2012. It took them only two years to return to the fore, as members of Bouteflika's picaresque campaign team in 2014. As for Khaled Nezzar, the iconic figure of the *éradicateurs*, he retired in 1994. Since then, he has resurfaced periodically to denounce Bouteflika or defend the honor of the army against its foreign enemies. The words used by Jean-Jacques Lavenue to describe the internal struggles in the FLN at the end of the 1980s thus come to mind:

> For almost fifteen years, the evolution of the FLN, and of Algeria more generally, suggests that it is doomed to reenact different versions of the same episode: "the succession of Boumediene." From the "victory of the Reformers" to the "revenge of the Orthodox," the public witnesses the rise, fall, and reappearance of heroes who have become genuine stereotypes, on a stage where the background never changes... Depending on the version of the episode, divas leave, resign in a dramatic manner, or plot on the ruins of their lost power.[126]

The rules may have changed, but the cyclical nature of the spectacle remained. With the political and media liberalization, new figures rose to prominence and criticism became fiercer. Crony capitalists, politicians, technocrats, and civil society leaders intervened in the country's political life. They praised or blamed the government and the army. Once again, the crisis proved instrumental to the reconfiguration of the political order and the broadening of the cartel.

3
Cronies and Labyrinths

The idea that there is, in a specific place, a thing called power, seems to me like a rigged analysis.... The reality is that power is based on relations, it is a more or less organized, more or less pyramidal, more or less coordinated network of relations.

—Michel Foucault

The Forum of Businessowners considers that the policy [of economic reforms] should continue vigorously. Thus, it supports Mr. Abdelaziz Bouteflika's program and will remain mobilized alongside public authorities, as has always been the case so far, in order to contribute positively to the edification of a prosperous, effective, and solidary economy.

—Statement released by the Forum of Businessowners

In the 1980s, the early stages of the process of political reconfiguration were accompanied by a broader economic restructuring. The reorganization of state-owned companies undertaken at the beginning of the decade resulted in their fragmentation into hundreds of disorganized structures.[1] In the meantime, the reform of agriculture led to a dismantling of self-managed production units, a decrease in food subsidies, and a distribution of public lands according to opaque criteria.[2]

These adjustments fueled discontent. Several years before becoming minister of finance under Bouteflika, the economist Abdelaziz Benachenhou underlined the hostility of the macroeconomic environment, the brutality of the reforms already undertaken, and the profound de-structuring to come.³ Despite its dreaded social consequences, the process of economic liberalization was nonetheless portrayed as a necessary evil, the impact of which was to be borne by the entire population.⁴

In April 1994, the government signed an agreement with the International Monetary Fund (IMF) for the implementation of a structural adjustment program (SAP). The subsequent devaluation of the Algerian dinar (dinar algérien, DA) by 50 percent resulted automatically in an increase in the amount of foreign debt held by public companies. Their accumulated deficit rose from 10 billion DA at the end of 1994 to more than 100 billion DA in June 1996. In this context, the public sector, already bled dry, was to be thoroughly dismantled. International financial institutions supported this option, as the sale of public assets brought the prospect of substantial revenues. The SAP also led to a revision of government priorities. While the state remained omnipresent in the security and hydrocarbon sectors, it partially withdrew from its role as a provider of public services, notably public health and education.⁵

The Dark Decade offered substantial opportunities linked to the growth of the informal economy and the opening of new markets. The SAP authorized a process of privatization that brought together governing elites and parasitic actors. The economic liberalization thus fostered a reconfiguration in which crony capitalists, enriched by privileges and monopolies, were to enjoy a privileged position, following a pattern common to other developing countries in the region and beyond.⁶ During the 1990s, widespread violence enabled the redistribution and accumulation of political, social, and economic capital. The combination of physical and economic violence was thus central to the (re)foundation of the political order and the (re)structuring of the state.⁷

To understand the combined reconfiguration of the state apparatus and the system of production, Bradford L. Dillman describes a transition in three steps, from "state dirigisme" under Boumediene, to "state reformism" under Chadli, and eventually the advent of the "rentier state" in the 1990s. If this periodization suggests a normative analytical framework in which "successful" economic liberalization is associated with democratization, Dillman nonetheless grasps the detrimental consequences resulting from the process of restructuring. Indeed, the SAP contributed to the formation of a predatory class alliance bringing together members of the military aristocracy, civilian officials (technocrats and politicians), and business elites.[8]

Overall, the Algerian trajectory followed a well-known pattern combining a form of "neoliberalization" with "authoritarian resilience." As in other countries in the region, economic reforms served the establishment of state-business networks and the construction of a new political economy aimed at maintaining the status quo.[9] Core elites reaped the benefits of these selective reforms and maintained their hold on strategic economic sectors.[10] At the same time, the reconfiguration of the political and economic orders allowed for the progressive incorporation of upwardly mobile elites (business, religious, etc.).[11]

This chapter therefore looks at the restructuring of the cartel from its margins rather than its core. It shows that the social groups participating in the reproduction of the status quo were much more diverse than the usual focus on a handful of obscure and omnipotent actors would normally suggest. Far from being limited to a "deep state," the cartel was reminiscent of Gramsci's notion of the "integral state," which describes the symbiotic relation between civil and political societies.[12] In the following pages, I look at the function of secondary actors and institutions in the state field (technocrats, magistrates, etc.). I also present the groups and individuals located on the periphery of the state who contributed to the diversification of the cartel's constituency (civil society organizations, businessmen, etc.). In this way, the chapter aims to uncover the mechanisms that enabled the production of vertical and horizontal linkages that stabilized the political order in a catastrophized environment. Finally, it contextualizes the role of corruption and clientelism, while showing the inadequateness of ethnocentric and particularistic analytical frameworks.

The State Field

A differentiated entity such as a nation-state requires a broad range of specific skills, adapted to each sector of the state apparatus. Various institutions cohabit. Their rationales are different and complementary, and the knowledge they require from their employees is the outcome of specific training and forms of socialization. Government agencies draw on diverse combinations of agents (technocrats, engineers, magistrates, economists, military officers, etc.) who learn to accomplish their official and unofficial tasks. Agencies and agents are nonetheless linked by common interests and holistic dynamics. Groups can compete while sharing the higher motivation of maintaining the established order. Securing benefits for oneself requires competition as well as cooperation. As networks connect the government agencies that constitute the ruling coalition, a situation of tense interdependence emerges at the heart of the state.[13] In Algeria, specialized state agents were also instrumental in crafting and implementing reforms aimed at regulating the polity after the Dark Decade.

TECHNICIANS OF THE STATE

In an open letter published in 2013, Hocine Malti, the former vice president of Sonatrach, addressed Toufik Mediene, calling him *Rab Dzayer* (lord of Algiers).[14] The term was often used in reference to the head of the DRS, an expression of his alleged omnipotence and ubiquity. Strictly speaking, though, it was impossible for Toufik, a single individual, to control all the activities of all the sectors in a differentiated state apparatus. There was a considerable gap between the power often attributed to the Machiavellian agents of the "deep state" and their actual capacity to influence decisions requiring specific technical knowledge.

> Everybody knows [Yazid] Zerhouni, the ex-member of the DRS, but he wasn't the worst. The really funny guy, who was all smug, was his general secretary [at the Ministry of Interior]. A guy with a moustache, without any knowledge, probably also a former military man. He used to come alone, with his authority, and he told us what he wanted here and there, without understanding a thing about technical issues. We discussed a technique for external siding called a "ventilated wall," and he responded that he didn't want this type of floor tiles.... We tried to tell him that this was completely different, but he persisted. Normally, this is not his business. There is a technical committee with real competence, and the order was already placed by the Directorate of Public Works [Direction des Ouvrages Publics].... Obviously, it's not going to happen

the way he wants it to. When we receive politicians, it's just a formal thing. They don't sign any contract, or official paper. The only thing that you have to do is focus on what was initially planned.

(ABDELHAKIM, GRADUATE OF ALGIERS POLYTECHNIC
SCHOOL OF ARCHITECTURE, PARIS, SUMMER 2010)

Before coming to France to finish his studies, this young architect worked for Cosider, a public construction company. His experience fueled his contempt for the ignorance of the *décideurs*, stripping them in his eyes of whatever omnipotence they were said to possess. According to him, the general secretary of the powerful Interior Ministry was certainly free to monitor the site chosen for the new national center for the production of identity documents, but his limited knowledge prevented him from making any architectural decisions. This type of technical choice was the prerogative of competent public servants, engineers, and architects. While situated at the highest level in the decision-making process, a minister or a general couldn't micromanage specialized government agencies. Beyond the narrative of the omnipotent deep state, an official's ability to decide was in reality limited by technical constraints and individual skills. Indeed, since the second half of the nineteenth century, technocrats have come to play an essential role around the world as a result of the increased specialization and diversification of state institutions.

In Algeria, many senior technocrats entered government service during the period of the planned economy, as administrators of the means of production in state-owned companies. As such, they represent an archetype of the state class.[15] Indeed, the policy of industrialization and state-centered development implemented in the 1970s gave a central role to administrators in the decision making-process.[16] Under Bouteflika, high-level public servants remained influential in what Werenfels characterizes as the first and second circles of "politically relevant elites."[17]

These technicians of the state share a common training in elite schools, in Algeria and abroad. The National School of Administration (École Nationale d'Administration) was founded in 1964 on the model of the eponymous French institution, with which it still has an exchange program. It has trained many ministers and *walis*, and several prime ministers have attended the diplomacy section (Ahmed Ouyahia, Abdelmalek Sellal). Former CEOs of Sonatrach were trained in prestigious institutions such as the

Algerian Institute of Hydrocarbons (Abdelhamid Zerguine, Rachid Hachichi) or the National Polytechnic School (Noureddine Cherouati, Abdelmoumene Ould Kaddour). Some prominent government officials who inherited strategic ministries, such as Finance or Energy and Mines, also attended foreign universities, some in France (Youcef Yousfi, Karim Djoudi) and some in the United States (Chakib Khelil). During the Hirak, representatives of the state class have been instrumental in managing the crisis and containing the revolutionary mobilization. Since 2019, three successive prime ministers (Noureddine Bedoui, Abdelaziz Djerad, and Aïmene Benabderrahmane) and the president elected to replace Boutelika (Abdelmajid Tebboune) have all been alumni of the National School of Administration.

Under Bouteflika, the state class intervened in the daily management of the state apparatus, in the implementation of repressive and redistributive policies, and in various embezzlement schemes.[18] In the 1990s, during the climax of the crisis, it was also instrumental in conceptualizing the economic restructuring. Its members organized economic reforms, facilitated the privatization of various state firms, and negotiated the restructuration of the country's foreign debt. Refusing to limit his analysis of the 1990s to *janviéristes* (the generals who led the 1992 coup), Hugh Roberts rightfully underlines the key position of the senior public servants who crafted and implemented pro-market reforms during the same period.[19] High-level technocrats heading state companies progressively developed pro-business ethics, especially those who were trained abroad. Thus, they acted as promoters of pro-market policies while simultaneously merging their discourses on economic effectiveness and competitiveness with a still dominant socialist and populist imaginary.[20]

The memoirs of former prime minister Ahmed Benbitour (1999–2000) offers an overview of the principal tasks undertaken by experienced technicians of the state, particularly debt restructuring.[21] They also illustrate the widespread tendency of these key actors to distance themselves from an opaque and malevolent *Pouvoir*. In so doing, influential public servants contributed to the illegibility of institutional politics under Bouteflika. Indeed, Benbitour's narrative echoes Werenfels's diagnosis, according to which references to the *Pouvoir* were not only a way to denounce an omnipotent and shadowy cartel. Blaming the *Pouvoir* was also a convenient way for members of the ruling elite to deny their responsibilities, as these discourses prevented a more critical analysis of the power structure.[22]

CONSERVATION AND COERCION

Even in states built on a revolutionary legacy, the circular nature of state power fuels a conservative logic among public servants. Algeria is no exception.[23] After the transition to political pluralism, the centralized bureaucracy worked to limit the possibilities of local opponents.

> The problem for us is that once we see that a local administrator doesn't work well, we can't do anything. They will systematically refuse an investigation committee. And if the government ever accepts sacking this person, it will take time for this file to be double-checked by all the security agencies for their own investigations. It will take two or three years before this administrator is eventually sacked. . . . In a way, we are all taken hostage, we face a kind of administrative terrorism. All key prerogatives in the sectors of housing, economics, social issues, culture are the exclusive privilege of the administration.
>
> (HAMID FERHAT, PRESIDENT OF THE APW
> AND MEMBER OF THE FFS, BEJAÏA, AUTUMN 2010)

During our discussion, Hamid Ferhat castigated the government's centralism. He was so infuriated by the bureaucratic obstacles preventing local governments from operating that he had given the *wali* the nickname "the Eye of Moscow." Violent repression was unnecessary, since mundane administrative procedures demonstrated the overwhelming power disparity between those who controlled the state and their peripheral challengers. Like Hamid Ferhat, many politicians and activists recounted how university managers or the services of a *wilaya* impeded their efforts by delaying the legalization of their association or cancelling their reservation of a meeting hall.

Other sectors of the state apparatus were structurally interested in the reproduction of the established order, starting with the judiciary. Magistrates enjoyed various benefits (allocated accommodation, generous housing and transportation bonuses, credit to buy a car). These economic advantages served as rewards for their active participation in mundane and extralegal displays of state power. During the 1990s, they were central in the "eradicating" apparatus targeting Islamist militants, tolerating confessions obtained through torture and accelerating cases involving the death penalty.[24] Under Bouteflika, they kept peaceful activists in pretrial custody and occasionally gave them punitive prison sentences. Judges also contributed to the daily management of socioeconomic unrest. While Algerian labor laws are relatively favorable to workers, social conflicts could result in exemplary punishments for labor organizers. At times, judges outlawed social movements in the name of "public order" or the "interest of citizens," despite the fact that the right to strike was enshrined in the constitution.[25] Prosecutors were also essential in the instrumentalization of financial crimes, which served to protect the monopolies of well-connected businessmen as well as to punish certain factions within the cartel. Moreover, magistrates also played a key role in the organization of successive elections (a key normalizing process), most notably by supervising electoral databases and collecting votes at the local level. Since Bouteflika's resignation in April 2019, magistrates have been involved in a reordering effort, through the judicial harassment of pro-Hirak activists and the prosecution of former members of Bouteflika's entourage. Some have nonetheless demonstrated a desire to regain their autonomy by demanding a separation between judicial and executive powers and launching a historic judicial boycott, which received the surprise support of the Superior Council of Magistrates.[26]

In addition to the DRS, the cartel also included powerful security agencies such as the DGSN and the National Gendarmerie, both of which were led by prominent praetorian figures. Between 2010 and 2018, the DGSN was under the command of retired general Abdelghani Hamel, sometimes portrayed as a potential heir to Bouteflika. The institution's manpower steadily increased under the president's tenure. In 2018, the total number of police amounted to more than 210,000 men and women. These inflated numbers reflected an attempt to transition away from military violence in favor of the nonlethal management of socioeconomic and political unrest, principally through the use of antiriot police forces. As for the gendarmerie, it remained under the command of General Ahmed Boustila from 2000 to 2015. Affiliated with the Ministry of Defense, it employed some 180,000 gendarmes in 2018. Both the DGSN and the gendarmerie acted as semiautonomous agencies with extended powers of investigation. They occasionally confronted each other, notably during the so-called Bouchi Affair, a drug trafficking scandal—exposed by the gendarmerie—that led to Hamel's fall in June 2018.[27]

These "regular" security agencies were complemented by paramilitary groups created during the 1990s. The Communal Guard Corps was founded in 1994 as a complementary counterinsurgency force. It was progressively restructured after the Dark Decade but still included some 90,000 men when it was eventually dissolved in 2012. The government also fostered the creation of self-defense groups, which acted outside of any legal framework until their legalization in 1997. At the peak of the conflict, these groups of "patriots" (waṭaniyyīn) amounted to 200,000 men. While they actively participated in the dismantling of jihadi guerrilla groups, they also contributed to the spiral of extreme violence that took place in the 1990s.[28] These militias were progressively dissolved after 1999. Both groups contributed to the integration of new constituencies, especially in rural parts of the country. Former militiamen were courted during elections. Some of these new agents of violence transitioned from counterinsurgency to private security. Others, especially among the communal guards (shanbīṭ), partook in various forms of social unrest and became a lasting thorn in the side of the government. At the end of 2018, Azouz Amar, a spokesman of the communal guards, announced that, after fighting terrorism, they were now "at war with the regime."[29]

The proliferation of security agencies also contributed to the illegibility of state policies. In 2012, I met a senior representative of the Catholic Church who had lived in Algeria for more than forty years. He shared the following anecdote with me in confidence. During the 2000s, he had received several letters from the Directorate of Planning and Training Studies (Direction des études chargée de la Programmation et de la Formation) demanding the departure of foreign students linked to the church. According to the letterhead, the office that had sent these missives was attached to the DGSN. Following another request targeting newly arrived Portuguese students, the clergyman decided to use his connections to meet with Ali Tounsi, then the director of Algerian police. Once in his office, he asked about the motives that had led the directorate to demand the immediate removal of students who had followed all the necessary legal proceedings and whose visas were perfectly valid. The head of the police took the letter. After exchanging some hushed words with his aides, he apologized for not being able to fix the problem. His subsequent explanation left the Catholic representative speechless: according to Ali Tounsi, neither he nor his aides had ever heard of such a directorate. It wasn't attached to the DGSN, and yet it was using its letterhead to threaten people legally present in the country with deportation. After concluding his story, the clergyman asked me with a smile, "Who do you think is behind this office? Does it even exist?"

DISTRIBUTING RENTS

Actors in the state field gained access to various key resources, starting with hydrocarbon rents. Since their nationalization on February 24, 1971, hydrocarbons have generated the majority of the state's income. In 2007, the sector generated US$58.2 billion, accounting for 97.8 percent of total exports (or 45.9 percent of GDP, while the entire industrial sector represented less than 5 percent).[30] In 2014, the drop in hydrocarbon prices resulted in a slight reduction in the country's dependence on oil and gas, but the sector still represented 98 percent of its exports, 30 percent of its GDP, and 60 percent of total government incomes.[31] Before that, this steady source of revenue allowed the government to hoard a considerable amount of cash. In 2012, the country had a total of US$182 billion in currency reserves; that same year, it even loaned US$5 billion to the IMF.[32]

As a result, Sonatrach remained "Algeria's largest and most lucrative source of patronage, privilege, and power."[33] In 1990, reformers rallied behind Mouloud Hamrouche tried to put an end to the opaque management of the largest company in Africa. Portrayed retrospectively as "unrealistic," their attempt was rapidly aborted, and the status quo prevailed.[34] The reform of the hydrocarbon sector remained a particularly sensitive topic in the decades that followed. As Entelis puts it, Sonatrach was "a fully integrated part of the national governmental structure."[35] The technocrats in charge of the company often joined the strategic Ministry of Energy and Mines, and some even became prime ministers during the Dark Decade (Belaïd Abdessalam, Mokdad Sifi). As the control of hydrocarbon resources remained a major political stake, senior public servants and government officials frequently switched places.[36] Under Bouteflika, high-level managers of Sonatrach were thus key players in the cartel.

After their extraction, the government ensured the distribution of resources through the allocation of budgets to the various sectors of the state apparatus. Each ministry maintained a relative degree of autonomy, such that the bureaucratic machine was frequently torn apart because of conflicting prerogatives.[37] The government remained the source toward which local officials directed their funding requests, in a vertical and centralized fashion.

> The report of the [Joint Commission for Land-Use Planning] has been transmitted to the *wilaya*, which will then hand it over to the ministry. Everything is decided at the level of the ministry because this is where the money comes from. Once we have their agreement, we will start the market studies and, sooner or later, the project will come to life.
>
> (MANSOUR, ELECTED MEMBER OF THE APW AND
> MEMBER OF JABHAT AL-MUSTAQBAL, CHLEF, SPRING 2014)

Having recently joined the APW, Mansour accepted his new role as a mediator. If he complained about the difficulties encountered by local officials when they interacted with the administration, he was nonetheless aware that it was standard procedure for a request to be communicated to the ministry. It was the best way for him to receive funding and respond to the demands of his constituency in Chlef. The rules were clear and the resources available, if one agreed to play by the rules dictated by the state apparatus. This vertical logic shaped what Mohammed Hachemaoui describes as a system of "clientelistic mediation" (*médiation clientélaire*), starting at the local level, where political life remained competitive and relatively open. There, elected officials had to demonstrate their ability to attract resources.[38] This centralized redistribution also served to punish the *wilayas* controlled by opposition forces. In that case, funds were given out in a way that prevented the local government from functioning properly. The administration hindered their distribution and surpluses had to be returned.

> I was elected to the APW and I saw tremendous amounts of cash come in just before the end of the administrative year, so we weren't able to spend them. Don't tell me that they are not aware of the time it takes to spend money in the administration, between the committees, the

tendering procedures, etc. They know very well what they are doing. It's unacceptable to distribute money while making sure that it will return to the government's treasury.

(MOHAND, FORMER OFFICIAL OF THE FFS AND THE RCD, TIZI OUZOU, SPRING 2011)

In addition to the allocation of public funds through proper administrative channels, the redistribution of rents also relied on another key institution: namely, public banks. The presidency directly appointed the technicians who controlled the public banking system and allotted fractions of the country's monetary reserves to well-connected entrepreneurs and ordinary citizens. This resulted in massive cash injections, in the name of "correcting the excess liquidity of the banking sector," in the form of credits for struggling small and medium-sized enterprises (SMEs), the creation of microenterprises by the youth, or affordable housing. Yet in the latter years of Bouteflika's tenure, no less an institution than the country's central bank warned against the proliferation of nonperforming loans benefiting a small number of "economically intertwined borrowers."[39] Indeed, public banks also massively financed the investments of crony capitalists.

The control of government agencies was a major issue. For instance, Bouteflika appointed Yazid Zerhouni as interior minister in 1999 with the objective of strengthening his influence over the DGSN. At the same time, the individuals heading these agencies took advantage of their relative autonomy. During their tenures, Generals Hamel and Boustila were among the most powerful men in Algeria. While interdependent, government agencies also participated in internal power struggles. They were instrumentalized to serve vested interests. Their unofficial functions became public knowledge, which progressively resulted in a crisis of state institutions.

We are all conscious of the bases on which the Algerian regime rests: these are violence, corruption, mystification, and lies. Society is subjected to a tyranny that has turned lies and corruption into a mode of governance.

(HAMID FERHAT, PRESIDENT OF THE APW AND
MEMBER OF THE FFS, BEJAÏA, AUTUMN 2010)

Hamid Ferhat argued that the "System" had betrayed the promises of 1962. He described a scheme of systematic embezzlement in which official discourses had no other function but to conceal their unavowable actions. During the last years of Bouteflika's reign, the succession of scandals and Olympian conflicts undermined the already weakened fiction of state neutrality. The resulting "de-objectivation" of state institutions demonstrated the persistence of the crisis.[40] Indeed, the apparent fragility of the institutional order seemed to fuel the possibility of another episode of "anomic terror."[41]

At the Periphery of the State

Beyond the state field, economic, media, and political liberalization resulted in the inclusion of new actors in decision-making processes. In this section, I look at the groups situated at the periphery of the state and whose leading elites became an integral part of the cartel under Bouteflika. While they all took part in the perpetuation of the political equilibrium and profit taking, the genuine diversity of these groups reveals a plurality of co-option mechanisms.

CARTEL PARTIES

I will only briefly comment on the issue of political parties, which will be discussed in greater depth in the following chapter. For now, let it be said that the FLN and the RND were proper "cartel parties." This notion underlines the collusion between their respective leaderships and members of the state apparatus to secure the benefits resulting from their participation in the government. As in Europe, cartel parties are in a position of mediation between society, which they claim to represent, and the state, on which they are structurally dependent.[42] This mediating function appeared clearly in Mansour's testimony, quoted already. During our discussion, he explained that members of the APW belonging to minority parties such as Jabhat Al-Mustaqbal sought the support of politicians attached to cartel parties. In his words, members of the APW in Chlef "benefit[ed] from the fact that the deputies belong[ed] to the FLN and the RND," and that "the ministry [was] listening to them." The two main nationalist parties therefore contributed to both political integration and social mediation, by co-opting local figures and distributing material and symbolic resources.

Since the Algerian political field had been especially fragmented since the early phase of liberalization in the late 1980s, the two cartel parties were complemented by a myriad of political organizations. These varied greatly in ideological alignment, size, autonomy, and relevance. Some joined the so-called Presidential Alliance and claimed a form of semiautonomy while offering their full support to the president. Others tried to advocate for a strategy of "opposition within the regime." I will explain these nuances in the next chapter.

SATELLITE ORGANIZATIONS

The cartel also integrated many leaders of so-called civil society organizations, which gravitated around the state and provided the ruling coalition with an extended social basis. They had a similar function of integration/representation and mediation. When mobilized as one, they performed the fictitious unanimity of "the people," thus validating key political decisions (reelection of the president, national reconciliation).

The General Union of Algerian Workers (Union Générale des Travailleurs Algériens, UGTA) was historically the most important of these organizations. Founded in 1956, the national labor union was rapidly deprived of any autonomy by the FLN's political bureau after independence.[43] During the period of single-party rule, the union's leadership was increasingly cut off from the working classes. It turned into an appendage of the FLN and undermined any meaningful worker mobilization. During the 1990s, the UGTA expressed an unwavering support for the strategy of eradication. Its general secretary, Abdelhak Benhamouda, became the head of the National Committee for the Safeguarding of Algeria, which demanded the cancellation of the legislative elections and the military coup in January 1992. In 1997, Benhamouda was assassinated by the GIA outside the People's House, the UGTA's headquarters in Algiers. He has since remained an iconic "martyr" of the struggle against terrorism.

After the end of the Dark Decade, the UGTA returned to a more mundane role as a peripheral actor in internal power struggles. During Bouteflika's first term, it denounced the privatizations pushed forward by the government. On February 23, 2003, it launched a two-day general strike, its first since 1991. The union was nonetheless disciplined after the 2004 presidential elections.[44] For the rest of the Bouteflika era, it adopted a position merging the traditional defense of the workers, defensive nationalism, and support for the president. Its privileged relationship with the government was emphasized by its members:

> The UGTA is not an autonomous trade union, but a union attached to the state. We are very organized. We, members of the UGTA-PTT [the section covering postal workers] of the Grande Poste, follow the hierarchy. We work with the coordination office for the Wilaya of Algiers, which then contacts the federal level. They are the ones who have contacts with the ministry and who will find a way to solve problems that arise at the local level. We are more efficient in this kind of negotiation because we have this organization with the state.
>
> (KAMEL, UNION REPRESENTATIVE UGTA-PTT, ALGIERS, AUTUMN 2010)

During our conversation, Kamel argued that the UGTA's structural relationship with the state was its main strength. Rather than a contentious defense of workers' interests, he presented a logic of negotiation between apparatuses. This mediation system echoed the description given earlier by Mansour. At the level of the UGTA-PTT in Algiers, or the APW in Chlef, requests were processed vertically by representatives belonging to cartelized organizations (party, union). These actors derived their legitimacy from their ability to negotiate directly with the relevant government agency to obtain concessions. This system of bureaucratic redistribution mitigated the impact of socioeconomic hardship.

Despite growing competition from autonomous unions, the UGTA benefited from its historical relationship with public authorities. "[Our union] has been part of the FLN for a long time," said Kamel. "This is the only union that has the power to represent the worker." As a matter of fact, the UGTA represented Algerian workers during tripartite negotiations with the government and business organizations. It has intervened as a mediator during conciliation procedures and, occasionally, when litigious cases ended up in court. As such, it also served to defuse and contain social unrest.

In addition to the UGTA's mediation function, the government could count on its political support.[45] The union's official position was identified with the voice of the "Algerian worker." As ruling elites drew on populist and democratic narratives to produce legitimacy, the support it offered responded to their need for representativeness. The UGTA's leadership was thus an integral part of the cartel. Its general secretary for more than twenty years, Abdelmadjid Sidi Saïd (1997–2019), was an outspoken supporter of Bouteflika. In 2014, he campaigned in support of the latter's fourth mandate, and even went so far as to compare the president to Mandela.[46]

Networks of power also permeated the university, notoriously a space for early politicization and social unrest.[47] As a result, structures linked to the political parties within the Presidential Alliance recruited new members among students. The three largest student unions in the country were the General Union of Algerian Students, affiliated with the RND, the FLN-linked National Union of Algerian Students, and the General Union of Free Students (Union Générale des Étudiants Libres, UGEL). The UGEL was associated with Islamo-conservative political movements, even though its exact affiliation fluctuated according to the cycle of defections that characterized this tendency under Bouteflika. In addition to its vocal denunciation of Palestinian suffering, this union was especially engaged in charitable work and echoed more sensitive claims such as the quality of student housing. While the UGEL could distance itself from the cartel depending on the state of political alliances, this was not the case for the two other unions. These organizations provided a base of young activists who could campaign during referendums and presidential elections. Indeed, in a country where more than 50 percent of the population was under the age of thirty, the support of student unions was key to preserving what little credibility these electoral consultations still enjoyed.

Satellite organizations belonging to so-called civil society thus allowed for the limited mobilization of different sectors of society. In January 2009, a few months before the presidential elections, the daily *La Tribune* dedicated its front page to the "millions of young signatories in favor of the third mandate," while page 2 was given over to expressions of support from the UGTA and the Business Owners Forum (Forum des Chefs d'Entreprise, or FCE). The nation's vital forces—students, workers, and businessmen—seemed united in their support for Bouteflika. Only the irreducible Abdallah Djaballah was mentioned as the last Islamist opponent calling for an electoral boycott.[48] The mobilization of these peripheral forces failed to hide an obvious truth: Bouteflika's reelection was a done deal months before the campaign even started.

THE REVOLUTIONARY FAMILY

In order to ensure both political representation and socioeconomic mediation, the cartel also relied on a historical social group called the "Revolutionary Family" (*Al-Usra Ath-Thawriyya*). The Revolutionary Family is at once a generation constituted by a common life experience, the War of Liberation, and a more limited group of actors who turned this conflict into a source of authority legitimizing political, material, and symbolic privileges. To understand this generation's crucial position in Bouteflika's Algeria, one must keep in mind Omar Carlier's diagnosis, according to which "there is no other contemporary society . . . that had its destiny so profoundly shaped by colonization and decolonization, and where identities and behaviors owe so much to the War [of Liberation]."[49]

The ritual invocation of the "martyrs" is reflective of the crucial place of the Revolutionary Family in Algerian politics. Under Bouteflika, it was also associated with the *tab jananu* generation, whose departure was long overdue. While the Revolutionary Family remained a pillar of the Algerian necropolis because of the blood its members had shed for independence, the ruling elite was nonetheless subject to a progressive generational renewal. Behind the image of a gerontocratic clique, actors born after the revolution, trained by the developmental state, and socialized during the Dark Decade, also became major players in the cartel.[50] Even still, the revolution remained a key marker of political legitimacy. To run for president, a citizen who was not himself a mujahid is expected to submit a certificate testifying to their parents' participation in the revolution; if they were born after 1942, the candidate should demonstrate their "non-involvement" in "hostile actions."[51] One's belonging to the Revolutionary Family was also a way of maintaining cohesion among ruling elites. For instance, the eight senators appointed by Bouteflika in January 2007 were all mujahideen, like him.

However, not all branches of the Revolutionary Family are equal, and some routinely provided the cartel with leading figures more than others. This was notably the case for what was formerly the Ministry of Weapons and General Liaisons (Ministère de l'Armement et des Liaisons Générales), the ALN's intelligence wing during the revolution. According to Daho Ould Kablia, the then president of the association representing its former members, the ministry had given Algeria no less than three heads of government, twenty ministers, and dozens of high-ranking officers as of 2004.[52] Ould Kablia himself soon joined their ranks, serving as interior minister between 2011 and 2013. Indeed, the *Malgaches* (the name derives from the ministry's French-language abbreviation) were a separate caste in the Revolutionary Family, one that was notably in charge of the security agencies.

Prominent associations defended the interests of the Revolutionary Family at the national level, including the National Organization of Mujahideen, the National Organization of the Children of Mujahideen, and the National Organization of the Children of Martyrs. In 2012, the Interior Ministry recognized the existence of nine national associations officially representing the various branches of the Revolutionary Family. This tally demonstrated the degree to which such belonging had been institutionalized. Similarly, to be recognized as a mujahid, one had to present an official application with three sworn witness statements, which then had to be validated by the Ministry of the Mujahideen. Indeed, the Revolutionary Family had not only produced the state—it was itself also produced and reproduced at the heart of the state apparatus, through the intermediation of official stamps and commissions. Unsurprisingly, the associations mentioned here mobilized during successive electoral campaigns to express their support for one of their most notorious representatives: Si Abdelkader El Mali, a.k.a. Abdelaziz Bouteflika.

Beyond its political support for the cartel, the Revolutionary Family also served to effect a degree of economic redistribution. The mujahideen and the widows and children of martyrs benefited from numerous material and symbolic advantages. Moreover, the number of beneficiaries increased over time, echoing a notable historical trend whereby the number of casualties resulting from the—already quite violent—War of Liberation was steadily inflated. With more than 1.5 million martyrs according to official numbers, revolutionary legitimacy was potentially present in every sector of society. As the members of the Revolutionary Family were entitled to political and economic privileges, they allied with the state to defend the political order during the Dark Decade. Mujahideen thus notoriously joined the patriotic militias formed to support the security forces.[53]

This ubiquitous social group appeared to be involved in both predation and coercion, a state of affairs that undermined its legitimacy. In Bouteflika's Algeria, not all mujahideen were heroes. The most prestigious cohort in the country had been contaminated, a symptom of the mistrust generated by social institutions, even those that were thought to be beyond reproach. The figure of the "fake mujahid" thus became one of the symbols of a society in which history had been manipulated and discredited.[54] If colonization and decolonization played a crucial part in shaping political "identities and behaviors," the widespread sense of historical falsification echoed the dominant political rationale of suspicion. As the cartel turned this heroic social group into one of its pillars, it also undermined the country's founding myth.

SUFI BROTHERHOODS

To compensate for the weakening of historical legitimacy, networks of power spread in other directions. From the early 1990s, Sufi brotherhoods (zāwya, pl. zawāyā) have been progressively integrated into the power structure, with a similar double objective of political integration and economic redistribution. This evolution has been studied by Werenfels[55] and Hachemaoui,[56] whose approaches are complementary.

Isabelle Werenfels looks at the circumstances that led to the reintegration of religious brotherhoods into the power structures of various North African political orders. She suggests that Sufi orders have proved useful for three reasons. First, they have countered the growing influence of political Islam and Salafism by opposing these allegedly "imported" religious movements with a "traditional and national Islam" more prone to obedience. Second, they have also permitted the inclusion of a larger social base in rural areas, which has contributed to the electoral successes required in the name of democratization. Finally, these brotherhoods have also been instrumental in the demobilization of the margins of society through their charitable activities. The restructuring of the established order thus relied on the insertion of semiautonomous actors who could address a set of new opportunities and constraints. In exchange for their support, these actors have acquired a bargaining position that has allowed them to gain political influence.

Mohammed Hachemaoui's analysis relies on ethnographic observations conducted in the Wilaya of Adrar, in the southwest of the country, in the early 2000s. He shows that the reinforcement of Sufi orders responded to the specificities of local social life. Actors competing at the national level, either in cartel parties or opposition movements, had to adapt to regional conditions. Electoral competition contributed to the revitalization of traditional structures such as the *zāwya* because of the convergence between collective strategies aiming to secure a social base and individual strategies seeking to monetize notability and fame. Clientelist networks thus became essential factors in electoral calculations and allowed local religious figures to position themselves as interlocutors vis-à-vis central authorities.

Sufi brotherhoods also offered opportunities for social, economic, and cultural integration where few otherwise existed. As appeasing the anger of the youth and compensating for their disaffection became major imperatives for ruling elites, *zawāyā* helped contain these tensions. Because of their charitable works and their extended social basis, religious organizations thus supported the overhaul of the political order while reinforcing their own autonomy.[57] By integrating Sufi brotherhoods, the cartel added valuable auxiliaries to its power structure. In exchange, successive ministers of religious affairs did not miss an opportunity to congratulate the *zawāyā* for their role in preserving the stability of the country. As one could expect, this recognition came with generous financial stipends.

Bouteflika's tenure was associated with the resurgence of Sufi brotherhoods, and the latter therefore oscillated between benevolent neutrality and outright support. In 2009, for example, journalist Mustapha Benfodil pointed out acerbically that the complacency displayed by the *shuyūkh* (leaders) of the Alawiyya brotherhood toward "Sidi" Bouteflika was at odds with their allegedly apolitical stance.[58] The leadership of the National Union of Algerian Zawāyā was not always that cautious. In 2014, the union's president, Mahmoud Omar Chaalal, expressed his support for the head of state and called for a massive mobilization for the upcoming presidential election.

CRONY CAPITALISTS

As one might expect, the cartel also projected its influence toward the economic field. During the premises and the climax of the crisis, the transition to a market economy benefited those with the right connections. As in other countries in the region, economic restructuring allowed for a redistribution of national wealth among different groups and the inclusion of new partners in the private sector.[59] In the 1980s, Chadli allowed a "small, but energetic, private sector to expand in the retail, housing and tourism industry."[60] The executive order of August 26, 1995, accelerated the privatization of public companies. Amid the implementation of the 1994 SAP, it created a new strategic body: the National Council of Privatizations. Placed under the control of the government, this body was in charge of setting prices and accepting bids for the acquisition of public companies. It also had the power to negotiate over-the-counter deals.[61] While this last practice was in theory exceptional, the legal framework in which it took place was designed in a way that facilitated the low-cost appropriation of public assets by well-connected entrepreneurs.

During the Dark Decade, the process of privatization provided new rents to be divided among ruling elites.[62] This redistribution benefited the private sector and foreign interests. It took place under the scrutiny of state actors who acquired discretionary powers to carry out the process of dismantling state-owned industries. This sparked the usual conflicts between members of the ruling elites. For instance, the 2000 feud between Bouteflika and his ephemeral prime minister, Ahmed Benbitour, was partly a consequence of the presidency's claim that it had the right to nominate members of the highly strategic National Council of Privatizations.

The dismantling of the public sector and the growth of the informal economy also contributed to the rise of a commercial bourgeoisie. New businessmen left senior management positions in state companies, the administration, or the army, and were able to monetize their contacts with the government. Meanwhile, *affairistes* (cronies) profited from the opening of new and lucrative markets in construction, as well as the food and drug industries. Some progressively acquired political influence, especially after the creation of businessowners associations.[63] Abdeslam Bouchouareb was one of them. Benefiting from the early phase of liberalization in the 1980s and from his connection with the military (two of his brothers were officers), this son of a wealthy Chaoui family made his fortune in the food industry, notably by selling potato-based products. After founding the country's first businessowners association, he was appointed head of the National Social and Economic Council in 1995 and became minister of industry the following year. He remained an influential member of Bouteflika's entourage throughout the 2000s and again served as minister of industry from 2014 to 2017.

Moguls and golden boys became familiar figures to the Algerian public in the early years of Bouteflika's rule. Their rapid rise was often linked to their status as figureheads supported by prominent state actors, notably in the military. In less than a decade, a young entrepreneur from El Biar named Abdelghani Djerrar rose to be the wealthy CEO of Tonic Emballage. In 2005, this paper-making company employed thirty-five hundred people, dominated almost 60 percent of the Algerian packaging market, and declared an export turnover of US$45 million.[64] Djerrar was also a close friend of Mohamed Lamari's son. Benefiting from the support of the ANP's chief of staff, the entrepreneur built his company thanks to a massive loan granted by the publicly owned Bank of Agriculture and Rural Development (Banque de l'Agriculture et du Développement Rural). Naturally, Djerrar joined Lamari in his feud against Bouteflika, notably by expressing his support for Ali Benflis before the 2004 presidential election. Following the president's reelection and Lamari's dismissal, Tonic Emballage was thus required to repay its debt. The entire empire soon collapsed. Djerrar spent a couple of weeks in jail in 2007, and the "largest paper company in Africa" was eventually nationalized.

Rafik Khalifa was another golden boy whose rise and fall made the headlines around the same period. Born in Bejaïa, Kabylia, the young man built his wealth during the Dark Decade. At his apogee in the early 2000s, his business empire employed more than twelve thousand people and had a turnover valued at US$1 billion.[65] Like Djerrar, Khalifa benefited from a large loan generously granted by a public bank. Like Djerrar, he enjoyed the support of high-ranking members of the bureaucratic military apparatus. His father, Laroussi Khalifa, was a prominent *malgache*, the first minister of industry after independence, and a founding father of the Military Security. By turning a blind eye to rates of return that defied any economic logic, regulators allowed Khalifa to attract investment from private individuals and public institutions. His bank also took part in money laundering and offered suspiciously cheap credit (benefiting Bouchouareb, among others). Once again, the tycoon's scheming came to an end after he attracted the presidency's wrath in 2002: his assets were frozen and his empire went into compulsory liquidation, resulting in record losses for the state. Khalifa fled to England, but he was eventually extradited and sentenced to eighteen years in prison in 2015.

These chaotic trajectories of enrichment and bankruptcy popularized the idea of an organized plundering of the country's wealth. Echoing this idea, activist Lyes Laribi described the 1990s as a "feast" bringing together the *décideurs* and armed factions.[66] In addition to the spectacular falls of Djerrar and Khalifa, more successful figures such as Ali Haddad (ETRHB), Mahieddine Tahkout (Group Tahkout), or the Kouninef brothers (KouGC) were emblematic of a larger trend. Indeed, these upwardly mobile businessmen built their successes on their connections at the pinnacle of the state. Unlike Djerrar and Khalifa, these crony capitalists were cautious enough not to alienate the presidency. Some became prominent members of the FCE, the main businessowners association, and raised funds to support Boutefika's presidential bids.

Algerian tycoons naturally supported a stability that favored their operations. Behind their widespread talk of "good governance," they benefited from continuous public investments that financed their nonproductive commercial practices (imports, speculation). Moreover, the health of their businesses was often dependent on the government's goodwill. Businessmen were therefore compelled to maintain their ties with the administration and the military for both opportunistic and pragmatic reasons.[67] This does not mean that they had no other choice but to support the president. Indeed, several members of the FCE were outspoken opponents of the fourth mandate. Slim Othmani (Rouiba) and Issad Rebrab (Cevital), for example, left the organization during the 2014 campaign. The resulting leadership crisis led to the eviction of Réda Hamiani, a rather cautious figure, and the election of Ali Haddad. A close associate of Saïd Bouteflika, Haddad thus became the representative of the cartel in business circles (or vice versa) and advocated loudly for an acceleration of the process of economic restructuring.

Despite the primacy of the state field, prominent capitalists who benefited from privatizations and monopolies managed to increase their influence significantly. Tycoons invested in the media field, first in the printed press and later in television and online media. Issad Rebrab acquired the newspaper *Liberté* and the satellite channel KBC, while Ali Haddad owned the dailies *Waqt al-Jazāʾr* and *Le Temps d'Algérie*, as well as the channel Dzaïr TV. As for the food, drug, and transportation magnate Ahmed Mazouz, he purchased shares in Echorouk, the most influential private media group in the country. Thanks to these outlets, capitalists positioned themselves both as supporters of the political order and promoters of an economic *aggiornamento*.[68] After 2013, with the decline of hydrocarbon rents, they exercised their influence in different ways. While Ali Haddad worked with more liberal members of the government to conceptualize pro-market reforms, Slim Othmani headed a "task force" in charge of drafting a governance code for Algerian enterprises, in collaboration with the FCE and international donors (notably the European Union and the IMF). In their own way, both men participated in the process of neoliberalization.

To weather the crisis, the cartel drew increasingly on crony capitalism as well as religious brotherhoods. The stabilization of the order resulted in the integration of new elements with their own political and economic agendas, as was the case in Syria at the same time.[69] These actors maintained their relative autonomy, as shown by the seemingly "apolitical" stance of most Sufi brotherhoods and the defections of members of the FCE during the 2014 presidential race. Yet the shared objective of maintaining the overall equilibrium did not prevent the expression of multiple contradictions. For instance, the rise of the crony capitalists led to an unsustainable mixed economy based on the distribution of rents.[70] These figures benefited from the flaws in the system of extraction, production, and distribution, while promoting additional neoliberal reforms in the name of postponing a potential economic collapse. Acting both as mitigating and catastrophizing actors, they were integral to the suspension of the disaster.

The Power Structure

Networks centered on the state penetrated surrounding social fields (economic, political, religious, etc.). In so doing, they allowed for the distribution of the immense resources extracted by the state apparatus and the constitution of a diversified constituency. Various peripheral organizations provided the cartel with new, upwardly mobile elites, who then took part in internal competition, following their own calculations and using the means at their disposal. Given this growing heterogeneity and pervasive concurrence, the cohesion of the existing order relied on the establishment of vertical as well as horizontal linkages between individual and social groups. Indeed, the reconfiguration that accompanied the crisis both fragmented the ruling elites and bound them together, as they complied with the rules of profiteering.[71] At the same time, practices such as clientelism and corruption not only contributed to the stabilization of the political order but also responded to grassroots demands for redistribution.

THE CEMENT OF CORRUPTION

During a conference organized by the daily *El Watan* in July 2012 near the Maqām ash-Shahīd, political scientist Mohammed Hachemaoui expressed his passionate conviction that "corruption [had] been located at the heart of the system since its origin." His talk ended with a standing ovation. Undoubtedly, corruption was generally viewed in the press and beyond as a widespread phenomenon that had contaminated even the most inconspicuous institutions. In Chlef in 2014, for example, the talk of the town was a corruption scandal involving the local Office of Religious Affairs. The imam of the Great Mosque and the office's interim director had been caught red-handed while asking an agent for 50,000 DA in exchange for facilitating his transfer. As I discussed the issue with Karim, the architect who kindly introduced me to the secrets of local urbanism, he simply brushed off my question, saying, "this doesn't surprise anybody anymore!"

According to the canonic definition given by Susan Rose-Ackermann, corruption is the misappropriation of power for the benefit of a third party in exchange for remuneration.[72] From the perspective of the state, it is rather an "abuse of public authority in favor of private interests."[73] As such, corruption is often conceived as a practice that departs from the institutional norms of the modern state and the regulated market economy. Yet ethnographic observations show that corruption is also central to these institutions. It allows for the development of affective relations, shapes the implementation of policies, and produces modes of belonging, all of which condition how grassroots actors experience these institutions.[74] Under Bouteflika, corruption was both structural, in the sense that it resulted from the routinized commodification of the discretionary powers of state agents, and structuring, as it shaped citizens' relationships with central and local administrations as well as interactions within the cartel.

On a daily basis, corruption results in the establishment of horizontal relationships between social fields. For economic actors, it is a way to "avoid being confronted with the hostile behaviors" of state agents and politicians.⁷⁵ With the support of their partners positioned in various economy-related ministries (SMEs, Public Works, Fishing, Trade), Algerian entrepreneurs were thus able to secure much-needed permits and otherwise sidestep certain bureaucratic obstacles. At the local level, the removal of such obstacles required good relationships with state bureaucrats. Their acquaintance (*ma'arifa*) was essential to facilitate interactions with the administration. For example, a bribe could shorten the six-month waiting time sometimes required to receive the administration's approval for starting a business in the field of health care.

While it can be studied by anthropologists adopting a grassroots perspective, assessing the depth and scale of corruption at the macroscopic level is a more complicated task. Given the difficulty of quantifying the practice in an objective manner, the existing data merely documents the feelings of economic actors, following a dominant doxa that sees corruption as being opposed to the modern state and the market. Therefore, these data offer a somewhat limited view of the phenomenon. In 2014, Algeria was ranked 100th in the annual report compiled by the NGO Transparency International, which evaluated the perceived level of corruption in the public sector in more than 170 countries. It came after Tunisia (79), Morocco (80), and even Egypt (94). Libya was the only North African country with a lower score (166).⁷⁶

In practice, corruption is a contradictory phenomenon; it can contribute to social integration or reinforce domination, mitigate social inequalities or exacerbate existing divides.⁷⁷ Under Bouteflika, this ambiguity nonetheless gave way to a relatively coherent discourse on corruption that functioned as a "diagnosis of the state."⁷⁸ The public institutions created after independence came to be imagined as having been captured by rogue actors, resulting in a deep-seated sense of political anomie. Because of its negative valence, the discourse on corruption thus served "to identify and condemn social ills of all sorts."⁷⁹

Undoubtedly, the embezzlement of public money by political figures fostered this discourse. The infamous scandals involving leading figures of the cartel (Chakib Khelil, Amar Ghoul) suggested the institutionalized nature of corruption. The diplomatic cables emanating from the American embassy and released by WikiLeaks in 2011 underlined the depth of the phenomenon and emphasized the involvement of the presidential entourage and the army command.⁸⁰ After Bouteflika's resignation in

April 2019, the sweeping judicial procedures that led to the arrests of major government figures (Ouyahia, Sellal, Ould Abbes) and prominent cronies (Haddad, Mazouz, Tahkout, Kouninef) confirmed the widespread character of corruption and its regulatory function. The embezzlement machine was seemingly located at every level of the state apparatus, from the senior management of Sonatrach to the imam of the Great Mosque in Chlef. The daily *Le Soir d'Algérie* dedicated a recurring two-page feature to the issue, entitled "Soir Corruption" (evening corruption). Occasionally, it included a small glossary, where one could learn that the word *qahwa* (coffee) can be used to refer to a bribe, as well as comparisons with other countries.

The government went out of its way to address the problem, including by passing a 2006 law introducing tough legal sanctions, such as a prison sentence of two to ten years and hefty fines (up to 1 million DA), for corruption charges.[81] Prosecutions were nonetheless limited mainly to low-level actors. Moreover, the public denunciation of reprehensible practices could also backfire as whistle-blowers could be punished for failing to maintain solidarity. The scandal of the so-called magistrate-counterfeiters (*magistrats faussaires*) offers a telling example. In 1992, Benyoucef Mellouk, an employee at the Ministry of Justice, revealed that prominent magistrates had obtained the status of mujahideen by resorting to corruption. After receiving a suspended prison sentence in 1997, he was eventually convicted of slander and sentenced to four months in prison in 2008, following complaints that were filed by two former ministers.

In fact, corruption and embezzlement were instrumental to the workings of the state apparatus, as they justified acts of regulation and reorganization. The prosecutions that followed Bouteflika's fall are another spectacular demonstration of such a judicial reordering. They were actively supported by the army command in order to limit the consequences of the Hirak and preserve the military's status. Before 2019, anticorruption laws had long been used to arbitrate conflicts within the state, as was the case, for instance, during the Betchine-Adami or Sonatrach scandals. In Fatiha Talahite's words, "control, which is in fact a form of self-control, [became] formal and bureaucratic. Ineffective at preventing misappropriations, it could be instrumentalized for personal and political purposes."[82] The struggle against corruption was therefore weaponized to settle internal conflicts and to control the course and pace of institutional change. In a turn of affairs common throughout the world, purges were presented as "clean hands operations."[83] The entanglement between acts of regulation and patterns of embezzlement demonstrates the existence of a "corruption/anti-corruption complex," which is "the site for two contradictory sets of desires: on one hand, for the rule of law, proceduralism, and justice, and, on the other hand, for modes of sociality, discretion, and intimacy that exceed the law."[84]

As a self-sustained process, corruption results in the increasing participation of various actors in society.[85] In 2011, student organizer Hocine told me that he had been offered good grades and a job in exchange for undermining a strike at the University of Tizi Ouzou. "I'm barely twenty years old and they are already trying to corrupt me," he said. His vocal rejection of corruption was part of his political identity, a conflictual way to interact with the state and advance his claims. Hocine was bitter because some of his comrades had seized this opportunity to negotiate with the university administration. As a routinized social practice, corruption thus served to include some and exclude others. Common in ruling circles and integral to the functioning of the bureaucracy, it acted as a sort of cement, thereby increasing social and political cohesion. At the same time, as a contentious narrative, corruption was also a crucial discourse articulating grievances against the state apparatus.

THE FRAMEWORK OF CLIENTELISM

Clientelism was another key mechanism structuring the order. Taking the shape of a "dyadic vertical relationship," this type of social relation is based on the proximity between unequal actors engaging in a reciprocal exchange of services.[86] Clientelism enables the redistribution of resources and the institutionalization of interpersonal loyalties. Patron and client recognize each other, repeat their exchanges, and enhance their relationship with a dose of affect. Such patronage can therefore be perceived as less detrimental than corruption, as it is entangled with legitimate interpersonal relations. In addition to his or her role as a protector, the patron can be viewed as a role model and associated with positive social values. Moreover, the cooperation between patron and client can also be portrayed as beneficial for society.[87] Nevertheless, once it permeates the public sector, clientelism becomes intertwined with corruption, as the former charts the path that the latter will then take.[88]

In practice, the benefits traded through clientelism are diverse. These can take the form of a place at university or the support of a certain social group for a political candidate. The value of the trade increases in the face of scarcity—for example, a job in a context of high unemployment. The social role of clientelism is thus reinforced during times of economic hardship. Individuals with limited resources will then tend to become dependent on well-connected actors within the state field, from where most resources can be obtained. Such dependency is a recurring topic in the literature on the political impact of clientelism, particularly in Latin America. Clientelism is sometimes framed as a perverting mechanism that can hold voters captive and allow party apparatuses to turn the "virtuous" mechanism of electoral accountability on its head.[89] However, some authors have also shown that clientelism should not be reduced to a mechanism of domination. Indeed, clients can use these relationships to negotiate with their patrons, procure goods and services, and hold politicians accountable if they fail to deliver on their promises.[90]

The resurgence of clientelism can also be portrayed as sign of the alleged persistence of "archaic" behaviors and a "premodern mentality." In the small artistic and intellectual scene of downtown Algiers, where expatriates mingle with the francophone intelligentsia, it was thus quite common to hear a bitter depiction of society voiced in culturalist terms. "The problem with Algerians is that they still live in a feudal system," explained a musician from Annaba, glass of wine in hand, as we talked on a balcony overlooking the capital in 2012. He continued by denouncing the hierarchical reflexes of his fellow citizens, arguing that "when they want to do something, they'll ask their father, who will ask his superior, and so on." This highlights another problem inherent to the discussion of clientelism: its significance for modernization theory as a marker of underdevelopment. Approaches based on rational choice thus associate the phenomenon with poverty and a lack of political options, while economic development and political competition are expected to foster program-based electoral behaviors.[91] Scholars studying the "quality of democracy" also start with the normative assumption that clientelism is a "challenge" to overcome for "aspirational" democracies (i.e., those states outside of the Organisation for Economic Co-operation and Development). Yet relations of patronage are also embedded in society, where they are essential for economic redistribution and ultimately play an instrumental role in state formation and the stabilization of recently established political orders.[92] In any case, the discourse on clientelism, formulated by social scientists, among others, is also an accusation that focuses on a polity's alleged civic deficits.[93] Because it looks at socially legitimate and embedded relationships, this discourse is not only a diagnosis of the state. It is a diagnosis of society.

Under Bouteflika, the structure of the political order was often interpreted by way of a dichotomy opposing the modern to the traditional. According to anthropologist Abderrahmane Moussaoui, the state's failure to erect a model of society based on "modern norms" led it to appropriate "communitarian norms" that served as a framework for predation and the distribution of resources.[94] Yet the idea of such a "failure" is contradicted by John Entelis, who noticed a growing institutionalization and regularization of political life in the early 1980s, despite the continuous relevance of patronage networks.[95] Thus, the opposition between communitarian and clientelistic strategies and modernity is far from obvious. The type of clientelism observed in developing countries is itself the product of modern capitalism, which has resulted in "the marketization of patronage relations and the rise of individualism."[96] Moreover, there is nothing traditional about the bureaucratic circuits that clientelism often follows. The discourses on clientelism and modernity are nonetheless fueled by exclusionary representations of the universal and the particular. This is especially the case when the recipient of said discourses is a Frenchman in Algeria.

Hachemaoui rightly points out that the resurgence of communitarian reflexes was a consequence of the successive upheavals experienced by the country. Drawing on the tribe as a relational strategy was a kind of reinvention of tradition in the face of a brutal de-structuring.[97] In a context of continuous scarcity, clientelistic networks provided practical responses to unemployment or social fragmentation. At the same time, the cartel espoused these social relations in an attempt to compensate for its lack of legitimacy. Intermediaries of all kinds could mobilize their social bases and act as mediators for central authorities: a local politician belonging to a prominent tribe, a former mujahid who became the leader of a militia, a prominent businessman with his employees, or the sheikh of a *zāwya*. These identities were also potentially cumulative, which provided some actors with a diverse repertoire of action through which to monetize the social capital in their possession. Yet clientelism was not synonymous with neo-patrimonialism. A close look at the Algerian situation before the 2019 Hirak reveals the rejection of authority figures and the ubiquity of social unrest. The paternalistic representations promoted by dominant figures collided with long-standing political grievances.[98]

As Leca and Schemeil point out, clientelism exists in one way or another in every society.[99] Consequently, the idea that it is an apolitical and archaic behavior does not hold water.[100] Much like the interior frame of a house, clientelism supported the overall power structure under Bouteflika, from the tip of the roof to the very foundation. As a structural phenomenon, the reliance on clientelism and patronage was an objective manifestation of the crisis. It compensated for the scarcity of resources and social fragmentation. As a structuring phenomenon, it participated in the reactivation of familiar communitarian forms (tribe, Sufi brotherhood, Revolutionary Family) that completed the state apparatus. Networks of power thus reproduced communitarian reflexes, adhering to well-worn social channels as a mineral spring gushes from the ground and follows the bed of a dried-up river. Yet while relations of patronage consolidated the established order, such behaviors remained widely associated with the predation of a privileged clique. The discourse on clientelism thus promoted representations of the ruling elites as "feudal," "regionalist," or even "mafia-like."

WAS THE ALGERIAN POLITICAL ORDER EXCEPTIONAL?

In this chapter, I have studied the structure of the Algerian order while trying to move away from the cartel's centers of gravity (the army staff, the presidency, the DRS). This power structure was fragmented by the multiplication of state and non-state agencies and the penetration of its networks into various social fields. It relied on vertical and horizontal linkages, and on multimodal exchanges of services. Consequently, the *Pouvoir* matched Foucault's description of "a more or less organized, more or less pyramidal, more or less coordinated network of relations."[101] This ability to visualize the skeleton of this system of domination illustrates the revelatory power of the crisis. The forms of collusion that should have been hidden became visible.

In light of this, the idea of an "accentuated autonomization of the state"[102] in North Africa seems obsolete. The climax of the crisis led to a growing integration of peripheral actors in benefit-taking and decision-making processes. Categorizing Bouteflika's Algeria as a "bunker state" therefore seems to miss the mark. In their analysis, Henry and Springborg rightfully emphasize the central role of the security apparatus and the army. Yet their reading of the political configuration in terms of "clans" inherited from the War of Liberation seems far too rigid.[103] This caricature can be explained by their extensive use of the memoirs of Ghazi Hidouci, a pro-market minister who opposed the FLN's Boumedienist faction. The notion of a bunker thus gives the impression of a narrow and relatively stable coalition of military actors, and partially absolves the reformers of their responsibility in fostering the crisis. While they underline accurately the instrumentalization of the economic restructuring by the cartel, Springborg and Henry systematically underestimate the role of non-state actors. "Civil society" is depicted as impoverished and separated from the country's elites by successive political upheavals, and therefore unable to influence policy making.[104] In the model of the bunker state, the autonomy of civilian and non-state actors is denied. They remain captives of almighty praetorian forces that manipulate politics and monopolize rents.[105] As I have shown in this chapter, one should not underestimate the contribution of non-state actors to the reconfiguration of the Algerian order since the late 1980s. Despite the dominant position of an entrenched core of elites, the power structure was labile and gave a more prominent role to representatives of so-called civil society.

Another recurring analysis of "Arab authoritarian regimes" focuses on the well-known theme of the resilience of the rentier state. Authors have explained the Algerian order's resistance to institutional change by emphasizing the role of hydrocarbon rents.[106] This assertion must be qualified, as institutional changes were essential to ruling elites' ability to weather successive upheavals since the 1980s. These resources were nevertheless essential in redistributing wealth by drawing on clientelist networks, financing associations reactivated opportunistically before an election, or buying political support.[107] In his comparison of Algeria with the Libyan and Iraqi cases, Martinez insists on the role of hydrocarbons in the consolidation of ruling coalitions. Rents certainly finance coercion and the integration of new groups. As I have noticed already, the crisis accentuates the attractiveness of the capital resulting from the extraction of hydrocarbons, thus making the institutionalized appropriation of this resource a key factor in the resilience of the ruling coalition in a period of scarcity.[108] It is nonetheless insufficient to claim that these resources are a blessing for "authoritarian regimes." Beyond the financing of repression and integration, hydrocarbon wealth has also fueled internal competition and the grievances of precarious actors on the margins. From this perspective, the Algerian case evokes that of Venezuela, where political and economic struggles progressively merged, leading to recurring upheavals that unveiled the unspeakable practices of ruling elites.[109] Combined with the revelatory power of the crisis, hydrocarbon rents were not merely a blessing for ruling elites. They also accentuated antagonisms within and around the state field, thus accentuating the image of a motley clique of oil thieves.

The question of hydrocarbons is important for another reason. Indeed, in focusing on the local misappropriation of rents, observers tend to overlook the crucial role of the foreign partners who provide local elites with economic and technical assistance. Behind the myth of national independence willingly promoted by oil states, the latter are deeply implicated in transnational networks of power.[110] These more or less autocratic systems exist within a global market where the political stability of some is intrinsically linked with the economic prosperity of others. Thus, to avoid the unproductive comparison between "Western democracies" and "Arab authoritarianism," one must remember that hydrocarbons are essential to the preservation of internal stability and vested economic interests in both cases.[111] Ultimately, contrary to the particularistic argument centered on the rentier state, the insertion of nation-states into the world system remains an inescapable fact. The difficulty arises when we try to reconcile this insertion with the fact that these states also have autochthonous bases.[112]

The proponents of the local order are the mediators of a global order that is at once political, securitizing, spatial, and economic. North African ruling elites have thus become the partners of the European Union in such crucial matters as antiterrorism, undocumented migration, and energy. This position fosters mechanisms of solidarity. For instance, the French state has actively participated in the training of Maghrebi police forces over the past twenty years. International financial institutions have also supported and shaped processes of state restructuring that benefited local ruling elites. This phenomenon is not particular to the region. In the 1990s, the IMF and the World Bank played the same role in Russia. There, they facilitated a wave of privatizations and the penetration of foreign capital, enabling a minority to confiscate national wealth.[113] Similarly, the Algerian cartel found some of the resources that allowed for the perpetuation of its domination at the international level.

Viewed from a relational perspective, the particularistic argument crumbles. National orders may function according to their own historical trajectory and their role in globalized markets, but they are nonetheless subjected to the same process of "variegated neoliberalization" that accompanies structural crises and reshapes institutional arrangements around the world.[114] Consequently, local orders rely on similar mechanisms for cohesion and competition. The emergence of coalitions transcending institutional limits is not particular to any one region of the world. Unofficial alliances acting outside the control of the citizenry also exist in countries that enjoy the flattering label of "democracies." Once again, the revelatory power of the crisis proves useful. In Italy, the infamous *Tangentopoli* scandal unveiled the existence of a caste of businessmen-politicians and the establishment of a "crypto-government behind the scenes," which made strategic decisions outside of the institutional framework.[115] These actors were linked by the immense benefits resulting from their monopoly on meta-power. Throughout the world, one can witness such alliances bringing together senior technocrats and government officials, crony capitalists and security agencies, consulting firms and media pundits. Their relative solidarity aims primarily at guaranteeing the stability of local arrangements and the short-term benefits derived therefrom, echoing the guiding logic of the cartel presented in chapter 2. Thus, power structures fluctuate without changing fundamentally. The convergence between "liberal democracies" and "authoritarian regimes" fuels a widespread rejection of political parties and electoral processes.[116] Meanwhile, in the Global North as in the Global South, public policies are the outcome of a system of government that is "oligarchic, co-opted and entrenched . . . where elected officials are either marginalized or favorable to the cause of the coalition."[117]

In a new iteration of the monopoly mechanism exposed by Norbert Elias, the concentration of meta-power in the state encourages the establishment of networks that reinforce the interdependence of ruling elites.[118] Negotiation and the trading of services are the symptoms of this interdependence. They shape the relations among members of the cartel, their clients, and their foreign partners. In this context, the signal attribute of the ruling elites is precisely their ability to cross social and national borders to constitute their network of allies and affiliates.

The Order as a Labyrinth

This chapter studied the cartel as an evolving and relatively inclusive structure. This alliance shrank during the 1988–1992 period before expanding again. It assigned a key role to "consolidating actors," many of them situated on the periphery of the state.[119] This was the case, for example, with Abdeslam Bouchouareb or Ali Haddad, who became major figures in the presidential entourage. This transformation enabled the cartel to navigate the crisis. The resulting power structure was not invisible, however. Figures 3.1 and 3.2 (located at the end of this chapter) represent the cartel at the time of the 2011 revolutions and before the 2019 Hirak.

As already mentioned, visibility does not equate to legibility. In 2011, the most prominent figures in the cartel were a general whose face was unknown (Toufik) and a president whose mind seemed absent (Bouteflika). Eight years later, the former was in jail for endangering the state, while the latter remained hidden from the public eye after he was forced to resign. The secrets of meta-power were and remained illegible. Thus, rather than giving a definitive response to one of the recurring questions about Algeria (Who has the power?), one should admit that power is in essence capillary and diffuse, and that uncertainty and fragmentation are normal states of affairs.

The plurality of elite strategies added a new layer of mystery, as the ability of actors to insert themselves simultaneously into different fields increased in step with their rise through the social hierarchy. Their ubiquity, in the army and business circles, in politics and the media, enabled them to mobilize complementary forms of capital. Multi-positioning was essential in order to better monetize the available resources.[120] It also fueled ongoing questioning about the potential alliances, allegiances, and betrayals among notorious figures in the cartel.

The fluidity of the political conjuncture blurred social frontiers and reinforced the mysteries surrounding the labyrinthine spaces of the established order. These mysteries collided with the revelatory power of the crisis. If this collision was paradoxical, it was certainly not contradictory. Indeed, the crisis unveiled the mismanagement and predation of national resources, the precariousness and anger of the population, and the competitiveness and collusion of ruling elites. These revelations did not completely elucidate the structures of power. Members of the cartel were surely involved in embezzlement schemes, but this information was not enough to determine responsibility with certainty.

What, then, were the options left to profane observers, as they tried to decipher the secrets of the labyrinthine spaces of the order? The multi-positioning of actors made an analysis difficult. Take, for instance, the case of former DRS officer turned political commentator, Mohamed Chafik Mesbah. Mesbah gained a public reputation as someone who would intervene frequently in private media. In June 2012, in an interview with *Le Soir d'Algérie*, he was asked to comment on allegations of fraud during the legislative elections. Without surprise, he emphasized the opacity of the results while at the same time criticizing the opposition parties for their "empty discourses denouncing fraud."[121] As he blamed both the ruling coalition and its opponents, his ambiguous intervention also raised legitimate questions. Who could argue with absolute certainty that Mesbah had cut all ties with his former employer? Who could be sure that he hadn't?

In the maelstrom of state and economic restructuring, the blurring of limits and rules became a technique of government.[122] It enabled the reconfiguration of complex networks that evolved according to circumstances, inside the state field and beyond. Multi-positioned elites benefited from their "knowledge of these labyrinthine spaces, and their ability to orient themselves and use these spaces practically."[123] They mastered the rules of influence and movement, the secrets of meta-power, whereas the uninitiated failed to discern a guiding logic. Yet their privileged position was not enough to make them appear either benevolent or disinterested. The widespread discrediting of political actors prevented such a transubstantiation.

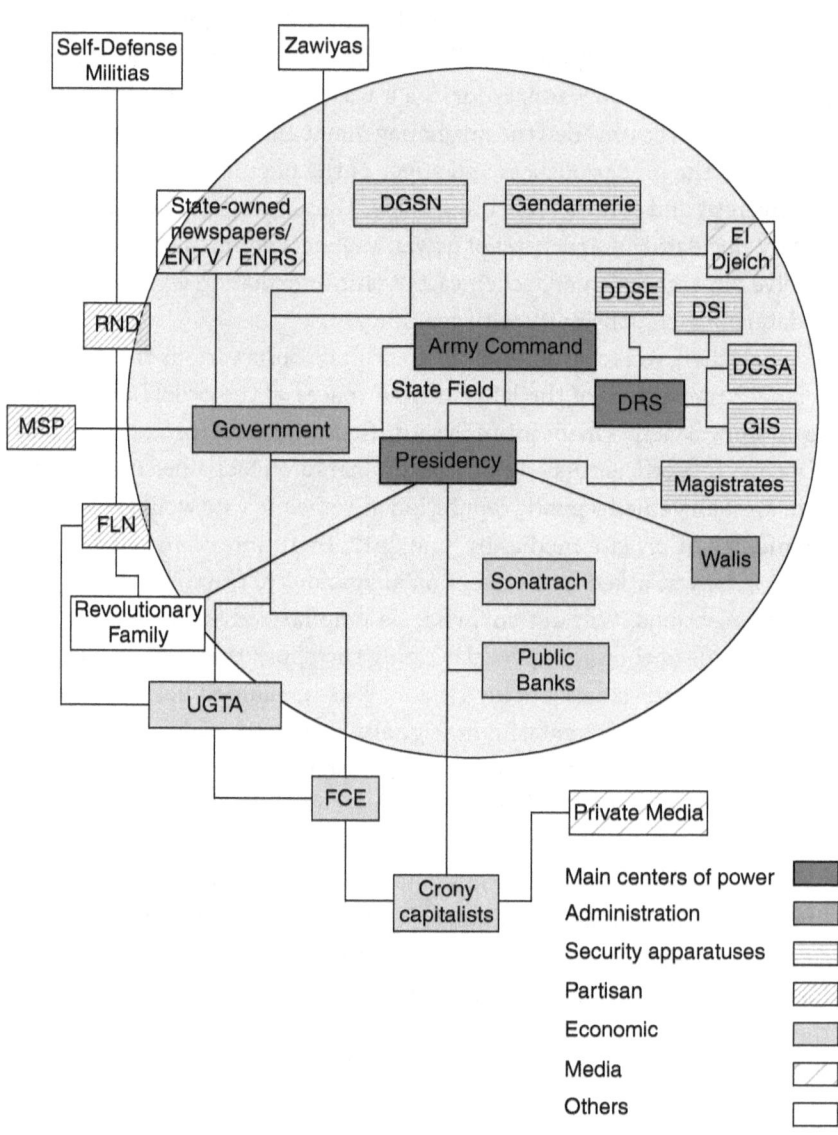

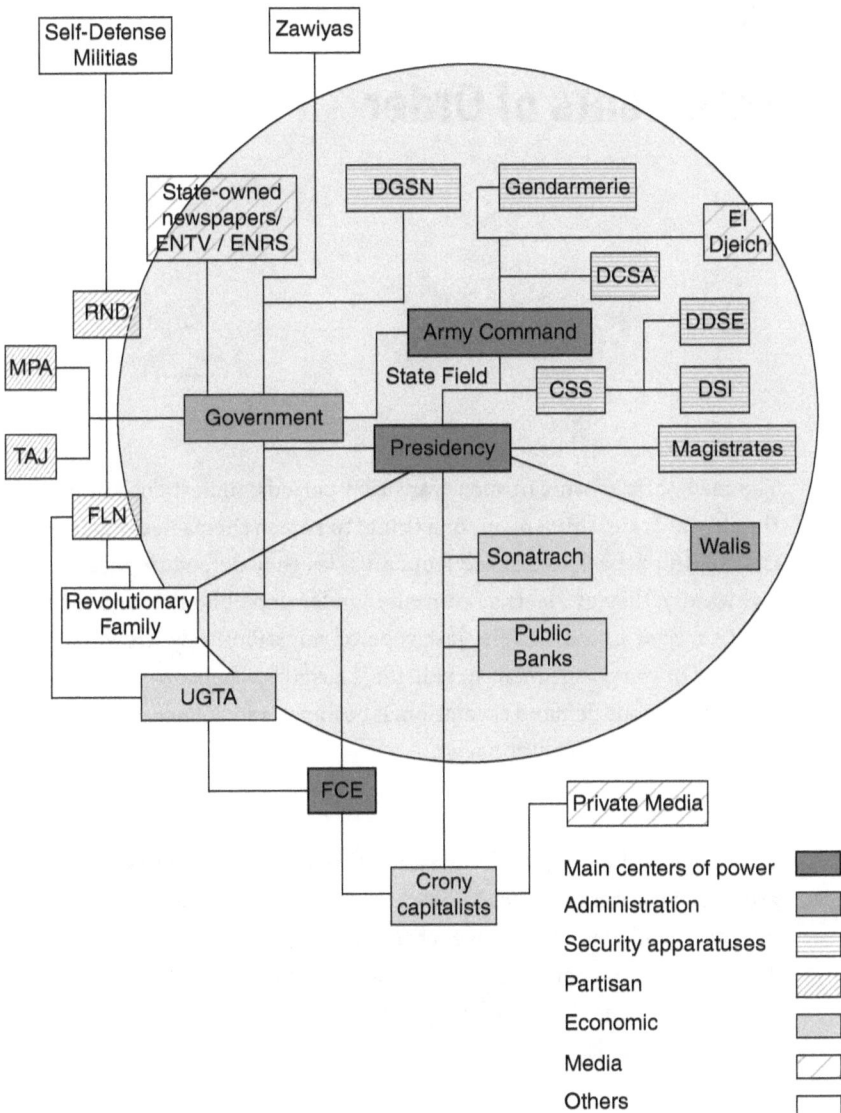

FIGURES 3.1 AND 3.2 Representations of the cartel in 2011 and 2019. (Diagram by author.)

4
Fragments of Order

The mediocrities who, in such transition periods, undertake to steer the ship of State, think of but one thing: to enrich themselves against the coming debacle. Attacked from all sides they defend themselves awkwardly, they evade, they commit blunder upon blunder, and they soon succeed in cutting the last rope of salvation; they drown the prestige of the government in ridicule, caused by their own incapacity. Such periods demand revolution. It becomes a social necessity; the situation itself is revolutionary.

—*Pyotr Kropotkin*

The image of the regime—for me and I think for most Algerians—is a group of gangsters who keep power for themselves and for their own interests, and who will do everything to keep it that way. It's Larbi Belkheir and co., really a group of gangsters whose names are known and who have been around for decades.

—*Abdelhakim*

The long periods of glaciation that have characterized the transformation of the Algerian order have nonetheless been punctuated by brief moments of opening. The 1989 constitution legalized political pluralism after almost thirty years of single-party rule and led to the creation of dozens of parties. But with the Dark Decade and Bouteflika's return, the status quo prevailed. Between 1999 and 2011, the Interior Ministry systematically withheld accreditation from newly founded organizations. It was only in 2011 that the ministry finally legalized multiple parties, some had been waiting for more than a decade for such recognition. This led to another rapid proliferation of political organizations, some of them without clear platforms or constituencies, which further destabilized the political field. These openings reflected the rhythm of the crisis, occurring as they did in the wake of the 1988 and 2011 uprisings.

Over the next two chapters, I look more closely at the transformation of the Algerian political order after the end of the Dark Decade. While the 1990s in Algeria certainly prefigured the gruesome reordering currently under way in Bashar al-Assad's Syria,[1] this transformation was also articulated by way of a long-standing process of "democratic globalization." Under Bouteflika, the efforts of transnational "democracy makers" overlapped with the survival strategies of local ruling elites.[2] At the same time, the uprisings of 2010–2011 have shown the limits of an analytical framework centered on authoritarian resilience and its other, democratization. This approach tends to emphasize the flexibility of local power structures and overlook the contradictory dynamics that accompany social, political, and economic restructurings.[3] Successive transformations do not only strengthen ruling coalitions, they also have unintended consequences and can fuel revolutionary mobilizations.

In Algeria, the restructuring of institutional politics resulted in the continuous domination of cartel parties. At the same time, it would be simplistic to limit our analysis to the critique of a "cosmetic democracy" (*démocratie de façade*) popular among opponents.[4] Following successive openings, the Algerian public sphere has undergone a virtually constant evolution. Under Boumediene, criticism was prohibited and dissidents severely punished. The state was able to mobilize political actors depending on its needs. This tight grip underwent a progressive loosening after Boumediene's death.[5] In the early 1980s, critical voices in various cultural and religious movements expressed their growing discontent. After the reforms of 1989–1990, newly created parties, associations, and newspapers echoed this feeling in a freshly liberalized public space.

Under Bouteflika, three levels of criticism were permitted in the public sphere, situated in different spaces and involving different actors. Grassroots criticism was rooted in the sociability of largely masculine spaces, such as the *cafés maures* studied by Omar Carlier,[6] but also in the back rooms of small shops and sidewalks where young Algerians tended to gather for lack of any better venues. While institutional politics were not a hot topic per se, the discussion of public life took the form of anecdotes, rumors, and jokes denouncing official privileges and fraud. The second level of criticism was mediatized, in the sense that it happened in the press and in social media. These spaces welcomed both profane and expert diagnoses that speculated on the alliances and feuds among ruling elites. There, cartoonists such as Dilem, Hic, or Ayoub described the sufferings of the population,[7] while ferocious homemade photomontages denounced the absurdity of politics. Finally, the third level of criticism was inherently linked to the public communication of politicized actors (members of the government, political opponents, labor organizers, etc.). It served to promote specific strategies and representations of the polity. It was also shaped by repetitive accusations of manipulation, betrayal, or corruption. These acrimonious exchanges reproduced the social and political fragmentation inherited from the 1990s. They also contributed to the latency of the crisis until 2019. As I have said previously, a rationality of suspicion and instrumentalization came to be dominant in the public space. This rationality shaped the three levels of public criticism. Activists, pundits, and politicians were thus compelled to use the same language of suspicion in order to remain audible.

This rationality of suspicion shaped the political spectacle discussed in this chapter, which starts with a presentation of the two ruling parties (the FLN and the RND). I then look at the trajectory of an Islamo-conservative party that was part of the Presidential Alliance from 1999 to 2012, the Movement for the Society of Peace (Mouvement pour la Société de la Paix, MSP). The last two sections, finally, describe the widespread discrediting of political actors and the persistent inability of ruling elites to generate legitimacy. As a result, the narratives of order took an increasingly patronizing stance, portraying the people as a childlike mass requiring discipline in order to maintain the nation on a path toward security and development.

The Presidential Alliance

The Presidential Alliance was the extension of the cartel in the political field. As its name indicates, it brought together various components supporting the presidency. In a context of crisis, the personalization of public debates and the coming together of parties of varying degrees of relevance contributed to the glaciation of politics. As it gave birth to heterogeneous governments made of technicians and politicians, the Presidential Alliance also served another objective: that of neutralizing pluralism and undermining the agonistic dimension of institutional politics in a way that has also become characteristic of many "democratic" systems.[8]

TWO CARTEL PARTIES

The FLN was formerly the country's sole political party and the recipient of a large share of revolutionary legitimacy. Its leaders were instrumental in the final phase of the War of Liberation against France, especially on the diplomatic front. They were also at the forefront of the institutionalization of the nation-state after 1962, which led Jean Leca to describe the party as "the State's midwife."[9] The FLN was nonetheless rapidly limited by its own political weaknesses and the rapid autonomization of the government. Boumediene once depicted it as a "body without a soul."[10] While Entelis concurred by presenting the FLN as a "receptacle of dead ideas,"[11] the party elite nonetheless strove to present a political alternative. This resulted in tensions between Boumedienist circles and Chadli's entourage throughout the 1980s, and a rebellion against the military aristocracy led by the FLN's general secretary, Abdelhamid Mehri, during the 1990s. In January 1995, representatives of the party joined the so-called Sant'Egidio Platform, which brought together supporters of a peaceful political settlement, including exiled leaders of the FIS. The FLN was then punished electorally during the legislative elections of 1997, before recovering its position as the leading party in the country in 2002. A couple of years later, the party's newfound autonomy was revoked and Bouteflika's entourage took over.

The cartel responded to the political vacuum resulting from the 1992 military coup and Mehri's dissidence by creating a brand-new organization made up of supporters of its "eradication" strategy: militiamen, members of the administration and security forces, and intransigent secularists. The RND notably received the support of the self-defense groups created during the Dark Decade.[12] The origin of the second cartel party thus resides in the opposition to "terrorism" and "fundamentalism." Strictly speaking, the RND was the party of dictatorship in the ancient Roman sense: it was formed to rescue the republic in a moment of emergency that warranted exceptional policies. Among the party's most prominent members were the veteran prime minister Ahmed Ouyahia and the long-standing president of the Council of the Nation, Abdelkader Bensalah, who succeeded Bouteflika as head of state in April 2019.

Both cartel parties maintained an organic relationship with the state, inherited from the War of Liberation (in the case of the FLN) and the Dark Decade (the RND). The idea of an exceptional nationalist legitimacy and a form of entitlement to state power permeated the statements of their members.

> The real Algerian party is the National Liberation Front. The others, the RCD, the FFS—it's not even politics. It's just rubbish. All this is just for money and power. They manipulate public opinion in some regions and cause riots. Because of them, Algeria is becoming regionalist... People are manipulated. In the FLN, at least, we are into real politics with President Abdelaziz Bouteflika, and for Algeria and the Algerian people.
>
> (MONCEF, MEMBER OF THE FLN, ALGIERS, AUTUMN 2010)

Moncef was a businessman in his late forties. He claimed to have been a member of the FLN since he turned eighteen, in the mid-1980s. He presented his political commitment as an obvious choice, resulting from the historical union between the party, the nation, and the people. Only the FLN could defend the public interest, because only the FLN had done so in the past. Here, one can recognize the tutelar narrative attached to the recipients of revolutionary legitimacy (army, Revolutionary Family, FLN). Moncef also insisted on the distinction between "real" and "fake" political parties, the latter being mostly comprised of Berberist organizations. His discourse thus reflected the rationality of suspicion and instrumentalization dominant in the public sphere.

I was among the first to join the RND in 1996 [in fact, the party wasn't formed until January 1997]. At that time, the situation was extremely bad in terms of security, and the RND is the party that fought the terrorists. It's a party that I love because it was here in these difficult moments. We are above all Algerian patriots, sons of mujahideen and *shuhadā'*.

(MUSTAFA, MEMBER OF THE RND, ALGIERS, AUTUMN 2010)

A member of the RND since its creation, Mustafa also had his "little place" in a local association that, he admitted, was an electoral appendix of the party. The association was reactivated when needed, in order to co-opt candidates that Mustafa depicted as "solid family men." In his forties as well, he was proud of his political commitment, which he linked to his economic success—a former truck driver, he was now the owner of his own transportation company. He viewed the mobilization of patriots during the 1990s as a continuation of the sacrifices made by the Revolutionary Family during the War of Liberation. Mustafa confirmed the association between the RND and the state. Seeking to provide me—the foreign researcher—with a consensual image of the party, he added, "we are for security and peace, and we want to be democrats. We want to work with the whole world, and to see Algeria take its rightful place in it."

Both the FLN and the RND echoed a defensive nationalism denouncing foreign interference and manipulations, a discourse that had been omnipresent since the early years of the developmental state.[13] Both spoke for "the people" and supported the president. Both relied on tropes that are common throughout the Global South (namely, stability and development) while occasionally adding a reference to the globalized themes of democracy and the war on terror. This ideological proximity engendered close competition among their members for public offices. When the FLN was brought back to the forefront in 2002, the RND lost more than a hundred seats in that year's legislative elections. In this context, supporters of one or the other also questioned the legitimacy of their competitor. After criticizing the Berberist parties, Moncef did not refrain from adding that "the RND is a party similar to the FLN, but it was created by people who wanted to benefit from the crisis. I mean Ahmed Ouyahia and Liamine Zeroual." On the other side, Mustafa was no less critical. Once I'd turned off my recorder, he castigated the FLN for signing on to the Sant'Egidio Platform with the "extremists" of the FIS in 1995. In their own way, both militants questioned the other party's fidelity to the nation and the people, thus revealing the competition between their organizations.

MISADVENTURES OF A *BARBÉFÉLÈNE*

The main difference between the two cartel parties was their different attitudes toward Islamism. This divergence found its superficial reflection in the styles of facial hair adopted by their figureheads in the 2000s. While Ahmed Ouyahia wore the large, Baathist-style mustache popular among military officers and senior public servants, Abdelaziz Belkhadem kept his beard trimmed in the Islamist fashion. The latter was an iconic representative of the *barbéfélènes*, a term used to designate the members of the Islamo-conservative faction in the FLN.

The trajectories of these two leading figures exemplify the deceptive and redundant spectacle of politics under Bouteflika. While politicians were often portrayed in the media as instruments of a military puppet master, whom they represented in the political field, they were also associated with stooges of their own who supposedly enabled their personal enrichment. For example, Ouyahia was thought to be the protector of transportation magnate Mahieddine Tahkout, despite the latter's denial.[14] He was also supposedly close to the military, and notably to Toufik. After being appointed prime minister in 2008, Ouyahia was depicted by a journalist as a counterweight to Bouteflika and a "phallic totem demonstrating the omnipotence of the army."[15] Six years later, having recently become the president's chief of staff, he was now presented as a potential heir facing the alleged hostility of the DRS.[16] As always, these diagnoses did not dispel the mysteries surrounding the cartel. Rather, they contributed to the promotion of an image of politics in which hidden agendas and sham appearances were the rule.

The misadventures of Abdelaziz Belkhadem are another illustration of the peculiar spectacle of politics under Bouteflika. A veteran of the FLN, Belkhadem became a deputy in the APN under Boumediene. He was instrumental in passing the contested Family Code in 1984, which earned him a reputation as a representative of the Islamo-conservative tendency within the FLN, as well as the lasting hostility of leftist, feminist, and secular activists. He became president of the APN in 1990 but was sidelined after the

1992 coup, when Islamo-conservatives fell into disfavor because of their alleged collusion with the FIS.[17] Belkhadem only returned to the fore in 2000, when he became minister of foreign affairs. In 2003, he led the "rectifiers" (known as *taqwīmīyin* in Arabic, or *redresseurs* French) of the FLN, who aimed to take over the party's leadership for Bouteflika. After this internal coup, he became the general secretary of the party and continued his ascension by being appointed prime minister; he subsequently returned to a "simple" position as minister of state and personal representative of the president. At this point, Belkhadem was added to the long list of Bouteflika's potential successors.

Internal conflicts within the FLN continued during Bouteflika's third term. The press covered these ongoing tensions in detail. Enjoying a dominant position after the party's Ninth Congress in 2010, Belkhadem threatened to discipline the leaders of yet another rectification movement. Fellow members of the government, such as Minister of Vocational Training El Hadi Khaldi, were already among the dissenters. Two years later, the rectifiers repeated their attempt. They accused Belkhadem of conspiring against the FLN and demanded that he be brought before the party's disciplinary board. During the 2012 legislative campaign, his opponents decided to defer their offensive, and the general secretary presented their rebellion as proof that democracy was alive and well inside the party. In the end, Belkhadem was "democratically" overthrown one evening in January 2013. This time, all the FLN-affiliated ministers had rallied against him.

Belkhadem's political resurrection wasn't long in coming, however. During the 2014 presidential campaign, he was recalled by the presidency to act as minister-adviser. His comeback immediately sparked further internal struggles for the control of the FLN. Shortly after Bouteflika's reelection, the "adviser" made his move, hoping to provoke the fall of Amar Saâdani and reclaim the position that he had lost eighteen months earlier. During a meeting of the party's Central Committee in June, a fistfight erupted and was subsequently broadcast on social media. The confusion inside the FLN kept growing. Belkhadem claimed to have the support of the presidency, an assertion that his adversaries rejected.[18] When he eventually attended a summer school organized by an Islamist party on the topic of political transition, this was the last straw. Belkhadem had attracted the Olympian wrath of El Mouradia (the presidential palace). The severity of the punishment was remarkable: the presidency released a statement announcing that he had lost his functions in the government and in the party, a double sanction viewed in the press as a political death sentence.[19]

We could limit our telling of Belkhadem's story to these basic facts. Yet in a public space infused with rumors and conspiracy theories, the *barbéfélène*'s misadventures fueled the proliferation of catastrophizing narratives in the media. For instance, a week after Belkhadem's sacking, a journalist for *Le Quotidien d'Oran* quoted an anonymous source who claimed to have "seen Belkhadem 'somewhere, discussing with prominent members of the Moroccan *makhzan* [state apparatus], and with senior operatives of the Islamic State of Iraq and the Levant.' "[20] At the heart of the Presidential Alliance, one thus found the same dynamics already highlighted in the state at large: illegibility, fear, and confusion. In the meantime, public critics described a political game in which manipulations and personal ambitions trumped public interest and threatened to destabilize the country.

FUNCTION AND CRITICISM OF THE TWO CARTEL PARTIES

Beyond the trajectories of headliners such as Ouyahia, Saâdani, or Belkhadem, both cartel parties suffered from the widespread sense that they had discredited themselves. This popular mistrust was a consequence of their function in the system of mobilization and redistribution described in the previous chapter. Within the discourse on corruption and clientelism, they were denounced for their role in maintaining a system of institutionalized predation. The FLN, because of its historical position, was a particular target of these attacks. Membership within the old nationalist party was often depicted as a sure path to various benefits. Indeed, in a 2010 interview published in *El Watan*, sociologist Abdelnasser Djabi described the party as a "folding seat for those who want to enjoy privileges and rapid social promotion."[21]

In other words, what was once a revolutionary movement had allegedly become the party of the *khobzistes* (bread eaters—that is, profiteers) and the *shiyyatin* (brushers—sycophants).[22] Certainly, it is quite common, even banal, for a political organization to attract members who are at least partially motivated by the material and symbolic benefits stemming from their commitment.[23] As the dominant party in the country, the FLN helped integrate diverse constituencies that could be mobilized during elections.

Because populism is not associated with any homogeneous social group, it facilitates the integration of different social classes.[24] Thus, the party benefited from its ideological flexibility (or inconsistency), thereby allowing it to fulfill a catch-all function: without a specific social base, it could attract people from all social groups and generate one-off support for state policies.[25]

Clientelistic mediation led to the creation of local "plutocracies." Politically connected businessmen competed for fiefdoms and reinforced the general fragmentation of the field, a situation comparable to the crisis of the Italian system at the beginning of the 1990s.[26] Baha-Eddine Tliba, a wealthy *affairiste* from Annaba, was one of these figures on the make. He had made his fortune in the real estate sector after benefiting from the privatization of a public company under the supervision of Belkhadem—then prime minister and as such in control of the National Council of Privatizations. Tliba had more than one protector, as his business partner was none other than the son of the army's chief of staff, Ahmed Gaïd Salah. He had earned the nickname the "Emir of Qatar of Annaba" because of his wealth and corpulent figure. He was first elected as an independent deputy in 2012, but soon benefited from Saâdani's support to join the FLN caucus and eventually became vice president of the APN between 2015 and 2017. He also caught the media's attention for calling his adversaries "mentally handicapped" in a debate in the National Assembly. In Annaba, he was accused of hiring thugs to threaten competitors and local officials, including the *wali*. In short, Tliba rapidly became the epitome of political ineptitude and corruption.

The role of cartel parties in allowing forms of economic redistribution fueled an internal competition that occasionally took violent forms. In the fall of 2010, following a reorganization of the FLN's local structures, rectifiers in Annaba occupied the party's *muḥāfaẓa* (local headquarters) to oppose senator and local strongman Mohamed-Salah Zitouni. After several months of sometimes violent confrontations, the senator himself pointed a rifle at his opponents. This type of conflict was a recurring feature of Algerian politics, especially before elections. In January 2012, members of the FLN clashed in Boumerdes, fifty kilometers east of Algiers. These conflicts could also erupt between members of the two cartel parties, notably when their candidates were in a tight race for office. In the Wilaya of Constantine, the 2012 local elections were marked by a series of pitched battles between supporters of the FLN and the RND. Electoral violence fueled media and grassroots depictions of a clique of "gangsters" turned politicians. Indeed, the frequent exchange of slurs and physical violence between the two sides was certainly incompatible with the image the RND and FLN had claimed for themselves as the "real" parties of the nation.

Both cartel parties enjoyed the administration's support as they sailed to electoral victories that were nothing less than suspicious. During the 1997 legislative elections, for instance, the RND benefited from such massive levels of fraud that the APN launched a commission of inquiry. While the final report was never released to the public, the reputation of a movement that had once been created to "save the nation from fundamentalism" deteriorated rapidly. In the words of one scholar:

> The party's discretion during the [2002] electoral campaign and its low score can be explained by the effect of many internal quarrels, which have made the front page for the last two years, and the indictment of dozens of mayors for corruption and mismanagement. The struggle for internal leadership, devoid of arguments, and the complete lack of attention to the public interest thus contributed to give a deplorable impression of the RND.[27]

This sharp diagnosis of the deterioration of the RND's reputation was echoed by the party's opponents, who denounced the fraud by which the cartel parties had repeatedly benefited. The different levels of public criticism (popular, journalistic, political) thus converged to condemn the manipulation of electoral process and the embezzlement of public resources. Of course, this did not prevent the Presidential Alliance from maintaining its attractiveness and thereby integrating new components.

The MSP and the Price of Co-option

The Presidential Alliance's domination cannot be explained solely by the behavior of the two cartel parties, even if they constantly secured an absolute majority in the parliament. In a context of post-conflict stabilization, the cartel also used co-option "as a means of averting threats to its stability and existence."[28] By integrating opposition movements, it was able to broaden its social basis, extend its circuits of redistribution, and prove its successful compliance with the globalized norms of democracy. Meanwhile, the seemingly never-ending crisis incentivized moderate organizations to make compromises and join the government in the name of pragmatism.

THE FRAGMENTED SUBFIELD OF ISLAMISM

The moniker "Islamist" is often wielded in a derogatory manner by secular actors and state officials—in Algeria and elsewhere. Crucially, Islamic activists themselves rarely use the Arabic equivalent of *islāmiyūn*. For the sake of argument, one can nonetheless describe Islamism as a divided political subfield where tendencies compete for hegemony.[29] To put it in simple terms, Islamists are political actors who present Islam as the main normative source guiding their approach to political questions. The range of religious and ideological references on which Islamists draw is nonetheless extremely diverse. Figures such as the Egyptians Hassan al-Banna and Sayyid Qutb, the Pakistani Abul Ala Maududi or the Iranian Ali Shariati have influenced revolutionary or reformist understandings of political action.[30] In Algeria, one must also take into consideration the role played by Abdelhamid Ben Badis and the Association of Ulema in the nationalist movement,[31] as well as the influence of philosopher Malek Bennabi and the so-called Algerianist movement (*Jaz'ara*).[32] Even from this rather limited list of seminal figures, one can infer that there is no such thing as a unified Islamist movement in Algeria or the wider region.

While Islamist politicians can underplay the plasticity of their doctrine, the idea of an intangible shariatic norm goes against the history of juridical practice. Islamic law provides a pragmatic and highly adaptable framework and enables the removal of most legal prohibitions when circumstances require. Rather than a rigid norm, sharia is the "flexible vocabulary of a 'moral economy' of claims and counter-claims between the classes and factions [in a society], and regarding the obligations of ruler and ruled."[33] The ensuing ideological plasticity offers Islamist movements a great deal of strategic flexibility.

This ability to adapt served the rise of Islamist movements in the 1980s, in a context marked by rapid economic, demographic, and political transformations. Throughout the Arab world, puritanism was a response to a growing sense of sociocultural anomie, while also allowing forms of solidarity that mitigated the effects of economic turmoil. Islamic activists also benefited from the benevolence of Arab governments hoping to offset the influence of Marxist activism on university campuses. Thanks to this support, as well as the broader discrediting of the Left, Islamist movements became the most visible counter-hegemonic forces in the region.

In Algeria, the FIS embodied a short-lived synthesis between diverse trends in political Islam until its dissolution in 1992. The movement echoed popular expressions of socioeconomic discontent, identity claims, and the rejection of the *ṭāghūt* (idolatrous) state in a context poisoned by the Gulf War.[34] Its young imams gained in popularity in working-class neighborhoods and attracted disenfranchised urban youth. Thanks to a discourse soaked in messianic radicalism that broke with the traditional Islamic intelligentsia, the FIS was able to attract more marginal groups, such as the Salafists and the "Afghans" recently returned from their jihad against the Soviet Union. In the meantime, the inclusion of the *Jaz'ara* provided the movement with a more pragmatic intellectual elite capable of attracting the conservative bourgeoisie.

The FIS thus brought together divergent subjectivities resulting from the contradictory socioeconomic transformations characteristic of Chadli's Algeria (pauperization of the urban working classes, emergence of a merchant bourgeoisie). As such, it should not be reduced to the image promoted by its adversaries of a totalitarian and violent party. The divisions in the movement illustrate the diversity of "Islamist" strategies. In the summer of 1991, after the arrest of its leaders Abassi Madani and Ali Belhadj, some senior members of the FIS were rapidly co-opted. Others were radicalized as a result of government repression. As for the intellectual elites, they rallied behind Abdelkader Hachani during the Congress of Batna, took over the party, and achieved a thunderous victory in the subsequent legislative elections.[35] Yet after the dissolution of the FIS in March 1992, Algerian Islamism was deprived of its main political force. Representing roughly four million voters, a lion's share of the electoral pie awaited seizure.

THE ROAD TO CO-OPTION

An Algerian offspring of the Muslim Brotherhood, the MSP became the dominant party in the Islamist subfield after 1992. Under Bouteflika, it was a long-standing pillar of the Presidential Alliance, which it provided with many ministers, often appointed to manage economic sectors (SMEs, Fishing, Tourism, Public Construction). In exchange for these lucrative ministries, the MSP contributed to the governmentalization of the cartel, which aimed to attenuate the image of a bureaucratic-military structure disconnected from society.[36]

An offspring of the association known as al-Irshād wa-l-Iṣlāḥ (Guidance and Reform), the party was founded in December 1990 under the name of Movement for the Society of Islam (MSI). Its leader, Mahfoudh Nahnah, stood apart from other Islamist figures. He had notoriously skipped the 1982 meeting in the Faculté Centrale in Algiers and didn't sign the founding petition proclaiming the birth of the Algerian Islamic movement.[37] Rather, Nahnah aligned himself with the strategy prioritized by the Muslim Brotherhood whenever possible: legalism, Islamization from below, compromise with governments. In Algeria, this reformist positioning fed the hostility of the MSI's Islamist rivals. The day after the creation of the MSI, Nahnah was literally chased out of a mosque by FIS supporters.[38] In return, MSI leaders did not hide their contempt for "populist autodidacts" like the self-educated preacher Ali Belhadj. There was undeniably a world of difference between Belhadj and Nahnah, who was sometimes portrayed as an "Islamist in an alpaca suit."[39]

During the 1990s, the MSI maintained its legalist approach. Refusing to join the *réconciliateurs* in signing on to the Sant'Egidio Platform, Nahnah echoed the dominant nationalist discourse by portraying the meeting as a result of foreign manipulation.[40] The movement was nonetheless subjected to threats coming from all sides. The abduction and execution of Mohamed Bouslimani, the president of al-Irshād wa-l-Iṣlāḥ, in January 1994 demonstrated the dangers stemming from nonalignment. The killing was claimed by both the Organization of Free Young Algerians (a pro-government terrorist group) and the GIA. In this violent context, co-option also meant protection. The MSI progressively made the defense of order its new motto, under the guise of "critical support."

> The crisis of the last two decades in Algeria has encouraged the party to disregard its own agenda and, with other political formations and the *Pouvoir* itself, focus on the priorities for the country. In order to come to a mutual agreement with these partners, while some of them refused to

engage in discussions with us, we had to make concessions, and to leave aside some of our convictions and concepts in order to get along.

(ABDELKRIM DAHMEN, MEMBER OF THE MSP'S NATIONAL COUNCIL,
FORMER DEPUTY OF TIPAZA, ALGIERS, AUTUMN 2008)

During our conversation, Abdelkrim repeatedly emphasized the key notions of "responsibility" and "priority," their role in the early formation of the MSI and their ongoing importance within the MSP. He considered that his party had done its duty by working with the *Pouvoir*. In his words, "it was better to have a tarnished legitimacy than no legitimacy at all." Indeed, the crisis had favored a pragmatic approach to politics characteristic of the bourgeois and reformist tendency that Samir Amghar calls "managerial Islamism."[41]

By participating in the 1995 election, the party had made a major step toward the cartel. Nahnah's standing allowed him to attract the support of some former FIS supporters and to ensure a voter turnout that strengthened Zeroual's legitimacy. In return, the MSI positioned itself as the main opposition party and the dominant force in the Islamist subfield. Naturally, this strategic choice was met with criticism. Cooperating with those who had annulled the results of an election won by an Islamist party and implemented a violent repression could be seen as a kind of betrayal.

> The choice of 1995 was poorly viewed by Muslim Brothers [outside the country] because they saw it as a sign of support for a regime that repressed Islamists. We had to defend our choices with our arguments, even with people whom we considered friends. The word "brothers" is not overrated, and we had to explain our choices. It was a difficult period, even on a personal level.

(NOUREDDINE AÏT MESSAOUDENE, MEMBER OF THE MSP'S NATIONAL COUNCIL, CHIEF
OF STAFF TO MINISTER OF STATE BOUGUERRA SOLTANI, ALGIERS, AUTUMN 2008)

The party's leaders had to revise their strategy continuously in the face of the constraints resulting from the crisis. This pragmatism had a cost, notably when it came to the party's relationship with foreign allies who did not perceive these constraints in a similar light. The party was also forced to change its name, as reflected in its switch to the MSP label, following a 1997 executive order prohibiting the instrumentalization of "fundamental components of national identity." The MSP was nonetheless rewarded with its first government positions in 1996, when party members were nominated for the offices of minister of SMEs and secretary of state for fisheries. The Islamist party also received 69 seats in the legislative elections of 1997, which, notoriously, were marked by high levels of fraud. While gaining significantly fewer deputies than the RND (at 155 seats), the MSP was nonetheless ahead of an FLN that had been punished for its rebellion (with just 64 seats). The party therefore settled into a position in which its support was critical. As moderate Islamists did not have the means to seize power on their own, they accepted an uneven partnership and contributed to the reconfiguration of the political order. In so doing, they were able to gain experience in management and policy making, which would have been impossible had they maintained a more radical stance or an exclusive focus on Islamization from below.[42]

> The MSP became a theoretical school by dealing with concrete action and abandoning a purely philosophical positioning. With its take on fundamental questions such as the place of religion, of international Islamism, or the necessity to accept the political other, whether he is Berberist or Communist, our Algerian experience was a very new thing.
> (ABDELKRIM DAHMEN, 2008)

Abdelkrim Dahmen underlined the pioneering position of the party and the necessity of innovating in order to deal with the crisis. This learning process also relied on the intervention of foreign actors. Abdelkrim himself benefited from training provided by an American NGO. His emphasis on the importance of pluralism and reasonable discussion thus resonated with mainstream liberal discourses. The appropriation of "democratic" norms accompanied the transformation of the MSP into a school of political action. But it also meant that the party embraced the objective of maintaining the renovated pluralist order. Despite the benefits that came with co-option, Abdelkrim admitted tacitly the cost of compromise when he argued that "the MSP has changed its ideological corpus enough ... for other political organizations to start doing the same thing."

INTEGRATION AND TENSION

As we have previously seen, the cartel's reconfiguration in the 1990s and 2000s relied on the inclusion of new constituencies. The MSP, for instance, offered access to a pool of pious middle- and upper-middle-class support as a dowry. It brought together the upwardly mobile bourgeoisie and the conservative intelligentsia, which were attracted by its discourse mixing responsibility, economic liberalism, and rigid religious standards.[43] As the urban working classes that had previously supported the FIS backed away from politics, the MSP became the flagship of a "respectable" Islamism, opposed to disorder and division. In so doing, it confirmed Rémy Leveau's intuition, namely, that bourgeois Islamists could be key to relegitimizing discredited Arab orders.[44]

The process of co-option "reflects a state of tension between formal authority and social power,"[45] which calls for the participation of newly integrated groups in the mediation of conflict. Islamo-conservatives contributed to such mediation by providing an additional gateway to student circles thanks to their affiliated union, the UGEL. As universities had faced increasingly difficult conditions since the 1980s, they became an ideal playground for the associative work traditionally characteristic of the Muslim Brotherhood. Consequently, the UGEL took part in the ongoing *protesta* movement and echoed a series of increasingly pressing claims, especially regarding the quality of life in student dorms. Yet while it denounced the mismanagement of universities, it remained cautious when it came to questioning the established order itself and supported Bouteflika until 2019.

Islamo-conservatives did not demand that *Raï* music be prohibited, or a strict Islamic dress code imposed. With their backgrounds as academics, doctors, architects, the MSP's spokespersons were eager to position themselves as "moderates." They claimed to defend human rights, democracy, and the market economy. Abdelkrim Dahmen underlined that he had worked abroad as an international observer in several foreign elections, having benefited from training provided by the U.S.-based National Democratic Institute. My interview with him certainly adhered to a similar logic: the NGO provided the know-how and certificate of good conduct, while the researcher contributed to the construction of Islamo-conservatives as key actors in the process of democratization.[46] While driven by different agendas, party, government, foreign NGOs, and experts coproduced the spectacle of "democratization through the inclusion of moderate Islamists." Supporters of the MSP were especially eager to demonstrate the existence of a "mature" Islamism. Potentially radical notions, such as *jāhiliyya* (ignorance), or God's *tawḥīd* (indivisibility) and *ḥākimiyya* (sovereignty), were reinterpreted in less exclusive ways. The religiously inspired discourse focused on compromise and the rejection of *fitna* (sedition, division). The radical and plebeian populism of the FIS was replaced by a consensual elitism associated with Nahnah's figure.

> In Algeria, we have a decent Islam, with real believers and an open mind. This is the kind of Islam that is promoted by the Hamas [an acronym for the MSP's Arabic name, Ḥarakat Mujtamaʿa as-Silm] and Sheikh Nahnah. He said that the Hamas was balancing things, as it was far from extremists on both sides: the secularists who ignore our culture and our Muslim tradition, and the radicals who want to destroy everything. Nahnah's was a language of tolerance and moderation.
>
> (YOUSSEF, LAWYER, MSP SUPPORTER, ALGIERS, AUTUMN 2010)

I met Youssef near the UGEL office in the Faculté Centrale. Upon learning about my research, he immediately emphasized the importance of a pragmatic Islamism open to the world and to difference. In our successive encounters, he repeatedly presented Nahnah as the embodiment of this "decent Islam," situated at an equal distance from all radical ideologies. In order to prove his tolerance, he explained that he had a homosexual friend and was tolerant of their lifestyle.

Yet this "respectable" Islamism also echoed some of the themes inherent to puritan demagoguery, especially when it castigated "deviant behavior" that allegedly insulted the faith of the majority. The MSP repeatedly denounced alcoholic beverages, Protestant evangelism, or the immorality of contestants in *Star Academy Arabia*, a popular television show in the region. And when I asked him about the severe sanctions leveled against those caught eating in public during Ramadan, Noureddine Aït Messaoudene developed the following argument:

> In this very precise case, it is about not attacking a society that is 99 percent Muslim with disrespectful behavior. Even foreigners are respectful of fasting. These people should have been hiding . . . As long as this issue is perceived as a question of public order, I can understand [why they deserve prison time].
>
> (NOUREDDINE AÏT MESSAOUDENE, 2008)

During its time in the government, the MSP positioned itself as an auxiliary of the state in its disciplinary undertaking. Echoing the dominant defensive nationalism, the party's puritan demagogy denounced foreign influences it claimed were endangering an Islamic society. Rather than mobilizing the population, both narratives prescribed vigilance and caution, in the name of defending the nation and Islam from external threats.

> Our society is like any society, even in the West. It has the right to defend its primary characteristics. It is normal to protect our features, especially when [Protestant] evangelists instrumentalize unrest and popular despair. The social situation is very difficult, and evangelists use this. We are extremely vigilant about this, because at stake is nothing less than the cohesion of the entire society.
>
> (NOUREDDINE AÏT MESSAOUDENE, 2008)

Noureddine's words illustrated the MSP's appropriation of a key catastrophizing narrative: that of the potential for social collapse. As beacons of respectability, morality, and cohesion, Islamist leaders claimed to act in defense of a population that could easily be manipulated. In their own way, they contributed to the suspension of the disaster.

THE BROTHERS DIVIDED

After joining the Presidential Alliance, Islamo-conservative leaders defended the compromises made in the name of emergency. Yet some observers have portrayed them as a new cartel party.[47] During our discussions, members of the MSP strove to articulate their message of "critical support."

> We can now witness a return to a strong presidential regime. It might be a choice that makes sense, but the boundaries with other branches of government are not clear anymore, which leads, notably, to the weakening of the legislative power. This is problematic. The disappearance of the distinction between the three powers reinforces the executive, and especially the figure of the president of the republic. It's a dangerous deviation. On the bright side, from the perspective of governance, at least we

can clearly situate responsibility. The tragedy of the era of the single party was that there was a dissolution of responsibility. One spoke about the *Pouvoir* as a kind of mysterious nebula bringing together clans and generals. Being able to clearly locate responsibility is a positive thing.

(NOUREDDINE AÏT MESSAOUDENE, 2008)

In denouncing a "dangerous deviation," Noureddine discussed the importance of constitutional checks in a purely liberal fashion. He demonstrated his relative autonomy by analyzing the process of presidentialization while recalling the pragmatic reasons for "critical support" that enabled the institutionalization of policy making. By drawing on the consensual and normative framework of democratic transition, he assessed the progress made in governance and underlined the limits of the process. The risk inherent to co-option was that one could be viewed as just another *khobziste*. As such, members of the MSP had to constantly prove their "pro-democracy" credentials to maintain a form of "subjective plausibility."[48]

The credibility of the notion of "critical support" nonetheless diminished after the Dark Decade, which after all had justified compromise in the first place. Meanwhile, the routinization of the crisis invalidated the promise of an improvement in governance. As the involvement of some MSP leaders in predatory schemes became obvious, the belief in the party's ability to offer a solution withered. Even long-standing supporters had to cope with disappointment.

> The discourse of "critical support" was made necessary by the civil war. We needed a strong state and the support of the intellectual elite represented by Hamas. The country still needs stability to bounce back. Now, there are very few people who actually understand this critical but free discourse since Nahnah died, including within the party.
>
> (YOUSSEF, 2010)

Youssef claimed never to have doubted the official line adopted by the MSP. He was proud to contribute to the strategy of critical support in his own way, as he had systematically voted for Bouteflika between 1999 and 2009. He nonetheless acknowledged the growing mistrust. In his mind, the death of the movement's founder resulted in an inability to make sense of its participation in government. The party might have been prone to staging its independence, but it was nevertheless difficult to remain credible after a decade spent feeding the government with ministers.

In 2008, political scientist Yahia Zoubir kindly agreed to enlighten me on the MSP's trajectory. According to him, the Islamist party had gone through a genuine process of "FLNization." It did so, of course, in a "specific way and with a different name," but as far as he was concerned the results were similar. This was evident first and foremost in the party's corruption. In his eyes, co-option came with the appropriation of certain dubious practices inherited from other cartel parties. A member of the MSP's national council, Abdelkrim Dahmen, viewed opportunistic behaviors as common among Algerian political organizations:

> People come and offer their name and popularity in exchange for the MSP label. There is political commitment and personal ambition. Those who do this kind of thing often end up in the party that best matches their ideas. But how many political parties can claim to act differently? Even the parties of the alliance cannot cover the entire country.
>
> (ABDELKRIM DAHMEN, 2008)

Abdelkrim considered that his movement had no choice but to adapt to the dominant practices in the political field. Changing the "System" from inside was made even more difficult by the fact that the MSP was never an essential component of the cartel. Its leaders were confined to socioeconomic ministries and remained complementary partners in the Presidential Alliance. As such, they were never in a position to challenge the pre-existing equilibrium.

The situation of the co-opted party was made even more precarious by the implication of its leaders in various public scandals. Nahnah's successor, Bouguerra Soltani, was mentioned during the trial of fallen golden boy Rafik Khalifa. A tuna-trafficking scheme also received substantial press coverage when he was minister of fisheries, and his chief of staff, also a member of the MSP, was subsequently indicted. This revealed a pattern of dysfunction under Soltani's stewardship of the ministry. In 2010, the granting of fraudulent public contracts for the construction of the East–West Highway and the Algiers Metro compromised the reputation of another figure in the party, Minister of Transportation Amar Ghoul, which once again led to the indictment of his chief of staff. Successive scandals undermined the MSP's image as a "party of responsibility," as it came increasingly to be associated in the public imagination with dirty money.[49]

Consequently, a profound crisis of leadership shook the party as Soltani's dominance was overtly challenged. The MSP's model of internal discipline proved to be closer to the FLN's than that of its Egyptian "brothers." During the 2006 National Congress, a group of rectifiers rallied behind Abdelmadjid Menasra, a former minister of industry in the Benbitour government (1999–2000). In response, Soltani tried to position himself as the herald of a new anticorruption struggle, publicly denouncing the "embezzlement of several billions of dinars in public money." This declaration led to a sharp rebuttal from Bouteflika, who ordered him to either release the files he claimed to have or get in line, which he did immediately.[50] After this failed attempt, Soltani and his supporters turned toward a new project: the unification of the Islamist subfield. This effort did not put a stop to the centrifugal forces within the MSP. Menasra and his followers eventually left to create their own party, the Front of Change.

At the end of 2011, the MSP, bolstered by the successes of other Islamist parties in Morocco, Tunisia, and Egypt, announced that it was leaving the Presidential Alliance. Soltani soon made official the creation of the Green Alliance, an Islamist coalition with Ennahḍa and Al-Iṣlaḥ, two minor parties that had also previously been co-opted. This strategic reorientation provoked a backlash among key MSP figures. After the 2012 elections, and despite the threats coming from the party's leadership, Mustapha Benbada welcomed his reappointment as minister of trade in Sellal's new government. A few days later, Amar Ghoul, still minister of transportation and freshly elected as a deputy, launched a dissident movement. This split gave birth to a new Islamist component in the Presidential Alliance, the Rally for Hope in Algeria (Tajama'a A'mal al-Jazāi'r, TAJ), which attracted a handful of MSP parliamentarians as well as the support of the UGEL. The following year, Abderrazak Makri replaced Soltani as leader of the party, with the goal of rebuilding its credibility as an opposition force. Justified in the name of saving the country, co-option came at a high price for the MSP.

After the abyss of the Dark Decade, twenty years of pluralism, dissidence, and participation in the government led to the shattering of the Islamist subfield into a myriad of reformist organizations who were met with deep popular mistrust. This does not mean that Islamism had lost its potential as a political contender. Under Bouteflika, some figures were still untarnished by compromise and collusion. Abdallah Djaballah was certainly the most iconic of these die-hard Islamist opponents, who rejected both the cartel and jihadi violence. The founder of Ennahḍa and Al-Iṣlaḥ, Djaballah was expelled from both parties in order to facilitate their co-option. He then created Al-ʿAdala, a political movement coupling religious conservatism with a sharp condemnation of elite corruption and calls for greater socioeconomic justice.[51] Djaballah's ability to bring together Islam, nationalism, and economic issues might support the notion of a filial relationship with the FIS. Yet he is the representative of a narrow elite linked to the Muslim Brotherhood, and the popular support he enjoys has been limited to the Wilaya of Constantine. Consequently, under Bouteflika, he remained an isolated opponent in a remarkably fragmented Islamist subfield. Al-Adala nonetheless won seven seats in the APN in 2012 and fifteen in 2017.

Until 2019, the mosaic of Islamist parties linked to the Muslim Brotherhood remained divided, unstable, and prone to dissidence and co-option. The circumstantial social alliance that once enabled the FIS to become a genuine challenger vis-à-vis the ruling coalition brought together upwardly mobile "counter-elites," the pious bourgeoisie, and the precarious urban working classes.[52] Under Bouteflika, such a broad coalition seemed out of the question. The social and political fragmentation made it seemingly unimaginable.

Pluralism and the Rejection of Politics

Given the dominance of cartel parties and the bureaucratic management of elections, it is tempting to apply Mohamed Tozy's notion of the "defused political field" to Algeria.[53] Yet the phrase does not capture the intensity of the struggles that occurred during electoral periods and inside partisan organizations. Successive campaigns opened a limited but very real horizon of possibility. In so doing, they fueled internal conflicts rooted in questions of ideology, strategy, organizational preeminence, and resources.[54] In order to perpetuate the status quo, the cartel drew on this competition to integrate, divide, and exclude.

INDEPENDENTS FOR SALE

The Algerian political field included a myriad of organizations whose ideological commitments, to the extent that they had any, were expressed in vague references to the dominant nationalist narrative. These parties provided the cartel with challengers for foregone elections (*lièvres*). During the 2009 presidential election, for instance, the general secretary of the Workers' Party (Parti des travailleurs, PT), Louisa Hanoune, was Bouteflika's main sparring partner. She was rewarded with an honorable second-place finish and 4.22 percent of the vote. One of many "opposition" movements in the country, the PT was the main force of the antiliberal Left. Party of the proletariat and the nation, it was and remains close to the UGTA. A herald of defensive nationalism, Louisa Hanoune was a vocal supporter of stability in the face of foreign conspiracies. She alternated between denunciation of the government's economic reforms and temporary alliances with the RND. She thus embodied the ambiguity characteristic of those partisan actors situated on the periphery of the cartel. In 2014, she repeatedly questioned Bouteflika's health before admitting that his victory was beyond dispute and praising him for being a "man of the Left."[55] Despite its ambiguity, the PT had solid relations with more radical opposition parties. A heavyweight among a fragmented Left, it was an indispensable partner. When I asked about the electoral alliance between his party and the PT for the 2012 legislatives, a member of the Trotskyist Socialist Workers' Party (Parti socialiste des travailleurs, PST) confessed, "We have no illusion about who we are dealing with, but it's the rule. We made this strategic choice so we can be heard."

The PT was far from being the only ambiguous organization. Moussa Touati's Algerian National Front (Front National Algérien, FNA) had a similarly opaque relationship with the cartel. Created in 1998 by former police officer Touati, the FNA offers a telling example of a party averse to categorization. An offspring of the National Organization of the Children of Shuhadā', the FNA gained traction in the early 2000s and peaked in 2007, when it received thirteen seats in the legislative elections. Despite its rhetoric mixing familiar themes (nation, people, crisis, reform, corruption), the movement was notorious for the vagueness of its political agenda, beyond its leitmotif of "giving power back to the people." Its main contribution to public debate was to fuel the speculations regarding its own positioning vis-à-vis the "System." This ambiguity was reinforced by recurring defections both originating from and in the direction of the cartel parties. In November 2007, for example, several RND dissidents joined Touati's party. A few years later, in May 2012, freshly elected FNA parliamentarians then swelled the ranks of TAJ. In both cases, these defections resulted from elections (local in 2007, legislative in 2012). Indeed, during an electoral campaign, the lack of a clear ideological line facilitated co-option. In order to better benefit from the opportunities available in the political marketplace, some actors simply avoided "being 'compromised' after taking a strong stance."[56]

The distribution of offices and nominations led to relatively banal forms of political horse trading. The exchange of different types of capital (organizational legitimacy, say, for popularity or money) was part of a pragmatic negotiation between parties and notables, each of them possessing what the other desired. The act of buying an office fell under the category of *shkara*, a term for corruption that refers to the plastic or paper bags in which cash bribes are often proffered. Nevertheless, political representation, as a sort of social magic trick, required that a minimal degree of respect was paid to formal etiquette to maintain popular belief.[57] The commodification of offices should have remained hidden. Yet the exact opposite happened when Touati publicly announced the auctioning of places on the FNA's list of candidates before the 2012 legislative elections.[58] Transgression was exposed in the public sphere, thereby eroding the belief essential to the illusion of political representation. When he published a document showing the cost of each position, the FNA's president renounced any pretense of a separation between economic wealth and political commitment. He dispelled the mystery and undermined the ministry. As affluence replaced genuine representation, it was not surprising to see a front-runner in the FNA primary in Souk-Ahras supplanted by a defeated challenger who had simply paid the amount requested by the party.[59] Commodified political offices thus became available to politico-economic actors seeking to accumulate capital in different fields, at the expense of the entire political class's credibility.

A well-negotiated political commitment could be bankable. Therefore, small independent organizations seeking easy profits proliferated. Before the local elections of 1990, more than sixty movements were created in less than a year. According to William Quandt, this was part of a strategy implemented by the reformist government in order to undermine the influence of the FLN's old guard.[60] This fragmentation persisted under Bouteflika despite repeated attempts to foster convergence. The plethora of independent parties, lacking any real guiding ideals besides claiming to support "the president," "concord" or "change," fueled a general suspicion toward politics, which became synonymous with collusion and opportunism.

The uninterrupted cycle of defections revealed the contradictions inherent to partisan organizations. Dissenters were labeled with the generic term "rectifiers," a euphemism that echoes the Revolutionary Correction (*at-Taṣḥīḥ ath-Thawrī*), the official name for the 1965 coup. Like the military, who once justified their putsch by accusing Ben Bella of monopolizing power, present-day rectifiers presented their rebellions as responses to authoritarian party executives. Indeed, party leaderships were frequently personalized. Following Michels's famous iron law of oligarchy, electoral competition and bureaucratization reinforced the tendency of political organizations to tame their plurality for the benefit of a homogenized executive.[61]

The combination of fictitious unanimity and public acts of rebellion prevented the emergence of stable currents capable of competing for power within their given political organization. Rather, executive bodies were under the control of a group in a dominant position, which aimed to prevent long-term competition between factions, and therefore to limit diversity within each party. Consequently, attempts to overthrow the leadership resulted in the exclusion of dissidents and the creation of new political organizations with similar goals and sociological bases. For instance, after a failed attempt to overthrow Moussa Touati, the short-lived president of the FNA, Mohamed Benhamou, created his own party, El-Karama, which received one seat in the 2012 legislative elections.

The succession of failed *redressements* turning into open dissidence made the mapping of the political field increasingly difficult. Movements with a strictly local basis and no legitimacy other than the social capital of a notable or the popularity of a local celebrity could nonetheless be represented in the APN. Fifteen parties each received less than 3 percent of the vote and at least one seat in the legislative elections of 2007. Five years later, in 2012, twenty-two organizations were in the same situation. In addition, dozens of elected independents proclaimed their support for the president as their sole political loyalty.

In return, the fragmentation of the field fueled stiff competition for political capital. Centrifugal dynamics ensured that parties were locked in a struggle for short-term survival, preventing them from offering a viable alternative to the cartel.[62] I have shown here that cartel parties faced their own rectifiers. While they were certainly no better disciplined than their competitors, the RND and the FLN nevertheless benefited from systemic advantages as well as significant material and organizational resources. In the meantime, the cycle of defections fueled the political marketplace with new candidates for co-option. Figure 4.1 and table 4.1 provide a more detailed picture of the extreme fragmentation of the Algerian political field during this period.

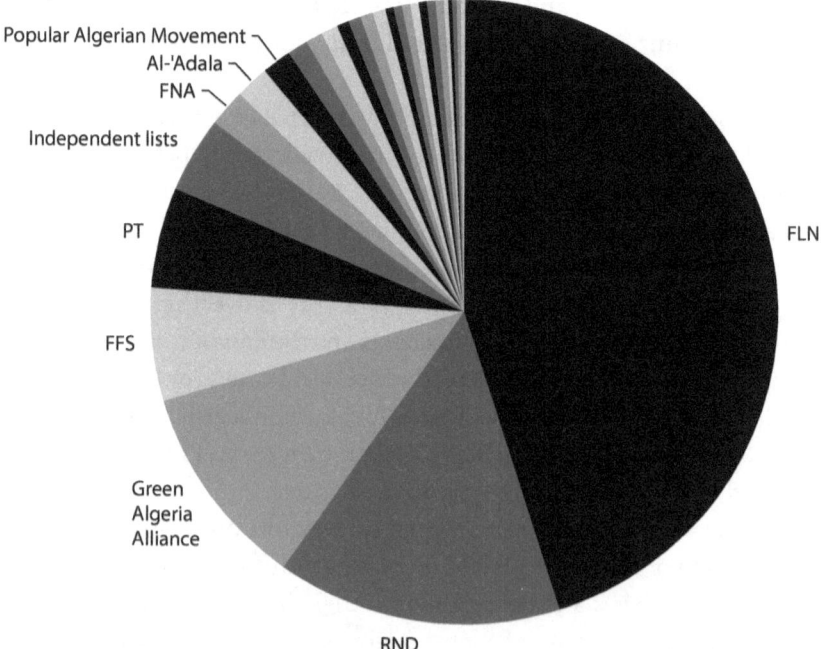

FIGURE 4.1 Composition of the People's National Assembly after the 2012 legislative elections. (Diagram by author.)

TABLE 4.1

Parties	Number of seats won	Percentage of total valid votes*
FLN	208	17.35
RND	68	6.86
Green Algeria Alliance	49	6.22
FFS	27	2.47
PT	24	3.71
Independent lists	18	8.79
FNA	9	2.6
Al-'Adala	8	3.05
Popular Algerian Movement	7	2.17
Al-Fajr al-Jadid Party	5	1.74
Front of Change	4	2.28
National Party for Solidarity and Development	4	1.5
Ahd 54	3	1.57
National Republican Alliance	3	1.43
National Front for Social Justice	3	1.84
Union of Democratic and Socialist Forces	3	1.5
Jabhat Al-Mustaqbal	2	2.29
National Movement of Hope	2	1.56
Youth Party	2	1.34
Al-Karama	2	1.7
Annur Al-Djazairi Party	2	0.64
Algerian Rally	2	1.54
Patriotic Republican Rally	2	1.5
National Democratic Front	1	1.33
National Front of Independents for Concord	1	1.41
Citizens' Movement	1	1.51
Al-Infitah	1	1.52
Algerian Renewal Party	1	1.46
Other parties	0	17.11

*18.25 percent of cast ballots were invalidated or blank.

Source: "Algeria: Al-Majlis Al-Chaabi Al-Watani (National People's Assembly); Elections in 2012," Inter-Parliamentary Union, accessed February 22, 2023, http://archive.ipu.org/parline-e/reports/arc/2003_12.htm.

POLITICS REJECTED

The engagement of notables and entrepreneurs in institutional politics compensated for a shortage of capital (both money and popularity). But it also reinforced the material dimension of the electoral competition at the expense of its ideological stakes.[63] Opportunistic and parasitic structures such as TAJ grew on the periphery of the cartel while undermining their respective subfields. Unsurprisingly, these defectors appeared in the public sphere as living proof of the alleged careerism of politicians, further eroding the representative system's credibility.

The creation of personal fiefdoms dominated by political businessmen—whether belonging to the *Pouvoir* or its opponents—fueled the denunciations of a mafia enriched by monopoly control and speculation (in public construction, private security, cement, food products). At the local level, detractors of a given party portrayed its big men as godfathers. In Tizi Ouzou, for example, student and supporter of the FFS Hocine described RCD deputy Nordine Aït Hamouda—son of the legendary colonel Amirouche[64]—as a genuine capo controlling the city with the support of militias founded during the 1990s. The competition between the two Berberist parties described in the next chapter was certainly an underlying motive in Hocine's depiction.

The pejorative representation of politics legitimized a widespread apoliticism.[65] It resulted in a contentious condemnation of all those considered complicit with the established order. As politics were routinely described as ḥarām, those elected to a public office were preemptively deprived of any kind of legitimacy. As such, abstention could not be reduced to the caricature of a lack of civic culture. People's indiscriminate rejection of politicians meant that in the popular imagination politics itself came increasingly to resemble an infamous bestiary populated by donkeys and hares. Arguably, avoiding politics was both a matter of morality and common sense.

> I never had any political commitment because I didn't want the FLN or RND tag. I would rather be an activist in an autonomous association, even if I know that politicians will try to control it for its experience or its reputation, for the benefit of their party or their career ... The worst thing would be to be seen as an association of the *Pouvoir*, or an association of

the president. Or, the other way around, to be seen as an association of the RCD [i.e., the opposition].

(YASMINE, GENERAL COORDINATOR FOR THE NGO TOUIZA, ALGIERS, AUTUMN 2010)

Yasmine's discourse and trajectory provided a telling example of the pejorative representation of institutional politics. Born in Oran, she had joined the Algerian Network of Young Activists, a program implemented by the German NGO Friedrich Ebert Stiftung, and had taken part in several rounds of training. With Touiza, she worked to promote the independence of women, and she was very proud of her job. While she was ready to work with foreign NGOs, Yasmine regarded political parties with suspicion and was weary of potential "manipulations." She agreed to collaborate with the state out of necessity but otherwise refused to have anything to do with the political field. In this sense, she was like many Algerians who sought to prevent their engagement from being tainted by politics. Some favored the generally antipolitical field of transnational NGOs specializing in development or the promotion of gender equality. Others remained active at the local level and emphasized the need to remain autonomous, even when they had personal connections with political organizations.

The CLE [Coordination locale des étudiants, or Local coordination of students] is autonomous both at the national level and at the political level. It doesn't belong to any political party even if there are political activists inside. But its members cannot be managed, manipulated, or co-opted by any political party. Students will decide. If there is a strategic decision to be made, we organize a general assembly. Parties must stay out of it. They must not decide for us.

(HOCINE, MEMBER OF THE LOCAL COORDINATION OF STUDENTS
AND FFS SUPPORTER, TIZI OUZOU, SPRING 2011)

Hocine was adamant in his rejection of political influence. He conceded that the goal was to avoid driving away fellow students, who might share the claims of the social movement to which he belonged but would have left if parties were involved. Hocine himself continuously denounced *khobzistes* of all kinds, including in the FFS, and understood the mistrust of his classmates. Under Bouteflika, the key to offering a credible discourse was to stay away from the political field. The avoidance of politics became

FIGURE 4.2 Photomontage posted on Facebook one month before the 2012 legislative elections showing candidates in the form of donkeys, hyenas, and chickens. (Screenshot by author.)

the rule, even as activists justified this in different ways, depending on their strategic goals, personal opinions, and the social context.[66]

While the rejection of politics is a common phenomenon around the world, the Algerian case was notable for the widely shared representation of electoral competition as little more than a cosmetic trick. During the Dark Decade, sociologist Rabeh Sebaa warned of a "reification of politics" that enabled the misappropriation of democratic ideals and the proliferation of opportunistic organizations.[67] The "cosmetic democracy" depicted by political opponents was allegedly populated by a clique of *khobzistes* and *shiyyatin* manipulated by the presidency and the DRS. While certainly simplistic, this representation revealed what Gramsci would characterize as a profound "crisis of hegemony on the part of the ruling class." The growing gap between rulers and subjects eroded the relevance of political parties. It also bolstered the influence of bureaucratic powers (civilian or military) and resulted in a precarious political equilibrium.[68] The photomontage depicted in figure 4.2 illustrates the very negative representations of the political field circulating on Algerian social media.

Narratives of Order

Crises of hegemony reshape the narratives that undergird the dominant order. Meanwhile, the dominant ideology smooths apparent contradictions and presents the prevailing sociopolitical order as a self-evident reality by invoking the alleged characteristics of the ruling elites and the population.[69] In Bouteflika's Algeria, dominant discourses thus merged a security-based rationale with elements of paternalism, populism, and conservatism. It evolved into a form of discursive catastrophization that opposed the alarming plurality of the masses with a fictitious unanimity. As the continuous existential threat justified obedience and discipline, "'endangerment' became a new operational baseline assumption for making the advances of 'development.'"[70]

CHAKIB'S DEFENSE OF THE ESTABLISHED ORDER

To understand the tension between the defenders and detractors of the political order, it is helpful to return to the local level, and more precisely to the city of Ghardaïa, situated six hundred kilometers south of Algiers, in the M'zab Valley, one of the gateways to the Sahara. There, half a dozen men were in the middle of a heated discussion when I joined them for tea in the autumn of 2011. Seated on the terrace of a café, these high-school teachers were on strike, and they proceeded to explain the reasons for their mobilization. Only one of them refused to blame the government: Chakib, a French teacher and father of two in his fifties. As he claimed to have always voted for the old nationalist party, his colleagues mocked him for being a *khobziste*. He tried to justify his allegiance by variously invoking the revolution, the historical accomplishments of the FLN, or Bouteflika's role in bringing back peace, but the others kept replying with the same outrageous argument: "if you support the FLN, it's for the money." More than a personal accusation, they weaponized the party's reputation to reject his claims, albeit in a friendly context. In response to his companions' mockery, Chakib distanced himself from the social movement and reversed the stigma:

> People who go on strike or who demonstrate against the regime because of what happened in Tunisia, they are not honest. What interests them is what they can get from it for themselves, not for the country. They do the same thing that the FFS folks did here. They fuel disorder for their own profit. This is what they call democracy.
>
> (CHAKIB, TEACHER AND FLN SUPPORTER, GHARDAÏA, AUTUMN 2011)

This sympathizer of the old nationalist party was convinced that only manipulation could explain the continuous wave of protests across the country. Annoyed by his colleagues' teasing, he enjoined me to disregard the disorder fueled by "Kabyles" who had come to the South to "spread" their regionalism. Drawing on the shared rationality of suspicion and instrumentalization, he insisted that the unity of the country was at stake. At his level, Chakib was thus invoking nothing less than an existential threat and therefore partaking in discursive catastrophization.

The discussion turned back to the central issues for these men: poor teaching conditions in high schools, lack of material resources, and the inadequate performance on the part of students. This dark depiction led one of the strikers, a math teacher, to speak about the despair of the youth and to present illegal emigration toward Europe (*harga*) as the consequence of a crumbling education system. Chakib was adamant in his disagreement:

> They call the government *khobzistes* but these people don't deserve better. They spend their days complaining, but these are lies and hypocrisy. In this country, we have money, cars, and jobs. All you need is not to be lazy and to have an entrepreneurial spirit. But if you don't want to do anything, and all you want is to go to Europe, you get what you deserve: unemployment ... The youth complain a lot, but what do they know about France, in reality? In fact, the main reason the youth want to leave the country is the false ideas they see on TV. The *harraga* [those who leave for Europe], what they are looking for in France is debauchery, pornography, and alcohol.
>
> (CHAKIB, 2011)

The teacher summarily dismissed the socioeconomic and political motives of undocumented migrants. As a supporter of a party that had been in government for forty of the last fifty years, he refused to acknowledge the reasons for an exile that he viewed as a sign of weakness. The *harga* could therefore be explained by morally despicable motives alone. In Chakib's account, the youth were both easily influenced by television and conditioned by their impulses. As is so often the case, hypersexualization served to disparage and incriminate problematic social groups.[71]

In Algeria, this paternalistic narrative castigating an amorphous youth all too ready to complain also echoed a looming generational conflict. The same evening, as we completed the crossword while enjoying a glass of fruit juice, Chakib returned to the morning's discussion. Again he deplored the immaturity of his fellow citizens, before underlining why the FLN was different from its challengers:

> Before, when we had only the FLN, things were easier. It's the party that fought France and enabled the birth of Algeria. It's the party that made Algeria grow until 1988. All these new parties, they criticize a lot, but if they want power, it's not for the Algerian people, but for the money.
>
> (CHAKIB, 2011)

Chakib echoed the widespread rejection of parties and the value judgments inherent to the discourse on corruption. In his eyes, the simplicity and honesty of the era of single-party rule was opposed to the current state of sociopolitical anomie. Nostalgia for a lost political clarity contrasted with an opaque present plagued by cynical calculations. He viewed the resilience of the FLN as an appropriate response to the chaos resulting from multipartyism.

DEFENDING NATIONAL UNITY

In their political communication, the cartel spokespersons claimed to be the sole guarantors of national unity and the protectors of the people against itself. Initially crafted by the developmental state after 1962, this rhetoric based on unanimity and paternalism was reinforced by the events of the 1990s. Eventually, it became an essential feature in discursive catastrophization under Bouteflika.

As I showed in chapter 2, pacification was an essential feature in Bouteflika's strategy of legitimation. It addressed socially shared expectations following the Dark Decade and justified constant calls for unity and discipline. During the campaign for the 2005 referendum, Belkhadem could thus claim that no FLN member was against the Charter for Peace and National Reconciliation.[72] The plebiscite organized by the presidency and its entourage prevented the expression of dissenting voices. The project of reconciliation did not tolerate any contradictory debate in the public sphere. Yet the reunification of the "Algerian Family" also drew on exclusionary procedures. In addition to the protection granted to former perpetrators of violence on behalf of the state, the executive order of February 2006 stipulated that "the exercise of political activity is prohibited, in whatever form, for any individual responsible for the instrumentalization of religion that led to the National Tragedy [the civil war]."⁷³ In the name of reconciliation, radical opponents—particularly those who rejected the charter's program of amnesia and amnesty—were banned from politics, even when they did not directly partake in violence, as was the case for many senior members of the FIS in exile.

The suspension of the disaster allowed for the repetition of a security-based narrative. Following the Arab uprisings of 2010–2011, Prime Minister Ouyahia repeatedly cast the regional upheaval as an "Arab Winter" or an "Arab Downfall." In a similar vein, the government-owned magazine *El-Djezair* dedicated a full issue to the "Spring of the Arab Curse," which it also described as a "Spring of the Graveyards," in May 2013. These transparent warnings echoed a recurring diagnosis that presented October 1988 as the original sin that led to the "National Tragedy." These uprisings were depicted as a mix of childish resentment and obscure manipulation that resulted in mass terrorism. In the words of Lakehal Ayat, the head of the intelligence services at the time, "October was the beginning of disobedience in Algeria, of the contempt for values, of the negation of institutions... A troublemaker gets used to confrontation. He just needs the means to turn into a terrorist, especially if he is supported by the dreadful enemies of Algeria."⁷⁴ In 2018, Ouyahia read the events in a similar fashion, declaring the 1988 uprising the beginning of chaos, lawlessness, and terrorism.⁷⁵ Indeed, in a critical configuration, radical critique is portrayed as inherently untimely.⁷⁶ This allegedly childish impulse contradicts the need to act in an orderly fashion, which is to say within the civil and regulated framework crafted by the ruling classes.

In the troubled regional context of the early 2010s, the FLN's victory in the 2012 legislative elections was cast as a "shelter vote" (*vote refuge*) by Minister of Interior Ould Kablia.⁷⁷ And when the time came to promote Bouteflika's fourth term, his supporters in the executive circles of the cartel parties portrayed him as the sole guarantor of stability and security.⁷⁸ Political competition was thus subordinated to the higher imperative of short-term survival.

While the proponents of the existing order monopolized the values of security and unity, their most virulent detractors were accused of harboring seditious aims. Uncompromising dissent was equated to national disintegration. As we saw in Chakib's account, Kabylia was often perceived as the Achilles' heel of national unity. As the epicenter of Algerian Berberism, the region had long been portrayed as a security hazard. Nationalist figures accused opposition parties such as the FFS of ethnic discrimination and, in some cases, of racism. Berberism was an alleged threat to the nation because it divided the people. As a result, ambiguous personalities such as Louisa Hanoune could speak of Kabyle activism with the zeal of a prosecutor. During the 2004 presidential campaign, the general secretary of the PT adopted a fiercely nationalistic rhetoric. After warning against the shenanigans of "foreign personalities representing the alliance against Iraq and the Palestinian people," she denounced the Citizens' Movement born in Kabylia in harsh terms. According to her, "the political movement that [called] itself '*archs*' [was] threatening the foundations of the Republic, because it [was] based on a form of regional and ethnical representation."[79]

Hanoune constantly traced Berberist unrest back to foreign conspiracies. Occasionally, she went so far as to link Kabyle autonomists to the jihadis who had found shelter in the neighboring Djurdjura Mountains. Meanwhile, government officials and affiliates raised the specter of Western imperialism, thus performing a script similar to their counterparts in Syria or Egypt.[80] Yet the case of Kabylia demonstrates that these defensive narratives also reinforced the opposition between two naturalized spatial units (the region and the nation). Nationalist anathemas thus contributed to the birth of marginal separatist movements.

In the mid-2000s, the regionalist threat progressively moved toward the South, from Tizi Ouzou and Bejaïa to Ghardaïa and Ouargla. As we will see in chapter 6, this displacement accompanied the revival of social movements denouncing the misappropriation of the country's natural resources. After Western military interventions in Libya and Mali, the geopolitical and socioeconomic dimensions of the crisis merged to displace the traditional epicenter of sedition. The South was increasingly viewed through the lens of security and national unity.[81] While visiting Tamanrasset in 2012, for example, Prime Minister Ouyahia denounced the "conspiracies fomented in the name of democracy" and the "foreign appetites targeting oil, gas, and uranium." He continued his speech in a vein characteristic of state paternalism: "What is happening in neighboring countries is an opportunity to close our ranks and become aware of the value of independence, territorial integrity, national unity, and the value of peace . . . There is no place for those who want to cause a revolution in Algeria under the pretext of disparities and discrimination in development. The state ensures the development of all regions in the country without any discrimination."[82]

Ouyahia finished his speech with a warning: "We are one single people, but vigilance is still needed." After dismissing the reasons for unrest in the South, the prime minister repeated a well-known security- and unanimity-centered narrative. This commonplace was also directed at foreign partners. One day before this trip, Ouyahia was interviewed in the French daily *Le Monde*. There, he emphasized the disorder resulting from the Arab uprisings and underplayed the protest movement in Algeria, which he portrayed as a mere form of "agitation." According to him, the Algerian people knew "the price of anarchy too well."[83]

THREE NATURES OF THE PEOPLE

In keeping with a long-standing populist tradition, the people occupied a central role in the dominant ideology, both as an ideal revolutionary subject and an infantilized mass. As abstention remained a thorn in the cartel's side, its spokespersons became increasingly critical of the population. Indeed, "the people" that should be democratized was not the heroic totality that had achieved independence. This tension also echoed the successive transformations of the political order. The original nature of the people, the *people-as-class*, appeared during the anticolonial struggle. As an empty signifier, the term "the people" allowed for the aggregation of diverse social groups in a context of intense political conflict.[84] During the revolution, an antagonistic and unanimity-driven mobilization successfully turned the people into a totality by overshadowing social fragmentation. The people-as-class was therefore "neither the addition of social partners or the collection of difference but rather the power to undo partnerships, collections, ordinations."[85] Its main features were its "collective vitality," its "worrying strangeness," and its ability to "destroy all kinds of regimes."[86] It is through this process of claiming to represent the totality of the nation that a fraction of the Algerian population was able to defeat the colonial order during the War of Liberation. Likewise, it is by "turning into a people" that temporary social coalitions gave birth to the revolutionary movements of 2010–2011 in Tunisia, Syria, and Egypt.

The materialization of the people-as-class is a decisive yet ephemeral phenomenon. If the mythical motto of *El Moudjahid* proclaims that the revolution was made "by the people and for the people," the latter was never meant to govern. After 1962, the new ruling elites organized the dissipation of the people-as-class. This is the process identified by Castoriadis when he describes the Jacobin takeover during the French Revolution as the rise of a specific bureaucracy that pushed the people away to only preserve an abstract link between the national community and its representatives.[87] This evolution came with a shift to a coercive approach whereby the new leadership designated the enemies of the people. As such, the reordering relied on the erection of a new sociopolitical hierarchy by way of a shift in values.[88]

Algerian Third Worldism displayed a similarly Jacobin view of the relationship between the people and those who serve them.[89] For the bureaucratic-military apparatus that took over after 1962, the people were no longer central in the political struggle. They were a mass that should be acted upon through a mix of coercion and redistribution, and mobilized punctually to serve state-driven projects. This gave birth to the *people-as-object*, a characteristic feature of what Lahouari Addi labels a form of "authoritarian populism."[90] Under Boumediene, the masses were expected to support developmental policies through the mediation of the leader. In his PhD dissertation, the future deputy and ambassador Khalfa Mameri argued that "there is no valid and viable government if there is not a community and an intimacy of thought between the people and its leader."[91] As a matter of fact, the people-as-object was expected to delegate its entire sovereignty to the ANP-FLN-state trio.

This dispossession was not definitive. With the advent of the crisis from the mid-1980s onward, the ability to legitimate obedience decreased. The social hierarchy and the categories enforced by the proponents of the postcolonial order were challenged by new contentious discourses. Algeria thus witnessed the resurgence of the people-as-class under the guise of the "Muslim people" invoked by the FIS. A paradigm shift occurred at the level of the ruling elites, as they were seemingly "betrayed" by the population they had tried to uplift through their developmental policies. The people therefore became an unstable, childish, and ultimately dangerous entity that was to be disciplined, coerced, and educated to contain its chaotic passions. In the mind of the proponents of the established order, this was the *people-as-child*. Confronted with the wave of uprisings that shook France in 1793, the Jacobins responded with a similar reversal: they argued that popular bewilderment and immaturity justified repression.[92] In both cases, the people-as-child legitimized the elites' shift to mass coercion in the name of progress.

Class, object, and child: the people appeared alternately in each of these guises depending on the pace of the critical process. In the last years of Bouteflika's rule, they were intertwined in public discourses. Protests, abstention, and riots demonstrated a transverse anger expressed in populist terms. At the same time, these performances of dissent resonated with the paternalistic subjectivity of the ruling elites: they were proof that the population needed to learn the virtues of civility. In the name of saving the population from itself, discontent was systematically dismissed. To explain the urban uprisings of January 2011, the *barbéfélène* Abdelaziz Belkhadem argued that rioters were merely repeating slogans heard in football stadiums and deplored a general lack of civic consciousness.[93] The people-as-child had become the target of a new civilizing mission: the population should be democratized and normalized. It should act civically by putting a ballot—the right one—in the box. It should accept budgetary austerity and pension reform to compensate for decades of mismanagement. It should submit to police authority and leave public space untroubled by its childish impulses. Nevertheless, the limits of these disciplinary narratives were clear. In February 2019, the massive resurgence of the people-as-class during the Hirak invalidated the paternalistic approach of ruling elites, at least temporarily.

REALITY CHECK

The proponents of order turned the latency of the crisis into a discursive resource. To produce legitimacy, they defended Islam, the memory of the revolution, the economy, the country, and, above all, the people (from itself). This legitimacy was nonetheless partial, precarious, and constantly challenged. Social and political fragmentation limited the ability of the cartel's spokespersons to be credible in their self-assigned role as protectors.

Take, for instance, Ahmed Ouyahia. In 2012, as he called for unity and obedience in Tamanrasset, the prime minister also faced internal dissent. In the midst of the legislative campaign, Nouria Hasfi, the general secretary of the Union of Algerian Women (an association of the Revolutionary Family), announced a movement of rectification targeting Ouyahia.

According to her, the RND was a "National Dictatorial Rally . . . managed like a barrack." She presented the prime minister as a "danger for Algeria" whose ambitions might "cause havoc."[94] There was certainly a kind of irony in this depiction of one of the most prominent despisers of popular agitation as himself a national threat.

In this context, relativity was key. When compared with their challengers, the FLN and the RND gained not credibility but normalcy. Indeed, the dominance of cartel parties was a matter of preexisting equilibrium: they prevailed because they had readier access to meta-power, because they were essential in the clientelist system of socioeconomic redistribution and mediation, and because they were supported by nonpartisan components of the cartel. The FLN won elections because it was what it was. In comparison, its competitors had to survive in a plural yet fragmented partisan framework, while being associated with one of many derogatory political categories: *shiyyatin*, fundamentalists, *khobzistes*, regionalists. Opposition parties struggled for their own survival in a system that weakened its own components. Given the accumulation of difficulties, political capital was extremely hard to preserve, let alone to accumulate. Consequently, "no political party, no public figure [could] emerge in a sufficiently decisive fashion to appear as a solid challenger."[95] The discredit that plagued the whole political field prevented the constitution of viable alternatives, while the narratives of order never managed to hide the arbitrariness of the entire power structure.

Vox Populi

In one of the epigraphs that start this chapter, the words of the young architect Abdelhakim revealed a very negative representation of the ruling coalition as a "group of gangsters." The following joke illustrates the accusation perennially targeting those who controlled the Algerian state:

> The godfather of Cosa Nostra keeps hearing reports about a powerful Algerian mafia. Eventually, these rumors get on his nerves, and he decides to find out if his competitors are as strong as people say. He sends one of his men to Algeria to collect information. When the man comes back, he

looks embarrassed and says, "I am sorry, boss, but these Algerians are just too strong for us."

"How is this even possible?" says the boss. "They cannot be stronger than Cosa Nostra."

"Boss, they have an army, a flag, and ambassadors. They even have their own police, justice system, a National Assembly, and a government!"

The Algerian vox populi seemed to confirm Charles Tilly's remarkable intuition: states can be compared to criminal organizations, notably because of their core functions of extraction and protection.[96] Obviously, portraying the cartel merely as a mafia that seized a state is a caricature. Yet this widespread diagnosis testified to the limited reach of the narratives of order. As the main figure in the cartel, Bouteflika was particularly targeted. Given his precarious health, the president was portrayed as an absent, benevolent, yet unchallengeable figure, following the canon of traditional patriarchal authority. He was nonetheless systematically derided in jokes and rumors. His sustained celibacy generated comments about his relationship with his mother and his sexual preferences. More importantly, the corruption of his entourage was also a hot topic for mockery. The president himself was nicknamed "Boutesriqa" (the father in thief). The caustic irony in which these rejections of presidential authority were expressed made them even more damaging. Without ignoring the fatalism inherent to this register of popular humor,[97] it was also part of a diffuse resistance that maintained the possibility of a transition to mass public dissent.[98]

During the Hirak, the jokes and signs depicting an impotent president and a gang ('iṣāba) who had seized the state demonstrated the weakness of the cartel's legitimacy and the irrelevance of its core authorities. In the language of protesters, the 'iṣāba comprised the presidential entourage, well-known crony capitalists, as well as military officers and party leaders. All of them were associated with the infamous practice of shkara, the systematic commodification of public offices and state power. The first year of the movement also demonstrated the spectacular hostility toward a pluralist institutional framework conceived in the name of democracy to effectively limit popular sovereignty. The key motive behind the peaceful uprising was the rejection of a presidential election meant to secure Bouteflika's fifth term. The inability of the FLN and the RND to offer a credible alternative to the ailing president, even after his resignation in early

April 2019, testified to their profound lack of legitimacy and internal divisions. Meanwhile "pragmatic" Islamo-conservative parties, such as the MSP, continued to oscillate between cooperation with the cartel and efforts to regain their credibility as opponents. In other words, from the perspective of the political field, the storm associated with the Hirak merely exacerbated some of the dynamics outlined in this chapter.

The uprising of February 2019 collided with the public performances of dominant actors who posed as the sole guarantors of the country's stability in the face of the suspended disaster. While such euphemizing discourses aim to mask the power imbalances and arbitrariness that are the root of all political orders,[99] they are by themselves not enough to prove that the state is neutral, that the party is united, or that the president preserves peace. For the magic to work, the actors' performances must be credible. This is true for the leader of a sect as much as for a head of state. The internal conflicts fracturing the ruling classes undermine their ability to maintain "the smooth surface of euphemized power."[100] Moreover, for this social magic to operate, the sociopolitical context must confirm that domination is being exercised for benevolent ends. This is obviously not the case when the latent crisis turns endangerment, suspicion, and precariousness into daily facts of life. Consequently, the narratives of order clashed with representations depicting military officers as brutes, ministers as ignorant crooks, and the presidential entourage as a corrupt clique. But if the proponents of order were portrayed in such derogatory terms, if their position of power was seen as the fruit of spoliation, it is also vital to study the mechanisms that limited the efficacy of criticism and reproduced the powerlessness of the cartel's opponents before the advent of the Hirak.

5

The Regulation of Freedoms

The sovereign nomos is the principle that, joining law and violence, threatens them with indistinction.... The sovereign is the point of indistinction between violence and law, the threshold on which violence passes over into law and law passes into violence.

—*Giorgio Agamben*

The invisibility of the opposition represents a genuine threat for democracy. Some tend to blame the *Pouvoir* for this state of affairs, but should we expect it to support its opponents? The evolution of the situation demonstrates that responsibilities are shared and the blame for the opposition's lack of audibility should not lie uniquely with the *Pouvoir*.

—*Noureddine Aït-Messaoudene*

With the increasing complexity of the system of domination, public criticism became a mundane feature of Bouteflika's Algeria. According to Luc Boltanski, the tolerance of dissent is intimately linked to the progressive transition toward a "capitalist-democratic" society.[1] Of course, this process of democratization can serve to preserve the preexisting equilibrium.[2] While the restructuring of the

Algerian political order resulted in a selective appropriation of globalized norms, political rights were routinely limited in the name of security. Despite these limitations, one should not overlook the possibilities offered by this transformation: over the past thirty years, Algerians gained access to new social and political channels through which to express their grievances.

All the same, the cartel was successful in containing discontent until 2019. Criticism was systematically framed by a set of legal and extralegal practices. Freedoms were tolerated and regulated by the authorities in the name of the suspended disaster. This management of the right to speak or to assemble demonstrated the growing conformity of the Algerian authorities to the "culture of danger" inherent in liberal governmentality, which allows the monitoring and limitation of freedoms by security apparatuses.[3]

This chapter analyzes the regulation of dissent in an environment of political pluralism. Rather than propose a normative liberal critique of a "failed democratization," it seeks to understand how democratic globalization and the generalization of exception work hand in hand. This results in an indetermination between political forms,[4] which renders stable normative categories such as democracy or authoritarianism increasingly inadequate and calls for a critical analysis of these dynamic processes. In the following pages, I first propose an overview of the key role assigned by the government to the 2012 legislative elections in the aftermath of the Arab uprisings of 2010–2011. Looking at the place of criticism and its main vectors in the Algerian public sphere, the chapter then presents the possibilities offered to politicians, labor organizers, and pundits, and the control measures that framed their contentious practices. As repressive tactics proved unpredictable and selective, I investigate the entanglements between regulation and exception. Indeed, the tools enabling various forms of censorship brought together the globalized trends of counterterrorism and political pluralism. Meanwhile, Berberist movements were increasingly trapped in a routine of "contentious insularity" in their stronghold of Kabylia. Limited to this oppositional enclave, their radical denunciation of the central state was isolated from the rest of the country. In short, this chapter explains how the convergence of democracy and security, regulation and exception, made public criticism both mundane and seemingly toothless.

An Algerian Spring

Algeria did not remain idle during the uprisings of 2010–2011 any more than Morocco or Jordan had. Indeed, each country "responded to its own logic according to a regional rhythm."[5] Algeria accompanied the succession of upheavals with its own dynamic, marked by an intense moment of sociopolitical unrest in early 2011 followed by a return to a more consensual and disciplinary iteration of "democratic transition." To contain the revolutionary threat, the cartel relied on some of the tools associated with the globalized theme of democratization (consolidation, elections, institutional reforms).

OPENING AND TIGHTENING

In early January 2011, as the Tunisian ruling coalition was on the brink of collapse, a wave of riots started in the northern Wilayas of Tipaza and Oran. In the capital, the urban uprising soon reached the iconic working-class neighborhood of Bab El-Oued, situated within walking distance of Parliament and Government Palace. In response, several autonomous unions joined the Algerian League for the Defense of Human Rights (Ligue Algérienne pour la Défense des Droits de l'Homme, LADDH) in announcing that they were "taking up the cause of the Algerian youth."[6] A group of parties, associations, and unions founded the National Coordination for Change and Democracy (Coordination Nationale pour le Changement et la Démocratie, CNCD). Yet the coalition was rapidly weakened by disagreements between its social and political wings over the objectives of the movement and the strategies for implementing them. Eventually, the coalition split into two CNCDs (one composed of political parties and the other made up of civil society organizations). Once again, social and political fragmentation prevented a sustained convergence of struggles.[7]

The most enduring expression of discontent came from students. Since the beginning of the 2010–2011 academic year, university students had protested the adoption of the license-master's-doctorate system following European standards. Local student committees sprouted up throughout the country. The movement focused on "pedagogical" demands and rejected any partisan influence. Yet beyond this self-limitation, it had a thoroughly political nature, notably because some of its core activists were also members of opposition parties.[8] After January 2011, its slogans targeting the government, and specifically the Ministry of Higher Education, became increasingly contentious (*"wizāra irhābiyya!"* [terrorist ministry!]). On April 12 of that year a massive demonstration in Algiers resulted in clashes with police. While prevented from reaching either the Government Palace or El Mouradia, thousands of students shouted slogans (some of them quite radical) and marched in a once forbidden space. At the peak of the movement, one of these slogans—"The people want the fall of the regime!"—resounded throughout the boulevards of Algiers. The agitation then slowly receded with the end of the academic year. Two weeks after the protests, Hocine and Abdou were back in their dormitories of Boukhalfa 2, at the University of Tizi Ouzou, when they told me about the day on which they had joined their fellow students to challenge the *Pouvoir*. "After experiencing this, I can die peacefully!" said Hocine, as he packed a small ball of *chemma*, a type of chewing tobacco, between his teeth and cheeks. Demonstrations had been banned in the capital for ten years.

After the riots of January and the student movement, the protests receded. The memories of the Dark Decade were still vivid, and many commentators suggested that a popular uprising could very well end up in a bloodbath.[9] To avoid a second "National Tragedy," the government proposed another series of reforms. As in 1988–1989, the intensification of the crisis led to the reconfiguration of the political order. On February 23, the government lifted the state of emergency, originally proclaimed in 1992, in the name of "restoring the rule of law." On April 15, a weakened Abdelaziz Bouteflika appeared on television to announce a series of reforms aimed at "reinforcing democracy," among them another revision of the constitution, a modification of the law on political parties, and the loosening of restrictions on television, radio, and online news. A national commission for political reforms was created. The ANP was involved in the process, as the retired major general Mohamed Touati, one of the army's top leaders during the 1990s, was appointed to lead the commission. The presidency nonetheless remained technically in control, as the civilian pole in charge of guaranteeing the consolidation of democracy.

None of the reforms truly challenged the overall balance of power. Some even opened the door for new repressive measures, such as a law on associations that prohibited any interference with state affairs and limited the possibility of foreign funding. Most institutional fixes were thus viewed with suspicion, especially the new law on information, which journalists described as a dangerous regression.[10] Others had a more significant impact, notably the birth and rapid expansion of private TV networks. The state monopoly on public audiovisual media had already been seriously eroded since the late 1980s, as viewers increasingly relied on foreign TV channels. The rise of satellite television contributed to the growing mistrust toward state-owned outlets and the rise of critical responses to official discourses.[11] The reform introduced in 2011 thus increased media pluralism by allowing private networks.[12] Yet after this date, prominent privately owned channels, such as Ennahar TV and Echorouk TV, were often suspected of conniving with the presidency and the military.

The cartel also responded to popular pressures by mobilizing its security apparatus. Arriving in Algiers a few days after the student march, in mid-April 2011, I found the city saturated with police forces. For International Workers' Day, the National Committee for the Defense of the Rights of the Unemployed had organized a rally in May 1st Square. Its members and supporters numbered roughly fifty as the protest began. Facing this modest assembly, the *wali* had summoned more than a hundred members of the antiriot police. After singing their slogans for about an hour, the protesters were overwhelmed by a tide of men in navy blue uniforms and scattered throughout the neighboring streets. The spectacular disproportion of this deployment testified to a huge disparity in power. At the same time, many of the bystanders in the area expressed a form of mistrust toward the protesters. Some mentioned the unfolding violence in Libya. "Here, it will be worse," one of them said. Others criticized the alleged laziness or greed of the unemployed, or their potential manipulation by certain opaque forces ("They are just here for the money," or, "They were paid to cause problems"). The securitization of socioeconomic unrest thus found its justification in the rationality of suspicion and the shadow of the suspended disaster.

Despite the end of the state of emergency, Algiers remained off-limits to protesters. The police were present in large numbers, yet they constantly changed their appearance and tactics. On October 5, 2011, on the occasion of the annual commemoration of the uprising of 1988, the DGSN's henchmen were mostly dressed as civilians and scattered through the crowd. Two hours before the beginning of one protest action, scheduled for 11:00 a.m. near Martyrs' Square, two senior members of the youth movement RAJ were arrested at their doorsteps. This preventive move forced the remaining activists to improvise. They split up into small groups to avoid being seen. After debating if they should maintain their action as planned, they eventually decided to join other opposition organizations in front of the Algerian National Theater. Despite many obstacles, the commemoration took place in a slightly different form than expected. The arrested activists were released before lunchtime. Police harassment and the threat posed by plainclothes policemen had nonetheless turned the morning into an exhausting game of cat and mouse.

By drawing on a mix of repression and reform, the cartel navigated 2011 without being fundamentally threatened. Instrumentalizing the horrific images coming from Syria and Libya, its spokespersons demanded the unity of the people in the face of foreign conspiracies. In the name of preventing the catastrophe, Algeria was removed from the regional revolutionary temporality and reintegrated into the steady continuum of a never-ending democratic consolidation. As the legislative elections of May 2012 became the country's new political horizon, injunctions to vote resounded throughout the public sphere. Farouk Ksentini, the head of the National Consultative Commission for the Promotion and the Defense of Human Rights, called for abstainers to be punished. A few days later, Tarek Mameri, a young man living in the working-class neighborhood of Belcourt in Algiers who had called for an electoral boycott in several widely viewed YouTube videos, was abducted in the middle of the night by police. Indeed, while the cartel generally tolerated criticism from political parties, individual advocates of a boycott were targeted in ways that were reminiscent of the enforced disappearances of Islamists during the Dark Decade. The Leviathan showed its fangs by demonstrating its ability to arbitrarily strike isolated opponents, before reminding the public of the importance of the upcoming election.

ELECTION AND ABSTENTION

The government portrayed the 2012 legislatives as an "Algerian Spring." After many newly legalized organizations joined the competition, the campaign seemed to proclaim the end of political glaciation. In Algiers, no less than thirty-eight lists jostled for position on the electoral leadership boards. Some campaigned for change, others supported the president, and yet another category advocated for both without worrying about the contradiction. As for the two cartel parties, they repeated the well-known melody of "consolidation." Near the Grande Poste in Algiers, a few days before the election, a group of RND campaigners were trying to engage with bystanders, without much success. The six young men were dressed up to the nines and neatly shaven, perfect embodiments of the RND as a party of order. The one who spoke for the group was a student at the National School of Administration. As I asked my questions, he and his companions oscillated between caution and a visible pleasure in recapitulating the party's slogans. The spokesman explained that, even in downtown Algiers, the people were either in a hurry or hostile. After I inquired about the reasons that could motivate a voter to choose their party, they conferred among themselves. Eventually, the improvised spokesman responded as follows:

> It's necessary to support the RND because it's the party that makes sure the country will stay stable and united, and that has worked for national reconstruction for fifteen years. When you start to rebuild a house that has been destroyed by a disaster, you cannot change everything once you have reached the third floor. This is the same thing for the development of Algeria. We are done with the foundations, we have solid walls, but we need to continue to draw on this if we don't want to ruin everything.

The task undertaken since 1997 had not been completed yet and continuity was essential to preserve what had already been achieved. The responsible choice seemed obvious. The spokesperson for the group continued to draw on analogies, this time to propose a critique of the Green Algeria Alliance and its inexperience: "If you have a field and you are sowing seeds, you cannot give the tractor to somebody who has not been trained just before the harvest or he is going to destroy everything." Once again, the theme of destruction recalled the underlying existential stake.

During the campaign, the Green Algeria Alliance assumed the role of challenger. European media speculated on the Islamist coalition's chances. Two days before the elections, I was leaving the diocesan study center located in El-Biar, in the hills above Algiers. Before I passed through the gates, one of the priests jokingly suggested that embassies were getting ready for a "green wave" and recommended that the *gaouris* (Europeans) remain in lockdown. Yet the members of the FFS and the PST whom I met over the following days did not give much credit to the alliance. An Islamist landslide was certainly difficult to imagine. In Algiers, the coalition had to make up for its lack of campaigners by paying young men who seemed so eager to rid themselves of their duty that they distributed their leaflets to foreigners and children. Compared with the charity networks that were once essential to the FIS's success,[13] the social outreach of these reformist Islamist parties seemed negligible.

Some opposition parties joined the race. After boycotting national elections for ten years, the FFS decided to participate in the 2012 legislatives. Its old leader, Hocine Aït Ahmed, announced from his Swiss exile that "taking part in these elections [was] a tactical necessity."[14] It was the occasion to remobilize the population and spread the party's message. The boycott strategy had proven to be costly from a political (withdrawal from national arenas), financial (loss of the fees paid by elected representatives), human (defections), and symbolic (accusations of irresponsibility) perspective. Remaining on the margins indefinitely was especially difficult. Moreover, opponents had no choice but to address the existential threat resulting from popular discontent. During a meeting organized in the suburbs of Algiers at the end of April, FFS candidate and president of the LADDH Mostefa Bouchachi expressed his deep concern. He had heard young men in the South claiming that, if the French ever came back, they would be "the first among the *harkis*."[15] For the lead candidate on the FFS's list in the capital, the risk of seeing the country explode was real and legitimized participation. Yet this choice fueled tensions in the party. The strategic calculations of the executive collided with the moral positioning of grassroots activists, as well as the competing ambitions of aspiring candidates. While electoral participation was appealing, it nonetheless undermined the cohesion of the oldest opposition party.[16]

The electoral "spring" organized by the cartel did not generate much enthusiasm. Meetings were interrupted in several *wilayas* and the leaders of former parties of the Presidential Alliance encountered virulent protests led by unhappy citizens. An observer for an American NGO confessed to me that the mission's official report had been redacted for diplomatic reasons. The text nevertheless described a campaign that happened "without enthusiasm from political parties and with a weak voter involvement."[17] During the last days of the campaign, the Algerians I met often appeared annoyed by the spectacle of politics. A couple from the neighborhood of Bouzareah explained that they did not plan to vote. He was a manager and she was a nurse, and both described the National Assembly as a tool for the *décideurs* and a foreign institution. Later, as I discussed the tense atmosphere in the city with a university professor, she explained that "people are exhausted with these nonsensical elections. They just want one thing: to be left alone." The Algerian political system under Bouteflika had a fascinating particularity: electoral choices were at once undeniably plural and utterly meaningless, which made the act of voting difficult to endorse.

The president himself rose from the dead for the occasion. On May 8, 2012, he delivered a speech in Sétif in which he compared the upcoming elections to November 1, 1954, the start of the insurrection against the French. He then pronounced the famous words "Jili tab jnanu" (My generation has given everything). Youth and women were invited to take over and vote in huge numbers. Other political figures strove to reinvigorate the belief in the magic of representation. As Bourdieu explains, "the problem is to make sure that the people are caught up in the game, that they are caught up by the political illusion." Yet the memories of past elections, rigged or canceled, made it difficult to preserve this belief. Indeed, "to be caught up in the political game, one needs to stand a chance."[18]

The day after the elections, Interior Minister Daho Ould Kablia announced that the FLN and the RND had secured a large majority in the APN, winning 273 of 462 seats. The Alliance for a Green Algeria ranked third with 49 deputies, while the FFS and the PT had elected just enough members to form their own parliamentary groups. The triumph of the two cartel parties surprised many observers, yet the results were far from abnormal. Indeed, the FLN earned its "sweeping" victory with 17.35 percent of the vote. Its domination resulted from a mix of gerrymandering, one-round majority voting, spoiled ballots, and political fragmentation (a more in-depth picture of these results can be seen in figure 4.1 and table 4.1 in chapter 4).

In the following days, government-owned newspapers and foreign partners immediately celebrated a "free, transparent, orderly and fair ballot," in the words of the head of the African Union observation mission.[19] Some private newspapers joined the choir by echoing international congratulations.[20] Meanwhile, opposition parties and critical newspapers focused their attention on suspected fraud. In Algiers, senior party officials browsed the available electoral protocols and sent their findings to the journalists among their contacts. *El Watan* published a two-page centerfold dedicated to instances of electoral fraud, with supporting evidence. Yet administrative support was not the sole explanation behind the success of the two cartel parties. The mosaic of opposition parties had proven unable to mobilize voters, who often viewed potential alternatives as just as "corrupt" and "incompetent" as those in charge.

Presented with personal quarrels, co-option, and unrealistic promises, Algerians chose to support the party of abstention, by far the most powerful. On the day of the elections, the private network Ennahar TV broadcast street interviews showing Algerians defiantly proclaiming "Manvotech" (I don't vote). The official voter turnout, at 42 percent, was painfully low. Responding to a journalist who asked about the high abstention rate in the northern part of the country, Daho Ould Kablia complained that people "went to the beach, to camp, or to do anything else" rather than vote. Facing popular mistrust, the interior minister reverted to the paternalist stance of the former revolutionary elites. While watching this scene, the words of Juan Linz come to mind: deprived of mobilizing ideology, the cartel positioned itself as "a solution to a specific problem of a specific society at a specific time."[21] In the context of democratic globalization, the nature of the problem had changed though: it was not about fighting underdevelopment or Islamism as much as disciplining the people-as-child, who had to be taught the basics of political modernity.

The Ways of Criticism

At the end of June 2012, a short video circulated widely on Algerian social media. The scene showed the former chief of staff of the ANP, Khaled Nezzar, being challenged by members of the Movement of the Independent Youth for Change (Mouvement des Jeunes Indépendants pour le Changement) in El Alia, Algiers's most famous graveyard. On camera, a young man called the generals "murderers" and accused them of being responsible for the country's situation.[22] This confrontation illustrated the transformation of the system of domination. After his retirement, Nezzar himself became an unofficial spokesperson for the military in his books and a voice in public debates. The era of tight state control over public expression had passed. As the biographies of former ministers and generals depicted ongoing struggles within the state, it was now possible to denounce the government's flaws or the influence of crony capitalists. Critical actors nonetheless faced various obstacles aimed at regulating their freedom of speech.

VIRULENT CRITICISM AND DISPARITIES OF POWER

The political field was the main beneficiary of this increased tolerance of criticism. Denunciations of centralism, corruption, or police brutality were tolerated as long as they fit into the framework of institutional politics. Politicians were thus able to express their mistrust toward the "System." Eager to demonstrate his "activism without concessions," Hamid Ferhat, the president of the Bejaïa APW, never shied away from publicly denouncing the absolute corruption of the state:

> Once again, the highest authorities in the country persevere in excluding the population from controlling its destiny. If the objective of the revolution was free self-determination, one century later [sic], we are nowhere close.... The rule of lies, corruption, and violence has become the republican sport in our country. There is not a day without misleading promises, multiple corruption affairs, or violent social regulations. How can we explain the extreme impoverishment of entire parts of our society and the underdevelopment of our territories, despite our extraordinary wealth? This shows that our country is simply in a phase of non-governance.[23]

Coming from the president of one of the two regional assemblies controlled by opposition parties, such a statement was not surprising. Public displays had become part of the system of domination; they served as demonstration of the freedom granted to opposition figures.

In actuality, criticism was limited by the prevailing power disparity. The cartel tolerated the expression of defiance precisely because it had the legal means to put an end to it if necessary. For instance, the union field saw the proliferation of organizations defending the rights of workers without any organic links with the state, unlike the UGTA. Autonomous unions gained a genuine degree of influence in the public sector, with some of them attracting hundreds of thousands of members (for example, the National Autonomous Union for Employees of Public Administrations [Syndicat National Autonome des Personnels de l'Administration Publique, or SNAPAP], and the Conseil National Autonome des Professeurs de l'Enseignement Secondaire et Technique [National Autonomous Council of Professors in the Secondary and Technical Education]). Autonomous unions contributed to the routinization of social movements, while the most influential became models for the development of practices of outright resistance.[24] They made their claims in the public sphere through strikes, workplace occupations, and sit-ins. Their denunciation of public policies led to repeated clashes with the government. Consequently, these organizations faced administrative bans and the strikes they organized were often met with police repression, leading to formal complaints from the International Labour Organization.[25]

Opportunities for circumvention differed depending on the particular social field, person, or place involved, as well as the national and regional contexts. The case of the associative field, and more precisely of human rights associations such as the LADDH or the groups representing the families of victims of the Dark Decade, is exemplary. While advocates of National Reconciliation emphasize its role in pacifying the country and stabilizing the political system, Bouteflika's signature policy failed to respond to the appeals of the families of those who disappeared during the conflict.[26] Thus, organizations representing these families continued to denounce the government's avoidance of the truth and demanded the prosecution of military figures in the International Criminal Court for crimes against humanity. Some of their spokespersons, such as the former minister turned human rights lawyer Ali Yahia Abdennour, publicly and repeatedly accused the government of wrongdoing.[27] At the same time, the ability of this associative block to access public media was limited to the private press and foreign outlets. While the possibility of attacking the cartel demonstrated a tolerance in conformity with the norms of democratic globalization, in actuality the media space to which these voices had access was limited.

The limits of this apparent tolerance for criticism were defined by proponents of the order. After June 2010, organizations such as SOS Disparus or the Collective of Families of the Disappeared in Algeria were forbidden from holding their weekly sit-ins in front of public buildings in the capital. According to Farouk Ksentini, the cartel's mouthpiece for questions of human rights, the issue of the disappeared had been settled by the Charter for Peace and National Reconciliation and was no longer relevant.[28] Public discussion of this issue was now inappropriate. The power imbalance between the state and associations that could mobilize no more than a few dozen individuals allowed for such alternation between repression and tolerance. Activists therefore paid close attention to the mood of the *décideurs*, whom they portrayed as "panicked," "on edge," or "short of breath," and adapted their contentious practices accordingly.

CRITIQUE AND PUNISHMENT IN A LIBERALIZED ENVIRONMENT

In addition to the political field, criticism could also be expressed in virulent terms in the media, especially in the printed press. In 1989, the new law on parties legalized the publication of outlets linked to political organizations. For instance, the FIS created its own publication, *El Mounqidh*. Subsequently, the suppression of the Ministry of Information and the policies implemented by the Hamrouche government fueled a genuine "state of grace" that led to the emergence of dozens of private daily newspapers.[29] In the framework crafted by Law No. 90-07 of April 3, 1990, journalists who committed to creating their own media outlets received severance payments equal to three years of their regular salaries, as well as banking advantages, including reduced credit rates.

Despite terrorist attacks targeting journalists, and the censorship imposed in the name of counterterrorism, the printed press survived the Dark Decade and preserved a plurality of editorial approaches. Some outlets defend the interests of certain factions within the cartel (*El Moudjahid* for the FLN, *El Djeich* for the army). Others represent specific political tendencies, such as the Islamist-friendly *Ennahar* (Arabic). Some position themselves as liberal critics of the cartel, such as *El Khabar* (Arabic) and *El Watan* (French).[30] Still other outlets favor a tabloid format and more conservative analysis, such as *Echorouk* (Arabic). Finally, under Bouteflika, some dailies belonged to prominent businessmen and defended their political and economic interests, such as the French-language *Liberté* (the property of Issad Rebrab) and *Le Temps* (which was owned by Ali Haddad), both of which are now defunct.

In 2002, Khaled Nezzar brought a defamation case against former special operations officer Habib Souaïdia in Paris. The press kit prepared by the human rights group Algeria Watch offers a telling example of the pluralism characteristic of national print media.[31] Quite logically, this sensitive episode led some outlets to revert to the old nationalist theme of a conspiracy bringing together NGOs, Berberists, deserters, and the French in order to destroy the country. They echoed the position of Nezzar himself, whose defense of the ANP drew on repeated denunciations of the interference of so-called *droits-de-l'hommistes* (human rights zealots).[32] Yet Algerian dailies also expressed contentious viewpoints about a wide range of heated issues, such as the role of France in the country's politics, the violence of the security forces during the Dark Decade, the conflicts between the presidency and praetorian figures, the cancellation of the electoral process in 1992, or the policy of National Reconciliation.

Private and public media were of course weaponized by groups competing within the cartel. I have already mentioned the 1998 media storm that led to the fall of key figures in Zeroual's entourage. Under Bouteflika, the press proved useful in settling internal disputes while preserving the fiction of state neutrality. Because of their duty of confidentiality, high-ranking members of the ANP have sometimes used journalists as unofficial mouthpieces.[33] In 2012, Khaled Nezzar's son, Lotfi, cofounded *Algérie patriotique*, an online francophone publication with a strong nationalist, pro-military, anti-Bouteflika, and anti-Islamist editorial line.

According to political scientist Chérif Dris, press pluralism assumed a "subtle mix of official discourse and free expression in order to make the audience less suspicious."[34] As in other pluralistic political orders, state and parastatal actors relied on the media to promote their views. Since the 1920s, the entanglement of public communication, marketing, and information has become a common feature of "democratic" polities. Around the world, the diffusion of deceptive messages benefits from the proximity between political and media elites.[35] The interdependence of different social spaces nourishes forms of collusion. Journalists rely on the funds, contacts, and clearances that emanate from the state, as well as from the political and economic fields. Yet the ability of those in power to impose their meanings in a top-down fashion didn't forestall the possibility of sharp criticism.

After the opening of 1990, editorial writers and political cartoonists became the pillars of print media. On paper, they expressed the resentment of the population toward the ruling elites, but also a wide array of feelings and anxieties resulting from the latency of the crisis experienced by the country. Cartoonist Ali Dilem became particularly famous for his biting caricatures published in *Le Matin* and *Liberté*. In his sketches, he presented various praetorian actors in composite, by way of a fat, mustachioed general wearing a skull-shaped medal. As for Bouteflika, he was drawn as a ridiculous little man with a ponytail tied with a pink knot. With a tender yet sour sense of humor, Dilem depicted the exhaustion and despair of the Algerian population, the epidemic of self-immolation, and the widespread desire to emigrate.[36]

Despite the space conceded to public criticism, the possibility of punishment persisted. Indeed, the state remained largely in control of the printing and publishing sectors, and thereby maintained pressure on journalists and editors. In the 1990s, steadily rising printing costs served to financially suffocate the printed press.[37] In August 2003, six dailies were prohibited from publishing unless they paid their outstanding bills to state printing houses. To shield themselves from this kind of threat, *El Watan* and *El Khabar* acquired their own shared printing operation. Located in Algiers, it was attacked by an angry mob aiming to set the building on fire in September 2011. This episode has sometimes been presented as retribution for the two dailies' desire to open their own TV channel.[38] The government also used more mundane tools to discipline private media, such as fiscal harassment or measures to limit advertising revenue. Both remained possible after the passing of the new law on information in 2012. In short, waves of liberalization led to a change in the tactics used to discipline the media, and notably the use of economic retaliation against unruly newspapers.

Censorship and Repression

Spaces of circumvention offered opportunities to question the legitimacy of the established order, while allowing new forms of intervention and regulation. Liberal normative discourses can thus be misleading. Similar to the sanctification of sharia law, which tends to obscure the debates that continuously transform this set of juridical norms over time, the idea that freedom of speech exists as a pure, essential, censorship-free principle ignores the constant struggles that shape the public sphere. Liberal representative systems have their own rules and exceptions, often justified in the name of security. Self-proclaimed "liberal" legal scholars can therefore support the limitation of free speech by invoking necessity.[39] In Bouteflika's pluralistic Algeria, the possibility of control persisted thanks to the constant blurring of the line between that which is permitted and that which is condemned, between the speakable and the unspeakable.

AN UNPREDICTABLE CENSORSHIP

The Algerian state is a signatory to the Universal Declaration of Human Rights and the International Covenant on Civil and Political Rights. The latter was ratified by the country in 1989 and comes with juridical obligations. At the national level, the revised version of the country's constitution guarantees freedom of conscience, opinion, and expression.[40] Under Bouteflika, the targeting of critical voices was therefore officially illegal—which doesn't mean that it was a bygone practice, including in its most brutal forms. Local strongmen could resort to gangster-like violence (kidnappings, beatings, murders) to silence local activists and journalists. For instance, journalist Abdelhaï Beliardouh, a local correspondent for *El Watan* in Tebessa, was abducted and tortured by the president of the local chamber of commerce in 2002, before committing suicide. Ten years later, Beliardouh's tormentor and his accomplices were eventually acquitted despite the testimony of numerous eyewitnesses.[41]

Nonetheless, the cartel had legal resources at its disposal that allowed for the coercion of its detractors without openly violating the expectation of pluralism. Dilem's caricatures, which spared none of the cartel's core institutions, earned him several convictions, each of them justified by the 2001 law on information. Once they had breached the accepted channels of circumvention, lawful criticisms became press offenses in the name of shoring up the pillars of the nation.

Mohamed Benchicou, the former editor of the opposition daily *Le Matin*, paid a high price for his virulent criticism of Bouteflika at a time when the president was still struggling to stabilize his position within the cartel.[42] The newspaper was eventually forced into bankruptcy after its tax status was reassessed in 2003. At the same time, Benchicou himself was arrested on arrival from Paris and indicted for a "breach of exchange rate controls." He was sentenced to two years in prison and a fine of 20 million DA. Because he had foreign currency in his possession, the editor was criminalized. His conviction for a financial infraction accredited Bouteflika's offensive discourse, as the president portrayed his critics in the media as "mercenaries of the pencil."[43] Released in 2008, Benchicou's *Journal d'un homme libre* (A free man's notebook) was seized at the printers at the request of Minister of Culture Khalida Toumi, who argued that it was subversive, antihistorical, and racist.

Adaptive censorship also targeted the academic field through acts of regulation that did not infringe on the shared norms of democratic globalization. For denouncing the research and teaching conditions in Algerian universities,[44] professor Ahmed Rouadjia was sentenced to a 25,000 DA fine following a defamation suit filed by the rector of the University of M'sila. After a new complaint, Rouadjia was fined another 20,000 DA and sentenced to six months in prison. He was also suspended for a year without salary, before being reintegrated upon request of the Ministry of Higher Education. Antidefamation legislation was useful for punishing discontent. Yet in most cases, the sword of Damocles remained suspended, or the sanctions were lifted as a result of pardons. Bouteflika himself frequently seized this opportunity to demonstrate his paternal benevolence while blaming those convicted for their indiscipline. In 2004, on World Press Freedom Day, the president declared that the press didn't suffer from censorship in Algeria but that it was its responsibility to "define appropriate practices and ethical rules."[45] Two years later, on the very same day, he used an executive order to pardon more than three hundred journalists indicted for defamation.

The treatment of journalists or academics was no different from that of the people-as-child. The freedoms granted after 1990 were also framed as potential vectors of instability if not properly managed. Thus, the press could be portrayed as a source of fanatic religious discourse and foreign proselytism, in need of training and scrutiny by the relevant authorities.[46] It needed to be educated and disciplined. While journalists were told to learn the norms framing supposedly decent public debate, the use of pardons reminded them of the arbitrary nature of sovereign power. Adaptive censorship was thus situated at the junction between the principles of regulation and exception.

Given the changing legal framework and the capriciousness of state control, sanctions responded to obscure criteria (type of offense, personal enmities, desire to make an example, or simply bad luck). "It is extremely difficult to know where they fix the threshold," a journalist for *El Watan* told me in 2012. For this reason, censorship was ubiquitous and lenient, protean and diffuse. It reminded the bearers of criticism that not every truth was fit to be told, without ever establishing clear limits between the speakable and the unspeakable. Given the prevailing indetermination, the threatening shadow of the state's imprimatur fueled self-censorship. Meanwhile, the opening of public space fostered both participation and restraint.

EVOLVING SPACES OF CIRCUMVENTION

To understand Bouteflika's Algeria, one must keep in mind the Foucauldian idea that "where there are legal rights, there are technologies of power."[47] Indeed, the sphere of legality was framed by the very security apparatuses that maintained the possibility of intervention. The proponents of the established order thus moved away from the mania of control to master the arts of regulation. They learned to sanction "excesses" of freedom in the name of protecting the nation, its institutions, people, and morals. Since no one should ignore the law, actors became responsible for their own adherence to the rules of a constantly changing game.

Legalization meant responsibilization. The first reforms introduced by the liberal government led by Mouloud Hamrouche included several provisions allowing for the repression of press offenses, especially if they came to "endanger" the sacred unity of the nation. For instance, article 86 of Law No. 90-07 of April 1990 stipulated that "anyone who publishes or spreads deliberately erroneous and biased information that could undermine state security and national unity will be sentenced to five to ten years in prison." After Bouteflika's election, the cartel continued its effort to regulate freedom of speech. The amendments to the penal code introduced in May 2001 sparked outrage among journalists, as the new provisions included exemplary punishments for "defamatory, insulting or humiliating statements" targeting the president or any public institution.[48] The regulatory framework was later complemented by the executive order introducing Bouteflika's National Reconciliation. Under the pretense of restoring national unity, the law promised three to five years in prison and a fine of 250,000 to 500,000 DA to any individual "who, through their statements, writings or other actions, instrumentalizes the wounds of the National Tragedy to undermine the institutions of the People's Democratic Republic of Algeria, weaken the State, affect the honor of its agents for serving it worthily, or tarnish the international image of Algeria."[49] The same year, a new legal provision penalized blasphemy, allowing the repression of religious offenses.[50] Protected under the heading of "Insults and Violence Targeting Public Servants and State Institutions," Islam thus became an alibi for a range of regulatory actions.

The crisis imposed its sinusoidal movement, a succession of openings and closures. After the repressive laws adopted during the phase of restoration, 2011 and 2012 saw a renewed effort to demonstrate the country's engagement on the path of "democratic consolidation." While the 2012 organic law preserved measures to regulate the media, it also removed prison terms for press offenses.[51]

The cartel adapted the repressive arsenal at its disposal to a changing public space. Its security apparatuses thus reinforced their ability to monitor and control the Internet. The gendarmerie and military intelligence created specialized units and acquired technologies of mass surveillance from China, Russia, Britain, and Denmark.[52] These technological and organizational shifts in the security apparatus accompanied the erection of a renewed legal framework, notably with the adoption of a law on "cybercrime."[53] After the beginning of the Hirak, the government announced its desire to crack down on "new forms criminality" and the penal code was amended to criminalize hate speech and the diffusion of fake news.[54] These measures allowed security apparatuses to selectively target online activists and random citizens, who were then punished for contributing to the vast amount of criticism spread online. After the conviction of Tarek Mameri in 2012, following his calls to boycott the elections, others faced a similar fate. In September 2013, blogger Abdelghani Aloui was arrested for his derogatory comments targeting Bouteflika and Sellal on Facebook. He was sent to Serkadji Prison, indicted for "contempt for the President of the Republic, insulting official bodies, and defending terrorism," and held captive while awaiting trial until March 2014. The arbitrariness of these interventions demonstrated the alleged omnipotence of the cartel. On the day in May 2014 when Bouteflika was sworn in, the weak Internet bandwidth in the capital was interpreted by some of my interlocutors as a conspiracy fomented by certain obscure forces. Some predicted an imminent coup, others a punishment targeting them personally, while a final group suggested that it was an attempt to preserve the impotent president from online mockery.

The evolving legal framework justified a seemingly erratic repression. In this context, mistrust could be voiced, sometimes in harsh terms, as long as critical actors "accepted an absolute asymmetry with the State's coercive apparatuses."[55] Successive liberalizations translated this asymmetry into legal norms, which in turn structured social and political conflicts. Beyond any transcendent idea of right or wrong, the violence of the law thus expressed a particular set of power relations.[56] Successive adjustments responded to sociopolitical transformation by allowing acts of regulation and maintaining enough latitude for the security apparatus. The exercise of domination relied on the hybridization of founding violence (or law-making violence—that is, the power that enables legal adjustments) and conservative violence (or law-preserving violence, which is to say law enforcement). The entanglement of these two types of violence extended the realm of security.[57] Security agencies thus inhabited an indeterminate space in constant expansion designed by law. Like Walter Benjamin's police, they were a "nowhere-tangible, all-pervasive, ghostly presence" able to supervise and regulate life.[58] Imbalance and indetermination were the bedrock of the tacit contract behind this controlled opening: the liberalized order could not be threatened, otherwise it risked a return to pure coercion, to the Leviathan, to the Dark Decade, and to outbursts of lawmaking violence.

TERRORISM AND THE STATE OF EXCEPTION

The crisis enabled the updating of repressive practices, from October 1988 to the beginning of the Hirak. In the early 1990s, the dramatization of politics resulted in a series of security measures aimed at "saving the nation." In 1991, Chadli signed a presidential decree that legalized forms of administrative detention outside of any legal scrutiny.[59] On February 9, 1992, newly appointed head of the HCE, Mohamed Boudiaf, promulgated a state of emergency in response to "serious threats to public order and the security of persons."[60] These two measures allowed for the repression and deportation of Islamist activists to camps located in the Sahara. In 1995, the unelected National Council of Transition expanded the legislative arsenal targeting "terrorist" and "subversive" acts.[61] This last round of measures also included penalties for interfering with the freedom of movement, unlawful public gatherings, insulting symbols of the nation, and obstructing the actions of security forces. Prison terms increased and sentences could now include the death penalty.

After the Dark Decade, the cartel converted its coercive potential into nonlethal methods of policing. This shift was tied to democratic globalization and demonstrated the country's insertion into the world system, with the support of international partners.[62] As in other parts of the region, the goal was to avoid the use of naked force in favor of a legalized and police-centered approach to coercion.[63] In his 2010 policy statement, Prime Minister Ouyahia announced the doubling of police and gendarmerie forces over the previous four years.[64] State violence evolved from counterinsurgency to policing, from the use of militias and special operations to an increased reliance on the blue uniforms of the DGSN. This transition happened under the supervision of former officers in military intelligence (Zerhouni, Tounsi). It accompanied the resurgence of socioeconomic unrest as Algeria earned a reputation as a police state constantly on edge. Following the 2010–2011 uprisings, a satirical map of the Arab world presented the country as the "headquarters of antiriot police."[65]

The existential threat persisted nonetheless. The ongoing clashes between the army and isolated groups of "terrorists" testified to this grim reality. Occasionally, more spectacular and dreadful events brought the issue of terrorism to the fore, as was the case, for example, after bloody attacks in Tingentourine (January 2013) and Iboudraren (April 2014). Exceptional tools of coercion thus remained on the table. According to the penal code, judges could order pretrial detention in cases where the alleged crime was punishable by three or more years in prison. This measure was in theory limited to four months, with two extensions of the same length validated by the investigating judge. For a crime related to "subversion" and "terrorism" (such as undermining the morale of the army, one of the cartel's favorites), the investigating judge could extend this detention up to five times. For a crime related to "transnational crime," provisional detention could be extended up to eleven times—thereby eroding entirely any pretense of provisionality.[66] Thanks to this change in the law, adopted at the height of the 2001 Kabyle Black Spring, an individual could thus be incarcerated legally for four years without a trial.

The removal of state protection was not limited to terrorists; it could apply to political activists too. This was especially the case for members of associations whose accreditation was repeatedly denied, such as RAJ, but who nonetheless kept protesting in public rather than joining the approved channels for proper political participation. In the era of nonlethal policing, the state's past ferocity remained a key marker for its long-standing opponents and a resource for the security forces under its remit. This state of exception kept alive the memories of the enforced disappearances of the 1990s. This was especially obvious in this experience shared by Nidhal a few weeks after we first met:

> First, they picked me up and threw me in a car with two cops. Then they started to drive around the city, without heading to the police station. I swear this time I thought that I was done, that they were going to make me disappear, as they did with other comrades. They continued to drive around, and when I asked them to go to the police station, they responded, "It's ok, brother, don't worry, relax." It must have lasted two or three hours, and finally they stopped and told me to get out and not do it again. When you get out of there, you think twice before going back to a protest.
>
> (NIDHAL, ELECTED OFFICIAL OF THE FFS, FOUNDING MEMBER OF RAJ, ALGIERS, AUTUMN 2010)

The possibility that one might be disappeared by agents of the state remained a tangible threat for activists who had experienced the Dark Decade: the loss of comrades and loved ones was a shared burden for those who were active politically during this troubled period.[67] Multiple sites synonymous with the brutality of the 1990s continued to haunt the country's urban spaces. In the capital, the Serkadji Prison, the Châteauneuf military barracks, and the Centre Principal Militaire d'Investigation in Ben Aknoun provided lasting proof of the state's potential ferocity. The policemen who had picked up Nidhal weaponized this shared memory and the legitimate fear resulting from it. Their feigned benevolence only reinforced the asymmetry between the state and its opponents. While rarely on full display, the potential for monstrous violence was evoked by each late-night arrest, or each time an ostensibly provisional detention was extended without motive. The state could always return to its Hobbesian nature should the crisis intensify once again.[68]

By no means did the mutation of repressive practices signify the end of violence. Despite the DGSN's claims that it was "putting citizens' dignity above everything else,"[69] police brutality remained a frequent cause of rioting. This state of affairs shaped the strategies of critical actors. In the spring of 2011, as we walked home from a small protest organized in the center of Algiers, Abdelouahab Fersaoui, the president of RAJ, explained that "we have to play the legalistic game because it is the only way to change things without having them shooting at the crowd." He continued by making an obvious reference to October 1988 and the Dark Decade: "We have seen what happens when the regime is challenged: it doesn't hesitate, it shoots." Thus, Fersaoui considered a legalist approach essential to avoid triggering the *décideurs*, given their past reactions. In the heated context of 2011, he knew that according to the discourse of order, a revolution would amount to a catastrophe. It could legitimize repression in the name of an existential threat to the established order. The yearly commemoration of October 1988 organized by RAJ was a reminder of this obvious possibility.

The normalization of exception served to regulate human life and manage the population. This allowed for the suppression of problematic groups,[70] notably radical Islamists and those calling for Kabyle independence, who were prevented from taking part in institutional politics. Such suppression was compatible with the adoption of nonlethal policing strategies. Describing what he proudly labeled "democratic crowd-management," Major General Hamel explained that this approach required "persuasion, psychology, a lot of nerve, a spirit of sacrifice and self-control, which is not an easy thing."[71] According to the head of the DGSN from 2010 to 2018, containing discontent required a careful dosage of nonlethal violence. This transformation of the police state benefited from the government's cooperation with European partners, who regularly praised the "level of professionalism of the Algerian police."[72]

Exception was the condition for maintaining the order's normalcy and facilitating its insertion into the world system. In the name of security, the Algerian cartel shares a global tendency to adapt liberal-democratic norms. Following a logic already highlighted by Arendt, bureaucratic governments draw on temporary decrees to adjust the law to singular challenges.[73] Thus, from Washington to Algiers, political elites share the same taste for emergency measures. After the Dark Decade, the proponents of the established order posed as precursors of the struggle against "fundamentalism." The connection between Algerian "residual" terrorism and global security issues allowed the cartel to enjoy a stable geopolitical resource, which notably benefited its security agencies.[74] After a moment of international disgrace, the 1990s became an asset. In 2013, for instance, the European Union's General Directorate for External Politics underlined the value of the Algerian experience in fighting terrorism when it came to promoting security in the Sahel.[75]

In order to debunk the myth of Arab authoritarianism, one should also recall that the technologies of power essential to the globalization of exception stem from a colonial tool kit based on the criminalization of subversion, the instrumentalization of the law, the militarization of repression, and the use of internment camps.[76] Rather than suggesting a cultural specificity, the repressive practices of the Algerian state are in fact largely indebted to the entangled dynamics of globalization and postcoloniality.

A VERY MODERN ALGERIAN SOVEREIGN

Particularistic explanations are nonetheless resilient. When looking at the Arab world, many explain the lack of democracy and freedom by pointing to the supposedly intrinsic limits of societies and their impact on state construction. Arab societies are portrayed as stuck in a "pre-political and pre-state" condition and paralyzed by a deep-seated preference for unanimity that prevents political pluralism.[77] Drawing from culturalist and liberal approaches, some authors diagnose the inadequacy of local structures when compared to Western political modernity, which allegedly is the sole pathway to individual freedom. While psychoanalysts emphasize the masses' submission to the figure of the leader,[78] jurists analyze the impossibility of establishing the rule of law given the prevalence of religious norms.[79] All nonetheless come to the same conclusion: the modern Arab state has failed. In so doing, these authors reproduce a normative approach that draws on an idealized and ideological representation of the political in the so-called West.[80]

The normalization of exception is not a sign of weakness. As Giorgio Agamben puts it, "the state of exception is neither external nor internal to the juridical order, and the problem of defining it concerns precisely a threshold, or a zone of indifference, where inside and outside do not exclude each other but rather blur with each other."[81] It is the suspension of the law as much as its enforcement that demonstrates the actuality of the juridical order. The possibility for the sovereign to fix the limits of what is acceptable, what is forgivable, and what is punishable rests on the potential that these limits might be lifted. The law on civil concord adopted in 1999 thus stipulated that insurgents might be pardoned if they joined the antiterrorist struggle. By bringing together a discourse on repentance, the necessity of ending the war, and the symbolic power of the state, the sovereign could then turn a "terrorist" into a "law enforcer." Making the law and breaching the law were part of the same process.

To be sovereign, one does not need to act legally. Sovereignty is situated precisely at the junction of the law and violence; it is established by the indetermination between these two constructs. In the Schmittian tradition, it is in its encounter with the state of exception that the sovereign reaffirms its capacity to decide.[82] Killing and pardoning, withholding and providing, jailing and tolerating—these are the core prerogatives of those who hold the state. Matters of collective well-being or individual freedom are secondary from the perspective of sovereignty. Thus, what better demonstration of what sovereignty meant under Bouteflika than the ruling coalition's ostentatious indifference to certain of its critics? In September 2011, Ali Dilem was the headliner at the Algiers International Book Fair, where he came to present his cartoon collection *Algérie, mon humour*. At a nearby stall, Mohamed Benchicou signed copies of his new book, *Le Mensonge de Dieu*. This event financed by the state welcomed two fierce critics of the political order. Symbols of the tolerance of a sovereign who constantly moved the cursor between permission and repression, these two men who once faced criminal prosecution were now met with indifference.

It is in the asymmetric and inescapable relationship to the law and violence that sovereignty materializes. At any moment, proponents of the order can reaffirm that freedom only exists as a concession, within the limits that they have set. While considering this ability on the part of the Algerian cartel to outlaw an online activist and protect a corrupt minister of energy—in short, to exercise sovereign power in all its unconditionality and unpredictability—one can only reject the idea of a failure of the state under Bouteflika. This did not make up for the cartel's inability to euphemize its domination, but it certainly increased its resilience.

Contentious Insularity

The regulation of public criticism relied on its containment in order to allow its routinization and prevent its expansion.[83] Expressions of dissent were normalized so long as they could be confined to an archipelago of contentious locations and portrayed as mere regional unrest. This strategy of dividing the national territory was particularly obvious in the Berberist case. Rather than a coherent ideology, Berberism is a heterogeneous subfield, marked by common historical references, which exists alongside other oppositional forces. In addition to the three "Berberist" movements that I will discuss in the following pages, the mosaic of Algerian opposition parties includes Islamist movements, leftist organizations, as well as more liberal-leaning parties. Berberism is nonetheless one of the oldest opposition forces in Algeria and has its roots in the 1963 insurrection denouncing Ben Bella's autocratic manners.

HOW MANY DIVISIONS FOR THE BERBERISTS?

In April 2011, the city of Tizi Ouzou commemorated the anniversary of the Kabyle Black Spring. On this occasion, the FFS did not take part in the "joint" demonstration that started in front of Mouloud Mammeri University. Rather, its members visited the grave of Massinissa Guermah, the young student whose murder in gendarmerie barracks sparked the 2001 regional uprising. As the rally began, members of the Movement for the Autonomy of Kabylia (Mouvement pour l'autonomie de la Kabylie, MAK— now known as the Movement for the Self-Determination of Kabylia) faced supporters of the RCD. While the former chanted pro-autonomy slogans, the latter responded by singing the national anthem. The two processions moved forward at a cautious distance from each other. While witnessing this display of division, I chatted with Lounes, a student in mechanics who came from Boumerdes, a town located halfway between Tizi Ouzou and Algiers. With a palpable bitterness in his voice, he explained, "I look at them fighting with their slogans, tearing down each other's posters, or demonstrating separately, and it breaks my heart. They're unable to talk to each other and they want us to follow them." A self-professed "progressive" and admirer of the iconic writer Tahar Djaout, Lounes found it impossible to endorse any of the contemporary avatars of Berberism. Ideological questions were secondary to his disaffection. His main concerns were the long-standing fractures within this characteristically North African political and cultural movement.

In Algeria, Berberists support the recognition of the Amazigh dimension of national culture and call for the adoption of Tamazight as an official language. Moreover, their long-standing opposition to bureaucratic centralism has often led them to advocate for democratic rights.[84] This advocacy sometimes causes tensions within Berberist organizations, which are often criticized by their own members for being bureaucratic or *za'aimist* (from *za'īm*, leader). While their representatives share common goals, they maintain strong disagreements when it comes to strategic orientation (temporary alliance with the cartel or the Islamists vs. autonomy) and economic views (liberal vs. socialist). Similar to Islamism, this second major subfield among the Algerian oppositions is fragmented, a state of affairs that worsened with the crisis.

The FFS is the oldest party in Algeria after the FLN. It was founded in 1963 in the lead-up to an insurgency that was rapidly crushed.[85] Its main leader, Hocine Aït Ahmed, was a nationalist militant during the revolution who remained an unchallengeable figure of authority until his death in 2015. During the Dark Decade, the FFS promoted a political settlement to the conflict, with the support of the other two fronts (FLN and FIS). Under Bouteflika, its spokespersons relentlessly denounced a kleptocratic and authoritarian system, and called for a "radical, nonviolent and democratic transformation."[86]

After the FFS, the second Berberist opposition party appeared with the transition to multipartyism in 1989. The RCD was founded by Saïd Saadi, a former member of the FFS, cofounder of the LADDH, and an activist with the Berber cultural movement who was imprisoned in the 1980s. The competition between the two parties started immediately. Their main strongholds are to be found along the northern coast, particularly in Kabylia and around Algiers. Both parties are the heirs of the Berberist resistance, even if the FFS adopted a populist orientation, while the RCD is more elitist and culturalist. It is also more economically liberal. More importantly, the RCD is a firmly secularist movement that supported the 1992 military coup. In interviews, its members presented the interruption of the electoral process as a moral choice to prevent "totalitarianism."[87] In opposition to this, critics of the RCD, especially among FFS supporters, often suggested that its creation itself was suspicious.

> Some create a party so one can see them, and they settle in a space that already exists for personal profit. This is what Saadi did with the RCD. He left the FFS, did some jail time in the 1980s, and decided to become famous with his own party. He is a traitor.
> (LOUBNA, FORMER JOURNALIST AND MEMBER OF THE FFS, PARIS, SUMMER 2010)

> The RCD was created by the *Pouvoir*. Together with the FIS, they are two extremes. General Toufik was a founding member of the RCD; he was there for their founding congress. Personally, I think that there is no honesty whatsoever in the RCD.
> (ABDELHAMID, MEMBER OF RAJ'S NATIONAL BUREAU, FFS SYMPATHIZER, TIZI OUZOU, SPRING 2011)

Loubna and Abdelhamid reproduced the commonplaces uttered by Moncef, the FLN supporter and critic of the RND whom we encountered in chapter 4. Following the dominant rationality of suspicion, they portrayed the organization competing with their "historical" party as a sham benefiting the personal interests of certain individuals (Zeroual and Ouyahia for the RND, Toufik and Saadi for the RCD).

While accused of being puppets in the hands of the cartel, RCD supporters made their own accusations. They notably denounced the FFS's collusion with Islamist actors and the irresponsibility of its leadership. During our discussion in Tizi Ouzou, Nassim, an RCD representative at the APW, explained the division within the Berberist movement by blaming the "fundamentalists in the FFS leadership." The continuous fragmentation of the subfield was therefore fueled by reciprocal accusations of instrumentalization and collusion.

The cartel took advantage of these divisions, as the RCD was briefly co-opted amid the emergency of the 1990s. After receiving two portfolios in the Benbitour government (the Ministries of Health and Transportation), the party justified its integration into the ruling coalition in the name of fighting the "rampant Islamization of institutions," here demonstrated by the inclusion of the MSP.[88]

> We are ready to go with the devil to save Algeria. We called for the cancellation of the electoral process, and we applauded this solution. We called for a resistance against this regression. After Bouteflika's arrival, we joined the government and provided two ministers. Unfortunately, we saw that this president was shooting at the people, and we left.
> (ASAF, LOCAL OFFICIAL OF THE RCD, TIZI OUZOU, SPRING 2011)

Asaf described the decision to participate in the government as a necessity aimed at saving Algeria from the political "regression" symbolized by Islamism. Co-opted during the Dark Decade, the RCD was forced to exit the ruling coalition by another critical event: the 2001 Black Spring. As in the case of the MSP (see chapter 4), this return to opposition fueled internal quarrels. Amara Benyounes, minister of health and vice president of the RCD at the time, announced the creation of his own organization in 2004. Accredited under the name of the Algerian People's Movement, it received seven seats during the 2012 legislative elections. For several years, Benyounes had been part of Bouteflika's campaign staff, in which he echoed the discourse of "consolidation." He was finally rewarded in September 2012 when he was appointed minister of territorial planning, environment, and the city. A rumor among Benyounes's detractors claimed that he had negotiated his betrayal in exchange for the right to create his own newspaper (*La Dépêche de Kabylie*). In any case, Berberist movements were not only internally divided—they also competed with entirely separate formations created by dissident members associated with the cartel.

THE CONFINEMENT OF "KABYLE PARTIES"

Kabylia is the historical stronghold of Algerian Berberism. On a map, the region is relatively close to Algiers. Boumerdes is only 50 kilometers away from the capital; Tizi Ouzou, 100 kilometers. Yet beyond this apparent geographical proximity, one needs to account for the region's uneven topography and its failing infrastructure. Thus, a 180-kilometer trip from Algiers to Bejaïa might take up to seven hours. While the East–West Highway opened up the southern part of the region (Bouira, Borj Bou Arrerij), the extensions connecting the two "rebel" *wilayas*, Tizi Ouzou and Bejaïa, were still unfinished in 2019. The region's isolation could therefore be partly explained by geography and infrastructure, even if political factors remained crucial.

While impacted by the national upheavals that have occurred since independence, Kabylia also followed a specific political trajectory marked by local mobilizations. Its temporality was affected by various singular events that shaped the experience of grassroots actors. During the Dark Decade, the school boycott of 1994–1995 and the riots that followed singer Lounes Matoub's assassination in 1998 were major landmarks. In 2001, the Black Spring formalized the break with a government that appeared both murderous and ignorant of the claims formulated by the protesters in the El Kseur Platform. In addition to the usual cultural and democratic claims, the Citizens' Movement demanded the withdrawal of the security apparatus, official apologies, the prosecution of those responsible for the repression, and the end of systemic injustice (*hogra* in Darija or *tamheqranit* in Tamazight).[89] Unable to echo the claims of this radical yet mostly peaceful grassroots mobilization, the FFS and the RCD both faced a major "crisis of representation," which in turn accentuated their rivalry.[90] Despite the genuine social proximity of their members, reconciliation between the two groups became increasingly out of reach:

> In Tigzirt, we had to enter into an alliance with the RND because the FFS refused [our offer]. There were three elected members of the RCD, one FLN, one RND, and two FFS [in the municipal council]. When I asked members of the FFS, they made morally unacceptable claims, notably protecting the incumbent mayor. We can have beers together, but when it comes to politics, it explodes. The guy from the RND, I went to school with him. I knew him. He left the FFS for the RND to have his little place, but without being RND in spirit.
>
> (AMEZZA, FORMER MEMBER OF THE RCD'S
> REGIONAL OFFICE IN TIZI OUZOU, PARIS, SPRING 2011)

Amezza's testimony was instructive on many levels. It underlined the diminished relevance of the opposition/regime dichotomy and the affective dimension of politics at the local level. Yet interpersonal connections didn't carry much weight in the face of the deep of organizational rivalry between the RCD and the FFS. It was simply easier for members of the former party to negotiate with the RND, especially given its outspoken secularism. The feud between Berberist movements thus allowed cartel parties to maintain their influence in a hostile environment.

The difficulties faced by Berberist parties were even greater at the national level. After 2001, the radicalized local climate nourished a constant struggle to define "the legitimate criteria for political participation."[91] The strategies of both parties evolved continuously, without generating the expected benefits. After leaving the government and boycotting the 2002 legislative elections, the RCD lost its nineteen deputies and faced a wave of defections. It reentered the APN in 2007 with the same number of deputies, just one seat short of the minimum needed to create its own parliamentary group and propose laws. Despite its limited influence, the party nonetheless announced that it was committed to its "tribunician function" in a resolution voted by its national council. Less than four years later, deputy Boussad Boudiaf welcomed me into his Tizi Ouzou office. "This is my first mandate as a deputy, and I'm telling you, it will be my last," he said. "I will not try to get a national elected mandate; it's pointless."[92] The RCD eventually returned to a boycott strategy in 2012. Shortly thereafter, it lost the only local assembly under its control, in Tizi Ouzou, to the FFS.

The oldest opposition party took a similarly rocky path. After 2001, the FFS opted for participation in local elections and a boycott of national polls. This different stance vis-à-vis the local and national levels was aimed at maintaining contact with grassroots activists while trying to harness the limited means of local institutions. Yet this strategy resulted in a lasting break between the party and the Citizens' Movement, which had placed the rejection of all electoral processes at the heart of its demands. According to members of the latter, the only way to combat the ruling coalition was to reject any kind of compromise, including voting (summed up in the phrase *ulach lvot ulach*—there will be no vote).[93] The FFS's participation in the local elections of 2002 thus resulted in violent confrontations, during which some of the party's offices were burnt down. As already mentioned, the strategy of national boycott ended in 2012, fueling internal tensions within the FFS. The list of candidates sparked dissent. Party officials also criticized the choice of campaign posters for being "too artistic" and lacking the signature sky-blue color. Some grassroots members in turn denounced the "politico-economic mafia" that had taken over the FFS, and, as we see in figure 5.1, dissidents held a meeting in Tizi Ouzou demanding a "return to the party's original line." By the end of the year, former general secretary Karim Tabbou and his supporters had left to create a new movement, the Democratic and Social Union.

The Wilayas of Bejaïa and Tizi Ouzou remained under the control of opposition forces. The FFS and the RCD were thus able to maintain their social bases and their capacity of action. Yet even in their fiefdoms, both parties were weakened by the overwhelming rejection of partisan politics supported by the Citizens' Movement. For that reason, they represented a minority of the population. Moreover, this regional anchoring earned them the unflattering reputation of "Kabyle parties," a liability at the national level. This situation also reinforced their vulnerability, as the region became a place of intense competition between various fractions of the subfield.[94]

FIGURE 5.1 A meeting of FFS dissidents. Tizi Ouzou, summer 2012. (Photograph by Hocine.)

FIGURE 5.2 MAK activists behind pictures of the martyrs of the 2001 Black Spring during that event's yearly commemoration. Tizi Ouzou, spring 2011. (Photograph by author.)

AUTONOMY AND ESSENTIALISM

The long-standing conflict between the region and the nation-state increased the radicalism of Berberist claims. As seen in figure 5.2, the memory of the victims of the 2001 Black Spring remained a crucial source of contention throughout Bouteflika's tenure. This resulted in the birth of the MAK, which nonetheless remained relatively marginal in the region. Mokrane, one of the group's founding members, argued that state violence played a key role in his decision. He recounted deciding to issue a "Call to the Kabyle People" in 2001, while at the hospital in Tizi Ouzou, where he was reviewing a list of victims of the repression. Since then, he had remained in favor of a pragmatic approach to autonomist claims, while acknowledging that others in the MAK supported a radical break.

> When some speak about a provisional government, we are not speaking about the same thing as the notion of autonomy. Economically speaking, the relationship is different, and the prerogatives of sovereignty that they want to exercise are those of an independent country. From a political perspective, there is a need to maintain a space for discussion with the

central government, because autonomy is only possible with the [support of the] central government.

(MOKRANE, FOUNDING MEMBER OF THE MAK, TIZI OUZOU, SPRING 2011)

Mokrane felt that claims to independence resulted from the lack of political prospects. He also blamed the influence of a faction within the leadership who had left the country for France. Illustrating this radicalization, the movement changed its name in 2013, replacing the term "autonomy" with "self-determination."

In this sense the ongoing conflict with the nation-state echoed the memories of colonization. Past references served the construction of a collective identity, namely, by drawing on a set of symbolic moments and allegedly inherent features.[95] Beyond autonomist circles, an essentialized representation of the group circulated. Breaking with the traditional Berberist argument presenting Arab-speaking citizens as Berbers in all but name, a sharp division between Kabyles and their "others" appeared.

> We are a rebel region that rejects any kind of control by a central authority, whether it is Roman, Turk, French, or allegedly Arab.... We have an Islam that is popular and based on brotherhoods and that stays away from secular issues. Religious figures have a spiritual approach, and they are not inherently opposed to the principle of laicity.... We have lived with our values that are, quote, "democratic." I mean that in our villages, there was no supreme authority, nobody who could decide for the others. In our region, the concentration of powers doesn't exist.
>
> (MOKRANE, 2011)

> There is a huge difference [between Kabyles and Arab Algerians]. There is nothing we can do about it. It's cultural, but also linked to choices made by individuals. I would not say this for all Arabs: some of them are not that different from Kabyles in practice. But in general, the place of religion is different in Kabylia. A religious preacher who comes to Tizi Ouzou to give a speech, he will preach alone. But in Algiers or Constantine, he will attract the whole region.
>
> (AMEZZA, 2011)

Kabyle culture was allegedly more resistant to fundamentalism and tyranny. In a more or less direct fashion, these discourses portrayed

Arab-speaking citizens as easily manipulated, even capable of falling for a kind of "Muslim totalitarianism." Both Mokrane and Amezza had appropriated an updated version of the "Kabyle myth" according to which the region's inhabitants possessed an innate attachment to liberty and equality and a cultural valorization of hard work—in short, a greater ability to adapt to European "modernity."[96] This myth was once formulated against the Arab population by the French colonial administration. Under Bouteflika, the rise of Kabyle essentialism responded to a new form of territorial conflict: in a situation of long-standing domination assimilated to an "Arabo-Islamic colonization," the revendication of an essential identity served to advance certain political and cultural claims. This form of "strategic essentialism"[97] legitimized autonomist discourses, presented as a response to Arabo-Islamic tyranny. Yet it also reinforced a contentious exclusionary dynamic, as it borrowed from French colonialism some of its preferential discriminatory concepts: modernity, laicity, and democracy. Sometimes presented as a form of racism targeting "Arabs," Kabyle essentialism echoed the idea of a break in the national community. Such a crystallization of political and cultural enmity logically supported catastrophist narratives.

The space of dissidence widened without completely escaping state control. The commemorations of the Black Spring that I witnessed in 2011 included a large crowd demonstrating its outright hostility toward the government. Yet the plainclothes police officers who monitored the protest did not miss the researcher who was—naively—taking pictures of the protest. After escorting me into an alley to check my identity, and even offering me some peanuts, one of the officers gave me a piece of advice: "You know, Kabyles are turbulent." Kabylia's apparently rebellious identity was here turned on its head to become a stigma. This portrayal of the region as a source of unrest and a threat—in a word, its securitization—also echoed the media's emphasis on real (yet very marginal) phenomena such as Christian evangelization.

The space of rebellion became a space of routinized dissidence. On election days, local and foreign journalists traveled from Algiers to Bouira or Bejaïa to be sure to collect striking images of boycott actions, whether it was riots targeting polling stations or a daring protester running away with a ballot box. Eventually, Kabylia was co-constructed as an island of radical dissent by the cartel, by Berberist factions, by the media, and by researchers who scrutinized an otherwise predictable display of unrest. A joke illustrates some of the caricatures that circulated in this context:

A traveling mattress salesman travels to Kabylia for business. Once in the marketplace, he decides to pose as a Kabyle to better sell his products. A threatening crowd gathers around him, and one of them yells out, "You're not a Kabyle, we can see it!

"I swear I am," says the salesman.

"If you really are one of us, why don't you say something in Tamazight?"

The salesman thinks for a second before responding, *"Pouvoir, assassin!"*

This humorous anecdote shows how criticism could be routinized. Indeed, a popular slogan in French was turned into a caricatural marker of Kabyle identity, an element of the region's folklore. Nevertheless, this routine was also synonymous with uncompromising contention. In Kabylia, as in other parts of the country, the illegitimacy of the ruling coalition was a given.

Oppositions Without Solutions?

The RCD oscillated between critical support of the ruling order and demands for radical political change, between participation and boycott. It earned a reputation for being an unreliable party, including among some of its former members. One of them, who later joined the leftist PST, explained that participating in the government at the end of the 1990s was the straw that broke the camel's back: "With this kind of government, there is nothing you can do. If you accept anything, you're opportunistic and worthless, you're anything but an activist."[98] Ideologically opposed to the Islamists, castigated by nationalists for its alleged "Kabyle" character, the RCD was also targeted by attacks coming from its own subfield. According to many of its Berberist competitors, the RCD was either a "right-wing party" or, even worse, a party of *"harkis* of the system."[99]

Thus, when the CNCD was created in January 2011, the participation of the RCD, disparagingly referred to as "Saadi's party," acted as a repellant. When the party tried to organize weekly marches on Saturdays, Saïd Saadi was nicknamed "Saïd Samedi." The CNCD became the C-RCD. Rather than the vanguard of a mass mobilization threatening the ruling order, the party was the scapegoat of an already divided movement.[100] Some counterprotestors chanted slogans targeting members of the RCD, whom they alternately labeled "dirty Kabyles," "dirty French," or "dirty Jews." According to officials within the party, their attempts to change the narrative were unsuccessful:

> We have never done anything in secret, whether it was participating or leaving, but the means by which we convey our discourses are too elitist.... We thought about doing and saying something else, but we're treading water. And I don't know if this is because we're incompetent or pretentious.
>
> (BOUSSAD BOUDIAF, DEPUTY AND MEMBER OF THE NATIONAL COUNCIL OF THE RCD, TIZI OUZOU, SPRING 2011)

Popular suspicion undermined the initiatives supported by the RCD. Ironically, it was Farouk Ksentini, the cartel's spokesperson for human rights, who lamented on public radio that such a "credible" party had decided to boycott the 2012 elections. Facing pervasive mistrust, RCD officials reaffirmed their belief in the necessity of the sacrifices of the 1990s. Commemorations of those who died fighting terrorism demonstrated the validity and morality of the choices made. Moreover, the alleged gap between the party's values and those of the "System," of the political field but also of the entire society writ large, explained its isolation. The RCD seemed to be alone against all, a stance that some members tried to depict in almost flattering terms:

> At the RCD, it is to our credit to have everybody agreeing to go against us, because we haven't developed a populist discourse. We tried to educate the people, but a comprehensive strategy has been set in motion to isolate us. We are in a ghetto, trapped by these discourses that label us as "Kabyles." And on the side of the *Pouvoir*, they have all the means—the ANP, Hassi Messaoud [the oil field], even Islam and Arabic are with them.
>
> (BOUSSAD BOUDIAF, 2011)

Notwithstanding Boussad's attempts to emphasize the RCD's independence, this was nevertheless a rather negative assessment of the party's situation. The cartel holding the state had huge material and symbolic resources at its disposal; opposition parties, conversely, struggled to preserve their political capital and merely survive. Even when protected by the formal opening of the field, partisan movements faced all kinds of impediments.

[The *Pouvoir*] has so many techniques of obstruction that they can let us speak in a vacuum, until they decide that this is not possible anymore. For example, we asked for permission to organize a meeting on May 7. They told us that the Harcha hall that we had booked was under construction. We asked for another venue: the Coupole. This time, they simply invented some phony judo championships.

(ASAF, 2011)

For this meeting cancelled at the last minute, the RCD had invited guest speakers from other North African countries. This could only clash with the government's desire to extract the country from the region's revolutionary temporality and maintain the national tempo of "democratic consolidation." The discrepancy in resources allowed the cartel to prevent what it regarded as reckless partisan initiatives. Security, bureaucratic, and economic hindrances represented a constant and unpredictable threat.[101] Opponents could proclaim their dissidence as long as the repressive arsenal at the disposal of the state guaranteed their relative powerlessness. By drawing on acts of regulation and exception, the cartel delimited the spaces in which criticism would be tolerated.

At the same time, and despite all their contradictions, Berberist, leftist, liberal, and Islamist movements could not be suppressed. While constantly under the shadow of a seemingly erratic repressive machine, individual activists sporadically denounced the dismal prospects confronting the country's youth and the absurdity of the electoral process. Cartoonists and editorialists published grim depictions of the country's ongoing crisis, undermining official discourses. Finally, despite the attempts to turn Kabylia into a ghetto of contestation, Kabyle protesters frequently took part in nationwide mobilizations. In 2001, 2011, and 2019, the security apparatus failed to prevent activists from traveling from Bejaïa, Tizi Ouzou, or Bouira and flooding the streets of Algiers.

In short, highly contentious discourses and practices persisted in the public sphere. Even if their fragmentation prevented them from presenting a credible alternative, the cartel's opponents challenged it and underlined the limits of its "upgrading."[102] The transformation of the system of domination allowed for the management and regulation of domestic political pressures, but criticism remained virulent. Meanwhile, pervasive socioeconomic unrest allowed the continuation of politics by other means.

6

The Crisis as a Lived Experience

The economic crisis is at the door, and behind it is the shadow of the approaching war. Holding on to things has become the monopoly of a few powerful people, who, God knows, are no more human than the many; for the most part, they are more barbaric, but not in the good way.
—*Walter Benjamin*

They don't want peace because they don't know our guerrilla.
In our head, it's always guerrilla, guerrilla, guerrilla.
—*Soolking*

On April 29, 2012, the self-immolation of Hamza Rechak sparked an urban uprising in Jijel, a city located three hundred kilometers east of Algiers renowned for its bungalows and scenic coastline. The young man was twenty-five years old. He owned and operated an informal market stall in a working-class neighborhood called Village Moussa. Selling cigarettes and cosmetic products, he was a minor actor in the parallel economy that allowed many Algerians to escape unemployment, an essential space of circumvention tolerated by the government in order to integrate the socioeconomic margins.[1] Yet the reformist agenda implemented in the name of preventing a budget crisis also called for the intermittent use of measures aimed at cracking down on this parallel economy. According to government officials, it was necessary to "clean up public spaces" and "regulate trade." On the morning of the twenty-ninth, Hamza was the target of one of these acts of regulation. Policemen ordered him to dismantle his stall. Harsh words were spoken. Hamza perceived this as a form of *hogra*: a display of contempt and injustice, a denial of his basic rights, a negation of his human dignity. He poured a gallon of gasoline on his body and his stall, and he tried to end his life. Soon after, the youth of Village Moussa gathered. They blocked the main road crossing the neighborhood. They fought the police, attacked government buildings, and burned tires and cars that were parked in the streets.[2] Hamza died from his injuries two days later, and once again the youth took to the streets of Jijel while the state sent antiriot units to back up local police forces. The story of Hamza Rechak is quite similar to that of Mohamed Bouazizi, the Tunisian street vendor whose own death by self-immolation had done so much to set off the wave of uprisings that would subsequently sweep through much of the region. In both cases, the suicide of a precarious young man unveiled the latent violence of the existing socioeconomic order and the depth of popular discontent. The legitimacy of state power was questioned publicly. Yet only Mohamed Bouazizi will be remembered as the original martyr who revived Tunisian history. As for Hamza Rechak and the hundreds of Algerians who resorted to self-immolation since the mid-2000s, their fate has been obscured by the ongoing routinization of the crisis.[3]

While the constant state of exception described in the previous chapter limits the possibilities for political action in theory,[4] it did not prevent contentious social movements in Bouteflika's Algeria. Indeed, the country displayed many of the hallmarks of a revolutionary situation. First and foremost, the latent yet persistent crisis undermined the cohesion among ruling elites and discredited state authorities, thus providing the structural conditions for radical social change.[5] Second, the country also conformed to a quintessentially Marxist model of revolutionary effervescence: the perceived sufferings of "the oppressed classes" seemed to result in "increased activities among the masses."[6] Yet for a very long time, no revolution occurred. While the catastrophized environment fueled various forms of contention, the seemingly never-ending crisis became a quotidian element in the lived experience of the population. This condition shaped the dialectical relationship linking forms of resistance and domination.

In this chapter, I analyze the tension between the lived experience of the crisis and the logic of governance by catastrophization by drawing on Walter Benjamin's "tradition of the oppressed." According to Benjamin, the catastrophe is not to be prevented in the future, as it is already happening in the present, as a condition of existence for the masses, a situation of emergency that has become the rule.[7] To this end, I describe a "state of social inequality" whereby apparent privileges undermined the postcolonial social contract and legitimized contentious subjectivities and practices. The trajectory of a social movement born in the southern part of the country, the National Committee for the Defense of the Rights of the Unemployed, offers a telling display of contentious performances that aimed to challenge the cartel and give voice to radical grievances in the public sphere. These performances contributed to the development of a modular repertoire of contention, which was in turn met with an evolving set of repressive strategies.[8] This situation of emergency also contributed to the edification of a political and moral economy of precariousness. Paternalist discourses and economic redistribution sought to limit dissent and prevent the country's descent into another period of chaos. Scarcity also had an impact on opposition activists and politicized artists, as they aimed to forestall exhaustion while testifying to the daily emergency faced by the people.

A State of Social Inequality

Under Bouteflika, the widely shared sense of a kleptocratic system cohabited with a routine marked by precariousness and boredom. Working-class youth knew all too well the gap between the egalitarian promises of state-led development and the reality of a political economy based on privileges. Displays of systemic injustice thus fueled an antagonistic version of Tocqueville's "egalitarian perception of social relations."[9] Contentious discourses expressed individual and collective experiences as non-life, an infra-human condition. This resulted in violent outbursts and the institutionalization of the riot.

FROM AÏN EL-TURK TO AÏN BESSEM

In the summer of 2006, I accompanied a friend who was visiting his family for the first time since the Dark Decade. We stayed at his uncle's apartment in Oran, but one of his cousins invited us to spend a week in his villa in Aïn El-Turk, a wealthy beach town situated nearby on the northwestern coast. In his early forties, Amine had made his fortune as a private contractor. Among other things, he provided catering services for the giant gas complex of Arzew. This year was an exciting one for him, as he had embarked on a new entrepreneurial adventure by opening a car dealership for Renault. During the week we spent in his company, Amine strove to demonstrate his success and differentiate himself from a population that he portrayed as complacently dependent on state welfare.

When we weren't touring the sites of his professional successes, Amine also made sure that we enjoyed our time with him and two of his friends. Both were entrepreneurs as well. One was a contractor working in public construction, the other dealt in imported goods. The three men spoke about the alleged laziness of Arabs or the role of personal contacts for successful businessmen like them. They also wanted us to go out to clubs, to see bike shows, and, more importantly, to find "girls." It was my first visit to Algeria, and I was intrigued by this discourse blaming the "masses" and the uninhibited quest for sex workers. I later came to understand that these were rather banal features in the lives of successful elites. Nonetheless, these particular elites did something that I was never to witness again: in the evening, before dinner, Amine and his friends sat at a table set up outside the villa, near the road. There, on their plastic seats, they opened a pack of cold Heinekens and drank openly. This type of conspicuous drinking usually happens after dark, in liminal spaces associated with anonymity, marginality, and insecurity (the Roman ruins in Annaba, the oasis in Taghit, the hill near the dam in Aïn Bessem). Yet in broad daylight, and in front of his villa, Amine displayed the confidence of someone who could bypass collective rules.

The value of such privilege becomes obvious in a different environment. Five years later, Hocine, whom I had met in the spring of 2011 in Tizi Ouzou, invited me to visit his hometown, Aïn Bessem. Located in the western part of the Wilaya of Bouira, this dry, midsize city was surrounded by potato fields. The bus stopped in a large, dusty square riddled with empty cardboard boxes. Piercing the monotony of an urban landscape comprised of standardized yellow residential complexes, an old grain silo built in the days of Boumediene dominated the horizon. The first night, Hocine introduced me to his childhood friends. Without hiding their bitterness, the group of young men told of the boredom they experienced in their day-to-day lives, which consisted mainly of playing dominoes, smoking hashish, chewing *chemma* tobacco,[10] and drinking coffee. One day, a stage actor from Bouira came to town to lead a theater workshop for teenagers. The group jumped at the occasion. While they were too old to join the workshop, they could at least attend rehearsals and chat with the actor about his experiences. As we left at the end of the day, one of the young men caustically invoked Khalida Toumi and her ironic relationship to Aïn Bessem. Indeed, while the minister of culture had been born in the city, the place was poorly equipped with leisure and cultural amenities.

When he was in town, Hocine stayed at his parents' home, even though living with his father was difficult. His friends did the same. They often shared their rooms with their brothers and sisters. In the morning, they left these apartments as soon possible and spent most of their days outside, "holding up the wall." They joked about the fact that it was my first experience as a *hitiste* (literally, a "wallist," from $ḥā^{ʾ}iṭ$ [wall]). This did not mean they were carefree: before sitting on a low wall, they used the cardboard left on the ground to protect their clothes. One of them had a car. Occasionally, he would take us on a "cruise" before improvising a rapid dash down a country road. We would also go to the nearby dam and throw rocks as far as we could. We were soon back to square one, however, idly drinking coffee and smoking hashish. For those who were stuck on the margins of working life without the social capital that would enable professional success, public space was an open-air waiting room rather than a place in which to showcase one's ability to bypass social norms.

Most of the group's members were precariously employed in the type of "jobs" that sometimes amounted to a sort of disguised unemployment. They complained about the difficulty of finding a stable position and the absence of social mobility ("When you're born in the shit, you'll stay in the shit," Hocine stated repeatedly). Some participated in the informal economy, which meant that they remained vulnerable and deprived of legal protection.[11] One of them took care of his father's sunglass stand in the city's souk. Another was a *pointeur* at the bus station: he organized the boarding of passengers on minibuses, depending on their order of arrival. He earned thirty dinars (about twenty-five cents) per bus. One night, he described his dream of becoming a fireman, but his friends quickly dismissed this wish as delusional: he smoked too much hashish to ever pass the fitness tests. A third one owned a small stationery and cosmetic shop bought with the support of the National Agency for Youth Employment. In the back room of the shop, an old foam mattress lay on the floor: the place also served as a *diki*, a hideout for more intimate encounters. This is where the group met at night, to chat, play dominoes, and smoke joints.

"It's not Ouyahia who is going to get me an apartment," said one of them as I explained that my job was researching politics. As the government routinely boasted of its $200 billion currency reserves, the young men contemplated their futures and saw a blocked horizon. Yet they didn't think of joining opposition parties. As a student delegate and FFS supporter, Hocine was the only one to proclaim an interest in politics. Nevertheless, when the town's mayor stopped him in the street to suggest that he should get involved in local public life, he politely rejected the offer. "He is corrupt," he explained with obvious contempt, as the mayor walked away.

Rather than speaking about institutional politics, the group spoke about girls and cars. Yet their caustic comments targeting Ouyahia or Toumi suggested deep underlying grievances against the country's ruling elites. In fact, the life of idleness to which so many young Algerians were condemned was often related to the shortcomings of the postcolonial state. Algerian *hitistes* thus became a symbol of the inescapable socioeconomic and political stagnation in the country's urban centers, which had in turn become sites for the management of the crisis.[12] Hocine was the most outspoken in his rejection of this grueling status quo:

> This is not a life. Nobody can accept this. Social misery is everywhere. There is no future for the youth, and it's almost worse for those who go to university like me. We're young, but we cannot find a place for ourselves. What am I going to do later? What am I going to do? Will I get married? Will I find a job? An apartment? A car? No. All doors are closed. Nobody is better off than before, except for those who belong to a very narrow class and find all the doors already open. For the others, there is nothing. How can you tolerate this? Everybody suffers from misery.
>
> (HOCINE, MEMBER OF THE LOCAL STUDENT COORDINATION AND FFS SUPPORTER, TIZI OUZOU, SPRING 2011)

196 THE CRISIS AS A LIVED EXPERIENCE

FIGURE 6.1 After a car accident, a riot targeted the *daïra* and locals installed improvised roadblocks. Aïn Bessem, autumn 2011. (Photograph by author.)

Discontent and socioeconomic stagnation didn't merely result in a form of idleness. In the bus that took us from Bouira to Aïn Bessem, Hocine pointed at several armored police vehicles speeding in the opposite direction. "These are mustache trucks," he explained, referring to the shape of the shield affixed to the front of each vehicle. "There is a riot happening not far away." Indeed, the Wilaya of Bouira had a flattering reputation in this regard. Later, as we walked in the shade of the giant grain silo, I noticed a couple of charred dumpsters and some rocks blocking the left side of the road. Hocine described the events that had happened a few days before: after another car accident on this dangerous bend, a small riot had started in the neighborhood. Infuriated by the lack of response from public authorities, residents installed the rocks shown in figure 6.1 to slow down traffic and then attacked the *daïra*'s headquarters.

PRIVILEGE, EXCLUSION, AND ALIENATION

From Aïn El-Turk to Aïn Bessem, the restructuring of the Algerian economy gave birth to a state of social inequality. On one hand, privatizations and "competitive" public markets offered opportunities for the rapid accumulation of wealth by a class of well-connected private actors. On the other, a large part of the population was negatively impacted by the dismantling of public services, successive waves of layoffs, wage stagnation, and the liberalization of prices. At the end of the 1990s, the country faced a decrease in its purchasing power, the end of social activities offered by public companies, and high rates of unemployment.[13] The decade-long restructuring engendered both growing precariousness and systematized privileges. While local and foreign capitalists fueled the market for corruption, bureaucratic control maintained the centrality of state agents, who could be permissive or prohibitive at will.

As shown in chapter 3, corruption and clientelism became structuring features of Bouteflika's Algeria. They were essential in reshaping networks of power, regulating state apparatuses, distributing wealth, and stabilizing the polity after the Dark Decade. Yet the discourse of corruption also reaffirmed the immoral and unfair nature of these widespread practices. Corruption was perceived simultaneously as "business as usual," which allowed for mundane forms of accumulation and regulation, and a symptom of social and political anomie.[14] Framed in moral terms, the phenomenon fed the widespread mistrust of rich and influential actors. Because privileges were ubiquitous, power and wealth were deemed suspicious. Without fully endorsing the idea that "all property [was] theft" under Bouteflika, one must admit that wealth was widely viewed as illegitimate.[15] Rapid social promotion was associated with being an *affairiste* or a *kachiriste*,[16] as success could only be explained by conformity to the predatory rules of politics and the economy.

While allegedly corrupt figures were the targets of grassroots criticism, young Algerians were also exposed to the fetishes of consumer society. In the back room where they played dominos and shared two seats for four, the group of friends from Aïn Bessem spoke about Japanese and German cars and compared the options available to the prospective buyer of each vehicle. Economic precariousness didn't shield them from the desires promoted by the globalized market economy. Each Lebanese music video was there to remind them that, somewhere, love stories were blossoming on yachts and in sumptuous villas. Whether in Milan or Aïn Bessem, consumption patterns are somewhat similar. The poor want to integrate into a society in which consumption has become a condition for participation. Eventually, these frustrated aspirations fuel grievances.[17]

The feeling of lack was also based on genuine material privation. The progressive improvement of macroeconomic indicators since the early 2000s had not put an end to ordinary Algerians' daily struggles. Despite an apparent recovery, newcomers on the job market were offered few opportunities. While official statistics indicated a sharp decline in youth unemployment since 2003 (a record year with a rate of 45 percent), it nevertheless remained more than two times greater than an already high general unemployment rate (respectively 29 percent and 12 percent in September 2018).[18] Official numbers ignored both the precarious nature of the jobs created and the growing role of the informal sector.[19] Economic hardship thus contributed to a form of generational stagnation associated with an "unemployment of despair" (biṭālat al-yā's).[20] The increase in the average age of marriage was a major sign of this delayed transition, as it remained a social milestone for achieving adulthood.[21] After finishing their studies, young people faced a long series of challenges affecting their personal lives (living with their parents, lack of employment, the impossibility of buying a car, a shortage of cultural and leisure activities). The promise of emancipation inherent to the Algerian revolution had withered, which brought a host of political consequences. At the beginning of the 1990s, Omar Carlier captured the growing disenfranchisement of a fraction of the urban youth: "Idleness, disillusionment and resentment are essential to the rejection of a society that has left them behind, a society of nouveaux riches and every man for himself. No, this state has certainly done nothing for them. It doesn't share their concerns, it doesn't speak their language, it is alien to them."[22]

With the collapse of the single-party system, these broken promises fueled a radicalism flavored with puritanism. But the wreckage of the 1990s dispelled any power of attraction once enjoyed by this alternative inspired by a transcendent morality. Earthly problems were an enduring feature of life. They shaped the experience of those living in crowded urban spaces where traditional social relations had been shattered and then reconfigured. In Algiers, the impoverishment of the city center came with the migration of the upper classes toward the residential periphery. The resistance emanating from commuter towns and slums coiled up the sides of gullies was a response to the creation of these bourgeois islands on the city's heights. The situation in the capital was a concentrated version of the contradictions that prevailed in Bouteflika's Algeria: it brought together large development projects and precarious public housing, crony entrepreneurs and *hitistes*, the cumulative logic of economic growth and the stagnating experience of the non-life.

In the different forms taken by boredom, despair, and the violence of urban life, one can recognize the *tufush* described by Pascal Ménoret in Riyadh.[23] This notion expresses the divergence between subjective expectations and objective reality, between hopes and opportunities, a divergence that results in a sense of powerlessness. In Algeria, this hiatus was apparent in the notion of *dégoûtage* and the phrase *rani karah hyati* (I'm disgusted by/bored with my life). Caught in the continuum of development and security, limited by the threat of the suspended disaster, the lived experience of many Algerians echoed Benjamin's depiction of the fragmented and melancholic individual, trapped in an anguished mental space (*denkraum*) created by war, technology, and poverty.[24] According to Benjamin's depiction of the alienated condition of modern individuals, "the purpose of [their] existence seems to have been reduced to the most distant vanishing point on an endless horizon."[25] In a world devoid of culture, the human experience is one of exhaustion and fascination, isolation and frustration. It is in this world that the act of self-immolation committed by Hamza Rechak makes sense, as "a testament to the absence of a collective movement and the helpless solitude experienced by an individual before an existing order."[26]

HOGRA AND RIOTS

Yet self-immolation precedes the riot, suggesting that there is a way out of alienation and isolation. Indeed, the act of self-killing is a form of necroresistance that "turns death against the power regime" and "transforms the body from a site of subjection to a site of insurgency."[27] Going back to Saudi Arabia, Ménoret underlines the conflictual value of *tufush* in the face of a Leviathan that obliterates the dreams of Saudi youth. He describes the desire to bite, crush, break, the need to rebel that is expressed in the nightly escapades of his "joyriders." The sense of "social inadequacy" thus becomes a "revolutionary feeling."[28] Similarly, the youth excluded by the Algerian order demanded what they considered to be rightfully theirs. Eventually, the cumulative temporality of the ruling elites and the fragmented temporality of their subjects collided. The publicized trajectory of corrupt ministers and the visible decay of public services generated grievances against a system of routinized despoliation. Various stories circulated illustrating the belief that national resources had been confiscated by shameless ruling elites. Take, for example, the following humorous anecdote, which—depending on the version—sometimes cast Bouteflika himself as the main character:

> An American minister welcomes his Algerian counterpart. The latter is impressed by the beauty of the country and the wealthy residence of his host. He asks how he managed to acquire such a nice house.
> "You see the highway over there," says the American minister. "When we finished it, I kept some of the money to build this house."
> Later, the American minister comes to Algeria for an official visit. He is invited to his counterpart's house and cannot believe what he sees: the residence is three times bigger than his. It's a palace made of marble and gold, with a big park full of animals.
> "How did you manage to get a house that is larger than mine?" he asks. "Algeria is certainly not wealthier than the United States."
> The Algerian minister brings him next to a window and points toward the horizon.
> "Do you see the highway over there?"
> "No," says the American, puzzled.
> "Well, this is how I found the money to build my palace."

Reminiscent of the East–West Highway scandal revealed in 2009, this story underlined the duplicity of foreign partners to better underline the Algerian minister's total lack of restraint. It also echoed the idea of a gap between what was owed and what was given.

Humor had long been a way to cope with economic hardship. The inflating price of essential products was a recurring theme in the jokes, memes, and chants circulating in the public sphere. At the end of 2009, for instance, football fans denounced the rising price of potatoes. In stadiums, they sang *batata seb'a alf!* (potato at seven thousand!—that is, seventy dinars per kilo). In 2012, following a further increase in the price of potatoes, a myriad of photomontages circulated on social media, one of them comparing potatoes with perfume. As a mundane ingredient was caustically compared to luxury items, the names of elite resorts reserved for the cartel and its affiliates (Le Club des Pins, Sidi Yahia) suggested the moral bankruptcy of a once revolutionary ruling class.

Bouteflika's Algeria was not, strictly speaking, a poor country. Annual economic growth was around 3 percent—in other words, steady, without matching the performance of emerging powers. Thanks to hydrocarbon rents, the government was able to repay its external debts, hoard some $200 billion in currency reserves, and even lend money to the IMF. Macroeconomic indicators suggested a more nuanced picture. Algeria's GDP per capita was that of a developing country, ranking around 100th worldwide depending on the agency and the data analyzed.[29] With the drop in hydrocarbon prices in 2014 and the ensuing budget crisis, the perceived gap between the alleged wealth of the country and its inhabitants' living conditions fueled outrage at the various forms of embezzlement benefiting remorseless *affairistes*. As the budget crisis lingered until 2019, this widespread hostility led to the rapid downfall of major figures of Algerian crony capitalism during the Hirak.

A key motive in the advent of the Hirak, *hogra* seemed ubiquitous under Bouteflika. Widely appropriated by social movements, the term echoed the "feeling of having one's rights violated and being victim of a fundamentally inegalitarian system based on privileges and impunity."[30] Facing systematic discrimination, the individual was diminished and trapped in a condition of nonbeing.[31] *Hogra* became a synonym for the state of social inequality. The denial of the right to live in dignity sparked widespread anger that targeted local politicians, low-level bureaucrats, businessmen, and above all the "System," this impersonal entity whose social function was seemingly to reproduce humiliation.

The rejection of *hogra* found its default form in the riots that came to characterize Bouteflika's Algeria. In the 1980s, social movements demanding public services and opportunities directed their rancor at older generations and the state, a feeling that was eventually echoed by the FIS.[32] The same decade saw urban uprisings become a major feature in the national repertoire of contention, a tendency that culminated in October 1988. After a pause during the Dark Decade, this type of mobilization again rose to prominence in the 2000s.[33] Riots then became part of a routine. Facing the deployment of antiriot units, rioters regularly attacked public and private buildings. In the smaller towns of the High Plateaus and the South, the population experienced scarcity in all its forms: power outages, water shortages, unemployment, lack of housing. There, popular violence responded to the socioeconomic and symbolic violence meted out by the state.

Riots occasionally took a form that was more threatening to the established order. The wave of urban clashes that swept the country in 2011 reached the capital on January 5. To contain discontent and negate its political valence, the cartel's mouthpieces portrayed this uprising as a mere "crisis of sugar and oil" that would be solved by acting upon the prices of food products. The media and peripheral organizations such as the UGTA echoed this version of events and placed the blame on "speculators" and "vandals."[34] Yet other defensive moves implemented by the government, such as the decision to restrict access to Twitter and Facebook when the clashes reached Algiers, betrayed the political nature of the unrest. Similarly, the massive deployment of police units in the streets of the capital after Friday prayers on January 7 illustrated the desire to contain the political discontent, as this moment of gathering has historically been associated with mass demonstrations.[35] Indeed, even though framed as a childish reaction to socioeconomic frustration, urban uprisings kept the possibility of a genuine insurrection alive.

From simple skirmishes to forms of popular manhunts, the riot itself yields ample variations of scale, intensity, and target. This versatility explains the difficulty of interpreting it as a social phenomenon.[36] Under Bouteflika, scarcity often acted as a trigger. Yet anger over water shortages, food prices, and deficient garbage collection was also symptomatic of broader social and political grievances, notably regarding the state's continuous shortcomings.

Far from being limited to irrational bursts of anger, riots also responded to practical imperatives. As a rapid and anonymous form of mobilization that does not require preexisting organization, a riot is structured by a set of constraints, notably social fragmentation.[37] It also proves to be an efficient mode of contention, inasmuch as public authorities are willing to compromise, within the framework of an extralegal yet institutionalized set of power relations. Indeed, compared to voting, seen as pointless under such conditions, riots can work as an alternative method for obtaining concessions from local officials.[38] Under Bouteflika, clashes frequently broke out following the publication of lists allocating public housing. This routine demonstrated the institutionalization of a contentious mechanism that allowed marginalized groups to demand a public service. Far from being another symptom of a premodern culture, the riot thus responded to the necessities of collective action as regards organization, interest, and occasion.[39] Moreover, both the growth of antiriot measures and the systematic concessions coming from government officials testify to the role of the state in regulating and legitimizing this type of collective action.

Even trapped in the catastrophic present of the never-ending crisis, Algerians were not "forced" into resistance. Social movements were strategic, often sectoral, and spatially limited. Violent or peaceful, they expressed long-standing socioeconomic and political claims. Popular demands put the government under constant pressure to redistribute national wealth. Precarious segments of society therefore received genuine benefits, notably through the progressive increase in the minimum wage, which rose from 8,000 DA to 18,000 DA per month in four successive increases between 2003 and 2011. These concessions were nonetheless inherently linked to a political economy based on scarcity, and they did not mitigate the overwhelming feeling of *hogra*.

THE SPACE OF CONTROL

To manage widespread discontent, state coercion delimited a space of control, notably centered on the capital. For the most part, protesters were banned from entering Algiers until 2019. The interdiction applied to those representing seemingly unruly social or cultural margins (Berberists, the unemployed) or groups committed to the publicization of a particular claim (as in the case of communal guards in 2011 and 2012). The gendarmerie and police checkpoints inherited from the 1990s were instrumental in preventing these sorts of incursions. They served to regulate human flows, filter traffic corridors, and delineate the striated space of control. The dissemination of mobile checkpoints did not require a permanent presence and allowed a more flexible and circumstantial form of coercion. Transportation toward the capital could be interrupted, and protesters intercepted in buses or at the station. When they managed to penetrate the securitized perimeter, activists could be arrested before attending a protest and sent back to their region of origin, as explained by a RAJ member from Bejaïa: "They take you to the police station for an identity check.

They see where you live and then they drop you off at [the Kharouba] bus station so you can go back to Bejaïa. And they tell you, 'It's over kids. Go back home now.'"

When protesters managed to overcome this first set of obstacles, they were targeted by a new round of dissuasive approaches. In October 2010, a policeman approached a group of young people who had joined the yearly commemoration of the uprising of 1988. In order to convince them to leave Martyrs' Square, he suggested that they seek shelter from the sun under a nearby set of arches. Another agent advised an elderly man to get refreshments in a café off the square. This was the initial stage in a multilevel approach to law enforcement, marked by negotiations with activists, patronizing recommendations, and identity checks.

The government could always take it to the next level and simply obliterate the possibility of accessing public spaces. By drawing on massive deployments of police, it remained able to canalize or disperse the few demonstrations organized in Algiers, especially when they targeted symbolic buildings (the APN, Government Palace, El Mouradia). Plainclothes officers and antiriot units would then complement uniformed policemen, and female officers would deal specifically with female protesters. The final level involved the frequent use of extralegal practices. In 2011, for instance, the cartel mobilized counterprotesters against the CNCD, thus adding a new layer of harassment to the obstacles already faced by protesters.[40]

Given the conjunction between a centralized political system and a working-class metropolis of symbolic importance, mobilizations in the capital represented an immediate danger to the political order.[41] While social movements proliferated on the periphery, notably in Kabylia, the High Plateaus, and the South, Algiers remained mostly out of reach for protesters. The national territory was thus divided and monitored as a mosaic. Crucial areas remained under strict control (symbolic political sites in the capital, embassies, state resorts, hydrocarbon-related infrastructure, military facilities, and sensitive border regions) while discontent could be expressed in the vast portions of the territory that served as spaces of circumvention. The development of the riot at the periphery was inseparable from the hyper-securitization of scattered centers of power. At the same time, we must avoid the old Moroccan dichotomy opposing *Blād al-Makhzan* to *Blād as-Sība*, "the land of government" and "the land of dissent." On the one hand, the dissemination of areas of control produced a discontinuous, securitized archipelago comprised of "sanctuary" spaces. On the other, contentious mobilizations responded to a myriad of motives that transcended the dichotomy opposing obedience and revolt.

Winds from the South

The connection between political and socioeconomic demands played a key role in the uprisings of 2011. In Tunisia, for instance, daily struggles fueled structural contradictions and strengthened the national repertoire of contention.[42] Similarly, the socioeconomic unrest that characterized Algeria under Bouteflika echoed various political grievances. The pervasive protest movement was perceived as a symptom of systemic injustice and unbearable violations of human dignity. Yet it was also instrumentalized to justify the securitization of political life. To understand the tension between the revolutionary situation and governance by catastrophization, this section studies the movement of the unemployed that emerged in the country's South.

THE CNDDC AGAINST INTERNAL COLONIALISM

From the mid-2000s, the defense of the rights of the unemployed came to occupy an increasingly prominent place in Algeria's contentious landscape. What was initially an informal social movement born in 2006 in the South had by February 2011 coalesced under the name of National Committee for the Defense of the Rights of the Unemployed (Comité national pour la défense des droits des chômeurs, CNDDC). The CNDDC decried the high unemployment rate, the exploitative practices of foreign companies extracting riches from the Sahara, and the state's failure to implement an egalitarian redistribution of the country's wealth. Moreover, its spokespersons blamed state officials for their alleged contempt for a particular social category, the unemployed, and a region, the South. In the face of this mobilization, the government alternated between minor concessions and repression. In the latter case, it relied on classic forms of state coercion: travel restrictions, police harassment and brutality, arbitrary arrests, unpredictable sentences. The dispute grew increasingly acrimonious. In June 2011, for example, a meeting between the minister of labor and a delegation from the CNDDC devolved into a verbal confrontation.[43] Consequently, the perceived *hogra* of the *Pouvoir* fueled regionalist discourses.

> The northerners, they feel that they are superior to us. They think that we are nomads, people who don't understand anything. Me, I don't believe in this border marking out what they call "Algeria." ... My opinion is that we in the South don't have anything in common with the North. We are culturally and historically different. Yesterday, I was with a friend from Ouargla who is also unemployed and who came with me. He said, "There is a Western Sahara. Why don't we try to make an Eastern Sahara?"
>
> (ABDELKADER, UNEMPLOYED WORKER FROM OUARGLA, MEMBER OF THE CNDDC, ALGIERS, SPRING 2011)

Abdelkader's statement illustrates the link between perceived contempt and regionalism. The combination of symbolic and economic violence led him to reaffirm an essential difference. This narrative was absent from the CNDDC's official statements, as its leaders instead emphasized the patriotic nature of their struggle. Nonetheless, Abdelkader's frustration was far from unique. Much like in the case of Kabylia, a sense of historical injustice could fuel centrifugal tendencies in the South, thereby contributing to the process of catastrophization.

The CNDDC presented the actors involved in the exploitation of the Saharan subsoil as foreign agents. Multinationals and "compradorized" elements, private contractors and members of the administration all benefited from the country's riches at the expense of local workers. While the Wilaya of Ouargla was often presented as the wealthiest in Algeria, its inhabitants were frustrated by a persistent lack of public services and economic opportunities.[44] This led the spokesperson and coordinator of the CNDDC, Tahar Belabbes, to describe a situation of internal colonialism and to repeatedly portray "those who possess the state" as mere invaders. Unemployment, bureaucratic hindrances, and poor infrastructure were proof of a violent extractivism reminiscent of the colonial exactions of the past. Indeed, "internal colonialism" was a recurring narrative wherever the betrayal and greed of centralist elites were denounced, from Kabyle autonomists in the North to unemployed activists in the South. This discourse condemned the persistence of ancient structures of domination, the marginalization of entire social groups, and the flaws in the "egalitarian process of development."[45]

Rather than simply echoing the narrow economic claims of a precarious group, the CNDDC came to express a deeper rejection of the transformation of the state since the 1980s.

> In our platform, we do not differentiate democratic claims from social claims. Because when we speak about liberalism and liberal globalization, we all know that in a country . . . like Algeria, economic liberalism and political repression go hand in hand. Here, corporate executives can be in the public or the private sector, they can be nationals or foreigners—they have no interest in a democratic state. They don't want the people to be in control of its resources and political power. The Algerian regime plays its role diligently. It crafts laws that are at the same time antisocial and hostile to freedom. It encourages the precariousness of workers and oppresses them.
>
> (SAMIR LARABI, SPOKESMAN OF THE CNDDC,
> MEMBER OF THE PST, ALGIERS, SPRING 2011)

While committed to upholding the distinction between his political and social activities, Samir Larabi maintained that the condition of workers could not be understood independently from the nature of the cartel, as a security-oriented entity acting as a local enforcer for the neoliberalized global order. From this perspective, the mobilization of the CNDDC was a thorn in the side of self-proclaimed nationalist ruling elites who claimed to protect the country from foreign interference and predation.

PACIFISM, PATRIOTISM, AND AUTONOMY FROM POLITICS

Members of the CNDDC personally faced the various forms of repression that made up the cartel's coercive tool kit. To overcome these challenges, the movement benefited from the experience of veterans of social and political struggles, such as Yacine Zaïd and Samir Larabi.[46] Moreover, the committee enjoyed the support of organizations with nationwide networks (SNAPAP, LADDH), as well as positive coverage from opposition newspapers (*El Watan, El Khabar*). As was the case in the early days of the Tunisian revolution, the long-standing proximity between social protest and political activism facilitated the expression of a highly contentious discourse.[47]

> The unemployed are the weak part of society. They live in precariousness and distress. They are destroyed socially and morally, but this doesn't mean that they cannot be heard. Quite the opposite: it's a part of society that can be mobilized to change things. . . . It's a segment that can be combative and that represents a reserve of activists. When I say activists, I am not speaking in terms of party, but rather about people who can commit and contribute to a power struggle against the *Pouvoir*, because they want favorable conditions for them and for all the workers.
>
> (SAMIR LARABI, 2011)

As a genuine Trotskyist, Samir praised the ability of the unemployed to advocate for radical change beyond their narrow class interests. Indeed, they did not have jobs to lose, were available to partake in public actions, and experienced *hogra* in its most blatant manifestations. Consequently, their actions could benefit the entire society. Public statements released by the CNDDC followed the same logic. A call released on May 1, 2011, put forth the following demands: the nationalization of strategic companies; the improvement of public services; the right to housing for all; and the protection of the freedoms of expression and protest. Rather than speaking in terms of "regime change," the unemployed based their discourse on socioeconomic claims. This, in turn, allowed them to express political discontent in a more socially acceptable idiom.

To preserve its place in the public sphere, the CNDDC had to overcome the usual challenges faced by activists. First and foremost, it hewed to the imperative of nonviolence in shaping its strategies, having emerged in a catastrophized environment where maintaining stability remained an absolute priority, even for opponents.[48] While some of its members had occasionally relied on rioting in their younger days,[49] the CNDDC's modus operandi espoused a nonviolent repertoire mixing symbolic actions and the occupation of public spaces.[50] Its spokespeople repeated their commitment to radical yet peaceful change and tried to turn the securitizing framework on its head by portraying the government as the source of violence. In March 2011, for instance, they denounced the "savage attacks" perpetrated by public authorities against a "peaceful demonstration of unemployed youth."[51]

The social movement also faced accusations of regionalism, given its strong anchoring in southern *wilayas*. In response, the CNDDC spokespersons combined their denunciation of internal colonialism with an emphasis on their movement's place in the national landscape. Their statements appealed to "all Algerians" and echoed a repeated demand for the South's deeper integration into the social and political fabric of the nation.[52] They also tried to expand their movement and occupy public spaces in northern *wilayas*, outside of their regional stronghold.

The CNDDC accounted for the widespread mistrust of political parties by demonstrating its organizational and political autonomy. In 2013, as they prepared for a massive demonstration in Ouargla, the spokespersons of the movement released a statement on Facebook in which they emphasized the grassroots nature of their mobilization and warned against any attempt to manipulate the upcoming protest. The CNDDC's contentious patriotic discourse certainly had a strong political edge. Moreover, many of its members were also linked to leftist organizations, such as the FFS or the PST. While remaining in dialog with these allies, however, the unemployed strove to demonstrate their independence at every turn. Indeed, staying away from the political field seemed, paradoxically, to be the best way to influence public debate.

With a strategy based on pacifism, patriotism, and autonomy from politics, the CNDDC navigated an environment shaped by the suspended disaster. On March 14, 2013, an estimated ten thousand protesters (according to the event's organizers) descended on Ouargla for the so-called March of the Million (*Miliyūniyya*). While employing highly contentious rhetoric, the demonstration was held without violence. Participants waved Algerian flags and sang the national anthem. In response, Prime Minister Sellal adapted his stance. While he had until then portrayed the unemployed as a bunch of thugs, he now praised them for their patriotism and promised "important announcements."[53]

The case of the CNDDC shows that the continuous socioeconomic unrest that took place during the 2000s and 2010s was far from a collection of depoliticized revolts. Resistance was systemic rather than episodic and evolved along with the forms of policing used by the ruling coalition, as was the case in other parts of the region.[54] Nonviolent strategies and patriotic discourses responded to an existential threat while aiming to prevent physical confrontations with the police. The unemployed also responded to the government's paternalism by demonstrating their civic-mindedness. Overall, the strategies used to occupy public spaces (demonstrations, sit-ins, public displays of patriotism) tested the cartel's ability to control and coerce. At the same time, they consolidated the national repertoire of contention, which was eventually put to use during the Hirak.

THE ROUTINIZATION OF SOCIAL MOVEMENTS

After the *Miliyūniyya*, the shadow of violence prevented an expansion of the CNDDC's movement toward the North. At the end of March 2013, a sit-in in Ouargla led to a violent confrontation with the police. At the beginning of April, the publication of the housing lists sparked a wave of rioting in the city. Following a well-known pattern, rioters denounced the obscure procedures used to allocate apartments and the priority given to "foreigners" coming from the North.[55] A few days later, similar clashes erupted in Illizi, near the Libyan border. The leaders of the CNDDC argued that these riots had been "sponsored" and called for the mediation of local "patriarchs."[56] The clashes nonetheless legitimized the securitization of social unrest in the South, a region that had already been under intense scrutiny since the beginning of 2013.

In January that year, the jihadi group Al-Muwaqqiʿūn bi-d-Dimāʾ, an offshoot of al-Qaeda in the Islamic Maghreb, had already launched a surprise operation targeting the Tinguentourine natural gas facility near In Amenas, in the Wilaya of Illizi. Given this regional context, the CNDDC was not only securitized as a regionalist movement. It was also associated with terrorist threats, an amalgam that was facilitated by the release of a statement in support of the protesters by al-Qaeda's local branch.[57] The amalgam was also justified by the historical precedent of the Movement for the Children of the South, which had advocated for equal development and economic opportunities at the beginning of the 2000s. Many of its members supported a peaceful approach, and some of these people were instrumental in creating the CNDDC, such as Tahar Belabbes. Others entered politics, notably by joining Abdallah Djaballah. Yet as the movement was met with fierce state coercion, a fraction of its members formed an armed group in the neighboring Tassili n'Ajjer Mountains. One of them participated in the terrorist assault on In Amenas. Memories of the 1990s, paranoid official discourses, and a limited yet genuine risk of radicalization converged to make the suspended disaster more tangible. After 2013, the South became a recurring element in conspiracy theories. The DRS, the United States, France, Morocco, or Israel were suspected of manipulating protests in the hope of destabilizing the country and plundering its riches.

In addition to the suspended disaster, the CNDDC soon faced another challenge: maintaining its relevance in a context of a latent crisis marked by a succession of events and nonevents. In order to promote the desired outcomes, the unemployed had to continuously demonstrate the relevance and urgency of their cause. Yet the country was caught up in a routinized succession of riots, strikes, terrorist attacks, and political upheavals. While the CNDDC strove to maintain the singular and subversive nature of its mobilization, it was slowly overwhelmed by the tide of events.

The crisis once again imposed its rhythm. As the leaders of the CNDDC were following up on their historical mobilization of March 2013 and preparing for the expansion of their movement toward the North, they met with a major disruption that would change everything. On April 27, Abdelaziz Bouteflika left the country for emergency medical treatment following a transient ischemic attack. Naturally, the resulting political uncertainty revived the specter of a descent into chaos. The existential stakes overtook any concerns for social justice. Sellal reverted to his litany of warnings to the people, claiming that Algeria was now "targeted at the level of its Republican foundations, its development and its security."[58] In the face of these alleged attempts to destabilize the country, socioeconomic unrest in the South was again portrayed as a result of manipulation at the hands of evil but opaque forces.

Meanwhile, the movement of the unemployed slowly drowned in an ocean of socioeconomic unrest. Between April and May, a massive strike by public servants paralyzed the High Plateaus and the South; this was followed by two further strikes by workers at Air Algérie and in public hospitals. Social issues competed with judicial developments as the Sonatrach scandal gave birth to yet another dramatic turn of events with the indictment and subsequent flight from the country of former minister of energy and mines Chakib Khelil. The CNDDC saw its ability to represent a singular challenge to the political order steadily erode during this period. Swallowed by the crisis and the successive upheavals it brought in its wake, the mobilization of the unemployed was now just one episode of socioeconomic unrest among many. At the end of May, an Algerian journalist and correspondent for a French radio station confessed to me that she had no idea when the next CNDDC demonstration was scheduled. In fact, it was supposed to occur two days later in Aïn Beïda. Yet it was as if the lack of media interest was premonitory: the protesters were in the end prevented from demonstrating. Some were arrested in buses as they made their way to Aïn Beïda, while others were attacked by local thugs. Without the protection of the public's gaze, the CNDDC's attempt to expand their scope of action faced the brutal reality of the DGSN's "democratic crowd management" (i.e., the sort of nonlethal policing described in chapter 5).

THE WAR OF THE POOR AGAINST THE POOR

Forms of social unrest motivated by exclusion and precariousness are not necessarily synonymous with resistance.[59] In some cases, long-standing grievances might lead to the horizontalization of popular violence. Riots do not always target the ruling order's symbols; often the target is other social groups. Competition between the most precarious members of society can thus pave the way for a war of the poor against the poor, in yet another symptom of the crisis.[60]

The South once again illustrates the way in which the latent crisis fractured urban spaces. In Ghardaïa, for instance, recurring conflicts pitted two communities against each other: the Mozabite (Tamazight-speaking Ibadites) and the Chambi (Arabic-speaking Sunnis). The conjunction of religious differences, old communal feuds, and a rapid and problematic urbanization gave birth to one of the longest-running series of urban clashes in Bouteflika's Algeria.[61] Once episodic, these clashes took on a systematic character as they spread across the entire *wilaya* after 2013. The government reacted by deploying antiriot police, but it was unable to prevent deadly confrontations. The continuous degradation of urban space had strengthened intercommunal hostility. In the autumn of 2011, a student representative of Beni Izguen (one of the five historical Mozabite citadels, or *qṣūr*) explained to me that the poor state of the city and its vital *oued* (river/riverbed) resulted from the presence of "Arabs." Yet he also blamed the state for doing nothing to facilitate the integration of newcomers and managing the city with a mix of "incompetence" and "ill will."

Indeed, the urban clashes in Ghardaïa exceeded mere communal acrimony. They also echoed a broader set of economic, political, and physical grievances targeting the established order and its local enforcers.[62]

Riots can occasionally take the form of punitive expeditions targeting vulnerable groups.[63] As the exploitation of hydrocarbons made some southern cities attractive for workers from the North, locals increasingly associated these "foreigners" with internal colonial despoliation. While movements such as the CNDDC tried to overcome these tensions, the competition between local and "foreign" workers fueled the war of the poor against the poor in its most gruesome form. The rash of violence targeting women in the city of Hassi Messaoud, in the Wilaya of Ouargla, was a particularly striking example of such a diversion. Hassi Messaoud is situated near the country's largest oil field. Since the 1970s, it has experienced tremendous demographic growth,[64] which has resulted in a deterioration of living conditions. This was also the occasion for a reorientation of socioeconomic grievances toward women who lived alone, worked for foreign or public companies, and were associated with an alleged moral deviance. The resulting riots saw multiple episodes of collective sexist violence inflamed by preachers who called for the cleansing of the city.

The South was far from the only place to witness bursts of horizontal violence. Indeed, the region enjoyed a flattering reputation as being relatively tolerant toward sub-Saharan migrants compared to northern *wilayas*. While migrants represented roughly 20 percent of the population in the Algerian Sahara, xenophobic discourses were more common in the North. There, racial prejudice could occasionally result in urban clashes targeting migrants.[65]

Thus, it appears that the shared denunciation of systemic injustice did not necessarily result in attacks targeting administrative buildings, police stations, and banks. Horizontal clashes echoing socioeconomic competition as well as cultural and political feuds seemed to undermine the potential for a revolutionary moment. A de-sectorization of popular struggle was unlikely, given the mosaic of contentious claims. Rather, the competition for state resources fueled the war of the poor against the poor and placed the cartel in the position of mediator.

Socioeconomic unrest of a unifying nature nevertheless persisted. Members of the CNDDC continued to use their bodies to advocate for human dignity in the public sphere, as they sewed their lips together or slashed their torsos with razorblades.⁶⁶ In the face of systemic *hogra*, the unemployed mobilized all available resources to build a peaceful repertoire of contention and renegotiate the postcolonial social contract.⁶⁷ At the same time, their discourse also amounted to a dichotomous call for unity. Interviewed by *El Watan* in 2014, the president of the CNDDC, Abdelmalek Aïbek, denounced private security companies working in Hassi Messaoud, whose employers "suck your blood" and act like "slave traders." He continued by calling for a "united social front including the unemployed, workers, students, lawyers, all social categories, in order to give new hope to the people."⁶⁸ In 2015, the CNDDC joined a broader social coalition denouncing the extension of fracking in the South. Once again, protesters maintained a long-running mobilization, this time culminating in a demonstration scheduled for March 14. Despite the tensions inherent to cross-class mobilizations, the unemployed positioned themselves as experienced "activists who [were] to be taken seriously and who managed to impose a certain subject and framing in the public sphere."⁶⁹ There remained, then, the potential for a convergence of struggles whose core contained a dichotomous discourse denouncing the "System"'s *hogra*.

The Crisis as a Routine

Faced with this succession of events and nonevents, social movements struggled to maintain their singularity. The routine of the crisis was accompanied by boredom and riots, scarcity and corruption, repression and redistribution, terrorist attacks and trivial events. It was at the same time an objective situation and a terrorizing spectacle. In response, the cartel implemented policies and formulated discourses for the daily management of the crisis: clientelism, state stipends, nonlethal policing, narratives of development and emergency.

MANAGEMENT BY SCARCITY

During the campaign for the 2012 legislative elections, the spokespersons of parties with various degrees of relevance were invited onto the francophone public radio station Chaîne 3 to present their programs. Some were more peculiar than others. One morning, an independent candidate proposed resurrecting the colonial dream of a canal linking the Mediterranean to the Sahara; the resulting inland sea would serve to dynamize the region. A few days later, another candidate suggested that each *wilaya* should specialize in the production and processing of one type of vegetable in order to provide jobs. Another called for the youth, notoriously underprivileged, to be offered jobs, political responsibilities, or low-interest loans. In the last case, this merely echoed one of the strategies already implemented by the National Agency for Youth Employment.

In a context marked by mass unemployment and precarious contracts, the public sector offered better work conditions. In 2014, data from the National Statistics Office showed that public sector wages were in general twice as high as in the private sector, with a monthly average of 51,000 DA against 29,200 DA. Trade unions were also more active as they benefited from job security to mobilize workers. In order to limit discontent, genuine financial advantages were granted to strategic components of the state apparatus. At the end of 2010, and while social unrest was on the rise, police officers were given a pay raise and a new severance package, both retroactive to two years. In a tense social climate, the hydrocarbon sector also benefited from state generosity. In 2011, Sonatrach employees received a substantial salary increase of 25 percent complemented by other benefits.

Security forces played a key role in integrating vast portions of the population. During the 1990s, militias were created as a response to both precariousness and insecurity. The *chambit* (communal guards) also integrated unemployed workers in rural areas impacted by terrorism.[70] Under Bouteflika, the ANP and the DGSN served similar goals. Between 2009 and 2014, the DGSN grew from 90,000 to 209,000 employees.[71] As for the ANP, it announced in 2011 the recruitment of additional personnel in order to compensate for the lack of places in universities.[72] The management of the precarious margins and the growth of the security apparatus thus walked hand in hand.

Meanwhile, scarcity also facilitated the co-option of once critical voices. Given the disarray of the political field and the daily difficulties encountered by activists, the cartel remained attractive by distributing positions and privileges.

> In all political parties, you have weak elements. The Algerian regime is precisely targeting these weak elements to undermine the opposition.

When they see that somebody can buy them, people sell themselves because it's the way to climb the ladder. The "System" fuels corruption, and as soon as it gets you into it, it controls you. The "System" says, "You'll serve us or you'll fall." Now, if people betray us, people who are very well-known like Khalida [Toumi], is it our fault? Is it the "System"? Or the person who betrayed us? I don't think that the RCD has anything to do with it.

(NASSIM, MEMBER OF THE COMMITTEE FOR SOCIAL AFFAIRS AND HEALTH AT THE APW OF TIZI OUZOU, RCD MEMBER, SPRING 2011)

What I find disgusting are the people who switch sides. People who were there in 1994 [for the school boycott], or who were in feminist movements, and who decided to be sellouts. The worst are those who become ministers overnight, when they used to defend the Berber cause. . . . I saw comrades doing jail time because they threw rocks at the presidential convoy. They did two years and then they were pardoned. These people were in the same associations as me, so it was a shock. But later, some of them took the jobs they were offered when they got out of jail. It really hurts to hear former comrades on the radio evoking a "historical correction" rather than a military coup when speaking about June 18 [1965].

(LOUBNA, FORMER JOURNALIST AND MEMBER OF THE FFS, PARIS, SUMMER 2010)

The RCD official and the former journalist both lamented the difficulty of maintaining radical opposition in the face of symbolic, material, and political rewards. Nassim was convinced that "oil is Algeria's curse" because it allowed the cartel to buy allegiances, while Loubna underlined the "poverty" and "vulnerability" of activists under Bouteflika. After facing repression and marginalization, stability seemed to offer an appeal that was impossible to counter. Widespread economic insecurity could thus serve to bolster the established order, as precariousness impacted the working classes as well as the intellectual, political, and economic elites. As in Tunisia before the revolution, this contributed to the edification of a political economy of domination based on uneven relations of exchange, which was not synonymous with absolute subjection and which served contradictory and conflicting interests.[73] Obedience was negotiated. It had a price, and a key feature of Bouteflika's Algeria was that management by scarcity significantly lowered this price.

A TERRORIZING SPECTACLE

The routine of the crisis was not only managed, it was also mediatized. Online rumors evoked bloody brawls between young football fans armed with swords. Newspapers depicted a litany of riots, state scandals, and strikes in a chronicle mixing fact and fiction. They told of the spectacular confrontation between the brutality of the system and that of the counter-system, thus demonstrating the potential collapse of both.[74] This is how the terrorist spirit of the crisis—in Baudrillard's sense—revealed itself, in the fascinating continuum of events and nonevents that announced anomie and shaped governance by catastrophization.

Indistinction is key to this fascinating if terrorizing spectacle.[75] At the end of 2011, the DGSN announced that it had been deployed eleven thousand times that year to "maintain public safety." Amalgamating all forms of protests into one single, crushing statistic prevented a more nuanced analysis of the causes of this unrest. The eleven thousand "gatherings, mobs, road blockage, sit-ins and non-authorized marches" were undifferentiated elements in the ongoing spectacle of the crisis, local evils monitored by the police and mediatized by the official news agency.[76] Under the scrutiny of the state, social movements were dispossessed of their singularity, which is to say their purpose. In the meantime, the statistics manufactured by the DGSN served to securitize socioeconomic unrest and objectivize the suspended disaster. Indeed, these eleven thousand interventions suggested that a threshold existed beyond which the catastrophe could no longer be mitigated.

Petty crimes gave form to a social malaise marked by seemingly deviant types of violence: sons hurting their fathers, groups of thugs brawling for the control of a given beach or parking lot. The sensationalist and depoliticized form of the spectacle, one that aims to become "the focal point of all vision and all consciousness,"[77] obscured the political nature of the conflicts fracturing the polity. Private newspapers depicted the mundane violence of a society plagued by anomie. Deviance appeared contagious, especially for a younger generation that had allegedly gone astray. A few days before the 2012 legislative elections, the daily *Liberté* dedicated its front page to "these Algerians who [were] beating their parents," revealing a "serious extension of the phenomenon."[78] National headlines deplored the growth of child trafficking and gang violence, while local reports chronicled the seemingly endless cycle of riots. Of course, the media and the state did not make all of this up; they merely accentuated a feeling of insecurity omnipresent among the urban public.

Security threats even appeared in the sports pages. In 2014, the death of football player Albert Ebossé after he was hit by a projectile thrown by a member of the crowd led the DGSN to raise the alarm about "a situation on the brink of chaos."[79] In January 2019, a month before the beginning of the Hirak, mobilized football fans were among the sharpest opponents of police brutality and the corruption of the cartel. In response, the DGSN strove to conflate their movement with forms of deviant violence. The police released a statement denouncing football fans' "deplorable deeds" and announced that 80 cases of violence had occurred over the first half of the season, causing 316 injuries (mostly to policemen) and 65 damaged cars (mostly police cars). Thousands of police officers were thus mobilized in stadiums throughout the year.[80] Once again, the conflation of various pieces of data fueled the process of catastrophization and legitimized the deployment of the security apparatus.

The law-preserving violence of the police defended a legal order seemingly on the brink of collapse, demonstrating that without obedience, the threat of anomie always looms large.[81] Paradoxically, the impending chaos served the interests of the cartel, whose figureheads weaponized socially shared anguish and posed as defenders of national and religious values. In a context of massive popular disaffiliation, the daily combination of physical and material insecurities, whether real or imagined, produced a desire for order that competed with more contentious demands for socioeconomic and political integration.

DUALIST REPRESENTATIONS OF THE POLITY

The crisis-as-routine also shaped forms of symbolic violence. Dominant discourses thus prescribed ways of thinking—the established order responds to threats to the nation; society is immature—and ways of acting—integrate redistribution networks; avoid radical dissent.[82] First and foremost, the portrayal of socioeconomic unrest as a cacophony of apolitical claims reinforced the depiction of the allegedly clientelized masses. This negative portrayal was sometimes appropriated by opponents of the ruling order, whose pro-democracy positions barely hid their mistrust of the people.

The crisis [affecting the CNCD in 2011] is above all the crisis of the elites who were supposed to lead the movement. These elites are unable to do so because they have no connection with society and never respond to its claims. This was obvious with the CNCD. I was in the first meetings as the representative of the PST. These guys, they'll tell you that people are digestive tracts [i.e., interested only in material issues], unlike those who fight for *nif* [honor] rather than for bread. They end up speaking about stupidity or a kind of anthropological flaw; the peasant spirit, if you will. They stigmatize their own people.

(SAMIR LARABI, SPOKESMAN OF THE CNDDC,
MEMBER OF THE PST, ALGIERS, SPRING 2011)

Samir lamented the elitist discourses of opposition figures. According to him, this explained the fractures within the CNCD. Surely, the self-imposed focus on social justice of most sectoral movements fueled a caricature of protesters as apolitical "digestive tracts." Far from being manufactured exclusively by the cartel's mouthpieces, this kind of prejudice was also shaped by the avoidance strategies inherent to the national repertoire of contention. The private press could also echo these representations by connecting precariousness and manipulation, thus objectivizing the link between discontent and the risk of destabilization. In an article dedicated to the spread of evangelical Christianity in Kabylia published in 2010, the daily *Ennahar* contended that foreign churches were offering visas and money to precarious youth.[83] Without looking at the political and economic reasons that could lead to such conversions (a marginal phenomenon, it must be said), the article identified two categories often associated with subversion—youth and Kabyles—as instrumentalized by foreign agents bent on fostering chaos.

Reproducing the dualist imaginary inherited from colonization and the developmental state, defensive redistributive policies were framed as proof of the cartel's responsible management of the people-as-child. At the end of February 2011, for instance, the presidency announced a series of economic gestures, including the cancellation of interest on youth loans and the distribution of 242,000 housing units in the coming year. Facing such a display of generosity, *Ennahar* could therefore argue that Bouteflika was "very aware of the aspirations of the youth," and that he was thus "very different from fallen Egyptian and Tunisian presidents . . . who did nothing to appease the anger of their citizens."[84] The representatives of the state class played a similar role, yet generosity was replaced by responsibility. For example, in 2012, Minister of Finance Karim Djoudi (in office from 2007 to 2014) explained that new economic regulations were necessary to clean up the balance sheets of private companies and monitor the price of essential products. In his technocratic jargon, he reaffirmed the necessity of continuing reforms in the name of the "good governance of public affairs" and the "prudential management of resources."[85] The dominant representation of the state apparatus thus brought together bureaucratic rationality (the state class) and paternal authority (the president). In so doing, it staged the dualist organization of the polity, as the ruling elites allegedly implemented a reasonable and benevolent process of modernization to mitigate the catastrophe, while the masses vehemently protested such measures out of a lack of maturity and composure.

Social Fatigue

The crisis-as-routine fueled widespread social fatigue. It resulted in a disaffection with politics, outbreaks of violence at the margins, and a continuous securitization of public affairs. The difficulty of mobilizing at the national level accompanied the scattering of social movements at the local and sectoral levels. As a result, social fatigue grew and seemed to limit the possibility of any major challenge to the cartel's grip on power.

THE DARK DECADE AND SOCIAL DEVIANCE

Terrorism in Algeria was not a mere "addition to the spectacle," as Baudrillard puts it. If he excels at highlighting the contradictions of the global system and their symbolic manifestations, the semiologist does not give a full account of the brutality of the phenomenon. After the 1990s, violence and insecurity remained palpably real. In previous chapters, I mentioned the lasting impact of the Dark Decade, which can only be understood in light of the widespread use of violence as a political resource and means for managing society.[86]

To understand how the civil conflict of the 1990s fueled the idea of a generalized deviance, a comparison with Colombia is enlightening. It provides us with a similar example of long-standing civil conflict and the neutralization of politics; it also helps avoid the exceptionalism endemic to commentaries on the Arab world and jihadi violence. Finally, fostering South-South comparison serves to "circumvent the Eurocentric gaze that usually accompanies studies of violence in the global South."[87]

Colombia has faced successive waves of violence, starting in 1948 with *La Violencia*, a civil war between two class coalitions dominated by liberal and conservative oligarchies, in addition to communist strongholds.[88] It then experienced a protracted asymmetric conflict marked by the fragmentation of Marxist guerrillas, the use of death squads, a rural exodus, and an economic crisis.[89] As in Algeria, these conflicts left many political issues unresolved and fueled residual forms of terrorism. In Colombia, too, the violence of the 1980s and 1990s saw a proliferation of violent actors (army, guerrillas, militias, criminal groups) and resulted in an increased illegibility. Consequently, violence occupied a growing place in popular subjectivities and seemed to permeate the entire society. Protracted conflicts naturalized the feeling of physical insecurity. The crippling and pervasive existential threat "suggested that social and political relations were continuously governed by violence."[90]

Similarly, in Bouteflika's Algeria, each petty crime harkened back to past episodes of fratricidal violence, thus reinforcing the idea of a deeply rooted and pathological aggressiveness. Society was seemingly plagued by deviance, starting with criminality and residual terrorism. At the end of the summer of 2012, *Le Quotidien d'Oran* published a special issue dedicated to a suggestive question: "Permanent Violence: Legitimate Revolt or Social Perversion?" In reference to French singer Michel Sardou, one journalist claimed that "it runs, it runs, the disease of violence." According to him, the degrees of violence that could be identified as intrinsic to different peoples resulted in different political systems.[91] Once naturalized, the alleged violence of the Algerian people could thus serve as an explanation for the resilience of the political order.

Rather than a new Dark Decade, the latency of the crisis could also result in a regression to pure savagery: bands of teenagers armed with clubs, setting up roadblocks, extorting money from their elders, burning cars and looting shops. The colonial image of feral street children (*yaouled*) certainly evoked some of the most mythical figures of the revolution (Ali la Pointe, Petit Omar), but it also referred to the threatening misery that the developmental state was supposed to eradicate in order to modernize the nation after 1962.[92] In many of the depictions of the 2011 urban uprising that I encountered, the chaotic figure of the lumpenized youth resurfaced. Society seemed under threat from a process of "decivilization," a regression that would reactivate the violent reflexes of the masses and annihilate collective and individual security.[93] For a country allegedly plagued by the "disease of violence," contentious and radical demands for change could seem like a perilous roll of dice. Some opponents could therefore suggest that one should wait for the cartel to reform itself.

> I don't think that [change] will come from the radicalism of the street, from violence or from any kind of unrest. We need to avoid falling back into these cyclical and nihilistic phenomena. If change must come, it will be the consequence of an internal evolution in the regime, and notably at the head of the army.
>
> (SOUFIANE DJILALI, FORMER GENERAL SECRETARY OF
> THE PARTY OF ALGERIAN RENEWAL, ALGIERS, AUTUMN 2010)

Like other critics of the cartel, Djilali, the future founder of the liberal party Jil Jadid, was weary of mass violence. He also underlined the need to educate the population in order to restrain its chaotic impulses. Under the threat of the suspended disaster, the masses were therefore declared unfit to emancipate themselves. The Dark Decade had surely proven the polity's fragility, especially after the outbreak of civilian massacres in 1997–1998.

THE SECURITY PACT

As political and media discourses presented violence as an essential feature of the Algerian character, they legitimated a type of governance by catastrophization that confined the polity to the narrow path of development and security. For many, the cartel was a default Leviathan, a deeply flawed sovereign whose function was to prevent Algerians from reverting to their chaotic impulses.

> Personally, I am completely anti-Bouteflika, but I wouldn't like him to fall today. Not now; it would be the worst thing that could happen. My problem is that the institution, good or evil, should not fall during a chaotic

period. And we are currently experiencing a period of extreme chaos. . . . The current regime has planned the chaos. I think that a chaotic society cannot start a revolution. It can rise up, but it won't produce change.

(MOHAND, FORMER OFFICIAL OF THE FFS
AND PAST MEMBER OF THE RCD, TIZI OUZOU, SPRING 2011)

Mohand confessed that he felt less and less like a "democrat." He was convinced that the upheavals in neighboring countries were mere "revolts guided by a desire for social revenge." While he rejoiced at the fall of Ben 'Ali in Tunisia, he also felt that these uprisings would only lead to more destruction, as he didn't see any credible alternatives in the Arab world.

By combining management by scarcity, nonlethal policing, and dualist discourses, the cartel laid the foundations of a "pact of security." Both physical and economic in nature, it responded to the vulnerabilities of the community and its members.[94] Such a pact might be understood from a "contractualist" perspective. Yet it also fits within the framework for securing popular support proposed by theorists of counterinsurrection.[95] Indeed, unlike a traditional social contract, the security pact doesn't enshrine consent as much as a reluctant obedience aimed at preserving one's life. It doesn't demonstrate legitimacy as much as popular exhaustion. During the Dark Decade, the combination of extreme violence and economic restructuring had increased the value of peace, to the benefit of the cartel. Under Bouteflika, the combination of precariousness, fear, and exhaustion bolstered the value of the stability proposed by the cartel through its security and redistributive policies.

Returning to the example of Colombia, the period of *La Violencia* that followed the murder of President Jorge Eliécer Gaitán resulted in the estrangement of society from politics. Meanwhile, armed factions sharing similar economic interests ensured the survival of the dominant order. After the formation of the Frente Nacional in 1958, ruling elites were able to weaponize Hobbes's *summum malum*, the threat of death, by claiming that their coalition was the population's only protection against a return to barbarism.[96] Yet the status quo remained fragile. While Hobsbawm viewed *La Violencia* as leading to the demoralization of the masses and the weakening of leftist parties, he also argued that the situation remained highly uncertain. "Superficially the situation looks stable, but this is plainly an illusory phenomenon," he wrote, adding that the possibility for "a social revolution both of the peasantry and of the urban poor is patently obvious."[97] Forty years later, the criminalization of social unrest and the securitization of politics by the Uribe government were still firmly opposed by the continuous mobilization of the socioeconomic fringes and Indigenous groups demanding radical change.[98]

Similarly, one could argue that the Dark Decade shaped the security pact under Bouteflika, but that the structural conditions for an uprising were nonetheless present. Until 2019, this pact revived the necropolitical paradigm inherited from the War of Liberation. Death was past, present, and future, the underlying argument of a political offer based on the prevention of the disaster. Monitoring and mitigating the threats, assessing the need for regulatory measures and exceptional punishments, the Algerian cartel thus pushed the government by insecurity to its extreme, without ever suppressing discontent.

CONTINUING THE STRUGGLE

Even in a period of peace and growth, death and misery remained default arguments in favor of obedience. The cartel's figureheads played the roles of both father and Leviathan. They repeated that the people knew the price of chaos and should not let itself be manipulated by Algeria's enemies. Meanwhile, their long-standing opponents aimed to outlive the crisis. For many, the price of political commitment and the lack of rewards led to a sense of exhaustion.

> At the end of the 1980s, we felt that a blow was coming, the masses were about to move. We ended up with these terrible years, and we continued our activism nonetheless. But at the end of the civil war, when you have lost comrades, after years of checkpoints and false checkpoints when you leave your house, you just feel exhausted. When I decided to stop, in 2002, it was because I didn't have the strength to do it anymore. I was drained. Socially, for me, the situation was very difficult. It was unsustainable. So I went back to work for the family business.
>
> (NACER, FOUNDING MEMBER OF THE PST, ALGIERS, SPRING 2012)

Nacer's hope of seeing the masses rise up vanished at the end of the Dark Decade. When I met him in Algiers, he was in a bar, downing beer after beer in rapid succession. He had come to Algiers in order to register a patent for an electrical generator powered by the tides. He had seized this opportunity to greet the younger PST members who had facilitated our encounter.

Between the late 1960s and the early 1990s, leftist movements in the Arab world faced a series of setbacks that fueled disenchantment and melancholy.[99] In Algeria, the political opening that followed October 1988 came with the questioning of the socialist legacy of the revolution, the ascendance of Islamist movements, and a rise in violence. According to a former mujahid and member of the Party of the Socialist Vanguard, Abdelalim Medjaoui, this led to the "political demoralization" of leftist activists.[100] Nacer continued to be active until the beginning of the 2000s, when the Kabyle Black Spring and economic hardships led him to abandon politics and seek what he described as a "normal life."

His personal story illustrated the fatigue generated by thirty years of crisis. As politics were viewed with suspicion and activism was felt to garner few tangible rewards, individuals had to ponder the cost of their commitment. Success in the short term seemed unlikely. Rather than offering a direct challenge to the cartel's grip on the state, resistance became ever more focused on ensuring that political organizations and individuals could preserve the idea of an alternative and promote counter-discourses to that end. Following Gramsci's recommendation, the priority was given to the war of position over the war of maneuver. Yet even this inscription in the long game was made uncertain by widespread exhaustion.

> One should not be afraid of self-criticism, including in RAJ, and we must admit that maybe we didn't give ourselves the means to come up with something new. The next stage is to be able to attract people, or resistance will only grow weaker. Let's take an image that I use often: the day before yesterday, there were 15 of us. Yesterday, there were 10 of us. Today, 5. Tomorrow, 3, and the next day, he will be alone. I'll stop here because I want to be positive.... It is demoralizing to see that we struggle to question ourselves and that we fail to move on to the next stage. I'm not demoralized yet, but many eventually give up. There is nevertheless a kind of satisfaction that counterbalances a potential demoralization: the fact that we have resisted this *Pouvoir* and the silence of the world for so long.
>
> (NIDHAL, ELECTED OFFICIAL OF THE FFS AND FOUNDING MEMBER OF RAJ, ALGIERS, AUTUMN 2010)

While some might find reward in the act of protesting publicly, this was not the case for Nidhal anymore. He was wary that an opposition that aims merely to survive might be progressively erased by the tide of social fatigue.

And yet despite these grim prospects, activists scrambled to create new possibilities and foster a convergence among struggles. Some, like Samir Larabi, strove to overcome the broad disaffection vis-à-vis politics by taking part in social movements, notably the CNDDC. Others, like Abdelouahab Fersaoui, the president of RAJ, aimed to promote better coordination between associations. As for Nidhal, he shared his experience with the younger generation and tried to develop forms of solidarity in Europe. Yet the passing of time did nothing to fuel his optimism. "In 1995, we were able to organize a concert for peace with ten thousand people that continued all night long. Today, we would have neither the venue, nor the people," he stated a few days before the 2014 presidential elections. Given their difficulty in mobilizing and occupying public spaces, opponents of the cartel often turned their gaze toward the struggles occurring within the labyrinthine spaces of the ruling order, as if liberation was to come from a spontaneous collapse.

TESTIFYING

Governance by catastrophization aimed to reinsert the country into the continuum of security and development. Yet from the perspective of the population, such a normalization was far from obvious. Rather than imagining some pacified future, pervasive uncertainty and precariousness kept many Algerians in a situation of emergency. Popular discourses did not describe the successful suspension of a potential disaster; rather, they unfolded in a catastrophic present separated from the nation's glorious past and in which the future seemed inaccessible.[101]

Algerian rap music was notoriously astute in its depiction of this constant state of emergency and the revolutionary potential resulting from it, both of which are at the heart of Benjamin's tradition of the oppressed.[102] In his song "Houkouma" (2011), Lotfi DK thus spoke of a "chained generation" abandoned by its government and hoping to find liberation through emigration. Many other songs described the absurd existence of a lost generation.[103] Far from accepting dominant discourses, these testimonies revealed the disjointed nature of time in Algeria. They depicted a reality that was neither cumulative nor progressive, but disarticulated, dislocated, and shattered.[104] Perhaps the most iconic depiction of this catastrophic experience is to be found in the song "La Casa Del Mouradia," which starts like this:

Sa'at lefjer w ma djani num
Rani nconsomi ghir bi shuya
Shkun esseba w shkun ellum
Melina lem'aicha hadia

Dawn is coming and I can't sleep
I'm doing [drugs] nice and slow
Who is right and who is to blame?
We're growing tired of this life

First performed in 2018 by Ouled el-Bahdja, a group of football fans, the song became one of the anthems of the 2019 Hirak. It expressed the entrapment and disillusionment of working-class youth, in a context of growing political absurdity and widespread economic predation.

This fractured existence was depicted in films centered on the vulnerability of the female body, the quest for recognition, and the difficulty to achieve social change.[105] Following figures such as Malek Bensmaïl or Habiba Djahnine, the burgeoning field of documentary film also played a central role in producing vivid testimonies of subaltern lived experiences.[106] When we first met in 2011, Habiba explained that she viewed her craft as providing a response to a grassroots need for representation, for depictions of the complexity of the Algerian reality.[107] Bringing together social realism and more symbolic forms, the visual testimonies of Algerian filmmakers reflect ordinary people's daily struggles, frustrations, and dreams. In *Of Sheep and Men* (2017), for instance, Karim Sayad looks at a group of men inhabiting the urban margins of the capital as they train their fighting rams and prepare for Aid al-Adha. He casts a poetic light on a society that could be at once caring and cruel, and where hopes for a distant future meet the inequalities of the present. Under no illusions as to the reality he inhabits, one of the documentary's main protagonists, Samir, explains that "in this country, the big fish eats the little one. If you have money, health, and power, you can do anything. If you don't have anything, like me, you eat bread and you shut up."

The theme of entrapment was a recurring feature of these subaltern chronicles. Beyond her proclaimed desire to fight negative representations of Algeria, Habiba Djahnine emphasized the weight of this entrapment, which she viewed as a legacy of the Dark Decade. "People suffocate. They can't do it anymore," she said. This feeling of social stagnation and forced immobility, of "confinement permeating day-to-day life spent in claustrophobic" environments, was summed up by Hakim Abderazzak as the *cementery*. Coupled with the need to risk one's life in order to escape entrapment, this is a central theme in many works of fiction and nonfiction depicting Bouteflika's Algeria.[108] In Hassan Ferhani's award-winning poetic documentary *A Roundabout in My Head* (2015), Youssef, a young man working in a slaughterhouse, explains the tension resulting from the need to flee a state of nonexistence. "Three things happen to any young Algerian: either you commit suicide, you fill your head with drugs and become a living dead, or you go do the *harga*. Any young person will tell you the same thing. Being a man from a respected family and working hard, that doesn't exist. Inshallah, I won't be a thug or a drug addict, but a *harrag*, that I'll do. I'll leave or kill myself. This plays like a loop in my head. Cross the sea or kill myself."

The experience of the crisis was therefore synonymous with a strong sense of unbearability. It fueled a longing for change expressed in the various cultural vectors used to testify to subaltern experiences. The ruling elites were especially targeted. A couple of months before Bouteflika's reelection for a fourth mandate, Lotfi DK released the song "Klehoua" (2014), a violent lyrical charge against a cartel that had "eaten" the country and stolen its wealth with the complicity of foreign companies. The catastrophic existence of the oppressed kept open the possibility of a messianic zero hour, a revolutionary moment connected to past struggles.[109] Algerian rap music notoriously appropriated the legacy of the War of Liberation to formulate a subversive counter-discourse.[110] For instance, Donquishoot and Diaz, both members of the group MBS, denounced the cartel's colonial-like domination in a song entitled "La bataille d'Alger" (2016). Reviving a revolutionary imaginary and weaponizing the heroic image of nationalist insurgent Ali la Pointe, the two rappers notably described an "administration dressed as paratroopers" (*al-i'dara labsa para*).

The emergency of the present demonstrated the necessity of a different socioeconomic and political system. As shown in Bahia Bencheikh El-Fegoun's documentary *Fragments de rêves* (2017), the desire for profound structural change remained acute, even after the backlash following the 2011 uprisings throughout the Arab world. In order to achieve such a change, pacifism was often presented as the only alternative. Even rappers who were virulent critics of the cartel repeatedly emphasized their rejection of violence in their songs.[111] By denouncing internal colonialism and advocating for nonviolence, these artistic testimonies contributed to the national repertoire of contention. Indeed, despite widespread social fatigue, the popular state of emergency laid the groundwork for the peaceful uprising of 2019.

The Absent Revolution

The lived experience of the crisis did not guarantee that a revolutionary moment would occur. Indeed, the Dark Decade had durably invalidated the use of violence. Moreover, opposition parties were profoundly discredited (see chapters 4 and 5). Undeniably, the revolutionary hypothesis did not only suffer from the inscrutability of the *Pouvoir*. It was also crippled by the absence of a coherent and organized alternative. Until 2019, socioeconomic mobilizations and the efforts of opposition parties failed to give birth to a "dual power" in Algeria.[112] Politicians and activists calling for radical change were never in a position to effectively threaten the cartel's domination. Because of their mutual distrust, as well as various repressive strategies, oppositional coalitions were short-lived.

Throughout the 2010s, the Algerian *Lumpenproletariat* and workers expressed their socioeconomic grievances by achieving greater levels of organization. In some cases, they benefited from the support of a politically diverse intelligentsia (human rights lawyers, critical journalists, academics with liberal, leftist, and Islamist sensibilities). This contentious configuration was also shaped by generational dynamics. Indeed, Algerian youth were increasingly defined by their experience of the crisis and in opposition to the ruling elites.[113] In short, despite the lack of a clear, unified, and organized alternative to the cartel, the social and political situation seemed ripe for a revolutionary mobilization.

Until February 2019, such an uprising was nonetheless considered unlikely by most observers, including myself. It is certainly not uncommon for a revolutionary movement to remain unthinkable until it occurs.[114] Revolutionary situations are unpredictable and undetermined. They bring together long-standing processes and chains of actions and decisions that can result in reformist, reactionary, or revolutionary outcomes.[115] In Algeria, the possibility of a disastrous turning point became a defining feature of governance: for two decades, reformist and repressive policies responded to the ever-present possibility of collapse. Thus, grassroots mobilizations made the imperative of avoiding a new episode of mass violence a key element of their strategies. As the case of the CNDDC demonstrates, poorly endowed protesters developed a repertoire of contention adapted to the suspended disaster and continued to make radical claims.

Yet radical change remained seemingly out of reach. The defensive policies implemented by the cartel allowed for the management of society through repression and redistribution, while derogatory discourses portrayed the masses as impatient and suggestible. The crisis continued. In its own way, the ongoing emergency called for diagnoses and the assignment of responsibility.[116] Efforts to conceptualize political action had once fueled the sacrificial violence of the Dark Decade by orienting the struggle toward a satanic pole situated within the *ṭāghūt* state. Under Bouteflika, opponents and intellectuals sought to make sense of a polity seemingly frozen in an existential crisis. As the next chapter shows, identifying the reasons for and the solutions to this continuing state of affairs became their central preoccupation.

7
In Search of Lost Meaning

When a polity is in crisis, the times are unhinged, running off course; time itself lacks its capacity to contain us and conjoin us.

—*Wendy Brown*

One only ceases to be colonized when one ceases being colonizable. This is an immutable law. And this grave problem cannot be resolved by drawing on simple aphorisms, or more or less coarse monologues, but rather by profound transformations of our being: each one of us must be re-adapted, progressively, to their social functions and their spiritual dignity.

—*Malek Bennabi*

From the onset of the Algerian crisis until February 2019, the idea that the country might fail was a recurring theme. In their memoirs, disillusioned high-ranking officials depicted this derailed historical trajectory as the consequence of the hijacking of the postindependence state and the systematic squandering of the country's national resources.[1] As this penultimate chapter will discuss negative representations of the polity, it is necessary to open with a few words about this narrative of failure. In fact, despite the setbacks of the 1980s and

1990s, Algeria's accomplishments as an independent postcolonial state remain unquestionable. The literacy rate has increased fourfold since 1962 to become one of the highest in Africa. Attendance rates in primary school exceed 97 percent and millions of students have gained access to publicly funded higher education. When they are duly enforced, Algerian labor rights remain more favorable to workers than in many countries in the Global North. The economic debacle of the 1980s and 1990s did not erase the spectacular improvement in living conditions that had taken place over the previous twenty years. Lastly, while the meaning of Algerianness remains a matter of debate, it is nonetheless a powerful vector of identification, which is an achievement for a formerly colonized nation. In short, the narrative of failure overshadows a record of genuine accomplishment. Yet at the same time, it testifies to the gap between the promises of 1962 and the state of the country in February 2019.

Fractured by contentious representations of national identity, Algeria has undoubtedly displayed some of the features of Mbembe's postcolony, starting with its "chaotic plurality" and "internal coherence."[2] As a specific system of signs, Algeria was shaped by the anti-imperialist, developmentalist, and populist mythology crafted in the 1960s. These themes remained central to public discourse. In May 2018, for instance, the general secretary of the FLN, Djamel Ould Abbes, praised the president who had saved the country from terrorism, reduced unemployment, and built millions of housing units for the people.[3] Turning these myths into accepted truths implied that they would become "part of the people's common sense" and an integral part of the "period's consciousness."[4] Yet the suspension of the disaster was unlikely to validate the grandiose claims made by Bouteflika's closest supporters.

As a result, this chapter analyzes the struggle for meaning within a postcolonial order in crisis and the competition between two profoundly contradictory narratives regarding the character of the people. The first one was based on the ideal of political sanctity inherited from the War of Liberation. This representation of the people was associated with various figures of martyrdom and exemplified the revolutionary potential inherent in the masses. It served a dichotomous discourse by pitting the people against the "gang" that had privatized the state and blaming the latter for Algeria's ills. A second depiction of the people echoed the narrative of cultural malaise widespread throughout the Arab world.[5] As experts, politicians, and journalists depicted a population that had failed to embrace the principles of political modernity, they described its alleged atavistic cultural features as the root cause of the crisis. Blaming the people or the "System" was an inherently political activity. After the identification of the problem (naming), and before the formulation of a proposition (claiming), blaming served to situate responsibility.[6] These public discussions aimed to identify culprits and political priorities. Eventually, the enduring ideal of political sanctity fashioned some of the counter-discourses that made the symbolic revolution of February 2019 possible.

The Rule of Uncertainty

Frantz Fanon once explained that the anticolonial struggle had produced a "very clear and comprehensible image for action, which could be appropriated by the individuals constituting the colonized people."[7] Yet the crisis weakened the stable framework inherited from the period of decolonization, as it made political processes seemingly autonomous and unpredictable.[8] The Dark Decade and the economic collapse of the 1980s–1990s confounded the prefabricated explanations proposed by great ideologies (socialism, Islamism, nationalism). With the disappearance of a political objectivity that mystified and reassured at the same time, the social world appeared artificial, unreliable, and saturated with contradictions.

THE RISE AND FALL OF THE THIRD WORLDIST EPISTEME

In 1962, the developmental state faced a dire situation. Yet the country had "unlimited expectations" and its leaders were committed to "achieving the impossible."[9] The new state pushed for the construction of a national economy liberated from foreign influence. Whereas Ben Bella tried to implement a "specific socialism" in a chaotic context, Boumediene pursued economic autonomy in a more organized fashion. After 1965, "the cycle for Algeria's evolution seemed perfectly planned; all things were coming together."[10]

With its ambition and urgency, this endeavor testified to the emergence of new conditions for truth production, the rise of a Third Worldist episteme. In the midst of decolonization, a newly born Algerian state scrambled to reinterpret the meaning of socialism, tradition, nationalism, self-management, and development in ways that were both unsettling and inspiring to foreign observers.[11] This new episteme shaped controversial education policies, such as the ban on colonial social sciences (ethnology and anthropology) and the program of Arabization.[12] Domestically, the state, the ANP, and the FLN embodied the public interest. Amid marked tensions, this triptych had to formulate a new way to think and be in the world. In 1971, the agrarian revolution and the nationalization of hydrocarbons concretized this effort based on the assertion of the rights of the once colonized people. In foreign affairs, Algeria was at the forefront of the struggle to rebalance the international system and create a world order freed from neocolonialist plots. In various international fora, summits, and at the UN General Assembly, its spokesmen advocated for the suppression of external debts and for sovereign control over national resources.[13] The country had by then become an international reference point, glorified for its revolution, respected for its diplomatic achievements, and scrutinized for its attempts to foster industrial modernity while reviving the "Algerian personality." The Third Worldist episteme made legible the new world born out of the ashes of colonialism.

These ambitions nonetheless collided with structural limits resulting from a century of foreign domination concluded by a violent war of liberation. Chief among the contradictions embodied by the new political order was its tendency to negate the multiple political sensibilities initially present within the FLN and instead promote the monolithic understanding of history and politics favored by bureaucratic-military apparatuses.[14] Initially latent, this postcolonial paradox soon appeared in broad daylight, as when Third Worldist discourses emphasizing emancipation, sovereignty, and authenticity encountered the primacy of bureaucratic-military apparatuses, dependency, and a profound acculturation. One hundred and thirty-two years of colonization were unlikely to bring about a tabula rasa. The population was impoverished and the economy turned outwards. Controlled by a divided elite, the state was dependent on foreign aid to train its police, military officers, and technocrats.[15]

Under Boumediene, the government spoke with a strong and relatively coherent voice in order to direct the energy of the state toward the development of productive means. Yet the rapid social and economic modernization favored by the advocates of Third Worldism had disruptive effects,[16] and many of the policies enacted between 1965 and 1978 helped to bring about the socioeconomic disorders that would subsequently afflict the country. While the sustainability of the entire developmental edifice rested on hydrocarbon rents, the resolutely industrialist and urban options prioritized by the government exacerbated the rural crisis. Facing rapid demographic growth and internal migration, public authorities struggled to provide new urban dwellers with services and opportunities to facilitate their socioeconomic insertion.[17] Initiated in a top-down fashion, the Arabization program also produced mixed results. Intended to counter acculturation, it accentuated Berberist grievances, crippled the education system, and reinforced social dualism by making French the language of the elites.[18] Finally, Third Worldist internationalism collapsed in the 1980s, as its beacons were undermined by their own shortcomings, their insertion into the global economic system, and a surge of new identity-based mobilizations.[19]

The crisis that culminated during the Dark Decade nonetheless contributed to a widespread representation of Boumediene's rule as a kind of golden age. The 1970s came to represent a moment of clarity before the collapse of the polity, a reminder of the faith that had once been placed in the project of national emancipation and community building.[20] This myth of a golden age accentuated the idea that Bouteflika's Algeria had somehow run aground. Yet beyond the discourse of failure, the modernizing and emancipatory ambitions situated at the core of the Third Worldist project carried the germs of disillusionment.

THE CIVIL WAR THAT WASN'T

The Dark Decade not only interrupted the anticipated trajectory of development; it also served as an epistemic vacuum, as the nature of what had happened to the country became a topic of controversy. Algerian officials still carefully avoid the label "civil war" (*ḥarb āʾhliyya*) and instead refer to the "National Tragedy" (*al-Māʾsāa al-Waṭaniyya*) or, more commonly, the Dark Decade (*al-ʿUshriyya as-Sawdāaʾ*). Indeed, acknowledging the occurrence of a civil war would undermine the unitarian narrative on which the state was built after 1954. It would also amount to recognizing the political nature of the violence perpetrated by Islamist groups, and therefore accepting the potential legitimacy of some of their claims. Consequently, from Zeroual's law on *rahma* (forgiveness) to Bouteflika's National Reconciliation, efforts to settle the conflict focused exclusively on material and judicial aspects at the expense of political issues. Islamist radicals were thus systematically criminalized and depoliticized.

From an academic standpoint, the notion of civil war is more commonly used in the francophone literature, following the seminal work of Luis Martinez.[21] This does not mean that such a frame has been universally accepted. The anthropologist Abderrahmane Moussaoui, for instance, another astute observer of the violence of the 1990s, remarks that the "civil war" moniker made little sense to the actors involved, and he generally avoids using it for that reason.[22] Most critiques of the notion come from anglophone scholars.[23] Some accurately underline the fact that the conflict did not oppose two delineated and territorialized groups waging war against each other.[24] This lack of clarity demonstrates the failure of the Islamist insurgents to durably secure any territorial foothold. As a result, if a revolutionary civil war is defined as an "organized and two-sided struggle" in which parties achieve a kind of parity,[25] such a conflict did not occur in Algeria. A second argument is somewhat more problematic. Its key proponent is Hugh Roberts, who argues that the violence of the 1990s had "no grounding in political principles." He explains the absence of a clash between two discrete, institutionalized sides, and the lack of cohesion among insurgent Islamist forces, by the fact that politics in Algeria are inherently nonideological and factionalized.[26] While competing groups certainly used violence to extract resources, this last line of argument invokes a well-known Orientalist and depoliticizing trope.

More recent academic works have rehabilitated the moniker and applied it to the Dark Decade and its aftermath.[27] In fact, the definition of a civil war is itself unstable and dependent on the political and cultural context in which such conflicts take place. A recurring feature is that actors claiming an uncontested political legitimacy, especially governments, refuse to view their adversaries as enemies in a civil war.[28] The Algerian Dark Decade would nevertheless match most civil war typologies, whether they are based on a minimalist definition of civil war as a conflict opposing organized groups who compete for power in a given region or country,[29] or on a more comprehensive set of criteria.[30] A clear dualism, with two politically coherent warring parties of roughly equal strength, is not necessary for a civil war to occur, as the case of Lebanon shows.[31] Moreover, with the factionalization and privatization of their military groups, their lack of political cohesion, and their shrinking social base, Islamist insurgents have displayed the key features of the ideal-typical losers of a revolutionary civil war.[32]

The rejection of the term in public discourses surely demonstrates a posteriori the insurgents' failure to secure popular support. Yet negating the civil and therefore political nature of the conflict in Algeria ignores the grievances formulated between 1988 and 1992. The desire to create an Islamic state, the rejection of a biased electoral law, the interruption of the electoral process, and the repression of the FIS were clear political motives behind the rise in violence, regardless of whether they were formulated in religious terms or denied by the state.[33] This does not mean that violence was not equally driven by material motives, starting with greed. But wars are complex social phenomena in which motives are entangled, and individual greed and deeper communal grievances often interact.[34] Eventually, this semantic choice reproduces a widespread tendency to silence Islamist actors. Insurrectional Islamism is always a matter of state sovereignty. Yet it is often demonized and *in fine* depoliticized.[35]

Crucially, the debate surrounding the use of the notion of civil war illustrates the epistemic instability that characterized Bouteflika's Algeria. Acute observers emphasized the shortcomings inherent in these normative efforts to categorize the conflict, which ended up forcing certain analytical frameworks onto the country and reproducing uncertainty.[36] Nevertheless, the lack of a socially shared explanation for the disintegration of the polity in the 1990s contributed to a broader state of mistrust and disbelief.

"QUI TUE QUI?"

In the 1980s, John Entelis explained that the country was "governed by a complex network of interactive structures that provide[d] institutional stability, direction, and predictability to the political system."[37] Some thirty-five years later, this statement seems to describe a different country. After October 1988, certainty vanished. In a book published in 1990, journalist Abed Charef strove to explain the events that had shaken the nation. Among other theses, he argued that the uprising could have been the result of foreign manipulation aimed at preventing the creation of an anti-Western Maghrebi front between Algeria and Libya. Referring to subversive actions perpetrated by the United States, France, or Saudi Arabia, Charef asked multiple questions ("Who benefits from the crime?," "Who paid?") without arriving at a definitive explanation.[38] In his eyes, the causes of the uprising remained uncertain. As Algeria strayed from the providential path laid out for it by revolutionaries and planners, the search for culprits intensified. Some twenty years later, suspicion persisted.

> I think that the events of October 5 were maybe encouraged to prevent the situation from maturing. It would explain why the *Pouvoir* reacted by letting the situation worsen. Some people connected to the "System" were leaders in these protests. There was something in this disorder that was a little too organized for me, and the question remains open.
>
> (ABDELKRIM DAHMEN, MEMBER OF THE NATIONAL COUNCIL OF THE MSP, FORMER DEPUTY OF TIPAZA, ALGIERS, AUTUMN 2008)

Abdelkrim was not alone in suggesting the potential manipulation of the October uprising. Berberist and leftist activists often pointed to the ambiguous role played by Islamist leaders who allegedly "disappeared" shortly before the army opened fire on a march they had organized on October 10. Opponents of all sides found the instrumentalization of protests by a faction in the cartel to be a plausible hypothesis. This idea had been echoed by high-ranking officers who commanded security organs at the time.[39] Former leaders of the FIS, including Madani, also argued that Islamist activists were manipulated by military intelligence. This narrative penetrated popular culture. In the movie *Bab El-Oued City* (1994), for instance, Merzak Allouache depicts the rise of fundamentalism while suggesting the implication of Machiavellian state actors. Radical contestation was thus increasingly associated with the suggestibility of the masses.

In 1994, political scientist Rachid Tlemçani explained that the political and criminal violence perpetrated by competing groups had become increasingly entangled and confusing.[40] Following a surge in political assassinations, the question of *qui tue qui?* (who kills whom?) appeared in public discussion. From President Mohamed Boudiaf to Islamist leader Abdelkader Hachani, general secretary of the UGTA Abdelhak Benhamouda or former head of military intelligence Kasdi Merbah, the list of prominent victims grew. Blurry motives, competing claims, denials by alleged perpetrators, and families of victims rejecting the official version—all conspired to lend these murders an enduring sense of mystery.

Speaking outside the country, military whistle-blowers nurtured the narrative of "who kills whom?" Mohamed Samraoui, a former number two within the Directorate of Counterintelligence who became a human rights activist in the 2000s, claimed that his former employer actively supported *takfiri* groups and manipulated Djamal Zitouni, the infamous emir of the GIA between 1994 and 1996.[41] The testimonies of whistle-blowers painted a particularly grim picture of the military leaders of the *éradicateurs* camp as a ruthless praetorian aristocracy. In his book *La sale guerre* (Dirty war), former special operations officer Habib Souaïdia wrote that the soldiers tasked with false flag "throat slitting missions" were given euphoria-inducing drugs to perform their criminal duties.[42] In a testimony broadcasted in 2010 on a Tunisian cable television channel, Karim Moulay, a former agent of the DRS, affirmed that the massacre of Beni Messous was perpetrated in September 1997 on the orders of General Toufik Mediene to facilitate the acquisition of vacated lands.[43] In these unprovable accounts, cold (albeit sordid) calculations and homicidal madness seemed to walk hand in hand. Mohamed Samraoui notoriously attributed the following line to Smaïn Lamari, his superior at the Directorate of Counterintelligence: "I am ready and committed to eliminate three million Algerians if needed, to maintain the order threatened by Islamists."[44]

In short, former officers depicted a military hierarchy that had actively massacred its own population for political and material reasons. We reconnect here with a central feature of Algerian necropolitics: the alleged ability of the security apparatus to plunge the country into extreme violence if people dared to oppose their agenda. This promise of a bloodbath suggested a dramatic imbalance between the unfathomable sovereign, who could slaughter large numbers of people at will in order to prevail, and its expendable subjects, who could be sacrificed for their insubordination.

The testimonies of these whistle-blowers also generated doubts, notably regarding their motives. Far from elucidating the past, they contributed to the proliferation of contradictory theories.

> The MOAL [sic],[45] it's a manipulation. It's the DRS, obviously. These officers who write books, they don't tell us anything new. A guy like Samraoui

changes his mind about the diplomat Hassani, who had been arrested for his role in the murder of Ali Mécili.[46] First, he says that it's him, then he says that it's not him anymore. One cannot trust these people. Everything that comes out of their mouths, you take it with extreme caution. Those who are close to the gods don't speak, or if they do, it's only to add more confusion.

(AMEZZA, FORMER MEMBER OF THE RCD'S
REGIONAL OFFICE IN TIZI OUZOU, PARIS, SPRING 2011)

Amezza's doubts were not uncommon. As they often contradicted each other, these "free" officers could be portrayed as yet another manipulation by the "deep state." Each book trying to uncover the dynamics at work during the Dark Decade was thus met with suspicion. Meanwhile, Khaled Nezzar portrayed the French publishers that released many of these books as serving the interests of human rights fundamentalists committed to decapitating the ANP.

As a result, a new line of questioning took shape, this one expressing mistrust toward those who interrogated the country's recent history. For instance, Mohamed Sifaoui, an independent journalist and the disgraced ghostwriter behind Souaïdia's book, dedicated several pages of one of his own volumes to the revelations of former ANP propagandist Hichem Aboud. According to Sifaoui, Aboud worked for the DRS in order to discredit those who tried to reveal the truth about the Dark Decade.[47] There is some irony in the fact that a member of the FFS told me the exact same thing about Sifaoui in 2012. Indeed, after "who kills whom?" came the theme of "who writes what?" The literary and media field were thus contaminated by the dominant political rationality of suspicion.

MANIPULITIS

Confusion was the result of the collapse of "the institutional order [that] represents a shield against terror" in the realm of meaning.[48] Much like the War of Liberation, the violence of the Dark Decade represented an epistemological break and invalidated the foundations of the preexisting political order. Underlining the continuities between the two conflicts experienced by Algeria over the past seventy years can be problematic, especially if it results in reading the 1990s as a mere consequence of the violent imposition of colonial modernity.[49] This can lead to an oversimplification of the 1990s as a conflict opposing society to a colonial-like state. The comparison was nonetheless central to the violent actors on all sides, as they often saw their struggle as a continuation of the war for national liberation.[50] There were also practical commonalities. Indeed, both asymmetric conflicts resulted in the use of similar forms of psychological warfare as a way to undermine the enemy's cohesion and secure the population's support.

During the War of Liberation, the French Army imported disinformation tactics that had previously been used in Indochina. To foster division within nationalist ranks, the French notably forwarded lists of "traitors" to the insurgents. The resulting paranoia was named *bleuite*, in reference to the fighters who were "turned" by the French and used to spread misinformation.[51] During the Dark Decade, the alleged manipulation of Islamist groups by the security apparatus led journalists Rabha Attaf and Fausto Giudice to speak of a "great blue fear." According to them, the conscious attempt to terrorize the population was part of a "sanitary program" that aimed to dissuade anyone from becoming involved in politics. The two authors saw a clear parallel between the actions of the ANP and the program of disinformation once implemented by the French Army.[52]

Under Bouteflika, many authors suggested the active support of the French state for the Algerian security services. One of the most convincing books in this regard is certainly Lounis Aggoun and Jean-Baptiste Rivoire's *Françalgérie, crimes et mensonges d'États* (Francealgeria, state crimes and lies), published in 2004. Yet while extremely well-documented, this book is also symptomatic of a vision of politics in which spontaneity and contingency vanish to make room for a rational world organized by sophisticated conspiracies. Such a depiction overlooks the fact that structural uncertainty also touched state actors. Despite their reliance on psychological warfare and violence, the ruling elites were also forced to improvise. The praetorians were not exempt from the very *bleuite* whose spread they enabled. Indeed, diplomatic cables sent by the American embassy in 2008 described the heads of the various parts of Algerian security apparatus as especially paranoid.[53]

The fear of manipulation fashioned oppositional strategies and the responses of public authorities. Even seemingly apolitical demands could appear suspicious.

> When I was in my second year in botany, I told my classmates that we should ask for the head of the department to integrate internships into the curriculum. When our cohort presented him with the letter we had written, he insisted on knowing who was behind the initiative. And when he discovered it was me, he told everyone that I was politicized, that I was here to manipulate people. Right away, I saw some classmates coming to me and asking questions. They became suspicious and distanced themselves from our initiative. It took a lot of time to make them understand that it was not about political manipulation but just a legitimate request.
>
> (ABDELHAMID, MEMBER OF RAJ'S NATIONAL OFFICE, FFS SYMPATHIZER, TIZI OUZOU, SPRING 2011)

While making what he viewed as was a purely pedagogical request, Abdelhamid had to defend himself against accusations of manipulation. Many student activists confirmed his testimony: *bleuite* was indeed widespread at the university. Among associations and labor unions, in the media and the political field, mistrust contaminated all sectors of social life. While not always unfounded, gossip accentuated the difficulty of formulating audible critiques. In an essay published in 2004, liberal politician Soufiane Djilali thus came to describe a kind of social disease, a "manipulitis" that systematically discredited public discourse. He viewed this flaw as a consequence of the "magical thinking" that still characterized the Algerian people.[54]

The Rejection of Cynicism

Despite successive pitfalls, the ruling elites didn't forgo the positivist and modernist narrative inherited from decolonization and Third Worldism. In 2014, Bouteflika's presidential program announced that the president would dedicate himself to "solidly anchoring the achievements linked to development and progress." The revived social pact would reflect "the new expectations and aspirations [of] the people" and "materialize the vision of a strong, prosperous, and fraternal Algeria." This type of discourse demonstrated not only the resistance of the Third Wordlist episteme but also the eternal return of unfulfilled promises. As daily experiences invalidated this narrative of triumphant progress, it became necessary to make sense of the disjunction between redundant promises and the world as it actually was.

THE MARTYRS OF THE "SYSTEM"

Echoing the theme of "who kills whom?," critical readings of national history came to focus on figures whose tragic fate demonstrated the seeming injustice of the established order. This martyrology operated as a contentious form of storytelling situated at the crossroads of necropolitics and the political rationality of suspicion. Renewed by the violence of the 1990s, it also served to highlight a set of values that had allegedly been obscured, such as honesty and tolerance.

When conducting semi-structured interviews, I would often encounter the name Abane Ramdane whenever my interlocutors wished to explain the betrayal of the promises of 1962. Abane is considered by many to be the "architect of the revolution" and the "champion of the preponderance of politics over the military." His death in 1957 became a symbol of the treachery of a faction in the FLN, that of the so-called three Bs: Abdelhafid Boussouf, Lakhdar Bentobal, and Krim Belkacem. These three figures of the armed struggle responded to Abane's criticism of their actions by organizing a trial in Morocco and sentencing him to death. His strangling was ordered by Boussouf, who is often viewed as the founder of the country's military intelligence. To a certain extent, the "System" was born on the Moroccan farm where Abane lost his life. Of course, the historical record is more complex. Abane was himself notoriously in favor of the unitarian and coercive orientation of the revolution. He notably supported violent purges against nationalist groups that competed with the FLN. Nonetheless, contemporary readings identify Abane's death as the original sin that led to the abandonment of revolutionary credentials and the development of a culture based on political assassination and military interference.[55]

Mohamed Boudiaf was another prominent nationalist figure. His murder in 1992 is often viewed as the act of a "mafia" capable of dire exactions to preserve its privileges. According to the official version, his killer was an isolated Islamist who infiltrated the security services. The investigation report released in 1992 nevertheless conceded that defects in the president's security detail pose serious questions about who was behind the killing, and Boudiaf's family rejects the official version of events. Instead, they have repeatedly pointed to Larbi Belkheir, one of the political figures of the ANP in the 1990s. The haziness that surrounds Boudiaf's murder is in stark contrast to his public image as an honest and principled man. While he supported the military coup and carried out a relentless crackdown on the FIS, he also announced deep structural reforms and a series of investigations into the embezzlement of public money. Having been exiled from the country between 1964 and 1992, he was not compromised by the collapse of the one-party system. A consequence of the crisis, his return to Algeria could be seen as his final sacrifice for the nation. Boudiaf thus remained a central figure in a shared political imaginary of injustice, which was synonymous with a nationalist commitment untarnished by corruption and dirty politics. Along with Boumediene and Bouteflika, his austere and emaciated face still figured prominently in the presidential pantheon displayed on the walls of cafés and shops before 2019.

> Boudiaf, I think that he was the only President we ever had, for real. In six months, he did what the others didn't do in fifty years. We will never know the truth about his murder. The people who killed him are still in place, whether they are Islamists or from the DRS. All we can say is that an honest man will necessarily infuriate the bastards [*salauds*]. As was the case with [the writer] Tahar Djaout. These people can only anger those who are beneath them, because they remind them to what extent they are bastards.
>
> (AMEZZA, FORMER MEMBER OF THE RCD'S
> REGIONAL OFFICE IN TIZI OUZOU, PARIS, SPRING 2011)

The martyr's testimony reaffirms the validity of transcendent values, and the ongoing Manichean struggle between "honest men" and "bastards." Yet Boudiaf's death also remained a powerful symbol of the triumph of malevolent forces. While Abane's assassination had provided early proof of the revolution's hijacking, Boudiaf's fate suggested the unlimited Machiavellianism of the cartel. The perverse sophistication of the *décideurs* seemed to go one step further. While Boussouf was on-site to witness

Abane's execution, Toufik and Lamari had allegedly put in place an "Operation Boudiaf" to eliminate the president without having to leave the labyrinthine spaces they inhabited.[56] The raw brutality that once brought together the perpetrator and their victim had been replaced by a chilling power, one that resorted to telekinesis in order to kill. In short, Boudiaf's assassination was at once the demonstration of the permanent opposition between good and evil, and proof of the omnipotent perversion that led to the collapse of the polity in the 1990s.

Specific causes had their own martyrs. In the Berberist case, cultural figures such as the writer Tahar Djaout or the singer Lounes Matoub are essential. Matoub, in particular, has remained an iconic figurehead of Berber music and politics. After being injured in October 1988, he was among the advocates of a peaceful settlement to the Dark Decade. He was eventually assassinated in hazy circumstances in 1998. Since then, his villa, situated in his hometown of Taourirt Moussa, has been treated as a "museum." There, one can contemplate the car he was driving when he was killed and countless posters, photographs, and other signs calling for the "seekers of truth" to continue their quest (see figures 7.1 and 7.2). As I was exiting the villa in 2011, I came across a noisy group of middle schoolers who had just spilled out of a bus. Surprised, I asked the villa's custodian if these sorts of school visits were common. "They come from all over the region," he replied. "Because they come to learn a part of their history. Matoub is a martyr of Kabylia. He deserves the same respect as the martyrs of the revolution." The singer could certainly be portrayed as another victim of a corrupt "System." Yet Matoub also embodied the specificity of the Berberist struggle for the defense of cultural pluralism in the face of an "Arabo-Islamist" oppression.

These iconic figures were invoked in order to locate the causes of the crisis in the army's predilection for political interference, in the cartel's drift toward criminality, and in the general sense of cultural intolerance. These murders illustrated the murkiness associated with Algerian necropolitics. They also served to reaffirm values that had the power to restore the community: the primacy of civilian power, moral integrity, and cultural pluralism. In other words, these martyrs did not only denounce the falsehoods of official discourses; they also resurrected the ideal of independence and political sanctity on which the nation-state had been built after 1962.[57]

FIGURE 7.1 The car in which Lounes Matoub lost his life, on display in his former villa. Taourirt Moussa, spring 2011. (Photograph by author.)

FIGURE 7.2 The memorial marking the place where Matoub was ambushed calls for the truth to be revealed. Near Taourirt Moussa, spring 2011. (Photograph by author.)

RUMORS, CONSPIRACY THEORIES, AND THE FOREIGNNESS OF RULING ELITES

A society in crisis is rife with rumors and conspiracy theories, whose propagators become the organizers of an uncertain world. While the spreading of rumor and hearsay contributes to the making of history from below, conspiracy theorizing, as a form of grassroot politicization, results in the construction of relatively coherent and organized contentious narratives.[58] Rumors and conspiracy theories are the "silent partner of a loud form of public resistance," and thus are inherently infra-political in nature.[59] Under Bouteflika, these meaning-making activities served to denounce military interference in politics or the alleged foreignness of the country's ruling elites. Conspiracy theories also served as a regime of truth through which individuals could disentangle the threads of an uncertain social world.[60] They clarified and simplified the country's historical trajectory by postulating the intentionality of all acts.

Former officials traded in narratives that blamed certain compromised renegades for the country's ills. For instance, former prime minister Abdelhamid Brahimi (1984–1988) released a memoir describing the wrongdoings of the "Party of France" (Ḥizb Fransā), which he blamed for the crisis of the late 1980s. According to him, the former colonizer's minions—led by Larbi Belkheir—had notably framed the ANP's chief of staff, Mostefa Beloucif, after he had prevented the signing of an arms deal that would have been detrimental to the country.[61] While the proximity between the French government and key members of the Algerian security apparatus is beyond doubt, an exclusive focus on Ḥizb Fransā overlooks the complex sociopolitical dynamics that led to the violence of the 1990s. Brahimi was certainly aware of the tensions unsettling the ruling coalition, as he himself became close to the FIS.

While rumors were often less than coherent, to say the least, they could nonetheless suggest relatively credible explanations for the state of the country. The case of former minister of education Boubekeur Benbouzid is a telling example. Benbouzid joined the government in 1993, and he remained for the most part in charge of the same ministry until 2012. Over time, he acquired a solid reputation for ineptitude. Among teachers, the man embodied the mismanagement of public education. He faced yearly strikes denouncing degrading material conditions and inadequate pedagogical objectives. Despite this unflattering record, Benbouzid remained in charge of education for sixteen years. This was the context in which an enduring rumor took hold according to which his wife was said to be the sister of none other than Vladimir Putin. In this case the claim was not completely disconnected from reality, for Benbouzid had indeed studied in Odessa and married a woman of Russian origin, though of course she had no personal links to Putin. The rumor nevertheless served to rationalize the ongoing mismanagement of the country's educational system: How else, aside from a family connection with a powerful foreign leader, to explain the resilience of an allegedly incompetent official? And the claim of foreign influence was not completely off base. The structural adjustment program supported by international financial institutions had indeed played a central role in weakening the public education system in Algeria. In this sense, the rumor echoed the familiar idea that ruling elites serving foreign interests have mortgaged the country's future. Under Bouteflika, the accusation of internal colonialism was never far off, and during the 2019 Hirak protesters made this explicit by denouncing the ruling elites as *wlad Fransa* (children of France).

Narratives of foreign intrusion did not only target despised ministers. In February 2008, Bouteflika presided over the opening of a giant desalination plant that was to provide the Algiers region with drinkable water. Official statements emphasized the priority given to water quality and described the safety measures implemented along the distribution chain.[62] Yet in the fall of 2008, several of my interlocutors wondered why, following an open bidding process, the municipality had selected an American company to build and manage the plant. According to them, the Americans were working with Algerian authorities to poison the region's water. It is worth noting that Algiers does not have an elected mayor and that local executive power rests in the hands of the civil administration. A few years later, I noted a different rumor that I heard first in Algiers in 2010, and then on a bus to Ghardaïa in 2011. This time, my interlocutors focused on Chinese goods sold in local souks. They told the story of a trader who had encountered great success in selling cheap ballerina shoes for little girls. Soon, however, many of the children were taken to hospital with rashes on their feet. It turned out that the shoes were made of rat skin. While seemingly different, these two stories insisted on the malevolence of foreign capitalists and their local intermediaries, all of whom profited from the population's vulnerability.

However, these two rumors are not simply concerned with denouncing foreign aggression and domestic treason. A rumor expresses multiple anxieties and contrasting political messages. In addition to the theme of foreign malevolence, these stories shared at least two other commonalities. First, both evoked the reliance on foreign expertise and industry over local know-how and production capacity. In this way, they suggested not just treason but also a crippling dependence on the part of the community, which seemed unable to make its own shoes and treat its own water. In opposition to the promise of national development inherent to Third Worldism, the country seemed dependent and vulnerable. The second commonality was the theme of contamination (whether in the water or on the skin). Perceived foreign aggression resonated with another recurring concern under Bouteflika—that of a national pathology. These rumors were therefore ambiguous. They expressed mistrust of malevolent neocolonial actors as well as a feeling of collective crisis. Eventually, these more or less coherent attempts to narrate the crisis contributed to an overdose of meaning.

BLED MIKI

In January 2014, the former head the Autonomous Zone of Algiers during the revolution, Yacef Saadi, accused honored mujahida Zohra Drif of selling out fellow nationalists to the French during the Battle of Algiers.[63] As surviving revolutionary heroes vented their acrimony, the resplendent image of the people-as-class, united in the struggle against the colonizer, was suddenly shattered. Even within the Revolutionary Family, suspicion was widespread and seemed capable of implicating anyone, regardless of whether they were dead or alive.

Structural uncertainty fueled a profusion of theories and counternarratives. Such disenchantment could have been emancipatory, but critics of modernity also know that an "oppressive wealth of ideas" can "swamp the people entirely."[64] Indeed, under Bouteflika, uncertainty amplified the epistemic violence of the "System." The disappearance of meaning produced absolute insecurity.[65] The illegibility of the world became intertwined with the illegibility of power. While critical voices expressed their mistrust toward the *Pouvoir*, they failed to promote an alternative truth. Irreconcilable narratives confirmed social fragmentation. "Theories float[ed]" and "no matter how the analysis proceed[ed], it proceed[ed] toward the freezing over of meaning."⁶⁶ In op-eds, in books published by former officers, in official statements, the past and the present collided. Eventually, the seemingly artificial nature of public discourse fed a cautious distancing, especially for those who had left the country.

> In France, I can say that I am taking a break from news coming from Algeria; I am letting my mind rest a little. I focus much more on myself than on what happens in Algeria because it is just too much. I speak with my family. They say that things are calmer, that everything is all right. And in the next sentence, they say that there was a terrorist attack in Boumerdes and nobody knows who is responsible. Always this same mix of violence and lies. This doesn't make me want to receive more news.
> (RACHID, BAKER BORN IN THE REGION OF TIZI OUZOU, PARIS, SUMMER 2010)

Rachid chose to protect himself by distancing himself from his country's political life and rejecting a system in which cynicism and deception seemed ubiquitous. He affirmed that "those who make the real decisions cannot even write," hence their inability to produce a credible representation of reality. In his view, the cynicism of the ruling elites was intrinsically linked to their profound ignorance.

Narratives depicting an illiterate and brutish elite were widespread under Bouteflika, which went against the reputation the president enjoyed at the start of his tenure as an intelligent and capable leader (see chapter 2). During Abdelmalek Sellal's time as prime minister (2012–2017), the notion of *sellaliate* was commonly deployed to describe his inept attempts at humor, which were said to express his idiocy and contempt for the people. Among the most famous examples are Sellal's use of a racist slur in a joke about Chaoui Berbers, his invocation of the phrase *As-salām ʿalaykum ya l-baṭāṭā* (Peace be upon you, potato!) to address a Chinese woman, and the invention of the word *faqāqīr* as a plural form of *faqīr* (poor) rather than the standard *fuqarāʾ*. Sellal thus came to embody the clownish incompetence of a predatory clique. Coupled with the vulgarity and corruption of the *khobzistes* and other *kachiristes*, the alleged stupidity of prominent ministers and generals fueled the sense that the nation had been polluted by its ruling elites. Algerians used the word "Chkoupistan" to mock their country's moral degradation. It is a play on *chkoupi*, which technically describes a seaweed that spoils fishermen's catch, but which in this case also denotes trash or male genitals.⁶⁷

The political order was portrayed as ludicrous long before Bouteflika was propped up as a zombified candidate and portrayed as Algeria's sole safeguard against chaos. A sentence attributed to Chadli Bendjedid captures this deviation: in it, the former president is alleged to have said that "a country that doesn't have problems is not a real country, and, thank God, we don't have any problems." Some versions have Chadli saying, "thank God, we have plenty of problems," which is perhaps more coherent but certainly not more reassuring. This statement, illustrating a mix of thoughtlessness and mediocrity, was taken up by rapper Lotfi DK in a song entitled "Bled Miki" (2004):

Bled Miki bled ta'a tiki
Bled koulech faux koulech faha mfabriki
Bled limafihach machakil mocheha bled
Wahna lhamdulilah! kima gal wahd dab

Country of Mickey, country of cash
Country where everything is false, everything is made up.
A country that doesn't have problems is not a country
And us, thank God! As a bear once said.

Another name for the country, Bled Miki was a regime of absolute simulacra. This narrative denounced the instability of reality and the disappearance of values. In Bled Miki, the political system was a "cosmetic democracy," an exercise in smoke and mirrors where ruthless decision makers hid behind clownish straw men, where former government opponents became ministers, and where the heroes of the War of Liberation traded accusations of betrayal. When speaking about Bled Miki, Algerians described the tricks of a *Pouvoir* that could animate the dead, accelerate time or freeze it, and summon puppets to act out the same scenes over and over again. This narrative certainly expressed a form of powerlessness in the face of a senseless political spectacle; it also proclaimed a refusal to endorse the frail myths manufactured by official discourses.

There are many shady things, and we know that we cannot trust our government. You cannot cover the sun with a sieve. No need to be an expert to see that all their stories have holes ... Algeria is Bled Miki. It's Disneyland because it's like a cartoon. If you have the means, you can change it as you want. I like you, I give you a place. I don't like you, I erase you.

(RACHID, 2010)

While he was weary of the news coming from Algeria, Rachid was not depoliticized. We met during a demonstration organized in Paris by leftist Algerian parties in support of the women assaulted in Hassi Messaoud. During his years in high school in Tizi Ouzou, between 1998 and 2002, he had taken part in more than his share of skirmishes with law enforcement. A decade had passed, but he remained convinced that "Algerians are colonized by their own government." His understanding of Bled Miki was one of absolute rejection. Unlike the alienated man described by Benjamin,[68] he could not be fascinated by the world of Mickey Mouse. He could not abandon himself to a senseless life, nor could he find a false sense of comfort in a cartoonish illusion.

Bouteflika's Algeria was a postcolony based on simulacra. Yet unlike in Assad's Syria, the cartel proved unable to "compel people to say the ridiculous and to avow the absurd."[69] The fetishes of *commandement* were exposed as mere trickery. The ceremony, the staging of majesty, the grotesque spectacle of officiality, were deprived of their festive and inclusive nature. The real rulers failed to appear in public. Official performances did not have a corporeal or didactic form. Political authorities were ludicrous rather than baroque. These shortcomings made a mutual zombification impossible.[70]

As the fetishes of *commandement* failed to captivate the masses, they also proved to be unbearable. The narrative of Bled Miki expressed the rejection of an order based on nihilism and indistinction, the refusal to be fascinated, the impossibility of accepting the triumph of cynicism. Haunted by a rationality of suspicion and instrumentalization, Boutefika's Algeria was a postcolony whose myths had been debunked. In Baudrillard's words, "reality was not what it used to be." What was left was a suspicious reproduction, an "artificial resurrection" that was perceived and denounced as such.[71] While official performances failed to generate adhesion, they became the target of a popular humor that viewed politics as a freak show. The satirical website El Manchar or the YouTuber DZjoker, with their ferocious parodies, mocked the inconsistency of public policies and the chaotic communication of public figures. They covered a botched simulation with another layer of ostentatious absurdity, and in so doing highlighted the cartel's failure to convincingly embody the ideal of popular sanctity situated at the heart of the revolution.

The Reproduction of Culturalism

Rather than accepting the absurdity of politics, journalists, academics, and writers strove to recreate meaning. While novelists such as Rachid Boudjedra or scholars such as Mohammed Harbi had been influential in the 1960s and 1970s, intellectuals gradually lost their prestige. Expected to become a vanguard in service of the country's development after 1962, these individuals were profoundly impacted by the breakdown of the 1980s and 1990s.[72] Their socioeconomic status was undermined by the economic restructuring that took place in these years, and many were forced into exile. While their views of the masses can be perceived as paternalistic and elitist, one must be weary of a critique that ignores the historicity of their work.[73] Indeed, they responded to the material and symbolic violence that they had experienced over the past three decades. As they addressed a loss of intelligibility and a break in the continuity of time, their analyses also participated in the reconstruction of a polity in crisis.[74]

AN EPISTEMOLOGICAL DEADLOCK

In 1956, the Soummam Platform, the founding document of the postcolonial state, announced that soon the "Algerian people will reap the sweet fruits of its painful sacrifice." What was left of this promise at the end of Bouteflika's rule? On July 5, 2012, the fiftieth anniversary of independence, the headlines of several private francophone newspapers lamented the "Broken Dream" (*El Watan*) and "Sordid Reality" (*Le Soir d'Algérie*) to which the country's independence had given rise. The Third Worldist episteme had nonetheless left its imprint on Algeria's political culture. On July 5, the Arabic-language daily *El Khabar* ended its depiction of "the occasion that inhabit[ed] the hearts of all Algerians" by reminding its readers that colonial thought remained dominant in France. Yet in the same issue, another article discussed a PR campaign orchestrated by the presidency in the French press. Comparing this publicity stunt to the propaganda efforts of Arab powers after the defeat of 1967, journalist Saad Bouakba underlined the clumsiness of the presidency. Denouncing the lies of the government on this symbolic day, he finished by repeating a widely asked question: "What kind of independence is that?!"[75]

Making sense of Algeria's trajectory became increasingly difficult after October 1988. In 1993, sociologist Ali El Kenz described this confusion in a short and poignant confession:

> This pivotal period that was October '88 led Algeria from a guaranteed [political] cycle to another model that remains to this day unknown. Everyone follows the current events in Algeria with many more questions than answers. Algeria has become a stranger; she used to be, we thought that she was, one of the most transparent countries in the Third World. She has become in just a few months and until this day as mysterious as Burma or Afghanistan. That's it. I don't know what happened.[76]

Seeking an explanation for the unfolding tragedy, Ali El Kenz emphasized the opposition between acculturated elites and dominated masses, which, he argued, relied increasingly on "weak forms of resistance" inspired by religion. He observed the reproduction of this sociopolitical dualism within the state apparatus, with a division of labor between traditionalist ulema and modernist nationalists. Ultimately, he saw the ongoing conflict as resulting from the weak institutionalization of both the state and intermediary classes, a loss of meaning and a frontal collision between state and society.[77] This analysis, produced at the spur of the moment, illustrated the force of a dualist representation of the crisis. This dualism was at the heart of the final column written by the secular journalist Tahar Djaout, published at the end of May 1993, a couple of weeks before his assassination. In this piece, entitled "La famille qui avance et la famille qui recule" (The family that moves forward and the family that moves backward), Djaout combined his virulent critique of the *Pouvoir* with an elitist plea in favor of quality (the modernist vanguard) over quantity (the fanaticized masses).[78]

The fault lines apparent within each camp eventually demonstrated the shortcomings of binary representations of the civil conflict, forcing experts to revise their reading of the situation. In 1993, French historian Benjamin

IN SEARCH OF LOST MEANING   255

Stora described a "battle between the 'modernists' . . . and the Islamists who promote traditional community life as a model."[79] Four years later, after witnessing the exactions of "ninja" units affiliated with the security services, the horror of civilian massacres, and the institutionalization of moderate Islamism, the same author offered the following explanation: "the clear and straight lines that used to divide the main protagonists . . . and the obvious circles in which acts of wars were situated have decomposed progressively in dark pathways, in labyrinths whose mazes are inextricable."[80]

Historian Malika Rahal emphasizes the difficulty of thinking about the history of independent Algeria, especially after the crumbling of the relatively stable and predetermined world that emerged after 1962.[81] Indeed, under Bouteflika, the Third World had dissolved under successive waves of globalization, and Arab nationalism had replaced Nasser and Michel Aflaq with Mubarak and Bashar al-Assad. Great meta-narratives had lost their appeal. A major task was now to overcome the epistemological deadlock and elucidate the latent crisis. Following a long-standing tradition, Algerian intellectuals scrutinized the alleged features of their population.

A CONTINUUM OF BINARIES

In the summer of 2012, I was invited to a dinner party at the Aérohabitat, a building situated in the center of Algiers. There, I met with a group of Spanish expatriates who used the ubiquitous word *khuya* (Darija for "my brother") as an adverb. They described people "driving *khuya*-style" or "arguing *khuya*-style"—in short, behaving like a typically careless Algerian. This racist slur could be placed on a continuum of pejorative representations of the masses that can be traced back to the colonial era, when the world was "divided in two."[82]

French colonial racism was organized around a series of binaries (nature/culture, Islamism/republicanism, savagery/civilization) that naturalized the process of land grabbing. The modernity of the colonizers who domesticated the land confronted the backwardness of local populations who failed to dominate nature.[83] Settlers were transformative agents who grew vineyards. Meanwhile, natives were portrayed as children plagued by a series of racial flaws that rendered them "born slackers, born liars, born thieves, and born criminals."[84] Islam was a key marker of native inferiority, as French social scientists depicted an antirepublican religion based on superstition and submission. Ernest Renan famously contrasted the Muslim faith and its "eternal tautology" (God is God) with Europe and its rationality, which he claimed made civilization possible.[85] Countless sociologists and anthropologists subsequently echoed this dichotomous diagnosis by portraying Islam as a force of death contrary to republican values.[86]

Edward Said famously subsumed the imperial assemblage of power-knowledge situated at the crossroads of science, public administration, arts, and politics constituted since the eighteenth century under the term "Orientalism."[87] Orientalist practices, behaviors, and actors vary a great deal depending on the context. In Algeria, the so-called civilizing mission portrayed the dualistic social system as dedicated to the betterment of backward natives. Among the Pied-Noirs (settlers), Arabness evoked images of poverty, idleness, dishonesty, and filthiness. As education aimed to remedy the anthropological flaws of the colonized, it was thus conceptualized as a process of de-Arabization.[88] Racist binaries also affected the development policies implemented by the French, especially as Islam was associated with inefficient practices to be replaced by market-oriented and efficiency-driven behaviors.[89]

When conceptualizing their program for national liberation, nationalist elites relied on culturalist frameworks to think about the challenges ahead of them. In response to the alienation produced by colonization, nationalist and religious leaders developed a project of "cultural decolonization," which aimed to restore the country's authentic self, notably by insisting on its Arabness and on the place of Islam. The notion of an Algerian personality (shakhṣiyya jazāi'riyya), coined by Sheykh Mohamed El Bachir El Brahimi in 1944, thus became a key focus in the name of creating a "new man in a new society."[90] Yet attempts to foster cultural and political homogeneity faced the reality of a large and complex country. The coercive impulses of the military-bureaucratic apparatus soon found its justification in the culture of the masses. As early as 1960, then interior minister of the Provisional Government of the Algerian Republic Lakhdar Ben Tobbal justified the need for discipline within the national movement by Algerians' supposedly natural inclination toward anarchy.[91] The analyses of religious figures followed a similar path. Leaders of the Association of Ulema positioned themselves as the promoters of the true principles of religion, in opposition to the French, of course, but also to the "ignorant Muslim masses." They strove to "improve the cultural level of Algeria [so it could be] recognized as an Arab and Muslim country."[92] In their effort to transform the nation, these elites reproduced a dualistic representation of society, one that permeated such influential developmentalist policies as Arabization or the agrarian revolution. Later, the upheavals of the 1980s and 1990s found an explanation in the population's flaws. It is thus not surprising that, fifty years after independence, Interior Minister Daho Ould Kablia should react to the rise in social unrest by complaining that "the people [had] become whimsical, impatient and impulsive."[93]

The Dark Decade also revived imaginative geographies that portrayed Algeria as a land of violence and legitimated transnational security projects.[94] Foreign media played a key role in this process, as they depicted a "barbaric" country plagued by fundamentalist violence that Westerners should avoid.[95] The myth of national savagery persisted under Bouteflika, in contrast to the widespread rejection of violence on the part of the population.[96] Culturalist explanations of terrorism depicted a brutal and schizophrenic country, despite the fact that similar forms of bloodshed also occurred in Europe.[97] As a matter of fact, the stereotypes used by foreign media and local politicians seemed to be validated by the critical process. After the Tingentourine hostage crisis of January 2013, the British press reproduced such stereotypes, thus prompting a public rebuttal by historian James McDougall.[98] Yet imaginative geographies are not that easy to dispel. A few days later, the BBC broadcast a segment portraying Algeria as "a nation born in violence."

PATHOLOGY AND DISCIPLINE

Echoing the narrative of cultural and political malaise that became widespread throughout the Arab world after the 1967 defeat,[99] pathological readings of the crisis inundated the Algerian public space. As intellectuals looked for a way out of their epistemological deadlock, some promoted interpretations that naturalized domination. Advocating for reform and sociocultural uplift, journalists, academics, and novelists increasingly depicted a people that seemed either mentally ill or culturally backward.

During the Dark Decade, "emergency writings" testified to the intertwining of life and death, reality and fantasy.[100] A political and clinical literature described the ills and lost hopes of the postcolony. Award-winning francophone authors such as Yasmina Khadra (*Morituri* [1997], *À quoi rêvent les loups* [1999]) or Boualem Sansal (*Le serment des barbares* [1999], *Harraga* [2007]) depicted a society plagued by paranoia, sexual frustration, and intolerance. Among other prominent Arabic-language writers, Ahlem Mosteghanemi was also inspired by the events of the 1990s and offered a sharp political, social, and cultural critique of her home country (*Fawḍā al-ḥawās* [1997], *Al-āswad yalīqu bīki* [2012]). Sansal and Khadra are especially interesting because they were both trained in elite state schools: Khadra was a pupil at the military academy of Cherchell, and Sansal a student at Algiers Polytechnic School. They both worked for the state, the former as an officer in the ANP and the latter as an employee of the Ministry of Economy. Their social critique was thus informed by the Third Worldist episteme that dominated their secondary socialization. By depicting deviance, they also aimed to "bring back normalcy in a pathogenic and morbid postcolonial society."[101]

Fictional accounts sometimes overlapped with journalism, as many in the latter profession pursued parallel literary careers. One of the most famous among them, Chawki Amari, described in August 2011 a society in which violence, misery, and drug addiction were exacerbated during the month of Ramadan. Appropriating the narrative of schizophrenia, he described the return to a more soothing social life once the day of fasting was over.[102] As a moment of introspection, the holy month offered an occasion to scrutinize society, identify its flaws, and offer solutions. At the same time, the famous journalist Hafid Derradji called on his fellow citizens to think critically in *Echorouk*. After describing the "stagnation of cultural life" and the "aggravating moral crisis" among the youth, he invoked the need for social and political reform.[103] A few days later, anthropologist Zaïm Kenchelaoui explained in *El Khabar* that Muslim societies had been asleep for too long. He suggested finding inspiration in foreign models in order to overcome hypocrisy and "mental entrapment" (*al-inḥibās adh-dhihnī*).[104] According to all three authors, the root causes of these social pathologies were structural (unemployment, puritanism, education).

In the documentary *Aliénations* (2003), Malek Bensmaïl depicted the life of a psychiatric hospital in Constantine. The son of a founding figure of Algerian psychiatry, his approach was undoubtedly Fanonian. He patiently filmed his fellow citizens describing their mental sufferings. Through these testimonies, Bensmaïl strove to describe the distress generated by the violence of a system in crisis. Yet other readings relied on an analytical framework that seemed more inspired by Le Bon's *Psychology of Crowds* than Fanon. In these works, psychiatric jargon served to formulate a disciplinary project that would cure the moral flaws of the population. Interviewed by the pro-government daily *L'Expression*, therapist Salaheddine Menia explained the violence that occurred during Ramadan in 2011 in the following terms:

> People do not tolerate frustration. They are hypersensitive and allow themselves to constantly fight each other. All this is characteristic of a kind of emotional immaturity. Seemingly, you are dealing with adults, but from a behavioral perspective, they operate like children. They are egocentric, they reject discipline and order, and these are characteristics of a small child's behaviors . . . Culturally, brawling is a source of pride among ordinary people. The one who is tough, beats others, assaults them, refuses to be pushed around, is valorized socially. This might be a sign of virility, but in fact it's a form of deviance.

Menia echoed the discourse of order. After identifying the behavioral causes of unrest—the emotional immaturity of the population and the cultural valorization of violence—he recommended curative steps inspired by Western security policies: "Just look at [the 2011 riots] in England. The authorities reacted swiftly by seeking the advice of an American expert in violent behavior in order to counter, treat and overcome [such] new behavior . . . Our rulers must find the solution by relying on professionals who can understand what is happening and propose responses, [who can tell us] what we can do at the individual, social and family level to absorb this aggressiveness."[105] A decisive shift had occurred. Structural causes disappeared from the analysis in favor of a focus on a deviant culture in need of a cure. Positioned at the crossroads of behavioral sciences and culturalism, Menia recommended a cultural reform. To address the flaws of the average Algerian, this childish being driven by his or her "general tendency to nervousness and aggressiveness," one should rely on "professionals." Warning that these violent tendencies would only increase, the expert called for public authorities to act rapidly and to coerce, discipline, and lift up the population.

ETHNOGRAPHY AND DEMOCRACY

In academic works, culturalist approaches have often served to explain the country's trajectory. After 1962, some foreign observers accounted for the difficulties of the newly founded state by arguing that Algerians' apparently "extreme individualism and distaste for regimentation border[ed] on anarchy."[106] With the climax of the crisis, local scholars increasingly incriminated "a patriarchal culture" and "segmental and traditional structures" that shaped the behaviors of rulers and subjects alike.[107] Cultural evolutionism became a way for social scientists to frame the political situation as the product of atavistic behaviors.

In *La guerre civile en Algérie*, Luis Martinez presents the archetype of the "political bandit" as a model for social uplift deeply embedded in local political culture. According to him, a centuries-old "imaginary of warfare" gave a key role to violence and was in direct opposition to the values of liberal democracy. In this way, Martinez explained the failed "democratic transition" of the early 1990s. While he considered that the resurgence of this imaginary was intertwined with the context of civil war and structural adjustment, Martinez, a political scientist, nonetheless appropriated a dichotomy that pitted traditional culture against democratic modernity.[108] Other Algerian academics echoed this dualistic and evolutionist narrative. In an op-ed published after the legislative elections of 2012, economist Abderrahmane Mebtoul argued that the FLN's success was proof of Algeria's "weak political culture."[109] As for political scientist Mohammed Hachemaoui, he started his study of clientelism under Bouteflika by highlighting the plethora of different "cultural grammars" and the hybridity of social dynamics. Yet despite these precautions, the Maghrebi archetype of the *Makhzan* resurfaced at the end of his book, as he appropriated once again the dichotomy contrasting premodern social structures with democratic modernity.[110]

Using such binaries to understand Algerian culture, which they viewed as bolstering the political order's resilience, these authors often underplayed a set of more mundane factors (military radicalism, defensive nationalism, economic restructuring, democratic globalization). An analysis published by sociologist Lahouari Addi in 2014 illustrates this type of reasoning:

State power in Algeria is vacant because there are no ideological mechanisms to return it to its rightful owner: society. This is where the failure of the regime lies, and it is not a question of model or misguided implementation of a more or less coherent economic policy. It is about political representations where the individual, as a legal subject, does not exist, and where the group is represented through the leader, whose authority originates from outside the group. This brings us back to the ancient traditional political order where politics are negated and where the leader is in charge of righting wrongs rather than protecting the liberty of each individual. There is a culture to overcome, which is centered on justice and which must be replaced by one centered on liberty.[111]

Addi appropriated key themes of liberal philosophy in his diagnosis, such as individual freedoms and the neutrality of the political. He thus revived colonial binaries by opposing a normative understanding of "modern" liberal democracy to a "traditional" egalitarian Algerian political culture that allegedly encourages authoritarian populism. Here, it would be too easy to disregard such cultural criticism as a mere form of internalized racism.[112] Addi has long rejected essentialist discourses targeting Islam and Arabs. Thus, while he and others identified the alleged flaws of a "traditional" mentality and relied on seemingly endogenous notions to describe the political order, they did so as part of an effort to conceptualize the road to reform. Indeed, scholars lamenting the lack of political culture and individual autonomy in Algeria also reaffirmed the historical responsibility of the state in this process.[113]

This tradition of cultural criticism could be traced back to the era of the Nahdha in the nineteenth century.[114] Later, in the 1940s, sociologist Malek Bennabi proposed the notion of "colonizability." He notably explained subjection and underdevelopment in Algeria by denouncing rigid interpretations of Islam and comparing the colonized people to children in thrall to Western material fetishes. To overcome the crisis resulting from colonialism, Bennabi suggested that Algerian society undergo a profound process of cultural reform.[115] These intellectual efforts advocated conjoined political projects. After the Muslim reformers, the nationalist elites, and the FIS, opponents voiced similar concerns under Bouteflika. For instance, Soufiane Djilali, a liberal candidate in the 2014 presidential elections, called for terminating the "inflexible and anachronistic anthropological values that prevent[ed] any internal transformation."[116] When we spoke in 2010, he laid out an understanding of the psychosocial dynamics at work in Algeria, which was reminiscent of Bennabi's thought.

> We have continuously functioned with a mentality that can be traced back to the previous century, which gives a central role to irrational thinking, to supernatural beliefs. These were quite common among those who were destitute. But one cannot rule a country with such a mentality. After independence, this has led to a form of schizophrenia in our country . . . As we were not conscious of this distortion between a way of life that came from the outside and our anachronistic mindset, we were unable to make sense of the objects around us. Modernity came from the outside. It invaded us. This created grave distortions in the way in which we behave toward one another.
>
> (SOUFIANE DJILALI, FORMER GENERAL SECRETARY OF
> THE PARTY OF ALGERIAN RENEWAL, ALGIERS, AUTUMN 2010)

Soufiane viewed the political deadlock as a matter of sociocultural progress and generational transition. He argued that the youth "believed in the rule of law" when the old elites "still lived in the era of the revolution."[117] But his faith in the younger generation was not universally shared. Others reproduced the symbolic violence of the ruling order and proposed a project aimed at raising up the people-as-child.

CHANGING THE PEOPLE

Facing the allegedly antidemocratic culture of the masses, intellectuals proposed a sociocultural *aggiornamento*. A surprising continuity could thus be observed between the colonial civilizing mission, the paternalism of revolutionary elites, and the "anti-populist" reformism of liberal intellectuals. Sociologist Djamel Guerid has criticized the tendency of industrialist and modernist elites to impose their ahistorical understandings of development or democracy, and thus clash with society. For him, the solution is to adapt development policies to "real society."[118] Yet society itself has often been cast as a problem. Echoing the binaries of colonial administrators, government officials under Bouteflika were preoccupied with the atavistic impulses of the population. They demanded civic-mindedness and a spirit of enterprise. They lamented popular immaturity and impulsiveness. These discourses were replicated by prominent critiques of the "System," such as that advanced by journalist and award-winning novelist Kamel Daoud. In a column published in 2014, Daoud affirmed, for instance, the need to "change the people." In this text that denounced "widespread naive optimism [*angélisme*]" and "emotional populism," he portrayed a population without civic values, whose passivity was perfectly embodied by the impotent man that had just been reelected:

> Many find their happiness in submission, in predation [*dévoration*] and in corruption. Few are those who think about future generations and collective interest. This is the equation that we need to change. This is the responsibility that we need to accept and demonstrate. Continuing to speak about a people of victims and intellectuals who are traitors has become easy and annoying. What needs to change is this people. We must explain the difference between resignation and constitution. We must demonstrate that creating jobs is better than building mosques. That working is a duty. That effort is glory. That civic-mindedness [*civisme*] is not naivety.[119]

Drawing on the discourse of corruption to locate the unmodern and reassert a normative conception of progress,[120] Daoud emphasized the necessity of changing the people's ways before thinking about changing the government. The journalist had nonetheless written more than his share of stories lambasting the ruling elites, and he took part in protests in favor of regime change in 2011. However, after the electoral successes of Islamist parties in Egypt and Tunisia, his writings became increasingly critical of Arab peoples, who, he claimed, were unprepared for democracy. He notably portrayed his fellow citizens as "a people three-quarters ignorant, careless of the land to pass on, dirty, without public spirit and intolerant."[121] A people, in other words, in need of the enlightenment bestowed by an elite coterie of truth tellers.

Daoud was not alone in pleading for a project of sociocultural uplift. For instance, after the 2012 legislative elections, *El Khabar*'s Jalal Bouati explained that the priority was to change the "mentality of the people and party leaders."[122] Similarly, former governor of the Bank of Algeria Abderrahmane Hadj Nacer published an essay entitled *La Martingale Algérienne*, in which he reflected on the causes of and solutions to the ongoing crisis. With a preface by Daoud, the book advocated for greater self-consciousness, and it was received positively in liberal circles in Algiers. Hadj Nacer underscored the crucial role of cultural factors in explaining the "collective failure to develop the country."

> Over the past centuries, Algerians have often lacked self-discipline and self-control. And this is not only about their Amazigh or Mediterranean temperament . . . In sports competitions, Algeria often falls short of winning. In the majority of cases, what was missing was discipline. Conversely, the rare successes in football or handball were obtained thanks to coaches like Aziz Derouaz, who managed to create a sense of self-discipline among the players . . . We must also investigate the phenomenon of "chain" behaviors that has impacted the daily life of Algerians for so long. There are some countries where queuing is an organized activity that demonstrates public spirit, as when one boards a bus. Conversely, the vision of a group of packed passengers unable to behave with discipline often means that you are near the check-in counter of a flight heading to or leaving from Algeria.[123]

In addition to the need for Algerians to learn self-discipline, Hadj Nacer's prose also revealed the role of mobility. Many of the intellectuals mentioned in the previous pages wrote their books in French and enjoyed a preferential access to transnational spaces where cultural critique encountered the liberal doxa. Some worked for financial institutions or foreign universities; others acquired a reputation as "beacons of modernity" in France thanks to their denunciation of Islamic fundamentalism, as was the case for Daoud and Sansal. Portrayed as dissidents, they served as "token Muslim intellectuals," as their discourses were instrumentalized to validate racist prejudices in the former imperial power.[124] The challenge here is to account for the Algerian context informing these analyses, without overlooking their reliance on colonial binaries.

Toward a Symbolic Revolution

Culturalist stereotypes certainly demonstrated the pervasive paternalism of political and intellectual elites. Nevertheless, they also circulated horizontally in the public sphere. The symbolic violence of the established order was also epistemic, imposing its reality at the grassroots level and fashioning a shared understanding of the social world.[125] At the same time, pejorative representations competed with counter-discourses that invoked the ideal of political sanctity associated with the people. Eventually this struggle to reinvent the community opened the way for a symbolic revolution that turned the *hogra* inherent to the order on its head.

CONTRADICTORY CONSCIOUSNESS

Fanon explains that "the last resource of the colonized is to defend his personality against his peer" (*son congénère*).[126] Similarly, the seemingly never-ending crisis could be explained by reference to collective flaws from which individuals tried to distance themselves.

> George Bush, Jacques Chirac, and Abdelaziz Bouteflika are in a plane flying around the world. The American president puts his hand by the window and says, "I just touched the top of the Statue of Liberty. We are in America!"
>
> The trip continues, and it is Chirac's turn to put his hand outside the window. "We're flying over France," he says. "I could feel the Eiffel Tower with my fingers."
>
> Later, it is Bouteflika's turn to extend his arm outside the plane, under the questioning gaze of his two colleagues. "Well, we've arrived in Algeria," states Bouteflika.
>
> "But how could you know," ask the two others jointly. "There is no Eiffel Tower or Statue of Liberty in your country."
>
> "Yes, but somebody just stole my watch."

I heard this joke on a private beach in Aïn el-Turk in 2006. The narrator was a young man who had invited me to share a drink with a group of friends at the end of their workday. In his early twenties and residing in a working-class neighborhood in Oran, he was working there over the summer. He took care of the beach chairs used by wealthy families and brought drinks to paying customers. By telling this story, he wanted me to understand the "problem of mentality" in Algeria.

His joke illustrated the comparative mechanisms that served the reproduction of self-deprecating discourses. Algerians' flaws were contrasted with the achievements of more "developed" people. France and the United States served as markers of difference. These two countries had their world-famous national symbols. In comparison, Algeria's signature was a tendency to practice petty theft, signaling dishonesty as much as misery. The joke illustrated the resistance of an old representation of Algerian society, that of a mass made problematic by its destitute and criminogenic nature.[127] As such, it also expressed an awareness of a developmental gap that still appeared impossible to overcome, almost fifty years after decolonization.

Self-deprecation has been a long-standing feature in Algerian popular culture and humor. It can be traced back to the colonial era and was revisited during the Dark Decade, when it was used to cope with extreme violence and uncertainty.[128] Yet the appropriation of the discourse on backwardness under Bouteflika was more than a mere defense mechanism. Caricatures rationalized the crisis and recreated meaning. Stating that Algerians "have a feudal mindset" created a far-reaching interpretative framework. It could explain the role of clientelist networks and elucidate the struggles within the ruling coalition, notably by focusing on the role of regional coalitions such as the "Oujda clan" or the "BTS Chaoui triangle."[129] Struggles within the state field could then be depicted as mere clashes between rival ʿaṣabiyyāt (social groups). As the people's mentality allegedly matched the "feudal spirit of governance,"[130] a coherent representation of an underdeveloped nation emerged. After decades of Third Worldism, the era of catastrophization testified to the failure to fix the Algerian personality.

This narrative of collective failure contradicted that of betrayal, dispossession, and hogra exacerbated by the lived experience of the crisis. According to Gramsci, such tension creates a "contradictory consciousness," a complex mental state resulting in apathy and resistance.[131] For almost two decades, an apparent demoralization cohabited with profound grievances. Eventually, these contradictions were overcome, at least temporarily, in February 2019.

EXILE AND PATRIOTISM

The memories of the Dark Decade and the continuous crisis certainly undermined the ideal of "profound and horizontal comradeship" that underpins the imagined national community, following Anderson's famous formula.¹³² This does not mean that positive representations of the nation had completely disappeared. Contradictory consciousness also fueled contradictory discourses. Algeria could thus be depicted as both a beloved motherland and an open-air prison, a land crippled by absurdity but blessed by the potential of its youth. The culturalist narrative targeting national culture was therefore far from hegemonic.

Self-deprecation is ambiguous. In the discourse of colonized people, it was a response to the construction of the settler as an unattainable embodiment of European racial supremacy. Under Bouteflika, this unattainable other was an archetype of neoliberal globalization, an animated fetish produced by mass consumption and the exclusive luxury of transnational mobility. Young Algerians suffered from the closed-door policy enforced by restrictive visa regimes and the police state. They suffered in comparison with the ideal of the fulfilled consumer, the role model offered by the fascinating spectacle of dematerialized materialism. This simulated and unreachable archetype lived in Europe or in Lebanon; it thrived in luxury, enjoyed the blessings of capitalist modernity, and lived fairy-tale romances. This ideal clashed with the lived experience of scarcity and entrapment. It clashed with the possibility of exile, seen both as a necessity and a painful trial.¹³³ Denigrating one's fellow citizens could thus be a way to extract oneself from the national community, and thus reaffirm the legitimacy and urgency of a desire to emigrate ("I can't deal with the people around here anymore").

Undocumented migration manifested this rejection of an unfair sociopolitical order. Exile could therefore reassert a form of belonging, positioning the individual in a contentious political configuration and tense relationship to the motherland.¹³⁴ Despite *harga* and the disaffiliation of the youth, systemic violence did not obliterate patriotic feelings.¹³⁵ Discourses mocking or blaming the culture of Algerians thus cohabited with various forms of praise for the adventurous and untamed "spirit" of the people.

> A number of young Algerians are ready to risk their lives to cross the sea. This reveals a form of despair but also a more positive feature of [their] mentality: a taste for adventure, an audacious temper that might be excessive but encourages them to see the world. You can find Algerians everywhere across the world. This mentality is also strengthened by a patriotic feeling. We felt it during the [2009] football game against Egypt.

There was an incredible mobilization with more than fifteen thousand people who were ready to go to Sudan to support their team, in particularly difficult conditions. This feeling of fervent patriotism moved the youth who have nothing to do with the *Pouvoir*, people who have always looked at it with a lot of mistrust. Some of them only thought about leaving for Europe. But when they considered that the national flag had been soiled, they all came together to defend it. This is to say that, despite all their contradictions, Algerians remain a people that are alive, that can certainly become violent and brutal in their excesses, but that can also be especially benevolent.

(SOUFIANE DJILALI, FORMER GENERAL SECRETARY OF
THE PARTY OF ALGERIAN RENEWAL, ALGIERS, AUTUMN 2010)

Soufiane's analysis had something of a *mise en abyme*. Having himself emigrated to France, he returned in the early 1990s to become involved in politics. Following in the footsteps of Malek Bennabi and Noureddine Boukrouh, he called for a profound cultural overhaul to address a set of psychosocial flaws. Yet when speaking about his fellow citizens, he somehow underlined the paradoxes inherent in his own culturalist approach. The people could be portrayed as traumatized and schizophrenic, but also resourceful and full of love for the motherland. Under Bouteflika, youth activists continued to refer to the Proclamation to the Algerian People of 1954 and its promises of freedom and equality.[136] Indeed, while the crisis had certainly legitimated pathological representations of the masses, it did not fully erase the ideal of political sanctity inherited from the revolution. Algerianness remained synonymous with an ongoing quest for justice and emancipation.

BETWEEN CULTURAL REFORM AND SYMBOLIC REVOLUTION

Far from always taking part in discursive catastrophization, some intellectuals challenged securitizing representations of the masses. In 2011, *El Khabar*'s Saber Ayoub seized the opportunity of the London riots to underline the civility of Algerians living in England.[137] Likewise, Algerian novelists also strove to reinvent the world beyond the limits imposed by the established order. With novels such as Mustapha Benfodil's *Archéologie du chaos (amoureux)* (2007), Algerian fiction contributed to a utopian and romantic quest that revived the revolutionary legacy.[138] By challenging catastrophizing and paternalistic narratives, these authors maintained the possibility of a symbolic revolution that would destroy the dominant ideology.[139]

Some viewed such a revolution as a prerequisite for the formation of any efficient counter-discourse. In March 2011, for instance, Hocine Aït Ahmed, the historical leader of the FFS, wrote a letter to the party's national executive. In order to offer a credible political alternative, he argued that one should first remind the public that, "in our culture, there are not only honorable bandits, but also honorable men of culture, honorable men of religion, and honorable politicians."[140]

In addition to the rejection of negative representations of the elites, cultural resistance could also question the mistrust inherited from decades of crisis. Filmmaker Habiba Djahnine, for example, explained how her work challenged the political rationality of suspicion and instrumentalization.

> There is a conspiracy-oriented thinking that contaminates everything. I don't accept this political culture of manipulation, of mistrust. The way in which politics work, the way in which analytical frameworks are put in place, with this world that is ruled by politics—this kind of politics—with conspiracies and internal negotiations: I don't want this anymore. We have lost a huge part of what human beings produce, because we focus on values that don't mean anything, including their so-called democratic values. This tires me. There are many more things in Algerian society, things that are really interesting and that we are not yet able to conceive.
>
> (HABIBA DJAHNINE, DOCUMENTARY FILMMAKER,
> FORMER MEMBER OF THE PST, ALGIERS, SPRING 2011)

Habiba rejected a narrow vision of society that was disconnected from reality. She felt that political activism was not the best way to address the challenges faced by the country, and especially to testify to all the positive aspects that were hidden by catastrophizing discourses. In opposition to a Machiavellian approach that sensed hidden political agendas lurking around every corner, she decided to focus on documentary film. She created a successful workshop, Béjaïa Doc, that trained aspiring filmmakers. Over the years, it supported the production of dozens of documentaries, many of them intimist or ethnographic movies depicting a diverse and complex society.¹⁴¹ According to Habiba, this effort was the best response to the political rational of suspicion, as it demonstrated the resistance of "a profound, popular culture that is extraordinary and hasn't been destroyed."

The groundwork for a symbolic revolution didn't always occur through the promotion of clear and enthusiastic representations of the people. More modestly, it also relied on efforts to uncover the meaning of Algerianness. Architect Abdelhakim explained that while he had always been politicized, he steered clear of political parties. During his years at the Polytechnic School of Architecture in Algiers, he chose to prioritize fieldwork and concrete action with his classmates. It was his way to contribute to a broader quest for meaning.

> The way you inhabit a place, it speaks about you and it reflects who you are. For me, the current state of the Casbah is really the sign of the identity crisis we are going through. So we started a project in the port wastelands near the Casbah. We used these empty spaces to express Algerian identity through architecture. We wanted to use this historical neighborhood to connect the past and the present, but also to think about the future. It's important to try to recreate a dynamic in this neighborhood, which was the heart of Algiers but which has since been abandoned. It is by looking in the direction of culture that we can understand our identity, which is so difficult to pin down . . . I don't know if there is a miracle cure to the problems of today's Algeria. But for me, if there is one, it will necessarily require a massive investment in the cultural sector. We need a kind of cultural revolution to finally understand who we are.
>
> (ABDELHAKIM, GRADUATE OF ALGIERS POLYTECHNIC SCHOOL OF ARCHITECTURE, PARIS, SUMMER 2010)

The architect came to the conclusion that his country needed a radical break. Of all the questions posed by the crisis, the issue of identity seemed to assume a primordial status. There was certainly a continuity between Abdelhakim's statement and the effort of Muslim reformers who once tried to revive a lost identity in order to break free from colonial domination.¹⁴² This attempt to recreate a way to be in the world also invoked the epistemological framework once laid out by Third Worldist thinkers. The stakes seemed broadly similar: reaffirming the legitimate existence of an Algerian self. The context was nonetheless different, as uncertainty prevented the formulation of a straightforward dichotomy such as those that opposed Islam to Europe (for the reformists) or the colonizer to the colonized (in the Fanonian model).

Cultural and associative activities also served to normalize the community's image against the narratives of deviance and backwardness. Even after thirty years and many disillusions and setbacks, Wahiba continued to advocate for the "democratization of learning" and to portray a polity that was not exceptional in its aspirations.

> Things will come one at a time, as we propose new solutions and new experiences to the people to open their mind . . . People are inhibited by a single moralistic discourse that is not counterbalanced. It takes time for a counter-discourse to take shape, and more time for it to penetrate the public. Currently, the means by which we can present the citizens with some kind of choice are missing. But we are trying to make things happen, to create the tools for a plural society, especially for the youth. Here, as elsewhere, people want to flourish. Kids want books, and those who are older have the same kind of wish. Algeria is not different from other countries in the world. People just want a good life.
> (WAHIBA, FOUNDER OF SEVERAL CULTURAL ASSOCIATIONS, NOW EMPLOYED BY FRIEDRICH EBERT STIFTUNG [NGO], ALGIERS, AUTUMN 2010)

Wahiba began to promote reading among children in the early 1990s. In 1998, she had taken part in a "cultural caravan" that toured France to "say that our country [was] not only terrorism," and that Algerians "want[ed] their children to grow up in an open country." She devoted her life to the promotion of culture, which was, according to her, the way to reveal the normality of a society in which "women go to work" and the "youth want to be in a relationship and have a strong desire to live better." Despite her consensual tone, she blamed the government for its inability to respond to these aspirations.

These reflections on identity and normalcy certainly spoke to the legacy of the Dark Decade. They also resonated with Hannah Arendt's profession of faith: "if it were true that man is a being such as Hobbes would have him, he would be unable to found any body politic at all."[143] Certainly, these efforts to think about national identity in a non-catastrophizing way showed that the community had a future beyond the limits imposed by the narratives of immaturity and deviance. Algerianness continued to harbor the promise of emancipation. With its experience of catastrophe and rebellion, its never-ending state of exception, and its quest for normalcy, Algeria carried a message that could resonate well beyond the national borders. Even when it seemed plagued by absurdity and disorder, the postcolony could never be reduced to the monstrous images that blinded its rulers and observers. It was a mirror and a supersession; a space of becoming and of metamorphosis; it was a way "of summing up the world."[144]

Truth Reborn

In *Crises of the Republic*, Arendt writes that truth is the "chief stabilizing factor in the ever-changing affairs of men."[145] Algeria experienced first-hand the vanishing of this shared understanding of reality. The need to rationalize an unstable social world fueled fear and suspicion. Citizens rejected official discourses as a simulation (Bled Miki) or mere trash (Chkoupistan). This does not mean that Algeria had become the negationist society imagined by Baudrillard, a product of simulacrum wherein uncertainty leads to generalized cynicism.[146] Quite the contrary: this society, though subjected to terror, manipulation, absurdity, and predation, developed a moralistic and dichotomous rejection of the actors associated with cynicism. Even diminished, the revolutionary ideal of political sanctity survived the crisis.

Rather than seeing the crisis solely as an opportunity for authoritarian upgrading and accumulation by dispossession, one must revert to an etymological understanding of the word: a crisis is a moment of judgment and discernment, which fosters both comprehension and action. This effort led activists and intellectuals to propose recurring yet contradictory analyses: Algerians suffered from schizophrenia; the people-as-child was impatient; the *Pouvoir* was driven by ignorance and greed; the political order testified to the premodern political culture of the masses; the people was colonized by its government; the people remained the heroic bearer of a revolutionary tradition. The critical process did not only result in a struggle to appropriate resources and control institutions. It also had a symbolic dimension, which notably fostered debates on cultural reform and national identity. It fueled dualistic representations of society that borrowed from colonial racism, authoritarian developmentalism, and liberal progressivism. But many also rejected these caricatures. Their effort to challenge pessimistic narratives echoed the need to arrive at a "post-dramatic" understanding of Bouteflika's Algeria.[147]

Eventually, the symbolic revolution occurred in the first months of 2019, reviving the ideal of political sanctity attached to the people and turning the dominant ideology on its head. Those who had assumed the posture of benevolent fathers were portrayed as worthless thugs. The infantilized masses recovered their heroic and emancipatory potential. Merging with the long-standing effort of social movements to demonstrate popular maturity, civic-mindedness, and pacifism, the *shaʿab/ʿiṣāba* (people/gang) dichotomy encompassed the deep rejection of cynicism and offered clarity. In the early months of the Hirak, a qualitative break in time materialized. Meaning made its way back into Algerian politics.

Coda

The King: Kings should be immortal.
Marguerite: They have a provisional immortality.

—*Eugène Ionesco*

We the people, we have skills and value that some tried to hide. They always tried to portray us as a bad character, violent, aggressive. . . . If they give us the chance, we are capable of extraordinary and exceptional things.

—*Djamel Belmadi*

The first half of 2019 was indeed an exceptional time for Algeria. After Bouteflika announced that he would run for a fifth term in a written statement released on February 10, a revolutionary mobilization started in the Northeast and rapidly spread to the rest of the country. Videos circulated on social media of Algerians calling the Swiss hospital where Bouteflika was allegedly receiving treatment. Pranksters asked the ailing president to pay for the four pizzas he had ordered before getting a fifth one, or demanded that a nurse pull the plug on him. Bouteflika was abandoned by the army and forced to resign on April 2. The new figureheads of the cartel, notably the ANP chief of staff Ahmed Gaïd Salah and interim president Abdelkader Bensalah, immediately pushed to organize new elections in July. Once again, their plans were derailed by a massive mobilization, and the Constitutional Council subsequently postponed the election in early June. In less than five months, opponents of the cartel had exacted a series of concessions that had previously been unimaginable.

A month after the second postponement, the national football team reached the final in the African Cup of Nations. In France, media outlets and politicians portrayed this successful campaign as a security threat, denouncing the public display of patriotism by local Algerian fans and deploring the violence that would allegedly occur if *al-khaḍrā'* (the green) won the title. On July 19, after only two minutes of play, the striker Baghdad Bounedjah scored the only goal of the game against Senegal. Algerians were the champions of Africa for the first time since the triumph of the 1990 "Golden Generation." In Algeria and throughout the world, fans celebrated in the streets in large numbers. Very few violent incidents occurred. The national coach, Djamel Belmadi, born in France, in Champigny-sur-Marne (near Paris), embodied the success of a team composed of players from diverse backgrounds who honored their commitment to "represent the people." A few months later, as the Hirak continued, Belmadi seized the opportunity of a press conference to express his support for a population that had too often been caricatured. The Algerian people's unwavering self-control, he said, meant that their demands should be met.

These two successes certainly boosted the country's reputation globally. They demonstrated that the Algerian people could overcome the narratives of childishness and innate violence. At the same time, the resilience of the cartel also testified to the adaptability of its model of governance. To manage the anticipated catastrophe of another Dark Decade, or the real catastrophe of the Hirak, bureaucratic-military actors relied on similar strategies: nonlethal policing, laws of exception, democratic consolidation, and economic reforms. This resilience is certainly not specific to the Algerian cartel. Ruling coalitions throughout the world have developed powerful tools to manage and even benefit from crises. Indeed, in the wake of the multilayered emergency resulting from the COVID-19 pandemic, global warming, etc., catastrophization is more than ever a feature of global governance.

The Making of the Hirak

Bouteflika's fourth mandate accentuated many of the dynamics outlined in this book, especially the widespread popular discontent that hinted at a revolutionary situation. From 2014 to 2019, citizens denouncing the lack of housing, youth unemployment, and the inflated price of foodstuffs attacked state officials for their inability to provide public services and social justice. Drawing on the discourses of *hogra* and *shkara*, they described a system based on dispossession and contempt. In the South, contentious social movements made subversive claims. For instance, the mobilization against fracking that started in In-Salah in January 2015 included references to internal colonization by a "System" whose dangerous extractive policies echoed the nuclear tests earlier performed by the French. The government nonetheless pressed on, as it remained dependent on the exploitation of the country's hydrocarbon wealth to mitigate the suspended disaster.

The cartel continued to manage the crisis while actively taking part in the production of an unfolding catastrophe. Given free-falling crude oil prices, state officials implemented new economic reforms in an attempt to limit imports, attract foreign investments, and develop productive activities. This bureaucratic reformism, justified in the name of a "battle for development," offered more opportunities to notorious crony capitalists. Mahieddine Tahkout thus partnered with the Korean car manufacturer Hyundai to open a local factory, which benefited from the support of public banks and a lenient regulatory framework. Meanwhile, contradictory economic interests and internal competition within the cartel contributed to recurring political upheavals in the upper echelons of the state. In 2017, Bouteflika sacked two prime ministers in less than three months, the second of whom was no other than future president Abdelmajid Tebboune, who had the misfortune of clashing with FCE president Ali Haddad. In 2018, the powerful head of the police, Abdelghani Hamel, was forced to resign after the revelation of his possible involvement in a drug-trafficking scandal. Meanwhile, state officials continued to invoke the specter of chaos. A letter allegedly written by Bouteflika and released in November 2018 denounced the actions of internal saboteurs who were "hiding the sickles of massacre and [would] not hesitate to use them to drag the country into unknown territory."[1] In this context, the institutional framework seemed more than ever detached from its official goals. A moment of social magic expected to bestow legitimacy on the entire republican edifice, elections were openly vilified by those who repeated the phrase *manvotech* (I don't vote). With official voter turnout at 50 and 35 percent, respectively, the 2014 presidential election and the 2017 legislative elections faced record-breaking abstention.

From this perspective, the announcement of Bouteflika's candidacy was not the reason behind the uprising so much as a tipping point, an occasion that allowed for the coalescence of all the grievances accumulated over the previous decade.[2]

> Then comes the fifth mandate, and this was the ultimate insult, the straw that breaks the camel's back, or whatever you want to call it. We felt that something was happening, with the depth of anger, each time a little more. . . . So, some said that we were going out to protest on the twenty-second, others on the twenty-fourth. Some said that the Islamists were behind it. Others said that it was Toufik. But I thought, "I'll be out there on the twenty-second, even if it's just ten of us, even if I am with the Islamists, even with the Devil, I don't care, I'll be out on the twenty-second." I was about to explode.
>
> (MALIKA, MEMBER OF IBTIKAR AND THE LOCAL STUDENT COORDINATION AT THE UNIVERSITY OF ORAN, REMOTE INTERVIEW, WINTER 2021)

Malika was a local coordinator for the citizen-led movement Ibtikar, an organization founded in 2017 in response to the country's "unique crisis" with the aim of building a "democratic, pluralist, social, modern, and open Algerian republic." When discussing her state of mind before the beginning of the Hirak, she described a sense of accumulated anger and a growing feeling of urgency. When she evoked the continuing suspicion and the unsuccessful efforts of activists who tried to "shake the zombie's grip" during the fourth mandate, she emphasized the unexpected and liberating nature of this mobilization. Indeed, once a symbol of political dispossession and the epitome of institutionalized absurdity, the dreaded election gave rise to a cross-generational movement that brought together different sectors of society in a dichotomous yet nonviolent confrontation between the "people" and the "'iṣāba."

The notion of 'iṣāba echoes an imaginary of corruption and economic plunder that has become central to the politicization of Algerian social movements. Actors that rose to prominence throughout the 2000s and 2010s by voicing socioeconomic grievances emerged as natural vectors for calls to uproot the cartel. In April 2019, two weeks after Bouteflika's resignation, one of the country's most powerful autonomous trade unions, the SNAPAP, released a statement of support for the Hirak, calling for the "departure of all the symbols of the corrupt system" ("raḥīl kul rumūz an-niẓām al-fāsid"). In order to achieve this goal, the union pledged to go on periodic strikes, boycott the revision of electoral lists announced by the government, and reject the election now scheduled for July 2019.[3]

In opposition to the "corrupt system," the SNAPAP and many other organizations depicted the Hirak as "popular" (sha'abi). In so doing, they revived the dualistic imaginary inherited from colonialism in the framework of a continuing struggle against ruling elites likened to national "traitors" (ya khawana). As Patrick Wolfe explains, the regular inflection and reformulation of such settler binary imaginaries can become eminently subversive.[4] The symbolic violence of the crisis had long justified the securitizing and civilizing policies characteristic of the Algerian model of governance by catastrophization. As a long-awaited symbolic revolution, the Hirak was the consecration of an effort to reformulate the binary imaginary inherited from colonialism and fight the abjection of the masses. Indeed, revolt works "as a subjectifying force—that is, as a means through which those made abject attempt to reconstitute themselves not only as citizens with rights, but as subjects of value."[5]

The peaceful uprising was not only a response to the lived experience of the crisis; as a degrading and terrifying trial, it also reasserted norms in the face of perceived anomie.

> In 2017–2018, I kept repeating to myself that [the uprising] was too slow to come. February 22nd is the most normal thing that could have happened given the country's situation. Seeing the President's picture paraded during the celebration of November 1st was just too much. The Hirak took too long, because what happened after 2014 was unthinkable and unacceptable.
>
> (MALIKA, 2021)

While she blamed some of her fellow citizens for contributing to the "gangrene" that she associated with Bouteflika's fourth mandate, Malika also viewed the Hirak as a chance to reassert the "values of citizenship." This was one of the many normative claims that burgeoned after February 2019, in addition to references to the rule of law, human rights, labor rights, dignity, the revolutionary principles of November 1954, and Islamic values. Out of the indetermination and confusion that characterizes a lingering state of exception, a potentially universal normativity can indeed emerge.[6] In the case of Algeria, it also meant the collective affirmation of the ideal of political sanctity inherited from the revolution and associated with the people, as the heroic agent of its own emancipation.

The Golden Generation

Nidhal had discussed leaving Algeria for a long time. When we talked on the phone at the end of the summer of 2018, he said that he was ready. The political situation showed no signs of improvement, and he was tired of waiting. He found the routine of political activism in Algiers increasingly pointless. Moreover, his efforts to start his own business had failed because of bureaucratic obstacles. He had thus made the decision to settle in France, where he had found a job in a prominent antiracist organization. He was ready to live a simpler life, even if it meant that he would have to distance himself from Algeria and RAJ, the organization he had helped build. Because he was afraid that their distress might make him change his mind, he waited until the last minute before announcing his departure to the young members of the movement. It was, he said, admittedly heartbreaking.

Six months later, Nidhal was living his new life in Paris while keeping up with the Hirak. Like many expatriates, he traveled to Algeria to protest. With the support of his boss, he left Paris every Thursday evening to attend the Friday march in the center of Algiers. He would then spend three days organizing with fellow activists before returning to France on Monday morning, for the beginning of the work week. The rhythm was exhausting, but Nidhal simply could not miss out on a revolution in the making. He flooded social media with triumphant pictures of himself surrounded by young activists and old friends, reclaiming the public space of the capital awash in a tide of Algerian flags.

Nidhal also mobilized his networks on the other side of the Mediterranean. In July 2019, I found him at a rally organized in support of the Hirak in Paris. More than a thousand people had gathered for a classic Parisian march from Place de la République to Place de la Nation, two of the city's major squares. As in Algeria, the crowd was disciplined, and several attendees made explicit comparisons with the disorder associated with the recent "Yellow Vest" movement in France. Young men and women wearing orange vests (the so-called *gilets oranges*) organized the demonstration, directing protesters and facilitating the passage of cars in coordination with the police. The protest's radical message—calling for regime change—contrasted with its form, complying as it did with the law. Nidhal knew most of the organizers, many of whom also had one foot in France and the other in Algeria. His daughter, Fouzia, marched with a section of antiracist activists. Over the past year, she had taken up the torch of student and political organizing. Now she traveled back and forth between France and Algeria with her father. Nidhal was immensely proud as he recounted Fouzia's recent participation in a meeting of Algerian organizations in favor of peaceful change.

For a short period of time, the Hirak was dubbed "the Revolution of Smiles" (*Thawra al-Ibtisām*). It was then rebranded as "the Peaceful" (*Essilmiyya*), a term that emphasized a key strategic feature of an uprising committed to avoiding any form of destruction.[7] This pacifist mode of struggle testified to how the suspended disaster had influenced forms of popular resistance. It also suggested a generational shift. Indeed, the peaceful mobilization of hundreds of thousands of young Algerians reflected the decades-long effort of dozens of youth groups, including RAJ, to change the country's political life.[8] The security-based justifications of the status quo ceased to be effective for various reasons, including demographics: the civil conflict had ended almost twenty years earlier, and approximately 54 percent of the Algerian population was under the age of thirty.[9] While the Dark Decade had constantly limited the political possibilities offered to a new generation of citizens, this period of extreme violence was a distant experience for many. The past catastrophe had been replaced by a current economic and political catastrophe resulting from years of autocratic mismanagement.

A common generational experience didn't mean that protesters were in agreement, however, even if they all rejected a group of actors associated with predation and internal colonialism. As a grassroots performance of sovereignty, the Hirak glossed over existing divisions between revolutionaries and reformists, secularists and Islamists, leftists and neoliberals. As the outcome of a fragmented mobilization that had started in the streets, it reproduced grassroots resistance practices while lacking any clear ideological framework or unifying intellectual references, comparable to the likes of Lenin or Shariati. At the same time, the collective consciousness forged in the streets didn't give birth to mere "non-movements," to use Bayat's term.[10] As in the rest of the Arab world, previous mobilizations had in common radical demands for dignity, justice, and democracy. They resulted in extremely diverse practices of contention, including more formal engagements.[11] Groups as varied as RAJ, local student committees, the Rachad movement (Islamo-conservative), or the SNAPAP institutionalized political debates and modes of action. Reflecting on how they could revitalize the notion of citizenship, they published their ongoing reflections, organized conferences, and offered training sessions. It is out of this collective consciousness that the people-as-class materialized in February 2019. The "Algerian people," as an empty signifier, served as a symbolic container that allowed for contentious demands to coalesce in the public space. This representation and aggregation of multiple grievances was made possible by a populist tradition that brought coherence to the movement.[12]

The people-as-class relied on deeply ingrained forms of contention taken from a national repertoire built under Bouteflika. Yet given the rapidly evolving dynamics within groups, the changes in repressive strategies, and the reconfiguration of national politics, protesters involved in such revolutionary mobilizations have no choice but to reinterpret their repertoire of action and alter their political performances in real time.[13] Thus, official pictures of Bouteflika, which had once symbolized the glaciation of political time, became targets of popular wrath. In the town of Khenchela in February 2019, protesters forced local authorities to take down a giant poster of Bouteflika, which they then proceeded to trample on. While previously limited for strategic reasons, protests became multi-sectoral and cross-generational. Students, lawyers, football fans, and grandparents took to the streets together. In the center of Algiers, demonstrators came from the working-class neighborhoods of Bab El-Oued and Belouizdad. While demonstrating the patriotism and anti-imperialism dominant in Algerian politics and social movements, the Hirak also provided an opportunity for the reintegration of the diaspora. In addition to the rallies organized in Paris, Montreal, and London, movements founded abroad, such as Ibtikar and Rachad, also intervened in debates among revolutionaries. The Hirak also updated the national musical repertoire of contention, which integrated already existing protest songs ("La Casa del Mouradia" by Ouled el-Bahdja), new pieces written by expatriate singers in support of the uprising ("Liberté" by Soolking, "Allo le Système!" by Raja Meziane), and remixes of international hits ("Win biha win," based on "Win el-Malayeen" by the Lebanese singer Julia Boutros).

In "Liberté," Soolking asserts that his is the "Golden Generation." If the insurrection again devolves into violence, the singer says, the youth will work in favor of peace, but the status quo is over. At the end of the same song, the backing band, Ouled el-Bahdja, echoes this sentiment, pledging that their flame will not fade away (*en-nar 'indi ma tetfash*). Here we see that the experience of the oppressed can conjure up a revolutionary mobilization, because it renders "visible the catastrophic nature of contemporary predicaments of power."[14] The generational duty to avenge "millions" is synonymous with politicization and mobilization. In the early months of the Hirak, a sign in front of Algiers's École Normale Supérieure quoted Fanon: "Each generation discovers its mission, accomplishes or betrays it."

This messianic mission is sealed by a "secret agreement between past generations and the present one," as Benjamin puts it.[15] The centrality of the anticolonial revolution in Algerian political culture made such agreement both necessary and self-evident. In 2021, Nadir, a local leader of the Rachad movement in Paris explained,

> My main motivation is that I hate *hogra*. I can't stand the way Algerians are treated on a daily basis, by police agents or bureaucrats. . . . Then, the revolutionary feeling is also in my blood. My aunt died during the war of liberation. I also have an uncle who died between '54 and '62, and my grandfather too, my mother's father, he died for Algeria.
>
> (NADIR, MEMBER OF THE LOCAL OFFICE OF
> THE RACHAD MOVEMENT, PARIS, WINTER 2021)

Nadir was one of many to make a connection with the sacrifices of the "Revolutionary Family." In April 2019, the SNAPAP concluded its statement in support for the Hirak as follows: "Long live the people's Hirak, long live a free and independent Algeria and glory to our martyrs." The autonomous union linked the present mobilization to the past martyrdom of anticolonial insurgents. These two qualitative moments were part of a single struggle to free the nation. Unsurprisingly, the Hirak appropriated many of the symbols and figures of the nation's contentious past, and protesters repeatedly invoked the unfulfilled promises of 1962. Indeed, the messianic mission of the "Golden Generation" was both "the full actualization of the past's lost and oppressed potentialities" and an effort to "derail the catastrophic course of actual history."[16]

Emergency Management

At the end of the march in Paris, Nidhal looked at Fouzia as she walked toward a nearby metro station. "She is even more radical than I am," he said with obvious pride. Later the same evening, he admitted that he might have to wait a bit longer before seeing a red flag hoisted over El Mouradia, the presidential palace. He recognized that it was imperative to create consensus among opposition movements and to reach out to less radical actors. He focused his energy on the Pact for a Democratic Alternative, a coalition of parties, labor unions, and NGOs that was made official in September 2019. Situated on the left of the political spectrum, the pact advocated for a national conference and a constituent process that would lead to a Second Republic. Meanwhile, liberal and Islamist politicians left open the possibility of negotiating with the remaining components of the cartel in the name of ending the crisis.

Forms of discursive catastrophization continued after the beginning of the Hirak. First and foremost, Chief of Staff Ahmed Gaïd Salah, now the most powerful man in the country, positioned the ANP as the guardian of the constitutional order. In addition to safeguarding national sovereignty, the army was thus charged with the double task of fighting corruption and guiding the process of democratization. Despite Gaïd Salah's efforts to foster a rapid return to order, the election scheduled for July 4 had been cancelled. In a speech at the Military Academy of Cherchell at the end of June, the army's chief of staff warned that departing from the constitutional framework would lead to chaos. He portrayed an ANP dedicated to the struggle against "plotters" and presented the future president as a "sword against corruption and the corrupters" (*sayfan 'alā al-fasād wa-l-mufsidīn*).[17]

A new election was soon scheduled for the end of December. This time, the full weight of the state apparatus ensured that the electoral process would not be further delayed, even if this meant that popular sovereignty would be disregarded.

A few days after the demonstration, I met Nidhal and one of his friends, Smaïl, also a former member of RAJ, near the Canal de l'Ourcq in Paris. The discussion rapidly turned to politics. The two men were amazed by the discipline of the protesters from Bab el-Oued. They noted that even those who did not pray on Friday nevertheless waited for those who did before taking to the streets, showing the solidarity and cohesion of the movement. But despite their unwavering admiration for the Hirak, they also expressed their fear that some might try to manipulate the movement. The rationality of suspicion and instrumentalization had not disappeared. As the cartel strove to drive a wedge between protesters, activists remained cautious. As we discussed how the *Pouvoir* could manipulate the protests, Nidhal mentioned the emergence of a new slogan: *Rahu jay, rahu jay, al-'isyan al-madani* (It's coming, it's coming, the civil disobedience). While he supported the option, he also found the simultaneity of these expressions of radicalization troubling. Smaïl agreed, adding that Toufik was probably influencing people from his jail cell. While he had been arrested in May 2019, the former head of the DRS was still viewed as an omnipotent puppet master commanding a vast network of henchmen. As he finished his fries, Smaïl noted that "the 'System' is playing its hand."

After the fall of Bouteflika and his affiliates, the cartel reverted to its barest form: a coalition of military and bureaucratic actors within the state field. Catastrophizing policies met with mitigating efforts. On the one hand, a judicial crackdown decimated Bouteflika's close-knit guard in the name of purging the state of corrupt elements. Ali Haddad was notably arrested while trying to cross the Tunisian border. He was then sent to El Harrach Prison, with several other iconic associates of the presidency such as transportation tycoon Mahieddine Tahkout and former prime ministers Ouyahia and Sellal. These purges exposed the predatory practices of high-ranking officials, including those of the former head of the police, Abdelghani Hamel.[18] Nonetheless, these anticorruption procedures also served to facilitate a pragmatic reconfiguration of the cartel.

At the same time, Gaïd Salah made no mystery of his determination to criminalize the more radical protesters who allegedly threatened the integrity of national territory. The security apparatus swiftly responded to his command by relying on the strategy of "democratic crowd management" set up by Hamel. Bearers of the Amazigh flag and Berberist activists were portrayed as dangerous and immature troublemakers instrumentalized by Algeria's enemies. From the second half of June onward, the number of protesters detained on charges of "threatening state security" and "demoralizing the army" rose steadily, reaching 151 on the eve of the December election.[19] It thus became increasingly difficult to maintain the idea of a communion between the army and the people. Slogans targeted the chief of staff—*Gaïd Salah, shayyat al-Imarat* (Gaïd Salah, servant of the Emirates), or *Jaysh Sha'ab, khawa khawa, wa Gaïd Salah ma'a al-khawana* (The army and the people are brothers, and Gaïd Salah is with the traitors)—and demanded a civilian state—*Jumhuriyya mashi cazerna* (A republic is not a barrack), *Dawla madaniyya mashi 'askariyya* (A civil state, not a military one).

When I sat down with Nidhal at the end of August, he was preparing to return to Algeria. After six months of traveling back and forth, he was too tired to keep up with this rhythm. "I am fifty years old now," he joked. He was about to quit his job in France and move back into his apartment in the center of Algiers. There, he could dedicate himself solely to the success of this "beautiful revolution." He knew that repression was intensifying, but he was determined to prevent the presidential election that he saw as "an insult to the people." At the beginning of September, a leader of the movement of the unemployed, Tahar Belabbes, gave an interview to *L'Avant-Garde*, an online publication dedicated to the coverage of social and progressist movements. Rejecting the upcoming presidential election and a return to the status quo ante, Belabbes warned of the intensification of repression after activists had been physically abused near Ouargla.[20] The crackdown continued despite pervasive popular mobilization. After the mujahid Lakhdar Bouregaâ was arrested in June, opposition politician Karim Tabbou was also apprehended for allegedly undermining national unity and the army's morale. Nidhal nonetheless moved back to Algeria and resumed his life as a pillar of local activism. On Friday, October 4—the thirty-third week of peaceful protests—he was arrested with a group of comrades before the beginning of a march. They were released only to be arrested again the same day and questioned for several hours about the organization and funding of RAJ. On the eve of the anniversary of

October 1988, a date that Nidhal had commemorated for the past twenty years, he was transferred to El Harrach Prison.

While security and judicial apparatuses cracked down on those who opposed the upcoming presidential election, a government of unelected technocrats announced new reforms against the backdrop of a rapidly deteriorating economic situation and a complete lack of accountability. Prime Minister Noureddine Bedoui announced the end of the 51/49 rule limiting foreign ownership of nonstrategic sectors. Eager to secure the complicit silence of the state's Western partners, he also pushed for the adoption a new and highly controversial law on hydrocarbons, which among other things favored the interests of major foreign companies such as Total and ExxonMobil. In response, protesters gathered in front of the parliament chanting, "They sold the country, we won't vote!"[21]

An alumnus of the École Nationale d'Administration, Bedoui also supervised the preparations for the upcoming presidential election. Unsurprisingly, another graduate of the school and former minister under Bouteflika was anointed. Thanks to the support of Gaïd Salah, and despite a new all-time abstention record for a presidential election (with more than 60 percent of voters abstaining), Abdelmajid Tebboune was sworn in on December 19, 2019. After the surprise death of the ANP's chief of staff, who succumbed to a heart attack a week later, Tebboune positioned himself as the new main authority in the cartel. He restructured the ANP's key directorates and appointed a former director of the École Nationale d'Administration, Abdelaziz Djerad, as his prime minister. Meanwhile, at conferences organized by the FCE, former ministers and experts rejoiced in the fact that the aggravating budget crisis might represent an opportunity to further restructure the economy.[22] As was the case under Bouteflika, managing the political and economic emergency allowed for the mitigation of various threats (chiefly indebtedness and the revolutionary mobilization) and the reorganization of the ruling coalition.

Nidhal was provisionally released at the beginning of January 2020, after Tebboune announced his willingness to negotiate with opposition figures in order to draft a "consensual constitution" that would "dispel the specter of future crises."[23] While some personalities and party leaders accepted this offer, many others reaffirmed the illegitimacy of the "System" and renewed their calls for a national conference. The Hirak continued and celebrated its first anniversary on Friday 21, 2020. Nidhal was once again in the streets, wearing a red scarf. A few weeks later, the COVID-19 pandemic hit Algeria. By the end of March, the Hirakists announced the suspension of their movement in the name of safeguarding public health before the government imposed a lockdown. Rapidly, the authorities instrumentalized the confinement to crack down on individual activists. Several websites were also blocked.[24] As the pandemic added to the revolutionary mobilization and the economic emergency, the cartel benefited from its long-standing experience of governance by catastrophization to suspend what was now a staggering list of disasters.

A Return to the Routine of the Crisis?

When we talked on the phone at the end of April 2020, Nidhal was stunned by this turn of events. He had never trusted the *Pouvoir* to keep its word, but the pandemic was an unexpected blow. "I wonder what we have done to deserve this," he said bitterly. All wasn't lost, though. He mentioned the Hirak's achievements over the past year. He was also proud of Fouzia, who had taken a leading role agitating in favor of political detainees (including himself). Not only was she a relentless activist like her father, but her grades were also skyrocketing. Nonetheless, as he awaited his own trial, he couldn't hide a sense of powerlessness resulting from the combination of political uncertainty, legal precariousness, and a month of Ramadhan under curfew.

Another month passed. With the pandemic receding, activists discussed the possibility of reigniting the Hirak. They were split between their commitment to act responsibly and prevent a health disaster, and the risk of falling back into the routine of bureaucratic-military management. One morning in June 2020, as he was walking with a friend, Nidhal found himself surrounded by police officers dressed as civilians. Once again, he was arrested and charged, this time for "participation in an unarmed gathering" and for disseminating "publications [in this case, Facebook posts] jeopardizing national interest." Nidhal was in a position of absolute vulnerability. He was kept on a "threshold of indistinction between exclusion and inclusion," as a product of sovereign arbitrariness, as a *homo sacer*.[25] At this instant, a myriad of disasters converged around him, individual and collective, to reproduce the conditions of subjection.

At the national level, the cartel has reverted to its usual tactics to manage the crisis. In April 2020, a revision of the penal code criminalized the spreading of "disinformation." Then, in December 2021, another modification established harsh penalties for blocking access to government buildings and public establishments. In the name of protecting the public, these laws limit the possibilities for dissent and expand the sphere of police and judicial intervention. Individual activists charged under phony pretexts are thus routinely sentenced to a year in prison, before a presidential pardon then demonstrates the mercifulness of the sovereign. In the eyes of many Hirak activists, such legalized arbitrariness makes Tebboune's rule significantly more repressive than Bouteflika's. Yet the new president continues to play the refrain of democratic consolidation, with the tacit support of his international partners. In November 2020, he organized a referendum on a new constitutional amendment, which left the current order virtually unchanged. And in June 2021, legislative elections were held, resulting in another underwhelming victory for the FLN, which remained the dominant party in the country with 6.2 percent of the votes cast in a widely boycotted electoral process.[26] Meanwhile, the economy remains under duress as attempts to limit spending while maintaining the ANP's inflated budget continue to guide the government's technocratic reformism. The combination of austerity and the reduction of imports thus fuels inflation without containing indebtedness. Contradictory objectives result in erratic policies, such as the introduction of new taxes in the 2022 finance law and their nearly immediate suspension. In short, Tebboune's Algeria replicates and amplifies the pillars of governance by catastrophization: a repression combining exception and regulation that remains far less violent than that practiced in Egypt or Sudan; a top-down democratic consolidation relying on discredited institutions; and a bureaucratic reformism aiming to prevent an economic collapse while protecting vested interests.

Given the ability of the cartel to manage the crisis and the tangible threats facing the nation, the necessity to negotiate with the ruling elites resurfaced. Some, like Nadir from the Rachad movement, considered such a compromise unthinkable. Others, such as Malika from Ibtikar, confessed that a negotiation was "inevitable" in order to "prevent the state from collapsing."[27] As in the 1990s, the crisis opened a space for actors aiming to balance opposition and participation—as was the case, for instance, in the framework of the organization al-Massar al-Jadid.

With al-Massar al-Jadid, we have two forces that are reunited in one single movement: people who have always been opponents, and people who have always worked with the "System." We use the position of the latter, their acquaintances, their network within the Algerian state. And we also rely on the Hirak, on political activists, writers, professors. I think that this is the complementarity we need to change the feudal mode of governance. We need people in the "System" to promote a progressive discourse.

(MOUNIA, MEMBER AL-MASSAR AL-JADID, ALGIERS, REMOTE INTERVIEW, WINTER 2021)

In Mounia's eyes, al-Massar al-Jadid was a response to the shortcomings of the Hirak, which she saw as unable to fundamentally change the country. She presented the search for compromise as a matter of responsibility, a necessity in a moment of extreme uncertainty. While she was still critical of the corrupt actors who had mismanaged the country during Bouteflika's last mandate, she was also weary of what would happen if "radicals"—that is to say Islamists—were to benefit from the Hirak to seize power. At the same time, several activists involved in the Hirak, including Nidhal, portrayed al-Massar al-Jadid as another creation of the "System" designed to sow confusion.

As the cartel maintains its hold on the state, the clear binaries of the Hirak's early days have lost their luster and confusion reigns again. In late 2019, the slogan *Badissiyya-Novembriyya*, which referred to Abdelhamid Ben Badis (a nationalist icon and inspiration to Algerian Islamo-conservatives) and the insurrection of November 1954, was accused of conflating the values of Islamism with that of the revolution. It was portrayed as a ploy of the MSP and/or the cartel to hijack the popular mobilization and promote a reactionary agenda. More recently, the liberation of General-Major Toufik, whose initial condemnation for conspiring against the state and the army was invalidated, has confirmed that the networks of the DRS are far from dismantled. The rationality of suspicion and instrumentalization has returned, fueling divisions within the Hirak and facilitating the efforts of state officials to treat recalcitrant opponents as terrorists.

The progressive return to a routinized crisis also means that a conjectural intensification is possible and can be instrumentalized. In the summer of 2021, the crisis resulting from the combination of a deadly wave of

COVID-19, economic hardship, political uncertainty, and climate change reached its apex when a wave of wildfires swept the North, causing dozens of deaths. As Kabyle villages were surrounded by burning forests, the government accused local pyromaniacs of igniting the fires. In this apocalyptic context, a young man arrested by the police was mistakenly accused of being one of them (in fact, he had traveled as a volunteer from a neighboring *wilaya* to help his "Kabyle brothers"). He was subsequently lynched and burned alive by an angry mob. Government officials continued to look for additional scapegoats, as they promoted a conspiracy theory in which the Moroccan government, secessionists from the MAK, and Islamo-conservatives of the Rachad movement worked together to destroy the country. Such discursive catastrophization allowed the government to criminalize the two organizations, which were now identified as terrorist groups. Meanwhile, it also contributed to the production of another potential disaster—namely, the threat of war with Morocco.

The Hirak has emerged from and evolved in the context of governance by catastrophization. Even after two years of mobilization, the shadow of the 1990s continues to shape the strategies of various actors, sometimes in diametrically opposed ways.

> The threat, if we don't find a political solution, and if we don't give a chance to democracy, with the resulting accentuation of the social and economic crisis, and with the political maturity demonstrated by the majority of the Algerian people, is to go back to a form of violence like that of the 1990s. And violence will be catastrophic for Algeria and the region.
>
> (NADIR, 2021)

> If tomorrow we have a democracy that gives the people the freedom to make decisions, it will be like in 1992 all over again. People are indoctrinated. They're not conscious. I mean, the majority, not those who live in big cities—Algiers, Oran, Constantine—most of them don't grasp the notion of citizenship. They want Islamism and the establishment of the sharia. The solution is to invest in the individual first, to invest in culture.
>
> (MOUNIA, 2021)

Mounia and Nadir represent two irreconcilable extremes of the Hirak. Since February 2019, Mounia has been wary of mass violence and a return to terrorism. She is fundamentally secularist and would have rather preserved the status quo than risk an electoral triumph for the Islamists. Thus, she supported al-Massar al-Jadid's strategy of conciliation and repeated an elitist discourse about the need to educate the masses. Conversely, Nadir believes that the status quo could lead to a catastrophic rise in violence. And in order to avoid such a trap, he advocated for a patient, cautious, and nonviolent approach to ensure the departure of the "System." While an agreement between them was unlikely, their divergent strategies of nonviolent resistance and pragmatic negotiation were responses to the constant endangerment that is a key feature of catastrophization.

Catastrophization and the Future of Governance

Throughout the world, governance by catastrophization allows the radicalization of state institutions and the deployment of the "integrated biopolitical-sovereign" apparatus described by Ophir.[28] In the name of necessity, international partners, NGOs, and former opponents intervene to work with catastrophizing state actors and suspend the disaster. In so doing, they create the conditions for a lasting state of emergency, a seemingly never-ending crisis that becomes the dominant rationale for the management of the population, the economy, and the polity.

Bouteflika's Algeria was no exception. The model of governance based on the production, management, and suspension of multifaceted crises has become a widespread feature that transcends the North/South and democracy/authoritarianism dichotomies. From Nicolás Maduro in Venezuela to Donald Trump in the United States, from Benjamin Netanyahu in Israel to Narendra Modi in India, the list of leaders who have thrived in the systematic production of disaster is long. Critics of neoliberalism might explain the rise of governance by catastrophization as the outcome of a mix of denialism and opportunism that seeks to weather a crisis induced by poor policy choices.[29] This model of governance might also be understood as the result of the profound transformation of modern governments accelerated by the so-called war on terror, an expansion of the realm of sovereignty and biopolitics toward a general state of indetermination that blurs the limits between exception and normalcy, peace and war, inside and outside, legality and illegality.[30] Finally, it might also be a transitory step toward the advent of an apocalyptic world of petty fortresses shaped by the accumulation of crises and the hegemony of securitization.[31]

Each of these hypotheses seems valid, but what is certain is that even in the midst of chaos, and despite the intervention of multiple actors, nation-states remain central in the production and mitigation of the suspended disaster. Governance by catastrophization is shaped by specific historical trajectories, by particular class and racial formations, and by local repertoires of contention, which are all in one way or another organized and/or mediated by the nation-state. In a context of emergency, nation-states are not necessarily weakened by the intervention of foreign organizations and the call to action of local actors. They act more than ever as gatekeepers, reasserting their role as partners for security and intermediaries for the distribution of resources. What's more, the anticipation of the catastrophe resonates with a national imaginary and mobilizes key state actors. In Algeria, the suspended disaster echoed a postcolonial political culture shaped by defensive nationalism and developmentalism. It has also served the restructuring of the bureaucratic-military machine born during the revolution.

This mode of governance generates subjection, but it also collides with grassroots representations of the catastrophe and opens a space for competing claims to sovereignty. Indeed, lived experiences of catastrophization are not merely at odds with state narratives; they can also fuel an understanding of the situation that calls for immediate rebellion. From this perspective, the Hirak certainly represents a remarkable example of revolutionary mobilization motivated by a sense of collective emergency.

Moments of rebellion are nonetheless shaped by catastrophization and do not guarantee a supersession in the direction of actual revolution. Again, the Hirak provides a telling example, notably through the nonviolent commitment of its adherents. Indeed, the pacifism of the protesters has certainly served to forestall a rise in violence and a repetition of the Dark Decade. Nevertheless, it is also compatible with the strategies of nonlethal policing and co-option developed by the Algerian state over the past twenty years. Thus, one could argue that pacifism is a conformation as much as a challenge, the product of a tacit agreement between protesters and rulers to reject pure anomic violence and the messianic redemption it authorizes.

In order to prevent a catastrophic escalation, subversive actors create the conditions for their potential capture by the state.[32]

It would therefore be inexact to claim that governance by catastrophization sows the seeds of its own demise. This is not to say that the Hirak, as a way out of the catastrophic present, is destined to fail. The narrative of failure ignores the reality of what has already been accomplished, from the collective demonstration of popular sovereignty to the establishment of transnational networks of actors dedicated to radical political change. Moreover, inasmuch as public authorities have been clearly and loudly identified as active producers of the disaster, their illegitimacy is a given that will durably undermine the political order. Indetermination and confusion remain ubiquitous, limiting both the potential of emancipatory movements and the ability of the security apparatus to maintain control. Imagining clear futures liberated from the shackles of terror, scarcity, and emergency thus remains central to revealing a horizon beyond the suspended disaster.

Acknowledgments

Almost fourteen years have passed since I started this research project. In between, a first version of this book was published in French a few weeks after the beginning of the Hirak. The peaceful uprising of 2019 proved to be both a confirmation of some of my hypotheses and an inspiration to include fresh perspectives and tackles new issues. The present version of *The Suspended Disaster* is therefore more than a mere translation. It gives the book a second life. Crucially, it benefited from the efforts of activists and researchers to understand the Hirak in real time. The engagement and support of these friends and colleagues spanning three continents proved to be invaluable resources in bringing the present project to fruition.

First and foremost, this research was only possible thanks to the contributions of those who welcomed me in Algeria. This includes, obviously, Hakim, who is like family and who has the best taste when it comes to football, even if he should eat more vegetables. Without him, there would be no research, no book, and consequently no reason to write these acknowledgements. I am also indebted to all those who agreed to meet with me, to have a quick coffee or take me on a day-long tour, particularly Habiba, Hadj Ali, Samir, and the striking professors in Ghardaïa. And it goes without saying that the researcher must occasionally rest and eat, and for this I am immensely grateful to my hosts in Algeria, starting with Salim and his family, Oussama, along with his parents and friends, Père Guillaume and all the workers and guests at the Centre d'Études Diocésain des Glycines, and the Pères Blancs in Tizi Ouzou.

As a collective endeavor, thinking is certainly made easier when one is surrounded by smart and generous people. I was lucky enough to undertake my fieldwork at the same time as a group of accomplished social scientists whose research has been critical in shedding new light on Algeria's contemporary trajectory, including Layla Baamara, Tristan Leperlier, Farida Souiah, Naoual Belakhdar, Giulia Fabbiano and Malika Rahal. Exchanging impressions about the challenges we faced and reading each other's work not only helped me grow intellectually, it was also critical in overcoming the sense of isolation resulting from the peculiar rhythm of academic research. I was similarly fortunate to benefit from the insights of senior colleagues in Algeria, notably Louisa Dris-Aït Hamadouche, Yahia H. Zoubir, and Daho Djerbal, who were generous enough to take the time to chat with a young and still relatively clueless French researcher. I am also thankful to the director of the Centre d'Etudes Maghrébines en Algérie, Robert Parks, for sharing his encyclopedic knowledge of Algerian politics. The maturation of this project was facilitated by the generous feedback provided by Luis Martinez, Élizabeth Picard, Omar Carlier, and Gilles Bataillon. Lastly, I owe much debt to my mentor, Hamit Bozarslan, who saved this project when it was going astray and who has supported me during all these years.

Numerous colleagues helped me in the process of translating the book and incorporating the tectonic shock represented by the Hirak. Among them, I must first thank the anonymous reviewers whose thoughtful comments helped me update the manuscript. I am also particularly thankful to Pascal Ménoret for sharing his wisdom on how to write legible academic prose and keep a Mediterranean gaze in all circumstances. I am also grateful for the support and feedback provided by colleagues scattered across the immensity of North America, including Ratiba Hadj Moussa, John P. Entelis, Jacob Mundy, and Benoit Challand.

Before finding its way into the hands (or onto the screen) of the reader, this book was also the product of the labor of those involved in the system of academic production. As such, I can only claim partial responsibility for its making. Romain Costa and Karima Dirèche at the IRMC, Xavier Audrain and Jeannie Raymond at Karthala, and Caelyn Cobb, Marisa Lastres,

Monique Laban, Ryan Perks, and Marc Lynch at Columbia were all instrumental in the publication of *The Suspended Disaster*. In addition, Philip Grant's work as a line editor was a tremendous help in ironing out the manuscript.

Furthermore, I am indebted to a cohort of brilliant colleagues and friends at UC Santa Cruz and its environs, who continue to provide the most stimulating and benevolent intellectual environment I could hope for. I am particularly thankful to Matthew Sparke and Benjamin Read for their mentorship, and to Megan Thomas, Marc Matera, Hillary Angelo, Benjamin Breen, Martin Devecka, Hunter Bivens, Gregory O'Malley, Johanna Isaacson, Roya Pakzad, Elaine Sullivan, Yasmeen Daifallah, Alma Heckman, Vilashini Cooppan, and Nidhi Mahajan for their constant engagement and inspirational presence. Above all, I must thank Jennifer Derr, whose energy, brilliance, and charisma are a reminder that if the limits of humankind remain unexplored, some definitely get closer than others.

Finally, my family is the bedrock sustaining the entire edifice of this research. My parents, Marie-Christine and Frédéric, have allowed me to take the time to experiment and pursue the career of my choice, with only my well-being in mind for some thirty-eight years now. My sister, Laureline, read drafts of my MA and PhD theses, and fixed more mistakes than one could count. And my grandmother, Micheline, has provided me with a model of unwavering strength and vitality that one can only hope to emulate. Muriam Haleh Davis, finally, has read different versions of this manuscript, delt with most of my moments of frustration, and listened to lengthy exposés of less than cogent theories, all without ever losing her calm. Another book would not suffice to express how lucky I am to share ideas and many other things with her.

Appendix A
Methods of Inquiry

Interviews

The individuals quoted in this book were all informed beforehand of the reasons for my presence in Algeria and the goals of my research. Unless otherwise noted, the quotes were collected during semi-directed interviews, structured by a set of preestablished themes (usually the following: personal trajectory, experience in the 1990s, expectations at the beginning of Bouteflika's tenure, experience of political activism, experience of repression, vision of the future) and adapted depending on the interviewee's responses and personal focus. The recording of our discussions started after the interviewees expressed their informed consent. A minority refused to be recorded. In that case, I wrote their responses directly into my fieldwork notebooks during the interview. When possible, I sent them a transcription of the interview for review.

Anonymity and Protection of the Sources

Most interviewees in the book are anonymized, although a majority indicated that they agreed to have their name appear in full. When a real name appears, it is because that individual's position of leadership is essential to contextualize their statements, the content of the quotations does not present a risk to their security, and the interview was recorded before 2014. Before this date, interviewees often expressed a willingness to have their names appear in print. This changed after the 2014 presidential election and the subsequent degradation of the political atmosphere. An increasing number of interviewees were by this point refusing to be recorded, in addition to requesting anonymity. The growing intensity of repression in Algeria since 2019 suggests that anonymization is now systematically warranted for interviews collected after this date.

Observations In Situ

The semi-directed interviews are complemented by observations collected during successive rounds of fieldwork between 2008 and 2014. These observations include informal discussions, rumors, jokes, as well as participant observation conducted before, during, and after protests in Algiers, Tizi Ouzou, and Ghardaïa. All of these notes were compiled at the end of each day in fieldwork notebooks.

Appendix B

A Time Line for Bouteflika's Algeria

October 1988	A nationwide popular uprising leads to a violent military crackdown as well as a political opening and the end of the single-party system.
1989–1991	The adoption of a new pluralist constitution prompts the rise of a diverse press landscape and the formation of the Islamic Salvation Front, which dominates successive elections.
1992	The Dark Decade begins following a military coup, the interruption of legislative elections, the dissolution of the FIS, and the assassination of President Mohamed Boudiaf. The ensuing decade of violence will cause the deaths of 150,00 to 200,000 Algerians.
April 1994	The IMF and the government sign an agreement to implement a structural adjustment program.
1997–1998	A wave of civilian massacres is perpetrated by mostly unidentified terrorist groups.
September 1998	President Liamine Zeroual calls for a snap presidential election.
April 1999	Bouteflika wins the snap presidential election after the withdrawal of his opponents. Official voter turnout is at 61 percent.

September 1999	The Referendum on Civil Concord is held.
April 2001	Beginning of the Kabyle Black Spring following the murder of eighteen-year-old Massinissa Guermah in a gendarmerie station near Tizi Ouzou.
May 2002	Legislative elections see the return of the FLN as the dominant party in the country. Official voter turnout is at 46 percent.
May 2003	Bouteflika sacks Prime Minister Ali Benflis, who decides to run against him in the upcoming presidential election with the support of the FLN and military figures.
April 2004	Bouteflika is convincingly reelected, despite Benflis's challenge. Official voter turnout is at 58 percent.
July 2004	The presidency proceeds to force the retirement of dozens of military officers, including the army's chief of staff, Mohamed Lamari, who is replaced by Ahmed Gaïd Salah.
September 2005	The Referendum on National Reconciliation is held, followed by the promulgation of the Charter for Peace and National Reconciliation in February 2006.
May 2007	Legislative elections are held, with official voter turnout at 35 percent. The Interior Ministry sends three million letters to identified abstentionists.
April 2009	Bouteflika is reelected after a constitutional revision adopted in haste by the People's National Assembly revokes presidential term limits. Official voter turnout is at 75 percent.
October 2009	Revelation of the East–West Highway scandal after an investigation conducted by the DRS.
January 2010	Beginning of the so-called Sonatrach Affair after an investigation conducted by the DRS, which leads to the revelation of four corruption scandals linked to the national oil giant between 2010 and 2016, and the demise of the influential minister of energy and mines, Chakib Khelil.
February 2010	Assassination of Ali Tounsi, the director of the DGSN.

January 2011	Urban clashes following the uprising in Tunisia. Birth of the short-lived National Coordination for Change and Democracy.
February 2011	Creation of the National Committee for the Defense of the Rights of the Unemployed.
April 2011	A massive student demonstration in the capital results in clashes with the police.
May 2012	Legislative elections branded an "Algerian spring." Official voter turnout is at 42 percent.
July 2012	Fiftieth anniversary of independence.
January 2013	A raid by a group affiliated with al-Qaeda in the Islamic Maghreb on the Tingentourine gas processing complex, in the country's Southeast, leads to the deaths of dozens of hostages, including many foreigners.
March 2013	The CNDDC organizes the so-called *Miliyūniyya* in Ouargla, a rally attended by an estimated ten thousand protesters.
April 2013	Bouteflika suffers a transient ischemic attack. After this date, he is unable to talk or move, and remains under constant medical supervision.
September 2013	The presidency announces a restructuring of the DRS, taking control of some of its agencies and transferring others to the army's command.
January–February 2014	A public feud breaks out between supporters of the presidency and those of the DRS.
April 2014	Bouteflika is reelected but is unable to pronounce the presidential oath. Official voter turnout is at 50 percent.
May 2014	After an initial scare at the end of 2013, a sharp fall in hydrocarbon prices leads to a budget crisis.
January 2015	Beginning of the protest movement against fracking in In-Salah.
September–October 2015	The DRS is dismantled. Most of its agencies are henceforth placed under the control of the presidency. Toufik is forced to retire.

May 2017	Legislative elections result in an extreme fragmentation of the APN, with more than thirty-five parties represented. Official voter turnout is at 35 percent.
August 2017	Abdelmajid Tebboune is fired four months after being appointed prime minister. Ahmed Ouyahia becomes head of the government for the third time.
June 2018	The head of the DGSN, Abdelghani Hamel, is sacked following the revelation of an international drug trafficking scandal (known as the Bouchi Affair).
February 2019	Beginning of the Hirak.
April 2019	Resignation of Abdelaziz Bouteflika.
September 2019	Saïd Bouteflika is sentenced to fifteen years in prison.
December 2019	Abdelmajid Tebboune is elected president. Official voter turnout is at 40 percent.
March 2020	After fifty-six weeks of protests, the Hirak suspends its weekly marches because of the pandemic and before Tebboune announces a ban on all public gatherings.
November 2020	A referendum on constitutional amendments is held to "lay the foundations of a new Algeria." Official voter turnout is at 23 percent.
June 2021	Legislative elections are "won" by the FLN with 6.2 percent of the vote. Official voter turnout is at 23 percent.
August 2021	A dramatic summer is marked by a combination of wildfires and a deadly COVID wave. The government scapegoats the Rachad movement and the MAK, labeling them terrorist organizations, and accuses Morocco of supporting them.
September 2021	Former Algerian president Abdelaziz Bouteflika dies at the age of eighty-four.

Glossary of Terms and Abbreviations

affairistes: From the French *affaires*. Crony capitalists affiliated with the ruling coalition.
Al-ʿAdala: Islamo-conservative opposition party.
ALN: Armée de Libération Nationale, or National Liberation Army. The military wing of the FLN during the War of Liberation and predecessor to the ANP.
ANP: Armée Nationale Populaire, or National People's Army, whose leadership has been a pillar of the ruling coalition since 1962.
APN: Assemblée populaire nationale, or People's National Assembly. The lower legislative chamber whose members are elected for five years.
APW: Assemblée populaire de wilaya, or People's Assembly of Wilaya. A regional deliberative body whose members are elected for five years.
Barakat: "Enough" in Darija. Name of a grassroots movement founded in 2014 to oppose Bouteflika's bid for reelection.
Bled Miki: "Country of Mickey [Mouse]" in Darija. Term used to describe Algeria as a land of lies, absurdity, and simulation.
Chkoupistan: From *chkoupi*, Darija term for a type of seaweed. Used to describe Algeria as a land plagued by trash and corruption.
Citizens' Movement: Grassroots oppositional movement born from the 2001 Kabyle Black Spring and organized in local assemblies.
CNCD: Coordination Nationale pour le Changement et la Démocratie, or National Coordination for Change and Democracy, a short-lived oppositional coalition founded in 2011.
CNDDC: Comité national pour la défense des droits des chômeurs, or National Committee for the Defense of the Rights of the Unemployed, a social movement founded in 2011 in Ouargla and mostly led by activists originating from the South.

306 GLOSSARY OF TERMS AND ABBREVIATIONS

DA: Dinar algérien, or Algerian dinar. The national currency.
Darija: Algerian Arabic, which is different from Modern Standard Arabic.
***Décideurs*:** French for "decision makers." The term designates the high-ranking military officers who are the alleged unofficial rulers of the country.
DGSN: Direction Générale de la Sûreté Nationale, or General Directorate for National Safety. The Algerian national police.
DRS: Département du Renseignement et de la Sécurité, or Department of Intelligence and Security. An autonomous military intelligence agency that was one of the main centers of power until 2015.
El-Mouradia: The presidential palace in Algiers.
***Éradicateurs*:** French for "eradicators." The term used to refer to supporters of the violent suppression of the Islamist insurgency in the 1990s.
FCE: Forum des Chefs d'Entreprise, or Business Owners Forum. The main pro-business organization and an increasingly powerful lobby under Bouteflika.
FFS: Front des Forces Socialistes, or Socialist Forces Front. A Berberist movement and the oldest opposition party in the country.
FIS: Front Islamique du Salut, or Islamic Salvation Front. An Islamist coalition that became the dominant party in the country after the opening of 1989 before being banned following the 1992 military coup.
FLN: Front de Libération Nationale, or National Liberation Front. The nationalist party that led the anticolonial struggle against the French and became a catch-all populist structure under Bouteflika.
FNA: Front National Algérien, or Algerian National Front. Nationalist party born out of the Revolutionary Family.
GIA: Armed Islamic Group. A fusion of Islamic guerrilla movements that evolved into a brutal organization targeting civilians during the second half of the Dark Decade.
***harga*:** Darija term for the act of migrating across the Mediterranean without proper documentation. Derived from the Arabic *ḥaraqa*, which means burning, and in that case, burning the borders.
***harkis*:** Algerian volunteers fighting for the French Army during the revolution. In the Algerian political lexicon, it is a synonym for "traitor."
HCE: Haut Comité d'État, or High Committee of State. The executive body that replaced the presidency after the coup of January 1992.
***hitiste*:** Darija term derived from *ḥāʾiṭ*, wall. Literally a "wallist," somebody who hangs out in the streets for lack of better things to do.
***hogra*:** Darija term for systemic contempt, injustice, and denial of one's right to live in dignity.
IMF: International Monetary Fund.
***ʿiṣāba*:** Arabic for "gang." Term popularized during the Hirak in reference to the corrupt figures of the "System."
Jil Jadid: Liberal opposition party.
***kachiriste*:** *Kachir* is a type of Algerian salami. The Darija term *kachiriste* refers to those serving the cartel's interests in exchange for stipends.

karāma: Arabic for "dignity." Often opposed to the cartel's *hogra* in the contentious discourses of political and social movements.

khobziste: Darija term for "profiteers," those embedded in clientelist networks and dependent on the "System." From *khubz*, bread.

LADDH: Ligue Algérienne pour la Défense des Droits de l'Homme, or Algerian League for the Defense of Human Rights.

MAK: Mouvement pour l'autodétermination de la Kabylie, or Movement for the Autonomy of Kabylia (later known as the Movement for the Self-Determination of Kabylia). An autonomist Berberist organization born after the Kabyle Black Spring.

MAOL: Mouvement Algérien des Officiers Libres, or Algerian Movement of Free Officers. Opposition movement created by military officers exiled in Europe.

MSI: Mouvement de la Société de l'Islam, or Movement for the Society of Islam. Former name of the MSP.

MSP: Mouvement pour la Société de la Paix, or Movement for the Society of Peace (also known as Hamas in Arabic, for Ḥarakat Mujtamaʿa as-Silm). Islamo-conservative party that was formerly part of the Presidential Alliance, but which became one of the main opposition forces after 2012.

mujahid: Veteran of the war of liberation against the French.

National Reconciliation: Known in Arabic as *Al-Muṣālaḥa al-Waṭaniyya*, this was Bouteflika's signature policy, aiming to close the chapter of the Dark Decade with a mix of amnesia, amnesty, and compensation.

National Tragedy: *Al-Ma'sāa al-Waṭaniyya* in Arabic, this is the official euphemism for the Dark Decade.

Niẓām: Arabic for "System."

OAS: Organisation Armée Secrète, or Secret Armed Organization. A French terrorist group that opposed the independence of Algeria at the end of the War of Liberation.

Pouvoir: French word for the "System."

protesta: Darija word for the continuous movement of socioeconomic unrest.

PST: Parti Socialiste des Travailleurs, or Socialist Workers' Party. Trotskyist opposition party.

PT: Parti des Travailleurs, or Workers' Party. Trotskyist-nationalist party.

Rachad movement: Opposition movement founded abroad by a mix of human rights activists and former members of the FIS in exile.

RAJ: Rassemblement Action Jeunesse, or Youth Action Rally. A left-leaning youth organization that advocated for human rights and democracy. It was dissolved by the government in 2021.

RCD: Rassemblement pour la Culture et la Démocratie, or Rally for Culture and Democracy. Berberist and secularist opposition party.

rectifiers: *Taqwīmīyin* in Arabic, or *redresseurs* in French. Term used to designate members of a political organization engaged in an attempt to overthrow its leadership.

Revolutionary Family: *Al-U'sra Al-Thawriyya* in Arabic, this term used to designate the social groups who shared a portion of the legitimacy inherited from the revolution (mujahideen, families of martyrs, etc.).

RND: Rassemblement National Démocratique, or National Democratic Rally. Nationalist and secularist party created in the 1990s and the second party of the ruling coalition.

SAP: Structural adjustment program, a term outlining a set of neoliberal economic reforms implemented under the guidance of the IMF.

shiyyatin: Sycophants who flatter powerful individuals, notably Bouteflika, for personal benefits. From the Darija word *shita* (brush).

shkara: Darija for "corruption," in reference to the plastic or paper bag used to carry bribes.

SMEs: Small and medium-sized enterprises.

SNAPAP: Syndicat National Autonome des Personnels de l'Administration Publique, or National Autonomous Union for Employees of Public Administrations. The largest autonomous union in the country.

Sonatrach: Publicly owned hydrocarbon company and one of the largest corporations in Africa.

"System": Representation of the ruling coalition, as a ubiquitous, impersonal, and corrupting force.

tab jnanu: An expression in Darija taken from one of Bouteflika's speeches and used to refer to the gerontocracy that ruled the country until 2019.

TAJ: Tajama'a A'mal al-Jazāi'r, or Rally for Hope in Algeria. Islamo-conservative party created to compensate for the withdrawal of the MSP from the Presidential Alliance.

takfiri: From the Arabic *takfīr*, the act of calling another Muslim an apostate. Term used in a derogatory manner to describe armed groups such as the GIA that target civilians.

UGEL: Union Générale des Étudiants Libres, or General Union of Free Students. A student union historically close to the Islamo-conservative tendency.

UGTA: Union Générale des Travailleurs Algériens, or General Union of Algerian Workers. The historical nationalist trade union, which remains intimately linked to the state.

War of Liberation: Ḥarb at-taḥrīr in Arabic. The successful war that started in 1954 and eventually brought an end to the French colonial occupation in 1962. Algerians usually refer to this struggle as "the revolution."

Notes

Preface

1. "Interview d'Abdul Aziz Bouteflika," France 2, April 15, 1999, http://www.ina.fr/video/CAB99016695/interview-d-abdul-aziz-bouteflika-video.html. Unless otherwise noted, all translations from the French and Arabic are my own.
2. Abdou Semmar, "Affaire Général Toufik: Un parti politique accuse Amar Saâdani d'être un agent des services secrets français," *Algérie Focus*, February 5, 2014.
3. In addition to their defense of "democratic liberties," both movements advocated for a political rather than military settlement to the civil conflict of the 1990s.
4. Echorouk, "Hamrouche yad'aū ath-thulāthī Bouteflika, Gaïd Salah wa Toufik li-ijmā'a waṭanī," *Echorouk* (Algiers), March 30, 2014.
5. Ivan Martin, "Politique économique et stabilité de l'Etat," Centre de recherches internationales, March–April 2003, https://www.sciencespo.fr/ceri/sites/sciencespo.fr.ceri/files/artim_0.pdf.
6. Louisa Dris-Aït Hamadouche, "L'abstention en Algérie: Un autre mode de contestation politique," *L'Année du Maghreb* 5 (2009): 263–273.
7. Front-page editorial, *El Moudjahid* (Algiers), April 18, 2014.
8. Front-page editorial, *Liberté* (Algiers), April 18, 2014.
9. Ahmed Cheniki, "Amin Khan, auteur: Les territoires obscurs de l'illégitimité et le règne de l'argent," *Le Soir d'Algérie*, April 18–19, 2014.
10. On his blog, political analyst Baki Mansour evokes the risk of a "dislocation of the country" following a war between members of the "oligarchy." See "De la démocratie en Algérie," *Observations confidentielles* (blog), February 2, 2016, http://7our.wordpress.com/2014/03/23/de-la-democratie-en-algerie/.

11. Houari Kaddour, *Rapport sur les logements préfabriqués dans la Wilaya de Chlef* (Chlef: LADDH, 2014).
12. Mary Laforest and Diane Vincent, "La qualification péjorative dans tous ses états," *Langue française* 144 (2004): 59–81.
13. Dianna Taylor, "Hannah Arendt on Judgement: Thinking for Politics," *International Journal of Philosophical Studies* 10, no. 2 (2002): 151–169.
14. Nikolay Karkov and Jeffrey W. Robbins, "Decoloniality and Crisis," *Journal for Culture and Religious Theory* 13, no. 1 (2014): 1–10.
15. Farah Souames, "Indignity and Solidarity Are Being Televised in Algiers," *Africa Is a Country*, March 4, 2019, https://africasacountry.com/2019/03/indignity-and-solidarity-are-being-televised-in-algeria.
16. Craig Calhoun, "A World of Emergencies: Fear, Intervention, and the Limits of Cosmopolitan Order," *Canadian Review of Sociology* 41, no. 4 (2004): 373–395.

1. A Never-Ending Crisis?

1. Mohamed Harbi, *Les archives de la révolution algérienne* (Paris: Éditions Jeune Afrique, 1981).
2. Béatrice Hibou, *La force de l'obéissance. Economie politique de la répression en Tunisie* (Paris: La Découverte, 2006), 263–266.
3. Wendy Brown, *Edgework: Critical Essays on Knowledge and Politics* (Princeton, NJ: Princeton University Press, 2005), 5–7.
4. Abdellatif Benachenhou, *Takawūn at-takhaluf fī al-jazā'ir: Muḥāwala li-dirāsat at-tanmiyya al-rāsmāliya fī al-jazā'ir bayn 'aāmī 1830-1962* (Algiers: SNED, 1979).
5. Robert Malley, *The Call from Algeria: Third Worldism, Revolution and the Turn to Islam* (Berkeley: University of California Press, 1996); Jeffrey J. Byrne, *Mecca of Revolution: Algeria, Decolonization, and the Third World Order* (Oxford: Oxford University Press, 2016).
6. Georges Mutin, "Implantations industrielles et aménagements du territoire en Algérie," *Revue de géographie de Lyon* 55, no. 1 (1980): 5–37.
7. Gérard Destanne De Bernis, "Les problèmes pétroliers algériens," *Etudes internationales* 2, no. 4 (1971): 575–609.
8. Saïd Chikhi, "Question ouvrière et rapports sociaux en Algérie," *Fernand Braudel Center Review* 18, no. 3 (1995): 487–524.
9. William B. Quandt, *Between Ballots and Bullets: Algeria's Transition from Authoritarianism* (Washington, DC: Brookings Institution Press, 1998), 24.
10. Omar Carlier, *Entre Nation et Jihad. Histoire sociale des radicalismes algériens* (Paris: Presses de Sciences Po, 1995), 342–345.
11. Martin Evans and John Phillips, *Algeria: Anger of the Dispossessed* (New Haven, CT: Yale University Press, 2008), 129–132.
12. Djilali Sari, "Deux décennies d'urbanisation sans précédent en Algérie," in *Croissance démographique et urbanisation: Politique de peuplement et aménagement du*

territoire, ed. Association internationale des démographes de langue française (Paris: PUF, 1993), 371–377.

13. Omar Benderra, "Économie algérienne 1986/1998: Les réseaux aux commandes de l'État," in *La Méditerranée des réseaux. Marchands, entrepreneurs et migrants entre l'Europe et le Maghreb*, ed. Jocelyne Cesari (Paris: Maisonneuve & Larose, 2002), 231–266.
14. Myriam Aït Aoudia, *L'expérience démocratique en Algérie (1988-1992). Apprentissages politiques et changement de régime* (Paris: Les Presses de Sciences Po, 2015), 31–56.
15. Quoted by Mohamed Ghriss, "Le 19 septembre 1988: Le jour où Chadli . . . ," *Le Quotidien d'Oran*, September 19, 2009.
16. Official figures list 157 victims of state repression, while the National Association of October 88's Victims counts 314 deaths. Rabah Beldjena, "19e anniversaire du 5 octobre 1988," *El Watan* (Algiers), October 6, 2007.
17. Mahfoud Amara, *Sports, Politics and Society in the Arab World* (New York: Palgrave Macmillan, 2012), 41–45.
18. Saïd Chikhi, "Algérie: Du soulèvement populaire d'octobre 1988 aux contestations sociales des travailleurs," in *Mouvement social et modernité*, ed. Daho Djerbal and Mohamed Benguerna (Algiers: Naqd/SARP, 2001), 69–103.
19. Myriam Aït Aoudia, "La naissance du Front islamique du Salut: Une politisation conflictuelle (1988–1989)," *Critique internationale* 30 (2006): 129–144.
20. Aït Aoudia, *L'expérience démocratique en Algérie*; Luis Martinez, *La guerre civile en Algérie* (Paris: Khartala, 1998).
21. Michael Willis, *The Islamist Challenge in Algeria: A Political History* (New York: New York University Press, 1997), 224–226; James D. Le Sueur, *Between Terror and Democracy: Algeria since 1989* (London: Zed Books, 2010), 49–50.
22. Willis, *The Islamist Challenge in Algeria*, 236–239; John Ruedy, *Modern Algeria: The Origin and Development of a Nation* (Bloomington: Indiana University Press, 2005), 254–255.
23. Willis, *The Islamist Challenge in Algeria*, 253–255; Mohamed Samraoui, *Chroniques des années de sang* (Paris: Éditions Denoël, 2003), 142.
24. Mahfoud Bennoune, "Pourquoi Mohamed Boudiaf a-t-il été assassiné?," *Confluences Méditerranée* 25 (1998): 163.
25. Martinez, *La Guerre Civile en Algérie*; Abderrahmane Moussaoui, *De la Violence en Algérie* (Arles: Actes Sud, 2006); Rasmus Bozerup, "Violence as Politics: The Escalation and De-escalation of Political Violence in Algeria (1954–2007)" (PhD diss., EHESS Paris and University of Copenhagen, 2008).
26. Lise Garon, "Entre propagande et voix dissidentes: L'information internationale et ses sources; le cas de la crise algérienne," *Études internationales* 29, no. 3 (1998): 599–629.
27. For the 2000 statistics, see General Directorate for Economic and Financial Affairs, *Examen de la situation économique des partenaires méditerranéen de l'UE* (Brussels: European Commission, 2003), https://op.europa.eu/fr/publication-detail/-/publication/a1e17fbd-d3d9-4870-a9a0-e24af4a9f492/language-fr/format-PDF/source-28002

2220. For 2010, see the numbers published by the Algerian National Statistics Office, "Emploi & Chômage au 4ème Trimestre 2010," National Office of Statistics, accessed February 22, 2023, https://www.ons.dz/IMG/pdf/emploi_chomage_2010.pdf.
28. NABNI (Notre Algérie Bâtie sur de Nouvelles Idées), *Cinquantenaire de l'indépendance: Enseignement et vision pour l'Algérie de 2020* (January 2013), 27–29, http://nabni.org/wp-content/uploads/2012/12/Nabni-Economie-2020.pdf.
29. Jaime Semprun, *Apologie pour l'insurrection algérienne* (Paris: Éditions de l'encyclopédie des nuisances, 2001); Maxime Aït Kaki, *De la question berbère au dilemme Kabyle à l'aube du XXIème siècle* (Paris: L'Harmattan, 2004); Hamid Chabani, *Le printemps noir de 2001 en Kabylie: Le cas de la coordination communale d'Aïn-Zaouia* (Paris: L'Harmattan, 2011).
30. Chérif Bennadji, "Algérie: La fin de la crise politique?," *L'Année du Maghreb* 1 (2004): 175–206.
31. Sune Haugbolle and Andreas Bandak, "The Ends of Revolution: Rethinking Ideology and Time in the Arab Uprisings," *Middle East Critique* 26, no. 3 (2017): 191–204.
32. Salim Chena, "L'Algérie dans le 'Printemps arabe' entre espoirs, initiatives et blocages," *Confluences Méditerranée* 77, no. 2 (2011): 105–118; Layla Baamara, "Quand les protestataires s'autolimitent. Le cas des mobilisations étudiantes de 2011 en Algérie," in *Au coeur des révoltes arabes. Devenir révolutionnaires*, ed. Amine Allal and Thomas Pierret (Paris: Armand Collin, 2013), 137–159; Naoual Belakhdar, " 'L'éveil du Sud' ou quand la contestation vient de la marge. Une analyse du mouvement des chômeurs algériens," *Politique africaine* 137 (2015): 27–48.
33. Thomas Serres, "La 'jeunesse algérienne' en lutte. Du rôle politique conflictuel d'une catégorie sociale hétérogène," *Revue des mondes musulmans et de la Méditerranée* 134 (2013): 213–230.
34. Slimane Medhar, *La violence sociale en Algérie* (Algiers: Thala, 1997); Martinez, *La Guerre Civile en Algérie*; Moussaoui, *De la Violence en Algérie*.
35. Tristan Leperlier, *Algérie, Les écrivains de la décennie noire* (Paris: CNRS Éditions, 2018).
36. Jacob Mundy, *Imaginative Geographies of Algerian Violence: Conflict Science, Conflict Management, Antipolitics* (Stanford, CA: Stanford University Press, 2015).
37. Luis Martinez, *Violence de la rente pétrolière: Algérie-Irak-Libye* (Paris: Presses de Sciences Po, 2010); Sidi Mohammed Chekouri, Abderrahim Chibi, and Mohamed Benbouziane, "Algeria and the Natural Resource Curse: Oil Abundance and Economic Growth," *Middle East Development Journal* 9, no. 2 (2017): 233–255.
38. John P. Entelis, *Algeria: The Revolution Institutionalized* (Boulder, CO: Westview Press, 1986); Kay Adamson, *Algeria: A Study in Competing Ideologies* (London: Cassel, 1998).
39. Bradford L. Dillman, *State and Private Sector in Algeria: The Politics of Rent-Seeking and Failed Development* (Boulder, CO: Westview Press, 2000); Benderra, "Économie algérienne 1986/1998"; Omar Benderra, "Pétrole et pouvoir en Algérie," *Confluences Méditerranée* 53 (2005): 51–58; Fatiha Talahite, "Économie administrée, corruption et engrenage de la violence en Algérie," *Tiers Monde* 41, no. 161 (2000): 49–74; Fatiha

Talahite, "La rente et l'État rentier recouvrent-ils toute la réalité de l'Algérie d'aujourd'hui?," *Tiers Monde* 210 (2012): 143–160.
40. Séverine Labat, *Les Islamistes Algériens. Entre les urnes et le maquis* (Paris: Éditions du Seuil, 1995); Willis, *The Islamist Challenge in Algeria*.
41. Quandt, *Between Ballots and Bullets*.
42. Hugh Roberts, *The Battlefield: Algeria, 1988-2002* (London: Verso, 2003).
43. Francesco Cavatorta, *The International Dimension of the Failed Algerian Transition* (Manchester, UK: Manchester University Press, 2009).
44. Isabelle Werenfels, *Managing Instability: Elites and Political Change in Algeria* (London: Routledge, 2007); Louisa Dris-Aït Hamadouche, "Au cœur de la résilience algérienne: Un jeu calculé d'alliances," *Confluences Méditerranée* 106 (2018): 195–210.
45. Mohammed Hachemaoui, *Clientélisme et patronage dans l'Algérie contemporaine* (Paris: Karthala, 2013).
46. Aït Aoudia, *L'expérience démocratique en Algérie*.
47. Chérif Dris, "La nouvelle loi organique sur l'information de 2012 en Algérie: Vers un ordre médiatique néo-autoritaire?," *L'Année du Maghreb* 8 (2012): 303–320; Belkacem Benzenine, "Les femmes algériennes au Parlement: La question des quotas à l'épreuve des réformes politiques," *Égypte/Monde arabe* 10 (2013): https://doi.org/10.4000/ema.3196; Laqra' Ben Ali, "A'zmat at-taḥawūl naḥw ad-dīmuqrāṭiyya fī al-jazā'ir (1989–2014)," *Al-majala al-'arabiya al-'ulūm al-siyāsiya* 45–46 (2015): 57–70; Ahmed Aghrout and Yahia H. Zoubir, "Algeria: Reforms Without Change?," in *North African Politics: Change and Continuity*, ed. Yahia H. Zoubir and Gregory White (London: Routledge, 2016), 145–155.
48. Baamara, "Quand les protestataires s'autolimitent"; Belakhdar, " 'L'éveil du Sud' "; Farida Souiah, "Humoriste, journaliste et artiste engagé," *L'Année du Maghreb* 15 (2016): 97–113.
49. Ranjana Khanna, *Algeria Cuts: Women & Representation, 1830 to the Present* (Stanford, CA: Stanford University Press, 2007); Muriam H. Davis, *Markets of Civilization: Islam and Racial Capitalism in Algeria* (Durham, NC: Duke University Press, 2022).
50. Tarik Dahou, *Gouverner la mer en Algérie. Politique en eaux trouble* (Paris: Karthala, 2018); Patrick Crowley, *Algeria: Nation, Culture and Transnationalism, 1988-2015* (Liverpool, UK: Liverpool University Press, 2017).
51. For example, see Adam Arroudj, "Derrière la mobilisation populaire, le jeu ambigu des islamistes en Algérie," *Le Figaro*, March 15, 2019, and Sabina Henneberg, "Algeria's Bouteflika Is on His Way Out. Here's What's Next," *Foreign Policy*, April 2, 2019, https://foreignpolicy.com/2019/04/02/algeria-bouteflika-is-on-his-way-out-heres-whats-next-oil-russia-protest-army/.
52. Brown, *Edgework*, 15.
53. Howard Becker, *Le travail sociologique: Méthode et substance* (Fribourg, CH: Academic Press Fribourg, 2006), 13.
54. Pascal Ménoret, *Joyriding in Riyadh: Oil, Urbanism, and Road Revolt* (Cambridge: Cambridge University Press, 2014).
55. Becker, *Le travail sociologique*, 13.

1. A NEVER-ENDING CRISIS?

56. Howard S. Becker, *Tricks of the trade: How to Think About Your Research While Doing It* (Chicago: University of Chicago Press, 1998); Joost Beuving, "Problems of Evidence in Ethnography. A Methodological Reflection on the Goffman/Mead Controversies (with a Proposal for Rules of Thumb)," *Forum Qualitative Sozialforschung/Forum: Qualitative Social Research* 22 (2020): https://doi.org/10.17169/fqs-22.1.3567; David Sanson and Claire Le Breton, "Research Ties as Social Tales: Intimacy and Distance in Ethnography," *M@n@gement* 23, no. 3 (2020): 114–117.
57. Sylvain Laurens, "'Pourquoi' et 'comment' poser les questions qui fâchent? Réflexions sur les dilemmes récurrents que posent les entretiens avec des 'imposants,'" *Genèses* 69, no. 4 (2007): 112–127.
58. Georges Didi-Hubermann, *Devant le temps. Histoire de l'art et anachronisme de l'image* (Paris: Editions de Minuit, 2000), 99–111; Frederik Le Roy, "Ragpickers and Leftover Performances," *Performance Research* 22, no. 8 (2017): 127–134.
59. Edgar Morin, "Pour une crisologie," *Communications* 25 (1976): 149–163.
60. Brown, *Edgework*, 9–10; Hamit Bozarslan, *Révolution et état de violence. Moyen-Orient 2011-2015* (Paris: CNRS Éditions, 2015).
61. John B. Thompson, "The Metamorphosis of a Crisis," in *Aftermath: The Culture of Economic Crisis*, ed. Manuel Castells, Joao Caraça, and Gustavo Cardoso (Oxford: Oxford University Press, 2012), 59–81.
62. Michel Dobry, *Sociologie des crises politiques* (Paris: Presses de Sciences Po, 1986), 141.
63. Tatiana Charlier-Yannopoulou, "La crise politique grecque," *Revue française de science politique* 17, no. 1 (1967): 47–64; Benjamin Gourisse, *La violence politique en Turquie. L'État en jeu (1975-1980)* (Paris: Karthala, 2014).
64. Dobry, *Sociologie des crises politiques*, 150.
65. Gourisse, *La violence politique en Turquie*, 14.
66. Barry Buzan, Ole Wæver, and Jaap De Wilde, *Security: A New Framework for Analysis* (Boulder: Lynne Reiner Publishers, 1998); Thierry Balzacq, "The Three Faces of Securitization," *European Journal of International Relations* 11, no. 2 (2005): 171–201; Fred Vultee, "Securitization: A New Approach to the Framing of the War on Terror," *Journalism Practice* 4 (2010): 33–47; Ole Wæver, "Politics, Security, Theory," *Security Dialogue* 42, nos. 4–5 (2011): 465–480.
67. Dobry, *Sociologie des crises politiques*, 153.
68. Dobry, 241.
69. Antonio Gramsci, *Quaderni del carcere. Volume terzo. Quaderni 12-29* (Turin: Giulio Einaudi editore, 1977), 1603.
70. Gourisse, *La violence politique en Turquie*.
71. Marnia Lazreg "Islamism and the Recolonization of Algeria," in *Beyond Colonialism and Nationalism in the Maghreb*, ed. Ali Abdullatif Ahmida (New York: Palgrave, 2000), 148.
72. René Thom, "Crise et catastrophe," *Communications* 25 (1976): 35–36.
73. Michel Dobry, "Les voies incertaines de la transitologie: Choix stratégiques, séquences historiques, bifurcations et processus de path dependence," *Revue française de science politique* 4–5 (2000): 613.

74. Norberto Bobbio, "La crise permanente," *Pouvoir* 18 (1981): 19.
75. Isabelle Werenfels, *Managing Instability: Elites and Political Change in Algeria* (London: Routledge, 2007); Isabelle Werenfels, "Beyond Authoritarian Upgrading: The Reemergence of Sufi Orders in Maghrebi Politics," *Journal of North African Studies* 19, no. 3 (2014): 275–295.
76. Myriam Revault D'Allonnes, *La crise sans fin* (Paris: Éditions du Seuil, 2012).
77. Nicos Poulantzas, *La crise de l'Etat* (Paris: PUF, 1976), 28.
78. Adi Ophir, "The Politics of Catastrophization: Emergency and Exception," in *Contemporary States of Emergency: The Politics of Military and Humanitarian Interventions*, ed. Didier Fassin and Mariella Pandolfi (New York: Zone Books, 2010), 59–88.
79. Alexis de Tocqueville, *L'Ancien régime et la Révolution* (1856; Chicoutimi, QC: Éditions de l'UQAC, 2007).
80. Hamit Bozarslan, "Le chaos après le déluge: Notes sur la crise turque des années 70," *Culture & conflits* 24–25 (1997): 3.
81. For example, see Bruce Riedel, "Algeria Goes to the Polls—Why the United States and Europe Have a Stake in Its Stability," *Markaz* (blog), Brookings Institution, May 1, 2017, https://www.brookings.edu/blog/markaz/2017/05/01/algeria-goes-to-the-polls-why-the-united-states-and-europe-have-a-stake-in-its-stability/.
82. See, for example, Yahia H. Zoubir, "The Arab Spring: Is Algeria the Exception?," *IEMedsObs* 61 (2013), https://www.iemed.org/publication/the-arab-spring-is-algeria-the-exception/, and Malika Rahal, "Algeria Joins the Arab Spring," *Politico*, March 12, 2019, https://www.politico.eu/article/algeria-joins-the-arab-spring/.
83. Michel Foucault, *Naissance de la biopolitique. Cours au Collège de France (1978-1979)* (Paris: Seuil/Gallimard, 2004), 70–71.
84. Steven Heydemann, "Upgrading Authoritarianism in the Arab World," Analysis Paper No. 13, Saban Center for Middle East Policy at the Brookings Institute (October 2007), 1, https://www.brookings.edu/research/upgrading-authoritarianism-in-the-arab-world/.
85. Neil Brenner, Jamie Peck, and Nik Theodore, "Variegated Neoliberalization: Geographies, Modalities, Pathways," *Global Networks* 10, no. 2 (2010): 184.
86. Lesley J. Wood, *Crisis and Control: The Militarization of Protest Policing* (London: Pluto Press, 2014), 19.
87. Ulrich Beck, *Risk Societies: Towards a New Modernity* (London: Sage Publications, 1992), 49–50.
88. Mike Davis, *Ecology of Fear: Los Angeles and the Imagination of the Disaster* (New York: Metropolitan Books, 1998).
89. Philip Mirowki, *Never Let a Serious Crisis Go to Waste* (London: Verso, 2013).
90. David Harvey, *A Brief History of Neoliberalism* (Oxford: Oxford University Press, 2005); Naomi Klein, *The Shock Doctrine: The Rise of Disaster Capitalism* (Toronto: Knopf Canada, 2007).
91. Ophir, "The Politics of Catastrophization," 63–64.
92. René Riesel and Jaime Semprun, *Catastrophisme, administration du désastre et soumission durable* (Paris: Éditions de l'encyclopédie des nuisances, 2008).

1. A NEVER-ENDING CRISIS?

93. Ophir, "The Politics of Catastrophization," 70.
94. Ophir, 66–67.
95. Craig Calhoun, "A World of Emergencies: Fear, Intervention, and the Limits of Cosmopolitan Order," *Canadian Review of Sociology* 41, no. 4 (2004): 378–392.
96. Ophir, "The Politics of Catastrophization," 80–81.
97. Giorgio Agamben, *State of Exception* (Chicago: University of Chicago Press, 2005), 1–2, 22.
98. Orietta Ombrosi, "La dialectique de l'idée de catastrophe dans la pensée de W. Benjamin," *Archives de Philosophie* 69, no. 2 (2006): 63–64.
99. Bruno Gulli, "The Ontology and Politics of Exception: Reflections on the Work of Giorgio Agamben," in *Sovereignty & Life*, ed. Matthew Calarco and Steven DeCaroli (Stanford, CA: Stanford University Press, 2007), 220.
100. Stephen Humphreys, "Legalizing Lawlessness: On Giorgio Agamben's State of Exception," *European Journal of International Law* 17, no. 3 (2006): 681; Wendell Kisner, "Agamben, Hegel, and the State of Exception," *Cosmos and History: The Journal of Natural and Social Philosophy* 3, nos. 2–3 (2007): 250–251.
101. Walter Benjamin, *Selected Writings*, vol. 1, *1913–1926* (Cambridge, MA: Harvard University Press, 1996), 251–252.
102. Agamben, *State of Exception*, 60.
103. Walter Benjamin, *Selected Writings*, vol. 4, *1938–1940* (Cambridge, MA: Harvard University Press, 2003), 389–400.
104. Ariella Azoulay, "The Tradition of the Oppressed," *Qui Parle* 16, no. 2 (2007): 73–96.
105. Matthew Bowser, "Catastrophe in Permanence: Benjamin's Natural History of Environmental Crisis" (PhD diss., University of North Texas, 2017), 14, 19.
106. Ombrosi, "La dialectique de l'idée de catastrophe dans la pensée de W. Benjamin," 265–266.
107. The homogeneous empty time is a progressive and cumulative temporality, which is both the product of capitalist modernity and necessary for the development of the nation-state. See Benjamin, *Selected Writings*, 4:395, and Benedict Anderson, *Imagined Communities: Reflections on the Origin and Spread of Nationalism* (London: Verso, 1991), 24.

2. Struggles at the Heart of the State

1. Algerians use the Arabic word *Niẓām* or the French *Système*.
2. Lisa Weeden, *Ambiguities of Domination: Politics, Rhetoric and Symbols in Contemporary Syria* (Chicago: University of Chicago Press, 2015), 30.
3. Béatrice Hibou, *La force de l'obéissance. Économie politique de la répression en Tunisie* (Paris: La Découverte, 2006), 18.
4. François Bastien and Jacques Lagroye, *Sociologie politique* (Paris: Presses de Sciences Po, 2002), 128.

5. Jean-François Médard, "The Underdeveloped State in Tropical Africa: Political Clientelism or Neo-patrimonialism," in *Private Patronage and Public Power*, ed. Christopher Clapham (London: Frances Pinter, 1982), 162–192.
6. Luc Sindjoun, "Le Président de la République du Cameroun à l'épreuve de l'alternance néo-patrimoniale et de la 'transition démocratique,'" in *Les figures du politique en Afrique: Des pouvoirs hérités aux pouvoirs élus*, ed. Momar-Coumba Diop and Mamadou Diouf (Dakar: CODESRIA; Paris: Karthala: 1999), 63–101.
7. Franck Moderne, "Les avatars du présidentialisme dans les états latino-américains," *Pouvoirs* 98 (2001): 64.
8. William B. Quandt, *Revolution and Political Leadership: Algeria, 1954–1968* (Cambridge, MA: MIT Press, 1969), 234.
9. Mohammed Hachemaoui, "Permanence du jeu politique en Algérie," *Politique étrangère* 2 (2009): 313–314.
10. During the War of Liberation, the Algerian Liberation Army created six semiautonomous zones of operation (*wilayas*) in mainland Algeria, and a seventh one in France.
11. Luis Martinez, "L'après-guerre civile: Les étapes de la réconciliation nationale," Centre de recherches internationales, January 2000, https://hal-sciencespo.archives-ouvertes.fr/hal-01064877.
12. Chérif Bennadji, "Le 'retrait' des six candidats à l'élection présidentielle du 15 avril 1999," *Annuaire de l'Afrique du Nord* 38 (2002): 149–157.
13. Khaled Nezzar, *Bouteflika, l'homme et son bilan* (Algiers: Éditions APIC, 2003), 57.
14. "Portrait Abdul Aziz Bouteflika," France 3, April 15, 1999, https://www.ina.fr/video/CAC99016765/portrait-abdul-aziz-bouteflika-video.html.
15. Akram Belkaïd, "La diplomatie algérienne à la recherche de son âge d'or," *Politique étrangère* 2 (2009): 337–344.
16. Abderrahim Lamchichi, "Référendum sur la concorde civile, les leçons d'un scrutin," *Confluences Méditerranée* 32 (2000): 155–166; Rémy Leveau, "Esquisse d'un changement politique au Maghreb?," *Politique étrangère* 65, no. 2 (2000): 499–507.
17. "Interview d'Abdul Aziz Bouteflika," France 2, April 15, 1999, http://www.ina.fr/video/CAB99016695/interview-d-abdul-aziz-bouteflika-video.html.
18. Article 92 of the revised version of the Algerian Constitution of 1996.
19. Article 118 of the revised constitution.
20. Mohammed Hachemaoui, "La représentation politique en Algérie entre médiation clientélaire et prédation (1997–2002)," *Revue Française de science politique* 53, no. 1 (2003): 38.
21. According to information passed on by an Algerian journalist who covered Bensalah's reelection in 2007, no other candidate challenged him out of respect for Bouteflika, despite the senators' frustration. U.S. diplomatic cable released by Wikileaks, January 16, 2007 (reference 07ALGIERS45), https://wikileaks.org/plusd/cables/07ALGIERS45_a.html.
22. Louisa Dris-Aït Hamadouche and Yahia H. Zoubir, "Pouvoir et opposition en Algérie: Vers une transition prolongée?," *L'Année du Maghreb* 5 (2009):114.

23. Article 182 of the revised constitution.
24. Articles 173 and 174 of the revised constitution.
25. Chérif Bennadji, "De l'ambiguïté des rapports entre le président de la République et le pouvoir judiciaire en Algérie," *L'Année du Maghreb* 3 (2007): 155–162.
26. *Décideurs* (decision makers) designates the high-ranking military officers who are the alleged unofficial rulers of the country.
27. Ernst Kantorowicz, *The King's Two Bodies: A Study in Mediaeval Political Theology* (Princeton, NJ: Princeton University Press, 1957).
28. Fernando Coronil, *The Magical State: Nature, Money and Modernity in Venezuela* (Chicago: University of Chicago Press, 1997), 4.
29. Jocelyne Dakhlia, "Dans la mouvance du prince: La symbolique du pouvoir itinérant au Maghreb," *Annales, Économies, Sociétés, Civilisations* 43 (1988): 735–760; Jocelyne Dakhlia, *Le Divan des Rois: Le politique et le religieux dans l'islam* (Paris: Aubier, 1998).
30. Juan Linz, "The Perils of Presidentialism," *Journal of Democracy* 1 (1990): 52.
31. Austin Ranney, "Referendum et Démocratie," *Pouvoir* 77 (1996): 7–19.
32. International Crisis Group, *La Concorde Civile: Une initiative de paix manquée*, Afrique rapport No. 31 (Brussels: International Crisis Group, 2001); Lamchichi, "Référendum sur la concorde civile, les leçons d'un scrutin."
33. Chérif Bennadji, "Algérie: La fin de la crise politique?," *L'Année du Maghreb* 1 (2004): 181.
34. Daho Djerbal, "Algeria: Amnesty and Oligarchy," Carnegie Endowment for International Peace, August 20, 2008, https://carnegieendowment.org/sada/21119.
35. Giorgio Agamben, *State of Exception* (Chicago: University of Chicago Press, 2005), 80, 84.
36. John P. Entelis, "Algeria: Democracy Denied, and Revived?," *Journal of North African Studies* 16, no. 4 (2011): 660.
37. Rachid Sidi Boumedine, "L'urbanisme: Une prédation méthodique," *Naqd* 25 (2008): 123.
38. Article 74 of the original constitution of 1996.
39. *A Strong and Safe Algeria*, electoral program of Abdelaziz Bouteflika, 1 (in the author's possession).
40. Samir Bouaila, "Un blog à l'image du président algérien, la communication politique entre jeu de miroirs et 'Je0' de mémoire," *Horizons Maghrébins—Le droit à la mémoire* 62 (2010): 133.
41. Tahar Fattani, "Les Algériens plébiscitent Bouteflika à 90,24%," *L'Expression* (Algiers), April 11, 2009.
42. I explain the notion of "people-as-object" in chapter 4.
43. Rafael Bustos, "Le référendum sur la charte pour la réconciliation nationale en Algérie et ses textes d'application," *L'Année du Maghreb* 2 (2007): 223–229.
44. Adi Ophir, "The Politics of Catastrophization: Emergency and Exception," in *Contemporary States of Emergency: The Politics of Military and Humanitarian Interventions*, ed. Didier Fassin and Mariella Pandolfi (New York: Zone Books, 2010), 63.
45. Ali Haroun, *Algérie, 1962: La grande dérive* (Paris: L'Harmattan, 2005), 266.

46. For Berberist analyses, see Madjid Benchikh, *Algérie: Un système politique militarisé* (Paris: L'Harmattan, 2003); Lyes Laribi, *L'Algérie des Généraux* (Paris: Max Milo éditions, 2007). For an Islamist perspective: Ahmed Merah, *Une troïka de généraux* (Algiers: Merah éditions, 2000).
47. Habib Souaïdia, *La sale guerre* (Paris: Éditions La Découverte/Syros, 2001); Hichem Aboud, *La mafia des généraux* (Paris: Éditions J-C Lattès, 2002); Mohamed Samraoui, *Chroniques des années de sang* (Paris: Éditions Denoël, 2003).
48. Hamit Bozarslan, *Passions révolutionnaires. Amérique latine, Moyen-Orient, Inde* (Paris: Éditions de l'Ecole des Hautes Etudes en Sciences Sociales, 2011), 33.
49. Article 28 of the revised constitution.
50. Alain Rouquié, "Le camarade et le commandant: Réformisme militaire et légitimité institutionnelle," *Revue française de science politique* 29, no. 3 (1979): 381–401; Miles D. Wolpin, "Military Radicalism in Latin America," *Journal of Interamerican Studies and World Affairs* 23, no. 4 (1981): 395–428.
51. Josiane Criscuolo, "Armée et Nation dans les discours du Colonel Boumédiène" (PhD diss., University Paul Valéry, 1975), 217.
52. Rachid Mira, "Nouvelle stratégie industrielle en Algérie et soutien politique aux entreprises publiques: Une approche institutionnaliste par la recherche de rentes," in *L'Algérie au Présent*, ed. Karima Dirèche (Paris: Karthala, 2019), 228–230.
53. Samuel P. Huntington, *Political Order in Changing Societies* (New Haven, CT: Yale University Press, 1973 [1968]), 78–82.
54. Jean-Luc Racine, "Le Pakistan après le coup d'Etat militaire," *Critique internationale* 7 (2000): 22–29; Lionel Jaffrelot, *Le syndrome pakistanais* (Paris: Fayard, 2013).
55. Ahmet Insel, "'Cet État n'est pas sans propriétaire!' Forces prétoriennes et autoritarisme en Turquie," in *Autoritarismes démocratiques et démocraties autoritaires au XXIè siècle*, ed. Olivier Dabène, Vincent Geisser, and Gilles Massardier (Paris: La Découverte, 2008), 135.
56. Khaled Nezzar, *Mémoires du Général Khaled Nezzar* (Algiers: Chihab, 2000).
57. Jean Guisnel, "Interview: Le Général de corps d'armée Mohamed Lamari," *Le Point*, January 15, 2003.
58. Hamit Bozarslan, "Le chaos après le déluge: Notes sur la crise turque des années 70," *Culture & conflits* 24–25 (1997): 79–98.
59. Insel, "'Cet État n'est pas sans propriétaire!,'" 137.
60. William Hale, *Turkish Politics and the Military* (1994; London: Routledge, 2003), 305.
61. Alfred C. Stepan, *The Military in Politics: Changing Patterns in Brazil* (Princeton, NJ: Princeton University Press, 1971).
62. Contra Huntington, *Political Order in Changing Societies*.
63. Renaud Egreteau, *Histoire de la Birmanie contemporaine: Le pays des prétoriens* (Paris: Fayard, 2010).
64. Nezzar, *Bouteflika, l'homme et son bilan*, 51.
65. Khalfa Mameri, *Orientations politiques de l'Algérie* (Algiers: SNED, 1973), 43.
66. William Zartman, "L'armée dans la politique algérienne," *Annuaire de l'Afrique du Nord* 7 (1969): 275.

67. Quandt, *Revolution and Political Leadership*, 260.
68. This is the justification that Tahar Zbiri gave a posteriori. Belkacem Bellil, "Pour leur première sortie médiatique de retour en Algérie: De l'exil aux colonnes du Soir," *Le Soir d'Algérie* (Algiers), August 17, 2020.
69. Beloucif's fall is often presented as a consequence of his refusal to validate the purchase of a costly radar system from France, in a context marked by budget restrictions.
70. Souaïdia, *La sale guerre*, 60.
71. Mohamed Sifaoui, *Histoire secrète de l'Algérie indépendante* (Paris: Nouveau monde éditions, 2012), 219.
72. Lahouari Addi, "Army, State and Nation in Algeria," in *Political Armies: The Military and Nation Building in the Age of Democracy*, ed. Kees Koonings and Dirk Kruijt (London: Zed Books, 2002), 197.
73. In January 2013, a commando belonging to a split group from al-Qaeda in the Islamic Maghreb crossed the Libyan border and took over the Tingentourine gas facility, near the eastern city of In Amenas. The resulting hostage crisis led to a violent intervention of the Special Intervention Group, causing the death of nearly all members of the commando and more than thirty hostages (mostly foreigners). This botched rescue mission led to widespread criticism of the DRS.
74. Addi, "Army, State and Nation in Algeria," 196.
75. Karen Farsoun, "State Capitalism in Algeria," *MERIP* 35 (1975): 4.
76. Gérard Viratelle, "Algérie: Les impatiences de l'armée," *Le mois en Afrique*, December 1967, 2–7.
77. François Gèze, "Armée et nation en Algérie: L'irrémédiable divorce?," *Hérodote* 116 (2005): 183–184.
78. Elizabeth Picard, "Armée et sécurité au coeur de l'autoritarisme," in *Autoritarismes démocratiques et démocraties autoritaires au XXIè siècle*, ed. Olivier Dabène, Vincent Geisser, and Gilles Massardier (Paris: La Découverte, 2008), 322–323.
79. Ahmed Rouadjia, "L'Etat algérien et le problème du droit," *Politique étrangère* 2 (1995): 351–363; Khadidja Abada, "La fin d'un mythe," *Les Cahiers de l'Orient* 36–37 (1995): 127–143.
80. Aboud, *La mafia des généraux*, 257.
81. Yahia Rahal, *Histoire de Pouvoir. Un Général témoigne* (Algiers: Casbah éditions, 1997).
82. Yassin Temlali, "Algérie-Egypte: Le football, révélateur des identités refoulés," *Afkar/Idée* 25 (2010): 51–53.
83. According to the World Bank. See "Military Expenditure (% of GDP)," World Bank, accessed January 16, 2022, https://data.worldbank.org/indicator/MS.MIL.XPND.GD.ZS.
84. Fayçal Oukaci, "L'Armée s'implique," *L'Expression* (Algiers), January 30, 2005.
85. Kacem Houdjedje, "At-tadakhul al-Insānī li-l-jaysh al-waṭanī ash-sha'abī fī muwājahat al-kawārith aṭ-ṭabī'iyya: Dirāsa li-l-sharāka 'askarī-madanī khilāl fayaḍān wād Mzāb sanat 2008m," *Dafātīr al-siyāsa wa-l-qānūn* 8, no. 14 (2016): 1–30;

Aicha Abdelhamid, "Dawr al-mūa'ssasat al-'askariya fī tanmiyat al-manāṭiq al-ḥudūdiya ḍamf mutaṭallabāt al-mahām al-insāniyya li-l-jaysh al-waṭanī ash-sha'abī," *Majalat al-bāḥith al-ākādīmī fī al-'ulūm al-qānūniya wa-l-siyāsiya* 3, no. 2 (2020): 153–166.

86. Alexis Arieff, *Algeria: Current Issues*, CRS Report No. 7-5700 (Washington, DC: Congressional Research Service, 2013), 6, https://sgp.fas.org/crs/row/RS21532.pdf.
87. Pierre Bourdieu, *Sur l'Etat. Cours au Collège de France, 1989-1992* (Paris: Éditions du Seuil, 2012), 41.
88. Pierre Bourdieu, *Réponses. Pour une anthropologie réflexive* (Paris: Éditions du Seuil, 1992), 73.
89. Neil Fligstein and Doug McAdam, *A Theory of Field* (Oxford: Oxford University Press, 2012), 9.
90. Bourdieu, *Sur l'Etat*, 580.
91. Michel Camau, "L'exception autoritaire ou l'improbable point d'Archimède de la politique dans le monde arabe," in *La politique dans le monde arabe*, ed. Elizabeth Picard (Paris: Armand Colin, 2006), 43–44.
92. In "L'exception autoritaire," 77, Michel Camau calls this phenomenon "reinforced authoritarianism."
93. Hamit Bozarslan, "Les révolutions arabes. Entretien avec Hamit Bozarslan," *Sciences humaines* 226 (2011): 46.
94. Mancur Olson, *The Rise and Decline of Nations: Economic Growth, Stagflation and Social Rigidities* (New Haven, CT: Yale University Press, 1982); Robert B. Horwitz, "Understanding Deregulation," *Theory and society* 15 (1986): 139–174.
95. Richard S. Katz and Peter Mair, "Changing Models of Party Organization and Party Democracy: The Emergence of the Cartel Party," *Party Politics* 1 (1995): 5–28.
96. William C. Byrd, "Contre-performances économiques et fragilité institutionnelle," *Confluences Méditerranée* 45 (2003): 72.
97. Quandt, *Revolution and Political Leadership*; Jean Leca and Jean-Claude Vatin, "Le système politique algérien (1976–1978)," *Annuaire de l'Afrique du Nord* 16 (1978): 15–80.
98. International Crisis Group, *Elections présidentielles en Algérie: Les enjeux et les perspectives*, Algérie rapport No. 4 (Brussels: International Crisis Group, 1999), 6.
99. International Crisis Group, *La presse dans la tourmente électorale*, Algérie rapport No. 2 (Brussels: International Crisis Group, 1999), 3–6.
100. Nezzar, *Mémoires du Général Khaled Nezzar*, 39–40.
101. Nezzar, 69.
102. Laribi, *L'Algérie des Généraux*, 206.
103. François Frison-Roche, "Les chefs d'Etat dans les PECO," *Le courrier des pays de l'est* 1043 (2004): 64–65.
104. The Principal Military Center of Interrogation in Ben Aknoun was well-known to be a site of torture and extrajudicial killings during the Dark Decade. Since the beginning of the Hirak, it has also been associated with cases of activists tortured at the hands of military intelligence services.

105. "Bouteflika yudāfiʿa ʿan al-jaysh wa 'yadhbaḥ' Saâdani," *Echorouk* (Algiers), February 11, 2014; "Journée nationale du chahid: Déclaration du président de la République," Algérie Presse Service, February 18, 2014, https://www.aps.dz/algerie/69964-journee-nationale-du-chahid-message-du-president-abdelaziz-bouteflika.
106. Maxime Aït Kaki, "Armée, Pouvoir et processus de décision en Algérie," *Politique étrangère* 2 (2004): 427–439.
107. Salima Tlemçani, "Oultache a grièvement blessé Tounsi et d'autres l'ont achevé," *El Watan* (Algiers), February 24, 2011.
108. Bourdieu, *Sur l'Etat*, 502.
109. Lahouari Addi, "Deux grands perdants de ces élections: Bouteflika et le FFS," *Le Quotidien d'Algerie* (Algiers), May 13, 2012.
110. Mohamed Cherak, "Arqām at-tashrīʿaiyāt tukarris istimrār al-waḍaʿa al-qāiʾm," *El Khabar* (Algiers), May 12, 2012.
111. Benchikh, *Algérie: Un système politique militarisé*.
112. François Gèze and François Burgat, "L'Union européenne et les islamistes: Le cas de l'Algérie," *L'Année du Maghreb* 3 (2007): 656.
113. Jeremy Keenan, *The Dark Sahara: America's War on Terror in Africa* (London: Pluto Press, 2009).
114. Paul Silverstein, "An Excess of Truth: Violence, Conspiracy Theorizing and the Algerian Civil War," *Anthropological Quaterly* 75, no. 4 (2002): 643–674.
115. Emmanuel Taïeb, "Logiques politiques du conspirationnisme," *Sociologie et sociétés* 42, no. 2 (2010): 265–289.
116. Sifaoui, *Histoire secrète de l'Algérie indépendante*, 268.
117. Aïssa Khelladi, "Rire quand même: L'humour politique dans l'Algérie d'aujourd'hui," *Revue du monde musulman et de la Méditerranée* 77–78 (1995): 227.
118. Michel Foucault, *Il faut défendre la société* (Paris: Seuil/Gallimard, 1997), 221.
119. Steven DeCaroli, "Political Life: Giorgio Agamben and the Idea of Authority," *Research in Phenomenology* 43 (2013): 237–238.
120. Achille Mbembe, "Nécropolitique," *Raisons politiques* 21 (2006): 29–60.
121. Frantz Fanon, *Pour la révolution africaine. Écrits politiques* (1964; Paris: La Découverte, 2001), 28.
122. Frantz Fanon, *Les damnés de la Terre* (1961; Chicoutimi, QC: Éditions de l'UQAC, 2002), 74.
123. Makhlouf Mehenni, "Abdelmalek Sellal: 'La Conférence nationale aura lieu immédiatement après l'élection,' " *TSA*, February 16, 2019, https://www.tsa-algerie.com/abdelmalek-sellal-la-conference-nationale-aura-lieu-immediatement-apres-lelection/.
124. Mbembe, "Nécropolitique," 54.
125. Malika Rahal, "Fille d'Octobre. Générations, engagement et histoire," *L'Année du Maghreb* 10 (2014): 183–187.
126. Jean-Jacques Lavenue, *Algérie: La démocratie interdite* (Paris: L'Harmattan, 1993), 168–169.

3. Cronies and Labyrinths

1. Yasmine Boudjenah, "Le démantèlement du secteur public algérien," *Recherches internationales* 56–57 (1999): 177–179.
2. Will Swearingen, "Algeria's Food Security Crisis," *Middle East Report* 166 (1990): 21–25.
3. Abdellatif Benachenhou, "L'aventure de la désétatisation en Algérie," *Revue du monde musulman et de la Méditerranée* 65 (1992): 175–185.
4. Smaïl Goumeziane, "L'incontournable libéralisation," *Confluences Méditerranée* 11 (1994): 39–52.
5. Naoufel Brahimi El-Mili, "Algérie: Une économie entre libéralisation et attentes sociales," in *Afrique du Nord, Moyen-Orient, Espace et conflits*, ed. Rémy Leveau (Paris: La documentation française, 2003), 163–175.
6. Béatrice Hibou, *La privatisation des états* (Paris: Karthala, 1999); Steven Heydemann, *Networks of Privilege in the Middle East: The Politics of Economic Reform Revisited* (New York: Palgrave Macmillan, 2004).
7. On the link between coercion and capital accumulation in the process of state formation, see Charles Tilly, *Coercion, Capital and European States, AD 990-1990* (Cambridge: Blackwell, 1992).
8. Bradford L. Dillman, *State and Private Sector in Algeria* (Boulder, CO: Westview Press, 2000), 136.
9. Sufyan Alissa, "The Political Economy of Reform in Egypt," Carnegie Middle East Center, Carnegie Papers No. 5 (October 2007), https://carnegieendowment.org/files/cmec5_alissa_egypt_final.pdf, and Bassam Haddad, *Business Networks in Syria: The Political Economy of Authoritarian Resilience* (Stanford, CA: Stanford University Press, 2012).
10. Steven Heydemann, "Upgrading Authoritarianism in the Arab World," Saban Center for Middle East Policy at the Brookings Institution, Analysis Paper No. 13 (October 2007), 18, https://www.brookings.edu/wp-content/uploads/2016/06/10arabworld.pdf.
11. Raymond Hinnebusch, "Authoritarian Resilience and the Arab Uprising: Syria in a Comparative Perspective," *Ortadoğu Etütleri* 7 (2015): 20.
12. Gramsci argues that consent cannot be obtained by drawing exclusively on the state apparatus. The production of hegemony requires entanglements that overcome the dichotomy opposing state and society. Antonio Gramsci, *Quaderni del carcere. Volume terzo. Quaderni 12-29* (Turin: Giulio Einaudi editore, 1977), 763.
13. Michel Camau, "Globalisation démocratique et exception autoritaire arabe," *Critique internationale* 30 (2006): 77.
14. Hocine Malti, " Algérie: Lettre ouverte au général de corps d'armée Mohamed 'Tewfik' Médiène, Rab Dzayer," *Blog Mediapart*, February 17, 2013, https://blogs.mediapart.fr/hocine-malti/blog/170213/algerie-lettre-ouverte-au-general-de-corps-darmee-mohamed-tewfik-mediene-rab-dzayer.

15. Harmut Elsenhans, "Capitalisme d'État ou société bureaucratique de développement," *Études internationales* 13, no. 1 (1982): 3–21.
16. Kay Adamson, *Algeria: A Study in Competing Ideologies* (London: Cassel, 1998), 98–99, 170.
17. Isabelle Werenfels, *Managing Instability: Elites and Political Change in Algeria* (London: Routledge, 2007), 23–24
18. This is consistent with Theda Skocpol's depiction of the government as a semiautonomous entity working to preserve sociopolitical structures and the interests of the ruling classes in *States and Social Revolutions: A Comparative Analysis of France, Russia, and China* (Cambridge: Cambridge University Press, 1979), 27.
19. Hugh Roberts, *The Battlefield: Algeria, 1988-2002* (London: Verso, 2003), 92.
20. John P. Entelis, "Sonatrach: The Political Economy of an Algerian State Institution," *Middle East Journal* 53, no. 1 (1999): 9–27.
21. Ahmed Benbitour, *Radioscopie de la gouvernance algérienne* (Algiers: EDIF 2000, 2006).
22. Werenfels, *Managing Instability*, 133.
23. Rachid Tlemçani, *State and Revolution in Algeria* (Boulder, CO: Westview Press, 1986), 160.
24. Yahia Assam, "Les instruments juridiques de la répression," *Comité Justice pour l'Algérie* 15 (2004): 12–16.
25. Mohamed Nasr-Eddine Koriche, "Justice et règlement des conflits du travail en Algérie," *L'Année du Maghreb* 3 (2007): 53–54.
26. Ilham Bouthalji, "Lan namūt juw'an wa-lan naqbal al-i'hāna . . . wa-li-i'stiqlāliyyat al-'adāla ṭāmiḥūn," *Echorouk* (Algiers), October 29, 2019.
27. Hamid Yas, "Min fāi'dat al-qadā' wa-s-sulṭa adh-dhahāb ba'aīdān fi qaḍiyyat al-Bushi," *El Khabar* (Algiers) June 28, 2018.
28. Luis Martinez, "Algérie: Les massacres de civils dans la guerre," *Revue internationale de politique comparée* 8, no. 1 (2001): 57.
29. Omar Arbane, "Bouira: Les gardes communaux protestent," *El Watan* (Algiers), October 23, 2018.
30. Organisation for Economic Co-operation and Development, *Perspectives économiques en Afrique 2008* (Paris: OECD Publishing, 2008), https://doi.org/10.1787/aeo-2008-fr.
31. International Monetary Fund, *Algeria: Selected Issues*, IMF Country Report No. 14/342 (Washington, DC: IMF, 2014), 24, https://www.imf.org/external/pubs/ft/scr/2014/cr14342.pdf.
32. The official statement was on the home page of the Finance Ministry's website in October 2012 and was widely commented upon in the press.
33. Entelis, "Sonatrach," 10.
34. Omar Benderra, "Pétrole et pouvoir en Algérie," *Confluences Méditerranée* 53 (2005): 57.
35. Entelis, "Sonatrach," 10.
36. Entelis, 17–19.
37. Tarik Dahou, *Gouverner la mer en Algérie. Politique en eaux trouble* (Paris: Karthala, 2018).

38. Mohammed Hachemaoui, "La représentation politique en Algérie entre médiation clientélaire et prédation (1997–2002)," *Revue Française de science politique* 53, no. 1 (2003): 35–36.
39. Bank of Algeria, *Rapport sur la stabilité du secteur bancaire algérien (2009–2011)* (Algiers: Bank of Algeria, 2013), 26–27, https://www.bank-of-algeria.dz/rapport-sur-la-stabilite-du-secteur-bancaire-algerien/.
40. Michel Dobry, *Sociologie des crises politiques* (Paris: Presses de Sciences Po, 1986), 154.
41. On the relationship between the crisis of institutions and the possibility of chaos and anomie, see Peter L. Berger and Thomas Luckmann, *The Social Construction of Reality* (London: Penguin, 1991), 121.
42. Richard S. Katz and Peter Mair, "Changing Models of Party Organization and Party Democracy: The Emergence of the Cartel Party," *Party Politics* 1 (1995): 5–28; Yohann Aucante and Alexandre Deze, *Le système de partis dans les démocraties occidentales. Le modèle du parti cartel en question* (Paris: Presses de Sciences Po, 2013).
43. Amar Mohand-Amer, "L'Union Générale des Travailleurs Algériens dans le processus de transition (1962–1963)," in *Le Maghreb et l'indépendance de l'Algérie*, ed. Amar Mohand-Amer and Belkacem Benzenine (Oran: CRASC; Tunis: IRMC; Aix-en-Provence: Karthala, 2012), 39–49.
44. Benderra, "Pétrole et pouvoir en Algérie," 53–55.
45. Koriche, "Justice et règlement des conflits du travail en Algérie," 43–46.
46. Nadia Benakli, "Sidi Saïd renouvelle son soutien," *L'Expression* (Algiers), January 29, 2014.
47. Layla Baamara, "Quand les protestataires s'autolimitent. Le cas des mobilisations étudiantes de 2011 en Algérie," in *Au coeur des révoltes arabes. Devenir révolutionnaires*, ed. Amine Allal and Thomas Pierret (Paris: Armand Collin, 2013), 137–159.
48. See the weekend edition of *La Tribune* (Algiers), January 30–31, 2009.
49. Omar Carlier, "Mémoire, mythe et doxa de l'État en Algérie. L'Étoile nord-africaine et la religion du 'watan,'" *Vingtième Siècle* 30 (1991): 83.
50. Werenfels, *Managing Instability*, 79–118.
51. Article 87 of the revised constitution.
52. Noureddine Azzouz, "Le MALG se penche sur sa propre histoire," *Le Quotidien d'Oran*, December 15, 2004.
53. Luis Martinez, *Violence de la rente pétrolière: Algérie-Irak-Libye* (Paris: Presses de Sciences Po, 2010), 98–99.
54. James McDougall, "Savage Wars? Codes of Violence in Algeria, 1830s–1990s," *Third World Quarterly* 26, no. 1 (2005): 127.
55. Isabelle Werenfels, "Beyond Authoritarian Upgrading: The Re-emergence of Sufi Orders in Maghrebi Politics," *Journal of North African Studies* 19, no. 3 (2014): 275–295.
56. Mohammed Hachemaoui, *Clientélisme et patronage dans l'Algérie contemporaine* (Paris: Karthala, 2013), 95–144.
57. Similar dynamics have been observed in Syria and Morocco. See Mehdi Nabti, "Soufisme, métissage culturel et commerce du sacré. Les Aïssâwa marocains dans la modernité," *Insaniyat* 32–33 (2006): 173–195; Thomas Pierret and Kjetil Selvik, "Limit

of 'Authoritarian Upgrading' in Syria: Private Welfare, Islamic Charities, and the Rise of the Zayd Movement," *Journal of Middle Eastern Studies* 41 (2009): 595–614.
58. Mustapha Benfodil, "Mystique et politique au temps de 'Sidi' Bouteflika," *El Watan* (Algiers), March 21, 2009.
59. Heydemann, "Upgrading Authoritarianism in the Arab World," 14–15.
60. John P. Entelis, *Algeria: The Revolution Institutionalized* (Boulder, CO: Westview Press, 1986), 128.
61. Mamoun Aidoud, "La privatisation des entreprises publiques algériennes," *Revue internationale de droit comparé* 48, no. 1 (1996): 125–127.
62. Rachid Tlemçani, "Les conditions d'émergence d'un nouvel autoritarisme en Algérie," *Revue du monde musulman et de la Méditerranée* 72 (1994): 108–118.
63. Dillman, *State and Private Sector in Algeria*, 49.
64. Taïeb Belmadi, "Tonic, le Titanic algérien," *Jeune Afrique*, September 10, 2009, https://www.jeuneafrique.com/201237/economie/tonic-le-titanic-alg-rien/.
65. Rachid Tlemçani, "Reflections on the Question of Political Transition in Africa: The Police State," in *Liberal Democracy and its Critics in Africa*, ed. Tukumbi Lumumba-Kasongo (London: Zed Books, 2005), 38.
66. Lyes Laribi, *L'Algérie des Généraux* (Paris: Max Milo éditions, 2007), 183.
67. Samir Bellal, "Problématique du changement institutionnel en Algérie—Une lecture en termes de régulation," *Revue Algérienne de Sciences Juridiques, Economiques et Politiques* 1 (2011): 43–71.
68. Amel Boubekeur, "Rolling Either Way? Algeria Entrepreneurs as Both Agents of Change and Means of Preservation of the System," *Journal of North Africa Studies* 18, no. 3 (2013): 469–481.
69. Pierret and Selvik, "Limit of 'Authoritarian Upgrading' in Syria," 611.
70. Dillman, *State and Private Sector in Algeria*, 3
71. Werenfels, *Managing Instability*, 152–153.
72. Susan Rose-Ackerman, "The Economics of Corruption," *Journal of Public Economy* 4, no. 2 (1975): 187–203.
73. Jean Cartier-Bresson, "Corruption, libéralisation et démocratisation," *Tiers Monde* 41, no. 161 (2000): 14.
74. See Akhil Gupta, "Blurred Boundaries: The Discourse of Corruption, the Culture of Politics, and the Imagined State," *American Ethnologist* 22, no. 2 (1995): 375–402; Akhil Gupta and Aradhana Sharma, "Globalization and Postcolonial States," *Current Anthropology* 47, no. 2 (2006): 277–307; Sarah Muir and Akhil Gupta, "Rethinking the Anthropology of Corruption," *Current Anthropology* 59, no. 18 (2018): 4–15.
75. Luigi Musella, "Réseaux politiques et réseaux de corruption à Naples," *Politix* 12, no. 45 (1999): 41.
76. See "Corruption Perception Index, 2014," Transparency International, February 22, 2023, https://www.transparency.org/en/cpi/2014.
77. Muir and Gupta, "Rethinking the Anthropology of Corruption," 11.
78. Gupta, "Blurred Boundaries," 389.
79. Muir and Gupta, "Rethinking the Anthropology of Corruption," 6.

80. U.S. diplomatic cables sent by the American embassy December 19, 2007 (reference 07ALGIERS1806), https://wikileaks.org/plusd/cables/07ALGIERS1806_a.html, and January 25, 2008 (reference 08ALGIERS85), https://wikileaks.org/plusd/cables/08ALGIERS85_a.html, released by WikiLeaks in 2011.
81. Law No. 06-01 of February 20, 2006, on the prevention of and struggle against corruption, article 25.
82. Fatiha Talahite, "Économie administrée, corruption et engrenage de la violence en Algérie," *Tiers Monde* 41, no. 161 (2000): 59–60.
83. Béatrice Hibou and Mohamed Tozy, "Une lecture d'anthropologie politique de la corruption au Maroc: Fondement historique d'une prise de liberté avec le droit," *Tiers Monde* 41, no. 161 (2000): 23–47; Roderic Broadhurst and Pen Wang, "After the Bo Xilai Trial: Does Corruption Threaten China's Future?," *Survival: Global Politics and Strategy* 56, no. 3 (2013): 157–178; Jiangnan Zhu and Dong Zhang, "Weapons of the Powerful: Authoritarian Elite Competition and Politicized Anticorruption in China," *Comparative Political Studies* 50, no. 9 (2017): 1186–1220.
84. Muir and Gupta, "Rethinking the Anthropology of Corruption," 10.
85. Nicolas Jacquemet, "Micro-économie de la corruption," *Revue française d'économie* 20, no. 4 (2006): 140.
86. Jean Leca and Yves Schemeil, "Clientelisme et patrimonialisme dans le monde arabe," *Revue Internationale de science politique* 4, no. 4 (1983): 455–494.
87. Ayokunle O. Omobowale, "Clientelism and Social Structure: An Analysis of Patronage in Yoruba Social Thought," *Africa Spectrum* 43, no. 2 (2008): 203–224.
88. Jean-François Médard, "Clientélisme politique et corruption," *Tiers Monde* 41, no. 161 (2000): 75–87.
89. Susan Stokes, "Perverse Accountability: A Formal Model of Machine Politics with Evidence from Argentina," *American Political Science Review* 99, no. 3 (2005): 315–325.
90. Robert Gay, "The Broker and the Thief: A Parable (Reflections on Popular Politics in Brazil)," *Luso-Brazilian Review* 36, no. 1 (1999): 49–70; Simeon Nichter, *Votes for Survival: Relational Clientelism in Latin America* (Cambridge: Cambridge University Press, 2018).
91. Herbert Kitschelt and Steven I. Wilkinson, *Patrons, Clients, and Policies: Patterns of Democratic Accountability and Political Competition* (Cambridge: Cambridge University Press, 2007).
92. Diego A. Brun and Larry Diamond, *Clientelism, Social Policy, and the Quality of Democracy* (Baltimore: John Hopkins University Press, 2014).
93. Isabel Kusche, "The Accusation of Clientelism: On the Interplay Between Social Science, Mass Media, and Politics in the Critique of Irish Democracy," *Historical Social Research/Historische Sozialforschung* 42, no. 3 (2017): 172–195.
94. Abderrahmane Moussaoui, *De la Violence en Algérie* (Arles: Actes Sud, 2006), 73.
95. Entelis, *Algeria*, 169.
96. Omobowale, "Clientelism and Social Structure," 219.
97. Hachemaoui, *Clientélisme et patronage dans l'Algérie contemporaine*.

328   3. CRONIES AND LABYRINTHS

98. The notion of neo-patrimonialism appears especially suspect given that demographic changes across the Arab world have undermined traditional psychosocial structures. Michel Camau, "L'exception autoritaire ou l'improbable point d'Archimède de la politique dans le monde arabe," in *La politique dans le monde arabe*, ed. Elizabeth Picard (Paris: Armand Colin, 2006), 34.
99. Leca and Schemeil, "Clientelisme et patrimonialisme dans le monde arabe," 456.
100. Lamia Zaki, "Le clientélisme, vecteur de politisation en régime autoritaire?," in *Autoritarismes démocratiques et démocraties autoritaires au XXIè siècle*, ed. Olivier Dabène, Vincent Geisser, and Gilles Massardier (Paris: La Découverte, 2008), 178.
101. Michel Foucault, *Dits et écrits*, vol. 2, *1976-1988* (Paris: Gallimard, 2001), 302.
102. Michel Camau, *Pouvoir et institution au Maghreb* (Tunis: Céres Production, 1978), 196.
103. Clement M. Henry and Robert Springborg, *Globalization and the Politics of Development in the Middle East* (Cambridge: Cambridge University Press, 2010), 99.
104. Henry and Springborg, *Globalization and the Politics of Development in the Middle East*, 102–103.
105. Henry and Springborg, 130.
106. Larbi Talha, "Le régime rentier à l'épreuve de la transition institutionnelle: L'économie algérienne au milieu du gué," in *Où va l'Algérie?*, ed. Ahmed Mahiou and Jean-Robert Henry (Paris: Karthala, 2001), 125–159; Martinez, *Violence de la rente pétrolière*.
107. Hachemaoui, *Clientélisme et patronage dans l'Algérie contemporaine*, 175–176.
108. Martinez, *Violence de la rente pétrolière*, 211.
109. Fernando Coronil, *The Magical State: Nature, Money and Modernity in Venezuela* (Chicago: University of Chicago Press, 1997), 9.
110. Robert Vitalis, *America's Kingdom: Mythmaking and the Saudi Oil Frontier* (Stanford, CA: Stanford University Press, 2007).
111. Timothy Mitchell, *Carbon Democracy: Political Power in the Age of Oil* (New York: Verso, 2011).
112. Achille Mbembe, *On the Postcolony* (Berkeley: University of California Press, 2001), 41.
113. Denis Paillard, "La Russie après le 11 septembre: Poutine petit soldat de la mondialisation libérale," *Naqd* 19–20 (2004): 267–280.
114. Neil Brenner, Jamie Peck, and Nik Theodore, "Variegated Neoliberalization: Geographies, Modalities, Pathways," *Global Networks* 10, no. 2 (2010): 182–222.
115. Donatella Della Porta, "Les hommes politiques d'affaires. Partis politiques et corruption," *Politix* 30 (1995): 61–75.
116. Francesco Cavatorta, "The Convergence of Governance: Upgrading Authoritarianism in the Arab World and Downgrading Democracy Elsewhere?," *Middle East Critique* 19, no. 3 (2010): 217–232.
117. Gilles Massardier, "Les espaces non pluralistes dans les démocraties contemporaines," in *Autoritarismes démocratiques et démocraties autoritaires au XXIè siècle*, ed. Olivier Dabène, Vincent Geisser, and Gilles Massardier (Paris: La Découverte, 2008): 52.

118. Norbert Elias, *La dynamique de l'Occident* (1975; Paris: Calmann-Lévy Pocket, 1990), 25–26.
119. Louisa Dris-Aït Hamadouche, "Au cœur de la résilience algérienne: Un jeu calculé d'alliances," *Confluences Méditerranée* 106 (2018): 195–210.
120. Luc Boltanski, "L'espace positionnel: Multiplicité des positions institutionnelles et habitus de classe," *Revue française de sociologie* 14, no. 1 (1973): 3–26.
121. Tarek Hafid, "Mohamed Chafik Mesbah au Soir d'Algérie: 'Le système n'est pas mûr pour des élections libres,'" *Le Soir d'Algérie* (Algiers), June 20, 2012.
122. Hibou, *La privatisation des états*, 30.
123. Boltanski, "L'espace positionnel," 26.

4. Fragments of Order

1. Steven Heydemann, "After the Earthquake: Economic Governance and Mass Politics in the Middle East," *Critique internationale* 61, no. 4 (2013): 69–84.
2. Nicolas Guilhot, *The Democracy Makers: Human Rights and the Politics of the Global Order* (New York: Columbia University Press, 2005); Michel Camau, "Globalisation démocratique et exception autoritaire arabe," *Critique internationale* 30 (2006): 59–81.
3. Francesco Cavatorta and Rikke Hostrup Haugbølle, "The End of Authoritarian Rule and the Mythology of Tunisia Under Ben Ali," *Mediterranean Politics* 17, no. 2 (2012): 179–195; Raymond Hinnebusch, "Syria: From 'Authoritarian Upgrading' to Revolution?," *International Affairs* 88 (2012): 95–113.
4. Madjid Benchikh, "Constitutions démocratiques et réalité autoritaire au Maghreb: La démocratie de façade," in *Le Débat juridique au maghreb*, ed. Yadh Ben Achour, Jean-Robert Henry, and Rostane Medhi (Paris: Publisud, 2009), 242–259.
5. Omar Carlier, *Entre Nation et Jihad. Histoire sociale des radicalismes algériens* (Paris: Presses de Sciences Po, 1995), 75.
6. Omar Carlier, "Le café maure. Sociabilité masculine et effervescence citoyenne (Algérie XVIIe–XXe siècles)," *Annales. Économies, Sociétés, Civilisations* 45, no. 4 (1990): 975–1003.
7. Farida Souiah, "Humoriste, journaliste et artiste engagé," *L'Année du Maghreb* 15 (2016): 97–113.
8. Juan Linz, "Quel avenir pour les partis politiques dans les démocraties contemporaines?," *Pôle Sud* 21, no. 1 (2004): 55–68.
9. Jean Leca, "Parti et État en Algérie," *Annuaire de l'Afrique du Nord* 6 (1968): 13–41.
10. Paul Balta and Claudine Rulleau, *La stratégie de Boumédiène* (Paris: Sindbad, 1978), 121.
11. John P. Entelis, *Algeria: The Revolution Institutionalized* (Boulder, CO: Westview Press, 1986), 173.
12. According to Hadj Driss Zitoufi, the former head of Chlef self-defense group, "30% of the GLD are members of the RND, and nobody can deter them from their party.

The GLD existed before the creation of the party, and when the RND was created, in 1997, they all joined it willingly and with the strong will that was characteristic of this period." Fayçal Oukaci, "Nous sommes à 'terrorisme zéro' dans notre région," *L'Expression* (Algiers), April 21, 2006.

13. Josiane Criscuolo, "Armée et Nation dans les discours du Colonel Boumédiène" (PhD diss., University Paul Valéry, 1975), 198–199.
14. Abdou Semmar, "Tahkout: 'Ouyahia n'a jamais été mon associé et je n'ai jamais détourné d'argent public,'" *Algérie focus* (Algiers), August 29, 2013.
15. Quoted in Louisa Dris-Aït Hamadouche and Yahia H. Zoubir, "Pouvoir et opposition en Algérie: Vers une transition prolongée?," *L'Année du Maghreb* 5 (2009): 119.
16. Abdou Semmar, "Ouyahia: Un pied à la présidence en attendant le 2ème?," *Algérie focus* (Algiers), March 13, 2014.
17. Jean-Jacques Lavenue, *Algérie: La démocratie interdite* (Paris: L'Harmattan, 1993), 117.
18. Lakhdar Rezaoui, "Taḥāluf mufājī' bayna Saâdani wa 'Abāda," *Echorouk* (Algiers), June 13, 2014; Hamid Yas, "Belkhadem rafa'a taqrīrān li-Bouteflika 'an a'ḥdāth al-Aurāsī," *El Khabar* (Algiers), June 25, 2014.
19. Achira Mammeri, "Bouteflika signe la mort politique de Belkhadem, de plus en plus incontrôlable," *TSA*, August 26, 2014, http://archives2014.tsa-algerie.com/2014/08/26/bouteflika-signe-la-mort-politique-de-belkhadem-de-plus-en-plus-incontrolable/.
20. Ghania Oukazi, "Limogé par Bouteflika: Le dossier Belkhadem n'est pas clos," *Le Quotidien d'Oran*, September 3, 2014.
21. Mokrane Ait Ouarabi, "Bataille pour le contrôle du FLN," *El Watan* (Algiers), November 7, 2010.
22. *Khobziste* comes from *khobz* (bread) and is used to speak about those who serve the system for material reasons. *Shiyyatin* comes from *shita* (brush) and is an ironic way to describe Bouteflika's supporters.
23. Daniel Gaxie, "Économie des partis et rétributions du militantisme," *Revue française de science politique* 27, no. 1 (1977): 123–154.
24. Ania Tizziani, "Du péronisme au populisme: La conquête conceptuelle du 'gros animal' populaire," *Tiers Monde* 189 (2007): 175–193.
25. Otto Kirchheimer, "The Transformation of the Western European Party Systems," in *Political Parties and Political Development*, ed. Joseph La Palombara and Myron Weiner (Princeton, NJ: Princeton University Press, 1966), 177–200.
26. Donatella Della Porta, "Les hommes politiques d'affaires. Partis politiques et corruption," *Politix* 30 (1995): 61–75.
27. Emma Tilleli [Myriam Aït Aoudia], "Les transformations de la société au regard des élections législatives et municipales de 2002," Centre de recherches internationales, March–April 2003, 5, https://www.sciencespo.fr/ceri/sites/sciencespo.fr.ceri/files/artet.pdf.
28. Philip Selznick, *TVA and the Grass Roots* (Berkeley: University of California Press, 1949), 13.

29. Even in Egypt, where the Muslim Brotherhood has long been prevalent, the gains won by the Salafists of An-Nour and the liberal dissidents of Al-Wassat during the 2011–2012 legislative elections showed that heterogeneity remains the norm. See Clément Steuer, "Les partis politiques fréristes en Egypte à la veille des élections parlementaires," *Moyen-Orient* 13 (2012): 28–31.
30. Olivier Roy, *L'échec de l'islam politique* (Paris: Éditions du Seuil, 1992); William Shepard, "Sayyid Qutb's Doctrine of Jahiliyya," *International Journal of Middle Eastern Studies* 35, no. 4 (2003): 521–545; Hamit Bozarslan, "Le jihâd. Réceptions et usages d'une injonction coranique d'hier à aujourd'hui," *Vingtième Siècle* 82 (2004): 15–29; Andrea Mura, "A Genealogical Inquiry Into Early Islamism: The Discourse of Hasan al-Banna," *Journal of Political Ideologies* 17, no. 1 (2012): 61–85.
31. James McDougall, *History and the Culture of Nationalism in Algeria* (Cambridge: Cambridge University Press, 2006); Charlotte Courreye, *L'Algérie des oulémas. Une histoire de l'Algérie contemporaine, 1931-1991* (Paris: Éditions de la Sorbonne, 2020).
32. The *Jaz'ara* is a nationalist and intellectualist trend in the Algerian Islamic movement. Many of its members received academic training in education or the hard sciences. After the creation of the FIS, the *Jaz'ara* and its leader, Mohamed Saïd, played a key role in organizing the party before joining the insurrection in the 1990s.
33. Sami Zubaida, *Law and Power in the Islamic World* (London: I. B. Tauris, 2003), 11.
34. Hugh Roberts, *The Battlefield: Algeria, 1988-2002* (London: Verso, 2003), 63–81.
35. Brahim Younessi, "L'islamisme algérien: Nébuleuse ou mouvement social?," *Politique étrangère* 60, no. 2 (1995): 370–371.
36. Pierre-Robert Baduel, "Les partis politiques dans la gouvernementalisation de l'État des pays arabes," *Revue du monde musulman et de la Méditerranée* 81–82 (1996): 9–51; Yahia H. Zoubir and Louisa Dris-Aït Hamadouche, "L'islamisme en Algérie: Institutionnalisation du politique et déclin du militaire," *Maghreb-Machrek* 188 (2006): 63–86.
37. Mustafa Al-Ahnaf, Bernard Botiveau, and Franck Fregosi, *L'Algérie par ses islamistes* (Paris: Karthala, 1991), 37.
38. Al-Ahnaf, Botiveau, and Fregosi, 42.
39. Xavier Ternisien, *Les Frères musulmans* (Paris: Fayard, 2005), 183–184.
40. Zoubir and Dris-Aït Hamadouche, "L'islamisme en Algérie," 76.
41. Samir Amghar, "Les trois visages de l'islam politique en Afrique du Nord et au Moyen-Orient: Essai de typologie," *L'Année du Maghreb* 6 (2010): 529–541.
42. Noura Hamladji, "Co-optation, Repression and Authoritarian Regime's Survival: The Case of the Islamist MSP-Hamas in Algeria," European University Institute Working Paper SPS No. 2002/07 (2002), https://cadmus.eui.eu/bitstream/handle/1814/327/sps20027.pdf?sequence=1&isAllowed=y.
43. Samir Amghar and Amel Boubekeur, "Les partis islamistes en Algérie: Structures révolutionnaires ou partis de gouvernement," *Maghreb-Machrek* 194 (2008): 7–23.
44. Rémy Leveau, "Islamisme et populisme," *Vingtième Siècle* 56 (2007): 214–223.
45. Selznick, *TVA and the Grass Roots*, 15.

46. Olivier Roy, *L'islam mondialisé* (Paris: Éditions du Seuil, 2004), 45; Amel Boubekeur, "Les partis islamistes algériens et la démocratie: Vers une professionnalisation politique?," *L'Année du Maghreb* 4 (2008): 219–238.
47. Zoubir and Dris-Aït Hamadouche, "L'islamisme en Algérie"; Isabelle Werenfels, "Algeria's Legal Islamists: From 'Fifth Column' to a Pillar of the Regime," in *Moderate Islamists as Reform Actors*, ed. Muriel Asseburg (Berlin: SWP Research Paper, 2007), 39–44.
48. On the notion of "subjective plausibility," which refers to both the credibility of the institutional order and the ability of actors to explain their own motives, see Peter L. Berger and Thomas Luckmann, *The Social Construction of Reality* (London: Penguin, 1991), 110–111.
49. See, for example, Zouheir Aït Mouhoub, "L'argent: L'autre religion du Mouvement de la société pour la paix (MSP)," *El Watan* (Algiers), December 23, 2011.
50. Djamel Lalami, "Limādhā dāfaʿa Bouteflika ʿan ḥaṣīlatih wa-lawaḥ bi-riʾāsiyyāt musbaqat?," *Echorouk* (Algiers), December 10, 2006.
51. Amghar and Boubekeur, "Les partis islamistes en Algérie," 18.
52. Ghaouti Mekamcha, "Pouvoirs et recompositions en Algérie," in *Les figures du politique en Afrique: Des pouvoirs hérités aux pouvoirs élus*, ed. Momar-Coumba Diop and Mamadou Diouf (Dakar: CODESRIA; Paris: Karthala, 1999), 394–395.
53. Mohamed Tozy, "Représentations/intercessions. Les enjeux de pouvoir dans les champs politiques désamorcés au Maroc," in *Changements politiques au Maghreb*, ed. Michel Camau (Paris: CNRS Éditions, 1991), 153–168.
54. Layla Baamara "Une campagne 'à part, mais pour le parti.' Le cas d'un candidat FFS aux élections législatives de 2012 à Alger," in *Faire campagne, ici et ailleurs*, ed. Layla Baamara, Camille Floderer, and Marine Poirier (Aix-en-Provence: Karthala, 2016), 149–170.
55. Essaïd Wakli, "Louisa Hanoune: Ce que j'ai dit à Bouteflika," *Algérie focus* (Algiers), May 2, 2014.
56. Pierre Bourdieu, *Langage et Pouvoir Symbolique* (Paris: Éditions du Seuil, 2001), 221.
57. Bourdieu, 221.
58. The cost of a position could reach several million dinars. Mehdi Bsikri, "Moussa Touati ouvre son parti au 'plus offrant,'" *El Watan* (Algiers), March 18, 2012.
59. Mohamed Rahmani, "Algérie: Législatives à Souk-Ahras—Une primaire du FNA pervertie par la 'Ch'kara,'" *La Tribune* (Algiers), April 1, 2012.
60. William B. Quandt, *Between Ballots and Bullets* (Washington, DC: Brookings Institution Press, 1998), 133.
61. Robert Michels, *Les partis politiques. Essai sur les tendances oligarchiques des démocraties* (Paris: Flammarion, 1914), 277–279.
62. Dris-Aït Hamadouche and Zoubir, "Pouvoir et opposition en Algérie."
63. Della Porta, "Les hommes politiques d'affaires"; Myriam Catusse, "A propos de 'l'entrée en politique' des 'entrepreneurs' marocains," *Naqd* 19–20 (2004): 127–153.

64. Hamirouche Aït Hamouda, a.k.a. the Wolf of Akfadou, was the commander of the "glorious" Wilaya III during the revolution. One of the fiercest adversaries of the French occupying forces, he was eventually killed in action in 1959.
65. Arnaud Lionel and Christine Guionnet, *Les frontières du politique. Enquête sur les processus de politisation et de dépolitisation* (Rennes: Presses universitaires de Rennes, 2005), 21.
66. From this perspective, the Algerian case shares some commonalities with the American example studied by Nina Eliasoph in *Avoiding Politics: How Americans Produce Apathy in Everyday Life* (Cambridge: Cambridge University Press, 1998).
67. Rabeh Sebaa, "Les élections en Algérie ou la quête de fondements," *Confluences Méditerranée* 23 (1997): 106.
68. Antonio Gramsci, *Quaderni del carcere. Volume terzo. Quaderni 12–29* (Turin: Giulio Einaudi editore, 1977), 1603–1604.
69. Pierre Bourdieu and Luc Boltanski, "La production de l'idéologie dominante," *Actes de la recherche en sciences sociales* 2 (1976): 3–73.
70. T. W. Luke, "On Insurrectionality: Theses on Contemporary Revolts and Resilience," *Globalizations* 12, no. 6 (2015): 843.
71. Frantz Fanon, *Pour la révolution africaine. Écrits politiques* (1964; Paris: La Découverte, 2001), 25–26; Paul Amar, *Security Archipelago: Human-Security States, Sexuality Politics, and the End of Neoliberalism* (Durham, NC: Duke University Press, 2013), 93.
72. Hakim Kateb, "Nos militants sont tous pour la réconciliation," *L'Expression* (Algiers), September 17, 2005.
73. Article 26 of the Executive Order No. 06-01 of February 27, 2006.
74. Ahmed Semiane, *Octobre, ils parlent* (Algiers: Éditions Le Matin, 1998), 133.
75. Samira L. "Ouyahia: Āḥdāth u'ktūbar 1988 u'dkhilat Al-Jazāi'r fī 'ahd al-fawdā wa-ll-lā-i'stiqrār," *Ennahar* (Algiers), October 6, 2018.
76. Wendy Brown, *Edgework: Critical Essays on Knowledge and Politics* (Princeton, NJ: Princeton University Press, 2005), 4.
77. Mohamed Mehdi, "Les résultats des élections," *Le Quotidien d'Oran*, May 12, 2012.
78. "La candidature du président de la République pour un quatrième mandat, un gage de stabilité pour le pays (Saadani)," Algérie Presse Service, January 29, 2014, https://www.djazairess.com/fr/apsfr/343192.
79. The Citizens' Movement is a grassroot democratic movement that appeared in Kabylia during the 2001 Black Spring. Mohamed Abdoun, "Louisa Hanoune: 'L'Algérie est menacée d'éclatement,'" *L'Expression* (Algiers), February 26, 2004.
80. Hesham Sallam, "The New Iraq and Arab Political Reform: Drawing New Boundaries (and Reinforcing Old Ones)," in *Iraq, Its Neighbors and the United States*, ed. Henry J. Barkey, Scott B. Lasensky, and Phebe Marr (Washington, DC: U.S. Institute of Peace Press, 2011), 204.
81. Raouf Farrah, "Tin Zaoutine. Marginalisation et militarisation aux confins des frontières algériennes," *Jadaliyya*, July 15, 2020, https://www.jadaliyya.com/Details/41416.

82. "Personne n'a fait don à l'Algérie de la moindre parcelle de son territoire (Ouyahia)," Algérie Presse Service, Avril 7, 2012, https://www.djazairess.com/fr/apsfr/240807.
83. Sylvie Kauffmann and Isabelle Mandraud, "L'Algérie défend 'l'intégrité territoriale du Mali,'" *Le Monde* (Paris), April 6, 2012.
84. Ernesto Laclau, *On Populist Reason* (London: Verso, 2005).
85. Jacques Rancière, *Aux bords du politique* (Paris: La Fabrique, 1998), 50.
86. Christophe Premat, "La 'grogne du peuple,'" *Tracés* 5 (2004): 13.
87. Cornélius Castoriadis, *Le Monde morcelé* (Paris: Éditions du Seuil, 1990), 15.
88. Jean-Claude Monod, "La force du populisme: Une analyse philosophique," *Esprit* 351 (2009): 42–52.
89. Robert Malley, *The Call from Algeria: Third Worldism, Revolution and the Turn to Islam* (Berkeley: University of California Press, 1996), 48.
90. Lahouari Addi, "Sociologie politique d'un populisme autoritaire," *Confluences Méditerranée* 2, no. 81 (2012): 27–40.
91. Khalfa Mameri, *Orientations politiques de l'Algérie* (Algiers: SNED, 1973), 6.
92. Christian Alain Muller, "Du 'peuple égaré' au 'peuple enfant.' Le discours politique révolutionnaire à l'épreuve de la révolte populaire de 1793," *Revue d'histoire moderne et contemporaine* 47 (2000): 93–112.
93. Djilali Benyoub, "Belkhadem veut 'relégitimer' les marches pacifiques!," *Liberté* (Algiers), January 9, 2011.
94. Hacen Ouali, "Ouyahia est un despote, un danger pour le pays," *El Watan* (Algiers), March 28, 2012.
95. Dris-Aït Hamadouche and Zoubir, "Pouvoir et opposition en Algérie," 126.
96. Charles Tilly, "War Making and State Making as Organized Crime," in *Bringing the State Back in*, ed. Peter Evans, Dietrich Rueschemeyer, and Theda Skocpol (Cambridge: Cambridge University Press, 1985), 169–187.
97. Elizabeth Perego, "Laughing at the Victims: The Function of Popular Jokes During Algeria's 'Dark Decade,' 1991–2002," *Journal of North African Studies* 23, nos. 1–2 (2018): 191–207.
98. Amin Allal, "Becoming Revolutionary in Tunisia, 2007–2011," in *Social Movements, Mobilization, and Contestation in the Middle East and North Africa*, ed. Joel Beinin and Frédéric Vairel, 2nd ed. (Stanford, CA: Stanford University Press, 2013), 197.
99. Bourdieu, *Langage et Pouvoir Symbolique*, 210–211.
100. James C. Scott, *Domination and the Arts of Resistance: Hidden Transcripts* (New Haven, CT: Yale University Press, 1990), 56.

5. The Regulation of Freedoms

1. Luc Boltanski, *De la critique* (Paris: Gallimard, 2009), 190.
2. Thomas Carothers, "The End of the Transition Paradigm," *Journal of Democracy* 13, no. 1 (2002): 5–21.

5. THE REGULATION OF FREEDOMS   335

3. Michel Foucault, *Naissance de la biopolitique. Cours au Collège de France (1978-1979)* (Paris: Seuil/ Gallimard, 2004), 67–69.
4. Giorgio Agamben, *State of Exception* (Chicago: University of Chicago Press, 2005), 2.
5. Jean-François Bayart, "Retour sur les printemps arabes," *Politique Africaine* 133 (2014): 154.
6. "Déclaration commune: LADDH, CLA, SATEF, Coordination des sections CNES, SNAPAP," joint statement released on January 10, 2011, available at http://ffs1963.unblog.fr/2011/01/10/declaration-commune-laddh-cla-satef-coordination-des-sections-cnes-snapap/.
7. Layla Baamara, "Mésaventures d'une coalition contestataire: Le cas de la Coordination Nationale pour le Changement et la Démocratie (CNCD) en Algérie," *Année du Maghreb* 8 (2012): 161–179.
8. Layla Baamara, "Quand les protestataires s'autolimitent. Le cas des mobilisations étudiantes de 2011 en Algérie," in *Au coeur des révoltes arabes. Devenir révolutionnaires*, ed. Amine Allal and Thomas Pierret (Paris: Armand Collin, 2013), 137–159.
9. Yahia H. Zoubir, "The Arab Spring: Is Algeria the Exception?," *IEMedsObs* 61 (2013), https://www.iemed.org/publication/the-arab-spring-is-algeria-the-exception/.
10. Mohamed Cherak, Hamid Yas, and Atef Kedadra, "Mashrū'a qānūn al-I"alām yulghī i'rādat ar-rai'ys fī al-i'ṣlāḥāt," *El Khabar* (Algiers), August 20, 2011; Chérif Dris, "La nouvelle loi organique sur l'information de 2012 en Algérie: Vers un ordre médiatique néo-autoritaire?," *L'Année du Maghreb* 8 (2012): 303–320.
11. Belkacem Mostefaoui, "Algérie, l'espace du débat médiatique," *Réseaux* 88–89 (1998): 153–188; Ratiba Hadj Moussa, *La télévision par satellite au Maghreb et ses publics. Espaces de résistance, espaces critiques* (Grenoble: Presses universitaires de Grenoble, 2015).
12. Rasmus Bozerup, *Authoritarianism and Media in Algeria* (Copenhagen: International Media Support, 2013), https://www.mediasupport.org/publication/authoritarianism-and-media-in-algeria/.
13. Myriam Aït Aoudia, "La genèse d'une mobilisation partisane: Continuités et politisation du militantisme caritatif et religieux au sein du FIS," *Politix* 102 (2013): 129–146.
14. Nadjia Bouaricha, "Hocine Aït Ahmed: 'Remettre du mouvement dans le statu quo,'" *El Watan* (Algiers), March 3, 2012.
15. *Harkis* were Algerian volunteers who fought for the French Army. In the Algerian political lexicon, it is a synonym for traitor.
16. Layla Baamara, "Une campagne 'à part, mais pour le parti.' Le cas d'un candidat FFS aux élections législatives de 2012 à Alger," in *Faire campagne, ici et ailleurs*, ed. Layla Baamara, Camille Floderer, and Marine Poirier (Aix-en-Provence: Karthala, 2016), 149–170.
17. National Democratic Institute, *Rapport final sur les élections législatives en Algérie* (Washington, DC: National Democratic Institute, 2012), 8, https://www.ndi.org/sites/default/files/Algeria-Report-Leg-Elections-FRE.pdf.
18. Pierre Bourdieu, *Sur l'Etat. Cours au Collège de France, 1989-1992* (Paris: Éditions du Seuil, 2012), 564.

19. Sihem Oubraham, "La mission déclare le scrutin libre, transparent, régulier et équitable," *El Moudjahid* (Algiers), May 12, 2012.
20. Ennahar, "Al-mulāḥiẓūn ad-duwaliyūn yushīdūn bi-miṣdāqiyyat wa shafāfiyyat al-i'ntikhābāt at-tashrī'iyya al-jazāi'riyya," *Ennahar* (Algiers), May 12, 2012.
21. Juan Linz, "L'effondrement de la démocratie, autoritarisme et totalitarisme dans l'Europe de l'entre-deux-guerres," *Revue internationale de politique comparée* 11, no. 4 (2004): 584–585.
22. The video was also uploaded to YouTube. See Sky Land, "Abdou Bendjoudi-Khaled Nezzar: Le clash!," YouTube, June 30, 2012, 3:31, https://www.youtube.com/watch?v=nPTF8gtXQTs.
23. Public statement of Hamid Ferhat, president of the Bejaïa APW, October 4, 2010 (in author's possession).
24. Siham Beddoubia, "Les syndicats autonomes en Algérie, initiateurs des luttes démocratiques?," *Confluences Méditerranée* 111 (2019): 119–134.
25. International Labour Organization, *Rapport de la Commission d'experts pour l'application des conventions et recommandations* (Geneva: International Labour Organization, 2012), 53, https://www.ilo.org/public/libdoc/ilo/P/09662/09662(2012-101-1A).pdf.
26. Ahmed Kerbouche, "Dawr siyāsat al-muṣālaḥa al-waṭaniyya fī mu'ālajat al-a'zma al-a'mniya fī Al-Jazāi'r," *Al-Majala al-jazā'iriya li-l-siyāsa al-'aāma* 4, no. 2 (2016): 142–164.
27. Lahouari Addi, "Entretien avec Ali Yahya Abdennour," *Confluences Méditerranée* 51 (2004): 39–44.
28. M. Ben, "Ta'alīmat Ksentini nuffidhat bidāyiat juwān," *El Djazair El Djadida* (Algiers), August 27, 2010.
29. Belkacem Mostefaoui, "Professionnalisation et autonomie des Journalistes au Maghreb. Eléments de mise en situation des actions et conflits," *Réseaux* 51 (1992): 61–62.
30. Zinel Benaouda explains that *El Khabar* was particularly supportive of the 2011 revolution in Tunisia, featuring interviews of victims of repression and comparing the events with those of October 1988. Such enthusiasm was in stark contrast to the general skepticism of the Algerian press. Zineb Benaouda, "Al-fā 'ilūn fī al-a'ḥdāth allatī 'arafathā Tuns min dīsambar 2010 'ilā dīsambar 2011 min khilāl al-yaūmiya Al-Khabr," *Majala ar-risāla li-l-dirāsāt wa-l-buḥūth al-I'nsāniya* 4, no. 4 (2019): 69–90.
31. For the press kit, see Algeria Watch, *Le procès du général Khaled Nezzar contre l'ex-sous-lieutenant Habib Souaïdia* (Paris: Algeria Watch, 2002), http://www.algeria-watch.org/pdf/pdf_fr/Dossier_presse_proces_Nezzar_Souaidia.pdf.
32. Khaled Nezzar, *Le Procès de Paris: L'armée algérienne face à la désinformation* (Paris: Éditions Médiane, 2003).
33. Lahouari Addi, "Army, State and Nation in Algeria," in *Political Armies: The Military and Nation Building in the Age of Democracy*, ed. Kees Koonings and Dirk Kruijt (London: Zed Books, 2002), 197.

34. Dris, "La nouvelle loi organique sur l'information de 2012 en Algérie," 319.
35. Edward Bernays, *Propaganda* (New York: Horace Liveright, 1928); W. Lance Bennett, Regina G. Lawrence, and Steven Livingston, *When the Press Fails: Political Power and the News Media from Iraq to Katrina* (Chicago: University of Chicago Press, 2007); Philippe Riutort, *Sociologie de la communication politique* (Paris: La Découverte, 2007), 54–81.
36. Ali Dilem, *Algérie, mon humour* (Algiers: Casbah éditions, 2011).
37. Ghania Mouffok, *Être journaliste en Algérie* (Paris: RSF, 1995), 44.
38. Salim Mesbah, "Tentative d'incendie de l'imprimerie d'El Watan et d'El Khabar," *El Watan* (Algiers), September 16, 2011.
39. Jean Morange, "La protection constitutionnelle et civile de la liberté d'expression," *Revue internationale de droit comparé* 42, no. 2 (1990): 771–787.
40. Articles 42 and 48 of the revised version of the Algerian Constitution of 1996.
41. Amel B., "Abdelhaï Beliardouh a vécu le calvaire," *El Watan* (Algiers), December 16, 2012.
42. Mohamed Benchicou, *Bouteflika: Une imposture algérienne* (Algiers: Le Matin, 2003).
43. Aïda Touihri, "Médias sous pression," *Jeune Afrique* (Paris), July 19, 2004.
44. Ahmed Rouadjia, "Petit essai sur la sociologie de la misère à l'université de Msila," *Le Quotidien d'Algérie* (Algiers), July 13, 2010.
45. Arezki Louni, "Ethique et liberté de la presse ne sont pas antinomiques," *L'Expression* (Algiers), May 3, 2004.
46. Moustafa Saou and Hicham Betahar, "Dawr as-ṣaḥāfa al-maktūba fī ṣaddi al-marji'iyyāt ad-dīniyya bi-Al-Jazāi'r. Dirāsa taḥlīliyya 'alā 'ayn min ā''adād yaūmiyat Al-Khabr," *Al-majala ad-dawliyya li-i'ltiṣāl al-i'jtimā'aī* 7, no. 1 (2020): 106–127.
47. Gerald Turkel, "Michel Foucault: Law, Power and Knowledge," *Journal of Law and Society* 17, no. 2 (1990): 190.
48. Articles 144 bis, 144 bis1 and 146 of the Penal Code.
49. Article 46 of Executive Order No. 06-01 of February 27, 2006.
50. Article 144 bis2 of the penal code.
51. Dris, "La nouvelle loi organique sur l'information de 2012 en Algérie," 315–316.
52. Massinissa Mansour, "Atteinte à la vie privée: L'Algérie se dote d'un système de surveillance de masse," *Algérie Focus* (Algiers), June 15, 2017; Yacine Babouche, "L'Algérie utilise des outils de surveillance russe et chinois," *TSA*, September 21, 2019, https://www.tsa-algerie.com/lalgerie-utilise-des-outils-de-surveillance-russe-et-chinois/.
53. Law No. 09-04 of August 5, 2009.
54. Laws No. 20-05 and 20-06 of April 28, 2020.
55. Hamit Bozarslan, *Sociologie politique du Moyen-Orient* (Paris: La Découverte, 2011), 53.
56. Jacques Derrida, "Force de loi," *Cardozo Law Review* 11 (1990): 940.
57. Nick Vaughan-Williams, "Borders, Territory, Law," *International Political Sociology* 2 (2008): 322–338.

338   5. THE REGULATION OF FREEDOMS

58. Walter Benjamin, *Selected Writings*, vol. 1, *1913-1926* (Cambridge, MA: Harvard University Press, 1996), 243.
59. Presidential Decree No. 91-196 of June 4, 1991.
60. Yahia Assam, "Les instruments juridiques de la répression," Comité Justice pour l'Algérie, Dossier No. 15 (May 2004), 17, https://www.algerie-tpp.org/tpp/pdf/dossier_15_instruments_juridiques.pdf.
61. Article 87 bis of Executive Order No. 95-11 of February 25, 1995.
62. Francesco Cavatorta, *The International Dimension of the Failed Algerian Transition* (Manchester, UK: Manchester University Press, 2009).
63. Elizabeth Picard, "Armée et sécurité au cœur de l'autoritarisme," in *Autoritarismes démocratiques et démocraties autoritaires au XXIè siècle*, ed. Olivier Dabène, Vincent Geisser, and Gilles Massardier (Paris: La Découverte, 2008), 309–313.
64. Mohamed Koursi, "Ouyahia fait parler les chiffres," *El Moudjahid* (Algiers), December 20, 2010.
65. To view the map, see alphadesigner, "The Arab Spring, Hitchhiker's Guide to The Near and Middle East," Flickr, June 2, 2011, https://www.flickr.com/photos/alphadesigner/5791308632.
66. Articles 51 and 125 bis of the Penal Code modified by Law No. 01-08 of June 26, 2001.
67. Habiba Djahnine, *Avant de franchir la ligne d'horizon*, 2011.
68. Bozarslan, *Sociologie politique du Moyen-Orient*, 42.
69. "La DGSN dément toute violence policière," *Horizons* (Algiers), December 2, 2013.
70. Agamben, *State of Exception*, 3–4.
71. "Un choix délibéré pour éviter toute effusion de sang," *El Moudjahid* (Algiers), May 24, 2012.
72. "Formation de la police scientifique," *El Moudjahid* (Algiers), February 3, 2018.
73. Hannah Arendt, *The Origins of Totalitarianism* (Cleveland, OH: Meridian Books, 1962), 216.
74. Yahia H. Zoubir, "Algeria and U.S. Interests: Containing Radical Islamism and Promoting Democracy," *Middle East Policy Council* 9, no. 1 (2002), 64–81; Luis Martinez, "L'Algérie de l'Après–11 septembre 2001," in *Afrique du Nord, Moyen-Orient, Espace et conflits*, ed. Rémy Leveau (Paris: La Documentation française, 2003), 149–161; Lakhdar Benchiba, "Les mutations du terrorisme algérien," *Politique étrangère* 2 (2009): 345–352.
75. General Directorate for External Policies, *L'Algérie: Un potentiel sous-exploité pour la coopération en matière de sécurité dans la région du Sahel* (Brussels: European Parliament, 2013, 4, https://www.europarl.europa.eu/RegData/etudes/briefing_note/join/2013/491510/EXPO-AFET_SP(2013)491510_FR.pdf.
76. Olivier Le Cour Grandmaison, *De l'indigénat. Anatomie d'un monstre juridique: Le droit colonial en Algérie et dans l'empire français* (Paris: Éditions La Découverte, 2010); Emmanuel Blanchard, *La police parisienne et les Algériens, 1944-1962* (Paris: Nouveau Monde éditions, 2011); Laleh Khalili, *Times in the Shadow: Confinement in*

Counterinsurgencies (Stanford, CA: Stanford University Press, 2012); Sylvie Thénault, *Violence ordinaire dans l'Algérie coloniale* (Paris: Odile Jacob, 2012).

77. Lahouari Addi, "Pluralisme politique et islam dans le monde arabe," *Pouvoirs* 1, no. 104 (2003): 85–95.
78. Moustafa Safouan, *Pourquoi le monde arabe n'est pas libre?* (Paris: Éditions Denoël, 2008).
79. Ali Mezghani, *L'Etat inachevé* (Paris: Gallimard, 2011).
80. Olivier Nay, "La théorie des 'États fragiles': Un nouveau développementalisme politique?," *Gouvernement et action publique* 1 (2013): 139–151.
81. Agamben, *State of Exception*, 23.
82. Giorgio Agamben, *Homo Sacer: Sovereign Power and Bare Life* (Stanford, CA: Stanford University Press, 1998), 30–35; Agamben, *State of Exception*, 54–55.
83. Boltanski, *De la critique*, 193–194.
84. Maxime Aït Kaki, *De la question berbère au dilemme Kabyle à l'aube du XXIème siècle* (Paris: L'Harmattan, 2004).
85. Aït Kaki, *De la question berbère au dilemme Kabyle*, 55–57.
86. Hocine Aït Ahmed, "La troisième guerre d'Algérie," *Maroc Hebdo International* (Casablanca), November 15, 2001.
87. "A party that says on live TV that Algerians must get ready to change their eating habits and their dress code. A party that says 'Dimukratia Kufr.' It's exactly the same undertaking as Hitler." Nassim, member of the Committee on Social Affairs and Health at the APW, RCD member, Tizi Ouzou, spring 2011.
88. Lahouari Addi, "Les partis politiques en Algérie," *Revue des Mondes Musulmans et de la Méditerranée* 111–112 (2006): 147.
89. See the fifteen points presented in the El Kseur Platform of June 11, 2001, available in "Plate-forme de revendications dite Plate-forme d'El-Kseur," Algeria-Watch, last modified June 4, 2018, https://algeria-watch.org/?p=58360.
90. Emma Tilleli [Myriam Aït-Aoudia], "Le Mouvement Citoyen de Kabylie," *Pouvoirs* 106 (2003): 151–162; Aït Kaki, *De la question berbère au dilemme Kabyle*, 171–172.
91. Myriam Aït Aoudia (as Emma Tilleli), "Les transformations de la société au regard des élections législatives et municipales de 2002," Centre de recherches internationales, March–April 2003, 14, https://www.sciencespo.fr/ceri/sites/sciencespo.fr.ceri/files/artet.pdf.
92. Boussad Boudiaf, deputy and member of the national council of the RCD, Tizi Ouzou, Spring 2011.
93. "Call to Boycott the 2002 Legislative Elections" released by the coordination of Aârch, Daïra, and communes, March 8, 2002, as well as the points 5, 6, and 7 of the "Code of Honor" of the Citizens' Movement (in author's possession).
94. Ouali Ilikoud, "FFS et RCD: Partis nationaux ou partis kabyles," *Revue des mondes musulmans et de la Méditerranée* 111–112 (2006): 163–182.
95. Marie-Claire Lavabre, "Usages du passé, usages de la mémoire," *Revue française de science politique* 3 (1994): 483.

340   5. THE REGULATION OF FREEDOMS

96. Patricia M. E. Lorcin, *Kabyles, Arabes, Français: Identités coloniales* (Limoges: PULIM, 2005).
97. Gayatri Spivak, "Subaltern Studies: Deconstructing Historiography," in *The Spivak Reader*, ed. Donna Landry and Gerald MacLean (1985; London: Routledge, 1996), 214.
98. Samir Larabi, spokesman of the National Committee for the Defense of the Rights of the Unemployed, member of the PST, Algiers, spring 2011.
99. According to then general secretary of the FFS Ali Laskri. See R. M., "FFS: Ali Laskri qualifie le RCD de 'harki du système,'" *Le Matin d'Algérie*, March 4, 2012, https://www.lematindz.net/news/7524-ffs-ali-laskri-qualifie-le-rcd-de-harki-du-systeme.html.
100. Baamara, "Mésaventures d'une coalition contestataire."
101. It is worth noting that bureaucratic obstacles are not necessarily consciously deployed, and they can also indicate a mix of suspicion, incompetence, and bad faith among low-level state agents. For example, Wahiba, a long-standing employee in local and international NGOs, told me that "As soon as public or private interests are threatened by an association, one puts roadblocks in its way, and this is often enough to stop it . . . There is also a form of incomprehension and bad faith coming from those who are in charge of these issues. Some will say that you work in a for-profit organization even if this is obviously not the case. There is bad faith, for sure, but really the problem here is rather a lack of understanding of legal texts." Wahiba, founder of several cultural associations, now employed by Friedrich Ebert Stiftung (NGO), Algiers, autumn 2010.
102. Steven Heydemann, "Upgrading Authoritarianism in the Arab World," Saban Center for Middle East Policy at Brookings Institution, Analysis Paper No. 13 (October 2007)., https://www.brookings.edu/research/upgrading-authoritarianism-in-the-arab-world/.

6. The Crisis as a Lived Experience

1. Nora Semmoud, "'Clair-obscur' de l'informel. Contrôle des polarités urbaines informelles à Cherarba, périphérie sud-est d'Alger," *Les Cahiers d'EMAM* 26 (2015), https://journals.openedition.org/emam/983.
2. Mounir M., "Iḥtijājāt 'anīfa wasaṭ madīnat Jījal," *El Khabar* (Algiers), April 30, 2012.
3. *El Watan* traced the practice of self-immolation back to the case of Djamel Taleb, who committed suicide in 2004 in Algiers. The phenomenon became especially widespread in 2011–2012. Mustapha Benfodil, "Immolations: Ces Mohamed Bouazizi que l'Algérie ne veut pas voir," *El Watan* (Algiers), February 3, 2012.
4. Giorgio Agamben, *State of Exception* (Chicago: University of Chicago Press, 2005), 11.
5. Theda Skocpol, *States and Social Revolutions: A Comparative Analysis of France, Russia, and China* (Cambridge: Cambridge University Press, 1979).
6. Vladimir Ilitch Lenin, *The Collapse of the Second International* (Glasgow: Socialist Labour Press, 1920), 17.

7. Walter Benjamin, *Selected Writings*, vol. 4, *1938-1940* (Cambridge, MA: Harvard University Press, 2003), 392.
8. On the notion of a "repertoire of contention" and its evolving relationship with state repressive strategies, see Charles Tilly, *Contentious Performances* (Cambridge: Cambridge University Press, 2008); Sidney Tarrow, *Power in Movement: Social Movements and Contentious Politics* (Cambridge: Cambridge University Press, 2011), 98-99.
9. The term "egalitarian perception of social relations" is used by Tocqueville to describe a type of grassroots subjectivity that he views as the essence of American democracy. See *De la Démocratie en Amérique, Tome 1* (1835; Paris: Garnier-Flammarion, 1981), 31. In the Algerian context, a key difference is that such a perception is articulated in a contentious manner, against economic and political hierarchies that are presented as the outcome of undue privilege.
10. *Chemma* is a mix of chewing tobacco and fig tree ashes.
11. Robert P. Parks, "Local-National Relations and the Politics of Property Rights in Algeria and Tunisia" (PhD diss., University of Texas at Austin, 2011), 311.
12. For a similar reflection on Senegal, see Michael Ralph, "Killing Time," *Social Text* 26, no. 4 (2008): 1-29.
13. Yasmine Boudjenah, "Le démantèlement du secteur public algérien," *Recherches internationales* 56-57 (1999): 177-179; Ivan Martin, "Politique économique et stabilité de l'État," Centre de recherches internationales, March-April 2003, https://www.sciencespo.fr/ceri/sites/sciencespo.fr.ceri/files/artim_0.pdf; Jonathan N. C. Hill, "Challenging the Failed State Thesis: IMF and World Bank Intervention and the Algerian Civil War," *Civil Wars* 11, no. 1 (2009): 39-56.
14. Béatrice Hibou, *Anatomie de la domination* (Paris: La Découverte, 2011), 49-55.
15. Parks, *Local-National Relations*, 313.
16. *Kashir* is a type of Algerian salami. *Kashiriste* was used to refer to those serving the cartel's interests under Bouteflika.
17. Jeanne Lazarus, "Le Pauvre et la Consommation," *Vingtième Siècle* 91 (2006): 137-152.
18. "Le taux de chômage en Algérie à 11,7% en septembre 2018," Algérie Presse Service, February 10, 2019, https://www.aps.dz/economie/85301-le-taux-de-chomage-en-algerie-a-11-7-en-septembre-2018.
19. Lahcen Achy, "Substituer des emplois précaires à un chômage élevé. Les défis de l'emploi au Maghreb," Carnegie Middle East Center, Carnegie Papers No. 23 (November 2010), 10-12, https://carnegieendowment.org/publications/?fa=view&id=42103.
20. Rabah Belabbas, "Muḥāwalat binā' namūdhaj qīāsī li-tafsīr biṭālat al-yā's fī Al-Jazā'ir," *Majalat al-'ulūm al-iqtiṣādiyya wa-t-tasiyīr wa-l-'ulūm al-tijāriyya* 10 (2013): 15-31.
21. Bruno Schoumaker and Dominique Tabutin, "La démographie du monde arabe et du Moyen-Orient des années 1950 aux années 2000," *Population* 5-6 (2005): 611-724.
22. Omar Carlier, *Entre Nation et Jihad. Histoire sociale des radicalismes algériens* (Paris: Presses de Sciences Po, 1995), 346.

23. Pascal Ménoret, *Joyriding in Riyadh: Oil, Urbanism, and Road Revolt* (Cambridge: Cambridge University Press, 2014), 58–60.
24. Elizabeth Stewart, *Catastrophe and Survival: Walter Benjamin and Psychoanalysis* (New York: Continuum, 2010).
25. Walter Benjamin, *Selected Writings*, vol. 2, *1927-1934* (Cambridge, MA: Harvard University Press, 1999), 735.
26. Banu Bargu, "Why Did Bouazizi Burn Himself? The Politics of Fate and Fatal Politics," *Constellations* 23, no. 1 (2016): 28.
27. Banu Bargu, *Starve and Immolate: The Politics of Human Weapons* (New York: Columbia University Press, 2014), 85.
28. Ménoret, *Joyriding in Riyadh*, 59.
29. In 2015, the World Bank placed Algeria between China and Brazil.
30. Louisa Dris-Aït Hamadouche and Yahia H. Zoubir, "Pouvoir et opposition en Algérie: Vers une transition prolongée?," *L'Année du Maghreb* 5 (2009): 122.
31. Saïd Bouamama, "Le sentiment de 'hogra': Discrimination, négation du sujet et violences," *Hommes et Migrations* 1227 (2000): 38–50.
32. Abdelnacer Djabi, "Al-u'sṭūra, al-jīl wa-l-harakāt al-ijtimā'iyya fī Al-Jazāi'r. A'w al-ab 'al-fāshil' wa-l-ibn 'al-qāfiz,' " *Insaniyat* 25–26 (2004): 43–54.
33. Hugh Roberts, *The Battlefield: Algeria, 1988-2002* (London: Verso, 2003), 287–291; Chérif Bennadji, "Algérie 2010: L'année des mille et unes émeutes," *L'Année du Maghreb* 7 (2011): 263–269.
34. *Liberté*, "Déclaration du secrétariat national de l'UGTA," *Liberté* (Algiers), January 8, 2011.
35. As was the case on October 7, 1988, and again during the 2019 Hirak.
36. Michel Kokoreff, Odile Steinauer, and Pierre Barron, "Les émeutes urbaines à l'épreuve des situations locales," *SociologieS*, August 23, 2007, https://journals.openedition.org/sociologies/254.
37. James C. Scott, *Domination and the Arts of Resistance: Hidden Transcripts* (New Haven, CT: Yale University Press, 1990), 151.
38. Farhad Khosrokhavar, "La violence et ses avatars dans les quartiers sensibles," *Déviance et Société* 24, no. 4 (2000): 433.
39. Charles Tilly, *La France conteste de 1600 à nos jours* (Paris: Fayard, 1986), 13–15.
40. Ghania Mouffok, "Retour sur la marche d'Alger: La révolution de onze heures à midi," *Maghreb émergent*, February 15, 2011, https://maghrebemergent.net/retour-sur-la-marche-d-alger-la-revolution-de-onze-heures-a-midi/.
41. Tilly makes a similar argument about Paris in *La France conteste*, 399.
42. Amin Allal, "Becoming Revolutionary in Tunisia, 2007–2011," in *Social Movements, Mobilization, and Contestation in the Middle East and North Africa*, ed. Joel Beinin and Frédéric Vairel, 2nd ed. (Stanford, CA: Stanford University Press, 2013), 185–204; Allal, "Retour vers le futur. Les origines économiques de la révolution tunisienne," *Pouvoirs* 156 (2016): 17–29.
43. Spokesperson and coordinator of the unemployed Tahar Belabbes explained that the minister had called them "ill-bred" and "manipulated youth," before

threatening them. "Selon Tayeb Louh, les chômeurs sont 'manipulés' et 'mal-élevés!,'" *El Watan* (Algiers), June 26, 2011.

44. Naoual Belakhdar, "'L'éveil du Sud' ou quand la contestation vient de la marge. Une analyse du mouvement des chômeurs algériens," *Politique africaine* 137 (2015): 35–36.
45. On the meaning of internal colonialism in Latin America and notably in Mexico, see Pablo Gonzalez Casanova, "Société plurale, colonialisme interne et développement," *Tiers Monde* 5, no. 18 (1964): 291–295.
46. Larabi took part in the Citizens' Movement after 2001 and later led a mobilization for the defense of working conditions in public media. As for Zaïd, he has been a long-standing unionist and a human rights activist especially visible in the South. His actions led to a series of retaliatory measures, including several arrests and convictions, notably for his allegedly defamatory statements.
47. Choukri Hmed, "Réseaux dormants, contingence et structures. Genèses de la révolution tunisienne," *Revue française de science politique* 62, nos. 5–6 (2012): 797–820.
48. James McDougall, "After the War: Algeria's Transition to Uncertainty," *MERIP* 245 (2007), https://merip.org/2007/12/after-the-war/.
49. Belakhdar, "L'éveil du Sud," 30.
50. On these types of social movements, see Tarrow, *Power in Movement*, 102–103.
51. Khaled Haddag, "Les militants du comité des chômeurs dénoncent le harcèlement des autorités locales," *Le Temps d'Algérie* (Algiers), March 18, 2011.
52. Belakhdar, "L'éveil du Sud," 40–42.
53. Idir Tazerout, "Ayez confiance en votre pays," *Le Soir d'Algérie* (Algiers), March 17, 2013.
54. Charles Tripp, *The Power and the People: Path of Resistance in the Middle East* (Cambridge: Cambridge University Press, 2013).
55. "Ouargla: Une liste de bénéficiaires de logements provoque l'émeute," *El Watan* (Algiers), April 10, 2013.
56. Houria Alioua, "Les chômeurs déterminés à dénoncer la manipulation," *El Watan* (Algiers), April 18, 2013.
57. Nazim Fethi, "Algérie: Bras de fer entre les chômeurs et le gouvernement," *Magharebia*, March 26, 2013, https://www.courrierinternational.com/article/2013/03/26/bras-de-fer-entre-les-chomeurs-et-le-gouvernement.
58. "La maladie du président Bouteflika 'ne sera bientôt plus qu'un mauvais souvenir,'" Algérie Presse Service, May 20, 2013, https://www.djazairess.com/fr/apsfr/303358.
59. Lucien Bianco, "Armes des faibles, faibles armes," *Perspectives chinoises* 51 (1999): 4–16.
60. Grégoire Chamayou, *Les chasses à l'homme* (Paris: La Fabrique éditions, 2010), 159; Ménoret, *Joyriding in Riyadh*, 103–104.
61. On the issue of problematic urbanization, see Marc Côte, "Une ville remplit sa vallée: Ghardaïa (Note)," *Méditerranée* 99 (2002): 107–110.

62. Laurence Dufresne Aubertin, "Revendications morales et politiques d'une révolte. Les émeutes du Mzab en Algérie (2013–2015)," *L'Année du Maghreb* 16 (2017): 209–222.
63. Chamayou, *Les chasses à l'homme*, 151.
64. Kamel Kateb, "Population et organisation de l'espace en Algérie," *L'Espace Géographique* 32 (2003): 326.
65. Julien Brachet, Armelle Chopin, and Olivier Pliez, "Le Sahara entre espace de circulation et frontière migratoire de l'Europe," *Hérodote* 142 (2011): 163–182; Sylvie Bredeloup, "Sahara Transit: Times, Spaces, People," *Population, Space and Place* 18, no. 4 (2012): 457–467.
66. Mélanie Matarese, "Les chômeurs du Sud algérien: Le revers de la rente," *Middle East Eye*, March 1, 2016, https://www.middleeasteye.net/fr/reportages/les-chomeurs-du-sud-algerien-le-revers-de-la-rente.
67. Belakhdar, "L'éveil du Sud."
68. "Quand les chômeurs se muent en force politique," *El Watan* (Algiers), February 3, 2014.
69. Naoual Belakhdar, "When Unemployment Meets Environment. The Case of the Anti-fracking Coalition in Ouargla," *Mediterranean Politics* 24, no. 4 (2019): 438.
70. Abderrahmane Moussaoui, *De la Violence en Algérie* (Arles: Actes Sud, 2006), 226.
71. Aber Betache, "La DGSN triple ses effectifs en cinq ans," *Le Soir d'Algérie* (Algiers), October 23, 2014.
72. Khaled T., "Augmentation du taux de recrutement dans le rang de l'armée," *Ennaharonline*, April 24, 2011, https://www.vitaminedz.com/fr/Algerie/augmentation-du-taux-de-recrutement-dans-289880-Articles-0-18300-1.html.
73. Béatrice Hibou, *La force de l'obéissance. Économie politique de la répression en Tunisie* (Paris: La Découverte, 2006), 215–218, 290–291.
74. Jean Baudrillard, *The Spirit of Terrorism* (New York: Verso, 2003), 45.
75. Baudrillard, 73.
76. "11.000 interventions de maintien de la sécurité publique en 2011 (DGSN)," Algérie Presse Service, January 5, 2012, https://www.djazairess.com/fr/apsfr/228277.
77. Guy Debord, *La société du spectacle* (1967; Chicoutimi, QC: Éditions de l'UQAC, 2006), 10.
78. See edition of May 6, 2012.
79. Noureddine Bedouar, "La DGSN ne veut plus assumer seule la responsabilité," *El Watan* (Algiers), September 30, 2014.
80. "80 cas de violence enregistrés durant la phase aller de la saison footballistique," Algérie Presse Service, January 13, 2019, https://www.aps.dz/sport/83696-80-cas-de-violence-enregistres-durant-la-phase-aller-de-la-saison-footballistique.
81. Steven DeCaroli, "Political Life: Giorgio Agamben and the Idea of Authority," *Research in Phenomenology* 43 (2013): 240.
82. Hibou, *Anatomie de la domination*, 56–58.
83. Adisa Marzuq, "Al-lughāt al-a'jnabiyya wa-l-vīzā hakadhā yunasar al-jazāi'riyyūn," *Ennahar* (Algiers), August 16, 2010.

84. Mohamed Bousri, "Bouteflika répond à ses opposants," *Ennaharonline*, February 24, 2011, https://www.djazairess.com/fr/ennaharfr/6642.
85. Akila Demmad, "La baisse des prix du pétrole impose une prudence dans la conduite de nos affaires économiques," *El Moudjahid* (Algiers), July 9, 2012.
86. Luis Martinez, *La guerre civile en Algérie* (Paris: Khartala, 1998), 20.
87. Roosbelinda Cárdenas and Hiba Bou Akar, "Writing About Violence," *Middle East Report* 284–285 (2017), https://merip.org/2018/04/writing-about-violence/.
88. Paul H. Oquist, *Violence, Conflict, and Politics in Colombia* (New York: Academic Press, 1980).
89. Eric Lair, "La Colombie entre guerre et paix," *Politique étrangère* 66, no. 1 (2001): 109–121.
90. Gonzalo Sanchez, *Guerre et politique en Colombie* (Paris: L'Harmattan, 1998), 212; Daniel Pécaut, "Présent, passé, futur de la violence," in *La Colombie à l'aube du troisième millénaire*, ed. Christian Gros (Paris: IHEAL, 1996), 30–31.
91. Ali Brahimi, "Elle court, elle court, la maladie de la violence," *Le Quotidien d'Oran*, September 13, 2012.
92. Christelle Taraud, "Les *yaouleds*: Entre marginalisation sociale et sédition politique," *Revue d'histoire de l'enfance "irrégulière"* 10 (2008): 59–74.
93. On the process of "decivilization" theorized by Norbert Elias, see *The Germans: Power Struggles and the Development of Habitus in the Nineteenth and Twentieth Centuries* (New York: Columbia University Press, 1996).
94. Hibou, *La force de l'obéissance*, 220–251.
95. David Galula, *Pacification in Algeria, 1956-1958* (1963; Santa Monica: RAND Corporation, 2006), 246.
96. Daniel Pécaut, *L'ordre et la violence. Evolution socio-politique de la Colombie entre 1930 et 1953* (Paris: Éditions de l'EHESS, 1987).
97. Eric J. Hobsbawm, "The Revolutionary Situation in Colombia," *World Today* 19, no. 6 (1963): 249.
98. Cristina Rojas, "Securing the State and Developing Social Insecurities: The Securitisation of Citizenship in Contemporary Colombia," *Third World Quarterly* 30, no. 1 (2009): 227–245.
99. Fadi A. Bardawil, *Revolution and Disenchantment: Arab Marxism and the Binds of Emancipation* (Durham, NC: Duke University Press, 2020).
100. Abdel'alim Medjaoui, *Le Géant aux yeux bleus. Novembre, où en est ta victoire?* (Algiers: Casbah éditions, 2007).
101. Adi Ophir, "The Politics of Catastrophization: Emergency and Exception," in *Contemporary States of Emergency: The Politics of Military and Humanitarian Interventions*, ed. Didier Fassin and Mariella Pandolfi (New York: Zone Books, 2010), 61.
102. Benjamin, *Selected Writings*, 4:389–390, 392.
103. For example, Diaz's *#Civil fi bled el 3askar* (2015) or the more confidential *Jazayri* released by Black T (2017).
104. Wendy Brown, *Edgework: Critical Essays on Knowledge and Politics* (Princeton, NJ: Princeton University Press, 2005), 8.

105. Ratiba Hadj Moussa, "Marginality and Ordinary Memory: Body Centrality and the Plea for Recognition in Recent Algerian Films," *Journal of North African Studies* 13, no. 2 (2008): 187–199.
106. Peter Limbrick, "Spaces of Dispossession: Experiments with the Real in Contemporary Algerian Cinema," in *Histories of Arab Documentary*, ed. Viola Shafik (Cairo: University of Cairo Press, forthcoming).
107. "In the experience of image making, I discovered that people here didn't have their own image, a representation of what they are." Habiba Djahnine, documentary filmmaker, former member of the PST, Algiers, spring 2011.
108. Hakim Abderezzak, "The Mediterranean Seametery and Cementery in Leïla Kilani's and Tariq Teguia's Filmic Works," in *Critically Mediterranean: Temporality, Aesthetics and Deployments of a Sea in Crisis*, ed. Yasser Elhariry and Edwige Tamalet Talbayev (London: Palgrave Macmillan, 2018), 147–161.
109. Benjamin, *Selected Writings*, 4:396.
110. Luc Chauvin, "Rap algérien: D'une révolution culturelle à une autre," *Mouvements* 4, no. 96 (2018): 111–118.
111. For example, MBS in *Maquis bla sleh* (2005) and Lotfi DK in *Wesh heeb* (2013).
112. Lenin is adamant about the need to enter into a direct power struggle to overthrow the old regime, even in a period of crisis. See *The Collapse of the Second International*, 17. Tilly also considers that "a revolutionary situation begins when a government previously under the control of a single, sovereign polity becomes the object of effective, competing, mutually exclusive claims on the part of two or more distinct polities." See *From Mobilization to Revolution* (Reading, UK: Addison-Wesley, 1978), 192. The need for a preexisting "dual power" is nonetheless a matter of debate. Arendt thus contends that a crisis is what makes a revolution possible, and that revolutionaries are merely hoping to seize power when it breaks out. See *On Revolution* (London: Penguin Books, 1990), 259–260.
113. Thomas Serres, "La 'jeunesse algérienne' en lutte. Du rôle politique conflictuel d'une catégorie sociale hétérogène," *Revue des mondes musulmans et de la Méditerranée* 134 (2013): 213–230.
114. Charles Kurzman, *The Unthinkable Revolution in Iran* (Cambridge, MA: Harvard University Press, 2004).
115. Mounia Bennani-Chraïbi and Olivier Fillieule, "Pour une sociologie des situations révolutionnaires. Retour sur les révoltes arabes," *Revue française de science politique* 62, no. 5 (2012): 793.
116. Brian Milstein, "Thinking Politically About Crisis: A Pragmatist Perspective," *European Journal of Political Theory* 14, no. 2 (2015): 141–160.

7. In Search of Lost Meaning

1. Ferhat Abbas, *L'indépendance confisquée (1962-1978)* (Paris: Flammarion, 1984); Hassan, *Algérie. Histoire d'un naufrage* (Paris: Seuil, 1996); Abderrahmane Hadj Nacer, *La*

martingale algérienne. Réflexions sur une crise (Algiers: Éditions Barzakh, 2011); Hocine Malti, *Histoire secrète du pétrole algérien* (Paris: La Découverte, 2012).
2. Achille Mbembe, *On the Postcolony* (Berkeley: University of California Press, 2001), 102.
3. Houda Bouatih, "Ra'yis al-Jumhūriyya khaṭṭun a'ḥmar wa-lā naqbal al-misās bi-i'njāzātih," *Ech Cha'ab* (Algiers), May 12, 2018.
4. Mbembe, *On the Postcolony*, 103.
5. Samir Kassir, *Considérations sur le malheur arabe* (Arles: Actes Sud, 2004); Elizabeth S. Kassab, *Contemporary Arab Thought: Cultural Critique in Comparative Perspective* (New York: Columbia University Press, 2010).
6. William L. F. Felstiner, Richard L. Abel, and Austin Sarat, "The Emergence and Transformation of Disputes: Naming, Blaming, Claiming," *Law & Society Review* 15, nos. 3–4 (1980): 631–54.
7. Frantz Fanon, *Les damnés de la Terre* (1961; Chicoutimi, QC: Éditions de l'UQAC, 2002), 49.
8. Hamit Bozarslan, "Le chaos après le déluge: Notes sur la crise turque des années 70," *Culture & conflits* 24–25 (1997): 8.
9. Omar Carlier, *Entre Nation et Jihad. Histoire sociale des radicalismes algériens* (Paris: Presses de Sciences Po, 1995), 316.
10. Ali El Kenz, "Algérie, les deux paradigmes," *Revue du monde musulman et de la Méditerranée* 68–69 (1993): 79.
11. John R. Nellis, "Algerian Socialism and Its Critics," *Canadian Journal of Political Science* 13, no. 3 (1980): 481–507; Kay Adamson, *Algeria: A Study in Competing Ideologies* (London: Cassel, 1998); Jeffrey J. Byrne, *Mecca of Revolution: Algeria, Decolonization, and the Third World Order* (Oxford: Oxford University Press, 2016); Mohammed Lakhdar Ghettas, *Algeria and the Cold War: International Relations and the Struggle for Autonomy* (London: I. B. Tauris, 2018).
12. On this topic, see Susan Slyomovics, "'The Ethnologist-Spy Was Hanged, at that Time We Were a Little Savage': Anthropology in Algeria with Habib Tengour," *boundary 2*, December 10, 2018, https://www.boundary2.org/2018/12/susan-slyomovics-the-ethnologist-spy-was-hanged-at-that-time-we-were-a-little-savage-anthropology-in-algeria-with-habib-tengour/.
13. Robert Malley, *The Call from Algeria: Third Worldism, Revolution and the Turn to Islam* (Berkeley: University of California Press, 1996), 141–146.
14. Byrne, *Mecca of Revolution*, 17; Alina Sajed, "How We Fight: Anticolonial Imaginaries and the Question of National Liberation in the Algerian War," *Interventions* 21, no. 5 (2019): 635–651.
15. Hilderbert Isnard, "L'Algérie ou la décolonisation difficile," *Méditerranée* 3 (1969): 325–340; Catherine Simon, *Algérie, les années pieds-rouges. Des rêves de l'indépendance au désenchantement (1962-1969)* (Paris: La Découverte, 2011).
16. Samuel P. Huntington, *Political Order in Changing Societies* (1968; New Haven, CT: Yale University Press, 1973), 36.
17. Georges Mutin, "Implantations industrielles et aménagements du territoire en Algérie," *Revue de géographie de Lyon* 55, no. 1 (1980): 5–37.

18. Gilbert Grandguillaume, *Arabisation et politique linguistique au Maghreb* (Paris: Maisonneuve et Larose, 1995).
19. Mark T. Berger, "After the Third World? History, Destiny and the Fate of Third Worldism," *Third World Quarterly* 25, no. 1 (2004): 9–39.
20. Edward McAllister, "Nation-Building Remembered: Social Memory in Contemporary Algeria" (PhD diss., Oxford University, 2015).
21. Luis Martinez, *La guerre civile en Algérie* (Paris: Khartala, 1998).
22. Abderrahmane Moussaoui, "Algérie, la guerre rejouée," *La pensée de midi* 3 (2000): 28–37, and *De la Violence en Algérie* (Arles: Actes Sud, 2006). For an exception, see Moussaoui, "Algérie, la réconciliation entre espoirs et malentendus," *Politique étrangère* 2 (2007): 339–350.
23. Michael Willis, *The Islamist Challenge in Algeria: A Political History* (New York: New York University Press, 1997); Hugh Roberts, *The Battlefield: Algeria, 1988-2002* (London: Verso, 2003); Martin Evans and John Phillips, *Algeria: Anger of the Dispossessed* (New Haven, CT: Yale University Press, 2008).
24. Evans and Philips, *Anger of the Dispossessed*, 225.
25. David Wilkinson, *Revolutionary Civil War: The Elements of Victory and Defeat* (Palo Alto, CA: Page-Ficklin Publications, 1975), 2.
26. Roberts, *The Battlefield*, 353–354.
27. Jonathan N. C. Hill, "Challenging the Failed State Thesis: IMF and World Bank Intervention and the Algerian Civil War," *Civil Wars* 11, no. 1 (2009): 39–56; Elizabeth Perego, "Laughing in the Face of Death: Humor During the Algerian Civil War, 1991–2002" (PhD diss., Ohio State University, 2017); Sharon M. Bartlett, "Masculinities, Money, and Mosques in Algeria's Civil War," *Peace Review* 30, no. 4 (2018): 470–478; Tristan Leperlier, *Algérie, Les écrivains de la décennie noire* (Paris: CNRS Éditions, 2018); Thomas Serres, "After the Apocalypse: Catastrophizing Politics in Post–Civil War Algeria," *Interdisciplinary Political Studies* 5, no. 1 (2019): 55–87; Faouzia Zeraoulia, "The Memory of the Civil War in Algeria: Lessons from the Past with Reference to the Algerian Hirak," *Contemporary Review of the Middle East* 7, no. 1 (2020): 25–53.
28. David Armitage, *Civil War: A History in Ideas* (New York: Alfred A. Knopf, 2017).
29. James D. Fearon, "Iraq's Civil War," *Foreign Affairs* 86, no. 2 (2007): 4.
30. Michael W. Doyle and Nicholas Sambanis include the Dark Decade in their list of civil wars in *Making War and Building Peace: United Nations Peace Operations* (Princeton, NJ: Princeton University Press, 2006).
31. Itamar Rabinovich, *The War for Lebanon 1970-1985* (Ithaca, NY: Cornell University Press), 1985.
32. Wilkinson, *Revolutionary Civil War*, 118–123.
33. Moussaoui, *De la Violence en Algérie*.
34. David Keen, *Complex Emergencies* (Cambridge: Polity Press, 2008), 30.
35. David Thurfjell, "Is the Islamist Voice Subaltern?," in *Postcolonial Challenges to the Study of Religion*, ed. Willy Pfändtner and David Thurfjell (Uppsala: Swedish Science Press, 2008), 9–17; Darryl Li, "A Jihadism Anti-primer," *MERIP* 276 (2015), https://merip.org/2015/12/a-jihadism-anti-primer/.

36. Jacob Mundy, "Deconstructing Civil Wars: Beyond the New Wars Debate," *Security Dialogue* 42, no. 3 (2011): 279-295; James McDougall, *A History of Algeria* (Cambridge: Cambridge University Press, 2017), 318-319.
37. John P. Entelis, *Algeria: The Revolution Institutionalized* (Boulder, CO: Westview Press, 1986), 168.
38. Abed Charef, *Algérie '88. Un chahut de gamin* (Algiers: Laphomic, 1990), 260-270.
39. Ahmed Semiane, *Octobre, ils parlent* (Algiers: Éditions Le Matin, 1998), 127-134.
40. Rachid Tlemçani, "Les conditions d'émergence d'un nouvel autoritarisme en Algérie," *Revue du monde musulman et de la Méditerranée* 72 (1994): 110.
41. Mohamed Samraoui, *Chroniques des années de sang* (Paris: Éditions Denoël, 2003).
42. Habib Souaïdia, *La sale guerre* (Paris: Éditions La Découverte and Syros, 2001), 115-117, 147-149.
43. To watch the interview, see Algeriavlog, "Karim Moulai DRS 1/4 قناة الحوار: الحلقة الأولى كريم مولاي," YouTube, July 31, 2010, 14:30, https://www.youtube.com/watch?v=lOc5NukH-pM.
44. Samraoui, *Chroniques des années de sang*, 163.
45. In fact it is the MAOL, or Mouvement Algérien des Officiers Libres (Algerian Movement of Free Officers), an organization comprised of defectors from the ANP based abroad.
46. Human rights lawyer Ali Mécili was assassinated in 1987 in Paris. In 2003, Samraoui claimed Mécili's mysterious murderer was Mohamed Ziane Hassani, a man in charge of protocol at the Ministry of Foreign Affairs. Hichem Aboud testified in favor of Hassani's innocence and spoke of a manipulation. The police inquiry was in the end inconclusive.
47. Mohamed Sifaoui, *Histoire secrète de l'Algérie indépendante* (Paris: Nouveau monde éditions, 2012), 169-171.
48. Peter L. Berger and Thomas Luckmann, *The Social Construction of Reality* (London: Penguin, 1991), 111.
49. *Contra* Abdelmajid Hannoum, *Violent Modernity: France in Algeria* (Cambridge, MA: Harvard University Press, 2010).
50. Moussaoui, "Algérie, la guerre rejouée."
51. Charles-Robert Ageron, "Complots et purges dans l'armée de libération algérienne (1958-1961)," *Vingtième Siècle* 59 (1998): 15-27.
52. Rabha Attaf and Fausto Giudice, "La grande peur bleue, questions sur une guerre sans visage," *Les Cahiers de l'Orient* 39-40 (1995): 169-171.
53. Diplomatic cable sent by the American embassy February 22, 2008 (reference 08ALGIERS198), https://wikileaks.org/plusd/cables/08ALGIERS198_a.html, released by WikiLeaks in 2011.
54. Soufiane Djilali, *L'Algérie, une nation en chantier* (Algiers: Casbah éditions, 2004), 61-64.
55. Sadek Hadjeres, "Algérie: Violence et politique," *Hérodote* 77 (1995): 43-64; Khalfa Mameri, *Abane, le faux procès* (Tizi Ouzou: Éditions Mehdi, 2007).
56. This narrative surrounding Boudiaf's assassination is notably promoted by the MAOL.

57. Carlier, *Entre Nation et Jihad*, 311.
58. Emmanuel Taïeb, "Logiques politiques du conspirationnisme," *Sociologie et sociétés* 42, no. 2 (2010): 280–285.
59. James C. Scott, *Domination and the Arts of Resistance: Hidden Transcripts* (New Haven, CT: Yale University Press, 1990), 199.
60. Paul Silverstein, "An Excess of Truth: Violence, Conspiracy Theorizing and the Algerian Civil War," *Anthropological Quarterly* 75, no. 4 (2002): 643–674.
61. Abdelhamid Brahimi, *Aux origines de la tragédie algérienne (1958-2000)* (London: Hoggar and the Centre for Maghreb Studies, 2000), 217–222.
62. Muhammad, "Bouteflika a''aṭā a'ms al-ḍaw' al-a'khḍar li-bidāyat istighlāl miyāh maḥaṭṭat al-ḥāma," *Ennahar* (Algiers), February 24, 2008.
63. Drif had allegedly denounced Ali la Pointe and Hassiba Ben Bouali to the French. All were members of the FLN "bomb network" that was dismantled in 1957. On the controversy, see Mohammed Allal, "Yacef Saadi yataḥaddath ʻan dawrihi al-qiyādī fī al-ʻiḍrāb wa Zohra Drif tatajāhaluhu," *El Khabar* (Algiers), January 29, 2019.
64. Walter Benjamin, *Selected Writings*, vol. 2, *1927-1934* (Cambridge, MA: Harvard University Press, 1999), 732.
65. Jean Baudrillard, *The Spirit of Terrorism* (New York: Verso, 2003), 58–59.
66. Jean Baudrillard, *Simulacre et Simulations* (Paris: Éditions Galilée, 1981), 230.
67. Muriam Haleh Davis, Hiyem Cheurfa, and Thomas Serres, "A Hirak Glossary: Terms from Algeria and Morocco," *Jadaliyya*, June 13, 2019, https://www.jadaliyya.com/Details/38734.
68. Benjamin, *Selected Writings*, 2:735.
69. Lisa Weeden, *Ambiguities of Domination: Politics, Rhetoric and Symbols in Contemporary Syria* (Chicago: University of Chicago Press, 2015), 12.
70. Mbembe, *On the Postcolony*, 104–108.
71. Baudrillard, *Simulacre et Simulations*, 17, 227–234.
72. Ali El Kenz, "Les chercheurs africains, une élite?," *Revue Africaine des livres* 1, no. 1 (2004): 19–22.
73. Fadi A. Bardawil, *Revolution and Disenchantment: Arab Marxism and the Binds of Emancipation* (Durham, NC: Duke University Press, 2020), 20–21.
74. Wendy Brown, *Edgework: Critical Essays on Knowledge and Politics* (Princeton, NJ: Princeton University Press, 2005), 5–7.
75. Saad Bouakba, "'Aārunā wa faḍīḥatuhum," *El Khabar* (Algiers), July 5, 2012.
76. El Kenz, "Algérie, les deux paradigmes," 81.
77. El Kenz, 83–84.
78. Lazhari Labter, *Journalistes Algériens (1988-1998): Chronique des années d'espoir et de terreur* (Algiers: Chihab, 2005), 45–47.
79. Benjamin Stora, "L'islamisme algérien," *Esprit* 196 (1993): 165.
80. Benjamin Stora, "Ce que dévoile une guerre. Algérie, 1997," *Politique étrangère* 4 (1997): 488.
81. Malika Rahal, "Le temps arrêté. Un pays sans histoire. Algérie, 2011-2013," *Écrire l'histoire* 12 (2013): 27–36.

82. Fanon, *Les damnés de la Terre*, 47.
83. Guy Pervillé, "Qu'est-ce que la colonisation?," *Revue d'histoire moderne et contemporaine* 22 (1975): 321–368.
84. Fanon, *Les damnés de la Terre*, 87
85. Ernest Renan, *De la part des peuples sémitiques dans l'histoire de la civilisation* (Paris: Michel Lévy Frères, 1862), 27–28.
86. Emmanuelle Sibeud, "Un ethnographe face à la colonisation: Arnold Van Gennep en Algérie (1911–1912)," *Revue d'histoire des sciences humaines* 10 (2004): 79–103.
87. Edward W. Said, *Orientalism* (New York: Pantheon, 1978).
88. Emmanuel Sivan, "Colonialism and Popular Culture in Algeria," *Journal of Contemporary History* 14, no. 1 (1979): 21–53.
89. Muriam H. Davis, "'The Transformation of Man' in French Algeria: Economic Planning and the Postwar Social Sciences, 1958–62," *Journal of Contemporary History* 52, no. 1 (2017): 73–94, and *Markets of Civilization: Islam and Racial Capitalism in Algeria* (Durham, NC: Duke University Press, 2022).
90. Henri Sanson, "Les motivations de la personnalité algérienne en ce temps de décolonisation," *Annuaire de l'Afrique du Nord* 6 (1968): 13–20; Jean-Charles Scagnetti, "Identité ou personnalité algérienne? L'édification d'une algérianité (1962–1988)," *Cahiers de la Méditerranée* 66 (2003): 367–384; McDougall, *A History of Algeria*, 260–261.
91. Mohamed Harbi, *Les archives de la révolution algérienne* (Paris: Éditions Jeune Afrique, 1981), 290.
92. Charlotte Courreye, *L'Algérie des oulémas. Une histoire de l'Algérie contemporaine, 1931–1991* (Paris: Éditions de la Sorbonne, 2020), 117, 295.
93. Ilhem Tir, "4536 protestations ont eu lieu cette année dont 3029 de nature violente," *Le Temps d'Algérie* (Algiers), October 3, 2012.
94. Jacob Mundy, *Imaginative Geographies of Algerian Violence: Conflict Science, Conflict Management, Antipolitics* (Stanford, CA: Stanford University Press, 2015), 26–29.
95. Belkacem Mostefaoui, "Algérie, l'espace du débat médiatique," *Réseaux* 88–89 (1998): 179–180; Samira Belarbi, "Aṣ-ṣirāʻa as-siyāsī fī Al-Jazāi'r min khālal aṣ-ṣaḥāfa al-fransiyya: Dirāsa taṭbīqiyya li-muʻālaja yaūmiyya 'Le Figaro' li-tadāʻiyāt i'lghā' natāi'j tashrīʻiyyāt 26 dīsambar 1991," *Al-Miʻiyār* 24, no. 49 (2020): 506–520.
96. James McDougall, "Savage Wars? Codes of Violence in Algeria, 1830s–1990s," *Third World Quarterly* 26, no. 1 (2005): 117–131.
97. Stathis N. Kalyvas, "Wanton and Senseless? The Logic of Massacres in Algeria," *Rationality and Society* 11, no. 3 (1999): 243–285.
98. James McDougall, "Algeria's Terrorist Attacks Owe Little to Its 'Pathological' History," *The Guardian* (London), January 22, 2013.
99. Kassab, *Contemporary Arab Thought*, 48–115.
100. Soumya Ammar Khodja, "Écritures d'urgence de femmes algériennes," *Clio. Histoire, femmes et sociétés* 9 (1999): 1–11; Leperlier, *Les écrivains de la décennie noire*, 165.
101. Françoise Naudillon, "Le polar, un genre postcolonial?," in *Violences postcoloniales. Représentations littéraires et perceptions médiatiques*, ed. Isaac Bazié and Hans-Jürgen Lüsebrink (Berlin: Lit-Verlag, 2011), 141.

102. Chawki Amari, "Un ramadan algérien d'une rare violence," *SlateAfrique*, August 8, 2011, https://www.slateafrique.com/23677/algerie-ramadan-violences-drogue-pauvrete.
103. Hafid Derradji, "Qaswatunā laysat ḥiqdan," *Echorouk* (Algiers), August 20, 2011.
104. Noureddine Belhouari, "Sā'at al-muslimīn tawaqqafat fī al-qarn ar-rābi'a al-hijrī," *El Khabar* (Algiers), August 28, 2011.
105. Salaheddine Menia, "La société souffre d'immaturité affective," *L'Expression* (Algiers), August 27, 2011.
106. David Ottaway and Marina Ottaway, *Algeria: The Politics of a Socialist Revolution* (Berkeley: University of California Press, 1970), 48.
107. Hassan Remaoun, "La question de l'histoire dans le débat sur la violence en Algérie," *Insaniyat* 10 (2010): 31–43.
108. Martinez, *La guerre civile en Algérie*, 375–377.
109. Abderrahmane Mebtoul, "Que nous apprennent les résultats?," *La Nouvelle République* (Algiers), May 13, 2012.
110. Mohammed Hachemaoui, *Clientélisme et patronage dans l'Algérie contemporaine* (Paris: Karthala, 2013), 177–185.
111. Lahouari Addi, *L'Algérie d'hier à aujourd'hui: Quel bilan?* (Saint-Denis, FR: Éditions Bouchène, 2014), 74–75.
112. Bardawil, *Revolution and Disenchantment*, 185–186.
113. Rabah Ali Moussa, "Al-I'ṣlāḥ as-siyāssī wa ishkāliyyat tajdīd al-binā al-i'jtimā'iyya al-siyāssiyya," *Majala al-'ulūm al-i'jtimā'iyya wa-l-i'nsāniyya* 13 (2017): 112–148.
114. Kassab, *Contemporary Arab Thought*, 17.
115. Malek Bennabi, *Les conditions de la renaissance* (1949; Algiers: Éditions ANEP, 2005).
116. See the first part of Soufiane Djilali's program for the 2014 presidential election, "Programme de M. Soufiane Djilali pour les présidentielles de 2014, Première Partie: Les valeurs fondamentales," accessed February 23, 2023, http://web.archive.org/web/20131225225537/http://www.djilali2014.com/index.php/djilali-president/le-projet.
117. "Ḥarb at-taḥrīr ḥaqqaqat al-istiqlāl wa-lam tuḥaqqiq ad-dīmuqrāṭiyya," *El Khabar* (Algiers), July 5, 2011.
118. Djamel Guerid, *L'Exception Algérienne: La modernistation à l'épreuve de la société* (Algiers: Casbah éditions, 2007).
119. Kamel Daoud, "Oui, il faut changer le peuple!," *Le Quotidien d'Oran*, May 23, 2014.
120. Sarah Muir and Akhil Gupta, "Rethinking the Anthropology of Corruption," *Current Anthropology* 59, no. 18 (2018): 6.
121. Kamel Daoud, "Une Algérie incroyablement sale: L'autre peuple plastic," *Le Quotidien d'Oran*, August 18, 2014.
122. Jalal Bouati, "Ash-sha'ab yarfuḍ at-taghīīr," *El Khabar* (Algiers), May 13, 2012.
123. Hadj Nacer, *La martingale algérienne*, 52–53.

124. Vincent Geisser, "Des Voltaire, des Zola musulmans . . .? Réflexion sur les 'nouveaux dissidents' de l'islam," *Revue internationale et stratégique* 65 (2007): 143–156; Leperlier, *Les écrivains de la décennie noire*, 259–262, 269–270.
125. Gayatri Spivak, "Can the Subaltern Speak?," in *Marxism and the Interpretation of Culture*, ed. Cary Nelson and Lawrence Grossberg (Basingstoke, UK: Macmillan Education, 1988), 271–313.
126. Fanon, *Les damnés de la Terre*, 60.
127. Sivan, "Colonialism and Popular Culture in Algeria."
128. Aïssa Khelladi, "Rire quand même: L'humour politique dans l'Algérie d'aujourd'hui," *Revue du monde musulman et de la Méditerranée* 77–78 (1995): 225–237. See also Elizabeth Perego, "Laughing in the Face of Death: Humor During the Algerian Civil War, 1991–2002" (PhD diss., Ohio State University, 2017), and "Laughing at the Victims: The Function of Popular Jokes During Algeria's 'Dark Decade,' 1991–2002," *Journal of North African Studies* 23, nos. 1–2 (2018): 191–207.
129. BTS stands for Batna, Tebessa, and Souk-Ahras, three cities in the Aurès region, where many military figures of the 1990s originated, notably Khaled Nezzar and Liamine Zeroual.
130. The phrase is borrowed from Belkacem Mostefaoui, "Gouvernance féodale," *El Watan* (Algiers), June 1, 2006.
131. Antonio Gramsci, *Quaderni del carcere. Volume secondo. Quaderni 6–11* (Turin: Giulio Einaudi editore, 1975), 1385.
132. Benedict Anderson, *Imagined Communities: Reflections on the Origin and Spread of Nationalism* (London: Verso, 1991), 7.
133. Myriam Hachimi Alaoui, "L'Epreuve de l'exil. Le cas des Algériens installés à Paris et à Montréal," *Insaniyat* 27 (2005): 139–145.
134. Salim Chena, "Sidi Salem et el harga," *Hommes & Migrations* 1300, no. 6 (2012): 52–61; Farida Souiah, "Les harraga en Algérie: Émigration et contestation" (PhD diss., IEP Paris, 2014).
135. This ambiguous relationship to the community was superbly captured in Carlier's depiction of Algerian youth at the beginning of the 1990s: *Entre Nation et Jihad*, 351–352, 377.
136. Ratiba Hadj Moussa, "Youth and Activism in Algeria. The Question of Political Generations," *Journal of North African Studies* 26, no. 2 (2019): 19.
137. Saber Ayoub, "Scotland Yard tuḥyī indibāṭ al-jazāi'riyyīn khilāl a"amāl shaghab London," *El Khabar* (Algiers), August 13, 2011.
138. Corbin Treacy, "Writing in the Aftermath of Two Wars: Algerian Modernism and the Génération '88," in *Algeria: Nation, Culture and Transnationalism: 1988–2015*, ed. Patrick Crowley (Liverpool: Liverpool University Press, 2017), 123–139.
139. Pierre Bourdieu, *Réponses. Pour une anthropologie réflexive* (Paris: Éditions du Seuil, 1992), 149.
140. Letter sent by Hocine Aït Ahmed to the national board of the FFS, March 18, 2011 (hard copy in the author's possession).

141. Joël Danet, "Bejaia Doc: Co-construction d'un regard documentaire sur l'Algérie d'aujourd'hui," *Communication, technologies et développement* 7 (2019), https://journals.openedition.org/ctd/1372.
142. Charlotte Courreye, *L'Algérie des oulémas. Une histoire de l'Algérie contemporaine, 1931-1991* (Paris: Éditions de la Sorbonne, 2020), 514, 519.
143. Hannah Arendt, *The Origins of Totalitarianism* (Cleveland, OH: Meridian Books, 1962), 140.
144. Mbembe, *On the Postcolony*, 241–242.
145. Hannah Arendt, *Crises of the Republic: Lying in Politics; Civil Disobedience; On Violence; Thoughts on Politics and Revolution* (San Diego, CA: Harcourt Brace and Co., 1972), 7.
146. Baudrillard, *The Spirit of Terrorism*, 80–81.
147. Walid Benkhaled and Natalya Vince, "Afterword: Performing Algerianness: The National and Transnational Construction of Algeria's 'Culture Wars,'" in *Algeria: Nation, Culture and Transnationalism: 1988-2015*, ed. Patrick Crowley (Liverpool: Liverpool University Press, 2017), 265–266.

Coda

1. Khaled Boudia, "Al-khiṭāb an-nārī li-Bouteflika," *El Khabar* (Algiers), November 29, 2018.
2. Gianni Del Panta, "Defeating Autocrats from Below: Insights from the 2019 Algerian Uprising," *Contemporary Politics* 28, no. 5 (2022): 539–557.
3. Statement of the SNAPAP/CGATA (Confédération Générale Autonome des Travailleurs Algériens, or General Autonomous Confederation of Algerian Workers), April 15, 2019 (in author's possession).
4. Patrick Wolfe, "Recuperating Binarism: A Heretical Introduction," *Settler Colonial Studies* 3, nos. 3–4 (2013): 257–279.
5. Imogen Tyler, *Revolting Subjects: Social Abjection and Resistance in Neoliberal Britain* (London: Zed Books, 2013), 215.
6. Wendell Kisner, "Agamben, Hegel, and the State of Exception," *Cosmos and History: The Journal of Natural and Social Philosophy* 3, nos. 2–3 (2007): 222–253.
7. Akram Belkaid, "Hirak," *Orient XXI*, November 15, 2019, https://orientxxi.info/magazine/hirak,3418.
8. Ratiba Hadj Moussa, "Youth and Activism in Algeria. The Question of Political Generations," *Journal of North African Studies* 26, no. 2 (2019): 311–336.
9. According to a study released by the National Statistics Office in June 2018. See *Demographie Algerienne, 2018* (Algiers: National Statistics Office, 2018), https://www.ons.dz/IMG/pdf/demographie2018.pdf.
10. Asef Bayat, *Revolutions Without Revolutionaries: Making Sense of the Arab Spring* (Stanford, CA: Stanford University Press, 2017).

11. Steven Heydemann, "After the Earthquake: Economic Governance and Mass Politics in the Middle East," *Critique internationale* 61, no. 4 (2013): 69; Hadj Moussa, "Youth and activism in Algeria," 20.
12. Ernesto Laclau, *On Populist Reason* (London: Verso, 2005), 95, 130–131.
13. Charles Tilly, *Contentious Performances* (Cambridge: Cambridge University Press, 2008), 62–87; Mounia Bennani-Chraïbi and Olivier Fillieule, "Pour une sociologie des situations révolutionnaires. Retour sur les révoltes arabes," *Revue française de science politique* 62, no. 5 (2012): 767–796.
14. Antonio Y. Vázquez-Arroyo, "How Not to Learn from Catastrophe: Habermas, Critical Theory and the 'Catastrophization' of Political Life," *Political Theory* 41, no. 5 (2013): 757.
15. Walter Benjamin, *Selected Writings*, vol. 4, *1938-1940* (Cambridge, MA: Harvard University Press, 2003), 390.
16. Sami Khatib, "The Messianic Without Messianism," *Anthropology & Materialism* 1 (2013): 11.
17. "Al-farīq Gaïd Salah yushaddid 'alā a'nnah 'lā muhādana wa-lā tā'jīl li-mas'aā muḥārabat al-fasād,'" *Ech Cha'ab* (Algiers), June 27, 2019.
18. Salima Tlemçani, "Procès de l'ex-patron de la police Abdelghani Hamel: Des walis qui évoquent des pressions et des menaces," *El Watan* (Algiers), March 16, 2020.
19. Daikha Dridi, "Qui sont les prisonniers politiques algériens?," *Middle East Eye*, December 23, 2019, https://www.middleeasteye.net/fr/en-bref/qui-sont-les-prisonniers-politiques-algeriens.
20. Meziane Abane, "Tahar Belabbas, ancien leader du Mouvement des chômeurs dans le sud," *L'Avant-Garde*, September 3, 2019, https://www.lavantgarde-algerie.com/article/interviews/tahar-belabbas-ancien-leader-du-mouvement-des-chomeurs-dans-le-sud.
21. Farouk Djouadi "Manif à Alger contre la nouvelle loi sur les hydrocarbures," *El Watan* (Algiers), October 13, 2019.
22. Karim Aimeur, "L'Algérie peut rattraper le déficit budgétaire en deux ans," *Le Soir d'Algérie* (Algiers), January 22, 2020.
23. "Le Président Tebboune confirme la poursuite des consultations politiques pour parvenir à une 'Constitution consensuelle,'" Algérie Presse Service, 23 January 2020, https://www.aps.dz/algerie/100546-le-president-tebboune-confirme-la-poursuite-des-consultations-politiques-pour-parvenir-a-une-constitution-consensuelle.
24. Youcef Oussama Bounab, "As the Hirak Goes Online due to COVID-19, so Does Repression," *Jadaliyya*, May 25, 2020, https://www.jadaliyya.com/Details/41168.
25. Giorgio Agamben, *Homo Sacer: Sovereign Power and Bare Life* (Stanford, CA: Stanford University Press, 1998), 105, 148.
26. The FLN received 280,000 votes out of a total of 24 million eligible voters. Out of the 4.6 million votes cast, more than 70 percent went to a myriad of candidates and parties that failed to be elected.

27. Interviews with Nadir (Paris) and Malika (remote), winter 2021.
28. Adi Ophir, "The Politics of Catastrophization: Emergency and Exception," in *Contemporary States of Emergency: The Politics of Military and Humanitarian Interventions*, ed. Didier Fassin and Mariella Pandolfi (New York: Zone Books, 2010), 59–88.
29. Philip Mirowski, *Never Let a Serious Crisis Go to Waste* (London: Verso, 2013).
30. Giorgio Agamben, *State of Exception* (Chicago: University of Chicago Press, 2005); Vivienne Jabri, "War, Security and the Liberal State," *Security Dialogue* 37, no. 1 (2006): 47–64; Eyal Weizman, "Lethal Theory," *Log* 7 (2006): 53–77.
31. Fabien Georgi, "Toward Fortress Capitalism: The Restrictive Transformation of Migration and Border Regimes as a Reaction to the Capitalist Multicrisis," *Canadian Review of Sociology* 56, no. 4 (2019): 556–579.
32. Walter Benjamin, *Selected Writings*, vol. 1, *1913-1926* (Cambridge, MA: Harvard University Press, 1996), 247; Orietta Ombrosi, "La dialectique de l'idée de catastrophe dans la pensée de W. Benjamin," *Archives de Philosophie* 69, no. 2 (2006): 283.

Bibliography

Books and Academic Articles

Abada, Khadidja. "La fin d'un mythe." *Les Cahiers de l'Orient* 36–37 (1995): 127–143.
Abbas, Ferhat. *L'indépendance confisquée (1962-1978)*. Paris: Flammarion, 1984.
Abdelhamid, Aicha. "Dawr al-mūa'ssasat al-'askariya fī tanmiyat al-manāṭiq al-ḥudūdiya ḍamf mutaṭallabāt al-mahām al-insāniyya li-l-jaysh al-waṭanī ash-sha'abī." *Majalat al-bāḥith al-ākādīmī fī al-'ulūm al-qānūniya wa-l-siyāsīya* 3, no. 2 (2020): 153–166.
Abderezzak, Hakim. "The Mediterranean Seametery and Cementery in Leïla Kilani's and Tariq Teguia's Filmic Works." In *Critically Mediterranean: Temporality, Aesthetics and Deployments of a Sea in Crisis*, edited by Yasser Elhariry and Edwige Tamalet Talbayev, 147–161. London: Palgrave Macmillan, 2018.
Aboud, Hichem. *La mafia des généraux*. Paris: Éditions J.-C. Lattès, 2002.
Achy, Lahcen. "Substituer des emplois précaires à un chômage élevé. Les défis de l'emploi au Maghreb." Carnegie Middle East Center, Carnegie Papers No. 23 (November 2010). https://carnegie-mec.org/2010/11/15/fr-pub-42103.
Adamson, Kay. *Algeria: A Study in Competing Ideologies*. London: Cassel, 1998.
Addi, Lahouari. "Army, State and Nation in Algeria." In *Political Armies: The Military and Nation Building in the Age of Democracy*, edited by Kees Koonings and Dirk Kruijt, 179–203. London: Zed Books, 2002.
———. "Entretien avec Ali Yahya Abdennour." *Confluences Méditerranée* 51 (2004): 39–44.
———. *L'Algérie d'hier à aujourd'hui: quel bilan?* Saint-Denis, FR: Éditions Bouchène, 2014.
———. "Les partis politiques en Algérie." *Revue des Mondes Musulmans et de la Méditerranée* 111–112 (2006): 139–162.
———. "Pluralisme politique et islam dans le monde arabe." *Pouvoirs* 1, no. 104 (2003): 85–95.

——. "Sociologie politique d'un populisme autoritaire." *Confluences Méditerranée* 2, no. 81 (2012): 27–40.

Agamben, Giorgio. *Homo Sacer Sovereign Power and Bare Life*. Stanford, CA: Stanford University Press, 1998.

——. *State of Exception*. Chicago: University of Chicago Press, 2005.

Ageron, Charles-Robert. "Complots et purges dans l'armée de libération algérienne (1958–1961)." *Vingtième Siècle* 59 (1998): 15–27.

Aggoun, Lounis, and Jean-Baptiste Rivoire. *Françalgérie, crimes et mensonges d'états*. Paris: La Découverte, 2004.

Aghrout, Ahmed, and Yahia H. Zoubir. "Algeria: Reforms Without Change?" In *North African Politics: Change and Continuity*, edited by Yahia H. Zoubir and Gregory White, 145–155. London: Routledge, 2016.

Ahnaf, Mustafa Al-, Bernard Botiveau, and Franck Fregosi. *L'Algérie par ses islamistes*. Paris: Karthala, 1991.

Aidoud, Mamoun. "La privatisation des entreprises publiques algériennes." *Revue internationale de droit comparé* 48, no. 1 (1996): 125–127.

Aït Aoudia, Myriam. "La genèse d'une mobilisation partisane: Continuités et politisation du militantisme caritatif et religieux au sein du FIS." *Politix* 102 (2013): 129–146.

——. "La naissance du Front islamique du Salut: une politisation conflictuelle (1988–1989)." *Critique internationale* 30 (2006): 129–144.

—— [Emma Tilleli, pseud.]. "Le Mouvement Citoyen de Kabylie." *Pouvoirs* 106 (2003): 151–162.

——. [Emma Tilleli, pseud.]. "Les transformations de la société au regard des élections législatives et municipales de 2002." Centre de recherches internationales, March–April 2003. https://www.sciencespo.fr/ceri/sites/sciencespo.fr.ceri/files/artet.pdf.

——. *L'expérience démocratique en Algérie (1988–1992). Apprentissages politiques et changement de régime*. Paris: Les Presses de Sciences Po, 2015.

Aït Kaki, Maxime. "Armée, Pouvoir et processus de décision en Algérie." *Politique étrangère* 2 (2004): 427–439.

——. *De la question berbère au dilemme Kabyle à l'aube du XXIème siècle*. Paris: L'Harmattan, 2004.

Ali Moussa, Rabah. "Al-I'ṣlāḥ as-siyāssī wa ishkāliyyat tajdīd al-binā al-i'jtimā'iyya al-siyāssiyya." *Majala al-'ulūm al-i'jtimā'iyya wa-l-i'nsāniyya* 13 (2017): 112–148.

Alissa, Sufyan. "The Political Economy of Reform in Egypt: Understanding the Role of Institutions." Carnegie Middle East Center, Carnegie Papers No. 5 (October 2007). https://carnegieendowment.org/files/cmec5_alissa_egypt_final.pdf.

Allal, Amin. "Becoming Revolutionary in Tunisia, 2007–2011." In *Social Movements, Mobilization, and Contestation in the Middle East and North Africa*, edited by Joel Beinin and Frédéric Vairel, 185–204. 2nd ed. Stanford, CA: Stanford University Press, 2013.

——. "Retour vers le futur. Les origines économiques de la révolution tunisienne." *Pouvoirs* 156 (2016): 17–29.

Amar, Paul. *Security Archipelago: Human-Security States, Sexuality Politics, and the End of Neoliberalism*. Durham, NC: Duke University Press, 2013.

Amara, Mahfoud. *Sports, Politics and Society in the Arab World*. New York: Palgrave McMillan, 2012.
Amghar, Samir. "Les trois visages de l'islam politique en Afrique du Nord et au Moyen-Orient: Essai de typologie." *L'Année du Maghreb* 6 (2010): 529–541.
Amghar, Samir, and Amel Boubekeur. "Les partis islamistes en Algérie: Structures révolutionnaires ou partis de gouvernement." *Maghreb-Machrek* 194 (2008): 7–23.
Anderson, Benedict. *Imagined Communities: Reflections on the Origin and Spread of Nationalism*. London: Verso, 1991.
Arendt, Hannah. *Crises of the Republic: Lying in Politics; Civil Disobedience; On Violence; Thoughts on Politics and Revolution*. San Diego, CA: Harcourt Brace and Co., 1972.
———. *The Origins of Totalitarianism*. Cleveland, OH: Meridian Books, 1962.
———. *On Revolution*. London: Penguin Books, 1990.
Arieff, Alexis. *Algeria: Current Issues*. CRS Report No. 7-5700. Washington, DC: Congressional Research Service, 2013. https://sgp.fas.org/crs/row/RS21532.pdf.
Armitage, David. *Civil Wars: A History in Ideas*. New York: Alfred A. Knopf, 2017.
Attaf, Rabha, and Fausto Giudice. "La grande peur bleue, questions sur une guerre sans visage." *Les Cahiers de l'Orient* 39–40 (1995): 169–171.
Aucante, Yohann, and Alexandre Deze. *Le système de partis dans les démocraties occidentales. Le modèle du parti cartel en question*. Paris: Presses de Sciences Po, 2013.
Azoulay, Ariella. "The Tradition of the Oppressed." *Qui Parle* 16, no. 2 (2007): 73–96.
Baamara, Layla. "Mésaventures d'une coalition contestataire: Le cas de la Coordination Nationale pour le Changement et la Démocratie (CNCD) en Algérie." *Année du Maghreb* 8 (2012): 161–179.
———. "Quand les protestataires s'autolimitent. Le cas des mobilisations étudiantes de 2011 en Algérie." In *Au cœur des révoltes arabes. Devenir révolutionnaires*, edited by Amine Allal and Thomas Pierret, 137–159. Paris: Armand Collin, 2013.
———. "Une campagne 'à part, mais pour le parti.' Le cas d'un candidat FFS aux élections législatives de 2012 à Alger." In *Faire campagne, ici et ailleurs*, edited by Layla Baamara, Camille Floderer, and Marine Poirier, 149–170. Aix-en-Provence: Karthala, 2016.
Baduel, Pierre-Robert. "Les partis politiques dans la gouvernementalisation de l'État des pays arabes." *Revue du monde musulman et de la Méditerranée* 81–82 (1996): 9–51.
Balta, Paul, and Claudine Rulleau. *La stratégie de Boumédiène*. Paris: Sindbad, 1978.
Balzacq, Thierry. "The Three Faces of Securitization." *European Journal of International Relations* 11, no. 2 (2005): 171–201.
Bardawil, Fadi A. *Revolution and Disenchantment: Arab Marxism and the Binds of Emancipation*. Durham, NC: Duke University Press, 2020.
Bargu, Banu. *Starve and Immolate: The Politics of Human Weapons*. New York: Columbia University Press, 2014.
———. "Why Did Bouazizi Burn Himself? The Politics of Fate and Fatal Politics." *Constellations* 23, no. 1 (2016): 27–36.
Bartlett, Sharon M. "Masculinities, Money, and Mosques in Algeria's Civil War." *Peace Review* 30, no. 4 (2018): 470–478.

Bastien, François, and Jacques Lagroye. *Sociologie politique*. Paris: Presses de Sciences Po, 2002.
Baudrillard, Jean. *Simulacre et Simulations*. Paris: Éditions Galilée, 1981.
———. *The Spirit of Terrorism*. New York: Verso, 2003.
Bayart, Jean-François. "Retour sur les printemps arabes." *Politique Africaine* 133 (2014): 153–175.
Bayat, Asef. *Revolutions Without Revolutionaries: Making Sense of the Arab Spring*. Stanford, CA: Stanford University Press, 2017.
Beck, Ulrich. *Risk Society: Towards a New Modernity*. London: Sage Publications, 1992.
Becker, Howard S. *Tricks of the Trade: How to Think About Your Research While Doing It*. Chicago: University of Chicago Press, 1998.
———. *Le travail sociologique: Méthode et substance*. Translated by Diane Baechler, Stéphanie Emery Haenni, and Marc-Henry Soulet. Fribourg, CH: Academic Press Fribourg, 2006.
Beddoubia, Siham. "Les syndicats autonomes en Algérie, initiateurs des luttes démocratiques?" *Confluences Méditerranée* 111 (2019): 119–134.
Belabbas, Rabah. "Muḥāwalat binā' namūdhaj qīāsī li-tafsīr biṭālat al-yā's fī Al-Jazā'ir." *Majalat al-'ulūm al-iqtiṣādiyya wa-t-tasiyīr wa-l-'ulūm al-tijāriyya* 10 (2013): 15–31.
Belakhdar, Naoual. " 'L'éveil du Sud' ou quand la contestation vient de la marge. Une analyse du mouvement des chômeurs algériens." *Politique africaine* 137 (2015): 27–48.
———. "When Unemployment Meets Environment: The Case of the Anti-fracking Coalition in Ouargla." *Mediterranean Politics* 24, no. 4 (2019): 420–442.
Belarbi, Samira. "Aṣ-ṣirā'a as-siyāsī fī Al-Jazāi'r min khālal aṣ-ṣaḥāfa al-fransiyya: Dirāsa taṭbīqiyya li-mu'ālaja yaūmiyya 'Le Figaro' li-tadā'iyāt i'lghā' natāi'j tashrī'iyyāt 26 dīsambar 1991." *Al-Mi'iyār* 24, no. 49 (2020): 506–520.
Belkaïd, Akram. "La diplomatie algérienne à la recherche de son âge d'or." *Politique étrangère* 2 (2009): 337–344.
Bellal, Samir. "Problématique du changement institutionnel en Algérie—Une lecture en termes de régulation." *Revue Algérienne de Sciences Juridiques, Economiques et Politiques* 1 (2011): 43–71.
Ben Ali, Laqra. "A'zmat at-taḥawūl naḥw ad-dīmuqrāṭiyya fī al-jazā'ir (1989–2014)." *Al-majala al-'arabiya al-'ulūm al-siyāsiya* 45–46 (2015): 57–70.
Benachenhou, Abdellatif. "L'aventure de la désétatisation en Algérie." *Revue du monde musulman et de la Méditerranée* 65 (1992): 175–185.
———. *Takawūn at-takhaluf fī al-ja zā'ir: Muḥāwala li-dirāsat at-tanmiyya al-rāsmāliya fī al-jazā'ir bayn 'aāmī 1830–1962*. Algiers: SNED, 1979.
Benaouda, Zineb. "Al-fā 'ilūn fī al-a'ḥdāth allatī 'arafathā Tuns min dīsambar 2010 'ilā dīsambar 2011 min khilāl al-yaūmiya Al-Khabr." *Majala ar-risāla li-l-dirāsāt wa-l-buḥūth al-I'nsāniya* 4, no. 4 (2019): 69–90.
Benbitour, Ahmed. *Radioscopie de la gouvernance algérienne*. Algiers: EDIF 2000, 2006.
Benchiba, Lakhdar. "Les mutations du terrorisme algérien." *Politique étrangère* 2 (2009): 345–352.
Benchicou, Mohamed. *Bouteflika: Une imposture algérienne*. Algiers: Le Matin, 2003.
Benchikh, Madjid. *Algérie: Un système politique militarisé*. Paris: L'Harmattan, 2003.

——. "Constitutions démocratiques et réalité autoritaire au Maghreb: La démocratie de façade." In *Le Débat juridique au maghreb*, edited by Yadh Ben Achour, Jean-Robert Henry, and Rostane Medhi, 242–259. Paris: Publisud, 2009.

Benderra, Omar. "Économie algérienne 1986/1998: Les réseaux aux commandes de l'État." In *La Méditerranée des réseaux. Marchands, entrepreneurs et migrants entre l'Europe et le Maghreb*, edited by Jocelyne Cesari, 231–266. Paris: Maisonneuve and Larose, 2002.

——. "Pétrole et pouvoir en Algérie." *Confluences Méditerranée* 53 (2005): 51–58.

Benjamin, Walter. *Selected Writings*. Vol. 1, *1913-1926*. Cambridge, MA: Harvard University Press, 1996.

——. *Selected Writings*. Vol. 2, *1927-1934*. Cambridge, MA: Harvard University Press, 1999.

——. *Selected Writings*. Vol. 4, *1938-1940*. Cambridge, MA: Harvard University Press, 2003.

Benkhaled, Walid, and Natalya Vince. "Afterword: Performing Algerianness: The National and Transnational Construction of Algeria's 'Culture Wars.'" In *Algeria: Nation, Culture and Transnationalism: 1988-2015*, edited by Patrick Crowley, 243–270. Liverpool, UK: Liverpool University Press, 2017.

Bennabi, Malek. *Les conditions de la renaissance*. Algiers: Éditions ANEP, 2005. First published 1949.

Bennadji, Chérif. "Algérie: La fin de la crise politique?" *L'Année du Maghreb* 1 (2004): 175–206.

——. "Algérie 2010: L'année des mille et unes émeutes." *L'Année du Maghreb* 7 (2011): 263–269.

——. "De l'ambiguïté des rapports entre le président de la République et le pouvoir judiciaire en Algérie." *L'Année du Maghreb* 3 (2007): 155–162.

——. "Le 'retrait' des six candidats à l'élection présidentielle du 15 avril 1999." *Annuaire de l'Afrique du Nord* 38 (2002): 149–157.

Bennani-Chraïbi, Mounia, and Olivier Fillieule. "Pour une sociologie des situations révolutionnaires. Retour sur les révoltes arabes." *Revue française de science politique* 62, no. 5 (2012): 767–796.

Bennett, W. Lance, Regina G. Lawrence, Steven Livingston. *When the Press Fails: Political Power and the News Media from Iraq to Katrina*. Chicago: University of Chicago Press, 2007.

Bennoune, Mahfoud. "Pourquoi Mohamed Boudiaf a-t-il été assassiné?" *Confluences Méditerranée* 25 (1998): 159–166.

Benzenine, Belkacem. "Les femmes algériennes au Parlement: La question des quotas à l'épreuve des réformes politiques." *Égypte/Monde arabe* 10 (2013). https://doi.org/10.4000/ema.3196.

Berger, Mark T. "After the Third World? History, Destiny and the Fate of Third Worldism." *Third World Quarterly* 25, no. 1 (2004): 9–39.

Berger, Peter L., and Thomas Luckmann. *The Social Construction of Reality*. London: Penguin Books, 1991.

Bernays, Edward. *Propaganda*. New York: Horace Liveright, 1928.

Beuving, Joost. "Problems of Evidence in Ethnography. A Methodological Reflection on the Goffman/Mead Controversies (with a Proposal for Rules of Thumb)." *Forum*

Qualitative Sozialforschung/Forum: Qualitative Social Research 22 (2020). https://doi.org/10.17169/fqs-22.1.3567.

Bianco, Lucien. "Armes des faibles, faibles armes." *Perspectives chinoises* 51 (1999): 4–16.

Blanchard, Emmanuel. *La police parisienne et les Algériens, 1944-1962.* Paris: Nouveau Monde éditions, 2011.

Bobbio, Norberto. "La crise permanente." *Pouvoir* 18 (1981): 5–20.

Boltanski, Luc. *De la critique.* Paris: Gallimard, 2009.

———. "L'espace positionnel: Multiplicité des positions institutionnelles et habitus de classe." *Revue française de sociologie* 14, no. 1 (1973): 3–26.

Bouaila, Samir. "Un blog à l'image du président algérien, la communication politique entre jeu de miroirs et 'Je' de mémoire." *Horizons Maghrébins—Le droit à la mémoire* 62 (2010): 127–135.

Bouamama, Saïd. "Le sentiment de 'hogra': Discrimination, négation du sujet et violences." *Hommes et Migrations* 1227 (2000): 38–50.

Boubekeur, Amel. "Les partis islamistes algériens et la démocratie: Vers une professionnalisation politique?" *L'Année du Maghreb* 4 (2008): 219–238.

———. "Rolling Either Way? Algeria Entrepreneurs as Both Agents of Change and Means of Preservation of the System." *Journal of North Africa Studies* 18, no. 3 (2013): 469–481.

Boudjenah, Yasmine. "Le démantèlement du secteur public algérien." *Recherches internationales* 56–57 (1999): 177–179.

Bourdieu, Pierre. *Langage et Pouvoir Symbolique.* Paris: Éditions du Seuil, 2001.

———. *Réponses. Pour une anthropologie réflexive.* Paris: Éditions du Seuil, 1992.

———. *Sur l'Etat. Cours au Collège de France, 1989-1992.* Paris: Éditions du Seuil, 2012.

Bourdieu, Pierre, and Luc Boltanski. "La production de l'idéologie dominante." *Actes de la recherche en sciences sociales* 2 (1976): 3–73.

Bowser, Matthew. "Catastrophe in Permanence: Benjamin's Natural History of Environmental Crisis." PhD diss., University of North Texas, 2017.

Bozarslan, Hamit. "Le chaos après le déluge: Notes sur la crise turque des années 70." *Culture & conflits* 24–25 (1997): 79–98.

———. "Le jihâd. Réceptions et usages d'une injonction coranique d'hier à aujourd'hui." *Vingtième Siècle* 82 (2004): 15–29.

———. "Les révolutions arabes. Entretien avec Hamit Bozarslan." *Sciences humaines* 226 (2011): 46.

———. *Passions révolutionnaires. Amérique latine, Moyen-Orient, Inde.* Paris: Éditions de l'Ecole des Hautes Etudes en Sciences Sociales, 2011.

———. *Sociologie politique du Moyen-Orient.* Paris: La Découverte, 2011.

———. *Révolution et état de violence. Moyen-Orient 2011-2015.* Paris: CNRS Éditions, 2015.

Bozerup, Rasmus. "Violence as Politics. The Escalation and De-escalation of Political Violence in Algeria (1954-2007)." PhD diss., EHESS Paris and University of Copenhagen, 2008.

Brachet, Julien, Armelle Chopin, and Olivier Pliez. "Le Sahara entre espace de circulation et frontière migratoire de l'Europe." *Hérodote* 142 (2011): 163–182.

Brahimi, Abdelhamid. *Aux origines de la tragédie algérienne (1958-2000)*. London: Hoggar and the Centre for Maghreb Studies, 2000.

Brahimi El-Mili, Naoufel. "Algérie: Une économie entre libéralisation et attentes sociales." In *Afrique du Nord, Moyen-Orient, Espace et conflits*, edited by Rémy Leveau, 163-175. Paris: La documentation française, 2003.

Bredeloup, Sylvie. "Sahara Transit: Times, Spaces, People." *Population, Space and Place* 18, no. 4 (2012): 457-467.

Brenner, Neil, Jamie Peck, and Nik Theodore. "Variegated Neoliberalization: Geographies, Modalities, Pathways." *Global Networks* 10, no. 2 (2010): 182-222.

Broadhurst, Roderic, and Pen Wang. "After the Bo Xilai Trial: Does Corruption Threaten China's Future?" *Survival: Global Politics and Strategy* 56, no. 3 (2013): 157-178.

Brown, Wendy. *Edgework: Critical Essays on Knowledge and Politics*. Princeton, NJ: Princeton University Press, 2005.

Brun, Diego A., and Larry Diamond. *Clientelism, Social Policy, and the Quality of Democracy*. Baltimore: Johns Hopkins University Press, 2014.

Bustos, Rafael. "Le référendum sur la charte pour la réconciliation nationale en Algérie et ses textes d'application." *L'Année du Maghreb* 2 (2007): 223-229.

Buzan, Barry, Ole Wæver, and Jaap De Wilde. *Security: A New Framework for Analysis*. Boulder, CO: Lynne Reiner Publishers, 1998.

Byrd, William C. "Contre-performances économiques et fragilité institutionnelle." *Confluences Méditerranée* 45 (2003): 59-79.

Byrne, Jeffrey J. *Mecca of Revolution: Algeria, Decolonization, and the Third World Order*. Oxford: Oxford University Press, 2016.

Calhoun, Craig. "A World of Emergencies: Fear, Intervention, and the Limits of Cosmopolitan Order." *Canadian Review of Sociology* 41, no. 4 (2004): 373-395.

Camau, Michel. "L'exception autoritaire ou l'improbable point d'Archimède de la politique dans le monde arabe." In *La politique dans le monde arabe*, edited by Elizabeth Picard, 29-54. Paris: Armand Colin, 2006.

———. "Globalisation démocratique et exception autoritaire arabe." *Critique internationale* 30 (2006): 59-81.

———. *Pouvoir et institution au Maghreb*. Tunis: Céres Production, 1978.

Cárdenas, Roosbelinda, and Hiba Bou Akar. "Writing About Violence." *MERIP* 284-285 (2017). https://merip.org/2018/04/writing-about-violence/.

Carlier, Omar. *Entre Nation et Jihad. Histoire sociale des radicalismes algériens*. Paris: Presses de Sciences Po, 1995.

———. "Le café maure. Sociabilité masculine et effervescence citoyenne (Algérie XVIIe-XXe siècles)." *Annales. Économies, Sociétés, Civilisations* 45, no. 4 (1990): 975-1003.

———. "Mémoire, mythe et doxa de l'État en Algérie. L'Étoile nord-africaine et la religion du 'watan.' " *Vingtième Siècle* 30 (1991): 82-92.

Carothers, Thomas. "The End of the Transition Paradigm." *Journal of Democracy* 13, no. 1 (2002): 5-21.

Cartier-Bresson, Jean. "Corruption, libéralisation et démocratisation." *Tiers Monde* 41, no. 161 (2000): 9-22.

Castoriadis, Cornélius. *Le Monde morcelé*. Paris: Éditions du Seuil, 1990.
Catusse, Myriam. "A propos de 'l'entrée en politique' des 'entrepreneurs' marocains." *Naqd* 19–20 (2004): 127–153.
Cavatorta, Francesco. "The Convergence of Governance: Upgrading Authoritarianism in the Arab World and Downgrading Democracy Elsewhere?" *Middle East Critique* 19, no. 3 (2010): 217–232.
———. *The International Dimension of the Failed Algerian Transition*. Manchester, UK: Manchester University Press, 2009.
Cavatorta, Francesco, and Rikke Hostrup Haugbølle. "The End of Authoritarian Rule and the Mythology of Tunisia Under Ben Ali." *Mediterranean Politics* 17, no. 2 (2012): 179–195.
Chabani, Hamid. *Le printemps noir de 2001 en Kabylie: Le cas de la coordination communale d'Aïn-Zaouia*. Paris: L'Harmattan, 2011.
Chamayou, Grégoire. *Les chasses à l'homme*. Paris: La Fabrique éditions, 2010.
Charef, Abed. *Algérie '88. Un chahut de gamin*. Algiers: Laphomic, 1990.
Charlier-Yannopoulou, Tatiana. "La crise politique grecque." *Revue française de science politique* 17, no. 1 (1967): 47–64.
Chauvin, Luc. "Rap algérien: D'une révolution culturelle à une autre." *Mouvements* 4, no. 96 (2018): 111–118.
Chekouri, Sidi Mohammed, Abderrahim Chibi, and Mohamed Benbouziane. "Algeria and the Natural Resource Curse: Oil Abundance and Economic Growth." *Middle East Development Journal* 9, no. 2 (2017): 233–255.
Chena, Salim. "L'Algérie dans le 'Printemps arabe' entre espoirs, initiatives et blocages." *Confluences Méditerranée* 77, no. 2 (2011): 105–118.
———. "Sidi Salem et el harga." *Hommes & Migrations* 1300, no. 6 (2012): 52–61.
Chikhi, Saïd. "Algérie: Du soulèvement populaire d'octobre 1988 aux contestations sociales des travailleurs." In *Mouvement social et modernité*, edited by Daho Djerbal and Mohamed Benguerna, 69–103. Algiers: Naqd/SARP, 2001.
———. "Question ouvrière et rapports sociaux en Algérie." *Fernand Braudel Center Review* 18, no. 3 (1995): 487–524.
Coronil, Fernando. *The Magical State: Nature, Money and Modernity in Venezuela*. Chicago: University of Chicago Press, 1997.
Côte, Marc. "Une ville remplit sa vallée: Ghardaïa (Note)." *Méditerranée* 99 (2002): 107–110.
Courreye, Charlotte. *L'Algérie des oulémas. Une histoire de l'Algérie contemporaine, 1931-1991*. Paris: Éditions de la Sorbonne, 2020.
Criscuolo, Josiane. "Armée et Nation dans les discours du Colonel Boumédiène." PhD diss., University Paul Valéry, 1975.
Cristias, Panagiotis. *Krisis. Perspectives pour un monde aux alentours de 2010*. Paris: L'Harmattan, 2011.
Crowley, Patrick, ed. *Algeria: Nation, Culture and Transnationalism: 1988-2015*. Liverpool, UK: Liverpool University Press, 2017.
Dahou, Tarik. *Gouverner la mer en Algérie. Politique en eaux trouble*. Paris: Karthala, 2018.

Dakhlia, Jocelyne. "Dans la mouvance du prince: La symbolique du pouvoir itinérant au Maghreb." *Annales. Économies, Sociétés, Civilisations* 43 (1988): 735–760.

———. *Le Divan des Rois: Le politique et le religieux dans l'islam*. Paris: Aubier, 1998.

Danet, Joël. "Bejaia Doc: Co-construction d'un regard documentaire sur l'Algérie d'aujourd'hui." *Communication, technologies et développement* 7 (2019). http://journals.openedition.org/ctd/1372.

Davis, Mike. *Ecology of Fear: Los Angeles and the Imagination of the Disaster*. New York: Metropolitan Books, 1998.

Davis, Muriam H. *Markets of Civilization: Islam and Racial Capitalism in Algeria*. Durham, NC: Duke University Press, 2022.

———. "'The Transformation of Man' in French Algeria: Economic Planning and the Postwar Social Sciences, 1958–62." *Journal of Contemporary History* 52, no. 1 (2017): 73–94.

Debord, Guy. *La société du spectacle*. Chicoutimi, QC: Éditions de l'UQAC, 2006. First published 1967.

DeCaroli, Steven. "Political Life: Giorgio Agamben and the Idea of Authority." *Research in Phenomenology* 43 (2013): 220–242.

Della Porta, Donatella. "Les hommes politiques d'affaires. Partis politiques et corruption." *Politix* 30 (1995): 61–75.

Del Panta, Gianni. "Defeating Autocrats from Below: Insights from the 2019 Algerian Uprising." *Contemporary Politics* 28, no. 5 (2022), 539–557.

Derrida, Jacques. "Force de loi." *Cardozo Law Review* 11 (1990): 920–1046.

Destanne De Bernis, Gérard. "Les problèmes pétroliers algériens." *Etudes internationales* 2, no. 4 (1971): 575–609.

Didi-Hubermann, Georges. *Devant le temps. Histoire de l'art et anachronisme de l'image*. Paris: Éditions de Minuit, 2000.

Dilem, Ali. *Algérie, mon humour*. Algiers: Casbah éditions, 2011.

Dillman, Bradford L. *State and Private Sector in Algeria: The Politics of Rent-Seeking and Failed Development*. Boulder, CO: Westview Press, 2000.

Djabi, Abdelnacer. "Al-u'sṭūra, al-jīl wa-l-harakāt al-ijtimāʻiyya fī Al-Jazāi'r. A'w al-ab 'al-fāshil' wa-l-ibn 'al-qāfiz'." *Insaniyat* 25–26 (2004): 43–54.

Djerbal, Daho. "Algeria: Amnesty and Oligarchy." *Sada* (blog), Carnegie Endowment for International Peace, August 20, 2008. https://carnegieendowment.org/sada/21119.

Djilali, Soufiane. *L'Algérie, une nation en chantier*. Algiers: Casbah éditions, 2004.

Dobry, Michel. "Les voies incertaines de la transitologie: Choix stratégiques, séquences historiques, bifurcations et processus de path dependence." *Revue française de science politique* 4–5 (2000): 585–614.

———. *Sociologie des crises politiques*. Paris: Presses de Sciences Po, 1986.

Doyle, Michael W., and Nicholas Sambanis. *Making War and Building Peace: United Nations Peace Operations*. Princeton, NJ: Princeton University Press, 2006.

Dris, Chérif. "La nouvelle loi organique sur l'information de 2012 en Algérie: Vers un ordre médiatique néo-autoritaire?" *L'Année du Maghreb* 8 (2012): 303–320.

Dris-Aït Hamadouche, Louisa. "Au cœur de la résilience algérienne: Un jeu calculé d'alliances." *Confluences Méditerranée* 106 (2018): 195–210.

———. "L'abstention en Algérie: Un autre mode de contestation politique." *L'Année du Maghreb* 5 (2009): 263–273.

Dris-Aït Hamadouche, Louisa, and Yahia H. Zoubir. "Pouvoir et opposition en Algérie: Vers une transition prolongée?" *L'Année du Maghreb* 5 (2009): 111–127.

Dufresne Aubertin, Laurence. "Revendications morales et politiques d'une révolte. Les émeutes du Mzab en Algérie (2013–2015)." *L'Année du Maghreb* 16 (2017): 209–222.

Duprat, Anne. *Le roi décapité, essai sur les imaginaires politiques*. Paris: Cerf, 1992.

Egreteau, Renaud. *Histoire de la Birmanie contemporaine: Le pays des prétoriens*. Paris: Fayard, 2010.

Elias, Norbert. *La dynamique de l'Occident*. Paris: Calmann-Lévy Pocket, 1990. First published 1975.

———. *The Germans: Power Struggles and the Development of Habitus in the Nineteenth and Twentieth Centuries*. New York: Columbia University Press, 1996.

Eliasoph, Nina. *Avoiding Politics: How Americans Produce Apathy in Everyday Life*. Cambridge: Cambridge University Press, 1998.

Elsenhans, Harmut. "Capitalisme d'État ou société bureaucratique de développement." *Études internationales* 13, no. 1 (1982): 3–21.

Entelis, John P. "Algeria: Democracy Denied, and Revived?" *Journal of North African Studies* 16, no. 4 (2011): 653–678.

———. *Algeria: The Revolution Institutionalized*. Boulder, CO: Westview Press, 1986.

———. "Sonatrach: The Political Economy of an Algerian State Institution." *Middle East Journal* 53, no. 1 (1999): 9–27.

Evans, Martin, and John Phillips. *Algeria: Anger of the Dispossessed*. New Haven, CT: Yale University Press, 2008.

Fanon, Frantz. *Les damnés de la Terre*. Chicoutimi, QC: Éditions de l'UQAC, 2002. First published 1961.

———. *Pour la révolution africaine. Écrits politiques*. Paris: La Découverte, 2001. First published 1964.

Farsoun, Karen. "State Capitalism in Algeria." *MERIP* 35 (1975): 3–30.

Fearon, James D. "Iraq's Civil War." *Foreign Affairs* 86, no. 2 (2007): 2–15.

Felstiner, William L. F., Richard L. Abel, and Austin Sarat. "The Emergence and Transformation of Disputes: Naming, Blaming, Claiming." *Law & Society Review* 15, nos. 3–4 (1980): 631–654.

Fligstein, Neil, and Doug McAdam. *A Theory of Field*. Oxford: Oxford University Press, 2012.

Foucault, Michel. *Dits et écrits*. Vol. 2, *1976–1988*. Paris: Gallimard, 2001.

———. *Il faut défendre la société*. Paris: Seuil/Gallimard, 1997.

———. *Naissance de la biopolitique. Cours au Collège de France (1978–1979)*. Paris: Seuil/Gallimard, 2004.

Freund, Julien. "Observation sur deux catégories de la dynamique polémogène. De la crise au conflit." *Communications* 25 (1976): 102–112.

Frison-Roche, François. "Les chefs d'Etat dans les PECO." *Le courrier des pays de l'est* 1043 (2004): 52–66.

Galula, David. *Pacification in Algeria, 1956–1958*. Santa Monica, CA: RAND Corporation, 2006. First published 1963.
Garon, Lise. "Entre propagande et voix dissidentes: L'information internationale et ses sources; le cas de la crise algérienne." *Études internationales* 29, no. 3 (1998): 599–629.
Gaxie, Daniel. "Economie des partis et rétributions du militantisme." *Revue française de science politique* 27, no. 1 (1977): 123–154.
Gay, Robert. "The Broker and the Thief: A Parable (Reflections on Popular Politics in Brazil)." *Luso-Brazilian Review* 36, no. 1 (1999): 49–70.
Geisser, Vincent. "Des Voltaire, des Zola musulmans . . .? Réflexion sur les 'nouveaux dissidents' de l'islam." *Revue internationale et stratégique* 65 (2007): 143–156.
Georgi, Fabien. "Toward Fortress Capitalism: The Restrictive Transformation of Migration and Border Regimes as a Reaction to the Capitalist Multicrisis." *Canadian Review of Sociology* 56, no. 4 (2019): 556–579.
Gèze, François. "Armée et nation en Algérie: L'irrémédiable divorce?" *Hérodote* 116 (2005): 175–203.
Gèze, François, and François Burgat. "L'Union européenne et les islamistes: Le cas de l'Algérie." *L'Année du Maghreb* 3 (2007): 655–665.
Ghettas, Mohammed Lakhdar. *Algeria and the Cold War: International Relations and the Struggle for Autonomy*. London: I. B. Tauris, 2018.
Gonzalez Casanova, Pablo. "Société plurale, colonialisme interne et développement." *Tiers Monde* 5, no. 18 (1964): 291–295.
Goumeziane, Smaïl. "L'incontournable libéralisation." *Confluences Méditerranée* 11 (1994): 39–52.
Gourisse, Benjamin. *La violence politique en Turquie. L'Etat en jeu (1975–1980)*. Paris: Karthala, 2014.
Gramsci, Antonio. *Quaderni del carcere. Volume secondo. Quaderni 6–11*. Turin: Giulio Einaudi editore, 1975.
———. *Quaderni del carcere. Volume terzo. Quaderni 12–29*. Turin: Giulio Einaudi editore, 1977.
Grandguillaume, Gilbert. *Arabisation et politique linguistique au Maghreb*. Paris: Maisonneuve et Larose, 1995.
Guerid, Djamel. *L'Exception Algérienne: La modernistation à l'épreuve de la société*. Algiers: Casbah éditions, 2007.
Guilhot, Nicolas. *The Democracy Makers: Human Rights and the Politics of the Global Order*. New York: Columbia University Press, 2005.
Gulli, Bruno. "The Ontology and Politics of Exception: Reflections on the Work of Giorgio Agamben." In *Sovereignty & Life*, edited by Matthew Calarco and Steven DeCaroli, 219–242. Stanford, CA: Stanford University Press, 2007.
Gupta, Akhil. "Blurred Boundaries: The Discourse of Corruption, the Culture of Politics, and the Imagined State." *American Ethnologist* 22, no. 2 (1995): 375–402.
Gupta, Akhil, and Aradhana Sharma. "Globalization and Postcolonial States." *Current Anthropology* 47, no. 2 (2006): 277–307.
Hachemaoui, Mohammed. *Clientélisme et patronage dans l'Algérie contemporaine*. Paris: Karthala, 2013.

———. "La représentation politique en Algérie entre médiation clientélaire et prédation (1997-2002)." *Revue Française de science politique* 53, no. 1 (2003): 35-72.

———. "Permanence du jeu politique en Algérie." *Politique étrangère* 2 (2009): 309-321.

Hachimi Alaoui, Myriam. "L'Epreuve de l'exil. Le cas des Algériens installés à Paris et à Montréal." *Insaniyat* 27 (2005): 139-145.

Haddad, Bassam. *Business Networks in Syria: The Political Economy of Authoritarian Resilience.* Stanford, CA: Stanford University Press, 2012.

Hadj Moussa, Ratiba. *La télévision par satellite au Maghreb et ses publics. Espaces de résistance, espaces critiques.* Grenoble, FR: Presses universitaires de Grenoble, 2015.

———. "Marginality and Ordinary Memory: Body Centrality and the Plea for Recognition in Recent Algerian Films." *Journal of North African Studies* 13, no. 2 (2008): 187-199.

———. "Youth and Activism in Algeria. The Question of Political Generations." *Journal of North African Studies* 26, no. 2 (2019): 311-336.

Hadj Nacer, Abderrahmane. *La martingale algérienne. Réflexions sur une crise.* Algiers: Éditions Barzakh, 2011.

Hadjeres, Sadek. "Algérie: Violence et politique." *Hérodote* 77 (1995): 43-64.

Hale, William. *Turkish Politics and the Military.* London: Routledge, 2003. First published 1994.

Hamladji, Noura. "Co-optation, Repression and Authoritarian Regime's Survival. The Case of the Islamist MSP-Hamas in Algeria." European University Institute Working Paper SPS No. 2002/07 (2002). https://cadmus.eui.eu/bitstream/handle/1814/327/sps20027.pdf?sequence=1&isAllowed=y.

Hannoum, Abdelmajid. *Violent Modernity: France in Algeria.* Cambridge, MA: Harvard University Press, 2010.

Harbi, Mohamed. *Les archives de la révolution algérienne.* Paris: Éditions Jeune Afrique, 1981.

Haroun, Ali. *Algérie, 1962: La grande dérive.* Paris: L'Harmattan, 2005.

Harvey, David. *A Brief History of Neoliberalism.* Oxford: Oxford University Press, 2005.

Hassan. *Algérie. Histoire d'un naufrage.* Paris: Seuil, 1996.

Haugbolle, Sune, and Andreas Bandak. "The Ends of Revolution: Rethinking Ideology and Time in the Arab Uprisings." *Middle East Critique* 26, no. 3 (2017): 191-204.

Henry, Clement M., and Robert Springborg. *Globalization and the Politics of Development in the Middle East.* Cambridge: Cambridge University Press, 2010.

Heydemann, Steven. "After the Earthquake: Economic Governance and Mass Politics in the Middle East." *Critique internationale* 61, no. 4 (2013): 69-84.

———. *Networks of Privilege in the Middle East: The Politics of Economic Reform Revisited.* New York: Palgrave Macmillan, 2004.

———. "Upgrading Authoritarianism in the Arab World." Saban Center for Middle East Policy at Brookings Institution, Analysis Paper No. 13 (October 2007). https://www.brookings.edu/research/upgrading-authoritarianism-in-the-arab-world/.

Hibou, Béatrice. *Anatomie de la domination.* Paris: La Découverte, 2011.

———. *La force de l'obéissance. Economie politique de la répression en Tunisie.* Paris: La Découverte, 2006.

———. *La privatisation des états.* Paris: Karthala, 1999.

Hibou, Béatrice, and Mohamed Tozy. "La lutte contre la corruption au Maroc: Vers une pluralisation des modes de gouvernement?" *Droit et société* 72, no. 2 (2009): 339–357.

———. "Une lecture d'anthropologie politique de la corruption au Maroc: Fondement historique d'une prise de liberté avec le droit." *Tiers Monde* 41, no. 161 (2000): 23–47.

Hill, Jonathan N. C. "Challenging the Failed State Thesis: IMF and World Bank Intervention and the Algerian Civil War." *Civil Wars* 11, no. 1 (2009): 39–56.

Hinnebusch, Raymond. "Authoritarian Resilience and the Arab Uprising: Syria in a Comparative Perspective." *Ortadoğu Etütleri* 7 (2015): 16–36.

———. "Syria: From 'Authoritarian Upgrading' to Revolution?" *International Affairs* 88 (2012): 95–113.

Hmed, Choukri. "Réseaux dormants, contingence et structures. Genèses de la révolution tunisienne." *Revue française de science politique* 62, nos. 5–6 (2012): 797–820.

Hobsbawm, Eric J. "The Revolutionary Situation in Colombia." *World Today* 19, no. 6 (1963): 248–258.

Horwitz, Robert B. "Understanding Deregulation." *Theory and society* 15 (1986): 139–174.

Houdjedje, Kacem. "At-tadakhul al-Insānī li-l-jaysh al-waṭanī ash-shaʿabī fī muwājahat al-kawārith at-ṭabīʿiyya: Dirāsa li-l-sharāka ʿaskarī-madanī khilāl fayaḍān wād Mzāb sanat 2008m." *Dafātīr al-siyāsa wa-l-qānūn* 8, no. 14 (2016): 1–30.

Humphreys, Stephen. "Legalizing Lawlessness: On Giorgio Agamben's State of Exception." *European Journal of International Law* 17, no. 3 (2006): 677–687.

Huntington, Samuel P. *Political Order in Changing Societies*. New Haven, CT: Yale University Press, 1973. First published 1968.

Ilikoud, Ouali. "FFS et RCD: Partis nationaux ou partis kabyles." *Revue des mondes musulmans et de la Méditerranée* 111–112 (2006): 163–182.

Insel, Ahmet. "'Cet État n'est pas sans propriétaire!' Forces prétoriennes et autoritarisme en Turquie." In *Autoritarismes démocratiques et démocraties autoritaires au XXIè siècle*, edited by Olivier Dabène, Vincent Geisser, and Gilles Massardier, 133–153. Paris: La Découverte, 2008.

Isnard, Hilderbert. "L'Algérie ou la décolonisation difficile." *Méditerranée* 3 (1969): 325–340.

Jabri, Vivienne. "War, Security and the Liberal State." *Security Dialogue* 37, no. 1 (2006): 47–64.

Jacquemet, Nicolas. "Micro-économie de la corruption." *Revue française d'économie* 20, no. 4 (2006): 117–159.

Jaffrelot, Lionel. *Le syndrome pakistanais*. Paris: Fayard, 2013.

Kalyvas, Stathis N. "Wanton and Senseless? The Logic of Massacres in Algeria." *Rationality and Society* 11, no. 3 (1999): 243–285.

Kantorowicz, Ernst. *The King's Two Bodies: A Study in Mediaeval Political Theology*. Princeton, NJ: Princeton University Press, 1957.

Karkov, Nikolay, and Jeffrey W. Robbins. "Decoloniality and Crisis." *Journal for Culture and Religious Theory* 13, no. 1 (2014): 1–10.

Kassab, Elizabeth S. *Contemporary Arab Thought: Cultural Critique in Comparative Perspective*. New York: Columbia University Press, 2010.

Kassir, Samir. *Considérations sur le malheur arabe*. Arles: Actes Sud, 2004.
Kateb, Kamel. "Population et organisation de l'espace en Algérie." *L'Espace Géographique* 32 (2003): 311–331.
Katz, Richard S., and Peter Mair. "Changing Models of Party Organization and Party Democracy: The Emergence of the Cartel Party." *Party Politics* 1 (1995): 5–28.
Keen, David. *Complex Emergencies*. Cambridge: Polity Press, 2008.
Keenan, Jeremy. *The Dark Sahara: America's War on Terror in Africa*. London: Pluto Press, 2009.
Kenz, Ali El. "Algérie, les deux paradigmes." *Revue du monde musulman et de la Méditerranée* 68–69 (1993): 79–86.
———. "Les chercheurs africains, une élite?" *Revue Africaine des livres* 1, no. 1 (2004): 19–22.
Kerbouche, Ahmed. "Dawr siyāsat al-muṣālaḥa al-waṭaniyya fī muʻālajat al-aʼzma al-aʼmniya fī Al-Jazāiʼr." *Al-Majala al-jazāʼiriya li-l-siyāsa al-ʻāāma* 4, no. 2 (2016): 142–164.
Khalili, Laleh. *Times in the Shadow*. Stanford, CA: Stanford University Press, 2012.
Khanna, Ranjana. *Algeria Cuts: Women and Representation. 1830 to the Present*. Stanford, CA: Stanford University Press, 2017.
Khatib, Sami. "The Messianic Without Messianism." *Anthropology & Materialism* 1 (2013). http://journals.openedition.org/am/159.
Khelladi, Aïssa. "Rire quand même: L'humour politique dans l'Algérie d'aujourd'hui." *Revue du monde musulman et de la Méditerranée* 77–78 (1995): 225–237.
Khodja, Soumya Ammar. "Écritures d'urgence de femmes algériennes." *Clio. Histoire, femmes et sociétés* 9 (1999): 1–11.
Khosrokhavar, Farhad. "La violence et ses avatars dans les quartiers sensibles." *Déviance et Société* 24, no. 4 (2000): 425–440.
Kirchheimer, Otto. "The Transformation of the Western European Party Systems." In *Political Parties and Political Development*, edited by Joseph La Palombara and Myron Weiner, 177–200. Princeton, NJ: Princeton University Press, 1966.
Kisner, Wendell. "Agamben, Hegel, and the State of Exception." *Cosmos and History: The Journal of Natural and Social Philosophy* 3, nos. 2–3 (2007): 222–253.
Kitschelt, Herbert, and Steven I. Wilkinson. *Patrons, Clients, and Policies: Patterns of Democratic Accountability and Political Competition*. Cambridge: Cambridge University Press, 2007.
Klein, Naomi. *The Shock Doctrine: The Rise of Disaster Capitalism*. Toronto, ON: Knopf Canada, 2007.
Kokoreff Michel, Odile Steinauer, and Pierre Barron. "Les émeutes urbaines à l'épreuve des situations locales." *SociologieS*, August 23, 2007. https://journals.openedition.org/sociologies/254.
Konings, Martijn. *The Emotional Logic of Capitalism: What Progressives Have Missed*. Stanford, CA: Stanford University Press, 2015.
Koriche, Mohamed Nasr-Eddine. "Justice et règlement des conflits du travail en Algérie." *L'Année du Maghreb* 3 (2007): 39–54.
Kurzman, Charles. *The Unthinkable Revolution in Iran*. Cambridge, MA: Harvard University Press, 2004.

Kusche, Isabel. "The Accusation of Clientelism: On the Interplay Between Social Science, Mass Media, and Politics in the Critique of Irish Democracy." *Historical Social Research/ Historische Sozialforschung* 42, no. 3 (2017): 172-195.

Labat, Séverine. *Les Islamistes Algériens. Entre les urnes et le maquis*. Paris: Éditions du Seuil, 1995.

Labter, Lazhari. *Journalistes Algériens (1988-1998): Chronique des années d'espoir et de terreur*. Algiers: Chihab, 2005.

Laclau, Ernesto. *On Populist Reason*. London: Verso, 2005.

Laforest Mary, and Diane Vincent. "La qualification péjorative dans tous ses états." *Langue française* 144 (2004): 59-81.

Lair, Eric. "La Colombie entre guerre et paix." *Politique étrangère* 66, no. 1 (2001): 109-121.

Lamchichi, Abderrahim. "Référendum sur la concorde civile, les leçons d'un scrutin." *Confluences Méditerranée* 32 (2000): 155-166.

Laribi, Lyes. *L'Algérie des Généraux*. Paris: Max Milo éditions, 2007.

Laurens, Sylvain. " 'Pourquoi' et 'comment' poser les questions qui fâchent? Réflexions sur les dilemmes récurrents que posent les entretiens avec des 'imposants.' " *Genèses* 69, no. 4 (2007): 112-127.

Lavabre, Marie-Claire. "Usages du passé, usages de la mémoire." *Revue française de science politique* 3 (1994): 480-493.

Lavenue, Jean-Jacques. *Algérie: La démocratie interdite*. Paris: L'Harmattan, 1993.

Lazarus, Jeanne. "Le Pauvre et la Consommation." *Vingtième Siècle* 91 (2006): 137-152.

Lazreg, Marnia. "Islamism and the Recolonization of Algeria." In *Beyond Colonialism and Nationalism in the Maghreb*, edited by Ali Abdullatif Ahmida, 147-164. New York: Palgrave Macmillan, 2000.

Leca, Jean. "Parti et Etat en Algérie." *Annuaire de l'Afrique du Nord* 6 (1968): 13-41.

Leca, Jean, and Yves Schemeil. "Clientelisme et patrimonialisme dans le monde arabe." *Revue Internationale de science politique* 4, no. 4 (1983): 455-494.

Leca, Jean, and Jean-Claude Vatin. "Le système politique algérien (1976-1978)." *Annuaire de l'Afrique du Nord* 16 (1978): 15-80.

Le Cour Grandmaison, Olivier. *De l'indigénat. Anatomie d'un monstre juridique: Le droit colonial en Algérie et dans l'empire français*. Paris: Éditions La Découverte, 2010.

Lenin, Vladimir Ilitch. *The Collapse of the Second International*. Glasgow: Socialist Labour Press, 1920.

Leperlier, Tristan. *Algérie, Les écrivains de la décennie noire*. Paris: CNRS Éditions, 2018.

Le Roy, Frederik. "Ragpickers and Leftover Performances." *Performance Research* 22, no. 8 (2017): 127-134.

Le Sueur, James D. *Between Terror and Democracy: Algeria Since 1989*. London: Zed Books, 2010.

Leveau, Rémy. *Afrique du Nord, Moyen-Orient, Espace et conflits*. Paris: La documentation française, 2003.

———. "Esquisse d'un changement politique au Maghreb?" *Politique étrangère* 65, no. 2 (2000): 499-507.

———. "Islamisme et populisme." *Vingtième Siècle* 56 (2007): 214-223.

Li, Darryl. "A Jihadism Anti-primer." *MERIP* 276 (2015). https://merip.org/2015/12/a-jihadism-anti-primer/.

Limbrick, Peter. "Spaces of Dispossession: Experiments with the Real in Contemporary Algerian Cinema." In *Histories of Arab Documentary*, edited by Viola Shafik. Cairo: University of Cairo Press, forthcoming.

Linz, Juan. "L'effondrement de la démocratie, autoritarisme et totalitarisme dans l'Europe de l'entre-deux-guerres." *Revue internationale de politique comparée* 11, no. 4 (2004): 531–586.

———. "The Perils of Presidentialism." *Journal of Democracy* 1 (1990): 51–69.

———. "Quel avenir pour les partis politiques dans les démocraties contemporaines?" *Pôle Sud* 21, no. 1 (2004): 55–68.

Lionel, Arnaud, and Christine Guionnet. *Les frontières du politique. Enquête sur les processus de politisation et de dépolitisation*. Rennes, FR: Presses universitaires de Rennes, 2005.

Lorcin, Patricia M. E. *Kabyles, Arabes, Français: Identités coloniales*. Limoges, FR: PULIM, 2005.

Luke, T. W. "On Insurrectionality: Theses on Contemporary Revolts and Resilience." *Globalizations* 12, no. 6 (2015): 834–845.

Malley, Robert. *The Call from Algeria: Third Worldism, Revolution and the Turn to Islam*. Berkeley: University of California Press, 1996.

Malti, Hocine. *Histoire secrète du pétrole algérien*. Paris: La Découverte, 2012.

Mameri, Khalfa. *Abane, le faux procès*. Tizi Ouzou: Éditions Mehdi, 2007.

———. *Orientations politiques de l'Algérie*. Algiers: SNED, 1973.

Martin, Ivan. "Politique économique et stabilité de l'Etat." Centre de recherches internationales, March–April 2003. https://www.sciencespo.fr/ceri/sites/sciencespo.fr.ceri/files/artim_0.pdf.

Martinez, Luis. "Algérie: Les massacres de civils dans la guerre." *Revue internationale de politique comparée* 8, no. 1 (2001): 43–58.

———. *La guerre civile en Algérie*. Paris: Khartala, 1998.

———. "L'Algérie de l'Après-11 septembre 2001." In *Afrique du Nord, Moyen-Orient, Espace et conflits*, edited by Rémy Leveau, 149–161. Paris: La Documentation française, 2003.

———. "L'après-guerre civile: Les étapes de la réconciliation nationale." Centre de recherches internationales, January 2000. https://hal-sciencespo.archives-ouvertes.fr/hal-01064877.

———. *Violence de la rente pétrolière: Algérie-Irak-Libye*. Paris: Presses de Sciences Po, 2010.

Massardier, Gilles. "Les espaces non pluralistes dans les démocraties contemporaines." In *Autoritarismes démocratiques et démocraties autoritaires au XXIè siècle*, edited by Olivier Dabène, Vincent Geisser, and Gilles Massardier, 29–56. Paris: La Découverte, 2008.

Mbembe, Achille. "Nécropolitique." *Raisons politiques* 21 (2006): 29–60.

———. *On the Postcolony*. Berkeley: University of California Press, 2001.

McAllister, Edward. "Nation-Building Remembered: Social Memory in Contemporary Algeria." PhD diss., Oxford University, 2015.

McDougall, James. "After the War. Algeria's Transition to Uncertainty." *MERIP* 245 (2007). https://merip.org/2007/12/after-the-war/.

———. *A History of Algeria*. Cambridge: Cambridge University Press, 2017.

———. *History and the Culture of Nationalism in Algeria*. Cambridge: Cambridge University Press, 2006.
———. "Savage Wars? Codes of Violence in Algeria, 1830s–1990s." *Third World Quarterly* 26, no. 1 (2005): 117–131.
Médard, Jean-François. "Clientélisme politique et corruption." *Tiers Monde* 41, no. 161 (2000): 75–87.
———. "The Underdeveloped State in Tropical Africa: Political Clientelism or Neo-patrimonialism." In *Private Patronage and Public Power*, edited by Christopher Clapham, 162–192. London: Frances Pinter, 1982.
Medhar, Slimane. *La violence sociale en Algérie*. Algiers: Thala, 1997.
Medjaoui, Abdel'alim. *Le Géant aux yeux bleus. Novembre, où en est ta victoire?* Algiers: Casbah éditions, 2007.
Mekamcha, Ghaouti. "Pouvoirs et recompositions en Algérie." In *Les figures du politique en Afrique: Des pouvoirs hérités aux pouvoirs élus*, edited by Momar-Coumba Diop and Mamadou Diouf, 385–412. Dakar: CODESRIA; Paris: Karthala, 1999.
Ménoret, Pascal. *Joyriding in Riyadh: Oil, Urbanism, and Road Revolt*. Cambridge: Cambridge University Press, 2014.
Merah, Ahmed. *Une troïka de généraux*. Algiers: Merah éditions, 2000.
Mezghani, Ali. *L'Etat inachevé*. Paris: Gallimard, 2011.
Michels, Robert. *Les partis politiques. Essai sur les tendances oligarchiques des démocraties*. Paris: Flammarion, 1914.
Milstein, Brian. "Thinking Politically About Crisis: A Pragmatist Perspective." *European Journal of Political Theory* 14, no. 2 (2015): 141–160.
Mira, Rachid. "Nouvelle stratégie industrielle en Algérie et soutien politique aux entreprises publiques: Une approche institutionnaliste par la recherche de rentes." In *L'Algérie au Présent*, edited by Karima Dirèche, 227–232. Paris: Karthala, 2019.
Mirowski, Philip. *Never Let a Serious Crisis Go to Waste*. London: Verso, 2013.
Mitchell, Timothy. *Carbon Democracy: Political Power in the Age of Oil*. New York: Verso, 2011.
Moderne, Franck. "Les avatars du présidentialisme dans les états latino-américains." *Pouvoirs* 98 (2001): 63–87.
Mohand-Amer, Amar. "L'Union Générale des Travailleurs Algériens dans le processus de transition (1962–1963)." In *Le Maghreb et l'indépendance de l'Algérie*, edited by Amar Mohand-Amer and Belkacem Benzenine, 39–49. Oran: CRASC; Tunis: IRMC; Aix-en-Provence: Karthala, 2012.
Monod, Jean-Claude. "La force du populisme: Une analyse philosophique." *Esprit* 351 (2009): 42–52.
Morange, Jean. "La protection constitutionnelle et civile de la liberté d'expression." *Revue internationale de droit comparé* 42, no. 2 (1990): 771–787.
Morin, Edgar. "Pour une crisologie." *Communications* 25 (1976): 149–163.
Mostefaoui, Belkacem. "Algérie, l'espace du débat médiatique." *Réseaux* 88–89 (1998): 153–188.
———. "Professionnalisation et autonomie des Journalistes au Maghreb. Eléments de mise en situation des actions et conflits." *Réseaux* 51 (1992): 55–66.

Mouffe, Chantal. *On the Political*. Abingdon, UK: Routledge, 2005.
Mouffok, Ghania. *Être journaliste en Algérie*. Paris: RSF, 1995.
Moussaoui, Abderrahmane. "Algérie, la guerre rejouée." *La pensée de midi* 3 (2000): 28–37.
———. "Algérie, la réconciliation entre espoirs et malentendus." *Politique étrangère* 2 (2007): 339–350.
———. *De la Violence en Algérie*. Arles: Actes Sud, 2006.
Muir, Sarah, and Akhil Gupta. "Rethinking the Anthropology of Corruption." *Current Anthropology* 59, no. 18 (2018): 4–15.
Muller, Christian Alain. "Du 'peuple égaré' au 'peuple enfant.' Le discours politique révolutionnaire à l'épreuve de la révolte populaire de 1793." *Revue d'histoire moderne et contemporaine* 47 (2000): 93–112.
Mundy, Jacob. "Deconstructing Civil Wars: Beyond the New Wars Debate." *Security Dialogue* 42, no. 3 (2011): 279–295.
———. *Imaginative Geographies of Algerian Violence: Conflict Science, Conflict Management, Antipolitics*. Stanford, CA: Stanford University Press, 2015.
Mura, Andrea. "A Genealogical Inquiry Into Early Islamism: The Discourse of Hasan al-Banna." *Journal of Political Ideologies* 17, no. 1 (2012): 61–85.
Musella, Luigi. "Réseaux politiques et réseaux de corruption à Naples." *Politix* 12, no. 45 (1999): 39–55.
Mutin, Georges. "Implantations industrielles et aménagements du territoire en Algérie." *Revue de géographie de Lyon* 55, no. 1 (1980): 5–37.
Nabti, Mehdi. "Soufisme, métissage culturel et commerce du sacré. Les Aïssâwa marocains dans la modernité." *Insaniyat* 32–33 (2006): 173–195.
Naudillon, Françoise. "Le polar, un genre postcolonial?" In *Violences postcoloniales. Représentations littéraires et perceptions médiatiques*, edited by Isaac Bazié and Hans-Jürgen Lüsebrink, 131–143. Berlin: Lit-Verlag, 2011.
Nay, Olivier. "La théorie des 'États fragiles': Un nouveau développementalisme politique?" *Gouvernement et action publique* 1 (2013): 139–151.
Nellis, John R. "Algerian Socialism and Its Critics." *Canadian Journal of Political Science* 13, no. 3 (1980): 481–507.
Nezzar, Khaled. *Bouteflika, l'homme et son bilan*. Algiers: Éditions APIC, 2003.
———. *Mémoires du Général Khaled Nezzar*. Algiers: Chihab, 2000.
———. *Le Procès de Paris: L'armée algérienne face à la désinformation*. Paris: Éditions Médiane, 2003.
Nichter, Simeon. *Votes for Survival: Relational Clientelism in Latin America*. Cambridge: Cambridge University Press, 2018.
Olson, Mancur. *The Rise and Decline of Nations: Economic Growth, Stagflation and Social Rigidities*. New Haven, CT: Yale University Press, 1982.
Ombrosi, Orietta. "La dialectique de l'idée de catastrophe dans la pensée de W. Benjamin." *Archives de Philosophie* 69, no. 2 (2006): 263–284.
Omobowale, Ayokunle O. "Clientelism and Social Structure: An Analysis of Patronage in Yoruba Social Thought." *Africa Spectrum* 43, no. 2 (2008): 203–224.

Ophir, Adi. "The Politics of Catastrophization: Emergency and Exception." In *Contemporary States of Emergency: The Politics of Military and Humanitarian Interventions*, edited by Didier Fassin and Mariella Pandolfi, 59–88. New York: Zone Books, 2010.
Oquist, Paul H. *Violence, Conflict, and Politics in Colombia*. New York: Academic Press, 1980.
Ottaway, David, and Marina Ottaway. *Algeria: The Politics of a Socialist Revolution*. Berkeley: University of California Press, 1970.
Paillard, Denis. "La Russie après le 11 septembre: Poutine petit soldat de la mondialisation libérale." *Naqd* 19–20 (2004): 267–280.
Parks, Robert P. "Local-National Relations and the Politics of Property Rights in Algeria and Tunisia." PhD diss., University of Texas at Austin, 2011.
Pécaut, Daniel. *L'ordre et la violence. Evolution socio-politique de la Colombie entre 1930 et 1953*. Paris: Éditions de l'EHESS, 1987.
———. "Présent, passé, futur de la violence." In *La Colombie à l'aube du troisième millénaire*, edited by Christian Gros, 17–63. Paris: IHEAL, 1996.
Perego, Elizabeth. "Laughing at the Victims: The Function of Popular Jokes During Algeria's 'Dark Decade,' 1991–2002." *Journal of North African Studies* 23, nos. 1–2 (2018): 191–207.
———. "Laughing in the Face of Death: Humor During the Algerian Civil War, 1991–2002." PhD diss., Ohio State University, 2017.
Pervillé, Guy. "Qu'est-ce que la colonisation?" *Revue d'histoire moderne et contemporaine* 22 (1975): 321–368.
Picard, Elizabeth. "Armée et sécurité au cœur de l'autoritarisme." In *Autoritarismes démocratiques et démocraties autoritaires au XXIè siècle*, edited by Olivier Dabène, Vincent Geisser, and Gilles Massardier, 303–329. Paris: La Découverte, 2008.
Pierret, Thomas, and Kjetil Selvik. "Limit of 'Authoritarian Upgrading' in Syria: Private Welfare, Islamic Charities, and the Rise of the Zayd Movement." *Journal of Middle Eastern Studies* 41 (2009): 595–614.
Poulantzas, Nicos. *La crise de l'Etat*. Paris: PUF, 1976.
Premat, Christophe. "La 'grogne du peuple.' " *Tracés* 5 (2004): 13–32.
Quandt, William B. *Between Ballots and Bullets: Algeria's Transition from Authoritarianism*. Washington, DC: Brookings Institution Press, 1998.
———. *Revolution and Political Leadership: Algeria, 1954–1968*. Cambridge, MA: MIT Press, 1969.
Rabinovich, Itamar. *The War for Lebanon, 1970–1985*. Ithaca, NY: Cornell University Press, 1985.
Racine, Jean-Luc. "Le Pakistan après le coup d'Etat militaire." *Critique internationale* 7 (2000): 22–29.
Rahal, Malika. "Fille d'Octobre. Générations, engagement et histoire." *L'Année du Maghreb* 10 (2014): 183–187.
———. "Le temps arrêté. Un pays sans histoire. Algérie, 2011–2013." *Écrire l'histoire* 12 (2013): 27–36.
Rahal, Yahia. *Histoire de Pouvoir. Un Général témoigne*. Algiers: Casbah éditions, 1997.
Ralph, Michael. "Killing Time." *Social Text* 26, no. 4 (2008): 1–29.
Rancière, Jacques. *Aux bords du politique*. Paris: La Fabrique, 1998.

———. "Introducing Disagreement." *Angelaki* 9, no. 3 (2004): 3–9.
Ranney, Austin. "Referendum et Démocratie." *Pouvoir* 77 (1996): 7–19.
Remaoun, Hassan. "La question de l'histoire dans le débat sur la violence en Algérie." *Insaniyat* 10 (2010): 31–43.
Renan, Ernest. *De la part des peuples sémitiques dans l'histoire de la civilisation*. Paris: Michel Lévy Frères, 1862.
Revault D'Allonnes, Myriam. *La crise sans fin*. Paris: Éditions du Seuil, 2012.
Riedel, Bruce. "Algeria Goes to the Polls—Why the United States and Europe Have a Stake in Its Stability." *Markaz* (blog), Brookings Institution, May 1, 2017. https://www.brookings.edu/blog/markaz/2017/05/01/algeria-goes-to-the-polls-why-the-united-states-and-europe-have-a-stake-in-its-stability/.
Riesel, René, and Jaime Semprun. *Catastrophisme, administration du désastre et soumission durable*. Paris: Éditions de l'encyclopédie des nuisances, 2008.
Riutort, Philippe. *Sociologie de la communication politique*. Paris: La Découverte, 2007.
Roberts, Hugh. *The Battlefield: Algeria, 1988-2002*. London: Verso, 2003.
Rojas, Cristina. "Securing the State and Developing Social Insecurities: The Securitisation of Citizenship in Contemporary Colombia." *Third World Quarterly* 30, no. 1 (2009): 227–245.
Rose-Ackerman, Susan. "The Economics of Corruption." *Journal of Public Economy* 4, no. 2 (1975): 187–203.
Rouadjia, Ahmed. "L'Etat algérien et le problème du droit." *Politique étrangère* 2 (1995): 351–363.
Rouquié, Alain. "Le camarade et le commandant: Réformisme militaire et légitimité institutionnelle." *Revue française de science politique* 29, no. 3 (1979): 381–401.
Roy, Olivier. *L'échec de l'islam politique*. Paris: Éditions du Seuil, 1992.
———. *L'islam mondialisé*. Paris: Éditions du Seuil, 2004.
Ruedy, John. *Modern Algeria: The Origin and Development of a Nation*. Bloomington: Indiana University Press, 2005.
Safouan, Moustafa. *Pourquoi le monde arabe n'est pas libre?* Paris: Éditions Denoël, 2008.
Said, Edward W. *Orientalism*. New York: Pantheon Books, 1978.
Sajed, Alina. "How We Fight: Anticolonial Imaginaries and the Question of National Liberation in the Algerian War." *Interventions* 21, no. 5 (2019): 635–651.
Sallam, Hesham. "The New Iraq and Arab Political Reform: Drawing New Boundaries (and Reinforcing Old Ones)." In *Iraq, Its Neighbors and the United States*, edited by Henry J. Barkey, Scott B. Lasensky, and Phebe Marr. Washington, DC: U.S. Institute of Peace Press, 2011.
Samraoui, Mohamed. *Chroniques des années de sang*. Paris: Éditions Denoël, 2003.
Sanchez, Gonzalo. *Guerre et politique en Colombie*. Paris: L'Harmattan, 1998.
Sanson, David, and Claire Le Breton. "Research Ties as Social Tales: Intimacy and Distance in Ethnography." *M@n@gement* 23, no. 3 (2020): 114–117.
Sanson, Henri. "Les motivations de la personnalité algérienne en ce temps de décolonisation." *Annuaire de l'Afrique du Nord* 6 (1968): 13–20.

Saou, Moustafa, and Hicham Betahar. "Dawr aṣ-ṣaḥāfa al-maktūba fī ṣaddi al-marjiʾiyyāt ad-dīniyya bi-Al-Jazāiʾr. Dirāsa taḥlīliyya ʿalā ʿayn min āʿʾadād yaūmiyat Al-Khabr." *Al-majala ad-dawliyya li-iʾltiṣāl al-iʾjtimāʿaī* 7, no. 1 (2020): 106–127.

Sari, Djilali. "Deux décennies d'urbanisation sans précédent en Algérie." In *Croissance démographique et urbanisation: Politique de peuplement et aménagement du territoire*, edited by Association internationale des démographes de langue française, 371–377. Paris: PUF, 1993.

Scagnetti, Jean-Charles. "Identité ou personnalité algérienne? L'édification d'une algérianité (1962-1988)." *Cahiers de la Méditerranée* 66 (2003): 367–384.

Schoumaker, Bruno, and Dominique Tabutin. "La démographie du monde arabe et du Moyen-Orient des années 1950 aux années 2000." *Population* 5–6 (2005): 611–724.

Scott, James C. *Domination and the Arts of Resistance: Hidden Transcripts*. New Haven, CT: Yale University Press, 1990.

Sebaa, Rabeh. "Les élections en Algérie ou la quête de fondements." *Confluences Méditerranée* 23 (1997): 103–106.

Selznick, Philip. *TVA and the Grass Roots*. Berkeley: University of California Press, 1949.

Semiane, Ahmed. *Octobre, ils parlent*. Algiers: Éditions Le Matin, 1998.

Semmoud, Nora. " 'Clair-obscur' de l'informel. Contrôle des polarités urbaines informelles à Cherarba, périphérie sud-est d'Alger." *Les Cahiers d'EMAM* 26 (2015). https://journals.openedition.org/emam/983.

Semprun, Jaime. *Apologie pour l'insurrection algérienne*. Paris: Éditions de l'encyclopédie des nuisances, 2001.

Serres, Thomas. "After the Apocalypse: Catastrophizing Politics in Post–Civil War Algeria." *Interdisciplinary Political Studies* 5, no. 1 (2019): 55–87.

———. "La 'jeunesse algérienne' en lutte. Du rôle politique conflictuel d'une catégorie sociale hétérogène." *Revue des mondes musulmans et de la Méditerranée* 134 (2013): 213–230.

Shepard, William. "Sayyid Qutb's Doctrine of Jahiliyya." *International Journal of Middle Eastern Studies* 35, no. 4 (2003): 521–545.

Sibeud, Emmanuelle. "Un ethnographe face à la colonisation: Arnold Van Gennep en Algérie (1911-1912)." *Revue d'histoire des sciences humaines* 10 (2004): 79–103.

Sidi Boumedine, Rachid. "L'urbanisme: Une prédation méthodique." *Naqd* 25 (2008): 109–133.

Sifaoui, Mohamed. *Histoire secrète de l'Algérie indépendante*. Paris: Nouveau monde éditions, 2012.

Silverstein, Paul. "An Excess of Truth: Violence, Conspiracy Theorizing and the Algerian Civil War." *Anthropological Quarterly* 75, no. 4 (2002): 643–674.

Simon, Catherine. *Algérie, les années pieds-rouges. Des rêves de l'indépendance au désenchantement (1962-1969)*. Paris: La Découverte, 2011.

Sindjoun, Luc. "Le Président de la République du Cameroun à l'épreuve de l'alternance néo-patrimoniale et de la 'transition démocratique.' " In *Les figures du politique en Afrique: Des pouvoirs hérités aux pouvoirs élus*, edited by Momar-Coumba Diop and Mamadou Diouf, 63–101. Dakar: CODESRIA; Paris: Karthala: 1999.

Sivan, Emmanuel. "Colonialism and Popular Culture in Algeria." *Journal of Contemporary History* 14, no. 1 (1979): 21–53.

Skocpol, Theda. *States and Social Revolutions: A Comparative Analysis of France, Russia, and China*. Cambridge: Cambridge University Press, 1979.

Slyomovics, Susan. "'The Ethnologist-Spy Was Hanged, at that Time We Were a Little Savage': Anthropology in Algeria with Habib Tengour." *boundary 2*, December 10, 2018. https://www.boundary2.org/2018/12/susan-slyomovics-the-ethnologist-spy-was-hanged-at-that-time-we-were-a-little-savage-anthropology-in-algeria-with-habib-tengour/.

Souaïdia, Habib. *La sale guerre*. Paris: Éditions La Découverte and Syros, 2001.

Souiah, Farida. "Humoriste, journaliste et artiste engagé." *L'Année du Maghreb* 15 (2016): 97–113.

———. "Les harraga algériens." *Migrations Société* 5, no. 143 (2012): 105–120.

———. "Les harraga en Algérie: Émigration et contestation." PhD diss., IEP Paris, 2014.

———. "La pénalisation des 'brûleurs' de frontières en Algérie." *Après-demain* 3, no. 39 (2016): 19–21.

Spivak, Gayatri. "Can the Subaltern Speak?" In *Marxism and the Interpretation of Culture*, edited by Cary Nelson and Lawrence Grossberg, 271–313. Basingstoke, UK: Macmillan Education, 1988.

———. "Subaltern Studies: Deconstructing Historiography." In *The Spivak Reader*, edited by Donna Landry and Gerald MacLean, 203–236. London: Routledge, 1996. First published 1985.

Stepan, Alfred C. *The Military in Politics: Changing Patterns in Brazil*. Princeton, NJ: Princeton University Press, 1971.

Steuer, Clément. "Les partis politiques fréristes en Egypte à la veille des élections parlementaires." *Moyen-Orient* 13 (2012): 28–31.

Stewart, Elizabeth. *Catastrophe and Survival: Walter Benjamin and Psychoanalysis*. New York: Continuum, 2010.

Stokes, Susan. "Perverse Accountability: A Formal Model of Machine Politics with Evidence from Argentina." *American Political Science Review* 99, no. 3 (2005): 315–325.

Stora, Benjamin. "Ce que dévoile une guerre. Algérie, 1997." *Politique étrangère* 4 (1997): 487–497.

———. "L'islamisme algérien." *Esprit* 196 (1993): 163–168.

Swearingen, Will. "Algeria's Food Security Crisis." *MERIP* 166 (1990): 21–25.

Taïeb, Emmanuel. "Logiques politiques du conspirationnisme." *Sociologie et sociétés* 42, no. 2 (2010): 265–289.

Talahite, Fatiha. "Economie administrée, corruption et engrenage de la violence en Algérie." *Tiers Monde* 41, no. 161 (2000): 49–74.

———. "La rente et l'État rentier recouvrent-ils toute la réalité de l'Algérie d'aujourd'hui?" *Tiers Monde* 210 (2012): 143–160.

Talha, Larbi. "Le régime rentier à l'épreuve de la transition institutionnelle: L'économie algérienne au milieu du gué." In *Où va l'Algérie?*, edited by Ahmed Mahiou and Jean-Robert Henry, 125–159. Paris: Karthala, 2001.

Taraud, Christelle. "Les *yaouleds*: Entre marginalisation sociale et sédition politique." *Revue d'histoire de l'enfance "irrégulière"* 10 (2008): 59–74.
Tarrow, Sidney. *Power in Movement: Social Movements and Contentious Politics.* Cambridge: Cambridge University Press, 2011.
Taylor, Dianna. "Hannah Arendt on Judgement: Thinking for Politics." *International Journal of Philosophical Studies* 10, no. 2 (2002): 151–169.
Temlali, Yassin. "Algérie-Egypte: Le football, révélateur des identités refoulés." *Afkar/Idée* 25 (2010): 51–53.
Ternisien, Xavier. *Les Frères musulmans.* Paris: Fayard, 2005.
Thénault, Sylvie. *Violence ordinaire dans l'Algérie coloniale.* Paris: Odile Jacob, 2012.
Thom, René. "Crise et catastrophe." *Communications* 25 (1976): 34–38.
Thompson, John B. "The Metamorphosis of a Crisis." In *Aftermath: The Culture of Economic Crisis*, edited by Manuel Castells, Joao Caraça, and Gustavo Cardoso, 59–81. Oxford: Oxford University Press, 2012.
Thurfjell, David. "Is the Islamist Voice Subaltern?" In *Postcolonial Challenges to the Study of Religion*, edited by Willy Pfändtner and David Thurfjell, 9–17. Uppsala: Swedish Science Press, 2008.
Tilly, Charles. *Coercion, Capital and European States.* Cambridge: Blackwell, 1992.
———. *Contentious Performances.* Cambridge: Cambridge University Press, 2008.
———. *From Mobilization to Revolution.* Reading, UK: Addison-Wesley, 1978.
———. *La France conteste de 1600 à nos jours.* Paris: Fayard, 1986.
———. "War Making and State Making as Organized Crime." In *Bringing the State Back In*, edited by Peter Evans, Dietrich Rueschemeyer, and Theda Skocpol, 169–187. Cambridge: Cambridge University Press, 1985.
Tizziani, Ania. "Du péronisme au populisme: La conquête conceptuelle du 'gros animal' populaire." *Tiers Monde* 189 (2007): 175–193.
Tlemçani, Rachid. "Les conditions d'émergence d'un nouvel autoritarisme en Algérie." *Revue du monde musulman et de la Méditerranée* 72 (1994): 108–118.
———. "Reflections on the Question of Political Transition in Africa: The Police State." In *Liberal Democracy and Its Critics in Africa*, edited by Tukumbi Lumumba-Kasongo, 26–45. London: Zed Books, 2005.
———. *State and Revolution in Algeria.* Boulder, CO: West View Press, 1986.
Tocqueville, Alexis de. *De la Démocratie en Amérique*, book 1. Paris: Garnier-Flammarion, 1981. First published 1835.
———. *L'Ancien régime et la Révolution.* Chicoutimi, QC: Éditions de l'UQAC, 2007. First published 1856.
Tozy, Mohamed. "Représentations/intercessions. Les enjeux de pouvoir dans les champs politiques désamorcés au Maroc." In *Changements politiques au Maghreb*, edited by Michel Camau, 153–168. Paris: CNRS Éditions, 1991.
Treacy, Corbin. "Writing in the Aftermath of Two Wars: Algerian Modernism and the Génération '88." In *Algeria: Nation, Culture and Transnationalism: 1988-2015*, edited by Patrick Crowley, 123–139. Liverpool, UK: Liverpool University Press, 2017.

Tripp, Charles. *The Power and the People: Path of Resistance in the Middle East*. Cambridge: Cambridge University Press, 2013.
Turkel, Gerald. "Michel Foucault: Law, Power and Knowledge." *Journal of Law and Society* 17, no. 2 (1990): 170–193.
Tyler, Imogen. *Revolting Subjects: Social Abjection and Resistance in Neoliberal Britain*. London: Zed Books, 2013.
Vaughan-Williams, Nick. "Borders, Territory, Law." *International Political Sociology* 2 (2008): 322–338.
Vázquez-Arroyo, Antonio Y. "How Not to Learn from Catastrophe: Habermas, Critical Theory and the 'Catastrophization' of Political Life." *Political Theory* 41, no. 5 (2013): 738–765.
Viratelle, Gérard. "Algérie: Les impatiences de l'armée." *Le mois en Afrique* 24 (December 1967): 2–7.
Vitalis, Robert. *America's Kingdom: Mythmaking and the Saudi Oil Frontier*. Stanford, CA: Stanford University Press, 2007.
Vultee, Fred. "Securitization: A New Approach to the Framing of the War on Terror." *Journalism Practice* 4 (2010): 33–47.
Wæver, Ole. "Politics, Security, Theory." *Security Dialogue* 42, nos. 4–5 (2011): 465–480.
Weeden, Lisa. *Ambiguities of Domination: Politics, Rhetoric and Symbols in Contemporary Syria*. Chicago: University of Chicago Press, 2015.
Weizman, Eyal. "Lethal Theory." *Log* 7 (2006): 53–77.
Werenfels, Isabelle. "Algeria's Legal Islamists: From "Fifth Column" to a Pillar of the Regime." In *Moderate Islamists as Reform Actors*, edited by Muriel Asseburg, 39–44. Berlin: SWP Research Paper, 2007.
———. "Beyond Authoritarian Upgrading: The Re-emergence of Sufi Orders in Maghrebi Politics." *Journal of North African Studies* 19, no. 3 (2014): 275–295.
———. *Managing Instability: Elites and Political Change in Algeria*. London: Routledge, 2007.
Wilkinson, David. *Revolutionary Civil War: The Elements of Victory and Defeat*. Palo Alto, CA: Page-Ficklin Publications, 1975.
Willis, Michael. *The Islamist Challenge in Algeria: A Political History*. New York: New York University Press, 1997.
Wolfe, Patrick. "Recuperating Binarism: A Heretical Introduction." *Settler Colonial Studies* 3, nos. 3–4 (2013): 257–279.
Wolpin, Miles D. "Military Radicalism in Latin America." *Journal of Interamerican Studies and World Affairs* 23, no. 4 (1981): 395–428.
Wood, Lesley J. *Crisis and Control: The Militarization of Protest Policing*. London: Pluto Press, 2014.
Younessi, Brahim. "L'islamisme algérien: Nébuleuse ou mouvement social?" *Politique étrangère* 60, no. 2 (1995): 365–376.
Zaki, Lamia. "Le clientélisme, vecteur de politisation en régime autoritaire?" In *Autoritarismes démocratiques et démocraties autoritaires au XXIè siècle*, edited by Olivier Dabène, Vincent Geisser, and Gilles Massardier, 157–180. Paris: La Découverte, 2008.

Zartman, William. "L'armée dans la politique algérienne." *Annuaire de l'Afrique du Nord* 7 (1969): 268–278.

Zeraoulia, Faouzia. "The Memory of the Civil War in Algeria: Lessons from the Past with Reference to the Algerian Hirak." *Contemporary Review of the Middle East* 7, no. 1 (2020): 25–53.

Zhu, Jiangnan, and Dong Zhang. "Weapons of the Powerful: Authoritarian Elite Competition and Politicized Anticorruption in China." *Comparative Political Studies* 50, no. 9 (2017): 1186–1220.

Zoubir, Yahia H. "Algeria and U.S. Interests: Containing Radical Islamism and Promoting Democracy." *Middle East Policy Council* 9, no. 1 (2002): 64–81.

———. "The Arab Spring: Is Algeria the Exception?" *IEMedsObs* 61 (2013). https://www.iemed.org/publication/the-arab-spring-is-algeria-the-exception/.

Zoubir, Yahia H., and Louisa Dris-Aït Hamadouche. "L'islamisme en Algérie: Institutionnalisation du politique et déclin du militaire." *Maghreb-Machrek* 188 (2006): 63–86.

Zubaida, Sami. *Law and Power in the Islamic World*. London: I. B. Tauris, 2003.

Articles from Newspapers, Magazines, and Websites

Abane, Meziane. "Tahar Belabbas, ancien leader du Mouvement des chômeurs dans le sud." *L'Avant-Garde*, September 3, 2019. https://www.lavantgarde-algerie.com/article/interviews/tahar-belabbas-ancien-leader-du-mouvement-des-chomeurs-dans-le-sud.

Abdoun, Mohamed. "Louisa Hanoune: 'L'Algérie est menacée d'éclatement.' " *L'Expression* (Algiers), February 26, 2004.

Addi, Lahouari. "Deux grands perdants de ces élections: Bouteflika et le FFS." *Le Quotidien d'Algerie* (Algiers), May 13, 2012.

Aimeur, Karim. "L'Algérie peut rattraper le déficit budgétaire en deux ans." *Le Soir d'Algérie* (Algiers), January 22, 2020.

Aït Ahmed, Hocine. "La troisième guerre d'Algérie." *Maroc Hebdo International* (Casablanca), November 15, 2001.

Aït Mouhoub, Zouheir. "L'argent: L'autre religion du Mouvement de la société pour la paix (MSP)." *El Watan* (Algiers), December 23, 2011.

Ait Ouarabi, Mokrane. "Bataille pour le contrôle du FLN." *El Watan* (Algiers), November 7, 2010.

Algérie Presse Service. "80 cas de violence enregistrés durant la phase aller de la saison footballistique." January 13, 2019. https://www.aps.dz/sport/83696-80-cas-de-violence-enregistres-durant-la-phase-aller-de-la-saison-footballistique.

———. "11.000 interventions de maintien de la sécurité publique en 2011 (DGSN)." January 5, 2012. https://www.djazairess.com/fr/apsfr/228277.

———. "Journée nationale du chahid: Déclaration du président de la République." February 18, 2014. https://www.aps.dz/algerie/69964-journee-nationale-du-chahid-message-du-president-abdelaziz-bouteflika.

———. "La candidature du président de la République pour un quatrième mandat, un gage de stabilité pour le pays (Saadani)." January 29, 2014. https://www.djazairess.com/fr/apsfr/343192.

———. "La maladie du président Bouteflika 'ne sera bientôt plus qu'un mauvais souvenir.' " *APS*, May 20, 2013. https://www.djazairess.com/fr/apsfr/303358.

———. "Le Président Tebboune confirme la poursuite des consultations politiques pour parvenir à une 'Constitution consensuelle.' " January 23, 2020. https://www.aps.dz/algerie/100546-le-president-tebboune-confirme-la-poursuite-des-consultations-politiques-pour-parvenir-a-une-constitution-consensuelle.

———. "Le taux de chômage en Algérie à 11,7% en septembre 2018." February 10, 2019. https://www.aps.dz/economie/85301-le-taux-de-chomage-en-algerie-a-11-7-en-septembre-2018.

———. "Personne n'a fait don à l'Algérie de la moindre parcelle de son territoire (Ouyahia)." April 7, 2012. https://www.djazairess.com/fr/apsfr/240807.

Alioua, Houria. "Les chômeurs déterminés à dénoncer la manipulation." *El Watan* (Algiers), April 18, 2013.

Allal, Mohammed. "Yacef Saadi yataḥaddath 'an dawrihi al-qiyādī fī al-'iḍrāb wa Zohra Drif tatajāhaluhu." *El Khabar* (Algiers), January 29, 2019.

Amari, Chawki. "Un ramadan algérien d'une rare violence." *SlateAfrique*, August 8, 2011. https://www.slateafrique.com/23677/algerie-ramadan-violences-drogue-pauvrete.

Arbane, Omar. "Bouira: Les gardes communaux protestent." *El Watan* (Algiers), October 23, 2018.

Arroudj, Adam. "Derrière la mobilisation populaire, le jeu ambigu des islamistes en Algérie." *Le Figaro* (Paris), March 15, 2019.

Ayoub, Saber. "Scotland Yard tuḥyī inḍibāṭ al-jazā'iriyyīn khilāl a"amāl shaghab London." *El Khabar* (Algiers), August 13, 2011.

Azzouz, Noureddine Azzouz. "Le MALG se penche sur sa propre histoire." *Le Quotidien d'Oran*, December 15, 2004.

B., Amel. "Abdelhaï Beliardouh a vécu le calvaire." *El Watan* (Algiers), December 16, 2012.

Babouche, Yacine. "L'Algérie utilise des outils de surveillance russe et chinois." *TSA*, September 21, 2019. https://www.tsa-algerie.com/lalgerie-utilise-des-outils-de-surveillance-russe-et-chinois/.

Bedouar, Noureddine. "La DGSN ne veut plus assumer seule la responsabilité." *El Watan* (Algiers), September 30, 2014.

Beldjena, Rabah. "19e anniversaire du 5 octobre 1988." *El Watan* (Algiers), October 6, 2007.

Belhouari, Noureddine. "Sā'at al-muslimīn tawaqqafat fī al-qarn ar-rābi'a al-hijrī." *El Khabar* (Algiers), August 28, 2011.

Belkaid, Akram. "Hirak." *Orient XXI*, November 15, 2019. https://orientxxi.info/magazine/hirak,3418.

Bellil, Belkacem. "Pour leur première sortie médiatique de retour en Algérie: De l'exil aux colonnes du Soir." *Le Soir d'Algérie* (Algiers), August 17, 2020.

Belmadi, Taïeb. "Tonic, le Titanic algérien." *Jeune Afrique*, September 10, 2009. https://www.jeuneafrique.com/201237/economie/tonic-le-titanic-alg-rien/.

Ben, M. "Ta'alīmat Ksentini nuffidhat bidāyiat juwān." *El Djazair El Djadida* (Algiers), August 27, 2010.
Benakli, Nadia. "Sidi Saïd renouvelle son soutien." *L'Expression* (Algiers), January 29, 2014.
Benfodil, Mustapha. "Immolations: Ces Mohamed Bouazizi que l'Algérie ne veut pas voir." *El Watan* (Algiers), February 3, 2012.
———. "Mystique et politique au temps de 'Sidi' Bouteflika." *El Watan* (Algiers), March 21, 2009.
Benyoub, Djilali. "Belkhadem veut 'relégitimer' les marches pacifiques!" *Liberté* (Algiers), January 9, 2011.
Betache, Aber. "La DGSN triple ses effectifs en cinq ans." *Le Soir d'Algérie* (Algiers), October 23, 2014.
Bouakba, Saad. "'Aārunā wa faḍīḥatuhum." *El Khabar* (Algiers), July 5, 2012.
Bouaricha, Nadjia. "Hocine Aït Ahmed: 'Remettre du mouvement dans le statu quo.'" *El Watan* (Algiers), March 3, 2012.
Bouati, Jalal. "Ash-sha'ab yarfuḍ at-taghīīr." *El Khabar* (Algiers), May 13, 2012.
Bouatih, Houda. "Ra'yis al-Jumhūriyya khaṭṭun a'ḥmar wa-lā naqbal al-misās bi-i'njāzātih." *Ech Cha'ab* (Algiers), May 12, 2018.
Boudia, Khaled. "Al-khiṭāb an-nārī li-Bouteflika." *El Khabar* (Algiers), November 29, 2018.
Bounab, Youcef Oussama. "As the Hirak Goes Online Due to COVID-19, So Does Repression." *Jadaliyya*, May 25, 2020. https://www.jadaliyya.com/Details/41168.
Bousri, Mohamed. "Bouteflika répond à ses opposants." *Ennaharonline*, February 24, 2011. https://www.djazairess.com/fr/ennaharfr/6642.
Bouthalji, Ilham. "Lan namūt juw'an wa-lan naqbal al-i'hāna . . . wa-li-i'stiqlāliyyat al-'adāla ṭāmiḥūn." *Echorouk* (Algiers), October 29, 2019.
Brahimi, Ali. "Elle court, elle court, la maladie de la violence." *Le Quotidien d'Oran*, September 13, 2012.
Bsikri, Mehdi. "Moussa Touati ouvre son parti au 'plus offrant.'" *El Watan* (Algiers), March 18, 2012.
Cheniki, Ahmed. "Amin Khan, auteur: Les territoires obscurs de l'illégitimité et le règne de l'argent." *Le Soir d'Algérie* (Algiers), April 18–19, 2014.
Cherak, Mohamed. "Arqām at-tashrī'aiyāt tukarris istimrār al-waḍa'a al-qāi'm." *El Khabar* (Algiers), May 12, 2012.
Hamid, Yas, and Atef Kedadra. "Mashrū'a qānūn al-I''alām yulghī i'rādat ar-rai'ys fī al-i'ṣlāḥāt." *El Khabar* (Algiers), August 20, 2011
Daoud, Kamel. "Oui, il faut changer le peuple!" *Le Quotidien d'Oran*, May 23, 2014.
———. "Une Algérie incroyablement sale: L'autre peuple plastic." *Le Quotidien d'Oran*, August 18, 2014.
Davis, Muriam Haleh, Hiyem Cheurfa, and Thomas Serres. "A Hirak Glossary: Terms from Algeria and Morocco." *Jadaliyya*, June 13, 2019. https://www.jadaliyya.com/Details/38734.
Demmad, Akila. "La baisse des prix du pétrole impose une prudence dans la conduite de nos affaires économiques." *El Moudjahid* (Algiers), July 9, 2012.
Derradji, Hafid. "Qaswatunā laysat ḥiqdan." *Echorouk* (Algiers), August 20, 2011.

Djouadi, Farouk. "Manif à Alger contre la nouvelle loi sur les hydrocarbures." *El Watan* (Algiers), October 13, 2019.

Dridi, Daikha. "Qui sont les prisonniers politiques algériens?" *Middle East Eye*, December 23, 2019. https://www.middleeasteye.net/fr/en-bref/qui-sont-les-prisonniers-politiques-algeriens.

Ech Cha'ab. "Al-farīq Gaïd Salah yushaddid 'alā a'nnah 'lā muhādana wa-lā tā'jīl li-mas'aā muḥārabat al-fasād.'" *Ech Cha'ab* (Algiers), June 27, 2019.

Echorouk. "Bouteflika yudāfi'a 'an al-jaysh wa 'yadhbaḥ' Saâdani." *Echorouk* (Algiers), February 11, 2014.

———. "Hamrouche yad'aū ath-thulāthī Bouteflika, Gaïd Salah wa Toufik li-ijmā'a waṭanī." *Echorouk* (Algiers), March 30, 2014.

El Khabar. "Ḥarb at-taḥrīr ḥaqqaqat al-istiqlāl wa-lam tuḥaqqiq ad-dīmuqrāṭiyya." *El Khabar* (Algiers), July 5, 2011.

El Moudjahid. "Formation de la police scientifique." *El Moudjahid* (Algiers), February 3, 2018.

———. "Un choix délibéré pour éviter toute effusion de sang." *El Moudjahid* (Algiers), May 24, 2012.

El Watan. "Ouargla: Une liste de bénéficiaires de logements provoque l'émeute." *El Watan* (Algiers), April 10, 2013.

———. "Quand les chômeurs se muent en force politique." *El Watan* (Algiers), February 3, 2014.

———. "Selon Tayeb Louh, les chômeurs sont 'manipulés' et 'mal-élevés'!" *El Watan* (Algiers), June 26, 2012.

Ennahar. "Al-mulāḥiẓūn ad-duwaliyūn yushīdūn bi-miṣdāqiyyat wa shafāfiyyat al-i'ntikhābāt at-tashrī'iyya al-jazāi'riyya." *Ennahar* (Algiers), May 12, 2012.

Farrah, Raouf. "Tin Zaoutine. Marginalisation et militarisation aux confins des frontières algériennes." *Jadaliyya*, July 15, 2020. https://www.jadaliyya.com/Details/41416.

Fattani, Tahar. "Les Algériens plébiscitent Bouteflika à 90,24%." *L'Expression* (Algiers), April 11, 2009.

Fethi, Nazim. "Algérie: Bras de fer entre les chômeurs et le gouvernement." *Magharebia*, March 26, 2013. https://www.courrierinternational.com/article/2013/03/26/bras-de-fer-entre-les-chomeurs-et-le-gouvernement.

Ghriss, Mohamed. "Le 19 septembre 1988: Le jour où Chadli . . ." *Le Quotidien d'Oran*, September 19, 2009.

Guisnel, Jean. "Interview: Le Général de corps d'armée Mohamed Lamari." *Le Point* (Paris), January 15, 2003.

Haddag, Khaled. "Les militants du comité des chômeurs dénoncent le harcèlement des autorités locales." *Le Temps d'Algérie* (Algiers), March 18, 2011.

Hafid, Tarek. "Mohamed Chafik Mesbah au Soir d'Algérie: 'Le système n'est pas mûr pour des élections libres.'" *Le Soir d'Algérie* (Algiers), June 20, 2012.

Henneberg, Sabina. "Algeria's Bouteflika Is on His Way Out. Here's What's Next." *Foreign Policy*, April 2, 2019. https://foreignpolicy.com/2019/04/02/algeria-bouteflika-is-on-his-way-out-heres-whats-next-oil-russia-protest-army/.

Horizons. "La DGSN dement toute violence policière." *Horizons* (Algiers), December 2, 2013.
Kateb, Hakim. "Nos militants sont tous pour la réconciliation." *L'Expression* (Algiers), September 17, 2005.
Kauffmann, Sylvie, and Isabelle Mandraud. "L'Algérie défend 'l'intégrité territoriale du Mali.' " *Le Monde* (Paris), April 6, 2012.
Koursi, Mohamed. "Ouyahia fait parler les chiffres." *El Moudjahid* (Algiers), December 20, 2010.
L., Samira. "Ouyahia: Āḥdāth u'ktūbar 1988 u'dkhilat Al-Jazāi'r fī 'ahd al-fawḍā wa-llā-i'stiqrār." *Ennahar* (Algiers), October 6, 2018.
Lalami, Djamel. "Limādhā dāfa'a Bouteflika 'an ḥaṣīlatih wa-lawaḥ bi-ri'āsiyyāt musbaqat?" *Echorouk* (Algiers), December 10, 2006.
Liberté. "Déclaration du secrétariat national de l'UGTA." *Liberté* (Algiers), January 8, 2011.
Louni, Arezki. "Ethique et liberté de la presse ne sont pas antinomiques." *L'Expression* (Algiers), May 3, 2004.
M., Mounir. "Iḥtijājāt 'anīfa wasaṭ madīnat Jījal." *El Khabar* (Algiers), April 30, 2012.
Malti, Hocine. " Algérie: Lettre ouverte au général de corps d'armée Mohamed 'Tewfik' Médiène, Rab Dzayer." *Blog Mediapart*, February 17, 2013. https://blogs.mediapart.fr/hocine-malti/blog/170213/algerie-lettre-ouverte-au-general-de-corps-darmee-mohamed-tewfik-mediene-rab-dzayer.
Mammeri, Achira. "Bouteflika signe la mort politique de Belkhadem, de plus en plus incontrôlable." *TSA*, August 26, 2014. http://archives2014.tsa-algerie.com/2014/08/26/bouteflika-signe-la-mort-politique-de-belkhadem-de-plus-en-plus-incontrolable/.
Mansour, Massinissa. "Atteinte à la vie privée: L'Algérie se dote d'un système de surveillance de masse." *Algérie Focus* (Algiers), June 15, 2017.
Marzuq, Adisa. "Al-lughāt al-a'jnabiyya wa-l-vīzā hakadhā yunasar al-jazāi'riyyūn." *Ennahar* (Algiers), August 16, 2010.
Matarese, Mélanie. "Les chômeurs du Sud algérien: Le revers de la rente." *Middle East Eye*, March 1, 2016. https://www.middleeasteye.net/fr/reportages/les-chomeurs-du-sud-algerien-le-revers-de-la-rente.
McDougall, James. "Algeria's Terrorist Attacks Owe Little to Its 'Pathological' History." *The Guardian* (London), January 22, 2013.
Mebtoul, Abderrahmane. "Que nous apprennent les résultats?," *La Nouvelle République* (Algiers), May 13, 2012.
Mehdi, Mohamed. "Les résultats des élections." *Le Quotidien d'Oran*, May 12, 2012.
Mehenni, Makhlouf. "Abdelmalek Sellal: 'La Conférence nationale aura lieu immédiatement après l'élection.' " *TSA*, February 16, 2019. https://www.tsa-algerie.com/abdelmalek-sellal-la-conference-nationale-aura-lieu-immediatement-apres-lelection/.
Menia, Salaheddine. "La société souffre d'immaturité affective." *L'Expression* (Algiers), August 27, 2011.

Mesbah, Salim. "Tentative d'incendie de l'imprimerie d'El Watan et d'El Khabar." *El Watan* (Algiers), September 16, 2011.

Mostefaoui, Belkacem. "Gouvernance féodale." *El Watan* (Algiers), June 1, 2006.

Mouffok, Ghania. "Retour sur la marche d'Alger: La révolution de onze heures à midi." *Maghreb émergent*, February 15, 2011. https://maghrebemergent.net/retour-sur-la-marche-d-alger-la-revolution-de-onze-heures-a-midi/.

Muhammad. "Bouteflika a"aṭā a'ms al-ḍaw' al-a'khḍar li-bidāyat istighlāl miyāh maḥaṭṭat al-ḥāma." *Ennahar* (Algiers), February 24, 2008.

Ouali, Hacen. "Ouyahia est un despote, un danger pour le pays." *El Watan* (Algiers), March 28, 2012.

Oubraham, Sihem. "La mission déclare le scrutin libre, transparent, régulier et équitable." *El Moudjahid* (Algiers), May 12, 2012.

Oukaci, Fayçal. "L'Armée s'implique." *L'Expression* (Algiers), January 30, 2005.

———. "Nous sommes à 'terrorisme zéro' dans notre région." *L'Expression* (Algiers), April 21, 2006.

Oukazi, Ghania. "Limogé par Bouteflika: Le dossier Belkhadem n'est pas clos." *Le Quotidien d'Oran*, September 3, 2014.

Rahal, Malika. "Algeria Joins the Arab Spring." *Politico*, March 12, 2019. https://www.politico.eu/article/algeria-joins-the-arab-spring/.

Rahmani, Mohamed. "Algérie: Législatives à Souk-Ahras—Une primaire du FNA pervertie par la 'Ch'kara.'" *La Tribune* (Algiers), April 1, 2012.

Rezaoui, Lakhdar. "Taḥāluf mufājī' bayna Saâdani wa 'Abāda." *Echorouk* (Algiers), June 13, 2014.

R. M. "FFS: Ali Laskri qualifie le RCD de 'harki du système.'" *Le Matin d'Algérie*, March 4, 2012. https://www.lematindz.net/news/7524-ffs-ali-laskri-qualifie-le-rcd-de-harki-du-systeme.html.

Rouadjia, Ahmed. "Petit essai sur la sociologie de la misère à l'université de Msila." *Le Quotidien d'Algérie* (Algiers), July 13, 2010.

Semmar, Abdou. "Affaire Général Toufik: Un parti politique accuse Amar Saâdani d'être un agent des services secrets français." *Algérie Focus* (Algiers), February 5, 2014.

———. "Ouyahia: Un pied à la présidence en attendant le 2ème?" *Algérie Focus* (Algiers), March 13, 2014.

———. "Tahkout: 'Ouyahia n'a jamais été mon associé et je n'ai jamais détourné d'argent public.'" *Algérie Focus* (Algiers), August 29, 2013.

Souames, Farah. "Indignity and Solidarity Are Being Televised in Algiers." *Africa Is a Country*, March 4, 2019. https://africasacountry.com/2019/03/indignity-and-solidarity-are-being-televised-in-algeria.

T., Khaled. "Augmentation du taux de recrutement dans le rang de l'armée." *Ennaharonline*, April 24, 2011. https://www.vitaminedz.com/fr/Algerie/augmentation-du-taux-de-recrutement-dans-289880-Articles-0-18300-1.html.

Tazerout, Idir. "Ayez confiance en votre pays." *Le Soir d'Algérie* (Algiers), March 17, 2013.

Tir, Ilhem. "4536 protestations ont eu lieu cette année dont 3029 de nature violente." *Le Temps d'Algérie* (Algiers), October 3, 2012.

Tlemçani, Salima. "Oultache a grièvement blessé Tounsi et d'autres l'ont achevé." *El Watan* (Algiers), February 24, 2011.
———. "Procès de l'ex-patron de la police Abdelghani Hamel: Des walis qui évoquent des pressions et des menaces." *El Watan* (Algiers), March 16, 2020.
Touihri, Aïda. "Médias sous pression." *Jeune Afrique* (Paris), July 19, 2004.
Wakli, Essaïd. "Louisa Hanoune: Ce que j'ai dit à Bouteflika." *Algérie Focus* (Algiers), May 2, 2014.
Yas, Hamid. "Belkhadem rafaʻa taqrīrān li-Bouteflika ʻan aʼḥdāth al-Aurāsī." *El Khabar* (Algiers), June 25, 2014.
———. "Min fāiʻdat al-qadāʼ wa-s-sulṭa adh-dhahāb baʻaīdān fi qaḍiyyat al-Bushi." *El Khabar* (Algiers), June 28, 2018.

Reports from Governments, International Institutions, and NGOs

Assam, Yahia. "Les instruments juridiques de la répression." Comité Justice pour l'Algérie, Dossier No. 15 (May 2004). https://www.algerie-tpp.org/tpp/pdf/dossier_15 _instruments_juridiques.pdf.
Bank of Algeria. *Rapport sur la stabilité du secteur bancaire algérien (2009–2011)*. Algiers: Bank of Algeria, 2013. https://www.bank-of-algeria.dz/rapport-sur-la-stabilite-du-secteur -bancaire-algerien/.
Bozerup, Rasmus. *Authoritarianism and Media in Algeria*. Copenhagen: International Media Support, 2013. https://www.mediasupport.org/publication/authoritarianism-and -media-in-algeria/.
General Directorate for Economic and Financial Affairs. *Examen de la situation économique des partenaires méditerranéen de l'UE*. Brussels: European Commission, 2003. https:// op.europa.eu/fr/publication-detail/-/publication/a1e17fbd-d3d9-4870-a9a0 -e24af4a9f492/language-fr/format-PDF/source-280022220.
General Directorate for External Policies. *L'Algérie: Un potentiel sous-exploité pour la coopération en matière de sécurité dans la région du Sahel*. Brussels: European Parliament, 2013. https://www.europarl.europa.eu/RegData/etudes/briefing_note/join/2013 /491510/EXPO-AFET_SP(2013)491510_FR.pdf.
International Crisis Group. *Elections présidentielles en Algérie: Les enjeux et les perspectives*. Algérie rapport No. 4. Brussels: International Crisis Group, 1999.
———. *La Concorde Civile: Une initiative de paix manquée*. Afrique rapport No. 31. Brussels: International Crisis Group, 2001.
———. *La presse dans la tourmente électorale*. Algérie rapport No. 2. Brussels: International Crisis Group, 1999.
International Labour Organization. *Rapport de la Commission d'experts pour l'application des conventions et recommandations*. Geneva: International Labour Organization, 2012. https://www.ilo.org/public/libdoc/ilo/P/09662/09662(2012-101-1A).pdf.
International Monetary Fund. *Algeria: Selected Issues*. IMF Country Report No. 14/342. Washington, DC: IMF, 2014. https://www.imf.org/external/pubs/ft/scr/2014/cr14342.pdf.

Kaddour, Houari. *Rapport sur les logements préfabriqués dans la Wilaya de Chlef*. Chlef: LADDH, 2014.
NABNI (Notre Algérie Bâtie sur de Nouvelles Idées). *Cinquantenaire de l'indépendance: enseignement et vision pour l'Algérie de 2020*. January 2013. http://nabni.org/wp-content/uploads/2012/12/Nabni-Economie-2020.pdf.
National Democratic Institute. *Rapport final sur les élections législatives en Algérie*. Washington, DC: National Democratic Institute, 2012. https://www.ndi.org/sites/default/files/Algeria-Report-Leg-Elections-FRE.pdf.
Organisation for Economic Co-operation and Development. *Perspectives économiques en Afrique 2008* Paris: OECD Publishing, 2008. https://doi.org/10.1787/aeo-2008-fr.
——. *Rapport sur les perspectives économiques en Afrique*. 2012.
Transparency International. "Corruption Perception Index, 2014." Transparency International, accessed February 22, 2023. https://www.transparency.org/en/cpi/2014.

Documentaries and Films

Allouache, Merzak, dir. *Bal El-Oued City*. 1994; Algiers: Jacques Bidou, Jean-Pierre Gallèpe, and Yacine Djadi.
Bensmaïl, Malek, dir. *Aliénations*. 2004; Paris: Ina and France 5 unité documentaire; Dubai: O3 Productions; Genève: Télévision suisse romande.
Djahnine, Habiba, dir. *Avant de franchir la ligne d'horizon*. 2011; Montreuil, FR: Polygone étoilé.
Ferhani, Hassen, dir. *A Roundabout in my Head*. 2015; Paris: Centrale électrique; Algiers: Allers Retours Films.
Sayad, Karim, dir. *Of Sheep and Men*. 2017; Geneva: Close Up Films; Paris: Norte Productions; Doha: Doha Film Institute.

Index

Abdennour, Ali Yahia, 163
Aboud, Hichem, 240, 349n46
abstention, from elections, xiv, 138, 146, 148, 157–161, 277, 286
accumulation by dispossession, 28, 272
activism, 42, 171–173, 192, 239, 281
ᶜAdala, Al-, 132, 305
Adami, Mohamed, 59, 98
Addi, Lahouari, 63, 147, 260–261
affairistes (cronies), xi, 92, 98, 201, 305
African Cup of Nations, 275
Agamben, Giorgio, 29–30, 152, 175–176
agriculture, 72, 93, 234, 257
Aïbek, Abdelmalek, 214
Aïn Bessem, xxii, 193–196, *196*, 197
Aïn El-Turk, 193–196, 265
Aït Ahmed, Hocine, 159, 178, 269
Aït Hamouda, Amirouche (Amirouche, the Wolf of Akfadou), 138, 333n64
Aït Hamouda, Nordine, 138
Aït Messaoudene, Noureddine, 124, 127, 128–129, 152
Aït Ouarabi, Abdelkader (General), 62
Alawiyya brotherhood, 91

Algerian Institute of Hydrocarbons, 77
Algerian Network of Young Activists, 139
Algerian People's Movement, 180
Algerian personality (*shakhsiyya jazāi'riyya*), 30, 234, 256, 266
"Algerian Spring," 154–161
Algeria Watch, 165
Algérie patriotique (online news outlet), 165
Ali la Pointe (Ali Ammar), 228, 350n63
Allouache, Merzak, 238
ALN (Armée de Libération Nationale, National Liberation Army), 7, 46, 51, 52, 55, 60, 305
Aloui, Abdelghani, 170
al-Qaeda, 64, 210, 320n73
Amar, Azouz, 80
Amari, Chawki, 258
ANP (Armée Nationale Populaire, National People's Army), 7, 9, 147, 155, 234, 240, 305; cartelized power structure and, 283, 288; confronted on social media, 161; as criticized institution, 52–54; disinformation

ANP (*continued*)
    and, 241; employees, 215, 258; immune defense and, 45–47, 49; praetorianism and indispensable, 54–56; praetorianism contradictions and, 50–51; with weaponization of media, 165
APN (Assemblée populaire nationale, People's National Assembly), 43, 119, 132, 135, 160, 182, 305; Belkhadem and, 116–117; composition after 2012 legislative elections, *136, 137*; with fraud inquiry, 120; with laws, 38
APW (Assemblée populaire de wilaya, People's Assembly of Wilaya), xvii, 84, 179, 305
Arabization, 234, 235, 256, 257
Arab uprisings (2010–2011), x, 111, 144, 145–146, 153, 154
Arendt, Hannah, xix, 174, 271, 272, 346n112
Arkoun, Mohamed, 16
Armée de Libération Nationale. *See* ALN
Armée Nationale Populaire. *See* ANP
army, xx, 33, 35, 42, 50–54, 283. *See also* ANP; military
Assad, Bashar al-, 111, 255
Assemblée populaire de wilaya. *See* APW
Assemblée populaire nationale. *See* APN
Association of Ulema, 121, 256
austerity, 13, 148, 288
authoritarianism, 14–16, 27, 38, 74, 111, 147, 175
autonomy, 186, 187, 233; MAK, 177, *183*, 184–185, 290, 307; SNAPAP, 163, 278, 281, 282, 308
Ayat, Lakehal, 144

Bab El-Oued City (film), 238
Bab El-Oued neighborhood, xiv, 154, 281, 284
Banna, Hassan al-, 121

Banque de l'Agriculture et du Développement Rural (Bank of Agriculture and Rural Development), 93
Barakat ("Enough") movement, xii–xiii, 13, 305
barbéfélènes, 116–118, 148
"bataille d'Alger, La," 228
Battle of Algiers, 249
Baudrillard, Jean, 217, 220, 252, 272
Bedoui, Noureddine, 286
Béjaïa Doc (film workshop), 269–270
Belabbes, Tahar, 206, 210, 285, 342n43
Belhadj, Ali, 8, 122, 123
Beliardouh, Abdelhaï, 167
Belkacem, Krim, 243
Belkhadem, Abdelaziz, xxi, 70, 116–118, 148
Belkheir, Larbi, 61, 110, 244, 247
Belmadi, Djamel, 274, 275
Beloucif, Mostefa, 51, 247, 320n69
Ben 'Ali, Zine el-'Abidine, 32–33, 223
Benbada, Mustapha, 131
Ben Badis, Abdelhamid, 121, 289
Ben Bella, Ahmed, 34, 135, 177, 233
Benbitour, Ahmed, 77, 92
Ben Bouali, Hassiba, 350n63
Benbouzid, Boubekeur, 247–248
Benchicou, Mohamed, 167–168, 176
Benchikh, Madjid, 63
Bendjedid, Chadli, 4–7, 9–11, 34, 91–92, 171, 251
Benflis, Ali, xiv, xv, 6, 11, 42, 60, 93
Benfodil, Mustapha, 91, 268–269, 340n3
Benhadid, Hocine, 62
Benhamou, Mohamed, 135
Benhamouda, Abdelhak, 85, 238
Beni Messous massacre (1997), 239
Benjamin, Walter, 19, 29, 30, 171, 190, 192, 226, 252, 282
Bennabi, Malek, 16, 121, 231, 261, 262, 268
Bennadji, Chérif, 12

Bensalah, Abdelkader, 38, 114, 275, 317n21
Bensmaïl, Malek, 227, 258–259
Bentobal, Lakhdar, 243
Benyounes, Amara, 180
Berberism, 145, 153, 177–180, 182, 184, 189, 216, 245
Berber Spring (1980), 5, 11
Betchine, Mohamed, 35, 59, 98
Black Spring (2001), 42, 177–178, 180–181, *183*, 184, 186, 225, 333n79
Bled Miki ("Country of Mickey [Mouse]"), 249–253, 272, 305
"Bled Miki" (song), 251
bleuite (blue scare, paranoia), 62–63, 241, 242
Bouazizi, Mohamed, 191
Bouchachi, Mostefa, 159
Bouchouareb, Abdeslam, 92, 106
Boudiaf, Boussad, 182, 188, 339n92
Boudiaf, Mohamed, 9, 32, 34–35, 171, 238, 243–245, 349n56
Boukrouh, Noureddine, 268
Boumediene, Houari, 2, 4–5, 34, 36, 50–51, 111, 113, 233–235
Bounedjah, Baghdad, 275
Bourdieu, Pierre, 16, 57, 63, 160
Bouregaâ, Lakhdar, 285
Bouslimani, Mohamed, 123
Boussouf, Abdelhafid, 243–244
Boustila, Ahmed, 79, 83
Bouteflika, Abdelaziz, xiv, 33, 50, 92, 112, 114, 117, 237, 276; Algeria of, 3, 14–20; ANP and, 52, 56; Benflis and, 11, 42; Bled Miki and, 252; in cartoons, 166; clientelism under, 101, 102; corruption under, 96, 97, 150; criticism of, 60, 63, 66, 70, 150, 167–168, 250–251; elections, ix–xiii, 13, 41–44, 61, 87, 274, 281; with embezzlement, 5, 77, 84; after ischemic stroke, x, xi, xv, 12, 34, 39, 41, 66, 68, 211; joke, 265; MSP under, 122–123; National Tragedy and, 10, 43, 69; with presidency, 38, 39–40, 41–45; with reforms, 155–156; resignation of, 14, 79, 97–98, 150–151, 274, 278, 284; return of, 35–37; rumors and conspiracy theories under, 247, 248; social inequality under, 192, 201, 202; social pact of, 242; speeches, 70, 160; state technicians under, 76, 77; support for, 89, 129, 133
Bouteflika, Saïd, 37, 94
Bouyali, Moustafa, 5
Bozarslan, Hamit, 46, 57
Brahimi, Abdelhamid, 247
Brahimi, Mohamed El Bachir El, 256

capitalists, crony, 91–95
Carlier, Omar, 88, 112, 198, 353n135
cartelized power structure, 58, 107, 149–150, 277, 283, 288; clientelism and, 91, 99–102; components, xx–xxi, 73–74, 95–106; corruption and, 96–99; internal restructuring, 69–71, 276, 286; mobilization against, 274–275, 278; necropolitics and, 66–69; parties, 84–85, 87, 91, 111, 113–116, 118–120, 136; political order and, 102–106; political rationale of suspicion and, 62–65; Presidential Alliance and, xxi, 45, 85, 87, 112–120, 123, 128, 130–131, 159; with protesters, 284–285; quarrels, 59–62; ruling coalition as, xx, 33, 56–57; state field, 74–84; at state periphery, 84–95; in 2011, *108*; in 2019, *109*; with ways of criticism, 161–166
cartoons, 112, 166, 167, 176
catastrophization, 20–27. *See also* governance by catastrophization
censorship, repression and, 166–177
Center for Communication and Diffusion, 51

Chaalal, Mahmoud Omar, 91
Chambi, the, 212
Chaoui, 250; Chaoui triangle, 266, 353n129
Charef, Abed, 237–238
Charter for Peace and National Reconciliation, 42, 69, 143, 164
chemma (chewing tobacco and fig tree ashes), 155, 194, 341n10
Cherak, Mohamed, 63
Chikhi, Saïd, 5
children, 89, 133, 210, 221, 248; people-as-child, 147–148, 161, 168, 219, 262, 272; trafficking of, 217. *See also* youth
China, 170, 248, 342n29
Chkoupistan, 251, 272, 305
Chlef, xvi–xix, 19, 82, 84, 86, 88, 89
Citizens' Movement, 145, 181–183, 305, 333n79, 339n93, 343n46
"Civil Concord" (*al-Wi'ām al-Madanī*), 10, 41, 176
"civil war" (*ḥarb ā'hliyya*), 235–237. *See also* Dark Decade
class: middle, xii, 9, 126; people-as-class, 146–148, 249, 281; predatory alliance, 74; upper, 9, 54, 193, 198; working, 5, 7, 126. *See also* ruling class
CLE (Coordination locale des étudiants, Local Coordination of Students), 139
clientelism, 16, 91, 99–102, 197
"clientelistic mediation" (*médiation clientélaire*), 82
CNCD (Coordination Nationale pour le Changement et la Démocratie, National Coordination for Change and Democracy), 154, 187, 204, 219, 305
CNDDC (Comité national pour la défense des droits des chômeurs, National Committee for the Defense of the Rights of the Unemployed), xxii, 156, 192, 226, 230, 305; against internal colonialism, 205–207; with pacifism, patriotism and autonomy from politics, 207–210; at protests with bodies mutilated, 213–214; routinization of social movements and, 210–212
Collective of Families of the Disappeared in Algeria, 163–164
Colombia, 220–221, 223–224
colonialism, xix, 26, 68, 234, 261, 278; French, 4, 30, 186; internal, 205–207, 209, 213, 229, 248, 276, 280
Comité national pour la défense des droits des chômeurs. *See* CNDDC
communal guards (*shanbīṭ, chambit*), 80, 215
conspiracy theories, ruling elite and, 247–249
Constitutional Council, 39, 275
contradictory consciousness, 265–267
co-option, MSP and, 120–132
Coordination locale des étudiants. *See* CLE
Coordination Nationale pour le Changement et la Démocratie. *See* CNCD
Coronil, Fernando, 17, 40
corruption, 2, 16, 33, 59, 105, 131, 195, 197; cement of, 96–99; financial crimes, 79, 93–94; fraud, 35, 120, 130, 161; government, 5, 51, 61, 63; nepotism and, 52, 53, 54; *shkara*, 134, 150, 276, 308. *See also* embezzlement
"cosmetic democracy" (*démocratie de façade*), 111, 140, 251
Council of the Nation, 38, 114
COVID-19 pandemic, 275, 287, 290
criminalization, 175, 212, 224, 284–285, 287, 288
crisis, 20–22, 24, 47–51, 140, 278, 320n73
crisis, as lived experience, 190, 191, 199, 230; dualist representations of polity and, 218–220; with management by scarcity, 214–216, 223; social fatigue, 220–229; social

inequality and, xxii, 192–205, 265; the South, unemployment and, 205–214; terrorizing spectacle and, 217–218
crisis, historical overview, xx, 1, 2, 11; academic literature and, 15–17; Algeria of A. Bouteflika, 3, 14–20; to catastrophization, 20–27; climax, 6–10; governance by catastrophization, 27–31; the Hirak, 12–14; premises, 4–6; ragpicker and, 17–20
criticism, xv, 111, 149, 179, 180, 254; of cartel parties, 118–120; of A. Bouteflika, 60, 63, 66, 70, 150, 167–168, 250–251; public, 112, 120, 152, 153, 166, 177; ways of, 161–166
cronies (*affairistes*), xi, 92, 98, 201, 305
crony capitalists, 91–95
"cultural hegemony," 27, 267
culturalism, reproduction of: "changing the people," 262–264; continuum of binaries, 255–257; epistemological deadlock, 253–255; ethnography and democracy, 260–262; pathology and discipline, 257–259
cynicism, rejection of, 242–253

DA (dinar algérien, Algerian dinar), 98, 168, 170, 195, 203, 215, 306; corruption and, 96, 131; devaluation of, 73
Dahmen, Abdelkrim, 67, 123–124, 125, 126, 130, 238
Daoud, Kamel, 263, 264
Dark Decade (*al-ʿUshriyya as-Sawdāaʾ*) (1990s), 9, 14, 46, 73, 92, 114, 164, 309n3; Chlef in, xvii–xix; "civil war," 235–237; memories of, 25, 43, 155, 173–174, 266; National Tragedy, 10, 43, 69, 144, 155, 170, 235, 307; repetition of, xx, 28, 33, 292; social deviance and, 220–222; with torture, 321n104; violence of, xix, 15, 240–241

debt, 5, 73, 234
décideurs ("decision makers"): APN as tool for, 160; with assassination, 244–245; military officers as, 39, 45, 65, 68, 76, 94, 306, 318n26; as threat, 164, 174, 251
deep state, 64, 65, 74, 75, 76, 240
democracy, 2, 16, 126, 283, 341n9; CNCD, 154, 187, 204, 219, 305; cosmetic, 111, 140, 251; ethnography and, 260–262. *See also* RCD; RND
Democratic and Social Union, 183
democratic globalization, 111, 153, 161, 163, 168, 172
democratization, 27, 90, 153, 154, 271; authoritarian rule and, 14, 15, 111; economic liberalization and, 57, 73–74; process of, xxi, 126, 152, 283
demonstrations. *See* protests
Département du Renseignement et de la Sécurité. *See* DRS
Derradji, Hafid, 258
DGSN (Direction Générale de la Sûreté Nationale, General Directorate for National Safety), 63, 83, 215, 217, 218, 306; agents of, xii; Catholic Church and, 80–81; police, 79, 156
Diaz (rapper), 228
"dignity" (*karama*), 307
Dilem, Ali, 112, 166, 167, 176
Direction des études chargée de la Programmation et de la Formation (Directorate of Planning and Training Studies), 80
Direction Générale de la Sûreté Nationale. *See* DGSN
Directorate of Counterintelligence, 239
Directorate of Military Factories, 47
Directorate of Planning and Training Studies (Direction des études chargée de la Programmation et de la Formation), 80
disappeared, by state, 163–164, 173–174

disenchantment, 7, 64, 225, 249
disinformation, 241, 288
dispossession, accumulation by, 28, 272
Djaballah, Abdallah, 87, 132, 210
Djabi, Abdelnasser, 118
Djahnine, Habiba, 227, 228, 269–270, 346n107
Djaout, Tahar, 178, 244, 245, 254
Djerad, Abdelaziz, 77, 286
Djerrar, Abdelghani, 93, 94
Djilali, Soufiane, 222, 242, 261–262, 267–268
Djoudi, Karim, 77, 220
Dobry, Michel, 20–21, 23, 24
documentary films, 227–228, 229, 258–259, 269–270
Donquishoot (rapper), 228
Drif, Zohra, 249, 350n63
Dris, Chérif, 165
DRS (Département du Renseignement et de la Sécurité, Department of Intelligence and Security), xi, xiii, 140, 211, 239, 240, 306; FLN and, 61–62, 116; politics and, 63–65; Special Intervention Group, 51, 255, 320n73
drugs, 13, 58, 80, 239, 258, 276
"dual power," 229, 346n112
Dzaïr TV, 94
DZjoker (YouTuber), 252–253

East-West Highway, 10, 13, 61, 130, 180–181, 200
Ebossé, Albert, 218
Echorouk (newspaper), 164, 258
Echorouk (private media group), 94
Echorouk TV, 156
École Nationale d'Administration (National School of Administration), 76, 77, 158, 286
École Normale Supérieure, 282
economic liberalization, 57, 73–74
economy, x, 4, 27, 92–93, 156, 183, 199; *aggiornamento*, 5, 95, 262; austerity, 13, 148, 288; collapse, 28, 95, 233, 288; debt, 5, 73, 234; financial suffocation of media, 166, 167–168; GDP, 10, 55, 81, 201; inflation, 5–6, 9, 10, 13, 200–201, 276, 288; judicial branch with benefits, 78–79; national wealth, 13, 52, 91, 105, 203; with privilege, exclusion and alienation, 197–198; reforms, 73, 276
education, 54, 76, 181, 232, 282; Arabization and, 234, 235, 256, 257; Ministry of Higher Education, xvii, 155, 168; mismanagement, 247–248; students, 80–81, 87, 99, 126, 127, 131, 139, 142, 154–155, 177, 191, 308
"egalitarian perception of social relations," 192, 341n9
Egypt, 55, 97, 131, 145–146, 263, 288, 331n29
El Djeich (magazine), 42
El-Djezair (government-owned magazine), 144
elections, 16, 120; abstention from, xiv, 138, 146, 148, 157–161, 277, 286; legislative, *136*, *137*, *140*, 144, 277, 288, 355n26; presidential, ix–xiv, 13, 35, 41–44, 61–62, 87, 274–275, 277, 281
El Khabar (newspaper), 63, 164, 166, 253, 258, 263, 268, 336n30
El Manchar (website), 252–253
El Moudjahid (government-owned newspaper), xiv, 6, 146–147
El Mounqidh (newspaper), 164
El Watan (newspaper), 96, 118, 161, 164, 166, 167, 169, 340n3
embezzlement, 5, 61, 77, 107, 244; army with, 51, 52; systemic, 83–84, 97–99, 120, 131, 201
employment, youth, 195, 215
Ennahar (newspaper), 164, 219
Ennahar TV, xvii–xviii, 156, 161
Ennahḍa, 131, 132
Entelis, John, 81, 101, 113, 237

ENTV, 42, 108, 109
éradicateurs ("eradicators"), 60, 70, 239, 306
essentialism, autonomy and, 184–187
ethnography, democracy and, 260–262
EU (European Union), 104, 175
exception, state of, 171–176, 191
exclusion, with privilege and alienation, 196–199
exile, patriotism and, 266–268
existential threat, xi, 12, 62, 142, 159, 172, 210; of colonial space, xix; crisis and, 3–4; obedience and discipline with, 141; repression and, 174; violence and, 221

Facebook, *140*, 170, 209
Faculté Centrale, xii, 123, 127
false flag operations, 23, 62, 239
Family Code (1984), 116
Fanon, Frantz, 16, 233, 259, 265, 282
Fegoun, Bahia Bencheikh El-, 229
Ferhani, Hassan, 228
Ferhat, Hamid, 38, 78, 83–84, 162
Fersaoui, Abdelouahab, xv, 174, 226
FFS (Front des Forces Socialistes, Socialist Forces Front), xv, 114, 138, 159, 177–178, 240, 306; CNDDC and, 209; dissidents, *184*; RAJ and, xii; RCD and, 179, 181–182; supporters, 160, 183, 195
filmmakers, documentary, 227–228, 229, 258–259, 269–270
financial crimes, 79, 93–94. *See also* embezzlement
FIS (Front Islamique du Salut, Islamic Salvation Front), 8, 10, 42, 113, 123–124, 132, 144, 147, 179, 244, 306; banning of, 9; dissolution of, 122; Islamo-conservatives and, 117; with *El Mounqidh*, 164; repression of, 237; RND and, 116; M. Saïd and, 331n32; social outreach, 159

fitna (sedition), 13, 43, 127, 145
FLN (Front de Libération Nationale, National Liberation Front), xi, 7–8, 11, 60, 125, 130, 147, 181, 234, 306; Abane and, 243; *barbéfélènes* and, 116–118, 148; "bomb network," 350n63; A. Bouteflika and, 36, 42; as cartel party, 84; DRS and, 61–62, 116; illegitimacy of, 150–151; legacy, 143; legislative elections and, 144, 288, 355n26; *El Moudjahid* and, xiv; National Union of Algerian Students and, 87; Presidential Alliance and, 113–120; rectifiers of, 117, 119, 131, 135–136, 307; supporters of, 141, 149, 160, 179; UGTA and, 85, 86
FNA (Front National Algérien, Algerian National Front), 133–135, 306
food prices, inflation, 200–201, 276
football, 66, 200, 217–218, 227, 264, 275; patriotism, 267–268; stadiums, 7, 13–14, 45–46; World Cup, 55
foreign manipulation, 211, 238, 248–249
Forum des Chefs d'Entreprise (FCE, Business Owners Forum), 87, 94, 95, 276, 286, 306
Foucault, Michel, 72, 169
fracking, 214, 276
France, x–xi, 62, 147, 211, 238, 241, 265–266; colonialism, 4, 30, 186; the Hirak supporters in, 279–280; Maghrebi police and, 104–105; media, 37, 275; "Party of France," 247
fraud, 35, 120, 130, 161
freedom, 162, 166–171
freedoms, regulation of, xxi, 152; "Algerian Spring," 154–161; censorship and repression, 166–177; contentious insularity and, 153, 177–187; oppositions without solutions, 187–189; ways of criticism, 161–166

Friedrich Ebert Stiftung, 139, 271, 340n101
Front de Libération Nationale. *See* FLN
Front des Forces Socialistes. *See* FFS
Front Islamique du Salut. *See* FIS
Front National Algérien. *See* FNA

Gaïd Salah, Ahmed, 43, 52, 56, 61, 62, 274–275, 283–285
gas, 11, 51, 320n73
General Union of Algerian Students, 87
gerrymandering, 8, 160
Ghoul, Amar, 61, 130–131
Ghozali, Sid Ahmed, 65
GIA (Armed Islamic Group, Groupe Islamique Armé), 10, 11, 85, 123, 239, 306
GLD. *See groupes de légitime défense*
golden age, myth of, 235
"Golden Generation," 275, 279–283
"Gouvernance féodale" (Mostefaoui), 353n130
governance by catastrophization, 62, 66, 205, 217, 278; future of, 291–293; goal of, 226; as government principle and lived experience, xxi, xxii; historical overview of crisis and, 27–31; with repression, 287–288, 290; ruling coalition and, 33; security pact and, 222; "social imaginary of emergency" and, xix; "tradition of the oppressed" and, 192
government, 75, 76, 83, 86, 98, 224, 258; corruption, 5, 51, 61, 63; defined, 324n18; with private press, 44, 51, 59, 60, 63, 163, 219. *See also* cartelized power structure; state
Gramsci, Antonio, 27, 74, 140, 225, 266; on consent, 323n12; on crisis, 1, 23
Grande Poste, 85, 158
Great Mosque, xi, 66, 96, 98
Green Algeria Alliance, 131, 158, 160
Groupe Islamique Armé. *See* GIA

groupes de légitime défense (GLD, self-defense groups), 35, 80; RND and, 329n12
Guermah, Massinissa, 11, 177
Guidance and Reform (Irshād wa-l-Iṣlāḥ, al-), 123
Gulf War, 8, 122

Hachani, Abdelkader, 8–9, 122, 238
Hachemaoui, Mohammed, 38, 82, 90, 96, 101, 260
Haddad, Ali, xiv, 94, 95, 106, 276, 284
Hadj Nacer, Abderahmane, 263–264
Hamadouche, Louisa Dris-Aït, 39
Hamas, 127, 129. *See also* MSP
Hamel, Abdelghani, 13, 79, 80, 83, 175, 284, 285
Hamiani, Réda, 94
Hamrouche, Mouloud, xiii, xiv, xv, 6, 8, 81, 169
Hanoune, Louisa, 133, 145
Harbi, Mohammed, 1, 2, 16, 17, 253
harga (illegal immigration across Mediterranean), 142, 228, 267, 306
harkis (traitor), 159, 187, 306, 335n15
Harrach Prison, El, 284, 286
Hasfi, Nouria, 148–149
Hassani, Mohamed Ziane, 349n46
HCE (Haut Comité d'État, High Committee of State), 9, 10, 34, 35, 60, 171, 306
hegemony, 1, 13, 33, 58, 121–122, 292, 323n12; crisis of, 21, 140; "cultural," 27, 267
Henry, Clement M., 103
Hibou, Béatrice, 17
Hidouci, Ghazi, 103
High Committee of State. *See* HCE
Hirak, 12–14, 46, 227, 248, 287; cultural reform and symbolic revolution, 268–272; exile and patriotism, 266–268; governance by catastrophization and, 290, 292–293;

making of, 276–279; support for, 275, 278, 279–282, 284, 286; symbolic, 264–272
hitiste ("wallist"), 194, 195, 199, 306
Ḥizb Fransā ("Party of France") (Brahimi), 247
Hobbes, Thomas, 44, 223, 271
hogra (systemic contempt), xxii, 181, 208, 265, 266, 282, 306; police and, 191; of *Pouvoir*, 206; riots and, 199–203, 214; *shkara* and, 276
homogeneous empty time, 30, 316n107
hostage crisis (2013), 51, 320n73
housing, 4, 10, 202, 219, 276
human rights, xvi, 18, 165, 167, 188, 279; activists, 42, 239; LADDH, 154, 159, 163, 178, 307
hydrocarbons, 2, 77, 213, 215, 234, 286; oil, 5, 6, 11, 214, 276; prices, x, 13, 43; rents, 4, 5, 81–84, 92, 95, 103, 104, 201

Ibtikar (citizen-led movement), 277, 282, 288
IMF (International Monetary Fund), 10, 73, 81, 95, 105, 201, 306
immigration, 142, 228, 267, 306
immune defense, ANP and, 45–47, 49
imports, 5, 276, 288
inflation, 5–6, 9, 10, 13, 200–201, 276, 288
insularity, contentious: autonomy and essentialism, 184–187; Berberists and, 177–180; "Kabyle parties" and confinement, 180–183
Interior Ministry, 111
internal colonialism, 205–207, 229, 248, 280
International Monetary Fund. *See* IMF
International Workers' Day rally (2011), 156
Irshād wa-l-Iṣlāḥ, al- (Guidance and Reform), 123
'iṣāba (gang), 150, 273, 277–278, 306
Iṣlāḥ, Al-, 131, 132

Islam, 5, 7, 79, 122, 124, 170, 289; GIA, 10, 11, 85, 123, 239, 306; Rachad movement, 87, 117, 281, 282, 288, 290, 307; racism and, 255–256. *See also* FIS
Islamic Salvation Army, 10, 42
Islamic Salvation Front. *See* FIS
Islamism, 121–123, 126, 127, 171–172, 237
Islamists, 121, 126, 235, 238

Jabhat Al-Mustaqbal, 84
Jaz'ara, 121, 122, 331n32
jihadis, 5, 10, 80, 122, 221
Jil Jadid (Liberal opposition party), 222, 306
journalists, xii, xvii–xviii, 167–170, 258
judicial branch, 39, 78–79

"Kabyle parties," confinement of, 180–183
Kabylia, 11, 186, 290
kachiriste, 197, 250, 306
Kafi, Ali, 35
Karama, El-, 135
Kenz, Ali El, 254
Khadra, Yasmina, 258
Khaḍrā', Al- (Green, The), 275
Khaldi, El Hadi, 117
Khalifa, Laroussi, 93
Khalifa, Rafik, 93, 94, 130
Khan, Amin, xv
Khelil, Abdelmoumène, 39
Khelil, Chakib, 61, 211
Khenchela (town), 281
khobzistes (profiteers), 118, 129, 139–142, 149, 250, 307, 330n22
Kouninef brothers, 94
Ksentini, Farouk, 157, 164, 188

labor, 85, 163, 232, 279, 283; organizers, xviii, 19, 79, 153; wages, 39, 197, 203, 215. *See also* workers
"La Casa Del Mouradia" (song), 227
Lamari, Mohamed, 48–49, 60, 61, 93

Lamari, Smaïn, 239, 245
Larabi, Samir, 207, 208, 219, 226, 343n46
Laribi, Lyes, 94
La Tribune (newspaper), 87
La Violencia (Colombia), 221, 223–224
laws, 38, 56, 79, 98, 116, 164, 166–169, 176
Lazreg, Marnia, 23
legislative branch, 38, 277
Le Matin (newspaper), 60, 166–168
Le Monde (newspaper), 146
Le Quotidien d'Algerie (online news), 63, 118
Le Quotidien d'Oran (online news), 221
Le Soir d'Algérie (private daily newspaper), xv, 98, 107
Le Temps d'Algérie (newspaper), 94, 164
L'Expression (newspaper), 44, 56, 259
liberalization, 27, 57, 73–74, 95, 105
Liberté (private daily newspaper), xv, 94, 164, 166, 217
Libya, x, xvii, 13, 97, 145, 156, 210, 238
Ligue Algérienne pour la Défense des Droits de l'Homme (LADDH, Algerian League for the Defense of Human Rights), 154, 159, 163, 178, 307
Lotfi DK (rapper), 226, 228, 251, 346n111
Lumpenproletariat, 5, 229
lynchings, 290

Madani, Abassi, 8, 10, 122, 238
mafia, 52, 53, 102, 149, 150, 183, 243. See also "System"
MAK (Mouvement pour l'autodétermination de la Kabylie, Movement for the Autonomy of Kabylia), 177, *183*, 184–185, 290, 307
Makri, Abderrazak, 131
Malgaches, 89
Mali, x, xvii, 145
Malti, Hocine, 75
Mameri, Khalfa, 50, 147
Mameri, Tarek, 157, 170
management, by scarcity, 214–216, 223

"manipulitis," 240–242
Maqām ash-Shahīd, 47, *48*, 96
Martinez, Luis, 103, 236, 260
martyrs (*shuhadā'*, sing, *shahīd*), 46, 88–89, 115, *183*, 243–246, *246*; Maqām ash-Shahīd, 47, *48*, 96; with self-immolation, 191
Martyrs' Square, 68, *68*, 156, 204
massacres, 59, 239, 255
Massar al-Jadid, al-, 288–289, 291
Matoub, Lounes, 181, 245, *246*
Maurice Audin Square, xii, xvi
Mazouz, Ahmed, 94, 98
Mbembe, Achille, 17, 232
MBS (rap group), 228, 346n111
McDougall, James, 257
Mebtoul, Abderrahmane, 260
Mécili, Ali, 240, 349n46
media, 35, 37, 42, 112, 156, 164–165, 275; elections and, 160–161; financial suffocation of, 166, 167–168; government with private press, 44, 51, 59, 60, 63, 163, 219; journalists, xii, xvii–xviii, 167–170, 258
Mediene, Mohamed "Toufik," xiii, 13, 61, 64, 75, 239, 245; Ouyahia and, 116; RCD and, 179
Medjaoui, Abdelalim, 225
Mehri, Abdelhamid, 113
Mellouk, Benyoucef, 98
Menasra, Abdelmadjid, 131
Menia, Salaheddine, 259
Merbah, Kasdi, 238
Mesbah, Mohamed Chafik, 107
middle class, xii, 9, 126
migration, 4, 16, 104, 235, 267
military, 47, 49, 55, 62, 70; army, xx, 33, 35, 42, 50–54, 283; intelligence, xi, 13, 51, 59, 61, 63, 64, 170, 172, 238, 243, 321n104; officers as *décideurs*, 39, 45, 65, 68, 76, 94, 306, 318n26
Military Academy of Cherchell, 258, 283
Miliyūniyya (March of the Million), 209

Ministry of Defense, 79
Ministry of Energy and Mines, 61, 77, 81, 211
Ministry of Fisheries, 125, 130
Ministry of Foreign Affairs, 349n46
Ministry of Higher Education, xvii, 155, 168
Ministry of Justice, 98
Ministry of the Mujahideen, 89
Ministry of Weapons and General Liaisons, 88
Morocco, 37, 97, 131, 211, 243, 290, 325n57
Mostefaoui, Belkacem, 353n130
Mosteghanemi, Ahlem, 258
Mouffok, Ghania, ix
Moulay, Karim, 239
Mouradia, El (presidential palace, the), 117, 155, 227, 283, 306
Moussaoui, Abderrahmane, 101, 236
Mouvement Algérien des Officiers Libres (MAOL, Algerian Movement of Free Officers), 307, 349n45, 349n56
Mouvement de la Société de l'Islam. *See* MSI
Mouvement des Jeunes Indépendants pour le Changement (Movement of the Independent Youth for Change), 161
Mouvement pour la Société de la Paix. *See* MSP
Mouvement pour l'autodétermination de la Kabylie. *See* MAK
Movement for the Children of the South, 210
Mozabite, the, 212
MSI (Mouvement de la Société de l'Islam, Movement for the Society of Islam), 123–124, 307
MSP (Mouvement pour la Société de la Paix, Movement for the Society of Peace, Hamas), xxi, 67, 151, 180, 307; co-option and, 120–132; Presidential Alliance and, 112, 123, 128, 130–131

Mubarak, Hosni, 255
mujahid (anticolonial fighter), 5, 307
mujahideen, 89, 90, 98
music, 126, 226–227, 228, 229
musical repertoire of contention, national, 282
Muslim Brotherhood, 122, 123, 124, 126, 132, 331n29
Muwaqqiʿūn bi-d-Dimāʾ, Al-, 210

Nabni (think tank), 11
Nahnah, Mahfoudh, 123, 124, 127, 129, 130
National Agency for Youth Employment, 195, 215
National Association of October '88's Victims, 311n16
National Committee for the Safeguarding of Algeria, 85
National Council of Privatizations, 92
National Democratic Institute, 126
National Directorate of Cooperatives, ANP, 47
National Gendarmerie, 79–80, 107–108, 170
National Organization of Mujahideen, 89
National Organization of the Children of Martyrs, 89
National Organization of the Children of Mujahideen, 89
National Organization of the Children of Shuhadāʾ, 133
National People's Army. *See* ANP
National Polytechnic School, 77
National Reconciliation (*al-Muṣālaḥa al-Waṭaniyya*), 10, 69, 143, 169, 236, 307; criticism and, 163–165; National Tragedy and, 144, 170; presidency and, 41–42, 44
National Social and Economic Council, 92
National Statistics Office, 215

National Tragedy (*al-Ma'sāaal-Waṭaniyya*), 10, 43, 69, 144, 155, 170, 235, 307. *See also* Dark Decade
National Union of Algerian Students, 87
National Union of Algerian Zawāyā, 91
national unity, political order and, 143–146
necropolitics, 66–69
neoliberalization, 27, 74, 95, 105
neo-patrimonialism, 40, 102, 328n98
nepotism, corruption and, 52, 53, 54
Nezzar, Khaled, 52, 240, 353n129; confronted on social media, 161; with defamation case, 165; on military, 47, 50, 70; on A. Bouteflika, 36, 60, 70
Nezzar, Lotfi, 165
NGOs, 125–126, 139, 159, 165, 271, 283, 291, 340n101
"ninja" units, Special Intervention Group, 51, 255
nonlethal policing, xxi, 27, 79, 172–174, 214, 223, 275, 292
"non-movements," 281
nonviolence, at protests, 209–210

OAS (Organisation Armée Secrète, Secret Armed Organization), xiv, 307
October uprising (1988), xiii, xiv, 7, 311n16
oil, 5, 6, 11, 214, 276. *See also* hydrocarbons
oligarchy, 13, 105, 135, 221, 309n10
Ophir, Adi, 291
Organisation Armée Secrète. *See* OAS
Organization of Free Young Algerians, 123
Othmani, Slim, 94, 95
Ould Abbes, Djamel, 232
Ould Kablia, Daho, 88–89, 144, 160, 161, 257
Ouled el-Bahdja, 227, 282
Ouyahia, Ahmed, 13, 14, 37, 70, 116, 195, 284; on Arab uprisings, 144, 145–146; dissent and, 148–149; with police, 172; RND and, 114, 115

pacification, 37, 43, 143, 226
pacifism, xxii, 207–210, 229, 273, 280, 292
Pact for a Democratic Alternative, 283
Palestinians, 87, 145
Parti des Travailleurs. *See* PT
Parti Socialiste des Travailleurs. *See* PST
Party of the Socialist Vanguard, 225
patriotism, 207–210, 266–268
"patriots" (*waṭaniyyīn*), 35, 80, 115
people: "changing the," 262–264; as child, 147–148, 161, 168, 219, 262, 272; as class, 146–148, 249, 281; as object, 147, 148, 318n42; three natures of, 146–148
pluralism, politics and, xxi, 8, 16, 44, 111, 125, 150, 165; with independents for sale, 133–137; rejection of, 132–140
police, 7, 9, 191, 196, 215, 218, 288; checkpoints, 53, 203–204, 224; Maghrebi, 104–105; with nonlethal policing, xxi, 27, 79, 172–174, 214, 223, 275, 292; at protests, xii–xiii, 155, 156–157, 186, 204, 210
political life, securitization of, 205
political order, xxi, 22; defense of established, 141–143; as exceptional, 102–106; MSP and co-option, 120–132; narratives of, 140–149; national unity and, 143–146; Presidential Alliance and, 112, 113–120; reality check, 148–149; three natures of "the people," 146–148; transformation of, 110–112; vox populi, 149–151
politics, xx, 5, 88, 126, 167, 224; *Avoiding Politics*, 333n66; candidates as animals on social media, *140*; cartel parties, 84–85, 87, 91, 111, 113–116, 118–120, 136; DRS and, 63–65; instability and presidency, 34–35;

"Kabyle parties," 180–183; necro-, 66–69; pacifism with patriotism and autonomy from, 207–210; pluralism and, xxi, 8, 16, 44, 111, 125, 132–140, 150, 165; rationale of suspicion and, 62–65, 112; rejection of, 138–140, 250
popular culture, 226–229, 248–259, 269–270
Pouvoir, 33, 77, 138, 152, 208, 229, 287, 307; Bled Miki and, 251; criticism of, 254; foreign manipulation and, 238; *hogra* of, 206; mistrust of, 250; protests and, 284; RCD and, 179; with repression, 189; resistance against, 225; supporters, 188. *See also* "System"
poverty, 5, 199, 212–214
power, 162–164, 229, 288, 346n112; presidency with institutional and symbolic, 34, 37–41; structure, 95–106. *See also* cartelized power structure
praetorianism: with ANP as criticized organization, 52–54; with ANP as indispensable, 54–56; contradictions, 50–52; crisis and, 47–50; immune defense and ANP, 45–47, 49
praetorian systems, 49
presidency: army opposing, xx, 33, 42; of Bendjedid, 4–5, 6, 34; chaos and, 41–45; DRS and, 61, 140; institutional and symbolic bases of power, 34, 37–41; National Reconciliation and, 41–42, 44; paradox of, 40–41; political instability and, 34–35; with reforms, 155–156; return of A. Bouteflika, 35–37; "System" and, 33–45. *See also* Bouteflika, Abdelaziz; cartelized power structure
Presidential Alliance, xxi, 43, 85, 87, 159; *barbéfélènes* and, 116–118, 148; FLN and, 113–120; MSP and, 112, 123, 128, 130–131; political order and, 112, 113–120; RND and, 114–115, 118, 120. *See also* cartelized power structure
prisoners, xvi, 167–168, 170
prison sentences, 79, 172–173
privilege: with exclusion and alienation, 196–199; upper-class, 193
protesta movement, 126, 307
protesters: criminalization of, 212, 284–285, 287, 288; pacifism of, 292; space of control and, 203–205
protests, 126, 148, 166, 282, 286, 307; with bodies mutilated, 213–214; against fracking, 214, 276; the Hirak, 248, 279–280; March of the Million, 209; police at, xii–xiii, 155, 156–157, 186, 204, 210; *Pouvoir* and, 284; presidential elections, xii–xiii, 274, 281; sit-ins, xii, 163, 210, 217; strikes, xviii, 7, 85, 211; students, 154–155, 191; violence at, 208–209; workers, 5, 7, 214; "Yellow Vest," 280. *See also* uprisings
PST (Parti Socialiste des Travailleurs, Socialist Workers' Party), xv, 133, 159, 187, 209, 219, 225, 307
psychological warfare, 241
PT (Parti des Travailleurs, Workers' Party), 133, 145, 160, 307
public affairs, securitization of, 220
public life, 69, 112, 195
punishment, in liberalized environment, 164–166
puritanism, 121–122

qui tue qui? (who kills whom?), 237–240, 243
Qutb, Sayyid, 121

Rachad movement, 87, 117, 281, 282, 288, 290, 307
racism, 145, 186, 255–256, 261, 273
radicalization, 11, 185, 211, 284, 291

Rahal, Malika, 255
Rahal, Yahia (General), 54–55
raḥma (forgiveness), 10, 236
Raï music, 126
RAJ (Rassemblement Action Jeunesse, Youth Action Rally), xi, xv, 173–174, 203, 225–226, 279–280, 284, 307; activism of, 281; criminalization of, 285; FFS and, xii; with member arrested, xvi; protests, 156–157; in turmoil, xiii–xvi
Rally for Culture and Democracy. See RCD
Rally for Hope in Algeria. See TAJ
Ramdane, Abane, 243, 244, 245
rap music, 226, 228, 229
Rassemblement Action Jeunesse. See RAJ
Rassemblement National Démocratique. See RND
Rassemblement pour la Culture et la Démocratie. See RCD
rationale of suspicion, politics and, 62–65, 112
RCD (Rassemblement pour la Culture et la Démocratie, Rally for Culture and Democracy), 65, 114, 187, 307; criticism of, 179, 180; FFS and, 179, 181–182; founding of, 178, 179; MAK and, 177; supporters, 183, 188, 189
Rebrab, Issad, 94
Rechak, Hamza, 190–191, 199
rectifiers (*taqwīmīyīn, redresseurs*), 117, 119, 131, 135–136, 307
re-enchantment: crisis with revelation and, 26–27; disenchantment and, 64
reforms, 3, 7, 111, 123; agriculture, 72, 234; cartelized power structure with, 275, 276; economy, 73, 276; repression with, 155–156, 169–170; symbolic revolution and cultural, 268–272
religion, 170, 219. See also Islam
rentier state, 1, 15, 73, 103, 104
repression, 78, 104, 111, 237; of activism, 171–172, 173; censorship and, 166–177; governance by catastrophization with, 287–288, 290; of media, 156, 169–170; oppositions without solutions, 187–189; with reforms, 155–156, 169–170; with spaces of circumvention, 166, 169–171; state, 311n16; with terrorism and state of exception, 171–175
residual terrorism, 3, 11, 56, 175, 221
resistance, social unrest and, 212
reunification, of "Algerian family," 43, 143
revelation, 26–27, 58, 59, 65, 107, 240, 276
Revolutionary Correction (*Taṣḥīḥath-Thawrī, at-*), 135
Revolutionary Family (*Al-U'sra Al-Thawriyya*), 67, 88–90, 249, 308
rights: International Covenant on Civil and Political Rights, 167; labor, 232, 279; of workers, 208, 232. See also CNDDC; human rights
riots, 6, 192, 210, 218, 268; in Aïn Bessem, 196; antiriot police, 79, 172, 196; *hogra* and, 199–203, 214; poor against poor, 212–214. See also uprisings
RND (Rassemblement National Démocratique, National Democratic Rally), 35, 84, 125, 136, 182, 308; A. Bouteflika with support from, 36; criticism of, 149, 179; dissidents, 134; FIS and, 116; General Union of Algerian Students and, 87; GLD and, 329n12; illegitimacy of, 150–151; Presidential Alliance and, 114–115, 118, 120; supporters of, 149, 158, 160
Roberts, Hugh, 77, 236
Rouadjia, Ahmed, 168
Rougab, Mohamed, 37
Roundabout in My Head, A (documentary film), 228

ruling class, 4, 14, 140, 144, 151, 201, 324n18; corruption and, 99; divided, 5; elites, 16, 76, 88, 92, 104, 106, 112, 200, 242, 247–249; as "mafia-like," 102, 149
ruling coalition: ANP and, 45; as cartelized power structure, xx, 33, 56–57; governance by catastrophization and, 33; political collapse and, xx; under A. Bouteflika, 33. *See also* army; presidency
Russia, 105, 170

Saâdani, Amar, 61–62, 117, 119
Saadi, Saïd, 178, 179, 187
Saadi, Yacef, 249
Saïd, Abdelmadjid Sidi, 87
Saïd, Mohamed, 331n32
Salafist Group for Preaching and Combat (al-Jamā'a al-Salafiyya lil-Da'wa wal-Qitāl), 11
Salafists, 11, 122, 331n29
Samraoui, Mohamed, 239–240, 349n46
Sansal, Boualem, 258, 264
Sant'Egidio Platform, 113, 115–116, 123
satellite organizations, 85–87
Saudi Arabia, 199, 238
Sayad, Abdelmalek, 16
scarcity, 13, 20, 192, 203, 267, 293; management by, 214–216, 223; of resources, 100, 101, 102, 104, 202; with riots, 202, 214
school boycott (1994–1995), 181, 216
securitization, xxii, 22, 69, 204, 210, 224; hegemony of, 292; of Kabylia, 186; of political life, 205; of public affairs, 220; of socioeconomic unrest, 156; totalizing, 25, 28
security: forces, xvii, 39, 42, 66, 89, 114, 156, 165, 172–173, 215; mass surveillance, 170; pact and social fatigue, 222–224; threats, 11; violence and, 171. *See also* DGSN; DRS; police
self-deprecation, 265–266, 267
self-immolation, 190, 191, 199, 340n3
Sellal, Abdelmalek, 69, 131, 170, 209, 211, 250, 284
shakhsiyya jazāi'riyya. *See* Algerian personality
sharia law, 166
Shariati, Ali, 121
shiyyatin (sycophants), 118, 140, 149, 308, 330n22
shkara ("corruption"), 134, 150, 276, 308
Sifaoui, Mohamed, 240
sit-ins, xii, 163, 210, 217
SMEs (small and medium-sized enterprises), 83, 125, 308
SNAPAP (Syndicat National Autonome des Personnels de l'Administration Publique, National Autonomous Union for Employees of Public Administrations), 163, 278, 281, 282, 308
social deviance, Dark Decade and, 220–222
social fatigue: crisis as lived experience, 220–229; Dark Decade and social deviance, 220–222; security pact and, 222–224; with struggle ongoing, 224–226; testifying and popular culture, 226–229
"social imaginary of emergency," xix
social inequality: Aïn Bessem, xxii, 193–196, *196*, 197; Aïn Turk, 193–196, 265; CNDDC and, 192; crisis as lived experience and, 192–205; *hogra* and riots, 199–203; with privilege, exclusion and alienation, 196–199; space of control and, 203–205
Socialist Forces Front. *See* FFS
social media, 13, 63, 170, 200, 209; ANP confronted on, 161; A. Bouteflika pranked on, 274; criticism on, 112;

social media (*continued*)
  FLN on, 117; the Hirak on, 279; political candidates as animals on, 140
social movements: migrations and, 16; pacifism and, xxii; routinization of, 210–212
social system, 5, 20, 21–22, 24, 256
social unrest, xxii, 12, 28, 87, 102, 215, 257; communal guards with, 80; criminalization of, 224; resistance and forms of, 212; securitization of, 210; UGTA containing, 86. *See also* protests; uprisings
Soltani, Bouguerra, 124, 130, 131
Sonatrach, 61, 75–77, 81, 98, 211, 215, 308
Soolking, 190, 282
SOS Disparus, 163
Souaïdia, Habib, 60, 165, 239, 240
Soummam Platform, 253
South, with unemployment, 205–214
sovereignty, 3, 26, 29, 47, 66, 147, 150, 234, 280, 283, 284, 291–293; autonomy and, 184; Islamism and, 127, 237; repression and, 175–177
Special Intervention Group, DRS, 51, 255, 320n73
speech: freedom of, 162, 167, 168; hate, 170
spies, xvii–xviii
state: bunker, 103; cartel parties, 84–85, 87, 91, 111, 113–116, 118–120, 136; conservation and coercion, 78–81; crony capitalists, 91–95; deep, 64, 65, 74, 75, 76, 240; dirigisme, 73; disappeared by, 163–164, 173–174; of exception, 171–176, 191; field, 74–84; HCE, 9, 10, 34, 35, 60, 171, 306; hegemony with society and, 323n12; hydrocarbon rents and, 81–84; idolatrous, 122, 230; integral, 74; periphery of, 84–95; reformism, 3, 73; rentier, 1, 15, 73, 103, 104;

Revolutionary Family, 88–90; satellite organizations, 85–87; Sufi brotherhoods, 90–91; technicians of, 75–78; violence, 49, 172
state universalism, fiction of, 40
Stora, Benjamin, 254–255
strategies: crisis with representations and, 23–24; securitization as, 25
strikes, xviii, 7, 85, 211
structural adjustment program (SAP), 10, 28, 73–74, 92, 248, 308
students, 99, 139, 142; Guermah, 177; ouster of Catholic, 80–81; protests, 154–155, 191; UGEL, 87, 126, 127, 131, 308
"subjective plausibility," 129, 332n48
subversion, 56, 172, 175, 219
Sufi brotherhoods (*zāwya*, pl. *zawāyā*), 90–91
Superior Council of Magistrates, 39, 79
Syndicat National Autonome des Personnels de l'Administration Publique. *See* SNAPAP
Syria, 13, 95, 111, 145, 146, 157, 325n57
"System" (*Niẓām, Pouvoir*), xv, 14, 249, 316n1; cartelized power structure and, xx, 276–277; corruption of, 2, 33, 276; defined, 32, 307, 308; illegitimacy of, 286; as mafia-like, 52, 53, 102, 149, 150, 183, 243; martyrs of, 243–246; presidency and, 33–45; rejection of, xiv
systemic contempt. *See* hogra

Tabbou, Karim, 183, 285
ṭab jnanu, 70, 88, 160, 308
ṭāghūt (idolatrous) state, 122, 230
Tahkout, Mahieddine, 94, 116, 276, 284
TAJ (Tajama'a A'mal al-Jazāi'r, Rally for Hope in Algeria), 131, 134, 138, 308
Takfiri, 239, 308
Talahite, Fatiha, 98
Taleb, Djamel, 340n3

Tamazight language, 178, 187
taqwīmīyin. *See* rectifiers
Tartag, Athmane, 61, 62
Tebboune, Abdelmajid, 276, 286, 288
technicians, of state, 75–78
temporalities: crisis and, 24–26; homogeneous empty time, 30, 316n107
term limits, presidency, 43
terrorism, 48, 210, 220, 241; at Algiers International Airport, 9; anti-, 104; attacks, 9, 64, 211; counterterrorist operations, 51; DRS with, 64; Organization of Free Young Algerians, 123; residual, 3, 11, 56, 175, 221; spectacle of, 217–218; state of exception and, 171–175
testifying, popular culture, 226–229
Third Worldist episteme, 233–235, 242, 253, 258
Tilly, Charles, 150, 342n41, 346n112
Tingentourine gas facility, hostage crisis, 51, 320n73
Tlemçani, Rachid, 238
Tliba, Baha-Eddine, 119
Tocqueville, Alexis de, 26, 192, 341n9
Tonic Emballage, 93
torture, 167, 321n104
totalizing, securitization, 25, 28
Touati, Mohamed (General), 61, 70, 133, 134, 135, 155
Touiza (NGO), 139
Toumi, Khalida, 168, 194, 195, 216
Tounsi, Ali, 63, 80–81
Tozy, Mohamed, 132
"tradition of the oppressed," 30, 192, 226
Tunisia, 131, 205, 216, 263, 284, 336n30; corruption in, 97; fall of Ben 'Ali, 223; uprisings in 2010–2011, x, 146, 154
Turkey, 47, 49

UGEL (Union Générale des Étudiants Libres, General Union of Free Students), 87, 126, 127, 131, 308

UGTA (Union Générale des Travailleurs Algériens, General Union of Algerian Workers), xviii, 85–87, 133, 162, 202, 308
uncertainty, rule of: "civil war" and, 235–237; "manipulitis," 240–242; *qui tue qui?*, 237–240; Third Worldist episteme, 233–235
unemployment, 5, 100, 202; disguised, 194–195; internal colonialism and, 205–207; with patriotism, pacifism and autonomy from politics, 207–210; rates, 10, 13, 197, 205, 215; with routinization of social movements, 210–212; in rural areas, 215; the South and, 205–214; war of poor against poor, 212–214; youth, 198, 208–209, 276. *See also* CNDDC
UN General Assembly, 234
Union Générale des Étudiants Libres. *See* UGEL
Union Générale des Travailleurs Algériens. *See* UGTA
Union of Algerian Women, 148–149
United States, 125–126, 159, 211, 238, 248, 259, 265–266, 341n9
Universal Declaration of Human Rights, 167
unrest: political, 5; social, xxii, 12, 28, 80, 86, 87, 102, 210, 212, 215, 224, 257; socioeconomic, 156
upper class, 9, 54, 193, 198
uprisings, 3, 11; Arab, 144, 145–146, 153; against OAS in 1962, xiv; October, xiii, xiv, 7, 311n16; protesters, 203–205, 212, 284–285, 287, 288, 292; protests, xii–xiii, xviii, 5, 7, 85, 126, 148, 154–157, 163, 166, 186, 191, 204, 208–211, 213–214, 217, 248, 274, 276, 279–282, 284, 286, 307; riots, 6, 79, 172, 192, 196, *196*, 199–203, 210, 212–214, 218, 268; of 2010–2011, x, 111, 144, 145–146, 153, 154; unrest,

uprisings (*continued*)
xxii, 5, 12, 28, 80, 86, 87, 102, 156, 210, 212, 215, 224, 257
urban spaces, 5, 173, 198, 212

Venezuela, 40, 104, 291
violence: Agamben on, 29–30; in Colombia, 221, 223–224; crimes, 238; crisis with symbolic, 278; of Dark Decade, xix, 15, 240–241; elections with, 120; existential threat and, 221; gangster-like, 167; immunity and, 42; against Islamist groups, 235; jihadi, 221; law and, 176; in Libya, 156; lynchings, 290; mass, 28, 73, 222, 291; against media, 167; police, 174, 210; prevalence of, 243, 275; at protests, 208–209; protests and nonviolence, 209–210; psychological warfare and, 241; repression and, 78; riots, 210; rise in, 6, 9, 15, 25, 48, 58, 80; security and, 171; in social systems with crisis, 20, 21–22; state, 49, 172; symbolic, 17, 202; in Syria, 157; of "System," 249; systemic, 21–22, 267; against women, 213, 252
visas, 18, 80, 219, 267

wages, 39, 197, 203, 215
Waqt al-Jazāï'r (newspaper), 94
war crimes, 49
War of Liberation (1954–1962), xiv, xxii, 40, 46, 63, 89, 224, 232, 234, 240, 282, 308, 317n10; disinformation tactics and, 241; FLN and, 114; rap music and, 228
wealth, national, 13, 52, 91, 105, 203
Werenfels, Isabel, 76, 77, 90
whistle-blowers, 60, 98, 239
who kills whom?. *See qui tue qui?*

WikiLeaks, 97
women, 16, 55, 79, 89, 148–149, 213, 252
workers: exploitation of, 206, 207; hydrocarbons, 213; International Workers' Day rally, 156; *Lumpenproletariat* and, 5, 229; mobilization, 85, 215, 229; National Union of Algerian Workers, xviii; protests, 5, 7, 214; PST, xv, 133, 159, 187, 209, 219, 225, 307; PT, 133, 145, 160, 307; rights of, 208, 232; sex, 193; strikes, xviii, 7, 85, 211; teachers, 142; unemployment, 5, 215. *See also* UGTA
working class, 5, 7, 126
World Bank, 10, 105, 342n29
World Cup, 55

"Yellow Vest" movement, France, 280
youth, 14, 16, 353n135; children, 89, 133, 147–148, 161, 168, 210, 217, 219, 248, 262, 272; employment, 195, 215; with exclusion and alienation, 196–199; with *hogra* and riots, 199–203; LADDH, 154, 159, 163, 178, 307; Movement of the Independent Youth for Change, 161; with October uprisings of 1988, 7; unemployment, 198, 208–209, 276; working class, 7. *See also* RAJ

Zaïd, Yacine, 207, 343n46
Zbiri, Tahar, 51, 320n68
Zerhouni, Noureddine "Yazid," 60, 63, 75, 83
Zeroual, Liamine, 10, 35, 59, 115, 165, 236, 353n129
Zitoufi, Hadj Driss, 329n12
Zitouni, Djamal, 239
Zitouni, Mohamed-Salah, 119
Zoubir, Yahia, 39, 130

GPSR Authorized Representative: Easy Access System Europe, Mustamäe tee
50, 10621 Tallinn, Estonia, gpsr.requests@easproject.com

www.ingramcontent.com/pod-product-compliance
Lightning Source LLC
Chambersburg PA
CBHW031228290426
44109CB00012B/206